The Bloomsbury Handbook of Montessori Education

ALSO AVAILABLE FROM BLOOMSBURY

The Bloomsbury Handbook of Global Education and Learning, edited by Douglas Bourn
The Bloomsbury Handbook of Culture and Identity from Early Childhood to Early Adulthood, edited by Ruth Wills, Marian de Souza, Jennifer Mata-McMahon, Mukhlis Abu Bakar and Cornelia Roux
Historical Perspectives on Infant Care and Development, Amanda Norman
Observing Children From Birth to 6, Carole Sharman, Wendy Cross and Diana Vennis
Qualitative Studies of Exploration in Childhood Education, edited by Marilyn Fleer, Mariane Hedegaard, Elin Eriksen Ødegaard and Hanne Værum Sørensen
Reflective Teaching in Early Education, Jennifer Colwell and Amanda Ince with Helen Bradford, Helen Edwards, Julian Grenier, Eleanor Kitto, Eunice Lumsden, Catriona McDonald, Juliet Mickelburgh, Mary Moloney, Sheila Nutkins, Ioanna Palaiologou, Deborah Price and Rebecca Swindells
Postdevelopmental Approaches to Childhood Art, edited by Mona Sakr and Jayne Osgood
Education for Social Change, Douglas Bourn

The Bloomsbury Handbook of Montessori Education

EDITED BY
Angela K. Murray, Eva-Maria Tebano Ahlquist,
Maria K. McKenna, and Mira Debs

BLOOMSBURY ACADEMIC
LONDON • NEW YORK • OXFORD • NEW DELHI • SYDNEY

BLOOMSBURY ACADEMIC
Bloomsbury Publishing Plc
50 Bedford Square, London, WC1B 3DP, UK
1385 Broadway, New York, NY 10018, USA
29 Earlsfort Terrace, Dublin 2, Ireland

BLOOMSBURY, BLOOMSBURY ACADEMIC and the Diana logo are
trademarks of Bloomsbury Publishing Plc

First published in Great Britain 2023

Copyright © Angela K. Murray, Eva-Maria Tebano Ahlquist, Maria K. McKenna and
Mira Debs and contributors, 2023

Angela K. Murray, Eva-Maria Tebano Ahlquist, Maria K. McKenna and Mira Debs
have asserted their right under the Copyright, Designs and Patents Act, 1988,
to be identified as Author of this work.

For legal purposes the Acknowledgments on p. xxiii constitute
an extension of this copyright page.

Cover design: Grace Ridge
Cover image © Hilma af Klint artwork, The Ten Largest, No 3 Youth. steeve-x-art / Alamy Stock Photo

All rights reserved. No part of this publication may be reproduced or
transmitted in any form or by any means, electronic or mechanical, including
photocopying, recording, or any information storage or retrieval system,
without prior permission in writing from the publishers.

Bloomsbury Publishing Plc does not have any control over, or responsibility for,
any third-party websites referred to or in this book. All internet addresses given in this
book were correct at the time of going to press. The author and publisher regret any
inconvenience caused if addresses have changed or sites have ceased to exist,
but can accept no responsibility for any such changes.

A catalogue record for this book is available from the British Library.

A catalog record for this book is available from the Library of Congress.

ISBN: HB: 978-1-3502-7560-7
ePDF: 978-1-3502-7561-4
eBook: 978-1-3502-7562-1

Typeset by Integra Software Services Pvt. Ltd.

To find out more about our authors and books visit www.bloomsbury.com
and sign up for our newsletters.

Contents

List of Figures — xi

Foreword
Yong Zhao — xiv

Preface
Mira Debs, Angela K. Murray, Eva Maria Tebano Ahlquist, and Maria K. McKenna — xvi

Acknowledgments — xxiii

PART I FOUNDATIONS AND EVOLUTION OF MONTESSORI EDUCATION

Introduction: Foundations and Evolution of Montessori Education
Maria K. McKenna — 3

1 Maria Montessori: Life and Historical Context
   Christine Quarfood — 5

2 The Scientific Feminism of Maria Montessori
   Valeria P. Babini — 21

3 Cosmic Education: The Vital Center of the Montessori Perspective
   Rossella Raimondo — 29

4 The Philosophy of Maria Montessori
   Patrick R. Frierson — 37

PART II KEY WRITINGS OF MARIA MONTESSORI

Introduction: Key Writings of Maria Montessori
Eva-Maria Tebano Ahlquist — 49

5 Origins of the Pedagogy: *The Montessori Method* and *The Discovery of the Child*
   Paola Trabalzini — 53

6   School Years: *The Advanced Montessori Method* and *From Childhood to Adolescence*
     Clara Tornar   63

7   What Is Childhood? *The Child in the Family*, *The Secret of Childhood*,
     and *The Absorbent Mind*
     Carmela Franzese   71

8   Math and Grammar: *Psychoarithmetic, Psychogeometry,* and *Psychogrammar*
     Benedetto Scoppola and Clara Tornar   81

9   Peace Education: *Education and Peace*
     Stephanie Van Hook   91

10   Philosophical Writings: *Education for a New World, To Educate the Human Potential*, and *The Formation of Man*
     Raniero Regni   97

11   Societal Responsibility and the Child: *The Child, Society and the World: Unpublished Speeches and Writings*
     Per Gynther   105

PART III MONTESSORI PEDAGOGY ACROSS THE LIFESPAN

     Introduction: Montessori Pedagogy across the Lifespan
     Eva-Maria Tebano Ahlquist   115

12   Learning in the Montessori School Environment
     Eva-Maria Tebano Ahlquist   117

13   The Montessori Approach to Children 0–3 Years Based on Grazia Honegger Fresco's Studies
     Sara Honegger   129

14   The Children's House for Children Ages 3–6
     Uma Ramani   137

15   The Montessori Elementary School for Children Ages 6–12
     William (Biff) Maier   147

16   Erdkinder: An Educational Approach for Adolescents Ages 12–15
     Ela Eckert   157

17   Adult Formation to Transformation
     Jaroslaw Jendza   167

PART IV THE SCIENCE OF MONTESSORI EDUCATION

Introduction: The Science of Montessori Education
Angela K. Murray — 177

18 Revisiting the Foundations of Montessori Education from a Modern Neuroscience Perspective
Mara Fabri — 179

19 A Logic Model for Informing Montessori Research
Brooke Culclasure and Sally Morris Cote — 189

20 Fidelity Issues in Montessori Research
Angela K. Murray and Carolyn Daoust — 199

21 Evaluating the Efficacy of Montessori Education
Karen Manship — 209

22 Assessment in Montessori Education
Susan Zoll, Laura Saylor, and Arya Ansari — 219

23 Neuroscience of Error Monitoring in the Montessori Context
Solange Denervaud — 231

24 A Critical Consideration of Montessori Education in Its Relation to Cognitive Science and Concrete-to-Abstract Thinking
Elida V. Laski and Muanjing Julia Wang — 241

25 Executive Functions in Montessori Education
Jan Mallett — 251

26 Motivation and Self-Determination in Montessori Education
Abha Basargekar and Angeline S. Lillard — 261

27 Montessori Education, Optimal Experience, and Flow
Kevin Rathunde — 271

PART V GLOBAL MONTESSORI EDUCATION

Introduction: Global Montessori Education
Mira Debs — 283

28 Montessori Education in Italy
Erica Moretti — 291

29 Montessori Education in the Netherlands
    Jaap de Brouwer, Hélène Leenders, and Patrick Sins — 297

30 Montessori Education in the UK
    Barbara Isaacs and Hannah Baynham — 303

31 Montessori Education in Ireland
    Tia Williams and Kate Stephens — 309

32 Montessori Education in Nordic Countries
    Petter Sandgren and Eva-Maria Tebano Ahlquist — 315

33 Montessori Education in Germany
    Jörg Boysen — 321

34 Montessori Education in Eastern Europe
    Jaroslaw Jendza — 327

35 Montessori Education in Africa: Themes and Examples across the Continent
    Amelia J. Murray, Hala Aboulela, Aicha Sajid, Noyenum Emafo, and Mira Debs — 333

36 Montessori Education in Tanzania
    Kerstin Forsberg, Hans Forsberg, Joyce Mbuya, and Shose Ngowi — 343

37 Montessori Education in Kenya
    Francescah Kipsoi — 349

38 AMI Educateurs sans Frontières
    Fay Hendriksen, Joke Verheul, and Elske Voermans — 355

39 Montessori Education in Saudi Arabia
    Lila A. Alhashim and Ilene Berson — 361

40 Montessori Education in India
    Rukmini Ramachandran and Mira Debs — 365

41 Montessori Education in Southeast and East Asia
    Saket Malhotra, Kannekar Butt, and Mai P. Nghiêm — 371

42 Montessori Education in China
    Jie Chen and Yu Liu — 377

43 Montessori Education in Japan
    Kimiko Kai — 381

44 Montessori Education in Australia
    Lesley Payne — 387

45	Montessori Education in Canada *Margaret Whitley*	393
46	Montessori Education in the United States *Katie Brown and Richard Ungerer*	399
47	Montessori Education in Puerto Rico *Ana María García Blanco and Katherine Miranda*	405
48	Montessori Education in Mexico *Eder Cuevas*	411
49	Montessori Education in Latin America *Joel Parham, Maria K. McKenna, and Lesli Romero*	415
50	Montessori Education in Brazil *Marion Wallis and Paige Geiger*	425
51	Montessori Education in Argentina *Astrid Steverlynck*	429
52	Future Directions for Global Montessori Research *Joel Parham*	435

PART VI CONTEMPORARY CONSIDERATIONS REGARDING MONTESSORI EDUCATION

	Introduction: Contemporary Considerations Regarding Montessori Education *Maria K. McKenna*	445
53	Montessori Education in the Digital Age *Elizabeth K. Park and Angela K. Murray*	447
54	Interdependent Impact: Contemporary Teacher Education and Montessori Teacher Preparation *Gay C. Ward and Paige M. Bray*	457
55	Montessori Education and Gender: Recasting Gender in Montessori Contexts *Sid Mohandas*	469
56	Montessori Education and Inclusion *Jennifer D. Moss and Ann Epstein*	479
57	Montessori Education in a Plurilingual World *Susan Feez and Anne-Marie Morgan*	489

58 Montessori Education and Critical Race Theory in the United States
    Lucy Canzoneri-Golden and Juliet King — 503

59 Beyond Authenticity: Indigenizing Montessori Education in Settler Colonial United States
    Trisha Moquino, Nacole Walker, and Katie Kitchens — 513

60 Montessori Education and Multilingualism
    Kateri Carver — 525

61 Montessori Education–Based Interventions for Persons with Dementia
    Cameron J. Camp and Evan G. Shelton — 535

62 Montessori Education: Ecoliteracy, Sustainability, and Peace Education
    Maria K. McKenna — 545

List of Contributors — 553
Glossary — 559
Index — 563

Figures

1.1 Maria Montessori in Rome, 1914. Courtesy of the University of Wisconsin-Stevens Point Nelis R. Kampenga University Archives — 6
1.2 Maria Montessori leading a 1914 training course in Rome, reprinted in *Feminel: Illustrario Catalano*, July 26, 1914, 88: 3 — 10
1.3 Maria and Mario Montessori in India, 1940. Courtesy of the Maria Montessori Archives, Amsterdam — 15
5.1 Children in the original San Lorenzo Casa dei Bambini at work. Reproduced from the *Montessori Method*, 1913. Courtesy of Biblioteca dell'Opera Nazionale Montessori — 54
7.1 Child with cylinder blocks. Photo courtesy of Carmela Franzese — 73
8.1 Number Rods. Illustration by Eva-Maria Tebano Ahlquist — 83
8.2 The proof of Pythagoras's theorem. Illustration by Eva-Maria Tebano Ahlquist — 83
8.3 The noun family: Article noun adjective. Sketch by Maria Montessori. Courtesy of the Maria Montessori Archives, photo section, Amsterdam — 87
12.1 Girl working with bells, Holliday Montessori School, Kansas City, Missouri, USA. Courtesy of Jennifer Baker Powers — 119
12.2 The Montessori Lived Environment. Illustration by the author — 124
15.1 Elementary students at Lexington Montessori School practice multiplication with the decimal Checkerboard, 2019. Courtesy of Biff Maier — 149
16.1 Preparing a meal. Courtesy of Roman Klune — 163
19.1 Montessori logic model. Image courtesy of the author — 194
22.1 Adapted observation diagrams, or work curves, representing the three-hour work cycles of two students. Courtesy of the National Center for Montessori in the Public Sector (NCMPS), adapted from *Spontaneous Activity in Education*, Maria Montessori, 1917 — 224
23.1 Peer learning in a Montessori classroom, using self-correcting materials. Courtesy of Ecole Montessori Vevey — 232
24.1 Elementary student works on Math exercises at Fruitful Orchard School, Lagos, Nigeria. Courtesy of Junnifa Uzodike — 244
26.1 Types of motivation described by the self-determination theory. Image courtesy of the authors — 263
26.2 Montessori system's support for intrinsic motivation through the fulfillment of the three self-determination needs. Image courtesy of the authors — 264
V.1 A total of 148 countries in 2020 with Montessori schools. Courtesy of Association Montessori Internationale — 284

Figures

V.2 A student at Fruitful Orchard Montessori, Lagos, Nigeria, completes the Pink Tower Brown Stair extension, with some help from a teacher, while her classmates cheer her on. Photo courtesy of Junnifa Uzodike 285

28.1 Children's House in a popular building on via delle Rottole run by Umanitaria, Milan, 1913. Courtesy of Biblioteca dell'Opera Nazionale Montessori 292

29.1 Class photo from the sixth Montessori school, Amsterdam, 1938, by J. M. Bakels. Anne Frank was also a student at this school. Courtesy of the Jewish Museum, Amsterdam 298

30.1 Students at the Gatehouse school use the nave of the St. Bartholomew's church as a classroom. School founder and the rector's wife, Phyllis Wallbank, is in the back of the photo, 1951. Courtesy of Topfoto 305

30.2 Gatehouse Montessori classes are also held outside in the courtyard among the gravestones, 1951. Courtesy of Topfoto 306

31.1 Maria Montessori visits St. Otteran's school, Waterford, 1927. Courtesy of the Maria Montessori Archives, Amsterdam 310

32.1 Children in Ida Sjögren's Montessori school in Norrköping, Sweden, 1924. Courtesy of the Norrköping City Archives 316

32.2 Maria Montessori visits Sweden, 1950. Courtesy of the Stockholm City Museum 317

34.1 Two boys collaborating in Kaunas, Lithuania, 1931. Courtesy of the Lithuanian Museum of Educational History 328

35.1 Children working at a Montessori school in a Catholic convent in Calabar, Nigeria, 1927. Courtesy of the Maria Montessori Archives, photo section, Amsterdam 335

35.2 Guide Samwel Kuria works with students Junaid Mercier and Bashir Albretch at Moonflower Montessori school in the Gambia, 2021. Courtesy of Nnaceesay Marenah 336

35.3 Child working with materials at the Lynedoch Children's House, South Africa, 2021. Courtesy of the Indaba Institute 339

36.1 Sister Bertha Kira makes Montessori materials, 2021. Courtesy of Sister Christina Nakey 344

37.1 Students at Corner of Hope Montessori. Courtesy of Fay Hendriksen 350

37.2 A teacher makes Montessori materials at St. Ann's Montessori Teacher Training College in Nakuru, Kenya. Courtesy of Fay Hendriksen 351

38.1 A Corner of Hope Montessori classroom setup in a tent, Kenya. Courtesy of Fay Hendriksen 357

39.1 A child works on Arabic vowel letters and matches the words with the objects in a Montessori classroom, Saudi Arabia. Photo courtesy of Sara Aljindan 362

40.1 Children at the Women's Indian Association Montessori School work outside in the open-air classroom under the banyan trees, Chennai, 1928. Courtesy of the Maria Montessori Archives, Amsterdam 366

41.1	A preschool child in Vietnam peels a carrot as a Practical Life exercise. Courtesy of Vietnam AMI Montessori Initiative (VAMI) and Nebula Children's Home, Vietnam	374
43.1	Language activity in the early 1980s at the Fukakusa Children's House in Kyoto. Courtesy of Minako Negishi	383
43.2	Children playing in the bamboo grown at the Fukakusa Children's House in Kyoto. Courtesy of Minako Negishi	384
44.1	Children working independently at Blackfriars Practising School, 1914, New South Wales, Australia. Courtesy of the State Library of New South Wales	388
44.2	Growth of Australian Montessori Schools and Centers 1976–2021. Source: Cleverley 1978; Independent Schools Australia 2011 & 2021; ACECQA. Image courtesy of the author	390
45.1	Child in the Piruvik Preschool doing work learning Inuktitut. Courtesy of Tessa Lochhead, Piruvik Preschool	396
46.1	Children working at Nancy McCormick Rambusch's Whitby school, Greenwich, Connecticut, ca. 1959. Courtesy of the American Montessori Society Records, Archives & Special Collections, University of Connecticut Library	400
47.1	An assistant teacher with a student in Vieques. Courtesy of the Instituto Nueva Escuela	407
47.2	Teachers from schools across Puerto Rico demonstrate their support for public Montessori education in front of the Capitol, 2020. Courtesy of Instituto Nueva Escuela	408
48.1	Domingo Alba, the first AMI-trained elementary guide in Mexico, working with some of his students, 1980s. Courtesy of Montessori de Chihuahua	412
48.2	A student works with Math materials at Montessori de la Ciudad de México, date unknown. Courtesy of Montessori de la Ciudad de México	412
49.1	Rural Montessori school in Muquiyauyo, Peru, ca. 1948. Photo courtesy of the Gabriela Mistral Legacy Writer's Archive, National Library of Chile	417
51.1	Children reached by Montessori education in Argentina in 2020 (N = 2654). Image courtesy of Fundación Argentina María Montessori (FAMM)	432
52.1	Children in Sri Lanka work in a Montessori classroom, date unknown. Courtesy of the Maria Montessori Archives, photo section, Amsterdam	438
59.1	Tulalip children work with Montessori letters at the Tulalip boarding school, ca. 1919. From *the Indian School Journal*, 1904–1926, National Archives ID 2745572. Retrieved from the National Archives Catalog, Department of the Interior, Office of Indian Affairs	518
61.1	A senior with dementia works with the Montessori Binomial cube. Ryerson Clark, 2015. Courtesy of Leica Photo	538
62.1	Beekeeping in a Montessori Adolescent Farming Community courtesy of Good Shepherd Montessori School, South Bend, Indiana. Courtesy of Good Shepherd Montessori School	550

Foreword

Yong Zhao

How students are viewed in the education process defines two different paradigms. One paradigm views students as passive recipients of predetermined knowledge and skills. The other views them as agentic, autonomous, and natural learners with their own passions and interests. The former paradigm has dominated the majority of schools in the world despite decades of efforts to change it. The latter has survived but never achieved dominant status in mainstream schools, despite multiple efforts to promote it.

The past few decades have witnessed dramatic growth in the paradigm that treats students as agentic, autonomous, and natural learners for a number of reasons. First, the traditional, mainstream paradigm that delivers one-size-fits-all education has proven to not serve all children well and fails too many students. Second, the advancement of technology has drastically altered society and thus demands students to be equipped with new skills and knowledge. Third, our understanding of students has improved dramatically and today the idea that students are agentic, autonomous, and natural learners is more accepted.

In practice, we are witnessing increasing innovation following the paradigm focused on student-driven education. Personalization of learning has already become an aspiration for many schools (Zhao 2018). Creativity and entrepreneurial thinking have been generally accepted as necessary educational outcomes for all students (Zhao 2012; Zhao et al. 2019). Schools have begun to seriously consider students' social and emotional health and to work on teaching students to become owners of their learning as self-determined learners (Wehmeyer and Zhao 2020).

The COVID-19 pandemic has furthered the movement. It has significantly disrupted traditional education; forced teachers, students, and parents to work in new models of learning; created globally accessible educational opportunities; and highlighted the importance and potential of student-directed education. As the pandemic comes to an end, however, these changes may be lost, and schools may return to what they were before.

At this important moment in human history, we are facing two possibilities in education. One is to return to the past, and the other is to speed up the transformation. The publication of a handbook about Montessori education is certainly a tremendous effort to speed up the transformation.

The pedagogy and philosophy of Maria Montessori are not new. In fact, they appeared over 100 years ago. But the core values of Montessori education represent the guiding principles of the paradigm of education we desire: students as agentic, autonomous, and natural learners. The pedagogy of Montessori education puts these principles in practice by making students owners of their learning. Moreover, over the past 100 years, Montessori education has continued and even expanded globally, with followers around the world.

Research and scholarship on Montessori education have grown significantly in recent years as well, which makes *The Handbook of Montessori Education* possible. Edited by Drs. Angela K. Murray, Eva-Maria Tebano Ahlquist, Maria K. McKenna, and Mira Debs, this book is an amazing contribution. They have gathered contributions from a global network of scholars and practitioners in twenty-five countries. The contributions cover comprehensively the life and work of Montessori, the pedagogy of Montessori education, the adoption and spread of Montessori education, and the scientific connections of Montessori philosophy. Most important, while they faithfully present Montessori education, they are critical examiners. This book is thus much more than a promotion of Montessori education. It is a reconnection with education's past with the future of educational transformation.

Bio

Yong Zhao is a foundation distinguished professor in the School of Education at the University of Kansas and a professor of Educational Leadership at the Melbourne Graduate School of Education in Australia. He previously served as the presidential chair, associate dean, and director of the Institute for Global and Online Education in the College of Education, University of Oregon, where he was also a professor in the Department of Educational Measurement, Policy, and Leadership. Prior to his work in Oregon, Yong Zhao was university distinguished professor at the College of Education, Michigan State University, where he also served as the founding director of the Center for Teaching and Technology, executive director of the Confucius Institute, and executive director of the US-China Center for Research on Educational Excellence. He is an elected member of the National Academy of Education and a fellow of the International Academy of Education.

References

Wehmeyer, Michael, and Yong Zhao. 2020. *Teaching Students to Become Self-Determined Learners*. Alexandria, VA: ASCD.
Zhao, Yong. 2012. *World Class Learners: Educating Creative and Entrepreneurial Students*. Thousand Oaks, CA: Corwin.
Zhao, Yong. 2018. *Reach for Greatness: Personalizable Education for All Children*. Thousand Oaks, CA: Corwin.
Zhao, Yong, and Trina E. Emler, Anthony Snethen, and Danquig Yin. 2019. *An Education Crisis Is a Terrible Thing to Waste: How Radical Changes Can Spark Student Excitement and Success*. New York: Teachers College Press.

Preface

Mira Debs, Angela K. Murray, Eva Maria Tebano Ahlquist, and Maria K. McKenna

> From the extreme dangers of our days, the vision is born of the necessity that [humans] should with their conscious will and with their sentiment, seek to find the "adaptation" to present conditions, thus forming one universal harmonious society. This is the aspiration to which today humanity clings, urged by the supreme appeal of seeking its own salvation. But how to attain this if not through a "direct preparation" of the new generation, i.e., through education?
> —*Maria Montessori, The Child, Society and the World, 1989, 110*

With the multitude of crises facing education worldwide, this volume seeks to address the changing political, social, and technological terrain through the lens of one approach, Montessori education.[1] It is a compilation of works that traces Montessori education from its historical roots to current scholarship and contemporary issues of culture, social justice, and environmentalism. We hope it will inspire new research, expand practice, and serve a diverse and global population of children and families.

We begin by acknowledging the volatility of a world grappling with a global pandemic and ongoing geopolitical challenges. Over the past century, Montessori education has come to the forefront as a solution to education-based challenges as well as a response to a world in great need of peacemakers and innovators. From the outset, Maria Montessori wished for her model of education to be widely used and understood. Within a decade of the opening of her first Casa dei Bambini (Children's House) in Rome in 1907, her pedagogical tools and philosophy had reached across the globe. Historically, Montessori organizations have estimated upward of 22,000 Montessori schools globally (Whitescarver and Cossentino 2008). Today, one Montessori organization, the Association Montessori Internationale (AMI) documents Montessori schools in 148 countries, and a recent global census estimates nearly 15,800 Montessori schools around the world (Debs et al. 2022). The number of Montessori schools globally underscores the relevance of the approach as we continue to grapple with educational access and the fundamental purposes of schooling.

Montessori education is, in part, a response to twentieth-century efforts to model the classroom on factories delivering learning in efficient units to "raw materials (children)" (Cubberley 1916, 338). In contrast to this, a central tenet of Maria Montessori's work was that all children have the capacity to be independent and to contribute meaningfully to their communities—a view she shared with other contemporary education reformers around the world. Her first work was with children with cognitive delays; she then worked with children from low-income families. Building off many influences in the scientific, anthropological, and educational communities,

Montessori created classroom environments outfitted with inviting materials that could support children working on their own and with peers of multiple ages over an open-ended period (Tebano Ahlquist 2012). Simultaneously, she developed a system of teacher training that envisioned a radically different kind of teacher, one whose job was not to direct at the front of the classroom, but instead to be an observing guide who partnered with the child to create a learning environment and a series of learning repertoires that cultivated their unique development. For a variety of reasons, Montessori created an infrastructure to develop this training largely separate from traditional, university-based teacher training schools, while working to create a permanent university training program of her own.

Maria Montessori's pedagogy, as explained through her writings and lectures, is based on her scientific training, using systematic observation and careful documentation of children's behaviors, dispositions, and preferences in the educational environments she created. Yet despite the integrity of her work and the global spread of the Montessori method throughout much of the twentieth century, it is often disregarded or mentioned only in passing in traditional teacher training and in psychology, developmental theory, and educational philosophy courses. We further explore the reasons for this in Part V ("Global Reach of Montessori"). But it should be noted that even in her own time, Montessori's ideas were considered by many to be radical and controversial. She was simultaneously criticized for being *too liberal* by those who thought she gave children too much freedom and *too structured* by some of the other progressive or "new" educators, with the insistence that her learning materials be used in specifically prescribed ways and that she maintained direct oversight of teacher training. Other criticisms were that introducing reading, writing, and counting at preschool age was too early and that the focus on children working with real-life tasks limited their imaginative play.

It is also possible that Montessori's keen sense of interdisciplinary thinking, her writing that straddled academic, personal, and religious perspectives, and her ideas on the interconnectedness of curricula also kept her from holding the attention of scholars; and that being a woman and an avowed feminist in a sea of male philosophers, education researchers, and psychologists led her ideas to be marginalized, disregarded, or in some instances, co-opted without attribution (Quarfood 2017). In addition, she may have been ahead of her time in thinking of education as a means not only to becoming literate and economically self-sufficient but to cultivating a more peaceful and sustainable way of communal living. And as other authors in this handbook develop further, Montessori may also have contributed to her own isolation by being proprietary with her ideas and by frequently falling out with some of her most devoted students, and by developing educational terminology that could be inaccessible to others.

This handbook also documents how the most recent wave of interest in Montessori inspired efforts to create Montessori organizations in nations across the globe, new Montessori schools and networks, new training programs, and academic offerings focusing on Montessori education and principles. Along with this most recent wave are accompanying debates, with long historical antecedents, around the commercialization and marketing of Montessori's name, without a deeper engagement with the pedagogy. Essential critiques dealt with in the handbook include race, gender, language, ability, and economic-/colonial-based challenges of Montessori education that were not previously considered in as much detail in the academic literature.

Preface

Compiling the Handbook

Having worked for a number of years to raise the academic profile of Montessori research, in 2019, while at an academic conference, we were approached by a Bloomsbury Publishing editor about compiling a handbook. We had created and participated in several networks of American and European Montessori researchers including Montessori Europe and the Montessori Research Working Group; founded two Montessori academic journals and an academic center for Montessori research; written dissertations, articles, and books about Montessori; trained at various levels as Montessori educators, taught about Montessori education at the university level, and established a Montessori Special Interest group at the American Educational Research Association, the largest educational research organization in the world. Creating a handbook was an exciting next step to building an international community of Montessori researchers and academics across an array of disciplines, including education, psychology, sociology, philosophy, history, and ethnic studies, through sharing diverse perspectives and expertise. We see the growing interest in education policy in support of learner-centered education as an ideal time to engage policymakers and educational leaders by providing a comprehensive overview of Montessori's writings, philosophy, pedagogy, and implementation.

The handbook, as we conceived it, is not a manual or definitive guide to Montessori pedagogy but rather, an accessible resource on the theories involved in Montessori education, and a representation of the extensive history, impact, and relevance of the global, pedagogical phenomenon of Montessori education. We hoped to provide an opportunity for readers to delve deeply into Montessori education and inspire additional scholarship. As white, female editors from the United States and Europe, we are aware of our own positionality, and worked with intention to create a volume of diverse, global voices. This handbook has input from over 100 contributors, including academic researchers, trained Montessori practitioners, and Montessori leaders from a wide range of international Montessori organizations. We contacted authors through our own networks and through recommendations of our colleagues, and with the assistance of Montessori organizations with more than twenty-five affiliates worldwide. Some of the handbook authors have Montessori training and represent a number of global Montessori affiliations while others do not. The authors reflect the religious, racial, ethnic, gender, and socioeconomic diversity of Montessori around the globe. To the extent possible, we sought out authors and collaborators who could represent the communities they were writing about from a first-person perspective. Each chapter was edited by at least two co-editors of the handbook and often commented on by additional experts in the field.

In assembling this academic volume, it was important that Montessori education be represented in a broad and critical context. In the face of external criticism, Montessori educators have historically developed a fiercely protective and affirming culture around Montessori education, as well as a rich literature for fellow educators documenting Montessori's life, pedagogy, and the dissemination of her work. To outsiders, this culture can appear both worshipful and uncritical. In academia, by contrast, criticism and addressing limitations are considered hallmarks of objective research. Developing a robust field of Montessori research requires balancing these competing impulses to document, affirm, *and* critique. This handbook reflects these competing impulses. For example, some chapters affirm Montessori education's connection to cognitive science and child development while others point out limitations in the method's reach, the harmful ways educators have applied Montessori education in particular countries and communities, and the ways Montessori education might be changed to better serve contemporary understandings of gender, race, and ethnicity.

Regardless of attempts to be comprehensive in this volume, gaps are inevitable, given the reach of Montessori education worldwide, its history of grassroots diffusion, and the resulting complex patchwork of networks. We humbly acknowledge this fact and take full responsibility for the work presented. At the same time, our quest for the most comprehensive volume possible was limited by space and network constraints, especially in some of our global chapters. We have also been limited by consideration of sensitive political and cultural circumstances of some contributors. However, we see these gaps as opportunities to spur more research and publications about Montessori education.

Handbook Structure

Part I: The Foundations and Evolution of Montessori Education

The first part introduces fundamental aspects of Montessori pedagogy, philosophy, and education. We begin with a conversation around the life of Maria Montessori and important historical, political, and social contexts of her upbringing and adulthood. From there we consider the philosophical and spiritual contexts of her work over time. Our hope is that this part provides a brief primer to understanding Montessori's work as it became a global phenomenon. It forms the foundation for the following five parts of the handbook.

Part II: Key Writings of Maria Montessori

Montessori's writings, many based on her lectures and training, are central to her pedagogy. This part presents key works in chronological order alongside critical discussions, reinterpretations, and perspectives on the contemporary significance of these texts. The part also addresses some of the challenges in accessing Montessori's writings due to translation issues, as her writing style can come across as flowery, antiquated, and missing context. In addition, Part II addresses issues of authorship around Montessori's works: some books were written directly by Montessori; others are based on notes from her lectures and are written by people other than Montessori herself.

Part III: Montessori Pedagogy across the Lifespan

Montessori education encompasses philosophical aspects and theories such as developmental psychology, and cognitive, social, and didactic perspectives. Part III aims to link theory and practice and point out the continuity on which her pedagogy is based through its adaptation to children's development. The first chapter in this part focuses on the role of the Montessori environment and how it relates to learning. Subsequent chapters offer rich depictions of the pedagogy's practical application from infancy through adolescence, along with a conversation about the role of adults in the Montessori context.

Part IV: The Science of Montessori Education

Montessori approached the development of her method as a scientific endeavor. Part IV begins with a chapter exploring how Montessori's early insights predated many currently accepted ideas on educational psychology and the learning process. To contextualize a discussion of current Montessori research, the second chapter outlines the expected inputs, processes, and outputs of the Montessori method. The third chapter traces efforts to assess implementation fidelity, and how it matters for research and implementation, especially given commercial pressures and resource restrictions around the world. The remaining chapters in Part IV connect Montessori education to current research in the areas of neuroscience, cognitive psychology, assessment, and executive function as well as motivation and optimal learning experience.

Part V: Global Montessori Education

The question of how Montessori education has expanded globally while staying separate from mainstream education is addressed in chapters focusing on the globalization of Montessori. Part V follows with brief profiles of twenty-five countries and regions across the globe and identifies key themes in the diffusion, expansion, and contraction of Montessori education in those locales, both historically and currently.

Part VI: Contemporary Considerations Regarding Montessori Education

The final part of the handbook aims to inform readers about more recent research and practices within, and around, Montessori communities and Montessori education, with a focus on equity, inclusivity, accessibility, and ecological preservation. Chapters examine linguistic, cultural, and ethnic and racial diversity, particularly as applied to Montessori education in the United States. Additional inquiries into cognitive diversity, gender, technology in Montessori education and Montessori practices with dementia patients are also addressed. Finally, Montessori practices are framed in the context of eco-literacy, sustainability, and climate change.

A Note on Terms in the Handbook about Race, Ethnicity, Gender, and Disability

The terms we use to talk about various identities including race, ethnicity, gender, and disability within the handbook are constantly changing. Our aim is to use language to represent peoples' identities with respect and thoughtfulness. In 2023, authors in this handbook refer to specific racial and ethnic identities, for example Black, Latinx (the *x* reflects not putting people into male and female categories), and Asian Canadian rather than broader categories like "minority." Authors use "Indigenous" to refer to people native to a territory whose status as members of sovereign nations often distinguishes them from other communities of color. Authors use gender-neutral language like children or youth instead of boy or girl. Authors also use identity-first language to talk about disability (for example autistic person instead of person with autism) to reflect the fact that disability, like many other identities, is a "natural, innate aspect of human variation" (Josephine Steuer-Ingall, pers. comm.). The usage of "disability" and "disabled" instead of "special needs" and "exceptionalities" also represents the fact that these terms are linked to legal rights and have been reclaimed by the disability advocacy community.

Though this language may be new to some readers, we hope that it reflects the communities we write about with respect and nuance. We welcome conversations about these terms and encourage ongoing dialogue within the research community to continue to be respectful and inclusive with our work.

About the Cover

In searching for an image for the cover of this handbook, we grappled with many possibilities before finding one that we felt represented the diverse ages, ethnicities, countries, and applications of Montessori's ideas in the world and in research. Hilma af Klint (1862–1944), a pioneering Swedish modernist painter, was a contemporary of Maria Montessori, with overlapping interests in theosophy and spirituality. Montessori and af Klint were also similarly avant-garde women with interests in the male-dominated fields of science, mathematics, and the natural world. Both abandoned safe career paths for visionary endeavors. To us, af Klint's 1907 painting, *Group IV, The Ten Largest, No. 3, Youth*, evokes the geometric precision and beauty of Montessori materials and Montessori's holistic ideas.

Note

1. In this handbook, we refer to either Montessori education, the Montessori model, or Montessori pedagogy. The title of Montessori's first book, *Il metodo della pedagogia scientifica applicato all'educazione infantile nelle case dei bambini*, was translated into English as *The Montessori Method*. Montessori later criticized this for not highlighting the responsiveness of her philosophy to the needs of children and the ongoing development of the educator. As Montessori explained in *The Discovery of the Child*, she understood her work to be "based on having observed the development of psychological phenomena which had hitherto been unknown and unobserved" rather than a static, unchanging "method of education" (1967, 346).

References

Association Montessori Internationale. 2006. "Montessori Census." *Montessori Centenary*. Accessed August 19, 2021. http://montessoricentenary.org/.
Association Montessori Internationale. 2020. "Montessori Schools in 2020." Annual General Meeting.
Cubberley, Ellwood. 1916. *Public Schools Administration*. New York: Houghton Mifflin.

Debs, Mira, Jaap de Brouwer, Angela K. Murray, Lynne Lawrence, Megan Tyne, and Candice von der Wehl. 2022. "Global Diffusion of Montessori Schools: A Report From the 2022 Global Montessori Census." *Journal of Montessori Research* 8 (2): 1–15. https://doi.org/10.17161/jomr.v8i2.18675.

Montessori, Maria. 1967. *The Discovery of the Child*. Translated by M. Joseph Costelloe. Notre Dame, IN: Fides.

Montessori, Maria. 1989. *The Child, Society and the World: Unpublished Speeches and Writings*. Oxford: Clio.

Quarfood, Christine. 2017. Montessoris pedagogiska imperium: Kulturkritik och politik i *mellankrigstidens Montessorirörelse*. Göteborg: Daidalos.

Quarfood, Christine. 2022. *The Montessori Movement in Interwar Europe: New Perspectives*. Cham, Switzerland: Palgrave Macmillan.

Tebano Ahlquist, Eva-Maria. 2012. *Skolans Levda Rum och Lärandets Villkor*. PhD diss., Stockholm University.

Whitescarver, Keith, and Jacqueline Cossentino. 2008. "Montessori and the Mainstream: A Century of Reform on the Margins." *Teachers College Record* 110 (12): 2571–600.

Acknowledgments

In completing an edited volume on Montessori education, we were fortunate for the support of so many individuals and institutions who helped bring this project to fruition. Working with so many transnational collaborators, over 100 in total, during the COVID-19 pandemic and a time of limited travel, helped remind us of our global connectedness and brought a great deal of joy to the work. We are especially grateful for our authors' expertise, commitment to the project, patience, and good humor during this process.

The Montessori Research Working Group organized by the KU Center for Montessori Research was an early site for mapping out what this project would look like and finding chapter authors. We are grateful for the vision of the working group participants.

We gratefully acknowledge funding and material support from the Department of Education, Stockholm University, the Educational Research in Citizenship Competences (ERiCC), Stockholm University, the Frederick W. Hilles Publication Fund of Yale University, the Yale Education Studies Program and its Summer Experience funding supported by the Endeavor Foundation, the Nanovic Institute for European Studies at the University of Notre Dame, the University of Notre Dame Graduate School's Summer Research Opportunities Program, the Center for Montessori Research in the Achievement and Assessment Institute at the University of Kansas, and Wend Collective. These various entities helped us to hire research assistants, translators, and copyeditors; complete indexing; and acquire photo permissions for several historical photos along with other support.

Summer undergraduate research associates Saket Malhotra, Amelia J. Murray, Lesli Romero, and Tia R. Williams conducted foundational research and co-authored several of the global chapters.

Mira Debs assumed the role of photo editor of the handbook and is grateful for the support of Fay Hendriksen, Sid Mohandas, Joel Parham, Joke Verheul, and research assistant Josephine Steuer-Ingall for obtaining permission to reproduce so many historical and contemporary Montessori photos.

Harald Ludwig served as a reader on several chapters. Darwin Michener-Rutledge, Ariel Rothman, and Eva-Maria Tebano Ahlquist provided translations. Laurie Costlow, Jan Feeney, Karen Hellekson, Michael Knight, Marcy Krever, Isabelle Lahaie, Lisa Stephen, Josephine Steuer-Ingall, and Joke Verheul provided copyediting, language editing, and fact-checking assistance.

Dr. Iris Müller-Westermann, Museichef (Museum Director) of the Moderna Museet Malmö, shared valuable insights with us about the artist Hilma af Klimt whose work is featured on the cover of this volume.

We thank our families for their support during this enormous endeavor. Finally, we recognize and honor all of the educators and children around the world who have shown persistence and fortitude during the enormous educational challenges of the last several pandemic years. This book honors your work.

PART I

Foundations and Evolution of Montessori Education

Introduction: Foundations and Evolution of Montessori Education

Maria K. McKenna

Part I provides an overview to Maria Montessori's life and her intellectual ideas in the context of her contemporaries. While this part could easily be its own handbook, in making difficult choices about what to include, we expanded beyond Montessori as an educator toward a broader history of Montessori honoring her contributions as a philosopher, feminist, and political agent. The four chapters of Part I expand Montessori's intellectual and practical legacies beyond education alone by emphasizing the relationship of her work to contemporaries, philosophy, feminist paradigms, spiritual influences, and the varied political narratives around Montessori.

Biographies of Montessori and histories of her pedagogy are found in languages around the globe written by scholars from a wide variety of disciplines. Much of this work focuses, somewhat narrowly, on straightforward chronological narratives. Fewer scholarly sources exist focusing on her work related to philosophy and peace studies. Importantly, in recent years, European scholars including those writing in Italian, Swedish, and German have led a thoughtful reassessment of Montessori's life and work. This is especially true of the countless contributions from those scholars and pedagogues working within Italian language literature and history that often get overlooked in the English-speaking world. In a review of Erica Moretti's new book, *The Best Weapon for Peace*, Mira Debs writes, "[There is a] dynamism of research about Montessori's life and legacy happening in non-English sources. Moretti's book connecting this scholarship to English-language readers is a bridge. In recent years, European scholars including Valeria Babini, Luisa Lama, Letterio Todaro, and Christine Quarfood have been leading an academic reassessment in book-length monographs of Maria Montessori's life and intellectual legacy" (Debs 2022). These contributions add a great deal to the provenance of Montessori's ideas within the unfolding Italian and European social and intellectual history of the time. She was a child of both the Enlightenment and the Risorgimento and buffeted by late-nineteenth-century and early-twentieth-century events just as were her contemporaries such as Gramsci, Croce, and Gentile (Mira Debs, pers. comm.). The fact she, and her work, survived at all, unlike many, even if some events in her lifetime are a bit dubious is a testament to her capacity to navigate very difficult historical contexts. Moreover, while Montessori was a prolific writer of lectures and pedagogical training sessions she was not particularly adept at philosophically oriented writing though contemporary reports note that she was a very effective orator of philosophical and feminist thinking.

As editors, we paid particular attention to less prominent facets of Montessori's life. We begin with a chapter highlighting the significance of the historical and social contexts of her upbringing and adulthood. From there we move on to think about the philosophical, political, and spiritual contexts of her work over time. Our hope is that Part I of the handbook provides a brief primer to Montessori's work as it becomes a global phenomenon. It forms the foundation for the remaining five Parts of the handbook. Finally, we would be remiss if we didn't uplift the many Montessori scholars, historians, and philosophers cited within the chapters of Part I and throughout the handbook. These authors and their work play a significant role in the longevity of the Montessori pedagogy and philosophy. They were pioneering scholars when Montessori work was neither popular nor as well known as it is today. We encourage our readers to explore the extant body of work, to read the chapters herewith, and also to continue to envision new ways of seeing and exploring Montessori's life, connections, and the varied contexts surrounding her work and legacy.

Reference

Debs, Mira Catherine. 2022. "BOOK REVIEW The Best Weapon for Peace: Maria Montessori, Education and Children's Rights." *Journal of Montessori Research* 8 (1). https://doi.org/10.17161/jomr.v8i1.17113.

Chapter 1
Maria Montessori: Life and Historical Context

Christine Quarfood

The Italian doctor Maria Montessori (1870–1952) was a remarkable woman, a scientifically minded leader of an international reform movement. In a time of deep social and political unrest, Montessori's vision of the liberated child mobilized hopes for a brighter future. Concerned about children's place in society and the failures of an outmoded school system, she proposed new solutions to age-old problems of education. Montessori's radically innovative field-tested method, with its prepared environment and interactive materials, shifted focus from the teacher to the learner, thus challenging established notions of childhood and schooling. As a public intellectual in interwar Europe, Montessori delivered a cultural critique, which drew inspiration from many sources: feminism, pacifism, evolutionary biology, medical hygienism and psycho-dynamics. During her adventurous life journey, she lectured and held teacher training courses all over Europe and also in America and India, finding allies in diverse cultural milieus and ideological quarters.

Montessori's Early Medical Career

Maria Montessori was born in Italy on August 31, 1870, in the small town of Chiaravalle, near Ancona. She was the only child of civil servant Alessandro Montessori (1832–1915) and Renilde Montessori, born Stoppani (1840–1912), both fervent supporters of the new Italian nation-state. A few weeks after Montessori's birth, the unification of Italy was completed with the annexation of the Papal territory. Alessandro, who in his youth had fought against the Austrians, worked as accountant for the state-run tobacco industry. After some years of moving from region to region inspecting factories, Alessandro in 1875 obtained a post in the capital, at the Ministry of Finance (Kramer 1988).

The Italy in which Montessori grew up was newly politically unified, but sharply socially divided, with great tensions between state and church, the ruling elite and the common people, and the industrialized north and the poor agrarian south. Regional language barriers and widespread illiteracy did not facilitate integration. As statesman Massimo d'Azeglio put it in his memoirs, which were posthumously published in 1867, "Italy is made, but not the Italians." The ex-Minister of Public Education Ferdinando Martini reframed this phrase in 1896, saying, "We have made Italy. Now we must make Italians." The optimistic hope that it would be possible to create a new and superior kind of citizen was not only part of the Italian nation-building project, but typical for the general cultural climate in which Montessori's first impressions were formed (Hom 2013; Quarfood 2005).

Figure 1.1 Maria Montessori in Rome, 1914. Courtesy of the University of Wisconsin-Stevens Point Nelis R. Kampenga University Archives.

A new law in 1883 gave women access to technical secondary schools and made it possible for Montessori to study engineering. In 1890, further defying social conventions, she enrolled at La Sapienza (the University of Rome), opting for a medical career. At the time, only five Italian women had obtained a medical degree. Montessori's choice of profession was very likely socially motivated. In the fin de siècle Italian context, medicine and left-wing social liberalism went hand in hand. Several of the professors Montessori encountered at La Sapienza also pursued political careers, including Guido Baccelli, Angelo Celli, and Clodomiro Bonfigli (Babini 2000; Quarfood 2005).

The ethos of positivist human sciences and medicine, the physical and moral regeneration of the population, shaped Montessori's outlook on life during the formative years of her medical studies. To cure the ills of a nation savagely plagued by cholera, malaria, and pellagra, medical scientists like Angelo Celli mobilized experimental hygiene based on bacteriological research. Late-nineteenth-century preventive medicine also sought to combat social ills. Crime rates were alarmingly high in Italy, and scientists debated whether delinquency and antisocial behavior had its roots in environmental or hereditary factors (Quarfood 2005).

Inspired by concepts of mental hygiene, Montessori specialized in the field of neuropsychiatry. Her doctoral dissertation, which earned her a medical degree in 1896, brought new clinical material to the controversy regarding hallucinations. In accord with her supervisor, assistant professor Sante de Sanctis, Montessori argued for a psychological explanation of a special kind of hallucinations perceived by patients suffering from delusions of persecution. The patients she had observed experienced conflicting auditory and visual hallucinations, for instance, hearing threatening voices at the same time as more encouraging ones or having visions of devils and angels simultaneously. Overactivity of the associative capacity, rather than brain damage, was the most probable cause of such hallucinations, Montessori claimed (Montessori 1896; Quarfood 2005).

Alongside her scientific training, Montessori's outlook was also shaped by her commitment to the feminist cause. The first wave of feminism, with its demands for equal rights, reached Italy toward the turn of the century. Montessori became an eager protagonist, fiercely denouncing pseudo-scientific prejudices about female inferiority. As one of the Italian delegates at the 1896 International Women's Congress in Berlin, she described the predicament of Italian women workers, earning barely half the wages paid to men. In the name of justice, she motioned for "equal work, equal wages" (Montessori 1897, 212). Montessori's impassioned speech attracted the attention of the press, and in 1899 she represented Italy at the congress organized by the International Council of Women in London. She also took part in the campaign for women's suffrage, which gained momentum in 1904 in anticipation of the electoral reform planned by the Giolitti government. However, the results of that reform, presented in 1911, were disappointing. Only men gained universal suffrage, a severe blow to Italian feminism (Babini and Lama 2000; Quarfood 2005).

A much more successful campaign, backed by politicians and leading scientists, concerned the establishment of medical-pedagogical institutes for the rehabilitation of developmentally disabled children. The idea was to offer this disadvantaged group, which had previously been locked up in mental hospitals, a more professional care. Psychiatry professor Clodomiro Bonfigli had raised the issue in parliament in 1897. Montessori became a leading figure in the campaign that followed, in close cooperation with her colleague Giuseppe Montesano at the Roman psychiatric clinic. In lecture tours, articles, and at various conferences, she stressed the urgency of improving the quality of services offered to developmentally disabled children. School failures, asocial behavior, and delinquency were different manifestations of degenerative, hereditary deficiencies. Montessori and other scientists asserted that the constitutionally weak and disadvantaged could profit from corrective treatment, combining methods of sensory training and mental hygiene. As Montessori explained in an 1899 lecture, such treatments were given in medical-pedagogical institutes all over the world, and it was now time that Italians, "the proud protectors of posterity," should also "listen to the voice of the degenerate child" and "lead him to redemption and regeneration" (Babini and Lama 2000; Montessori 1899, 107; Quarfood 2005).

In 1900, Montessori and Montesano jointly opened an Orthophrenic School and teacher training center for mentally disabled children in Rome. The year before Montessori had visited the Bicêtre hospital in Paris, where the special education methods devised by Jean Itard (1774–1838) and Edouard Séguin (1812–1880) were further developed in a hygienistic direction by Désiré Magloire Bourneville (1840–1909), head of the Bicêtre department for mentally disabled children from 1879 onward. Central to Séguin's physiological method was a set of hands-on didactic tools, which, in a systematic and analytical way, stimulated the senses, thus strengthening cognitive capacity.

By the end of 1901, Montessori's collaboration with Montesano came to an end. Notably, their relationship had not been merely professional: they had a son together, born in 1898, who was hidden from the world and nursed in the countryside. Why they never married is not clear. Kramer believes that Montessori's mother Renilde thought marriage would have put an end to her daughter's career. According to Babini, Montessori's feminist politics may have informed her preference to remain unwed. When Montesano in 1901 married another woman, the situation proved untenable. Montessori left the Orthophrenic School (Babini and Lama 2000; Kramer 1988; Quarfood 2005).

Montessori subsequently decided to venture into the field of anthropology as applied to the school environment. With Giuseppe Sergi (1841–1936) as her mentor, she carried out research on school children, trying to establish connections between school performance, social status, and physiological factors such as craniometrical measures. Although an adherent of sociobiological Darwinism, Sergi's views on eugenics differed from those of Francis Galton; Sergi advocated not only repressive measures, but also a program of improvement through education. In 1904, Montessori earned the degree of *libera docenza* (private lecturer) in anthropology, qualifying her to teach the subject at the university level. From 1906 to 1910 she lectured in pedagogical anthropology at the recently created pedagogical department of the Sapienza University of Rome. She also lectured in hygiene and anthropology at the Regio Istituto Superiore di Magistero Femminile (Royal Higher Institute for Women Teachers), a teacher training college for women. As is obvious from Montessori's lectures, published in *Antropologia Pedagogica* (Pedagogical Anthropology) in 1910, her perspective as an anthropologist was firmly anchored in the paradigm of positivism. Her focus was on detecting anomalies, deviations from normal development. Like Sergi, she believed it was possible to counteract degenerative influences, social as well as biological, through rational methods of primary education strengthening cognitive capacity (Babini and Lama 2000; Quarfood 2005).

The Casa dei Bambini Experiment

In 1906, Montessori was invited to cooperate on a social housing project in the Roman slum district of San Lorenzo. Edoardo Talamo, manager of the real estate company Istituto Romano dei Beni Stabili (Roman Real Estate Association), intended to offer preschools to the projects' tenants as part of the housing facilities. On January 6, 1907, the first Casa dei Bambini (Children's House) opened at 58 Via dei Marsi. Given free rein to work out the educational program, Montessori initiated an experiment designed to answer questions of psychological as well as pedagogical relevance. On the one hand, she wanted the Children's House to be "an experimental field for the study of man" where children's normal tendencies, actions, and reactions could be observed (Montessori 1912, vii). This meant freedom of movement in an environment with child-sized furniture and with adult interference reduced to a minimum. On the other hand, freedom had to be combined with opportunities for self-development. To meet the educational needs of the preschool children, it was necessary to provide them with occasions for freely chosen work. But instead of just reproducing the standard curriculum of Froebelian inspiration, with its focus on fantasy play and group games with imaginative content, Montessori radically transformed preschool education (Foschi 2008; Quarfood 2005).

Particularly innovative, compared to traditional child-rearing methods, was the introduction of instruments and exercises that had previously only been used in the medical context of special education into the preschool context. Montessori's intention in transferring sensory education from the clinic to the nursery was to investigate the responses of ordinary children to a method that stimulated the cognitive development of children with learning difficulties. She wanted to test her hypothesis that "similar methods applied to normal children would develop or set free their personality in a marvelous and surprising way" (Montessori 1912, 33). During the first year of the Casa dei Bambini experiment, a vast variety of special educational tools were presented to the children, but only those awakening their spontaneous interest became part of the Montessori set of didactic materials. As Montessori also pointed out in the 1909 book that presented her method, *Il metodo della pedagogica scientifica applicato all'educazione infantile nelle Case dei bambini* (The Montessori Method: Scientific Pedagogy as Applied to Child Education in "The Children's Houses"), many modifications of the didactic materials once devised by Séguin had to be made during this process of experimentation (Montessori 1912).

As a result of her experiment, Montessori's whole worldview changed. Deeply impressed by the sustained attention and remarkable self-discipline of the Casa dei Bambini children, she questioned prevalent theories of child psychology, as well as outmoded pedagogical methods and stereotyped notions of kids as boisterous and messy. The sociobiological degeneration theory of Giuseppe Sergi and Herbert Spencer that she had previously embraced was now replaced by the concept of "biological liberty." This key concept was, as Montessori explained in *Il Metodo* (1909), inspired by the evolutionary theory of Hugo de Vries. In stressing the importance of internal genetic factors, de Vries had proved, Montessori claimed, that "environment is undoubtedly a *secondary* factor in the phenomenon of life: it can modify it in that it can help or hinder, but it can never *create*." From this followed that education could only support the creative life force by allowing children freedom to develop their innate potential. The ideal of normality remained paramount, but now in the context of furthering the normalization of the ordinary child, rather than applying corrective treatments to disabled children. Working diligently with the Montessori apparatus, children could develop their potential in an optimal way (Montessori 1912, 105–6; Quarfood 2005).

The Montessori Movement, 1911–1918

On the eve of the First World War, Montessori was quite well known around the globe. Her schools spread all over the world and Montessori societies were formed in the United States,

England, and Italy (see Part V: Global Montessori Education). Several factors contributed to the rapid internationalization. This was a time of accelerating modernization, with inventions like the telephone and automobile transforming everyday life almost overnight. Montessori's progressive, self-correcting educational tools enabling children to take command of their own learning process were hailed as yet another achievement of technical engineering. With this method, children at the preschool stage could acquire basic skills in counting, writing, and reading. Like other technical innovations, the method appeared to be applicable everywhere, regardless of cultural contexts. Montessori's scientific background was obviously an asset in the fierce competition with rival educational methods (Quarfood 2017).

Helpful in popularizing Montessori's message and establishing her image as "an educational wonder-worker" was, of course, the press. In America, the hype surrounding Montessori knew no bounds. *McClure's Magazine*'s Montessori promotion campaign, launched in 1911, led to the English translation of her book. The following year, *The Montessori Method* became a bestseller, and on tour in 1913, Montessori was greeted by the *New York Tribune* as "the most interesting woman in Europe" (Kramer 1988, 186–7). During the First World War, she returned several times to the United States, holding teacher training courses.

Figure 1.2 Maria Montessori leading a 1914 training course in Rome, reprinted in *Feminel: Illustrario Catalano*, July 26, 1914, 88: 3.

At the San Francisco Panama-Pacific Exposition, 1915, the live-model Montessori class exhibited behind a glass wall aroused great interest as one of the most popular attractions of the fair. However, this first wave of American enthusiasm for Montessori's ideas was a short-lived affair. Partly due to serious tensions between Montessori and the leaders of the Montessori Educational Association, the American Montessori movement collapsed after the war, not to be revived until the 1960s. Montessori also encountered competition from educational progressivists like John Dewey and William Heard Kilpatrick (1871–1965), who dominated the American public school scene. Montessori's reputation as a leading scientific educationalist suffered some damage due to the harsh critique delivered by Kilpatrick in 1914. He claimed that sensory training was based on an obsolete psychological theory and that Montessori's method was far too individualistic (Gutek and Gutek 2016, 2020; Kramer 1988; Quarfood 2017).

Just before the war, Montessori reunited with her son Mario, who had grown up in a foster home. In 1913, some months after her mother Renilde's death, she took charge of her son, who was publicly presented as her nephew. Mario M. Montessori (1898–1982) accompanied his mother to California in 1915, in all likelihood to avoid being drafted into the war. Italy had entered the First World War on the side of the Allied Powers in May that year. Mario followed his mother to Barcelona, where she held the Fifth International Montessori Course in 1916. A year later, in December of 1917, he married Montessori's American student Helen Christy in California. In 1918, Montessori moved to Barcelona, and the young couple joined her there. During the years that followed, Mario would become his mother's closest co-worker. Four children were born to Helen and Mario between 1919 and 1929, Marilena, Mario, Rolando, and Renilde (Cañigueral Viñals 2018; Kramer 1988).

For a few years Montessori cooperated with the Catalan government and representatives of the Catholic Church associated with the Barcelona orphanage La Maternidat (The Maternity). Montessori pioneer Anna Maria Maccheroni (1876–1965) had traveled to Barcelona in 1915 and founded the Escola Modelo Montessori (Montessori Model School). It was one of the first schools where Montessori's advanced method for the elementary school level was put into practice. An institute for teacher training and research in the Montessori method was also supported by the Catalan government. In 1916's *L'Autoeducazione nelle scuole elementari* (Auto-education in Elementary Schools), a book that the following year appeared in English as *The Advanced Montessori Method*, Montessori explained how self-education could be implemented in the elementary school without lowering school standards. Working with the advanced set of didactic materials, the schoolchildren studied grammar, reading, arithmetic, and geometry. Aesthetic subjects like drawing and music were also included in the school program. Montessori also experimented with religious instruction, preparing children for their first communion (Cañigueral Viñals 2018; Quarfood 2017).

European Interwar Montessorism

While Europe was almost torn apart in the protracted two-front war of 1914–1918, neutral Spain offered the budding Montessori movement a safe refuge. After the war, Montessori reconnected with Montessorians all over Europe, beginning with the British Montessori Society. Her 1919

London course met with enthusiastic response. Sheila Radice, assistant editor of *Times Educational Supplement*, published a series of interviews highlighting Montessori's importance as a leading cultural critic and intellectual. Radice's book *The New Children: Talks with Maria Montessori* presented Montessori education as a new philosophy of life (Radice 1920). In the press of the 1920s and 1930s, *Montessorism* was frequently used as a non-pejorative term by Montessorians and others to designate the wider worldview, social agenda, and spirit of Montessori education. In Britain, Montessorism was conceptualized as a liberal child-rearing method furthering individual independence, an alternative to the collectivistic school regime. "Individual work" became the catchphrase of the British Montessori debate (Brehony 1994; Quarfood 2017, 2021).

However, assuming control over a movement that for several years had developed freely was no easy task. Many British Montessorians believed that methodological pluralism must necessarily follow from Montessori's principle of freedom. Their Montessorism thus included educational ideas from a wide variety of sources. According to Montessori, it was the other way around: the liberation of the child could *only* be achieved through the correct application of her method. Eclecticism was doomed to fail. Whether the word "Montessori" should be considered a trademark or a broad label applicable to all those inspired by Montessori's writings was a subject of debate preceding the split of the British Montessori Society in 1921–1922 and remained a source of contention for years to come (Quarfood 2017, 2022).

With the eclectics finally outmaneuvered, the British Montessori Society was in 1923 granted permission to establish a Montessori Teacher Training College, which was first situated in Letchworth and then moved to London. Students dedicated the last term of their two years of study to Montessori's London course. At a time when the European Montessori movement was expanding in all directions, the regularly recurring London courses provided stability and secured fidelity to the method (Kramer 1988) (see Chapter 30: "Montessori Education in the UK").

Montessori's commitment to the fast-growing movement made her life almost nomadic. Four new Montessori societies emerged between 1917 and 1923, in the Netherlands, Denmark, Germany, and Austria, and Montessorism also had a stronghold in Switzerland. With all the traveling around, teaching courses, and giving lectures here and there, it was hardly surprising that Montessori lost control over the Barcelona school in 1921. Two years later, Primo de Rivera's dictatorship put an end to Catalan autonomy. For some years, Montessori, Mario, and his family lived alternately in Italy and England. In 1927, they finally settled down, returning to Barcelona where they rented a house at Calle Ganduxer 22 (Cañigueral Viñals 2018).

The transnational network of her movement allowed Montessori to gain access to a wide range of cultural milieus where different aspects of her educational program could be developed. In Spain, in cooperation with the Catholic Church, she began working out methods to facilitate children's understanding of church liturgy. In the Dutch context, where her method was applied in the higher school levels, she found scientists willing to cooperate in working out a curriculum suited to teenagers. In Austria, collaborating with psychoanalytically influenced educationalists, she developed guidelines for infant care.

Aiming higher than reform of teaching methods, the Montessori movement also had a social agenda, addressing questions about children's place in society and the generational gap. The movement gained momentum in the aftermath of the First World War, when there was growing dissatisfaction with authoritarian attitudes. So many young men had died in the trenches, and a vital component of Montessori's cultural critique focused on age-related power conflicts: the war between adults and children. Montessori had raised the issue of children's rights already in *L'Autoeducazione* (1916), describing children as a discriminated social class. She also took initiative to assist children traumatized by the war, suggesting a White Cross organization for this purpose. A similar organization was in fact created in 1920. Although not directly based on the plan sketched by Montessori, the Union international de sécours aux enfants (International Union of Care for Children), the UISE, worked in the same direction, and its work resulted in the Geneva Declaration of the Rights of the Child, adopted in 1924 (Moretti 2021; Quarfood 2017, 2022).

There was also a psycho-pedagogical dimension to Montessorism, articulated in *Das Kind in der Familie* (The Child in the Family), a series of lectures published in Vienna in 1923, as well as in *The Secret of Childhood* (1936). The subtitle of *The Call of Education*, the first international Montessori journal, published in Amsterdam in 1924–1925, was *Psycho-pedagogical Journal, International Organ of the Montessori Movement*. A cornerstone of Montessori's psycho-pedagogical doctrine was the concept of sensitive periods, a concept on which she elaborated on significantly in the mid-twenties. It was inspired by the Dutch biologist de Vries's theory about critical periods in the early development of organisms, the same source of inspiration, which in the 1940s and 1950s would guide Konrad Lorenz's experiments with goslings and John Bowlby's psychological attachment theory (Quarfood 2017).

Politicization of Italian Montessorism, 1924–1934

The impact of the Montessori movement on public opinion was partly due to its utopian message about new children in a new world, a message that responded to the hopes of many social, educational, and political groups. But the creed of Montessorism—that it was possible to regenerate society through educational means—lent itself to diverse ideological interpretations. During the turbulent interwar period, educational theories became increasingly mobilized for various political causes, from the left to the right. For a decade, between 1924 and 1934, the Italian fascist regime tried to install the Montessori method on a grand, national scale.

Montessori and Mario willingly cooperated with the regime. The Italian Montessori Society, reorganized as the Opera Nazionale Montessori (National Montessori Organization) in 1924, was from 1926 led by the right-wing neo-Hegelian philosopher Giovanni Gentile, with Mussolini as its honorary president. The years before the fascist takeover, the idealist Gentile school gradually came to reappraise Montessorism in line with their own cultural critique of positivism. Deeply rooted in the classical tradition of the humanities, with its emphasis on language, philosophy, and history, the Gentile school campaigned against the materialistic tendencies of positivist ideology, and its claims that the research method of the natural sciences—systematic factual observation and experimentation—should be applied in all fields of science, including pedagogy. *Autoeducazione*, the Italian term for self-guided education, was a key concept for the Gentilians as well as for the Montessorians. There were some similarities between Gentile's idealistic view of the process of becoming human and the spiritualist tenets of Montessori's cultural critique. As minister of education from 1922 to1924, Gentile included the Montessori primary school program as part of the major school reform he undertook (Quarfood 2017, 2022).

The Montessori-Mussolini alliance has been described as a marriage of convenience, where both partners, for pragmatic reasons, managed to overlook ideological differences. Montessori's international fame was of course prestigious for Mussolini, who could pose as the savior of the method, which for so long had been neglected in its homeland. With the patronage of Il Duce, new Montessori schools were opened in Italy, including, in 1928, a teacher training school in Rome, the Regia Scuola di Metodo Montessori (Royal Montessori Method School). Four Montessori journals were sponsored by the regime between 1927 and 1934, as well as two national teacher training courses offered in 1926–1927. The fifteenth and sixteenth international Montessori courses were held in Rome in 1930 and 1931. The grand finale of this problematic collaboration was the Fourth Montessori Congress, which took place in Rome in 1934 (Kramer 1988; Leenders 2001; Quarfood 2017, 2022).

But if the fascists supported Montessori, it was also because they realized the efficiency of her method as a means to combat illiteracy and to instill discipline at an early age. It was not a coincidence that the regime's interest in Montessorism increased in 1926, the year in which the fascist youth organization Opera Nazionale Balilla was launched. Although Italy by that time had developed into a totalitarian state, it was not yet a belligerent nation. Before the invasion of Ethiopia in 1935, it was still possible to misinterpret Mussolini's politics. Like many of their contemporaries, Montessori and her son Mario were impressed by the school reforms and social investments of the regime. In addition, the Lateran pact with the Catholic Church in 1929 gave the fascist regime a semblance of respectability. That year, Montessori and Mario consolidated the multifaceted Montessori movement with the creation of Association Montessori Internationale (AMI), hoping to make Italy the center of their movement. The headquarters of AMI moved from Rome to Berlin in 1932 and to Amsterdam in 1933 (Lama 2002; Mario M. Montessori 1952, 15; Quarfood 2017, 2022).

The turning point came in 1932, after Montessori's famous speech on Peace and Education at the disarmament conference in Geneva. The Swiss Montessori society was founded that year; Montessori refused to give in to fascist pressure and appointed peace activist Elisabeth Rotten to the post of vice president instead of the fascist Montessori pioneer Teresa Bontempi. She appointed child psychologist Jean Piaget president. Montessori had also announced that her next international teacher course, in 1933, would take place in republican Spain. All these factors might have contributed to the so-called Sorge Affair, when Montessori and her staff at the teacher training school in Rome came under surveillance by the fascist secret police. In what resembles a film noir, this affair led to increasing tension between the Montessorians and the fascist party, the latter suspecting Montessori of double-crossing them. In one of the spy reports she was nicknamed "Monterossi," probably as a hint about her red (*rosso*) left-wing political sympathies, alongside notes wishing for a "montessorism without Montessori." Montessori and Mario resigned from Opera Nazionale Montessori in 1933 and made their last appearance in fascist Italy during the 1934 Montessori Congress in Rome (Baumann 2007; Marazzi 2000; Quarfood 2017, 2022).

The Years in India, 1939–1946

The 1930s were hard times for the European Montessorians. In Nazi Germany the entire Montessori movement was banned in 1936. In Italy, now closely allied with Nazi Germany, Montessori schools were abolished the same year. The 1936–1939 civil war in Spain put an end to Spanish Montessorism. Montessori left Barcelona in all haste onboard a British battleship. With the annexation of Austria into Nazi Germany in 1938, Austrian Montessorians also had to go into exile. Exiled in the Netherlands, Montessori continued pleading for peace. At the 1937 sixth Montessori Congress in Copenhagen, she suggested the creation of a social party to defend the rights of children. The child was "the forgotten citizen" (Kramer 1988).

In 1938, Montessori received an invitation to lecture in India at the Theosophical Society's headquarter in Adyar (see Chapter 40: "Montessori Education in India"). Acquainted with both Mahatma Gandhi and Rabindranath Tagore, Montessori was well-aware of the growing Indian interest in her ideas, and gladly accepted the invitation. At the outbreak of World War II, Montessori and Mario left Europe, not to return until after the war in 1946. During their seven years' stay in India, about 1500 teachers were trained by Montessori. She closely cooperated with the directors of two art centers, who were striving to resurrect Indian traditional arts and folklore: Rukmini Devi Arundale in Adyar and Saraladevi Sarabhai in Ahmedabad. Numerous

Figure 1.3 Maria and Mario Montessori in India, 1940. Courtesy of the Maria Montessori Archives, Amsterdam

non-authorized Montessori groups had emerged in India between the establishment of the first Indian Montessori school in 1915 and Montessori's arrival in 1939. Notable among them was Tarabai Modak and Gijubhai Badheka's adaptation of the Montessori program with a particular emphasis on local languages, cultural traditions, and accessibility to poor and rural children (Kramer 1988; Moretti 2021; Trudeau 1984; Tschurenev 2021; Wilson 1987).

In India, Montessori's spiritual insights deepened. She developed ideas about cosmic education, reinterpreting theosophical concepts in an eco-pedagogical direction. Man's cosmic task was to continue the work of creation, taking care of the planet. Montessori also conducted observations of infants (Moretti 2021; Trudeau 1984). One of her major publications, *The Absorbent Mind* (1949), concerned the mysterious miracle of early childhood development. Montessori spent her last years in post-war Europe, reconstructing her movement. In 1949, 1950, and 1951, she was nominated for the Nobel Peace Prize. She worked closely with UNESCO in these last years. Montessori died on May 6, 1952, and was buried in the cemetery of Noordwijk, near the Hague on the Netherlands North Sea coast (Kramer 1988).

Posthumous Development of the Montessori Movement

In her will, Montessori appointed Mario as her successor, entrusting him to preserve her legacy and continue her life's work. She had for several decades worked in close collaboration with her son, who provided extensive support as the movement expanded. Mario handled all kinds of practicalities and administrative matters, and it was on his initiative that AMI was created in 1929. During their time in India, he became involved in teacher training, but also made important contributions to Montessori's plan for nature-study and cosmic education. Back in Europe and reunited with his four children, Mario, who was divorced from his first wife Helen, married Ada Pierson (1914–1988) in 1947. Their house at 161 Koninginneweg, Amsterdam, still functions today as the headquarters of AMI. For thirty years, Mario was the General Director of AMI, advocating a classic, unmodified Montessori approach. The organization furthered the diffusion of the Montessori movement, regulating and supervising affiliated Montessori societies, with the aim of safeguarding the integrity and coherence of Montessori's educational method (Kramer 1988).

A revival of Montessori education took place in the United States in the early 1960s (see Chapter 46: "Montessori in the United States"). Between 1958 and 1963, over 400 Montessori schools were established. Middle-class parents anxious to give their children the best possible education rediscovered the Montessori method as a more intellectually stimulating alternative to prevailing early childhood programs. The Cold War gave rise to increasing public concern about the decline of the American school system. With the Sputnik crisis of 1957, when Americans found themselves bypassed by the Russians in the technological space race, a paradigm shift occurred, promoting more scientific, skills-based educational approaches. The second wave of American Montessorism had as its leader Nancy McCormick Rambusch (1927–1994) who in 1954–1955 had completed the AMI teacher training course in London. In 1960, she founded the American Montessori Society (AMS), proposing a modernized version of the Montessori method modified to better suit the American cultural context (Povell 2010; Whitescarver and Cossentino 2008).

Tensions between AMS and AMI soon developed. The attempts to adapt the Montessori method to the American way of life clashed with AMI's more universalist and orthodox views. Mario Montessori feared that essential aspects of the method might be lost in translation. Central to the conflict was the issue of teacher training. John McDermott (1932–2018), a philosophy professor at the City University of New York, urged the Montessorians to update their training program to meet American professional standards so that it could be recognized by the state educational department and introduced into university-based schools of education. For instance, he argued, courses in developmental psychology and American educational history ought to be part of the curriculum. In 1962, the conflict escalated when AMS declined to certify the Washington teacher training course staffed by AMI due to its methodological orthodoxy. In 1963, AMS and AMI parted ways. A trademark dispute between AMS and AMI followed over exclusive rights to use the term "Montessori" for schools and teacher accreditation in the United States. The dispute was settled in 1967 by the US Patent and Trademark Office, which declared that Montessori only had a generic, descriptive significance and thus could be used freely by any organization (*AMS Inc. v. AMI* 1967; Povell 2010; Whitescarver and Cossentino 2008).

Consequently, the number of Montessori societies offering varying forms of teacher training multiplied, not only in the United States but globally. Although some efforts have been made in the 1990s to unite teachers from the most important Montessori organizations—for instance, International Association for Montessori Education (IAME) and its accreditation council Montessori Accreditation Council for Teacher Education (MACTE)—there is no longer a unified Montessori movement. However, the global diffusion of Montessori education is impressive. According to the 2020 AMI annual report, Montessori education, in one form or another, was present in 148 countries, and AMI teacher programs were offered in seventy-five training centers across thirty-three countries (*AMI Annual Report* 2020; Whitescarver and Cossentino 2008).

Conclusion: Montessori's Legacy

At least three aspects of Montessori's rich legacy are worthy of notice: the schools, the writings, and the movement. Although they are closely intertwined and complementary, it is still possible to distinguish them from each other. One can for instance focus on the practicality of her method—the very structured educational tools and school environment designed by Montessori. That this element of Montessori's educational program has stood the test of time is obvious from the international array of schools employing a Montessori approach today. But in order to truly understand the theory behind the method, one has to turn to Montessori's writings. Montessori's intellectual legacy adds another dimension to her life's work. She wanted to change the very way we conceptualize childhood. She had very definitive ideas about mind-body interaction, freedom, and discipline, work and play, war and peace, adults and children. The wider worldview, social agenda, and spirit of Montessori education—Montessorism—must be taken into account.

However, Montessorism did not develop in a vacuum. The historical context of Montessori's life and work, the many members of her movement, and the thinkers that inspired her ideas are of course factors of importance. Although Montessori had a solid training within the experimental sciences—medicine and anthropology—the quest she embarked upon when she decided to devote herself to the cause of children led her far away from the ivory tower of university life. As a freelance movement leader in direct contact with her supporting groups, her ideas had a significant impact on society during her lifetime, and many of her essays originated as lectures in her teacher training courses and at the conferences of her movement. Some of the contradictions and complexities of Montessorism can be explained against this background, including, for instance, her conviction that she had formulated the definitive, scientific method of child-rearing, which made her unwilling to accept any modifications. This attitude led to many schisms within the Montessori movement. Although she was very particular about attempts to modify her practical method, she was less clear-sighted when it came to ideological reinterpretations of Montessorism, as is obvious from her decade-long collaboration with the Italian fascist regime. One should keep in mind, however, how difficult it was to navigate the changing political landscape of interwar Europe. In the long run, it was the internationalism, humanism, and pacifism of Montessorism that secured the vitality of its legacy and its relevance for us today.

References

American Montessori Society Inc. v. Association Montessori Internationale. 1967. 155 U.S.P.Q., 591, 592.
Association Montessori Internationale. 2020. "AMI Annual Report." https://montessori-ami.org/news/2020-ami-annual-report.
Babini, Valeria. 2000. "Science, Feminism and Education: The Early Work of Maria Montessori." *History Workshop Journal* 49 (1): 45–67.
Babini, Valeria, and Luisa Lama. 2000. *Una Donna Nuova: Il Femminismo Scientifico di Maria Montessori*. Milan, Italy: Franco Angeli.
Baumann, Harold. 2007. *1907–2007—Hundert Jahre Montessori-Pädagogik. Eine Chronik der Montessori-Pädagogik in der Schweiz*. Bern, Switzerland: Haupt Verlag.
Brehony, Kevin. 1994. "Individual Work: Montessori and English Education Policy 1909–1934." Paper presented at the Annual Meeting of the American Education Research Association, April 4–8, New Orleans, LA.
Cañigureal Viñals, Dani. 2018. *The Story of Montessori in Barcelona: The Exceptional Story of Love and Affinity between Barcelona and Dr. Montessori*. Research paper for Montessori Elementary Training of Trainers Program.
Foschi, Renato. 2008. "Science and Culture around the Montessori's First Children Houses in Rome (1907–1915)." *Journal of the History of the Behavioral Sciences* 44 (3): 238–57.
Gutek, Gerald, and Patricia Gutek. 2016. *Bringing Montessori to America: S.S. McClure, Maria Montessori and the Campaign to Publicize Montessori Education*. Tuscaloosa, AL: University of Alabama Press.
Gutek, Gerald, and Patricia Gutek. 2020. *America's Early Montessorians: Anne George, Margaret Naumburg, Helen Parkhurst and Adelia Pyle*. Cham, Switzerland: Palgrave Macmillan.
Hom, Stephania Malia. 2013. "On the Origins of Making Italy: Massimo d'Azeglio and Fatta l'Italia Bisogna Fare gli Italiani." *Italian Culture* 13 (1): 1–16. https://doi.org/10.1179/0161462212Z.00000000012.
Kramer, Rita. 1988. *Maria Montessori: A Biography*. New York, NY: Addison Wesley Publishing Company.
Lama, Luisa. 2002. "Maria Montessori nell'Italia Fascista. Un Compromesso Fallito." *Il Risorgimento, Rivista di Storia del Risorgimento e di Storia contemporanea* 54 (2): 309–39.

Leenders, Hélène. 2001. *Der Fall Montessori. Die Geschichte einer Reformpädagogischen Erziehungskonzeption im Italienischen Faschismus*. Bad Heilbrunn, Germany: Verlag Julius Klinkhardt.

Marazzi, Giuliana. 2000. "Montessori e Mussolini: La Collaborazione e la Rottura." *Dimensioni e problemi della ricerca storica* 31 (1): 177–95.

Montessori, Maria. 1896. *Contributo Clinico allo Studio Delle Allucinazioni a Contenuto Antagonistico*. Thesis, Regia Università di Roma.

Montessori, Maria. 1897. "Über den Lohn der Arbeiterinnen." Presented at *Der Internationale Kongress für Frauenwerke und Frauenbestrebungen*, September 19–26. Reprinted in *Eine Sammlung der auf dem Kongress Gehaltenen Vorträge und Ansprachen* (ed. Rosalie Schoenflies), 202–12. Berlin, Germany: Hermann Walther.

Montessori, Maria. 1899. "Pei Fanciulli Infelici." *Rivista Politica Parlamentare* 2 (5): 102–7.

Montessori, Maria. 1912. *The Montessori Method*. New York, NY: Frederick A. Stokes Company.

Montessori, Mario M. 1952. "Che Cosa e l'A.M.I." *Vita dell'Infanzia* 1 (10–11): 14–15.

Moretti, Erica. 2021. *The Best Weapon for Peace. Maria Montessori, Education and Children's Rights*. Madison, WI: The University of Wisconsin Press.

Portielje, Bob. 1998. "Mario Montessori in his Own Right." *Communications: Association Montessori Internationale* 1: 4–11.

Povell, Phyllis. 2010. *Montessori Comes to America: The Leadership of Maria Montessori and Nancy McCormick Rambusch*. Lanham, MD: University Press of America.

Quarfood, Christine. 2005. *Positivism med Mänskligt Ansikte. Montessoripedagogikens Idéhistoriska Grunder*. Stockholm, Sweden: Östlings Bokförlag Symposion.

Quarfood, Christine. 2017. *Montessoris Pedagogiska Imperium. Kulturkritik och Politik i Mellankrigstidens Montessorirörelse*. Göteborg, Sweden: Daidalos.

Quarfood, Christine. 2021. "En Rörelse i Tiden. Montessori, Montessorismen och Montessorianerna." *Arr. Idéhistorisk tidsskrift* 23 (3–4): 135–45.

Radice, Sheila. 1920. *The New Children: Talks with Maria Montessori*. New York, NY: Frederick A. Stokes Company.

Trudeau, Christina. 1984. "A Study of the Development of the Educational Views of Dr. Maria Montessori Based on an Analysis of her Work and Lectures while in India, 1939–1946." PhD diss., University of Hawai'i at Manoa.

Tschurenev, Jana. 2021. "Montessori for All? Indian Experiments in 'Child Education,' 1920s–1970s." *Comparative Education* 57 (3): 1–19. https://doi.org/10.1080/03050068.2021.1888408.

Wilson, Carolie. 1987. "Montessori in India: A Study of the Application of Her Method in a Developing Country." PhD diss., University of Sydney.

Whitescarver, Keith, and Jacqueline Cossentino. 2008. "Montessori and the Mainstream: A Century of Reform on the Margins." *Teacher's College Record* 110 (12): 2571–600.

Chapter 2
The Scientific Feminism of Maria Montessori

Valeria P. Babini

It is a matter of historical record that Maria Montessori's first appearances on the public stage were political and that in the late nineteenth century she was active in both the national and the international arenas. Nonetheless, providing an account of her militant feminism requires that we do more than simply draw attention to her participation in the two international congresses held in Berlin in 1896 and London in 1899, where her role as speaker was followed with admiration by the press. We would, in fact, go so far as to assert that feminism, understood in the broadest sense as a concern with the condition of women in social, political, and even private political life, was the guiding thread of the intellectual and scientific formation of the young Montessori, furnishing also the inspiration for her crucial passage from medicine to pedagogy (Babini and Lama 2000; Babini 2000).

Even before obtaining her degree in medicine, awarded in Rome in 1896, Montessori was active in what was then known as practical and social feminism, alongside philanthropic noblewomen who were then taking an interest in the health and welfare of the capital city's women and children. Whereas women's emancipation (to use the term often employed in the Italian context) was concerned with the demand for rights, practical feminism represented a shift in the political strategy regarding the struggle for parity between man and woman. The strategy now involved demonstrating in the social sphere and in public health the capacity of women to assume roles of active management in, and through, the activities themselves. But practical feminism was also concerned with identifying the shortcomings in the social policy, which was of course male-dominated, deployed in the governance of the nation.

Within this current of Italian feminism, Maria Montessori developed her own particular slant, which we have dubbed "scientific feminism,"[1] a term drawn from a lecture given by the young doctor and serving to remind us of the role then attributed to science in the process by which women would be emancipated (Babini 2000). In this regard, it is worth noting that beginning in the 1890s, Montessori was actively involved in public health initiatives directed at women and infants and likewise in promoting the popularization of science in the female world, both with regard to the various kinds of knowledge involved and the intrinsically democratic nature of its procedures. Through her scientific feminism she hoped in particular to bring women closer to deductive scientific reasoning, a specific feature of science regarded as the most powerful weapon available for attaining complete autonomy of thought. Maria Montessori ascribed this emancipatory power of science to the democratic foundations of scientific reasoning but also recognized a fruitful tension between discipline (logical order) and creativity (freedom of thought), which may have furnished her with an important pedagogical insight, one that we encounter subsequently in the heart of her education method.

This occurred at a historic moment in the first few years of the twentieth century while the Italian public was debating female suffrage and politicians were divided between those who predicted that the votes of women would simply duplicate the votes of their husbands and others who feared clerical dominance through expanding suffrage. Instead, Maria Montessori invited women to draw closer to science in its guise as objective knowledge and therefore a genuine instrument of emancipation from the authority of the husband or the Catholic Church.

The strong tie between feminism and science likewise characterized Montessori's scientific publications from the outset, through which she promoted the Lega nazionale per l'educazione e la cura dei deficienti (National League for the Care and Education of Mentally Deficient Children) as a founding member in 1899. At that time, "degeneration," the supposed decline of a population of children born with disabilities, was at the center of European medical and scientific debate (Pick 1993). Indeed, in doctors' eyes, degeneration had assumed a real prominence, especially with regard to the health of any offspring. Maria Montessori sought to address this issue publicly, insisting on the role of preventive medicine and on the involvement of women in the battle to defeat degeneration. The lectures that she gave in the assembly rooms of various inns in the main Italian cities were always two in number: one on degeneration and the other on *the new woman*, focused on the role of women in a swiftly modernizing society. Montessori explained to future mothers the possible causes of the so-called degenerative stigmas that might mark their own children and damage future generations and indicated how to avoid them by having recourse to a scientifically informed pedagogy. Montessori's acute political insight was arguing that the responsible involvement of women could assist children's cognitive well-being.

"My wish is for women to fall in love with scientific reasoning," she declared in one lecture (Kramer 1988, 80). With this unusual but intentional wording Maria Montessori sought to identify rationality itself as a guide to female conduct, even in the most personal and intimate choices, including marriage. Consequently, she urged women wishing to become mothers to follow the dictates of medical science, informing themselves about the health of their own partners and about any possible hereditary illnesses. The choice of motherhood was thus referred back to a female consciousness "illuminated" by science.

Promoting the value of scientific authority to women in relation to maternity, mothering, and heredity entailed also pointing out to them their intellectual autonomy even regarding questions pertaining to the intimate sphere and their own sexuality. This autonomy of thought, along with economic independence, represented an indispensable instrument for the emancipation of the female world. Notably, her vision also included procreative autonomy. Thus, in 1902, Montessori wrote as follows:

> Women's social victory will be a maternal victory, one destined to ameliorate, to render stronger the human species. [A woman,] after having gone on to conquer social labour, will take a further step: she will conquer her biological labour, which is the true goal of feminism: the victory of her own children.
>
> *(206)*

This passage has been critiqued by Italian feminist historians for adhering to the eugenics movement, an integral aspect of social medicine at the time. Alongside this critique, however, it is possible to discern a clearly feminist stance, where Montessori assigns to women the unilateral decision to choose motherhood and, albeit implicitly, to manage their own sexuality.

From 1905 to 1906, Montessori was a lecturer in hygiene and anthropology, the only scientific subjects available at Rome's women's university, the Magistero Femminile. During this time, Italian feminists were responsible for an array of ideas and experiments, as militants engaged during that same period in several battles for women's suffrage and equality. Montessori was involved in the campaign for the vote and put her signature to the Italian women's petition to parliament promoted by thirty or so women known for their aristocratic origins and their talent, led by Annamaria Mozzoni. This was not all that Montessori did, however. Her lectureship at the Magistero also gave her abundant opportunities to recruit young women prepared to struggle for their emancipation and for the vote. Together they founded a society, Pensiero e Azione (Thought and Action), consisting of young women from secondary schools or universities who, once mobilized, proceeded to launch an Office of Intellectual Labor, a concrete example of the emancipation of female intellectual labor, something traditionally confined to a subaltern status. The society's program rested on two primary objectives: to render intellectual women visible and to conceive of their work as a collective response to historical oppression. Members of the society willingly provided translations of lectures, staged performances in private houses, and conducted bibliographical research for newspapers and reviews. Pensiero e Azione also promoted a suffrage proclamation, endorsed by Montessori and affixed to walls in Rome by female college students, urging women to vote at elections (Babini 2000; Montessori 1906a).

At the time of the ultimately unsuccessful campaign for women's suffrage (Italian women ultimately won the right to vote in 1945), Montessori in 1904 had already attained an important scientific objective: becoming qualified as a lecturer in anthropology. The examining committee, despite voicing a fair number of paltry objections and betraying ill-concealed embarrassment, was obliged to yield and ended up assigning her the task of conducting anthropological research into the physical characteristics of the women of Lazio (Babini 2011). The committee was presumably taking advantage of the rare opportunity offered through having a female anthropologist present, who might be able to obtain scientific data relating to the female population, about which almost nothing was known and was, in any case, highly reluctant, out of a sense of modesty, to be in contact with medical "measurers" (the majority of Italian anthropological inquiries at the time had to do with the military).

Despite the huge difficulties involved in "measuring" the women from the rural areas of Lazio, the young lecturer proved to be an assiduous and determined investigator aided in her inquiries by the close-knit network of feminists to which she belonged. Indeed, Maria Montessori managed to present some 200 case studies to the commission, twice the number stipulated. This was because those prepared to take part in the research included private clients who were students at the Magistero, ladies from the Roman upper bourgeoisie, and sisters from the Ricreatorio Femminile di Trastevere (Montessori 1906b).

The practice of science understood as a form of feminist militancy enabled Montessori to combat women's purported mental inferiority, an idea vested at the time with scientific legitimacy. In the second half of the nineteenth century, doctors and anthropologists, responding to a request made by jurists engaged in drafting the first civil and penal codes of united Italy, reinforced the stereotype of the inferiority of women. This was in the guise of the scientific construction of a female nature that was "by nature" lesser in intelligence and mental capacities. There was, in other words, a price to be paid for the high biological function of maternity, which was held to involve a great expenditure of physical and mental energy (Babini et al. 1986). Montessori attempted to scientifically refute that "bad science" in her lectures on anthropology at the University of Rome. In 1910 the lectures became a text in which she overturned the scientific preconceptions of her male colleagues, asserting the anthropological superiority of women (Montessori 1910).

Montessori understood motherhood as a critical space for women to gain rights and incorporated scientific feminism to argue it should be examined both socially and scientifically. Often historians have overemphasized her engagement with childhood as linked solely or even primarily to her personal experience of single motherhood. There is, however, sufficient historical evidence to suggest that Montessori's stance on mothering was consistent with that expressed by various exponents of female emancipation, including Anna Maria Mozzoni, founder of the women's movement in Italy. As early as 1864, Mozzoni asserted that, given the repressive laws regarding women in Italy at the time, "[a] woman should not subjugate herself to marriage," and in order to have a "maternal right … she must be mother only to illegitimate offspring" (Ramsey-Portolano 2020, 7). For Mozzoni and other Italian feminists of the time, motherhood and marriage were incompatible. Furthermore, if one places undue stress on Maria Montessori's personal life, it reduces her intellectual originality and philosophical power to being simply a compensatory reaction to her own maternal sacrifice (Babini 2015). For all of these reasons, her choice to advocate for maternal rights, which undoubtedly were personally painful, marked an important refusal to conform socially. It's important to note that Montessori's advocacy and evolving ideas of maternity were situated, and remained, at the center of her thinking from 1898 (the year in which her son Mario was born) until 1909 (the year in which the *Metodo* [Montessori Method] was published), even as she shifted her gaze from the sphere of politics to that of pedagogy (Babini 2014).

From the outset, Montessori observed the theme of motherhood in conjunction with the question of degeneration. Maternity therefore formed part of a discourse of eugenicist birth control that was inserted into a militant conception of health promoted in those years by advocates of social medicine. Here Montessori still spoke of modernity solely in terms of procreation, albeit of a responsible kind. With the introduction of the concept of social motherhood, however, the emphasis shifted from biological maternity to an extended (social) maternity, which, on the one hand, contemplated the care of children of others in need (thus, for example, the *Lega per la cura e l'educazione dei deficienti*) and, on the other hand, envisaged the moral education of her own biological child as the "new man" that every woman would like to have by her side. In parallel, she advocated for a sexual education under the banner of the female values of parity and respect, as she would explain in the report presented in Rome in 1908 at the national Convention of Italian Women, where, for the first time in Italy, the question of sexuality was raised.[2]

With the concept of social motherhood, Maria Montessori identified the contribution that women can and must make to the amelioration, if not to the salvation, of humanity. In some of her writings, and not by chance, the phrase *a truly human motherhood* became superimposed on social motherhood. It was as if she was concerned to indicate the attainment of a second level of procreation, which was human, above that of simple biological motherhood, which was animal. This change in the conception of motherhood as maternal sentiment is a nodal point in Montessori's definitive transition to pedagogy, resulting in her largely abandoning medicine and feminism.

To demonstrate this shift toward social motherhood, in a 1902 lecture Montessori used a biblical juxtaposition of Eve as a subjugated woman and Mary as a woman empowered by motherhood. Montessori referred to Mary in this instance as "social Mary," one who was able to elevate mothering to involve agency, but also where one must be open to shared responsibility for the education of the child. With a gaze directed at the immediate future, Montessori foresaw that social organization, the division of labor and industrial development that was gaining ground, would lead not only to the end of the patriarchal family but also to the end of the couple, in its guise as an economic and social cell.

According to Montessori, the question of the transformation of the woman would run parallel to the transformation of the family and the increasing significance of the Italian state in supporting the welfare of children. Just as in the past the dignity of woman—*domina* and *mater*—had rested on her capacity to transform primary materials into objects useful to the family (feeding, clothing), so too in the contemporary period, in which industrial progress was reabsorbing these forms of labor previously undertaken in the domestic sphere, a time was fast approaching in which the *domina* would no longer have any reason to exist. Indeed, Montessori advanced the hypothesis that the *mater* too would lose her centrality in the educative function because children's education "is more and more becoming a collective endeavor and the mission of the State" (Montessori 1902, 6).

A project that was both concrete and utopian, the San Lorenzo experiment would shortly afterward enable Montessori to give expression to all her ideals. Feminism, social medicine, utopian politics, and pedagogical concerns breathed life into the inaugural discourse given at the Casa dei Bambini (House of Children) in April 1907. Helping to raise up that part of the outcast world was only the first level at which her experiment was realized. Indeed, the Casa dei Bambini assumed the guise of a political laboratory in which it was a matter of refining a method that was pedagogical, but with which the intention was to save future humanity, not only the suffering humanity of San Lorenzo. We could define it as a pedagogy with a feminist matrix: The values of respectful listening, and therefore of awaiting the revelation of the human potential that every baby has within itself, are always, according to Maria Montessori, female values. As early as 1902 she had written that woman, in turning herself into a social worker, would have poured out into society something additional with respect to man. She would bring to it what had always been in the family, "the purificatory, the consoling, the source of love and peace." She would have socialized "the domestic virtues." Society, she concluded, "feels the need for the woman, who refines it with her work, for the mother who protects it" (Montessori 1902, 6).

In her discourse of 1907, Maria Montessori announced the advent of a new fact, shifting her attention from feminism and motherhood to the rights of the child. In the guise of a sort of community that offers a socialized infirmary and kitchen, the educationalist also prefigures a nursery school, but one that is so new in its goals as to require a new name: Casa dei Bambini. The difference, however, is not solely terminological; it serves to indicate, where education is concerned, the passage of custody from the familial milieu (protective and maternal) to the social or public one, where the new fact of the socialization of the maternal function would be tried out. However, Montessori would shortly afterward revolutionize this in an anti-institutional sense. One merely has to consider the passage from the *Metodo*, in which, after pointing the finger at a bench built to facilitate "the greatest possible immobility of the child or, if you will, [ensuring that the child is] spared all movement," she inveighs against the "bench of the soul" with which every adult treats the child in obeisance to a notion of education as taming: "Rewards and punishments are ... the *bench* of the soul, that is to say, the instrument enslaving the spirit" (Babini 2013; Montessori 1909, ch. 1). As noted earlier, Maria Montessori's attention and commitment have shifted from woman-mother to baby. There is more than one sign of this change of perspective in the report on sexual morality, presented at the National Women's Congress and in the first edition of the *Metodo*, in which, albeit with different aims in mind, Maria Montessori shifts the question of motherhood and sexual education to the universal plane of a new pedagogy for a new humanity.

In her discourse *Sulla Morale Sessuale* (On Sexual Morals), addressing the question of an education under the banner of female values, and emphasizing the importance of a sexuality founded on respect and equality, Montessori gives a definition of motherhood that does not fully correspond with the maternal affection but is defined by protection and preservation. From the pages of the *Metodo* we learn that her most original intuition had to do with the human potential present in every baby but repressed by the adult, both unconsciously and systematically.

The battle on behalf of motherhood and women henceforth shifted from the political to the educational plane. For Maria Montessori, no change in mentality and custom would be possible without a radical pedagogical reform requiring adults, whether educators, fathers, or mothers, to "limit themselves," "step back," and "disarm themselves" (as she would say in the 1930s and 1940s) to allow to grow freely, instead of suppressing, whatever was already potentially present in the baby. From now on, in Montessori's perspective, the infant was the future mother of humanity.

Notes

1. The term "scientific feminism" has subsequently been adopted in books published after the one from 2000 written with Luisa Lama. See, for example, Suzanne Stewart-Steinberg, *The Pinocchio Effect: On Making Italians, 1860–1920*, Chicago: University of Chicago Press, 2007.
2. The convention on sexuality promoted by Giuseppe Prezzolini's review, *La Voce*, was held in 1910.

References

Babini, Valeria. 2000. "Science, Feminism and Education: The Early Work of Maria Montessori." *History Workshop Journal* 49: 45–67.

Babini, Valeria. 2011. "'Le Donne Sono Antropologicamente Superiori.' Parola di una Donna di Genio." In *Se Vi Sono Donne Di Genio*, edited by Alessandro Volpone and Giovanni Destro-Bisol, 12–26. Rome: Centro Stampa Università degli Studi di Roma La Sapienza.

Babini, Valeria. 2013. "Maria Montessori: Nascita, Metodo e Rivelazioni Di Una Vera 'Pedagogia Scientifica.'" In *La Nascita Delle Scienze Umane Nell'Italia Post-Unitaria*, edited by Guido Cimino and Giovanni Pietro Lombardo, 295–312. Rome: Istituto Italiano di Studi Germanici.

Babini, Valeria. 2014. "Maria Montessori. Liberare la Madre: La Pedagogia Come Maternità Sociale." In *Di Generazione in Generazione: Le Italiane Dall'Unità a Oggi*, edited by Maria Teresa Mori, Alessandra Pescarolo, Anna Scattigno, and Simonetta Soldani, 167–79. Rome: Viella.

Babini, Valeria. 2015. "Between Public and Private. Sexuality and Maternity in Three 'New Women': Sibilla Aleramo, Maria Montessori, Linda Murri." In *Italian Sexualities Uncovered: 1789–1914*, edited by Valeria Babini, Chiara Beccalossi, and Lucy Riall, 162–81. London: Palgrave Macmillan.
Babini, Valeria, and Luisa Lama. 2000. *Una Donna Nuova: Il Femminismo Scientifico Di Maria Montessori*. Milan: Franco Angeli.
Babini, Valeria, Fernanda Minuz, and Annamaria Tagliavini. 1986. *La Donna Nelle Scienze Dell'uomo*. Milan: Franco Angeli.
Kramer, Rita. 1976/1988. *Maria Montessori: A Biography*. New York: Addison Wesley.
Montessori, Maria. 1902. "La Via e L'orizzonte Del Femminismo." *Cyrano de Bergerac* 6: 203–5.
Montessori, Maria. 1906a. "Proclama." *La Vita*, February 26.
Montessori, Maria. 1906b. "Caratteri Fisici Delle Giovani Donne Del Lazio." *Atti Della Società Romana Di Antropologia* 12: 1.
Montessori, Maria. 1909. *Il Metodo Della Pedagogia Scientifica*. Città di Castello: Lapi.
Montessori, Maria. 1910. *Antropologia Pedagogica*. Milan: Vallardi.
Pick, Daniel. 1993. *Faces of Degeneration: A European Disorder, 1848–1918*. Cambridge: Cambridge University Press.
Ramsey-Portolano, Catherine. 2020. *Nineteenth-Century Italian Women Writers and the Woman Question: The Case of Neera*. London: Routledge.

Chapter 3
Cosmic Education: The Vital Center of the Montessori Perspective

Rossella Raimondo

Starting with an analysis of the origins, the main characteristics, and the evolution of cosmic education, this chapter looks at the centrality cosmic education assumes in Montessori education for children ages 6 to 12. This work examines how cosmic fables, elaborated with Mario Montessori and other collaborators, allowed Maria Montessori to foster active and participatory experiences. More specifically, she believed cosmic fables allow children to better understand key concepts of scientific disciplines and to interpret the interdependencies, even the implicit ones, among the elements of creation (Montessori 1970a). Children can thus conceive themselves as parts of a whole, involved in common designs and purposes.

Cosmic education is a framework within which to insert the entire work of Montessori. It is the original nucleus of her thought, starting from the early years of the twentieth century. The subtly provocative question, "Philosophy or methodological suggestion?" guided the reflections of two well-respected Montessori educators, Maier and Breiman, during a workshop at the Montessori Congress in Rome in 1996. They defined cosmic education as an idea that goes beyond a set of philosophical elements, pedagogical indications, teaching strategies, and learning methods (Honegger Fresco 2000, 196).

The sphere of cosmic education is complex as it considers each aspect of a person in relation to every other living form on the planet; it includes the history of the world, of the cosmos, and of our role in it. By extension, it includes the history of civilizations and cultures, elaborating a holistic vision of phenomena. The goal of this philosophical framework is the activation of an education tending toward universal cooperation, the affirmation of democracy, of peace, and the construction of a new world (Montessori 1949).

Cosmic education is both multidisciplinary and interdisciplinary. It questions nature by investigating the interweaving of functions and relationships through which its elements live and transform themselves, and thus it guarantees the survival and development of ecosystems. In her work, Montessori's attention focused above all on the deep connections that link every living form. She wrote, "Everything is closely connected on this planet and every detail becomes interesting because it is connected to others. We can compare the whole to a canvas: every detail is an embroidery, the whole forms a magnificent fabric" (Montessori 1970b, 50).

Cosmic Plan

The word "cosmos" comes from the Greek "*kosmos*" meaning order. Applied to Montessori education, this order finds expression in the cosmic vision as a way of looking at the world in its unity on a very large scale. Within this unity all inorganic and organic beings are ecologically linked to each other in countless ways "to form a single whole" (Montessori 1970b, 19). Here, humanity is considered biologically and psychologically, consciously and unconsciously; it intersects ages, differences, affinities, and forms of sociality. Humans, animals, plants, and all other organic objects of creation inhabit the cosmic plane, which consists of an integrated structure (or cosmic organization). Thus, everything that exists has a task to accomplish—a cosmic task that follows a global design. Within this design, the sun, earth, water, and air act on a large scale, following cosmic laws according to their nature; plants and animals behave in the same way but in more limited environments, their actions guided by a universal intelligence that is characterized as an impulse, as craving, as an unconscious guide in the direction of evolution. Each cosmic agent, therefore, must fulfill a mandate, not autonomously but in correlation with a multitude of other mandates; here we are in continuity with the concept of telluric economy previously proposed by geologist Stoppani, who was "among the first—if not the first—to grasp the meaning of the balances between the different terrestrial, physical and biological, geological and climatic forces" (Honegger Fresco 2000, 163).

The Centrality of Cosmic Education in Childhood Pedagogy

By cosmic education, Montessori also meant the ambitious educational project that allows the child, during the second stage of development, between the ages of 6 and 12, to organize their own *abstract plan of the spirit* pursuing planetary and holistic dimensions. During this period, defined as *of culture*—of the sense of belonging and reasoned adhesion to the world of adults—physical and mental horizons open up, and there is no limit to what the child can explore. The scientific knowledge of phenomena and the understanding of how deeply the evolution of humanity, nature, and our cosmos are interconnected are what children most need at this stage; they are desirous of knowledge, understanding, finding answers to the great whys that animate the world, and intertwining interrelationships among the different elements.

> Why are there flies and whales, stars and flowers? Why are the leaves green? Why does the sun go there and the moon comes? Countless times children with their questions and reflections—often of a philosophical nature—ask us for answers on vital phenomena.
>
> *(Honegger Fresco 2000, 58)*

If the child had the opportunity to directly experience the surrounding world through the senses in the previous phase of early childhood, in this next phase the child wonders about the reasons that can explain the dynamics they grasped. The need to ask questions varies from subject to subject, growing in proportion to the intensity, depth, and frequency that had characterized earlier sensory experiments. As Montessori wrote in 1912, "[i]t is good to develop this feeling of trust and confidence in living beings, which is then a form of love and union with the universe" (Montessori 1912, 159). It is no coincidence that Montessori, precisely in reference to this evolutionary phase, spoke of an education capable of providing incentives to capture the child's imagination that supports the child's abstraction and reasoning ability.

> The very basis of the spirit [the imagination], however, needs to be built, organized with the exactness that the human mind always requires. It is not the idle daydreaming in the nonexistent, but thinking of a forest having discovered the life of a tree or of the ocean starting from a small lake in your region. Hence we give the Whole, presenting the particular as a means, that is, the world, the globe, the planisphere and together the earth, water, the blade of grass.
>
> *(Montessori 1970b, 56)*

Montessori urged adults not to present single fragments of knowledge, but to offer paths of reasoning where the topics can be understood in their totality and interdisciplinarity, in other words, a cosmic perspective. This period has been compared to a field destined for the sowing of wheat, able to accommodate quantities of seeds that are not possible in subsequent stages (Montessori 1970a).

Cosmic Fables

Montessori developed the concept of cosmic education most robustly during her stays in India, from 1939 to 1946 and again from 1947 to 1949. She collaborated with her son Mario, who as noted in previous chapters, was her supporter, adviser, and companion of studies and observations, but also her philosophical heir and interpreter. The figure of Mario assumes indisputable relevance. Apart from his familial connection, his observational work, critiques, and keen recording of data are notable. His desire for research and the need for additional information about the work of youth prompted his actions. Ultimately, he too assumes an authoritative position in the scientific field of education (Scocchera 1998). Mario Montessori's intuition and investment in his mother's legacy allowed him to devote himself to deepening the concept of cosmic education, adding the didactic proposal of the *materialized abstractions*.

To this end, he, together with his mother and their students, created a repertoire of stories based on various protagonists of creation. These are commonly called the cosmic fables or Great Lessons: the five themes are the creation of the universe, the coming of life to the universe, the coming of humans, communication in signs, and the story of numbers (see Chapter 15: "The Montessori Elementary School for Children Ages 6–12"). Each story is rich in mental images and is designed to awaken curiosity, arouse interest, and stimulate the imagination, which Montessori considered the "great power of this age" (Montessori 1994, 20). As Montessori said, "What [the child] learns must be interesting, it must fascinate him: we must offer him great things: to begin with, let us offer him the world" (Montessori 1970a, 45). It is in fact in the world, even in the entire universe, that life unfolds and that the answers to childhood questions are contained, ready to be revealed according to Mario and Maria's work. Active, participatory experiences can arise from cosmic tales. They can both bring children closer to the key concepts of scientific disciplines and help them understand and interpret the interdependencies among the elements of creation, even the implicit ones, as well as the cultivation of meaning. Cosmic education also elicits gratitude toward every living being. In this way, everyone, children included, can perceive themselves as part of a whole, on the basis of common purposes. The need for cosmic education, therefore, underlies its desirable connotation as a fulcrum within Montessori education around which to organize knowledge, so that children can experience their own harmony with all of creation.

The central idea behind the first Great Lesson, which is called "God with No Hands," refers to the story of the birth of the universe after the Big Bang (Lillard 1996, 61). In classrooms today, God is not named by the teachers who present this lesson to their pupils. The intent of the first cosmic lesson is to illustrate the succession of events that included the birth of the universe and the formation of natural environments, thus cultivating a sense of wonder, an engine to awaken students to how cosmic order is regulated by laws that are not abstract but functional to the harmony of the whole.

The second cosmic lesson, "The Coming of Life," follows the first, introducing the animal and plant worlds. In this case, single-celled organisms that lead, through processes of aggregation and disaggregation, to other, more complex forms of life (Lillard 1996, 61). In *How to Educate Human Potential*, Montessori argued that human intelligence has transformed and enriched the world.

> Of course, it is evident that man has a mission. He was able to draw from the earth hidden riches, marvelous energies, and created a superworld or, if you like, a supernature; and gradually building this supernature, man has elevated himself, and from a natural man he became a supernatural man. Nature is a plan that has existed for centuries, supernature is another plan that man has been building. Today's man no longer lives in nature, but in supernature. ... Man depends on man. How many men work for the bread we eat to reach us! And a fruit, which has come to us from distant lands, can represent a whole organization of men, a formidable and severe organization, which holds human society together.
> *(Montessori 1949, 98–9)*

In the third cosmic lesson, "The Coming of Human Beings," Montessori intended to lead children to understand that, for the protection of the common good, the laws regulating the functioning of social groups are founded on the need for a shared collaboration (Lillard 1996, 63). This theme is very similar to the cognitive and moral potential that children should reach during the second plane of development, from the age of 6 to 12 years, when they are immersed in an existential phase in which cooperation and dialectical exchange are attractive to the child.

Finally, the fourth and fifth cosmic lessons, "The Story of Communication in Signs" and "The Story of Numbers," refer to the invention of the first human alphabets and numbering systems, offering children the opportunity to get involved with ancient cuneiform scripts and personal languages (Lillard 1996, 65). Projects emerging from the Great Lessons can include history, geography, and natural sciences, through exploring concepts and experiential approaches. Narration can activate fantasy, curiosity, and imagination, especially when the teacher is not responsible for communicating all content, but just introducing concepts that invite further investigation. From there, children develop and deepen their learning by drawing on classroom and external resources or specific lessons.

Through cosmic lessons, Montessori did not want to exhaustively present concepts but aimed to widen knowledge gaps, excite curiosity, and direct students toward research paths. In fact, she argued, "But the simplest and most natural thing is the origin of things: as I always say, the child must have the origin of things because the origin is clearer and more natural for his mind. All we have to do is find a material that makes the origin accessible" (1931, n.p.). From a Montessori perspective, cosmic lessons should open fields of interest and create emotional connections, allowing teachers the opportunity to design educational paths that suit the interests and needs of the students, while combining scientific study with ethical reflection. Acting on the child's imagination, cosmic lessons encourage the emergence of individual representations of the world and others in which personal experiences are enriched with symbols and emotional tones, mutually enhancing each other. The deeper dimensions of the child are thus questioned, so they will be able to refine a critical spirit and the ability to elaborate comparisons.

Conclusion

The definitions of cosmic vision and cosmic plan are the necessary prerequisites for coming to understand cosmic education; at the same time, the plan is the tool through which it is possible to put these concepts into practice. Cosmic education is, as Augusto Scocchera wrote, "a new way of observing and interpreting the phenomena of life" (Scocchera 2005, 38); "by cosmic education we mean an effective preparation of the new generations to understand that the whole of humanity tends to unite in a single organism" (Montessori 2000, 165). In other words, cosmic education allows the children, through the global tasks and duties necessary for the functioning of the entire world system, to assume an ethic of responsibility in their daily behaviors, and to strengthen social structures, community, and interdependence. This type of vision allows the child to move in space and time, capturing the evolutionary changes of the world and its ecological functioning. Rita Scocchera as quoted in Augusto Scocchera's 2005 work wrote that Montessori

> assumes the new ecological perspective well in advance: interconnection and mutualism are evident, not only between living creatures, but—and this is even more disconcerting—between the different conditions of matter, inanimate and animate. Life itself is understood there through the notion of emergency, illustrated by the beautiful similarity of the fur that grows from the animal's body. The Earth therefore appears to her as a Gaian system, in which life determines the conditions of its own existence, always in the balance, in an indefatigable and unconscious search for balance.
>
> *(35–36)*

Similarly, Cambi (2005, 29–30) recognized in Montessori's reading that Montessori gave of the child a "utopian" and "ecological" perspective, characterized by the respect and strengthening of a cosmic order that is primarily physical-biological, but also spiritual. These are themes that, up to the present day, have continued to attract the interest of scholars, touching the boundaries of contemporary ecology: among the many it is possible to mention Gregory Bateson, Urie Bronfenbrenner, and Edgar Morin. Placing himself on this interpretative line, Fornaca (2005) argued that Montessori can be considered a significant point of reference for new reflections and comparisons on the origin of life, on research concerning the cosmos in all its dynamic manifestations, and on how the educational sciences can appropriate and rework this content especially in the service of children.

Montessori's invitation to see beyond and to perceive links finds a result in the reminder of the responsibility entrusted to cosmic education to build peace, which is understood as one of the main social issues involving the whole of humanity. She also stressed two different intellectual lines of thinking as a result: one that allows the development of human values, especially moral ones, and another that contributes to making people aware of the purposes of their work. It is therefore necessary to use the ideas of cosmic education to place peace and peacemaking at the center of educational processes. Thus formed, a better man can be an active citizen of a so-called unique nation, which is configured as a sort of organism that absorbs all of humanity into itself. In this way, people learn to act for the global interest, even before for their own individual purposes, feeling fully involved in their own cosmic mission as a subject at the service of humanity (Raimondo 2018).

Today cosmic education remains topical in at least two ways. First, the content aims to integrate various disciplines, like science education, history education, and geography education into a unitary vision of knowledge development. This is more relevant than ever in educational contexts in which knowledge bases increasingly overlap. As Montessori wrote in 1938 (published in the 1949 edition of *Education and Peace*),

> Studies separated from each other do not favor human intelligence that constantly seeks the relationship between things and unity or, if you like, every separate study is in a certain sense chaotic, while if we put order in the various sciences, we not only understand the ultimate purpose of all this, but we take advantage of it on the level of knowledge.
>
> *(64)*

The ability to place the results of her discoveries in deep relationship with the contents and developments of the other disciplines, in order to validate and support them, is peculiar to the personality, writing, and educational practices of Montessori who inserted them into a broader and more consolidated thought landscape. On the existential level, however, cosmic education embraces and incorporates the concepts of ecological education, education for peace, and education for the world and recalls implications of ethical and aesthetic education. As a "builder of humanity," cosmic education is therefore the education of whole being beginning in childhood and throughout a lifetime (Montessori 1949, 48).

References

Cambi, Franco. 2005. "L'Educazione Cosmica da Maria Montessori a Noi." *Vita dell'Infanzia* (3–4): 27–30. 10.13128/Studi_Formaz-24669.

Fornaca, Remo. 2005. "Montessori e l'Istanza dell'Educazione Cosmica." *Vita dell'Infanzia* (3–4): 18–21. doi.org/10.4454/rse.v6i1.182.

Honegger Fresco, Grazia. 2000. *Montessori: Perché No? Una Pedagogia per la Crescita*. Milan: FrancoAngeli.
Lillard, Paula Polk. 1996. *Montessori Today*. New York: Schocken Books.
Montessori, Maria. 1912. *The Montessori Method*. New York: Schocken Books.
Montessori, Maria. 1931. "Montessori International Course in Rome." *Extract from the Conference* May 5, 1931.
Montessori, Maria. 1949. *Educazione e Pace*. Rome: Opera Montessori.
Montessori, Maria. 1956. *Il Bambino in Famiglia*. Milan: Garzanti.
Montessori, Maria. 1970a. *Dall'Infanzia all'Adolescenza*. Milan: Garzanti.
Montessori, Maria. 1970b. *Come Educare il Potenziale Umano*. Milan: Garzanti.
Montessori, Maria. 1994. *From Childhood to Adolescence*. Oxford, England: Clio Press.
Montessori, Maria. 2000. "Che Cos'è l'Educazione Cosmica." In *Montessori Perché No?* edited by Grazia Honegger Fresco, 165–8. Turin: Il Leone Verde.
Raimondo, Rossella. 2018. "Cosmic Education in Maria Montessori: Arts and Sciences as Resources for Human Development." *Studi sulla Formazione* 21 (2): 249–06. http://dx.doi.org/10.13128/Studi_Formaz-24669
Scocchera, Augusto. 1998. *Introduzione a Mario Montessori*. Rome: Opera Nazionale Montessori.
Scocchera, Augusto. 2005. "Dentro l'Educazione Cosmica." *Vita dell'Infanzia* (3–4): 35–46.

Chapter 4
The Philosophy of Maria Montessori

Patrick R. Frierson

Maria Montessori was a scientist, social scientist, and philosopher in a truly transdiscipinarly manner. Having completed her medical degree, when Montessori "decided to study the education of normal children and the principles upon which it is based," she "enrolled as a student of *philosophy* at the university" (Montessori 2017/1936, 1; Montessori 2017/1909, 23, emphasis added). She studied with philosophers, including Giacomo Barzellotti (scholar of Kant, Schopenhauer, and Herbert Spencer), Luigi Credaro (translator of G. F. Herbart's educational philosophy), and the Hegelian Marxist, Antonio Labriola (Matellicani 2007; Trabalzini 2011). Simultaneously, she studied anthropology and psychology with Giuseppe Sergi, was influenced by "evolutionary positivism," and participated in a surge of Italian interest in American pragmatism, particularly that of William James.[1] Her corpus of work explicitly engages with James, Nietzsche, and Bergson and draws from philosophers such as Aristotle, Kant, Schopenhauer, and Hegel. This long and distinguished list of intellectual interlocutors indicates depth and the breadth of Montessori's influences and thought partners. Nonetheless, Montessori ascribes her philosophy to children rather than any historical philosopher or even to herself:

> Other methods are the result of the efforts of people … of genius … endowed with a great love of humanity. Although this method bears my name, it is not the result of the efforts of a great thinker who has developed his own ideas. My method is founded on the child himself. … The method has been achieved by following the child.
>
> *(Montessori 2012a, 7)*

The Discovery of the Child and *The Secret of Childhood* testify to the centrality of the child's perspective in shaping her philosophy (Montessori 2017, 2019a). She explains, "[In] an environment … conducive to the most perfect conditions of life, and the freedom which allows that life to develop," children "reveal to us the phases through which social [and intellectual] life must pass in the course of its natural unfolding" (Montessori 2013, 54; 2014, 212; see also Montessori 2012a, 81–2).

Historically, academic philosophy marginalizes children's insights. In the case of Montessori, this is especially true alongside her status as a female, Italian, and an engaged, global educator rather than an "ivory tower" academic. Montessori herself sometimes deprecates philosophy in favor of empirical, scientific investigation or real life, such as when she praises her mentor Sergi, who "like the scientists who preceded him … was led to substitute (in the field of pedagogy) *the human individual* in his lived reality, in place of general principles or abstract philosophical ideas" (Montessori 1913, 14). Similar to Sergi, Montessori places actual individuals—particularly children—ahead of abstract philosophies, and she insisted on drawing from the lives of children to illuminate every "branch of … philosophy" (Montessori 2019a, 1). The

Italian editors of her writings on peace correctly note, "Once a firm basis for her theories had been established through practical experience, [Montessori's] thoughts as an educator and a philosopher ranged further and unveiled new perspectives that seem broader and broader as time goes by" (Montessori 2007, vii).

Montessori's philosophical insights speak not only to central issues in metaphysics, epistemology, human nature, freedom, and morality but also to their application to child development. Her willingness to engage in deeply philosophical work but in the service of children makes her distinctive in the philosophical world. A series of philosophical themes emanate from Montessori's work.

1. Montessori's metaphysics, focusing on the central place of life in the universe.
2. Epistemology, which includes an accounting of the nature of human knowledge; here the important roles of the senses and of active interest in guiding human intellectual life are emphasized.
3. The philosophy of freedom in Montessori pedagogy emphasizing its nature and central importance for her philosophy.
4. Montessori's moral philosophy—including comments on character, mutual respect, and social solidarity.
5. Finally, the central role of *movement* and the *body* in every dimension of Montessori's philosophy calls for consideration; revealing how Montessori's emphasis on the body anticipates recent developments in the philosophy of mind.

Other chapters in this volume discuss further features of Montessori's philosophy, such as her feminism (see Chapter 2: "The Scientific Feminism of Maria Montessori") and the ways spirituality was emphasized in her work (see Chapter 3: "Cosmic Education: The Vital Center of the Montessori Perspective"). Her insights with respect to each of these philosophical themes warrant further consideration as her pedagogy and legacy continue to be examined and especially as her work is considered within the corpuses of twentieth-century philosophy, ethnic and gender studies, and educational studies.

Metaphysics of Life

In contemporary philosophy, metaphysics is the study of the basic nature of reality. For Montessori, the central category through which she interprets the world is life. In *Pedagogical Anthropology*, she praises her mentor Sergi, who "substitute[d] the human individual taken from actual life in place of ... abstract philosophical ideas" (Montessori 1913, 14). Montessori's pedagogy's central focus is children's *living* individuality.[2] Her curricular maps explain how science and history are "correlated to a central idea ... the Cosmic Plan in which all ... serve the great Purpose of Life" (Montessori 1913, 18, 2015b, vii). Rather than mere rational deduction or brute sense data Montessori drew from her medical and psychological background and saw the developing embryo as a model for understanding reality, formulating a metaphysics within which self-organization, growth, and development are part of the structure of reality itself.

Montessori's metaphysics involves two essential elements: teleology and interconnection. Teleology states that the work of living things "tend[s] towards a definite purpose" (Montessori

1913, 40). Montessori identified "embryolog[y]" and genetics as frameworks for understanding "nature's plan" (Montessori 2015b, 70).³ She even illustrates teleology with "the transformation of the fertilized ovum into the fully developed individual" (Montessori 1913, 40). Here a collection of cells does not merely move and change in accordance with laws of physics but builds structures, acting for a specific purpose, namely the development of the organism. The importance of teleology was central to Montessori's work. Attention to goal-directedness emerged from her fundamental pedagogical insight, namely that young children are spiritual embryos, seeking to develop for a specific purpose. In children, life's "creative energy ... has ... an unconscious directive ... to develop a normal person [or other organism]" (Montessori 2012a, 225). Because the child is teleologically ordered, pedagogy should respect life's teleology:

> Education must be ... active *help* given to the normal expansion of the life of the child. The ... body which grows and ... soul which develops ... have one eternal font, life itself. We must neither mar nor stifle the mysterious powers which lie within these two forms of growth.
>
> *(Montessori 1912, 59)*

Montessori's pedagogical practice and metaphysical insight mutually reinforce each other. She was attuned to how the child seeks purposeful growth and development and her metaphysical theories directed her attention to the importance of purposeful work for children.

Montessori consistently observed the interconnectedness of life. Her pedagogical methodology of indirect preparation noted how children engage with goal-directed activity and add complexity over time. For example, children strengthen their pincer grip through work with puzzles or cylinder blocks and separately develop an association between shapes of letters and their sounds. Eventually, these different capacities become interconnected in the child's capacity for writing. Similarly, children develop patterns of respectful work within a classroom to form a community of interdependent agents creating a common culture. Over time, internal and external interconnections are strengthened.

As Montessori developed curricula for older children, she noticed children were interested to learn about the world through understanding interconnectedness. Earth's biosphere comprises "this force which is life [which] reconstructs the world and at the same time perfects its functioning" (Montessori 2008, 56). Whereas plants and animals can be considered solely in terms of individual survival, one must also attend to "the cosmic function of each living being ... working in collaboration for the fulfillment of the Purpose of Life" (Montessori 2015b, 24–5). Just as the strengthened pincer grip from work with a puzzle serves a broader purpose (writing and the expression of ideas) in the eventual life of the child, so too can the individual purposes of each organism and species be seen as an integrated part of a broader cosmic whole. Within Montessori education, children themselves are invited to consider their place in the cosmic whole, which is intensely interesting to them. Within Montessori's metaphysics and pedagogy, life's teleological tendency to perfect individuals is subordinated to a more fundamental "cosmic charity"; she notes: "victory in self-fulfillment can only come to the All," in which "each individual is concerned more with the advantage of the evolution of the whole in which all take part than with its own salvation" (Montessori 2012a, 89; Montessori 2012b, 10; Montessori 2015a, 111; Montessori 2015b, 25).

Her metaphysical orientation allowed Montessori to focus on the way that natural teleology and interconnection permeate human life and the universe as a whole. Various forms of teleological metaphysics, including attempts to integrate a plausible account of nature with human minds and values, are important still today.[4] Montessori saw the importance of this development years ago and demonstrated how the lives of young children exhibit the teleological orientation of natural, living organisms. Moreover, her attention to interconnection anticipates the importance of ecology within contemporary biology (see Montessori 2012a, 87–90, 165) and ecological thinking within contemporary environmental philosophy. Her elementary curriculum cultivates increased awareness of this interconnection through study of human history and interdependence among living things and her recommendations for adolescence confirm this need (Montessori 2015b). Her teleological and ecological metaphysics grows out of and buoys a pedagogy that recognizes and appreciates a child striving for individual development while also promoting the sense of cosmic purpose and interconnection that are necessary to the common good.

Agential Empiricist Epistemology

Epistemology investigates human knowledge, understanding, and, in Montessori's case, intelligence. Montessori saw intelligence as malleable rather than fixed and her epistemology explains how to understand and promote intellectual excellence.

As an empiricist, Montessori understood knowledge as grounded in the senses. Senses are the "foundation of the entire intellectual organism," such that "[t]here can be neither ideas nor imagination, nor any intellectual construction, if we do not presuppose an activity of the senses" (Montessori 2013, 260; see also Montessori 2012a, 193–4). However, unlike classical empiricists Montessori does not see senses as passive, but rather as active capacities. As she explains, seeing, hearing, and smelling require active not passive engagement:

> The child actively takes from the environment. The old psychologists used to say that the child responded to sensory stimuli. ... This ... passive interpretation of psychic life ... is very different from the fact that the child actively takes for himself what he needs from the environment in order to construct his own psychic life.
>
> *(Montessori 2012a, 172–3)*

According to Montessori's *agential* empiricism, individuals direct their senses and imagination: "In the world around us, we do not see everything ... but only some things that suit us" (Montessori 2013, 185). Her view is that of an empiricist, in that all as knowledge starts from the senses, but her empiricism is *agential* in that our actions govern our interests. Montessori's attention to agency allowed her to recognize sensitive periods of development during which particular capacities are especially susceptible to improvement because during those stages, children are particularly interested in some sort of work.

Agential empiricism has implications for Montessori pedagogy and contemporary philosophy. Her empiricism is evident in the materials she designed to cultivate, refine, and order children's senses. Her focus on agency compels educators to create schools filled with materials to attract and hold student interest. This perspective offers an alternative to contemporary philosophy's thinking about sense perception by demonstrating that sensory perception is not passively given but cultivated.[5]

Philosophy of Freedom

Within much contemporary (and historical) philosophy, the concept of (human) freedom and agency features prominently, from metaphysical debates about the relationship between free will and determinism to moral philosophies that attend to the value of freedom to political theories within which political freedom is a central concern. For Montessori "freedom should be the basis of pedagogy" (Montessori 2013, 74). As an empiricist, Montessori saw that "the conditions of a real experiment and subsequently ... of observation are made of two elements: an environment conducive to the most perfect conditions of life and the freedom which allows that life to develop" (Montessori 2013, 54). Observing children in "public schools where [they] are repressed in the spontaneous expression of their personality till they are almost like dead beings" is comparable to studying butterflies' behavior when "mounted by means of pins, their outspread wings motionless" (Babini 2013, 18; Montessori 1912, 14). When we study children without consideration of the environment or circumstance, we remain blind to the effects of oppression on the actualization of their potential. To see true potential, one must investigate individuals in *freedom*. And because children's absorbent minds adapt psychologically to developmental conditions, freedom must begin from birth.

People often misinterpret Montessori's emphasis on freedom, taking it to imply neglect or reckless permissiveness or lawless behavior among children. For example,

> When teachers become weary of my observations [about the importance of giving children freedom], they begin to let the children do anything they pleased. I saw some of them ... pushing their companions about ... without the teacher paying the slightest attention.
>
> *(Montessori 2017, 54)*

Unlike whimsical license, "freedom in nature is order—the result of absolute obedience to laws of creation that bring about harmony and discipline" (Montessori 2013, 74). This freedom "should have as its limit the interests of the group to which [one] belongs" and should be oriented toward "work"; that is, children "must find a way of busying themselves in a manner adequate to the needs of their inner development" (Montessori 2013, 78; Montessori 2017, 50).

Promoting such freedom requires what Montessori called the prepared environment: "freedom includes all conditions ... favorable to its development" (Montessori 2013, 54). Freedom requires us to exist in a context rich with opportunities for activity and to be allowed to pursue the activities we choose. Children and adults should not only be free to "choose their work" and free from "the constant external influence of one who wishes to instruct him," but also free in "the environment most favorable to ... development" (Montessori 2013, 75–6).

Montessori's ideas about freedom have a lot to contribute to contemporary philosophical debates as well as to practical pedagogy. At the philosophical level, her emphasis on a freedom respectful of others and oriented toward community-oriented work in the world corrects widespread accounts of choice and freedom which assume it means the absence of any meaningful constraints on activity. Focusing on the conditions of freedom led Montessori to develop an empirical psychology that challenges methodological assumptions of psychology in her day and does so still. Moreover, her emphasis on the environment as related to freedom is helpful, extending discussions beyond internal capacities toward the outward conditions and realization of those capacities.

Moral Philosophy: Character, Respect, and Solidarity

Just as Montessori contributed ideas to metaphysics, epistemology, and discussions of freedom, she also developed important insights around key tenets of moral philosophy. Moral philosophy involves the study of human virtues, obligations, or goods. Moral philosophers typically seek to elucidate principles for making morally good choices or to lay out ideals of a morally good life. Montessori's writing emphasizes the value of a good, healthy, or flourishing human life and locates this flourishing in three main values: character, respect, and solidarity. The first of these values, character, has echoes in Nietzschean and perfectionist approaches to ethics (Conant 2010, 181–257; Rutherford 2018). The value of respect reflects concerns widely associated with Kantian moral theories (e.g., Korsgaard 2009; Wood 2007). The third value of solidarity echoes Hegelian and Marxist themes and has the potential to make significant contributions to recent debates about social and group agency.[6]

Montessori's moral philosophy begins where the previous section ended, with the centrality of freedom. Allowing children freedom provides conditions for what Montessori often calls *normalization*. This normalization is neither the conformity of the child to some fixed standard of normalcy nor an enforced standardization of children's behavior. Rather, Montessori sees normalization as the restoration of a person's authentic selfhood, free of the repressions and psychological disruptions that come from being inhibited in the exercise of one's life. As she puts it, normalization is "a psychological … return to normal conditions" (Montessori 2017, 133–4). Madonna Adams argues that "Montessori's goal is practical: to free human beings from a self-destructive and alienated state and to show how human development, freedom, and peace can be achieved by a radical transformation of the educational process based on a true science of human nature" (Adams 2005, 249). This practical philosophy grows from Montessori's metaphysical idea of life because, she notes, "we are immoral when we disobey the laws of life," such that "we should consider as good that which helps life and as bad that which hinders it …, the good [that] which causes a maximum degree of development and the evil [that] which … hinders development" (Montessori 1913, 27; Montessori 2013, 263). As such, her moral philosophy is an extension of her understanding of reality. Humans achieve goodness through promoting the development of living beings (themselves and others) and the world around them.

Montessori understands character to be the fundamental expression of life, a tendency toward self-perfection through active work. This character is a sort of normality in the operation of life already present in children. Character needs only to be "preserve[d]," and at the same time, it is "the source of those moral … values which could bring the whole world to a higher plane" (Montessori 2014, 217). Those with character pursue work they choose for themselves, in accordance with their guiding instincts and set high standards for themselves. When an individual's work adheres to such standards of excellence, this orients them toward continued excellence. To have character in this sense is to engage with the world in which one lives in a self-directed and excellence-oriented way.

The second pillar of Montessori's moral philosophy is respect for others. For Montessori, character naturally generates "respect for the work of others and consideration for the rights of others" (Montessori 2016, 70). This respect requires non-interruption—"never … intervene when the child is immersed in his work" (Montessori 2019b, 62)—and includes help. Montessori distinguishes respectful help from service because service acts *for* another, removing another's exercise of character, whereas genuine help promotes another's activity. "Help me to do it by myself" is the paradigm of respectful help within a Montessori classroom (Montessori 2017, 175).

Finally, Montessori recognizes the value of social solidarity and cohesion, going beyond mere respect or assistance. She understands social solidarity to involve acting *together* as a single organism (Montessori 2015a, 22). Solidarity occurs in many contexts, and a particularly vivid example is a classic Montessori activity called the Silence Game (Montessori 1912, 212–13, 364; Montessori 2014, 237). The teacher directs the class, often with a whisper, to be silent, and then silence sweeps over the children: "Fifty or sixty children from two and a half years to six years of age, all together and at a single time, know how to hold their peace so perfectly that the absolute silence seems that of a desert" (Montessori 1912, 116). Montessori elsewhere compares this immediate and felt cohesion with the warp in weaving:

> When a piece of cloth is to be woven, the warp is prepared first. All the threads lie close together, but parallel to each other. This is like the society by cohesion. ... The second stage is when the shuttle attaches all the threads together. This is like the work of the leader who connects all the people together. Yet it is necessary to have the warp, the society by cohesion, as a basis—or we could not weave a strong piece of cloth.
>
> *(Montessori 2012a, 237–8; cf. Montessori 2014, 214–15)*

Similar to cloth woven from misaligned threads, humans united only by leaders or organized structures are often poorly united. However, when individuals practice social solidarity from childhood they understand how to bind people together strongly, like well-woven cloth. Montessori's pedagogical concern with solidarity, even in the earliest years, provides the basis for children to develop into socially and politically conscientious adults.

In the end, Montessori's moral philosophy helps orient her pedagogy but can also be seen as outgrowth of her work. Through working with and observing children in conditions of freedom, she came to see the importance of character, respect, and solidarity in human life. Her pedagogy, in turn, increasingly became oriented toward cultivating these three features of human flourishing. Every Montessori classroom includes materials for children's active work, which cultivate character; contexts for social coordination and courtesy, which foster respect; and opportunities for profound degrees of working together, which promote solidarity.

Embodiment

One of the most important recent developments in philosophy is increased attention to the role of physicality in intelligence, cognition, mindedness, and action. Proponents of embodied or embedded cognition see the whole body, rather than merely the brain or nervous system, as involved in cognition. That is, the mind "is not disembodied [nor even merely neuronal] ... but arises from the nature of our brains, bodies, and bodily experience" (Lakoff and Johnson 1999, 4 and 555), such that even "perception is in part constituted by our possession and exercise of bodily skills" (Noë 2004, 25). Montessori was ahead of her time understanding this philosophical development; for her, knowledge and action, including sensory experience, is embodied movement and sensory experiences. Because of the essential "interconnection between mind and muscle," the mental network includes senses and motor functions (Montessori 1913, 222–3; Montessori 2014, 126). To know how to write, for example, is in part to have hands with the muscular coordination to hold a pencil and form letters. In recognizing the importance of this type of "embodied cognition,"[7] Montessori's approach impacts our understanding of the philosophy of mind as well as other areas of philosophy, including virtue epistemology and practical pedagogy (Frierson 2020, 48–58, 149–61).

Finally, Montessori's focus on embodiment is not limited to traditional epistemological concerns about acquiring knowledge. She also adopts a deeply embodied approach to ethical life. For example, to respect others is in part to "move gracefully and properly" and avoid "knocking against his companions, … stamping on their feet, … [or] overturning the table" (Montessori 1913, 84; Montessori 2016, 129–30). Lessons in grace and courtesy, along with an overall classroom environment fostering *active* and *embodied* forms of respect, illustrate Montessori's awareness that moral life is not merely a matter of having good intentions but also controlling our actions such that we foster certain sorts of habits of movement *and* the mind relative to others. Because contemporary moral philosophy has generally not emphasized literal embodiment in moral life Montessori's insights about embodied features of moral agency can make a real contribution to bringing embodied cognition and moral philosophy together (Frierson 2022, 175–99; Saito 2016, 225–42).

Conclusion

Montessori's return to Rome to study philosophy for the sake of her pedagogy was prescient. Over the course of developing her vision for children and education, she attended carefully to the free activities of children, opening her eyes to see traditional philosophical issues in new ways. Her study of philosophy, combined with her capacious mind and loving attention to children, led her to new approaches in epistemology, metaphysics, the philosophy of freedom, and moral philosophy. In a philosophical context, Montessori education remains an area ripe for study and further exploration.

Notes

1. For evolutionary positivism, see Cimino and Foschi (2012, 310); also see Foschi (2012), Foschi and Cicciola (2006), James (1906), and Santucci (1963).
2. The original wording is italicized.
3. See Hugo DeVries (Montessori 1913, 47), Carl Naegeli (Montessori 1913, 46), Gregor Mendel (Montessori 1913, 50–1), and Charles Manning Child (Montessori 2015b, 70).
4. See, for example, Thomas Nagel's *Mind and Cosmos* (2012).
5. For a detailed discussion of the implications of this epistemology for contemporary debates about reliabilism and responsibilism in virtue epistemology, see Frierson (2020).

6. For a brief introduction to Hegelian ethics, see Pippin (2008). For discussion of the social nature of agency, see Bratman (2013) and Gilbert (2006).
7. See Clark (2011), Lakoff and Johnson (1999), Noë (2009), Thelen and Smith (1994), and Varela et al. (1991).

References

Adams, Madonna. 2005. "The Concept of Work in Maria Montessori and Karl Marx." *Proceedings of the American Catholic Philosophical Association* 79: 247–60.
Babini, Valeria. 2013. "Scienze Umane e Pratica di Democrazia. Da Maria Montessori a Franco Basaglia." *Rivista Sperimentale di Freniatria* 137: 9–32. http://digital.casalini.it/10.3280/RSF2013-001002.
Bratman, Michael. 2013. *Shared Agency: A Planning Theory of Acting Together.* New York: Oxford University Press.
Cimino, Guido, and Renato Foschi. 2012. "Italy." In *The Oxford Handbook of the History of Psychology: Global Perspectives*, edited by D. B. Baker, 307–46. Oxford: Oxford University Press.
Clark, Andy. 2011. *Supersizing the Mind: Embodiment, Action, and Extension.* Oxford: Oxford University Press.
Conant, James. 2010. "Nietzsche's Perfectionism: A Reading of *Schopenhauer as Educator*." In *Nietzsche's Postmoralism: Essays on Nietzsche's Prelude to Philosophy's Future*, edited by R. Schacht, 181–257. Cambridge, UK: Cambridge University Press.
Foschi, Renato. 2012. *Maria Montessori*. Rome: Ediesse.
Foschi, Renato, and Elisabetta Cicciola. 2006. "Politics and Naturalism in the 20th Century Psychology of Alfred Binet." *History of Psychology* 9 (4): 267–89.
Frierson, Patrick. 2020. *Intellectual Agency and Virtue Epistemology: A Montessori Perspective*. London: Bloomsbury.
Frierson, Patrick. 2022. *The Moral Philosophy of Maria Montessori: Agency and Ethical Life*. London: Bloomsbury.
Gilbert, Margaret. 2006. *A Theory of Political Obligation: Membership, Commitment, and the Bonds of Society*. Oxford: Oxford University Press.
James, William. 1906. "G. Papini and the Pragmatist Movement in Italy." *The Journal of Philosophy, Psychology and Scientific Methods* 3 (13): 337–41. https://www.jstor.org/stable/2011869.
Korsgaard, Christine M. 2009. *Self-Constitution: Agency, Identity, and Integrity*. Oxford: Oxford University Press.
Lakoff, George, and Mark Johnson. 1999. *Philosophy in the Flesh: The Embodied Mind and Its Challenge to Western Thought*. New York: Basic Books.
Matellicani, Anna. 2007. *La "Sapienza" di Maria Montessori: Dagli Studi Universitari alla Docenza 1890–1919*. Rome: Arachne editrice.
Montessori, Maria. 1912. *The Montessori Method*. New York: Frederick A. Stokes and Co.
Montessori, Maria. 1913. *Pedagogical Anthropology*. New York: Frederick A. Stokes and Co.
Montessori, Maria. 2007. *To Educate the Human Potential*. Amsterdam: Montessori-Pierson Publishing. (originally 1948).
Montessori, Maria. 2008. "Cosmic Education: Lecture Four." *Communications* 2: 52–8.
Montessori, Maria. 2012a. *The 1946 London Lectures*. Amsterdam: Montessori-Pierson Publishing Company.
Montessori, Maria. 2012b. "The Unconscious in History." *NAMTA Journal* 37 (2): 7–25.
Montessori, Maria. 2013. *The 1913 Rome Lectures: First International Training Course*. Amsterdam: Montessori-Pierson Publishing Company.
Montessori, Maria. 2014. *The Absorbent Mind*. Amsterdam: Montessori-Pierson Publishing Company.
Montessori, Maria. 2015a. *Education and Peace*. Amsterdam: Montessori-Pierson Publishing Company.

Montessori, Maria. 2015b. *To Educate the Human Potential*. Amsterdam: Montessori-Pierson Publishing Company.
Montessori, Maria. 2016. *The Advanced Montessori Method, Volume 1: Scientific Pedagogy as Applied to the Education of Children*. Amsterdam: Montessori-Pierson Publishing Company.
Montessori, Maria. 2017. *The Discovery of the Child*. Amsterdam: Montessori-Pierson Publishing Company.
Montessori, Maria. 2019a. *The Secret of Childhood*. Amsterdam: Montessori-Pierson Publishing Company.
Montessori, Maria. 2019b. *Il Peccato Originale*, edited by Fulvio De Giorgi. Brescia, Italy: Scholé. http://www.cremit.it/wp-content/uploads/2019/04/0060-montessori.pdf
Nagel, Thomas. 2012. *Mind and Cosmos: Why the Materialist Neo-Darwinian Conception of Nature Is Almost Certainly False*. Oxford: Oxford University Press.
Noë, Alva. 2004. *Action in Perception*. Cambridge, MA: MIT Press.
Noë, Alva. 2009. *Out of Our Heads: Why You Are Not Your Brain, and Other Lessons from the Biology of Consciousness*. New York: Farrar, Straus, and Giroux.
Pippin, Robert. 2008. *Hegel's Practical Philosophy: Rational Agency as Ethical Life*. Cambridge: Cambridge University Press.
Rutherford, Donald. 2018. "Nietzsche as Perfectionist." *Inquiry: An Interdisciplinary Journal of Philosophy* 61 (1): 42–61.
Saito, Yuriko. 2016. "Body Aesthetics and the Cultivation of Moral Virtues." In *Body Aesthetics*, edited by Sherry Irvin, 225–42. Oxford: Oxford University Press.
Santucci, Antonio. 1963. *Il Pragmatismo in Italia*. Bologna: Il Mulino.
Thelen, Esther, and Linda B. Smith. 1994. *A Dynamic Systems Approach to the Development of Cognition and Action*. Cambridge, MA: MIT Press.
Trabalzini, Paola. 2011. "Maria Montessori through the Seasons of the Method." *The NAMTA Journal* 36: 1–218.
Varela, Francisco, Evan Thompson, and Eleanor Rosch. 1991. *The Embodied Mind: Cognitive Science and Human Experience*. Boston: MIT Press.
Wood, Alan. 2007. *Kantian Ethics*. Cambridge: Cambridge University Press.

PART II

Key Writings of Maria Montessori

Introduction: Key Writings of Maria Montessori

Eva-Maria Tebano Ahlquist

Montessori's extensive works cover a wide range of topics from the human prenatal stage to adulthood. Through her books, we can read her observations, her early educational research reports, and her experiences interspersed with anecdotes from observations of children. Her writings are multifaceted and sometimes challenging for today's readers because they contain philosophical expositions, almost arcane vocabulary, and even references to biblical texts. In prioritizing which of Montessori's works to include in *The Bloomsbury Handbook of Montessori Education*, we chose a selection of her key writings that reflect the broad range of her body of work and that represent ideas that are fundamental for Montessori education today. We should note that the chapters in Part II are more descriptive than critical in nature, intended to introduce readers to the texts and inspire further reading. Currently, text-critical publications are available in the German edition of the *Montessori Collected Works* (2010–2026[1]) and the Italian edition *Montessori Bibliografia Internationale 1896–2000* (2001).

Compiling a definitive overview of Montessori's writings is complicated by several factors. First, Montessori's own thinking evolved over her career so that later editions of her earlier works were reissued with modifications. In addition, first editions of her books were published in various languages. She lectured mainly in Italian and, more rarely, in French leading to multiple translations circulating around the world with the possibility of slightly differing interpretations. Finally, since Montessori herself did not write many books in the latter part of her career, the later books are transcripts from her lectures and documented by people other than herself. Some parts of the lectures represented recurring themes appearing in several books with terminology that may have shifted between them based on transcribers' understanding. Despite these challenges, Montessori provides, through her anecdotes, an understanding as she "penetrate[s] the layers of meaning of the concrete by tilling and turning the soil of daily existence" (van Manen 1990, 116). Her writing style offers considerable coherence and a clear understanding of a vision for a better educational system.

In Part II, the chapter sequence is generally organized by year of first publication to follow the evolution of Montessori's scholarly work. Part II of the handbook begins with a presentation with the most famous of Montessori's books *Il Metodo della Pedagogia Scientifica applicato all'educazione infantile nelle Case dei Bambini* known as *The Montessori Method*. The chapter compares the many revised editions, with the last edition entitled *The Discovery of the Child*, a title preferred by Montessori. She considered the term "method" to routinize the educational process into a packaged curriculum rather than reflecting the broad goals she sought, as she regarded her pedagogy to be a "means offered to deliver the human personality from the oppression of age-old prejudices regarding education" (Montessori 1989b, 6). This context is a fruitful framing for considering her other works and making them timeless.

In addition to considering Montessori's works chronologically, there is also value in considering organizing them by theme. The books which focus on theory are *The Advanced Montessori Method Volume I, The Child in the Family, The Secret of Childhood, Education for a New World, Formation of Man, Absorbent Mind,* and *The Child Society and the World. Education and Peace* can be considered to belong to the theory books. Philosophical themes are included in the theory books and Montessori's interest in psychoanalysis can be followed in several of these texts. The role of the teacher and the adult's approach to the child is always present. If the reader is interested in Montessori didactics, *The Advanced Montessori Method Volume II, Psychoarithmetic, Psychogeometry* and *Psychogrammar*, would be the choice. The books *Montessori Method/The Discovery of the Child, To Educate the Human Potential,* and *From Childhood to Adolescence* contain both theory and didactics.

Beyond educational philosophy and practice, these chapters illustrate how Montessori consistently centers the child's well-being when writing and speaking of child development, how the child should be taught, and how the adult should respond to the child's needs. She argued that children must not be oppressed, indoctrinated, or deprived of their integrity and independence. Understandably, Montessori education was banned after the mid-1930s by Nazi Germany and the fascist regime in Italy (see Chapter 1: "Maria Montessori: Life and Historical Context").

Montessori's ideas about how humanity should evolve to make the planet a peaceful place are found in almost all of her books, even if not always explicitly expressed (1992). She said the aim of education is "[t]he defence of the child, the scientific recognition of his nature, the social proclamation of his rights, [that] must replace the piecemeal ways of conceiving education" (Montessori 1989b, 6–7). With violence seemingly ever present in the world today, her ideas about how education has the potential to benefit humanity and bring about a more peaceful society and sustainable world are as relevant today as they were when she wrote them. In fact, today's readers can consider how Montessori's holistic approach to children can be applied in new ways in light of the challenges we face in developing critical thinkers who consider their place in an increasingly complex world where we strive for the child to become the new human (1989a).

Note

1. Maria Montessori—Collected works [Gesammelte werke], ed. Harlald Luwig, Friburg: Herder. Tentative date for completion of the series of approximately twenty books is 2026 (Harlald Luwig, pers. comm., April 25, 2022).

References

Montessori, Maria. 1989a. *Education for a New World*. Oxford: Clio.
Montessori, Maria. 1989b. *The Formation of Man*. Oxford: Clio.
Montessori, Maria. 1992. *Education and Peace*. Oxford: Clio.
Tornar, Clara. 2001. *Montessori Bibliografia Internationale 1896–2000*. Rome: Opera Nazionale Montessori.
Van Manen, Max. 1990. *Researching Lived Experience: Human Science for an Action Sensitive Pedagogy*. Albany, NY: State University of New York Press.

Chapter 5
Origins of the Pedagogy: *The Montessori Method* and *The Discovery of the Child*

Paola Trabalzini
Translation By: Darwin Michener-Rutledge

1909: The Scientific Pedagogy of Maria Montessori Is Born

Maria Montessori wrote with shaky handwriting in 1952 to her friend Sofia Ravasi Garzanti, "I wish I were young so that I could work more, and have more time to write and develop new ideas, and especially to write my book: Man. Help me as a friend, with your encouragement, your support" (Ravasi Garzanti 1965, 18). Sofia Ravasi Garzanti was the wife of Aldo Garzanti, the founder of the publishing house of the same name that has published Montessori books in Italy since 1950. From the title of the book, *Man*, we can advance the hypothesis that the book would have further deepened the goal of Montessori's research: a natural science of the formation of the human being from birth to adulthood. This research began in 1909 with the publication of the book *The Method of Scientific Pedagogy Applied to Infant Education in Children's Houses*[1] with, as expressed in the title, a study concerning the contribution that Montessori's Casa dei Bambini would give to the foundation of pedagogy as a science.

Maria Montessori published *The Method* five times: the first four editions in 1909, 1913, 1926, and 1935, and the fifth in 1950 with the title *The Discovery of the Child*. In each publication, she modified the text in various aspects: deleting, moving, and inserting new chapters, paragraphs, and individual terms, and deleting and adding names and images. In this contribution, the most significant variations are noted to pinpoint the identity of each edition of *The Method* and the main features of the evolution of Montessorian thought.[2]

In *The Method,* Montessori describes the experiments carried out in the Casa dei Bambini, the first of which was inaugurated on January 6, 1907, in the working-class district of San Lorenzo in Rome. Montessori had a working goal to experiment with the scientific education of the senses. Her experience from 1886 to 1902 with children with intellectual disability indicated that this approach was successful and instructive, hence her desire to replicate this with typically developing children.

The text was presented during the first Course of Scientific Pedagogy, which was, in fact, the first training course for Montessori teachers. This was held in Città di Castello, Perugia, at the residence of the Franchetti barons, in August 1909.[3] The barons were patrons of Montessori. Anna Maria Maccheroni, one of Montessori's first pupils, remembers that it was Baron Leopoldo

Figure 5.1 Children in the original San Lorenzo Casa dei Bambini at work. Reproduced from the *Montessori Method,* 1913. Courtesy of Biblioteca dell'Opera Nazionale Montessori.

Franchetti himself who, in 1909, arranged the most comfortable conditions for Montessori to write the book. It was later published by a printer—not a publisher—in Città di Castello with the order to print the book word for word without changing so much as a comma (Maccheroni 1956). Montessori dedicated the 1909 edition of *The Method* to the Franchettis: "I dedicate this book to the noble Baroness Alice Franchetti Hallgarten and to Baron Leopoldo Franchetti, Senator of the

Kingdom. It was their wish that it should be written and through their efforts it is released today in the world of thought, introducing the 'Case dei Bambini' into scientific literature" (translated paraphrasing) (Montessori 2000).

In 1912, *The Method* was published in the United States with the title *The Montessori Method*, and the first 5000 copies sold out in one week. In the first year in print in the United States, there were seven reprints.[4] Montessori dedicated the US edition of the book solely to Alice Franchetti Hallgarten, who died in Switzerland in 1911:

> I place at the beginning of this volume, now appearing in the United States, her fatherland, the dear name of ALICE HALLGARTEN of New York, who by her marriage to Baron Leopold Franchetti became by choice our compatriot. Ever a firm believer in the principles underlying the Case dei Bambini, she, with her husband, promoted the publication of this book in Italy, and throughout the last years of her short life, greatly desired the English translation which would introduce to the land of her birth the work so near to her heart. To her memory I dedicate this book, whose pages, like an ever-living flower, perpetuate the recollection of her beneficence.
>
> *(Montessori 1912, Acknowledgements)*

In the wake of the book's success, Montessori went to the United States for the first time in 1913. *The New York Tribune* called her "the most interesting woman of Europe" (Kramer 1988, 186).[5]

As mentioned, Montessori published five editions of *The Method*. In 2000, the Montessori National Opera—an Italian cultural institution founded by her will in 1924—published the critical edition of *The Method*, where each of the Italian editions is compared. Here we see the study of the variations and the evolution of the author's thoughts emerge along with the dynamism and openness of *The Method*. While structure of the text remains essentially the same, new observations, additions, and nuances highlight Montessori's continuous reflection (Cives 2000).

The variations in these editions indicate the progressive emergence of Montessori's interest in the study of the stages of development of children and their minds. This expands her initial attention given to educational pedagogy as a science. In the first two editions of *The Method*, Montessori writes about the use of teaching materials, while in subsequent editions, she moves on to the definition of development materials. In the third edition, she introduces references to sensitive periods—for example, that of language, movement, or the soul "in which [the child] has intuition and religious urges" (Montessori 2000, 469). In the fifth edition, whose title, uncoincidentally, is *The Discovery of the Child*, Montessori introduces the theme of the absorbent mind. At the end of the book, she highlights that "the method is the consequence of having assisted the development of psychological phenomena which had remained unobserved and hence unknown for thousands of years" (686–7). According to Montessori, the main psychological dispositions are free choice of activity, the polarization of attention, the repetition of an exercise, and spontaneous discipline.

The textual evolution and variation within constitute an "internal" evolution of Montessorian thought. Here we see the influence of the changing historical and cultural contexts into which the editions of *The Method* are inserted: the liberal Italy of 1909 and 1913, the fascist one of 1926 and 1935, and the republican and democratic one of 1950.

The Evolution of the Book

In 1909, Italy was heading toward a process of modernization and reforms, but not without contradictions. The title and dedication of the first edition and the title of the first training course in Città di Castello indicate the theoretical framework in which Montessori inserts *The Method*: the emergence of educational pedagogy as a science. Montessori asserts that this work is not possible in the traditional school framework but only when the school becomes a home where children experience an atmosphere of freedom, activity, and peace. In the first edition, Montessori writes that the birth of pedagogy as a science "of which we speak, but which does not, in reality, exist" and which "by the aid of the positive and experimental sciences that have renewed the thought of the nineteenth century, must emerge from the mist and clouds that have surrounded it" (70).

Montessori's writing is indicative of her medical training and her diverse and robust educational background in botany, zoology, experimental physics, comparative anatomy, physiology, and chemistry. During her years of study at the University of Rome (1890–1896), she connected the horizons of the nineteenth and twentieth centuries by marrying work in biology, anthropology, psychiatry, experimental psychology, and hygiene. The first edition of *The Method* mainly cites doctors, biologists, physiologists, psychologists, and psychiatrists. Citations from the French doctors and educators, Itard and Séguin, who inspired her work, recur about sixty times in the text. Among the great pedagogues, she cites only two: Froebel and Rousseau. Froebel is quoted fourteen times (the occurrences are halved in later editions) essentially concerning teaching materials, and Montessori underlines her different scientific position: the materials that she proposes are developmental materials; they are the property of the child. Rousseau is quoted twice, both times in a critical way: in the first occurrence, Montessori holds that Rousseau refers to infantile freedom without realizing it; in the second, Montessori quotes the famous aphorism, "*Tout est bien sortant des mains de l'Auteur des choses*, tout dégénère dans les mains de l'homme" (297). [Everything is good leaving the hands of the author of things, everything degenerates in the hands of Man.]" She observes that it is possible to derive that education is harmful.

At the same time, only five philosophers are named: Helvetius, Kant, and Nietzsche, each mentioned once, and then James (once) and Wundt (four times) who are often remembered more as psychologists than philosophers. These occurrences are sometimes random (Nietzsche), sometimes more significant. Montessori quotes Helvetius, who had absolute confidence in education ("man is nothing without the work of man"), because Itard was a follower of Helvetius. Montessori remembers Kant because she believes that her pedagogy is modeled on the concept expressed by Kant in the book *On Education*: perfect art returns to nature. Montessori quotes Nietzsche when she refers to the "new woman," and she recalls his creation of the woman of Zarathustra, who wants to be loved by man for herself and with him to procreate a better child than herself. In the first and second editions of *The Method*, James is mentioned for the psychological importance of religious conscience; the third edition eliminates his name in favor of a specific chapter on religious education. Finally, Wundt is cited concerning experimental psychology and the importance of the observation method.

In Italy, Montessori was criticized for her scientific and non-philosophical approach to pedagogy and her positivist training. This criticism grew with the emergence of neo-idealist philosophy, which criticized positivism, early in the twentieth century. Montessori took the critiques as an opportunity for clarity, examination, and verification. However, Fornaca noted, "[T]he limits of the old scientism on which she establishes a new scientific pedagogy, mindful of child psychology, but also of the environment and the new culture and in proposing a truly new educational and methodological model, sensitive to the demands of the real child, to his needs, to the learning processes" (Fornaca 1988, 346).

In the first edition of *The Method*, Montessori refers to science, not just scientists, as eight of the individuals cited are intellectuals, poets, and writers. Eight are sacred names. The painter Raffaello Sanzio is mentioned for painting the *Madonna della Seggiola*, which later became the symbol of the Case dei Bambini. The literary and religious references also reveal that Montessori's humanistic and spiritual formation are integrated into her scientific-pedagogical theory. She provides examples and metaphors to clarify the concepts. Montessori's scientific and humanistic training, therefore, merge in *The Method*.[6]

The scientific pedagogy proposed by Montessori is attentive to the constructive subjectivity of children and the fundamental relationship they have with their environment; it promotes a new culture of childhood and its rights. This latter feature allows Montessori to avoid a rigid and mechanical scientificity and to remain open to the ecological conception of human development.

The 1909 edition ends with twenty-two illustrations that have the educative function of presenting the materials rather than the educational environment. In fact, only the first eight photographs show children of San Lorenzo at work. Particular attention is paid to materials for learning reading and writing as literacy acquisition by children between the ages of 4 and 5, which aroused the admiration of visitors to the Casa dei Bambini.

In 1913, the second Italian edition of *The Method* was published with few variations save for the presence of two new chapters: "Sequence and Grades in the Presentation of Material and in the Exercises" and "General Review of Discipline," which appeared for the first time in the US edition. The variations presented in the second Italian edition of *The Method* mainly indicate two aspects: greater attention to the psychological life of the infant and the international diffusion of the method. The number of photographs increased to forty-two and testified to the international expansion of the Montessori method with images of Casa dei Bambini in France, England, and the United States.

After the First World War, Montessori saw her work recognized in Italy on both cultural and practical levels with an increased number of schools. This success forced her to have her first contact with the liberal government in the 1920s and subsequently in 1922 with Mussolini's government. Here she tried to open a dialogue between the Catholic Church and fascism to reconcile some political and educational issues. The achievement of this aim compelled her to start a dialogue with the Italian political and cultural forces. This contextualizes the "softening of the positivistic" and political-reformist tones in the 1926 edition of *The Method* without conceding anything to the regime's ideology (Cives 2000).

For example, in 1909, Montessori wrote that the San Lorenzo experiment "would seem to open up a way for the practical application of new *principles*, capable of *rebuilding Pedagogy*. Much has been said in the past decade concerning the tendency of pedagogy, following in the footsteps of Medicine, to pass beyond the purely speculative stage and base its conclusions on the positive results of *experimentation*" (Montessori 2000, 69). In the 1926 edition, in contrast, this sentence was changed to reflect that the experiments in the Case dei Bambini seem to open up a way for the practical application of new methods, capable of giving to pedagogy a wider application of scientific experiments without removing it of its natural bases on theoretical principles (translated paraphrase). Here we see Montessori writing in a softer manner about methods, not principles, and about the use of *scientific experiences* instead of a reconstruction of pedagogy that remains on its natural foundations of speculative principles. This variation does not testify to a philosophical conversion of any kind but rather Montessori's attempt to protect herself from accusations of positivism.

Furthermore, the introduction to the 1926 edition begins with the blessing of the book by Pope Benedict XV, which Montessori had received in 1918 but only made public in 1926.[7] She wanted to emphasize that the spiritual vision of man was not in contrast with scientific pedagogy. In 1926, a chapter on Catholic religious education was also introduced for the first time, in which Montessori reports on the experiment carried out from 1915 in Barcelona. She also dilutes references to the naturalistic-biological matrix, retouching or replacing the passages that might lead the reader to think she was advocating almost unconditional freedom. For instance, the title of the paragraph "Biological concept of liberty in pedagogy" becomes in 1926 "Liberty of development" (2000, 215, note 279). The title of the paragraph "Abolition of prizes and external forms of punishment" in 1926 becomes "Our children face to face with prizes and punishments" (2000, 211, note 257).

Despite Montessori's intentionality in this edition, the criticisms were renewed both by the neo-idealists and by some Catholics, testifying to a challenging cultural climate unfavorable to Montessorian thought in Italy. Strengthened with international success and a newly buoyed reputation for her methods, she drew additional attention from the Italian people but also from the government. From 1932, Montessori and her son Mario were subjected to the surveillance of the fascist police. During that same year in Geneva, she exposed her pacifist thinking in the conference Peace and Education. Just the year before, however, Mussolini wrote that "only war brings all human energies to the maximum tension and gives a seal of nobility to the peoples who have the virtue of facing it" (Mack Smith 1997, 477). It is during this time that Montessori also opposed the regime's interference in the choice of teachers for the Regia Scuola di Metodo, the school that she directed in Rome for the training of Casa dei Bambini teachers.

These examples are just a few of the events that precipitated the relationship between Montessori the scientist and fascism. Montessori did not want to give up her projects and independence in her work, so she left Italy in 1934. She returned in 1947, and on May 3, she was received with full honors by the nascent Constituent Assembly, which, on June 25, 1946, began its work to give the Italian Republic its first constitution.

In 1950, Montessori resumed teaching courses in Italy, and it was necessary to republish her fundamental book. Hence, she published the fifth edition of *The Method* with the title *The Discovery of the Child*. In the 1950 book, Montessori limits herself to clarifying only a few aspects of the text, given that "it was impossible to bring this book up-to-date without re-writing it completely, not only as far as its contents, but also as far as the wording is concerned" (Montessori 2000, 67). Montessori makes it clear that in order to get a full picture of her work, reading *The Discovery of the Child* must be integrated with the reading of her other texts produced over the fifteen years since the previous printing of the work. She emphasizes strongly that "the result of our work has been more than the creation of a new method of education. The conclusions reached are expressed in the new title" (67).

Montessori explained the change in titles and the centrality of the revelation of the "new child" as a result of psychological phenomena never observed and studied before, but nonetheless important. "They are the exponent of a special mental form, of psychological sensibilities found only in the creative period of growth" (686). The child, then, is the fulcrum of Montessori's work in relation to how her scientific method of educational pedagogy develops and aims to transform the way of teaching in school and the adult-child relationship. Montessori continued by noting the experimental method and scientific pedagogy emphasizing the perspective the reader must consider: the psychological study of the natural laws of childhood life. Also, in part of the 1950 book, Montessori speaks of "psychological discovery" regarding the characteristics and mental formation of childhood, writing that "this is the real basis of our whole work because it was developed around and inspired by these phenomena" (82).

Finally, in the 1950 edition, in her chapter on religious education, Montessori specifies that the experiment in religious education was abolished in the Casa dei Bambini "because it referred solely to Catholic religious education, in which it is possible to make the preparation active by means of movements of the body and of objects, that is 'material'; whilst that cannot be done with other religions which are quite abstract. ... But these practical attempts, being beyond common use, cannot be disseminated" (658). The period spent continuously in India from 1939 to 1946 and the work in a new cultural and religious environment, the deepening of the theme of the "cosmic plan," and the disappearance of the concerns and objectives that accompanied the third edition of the book must have given Montessori the sense of overcoming a somewhat narrow and specific confessional Catholic perspective.

The 1926 edition had more photographs—totaling sixty-two—than the previous editions; the captions allowed Montessori to comment and specify various aspects of her pedagogical proposal. Notably, in the 1950 edition, there are twenty-two illustrations concerning educational life in the Children's Houses rather than the presentation materials. Scocchera implies that Montessori "prefers to communicate the relevant psychic phenomena: especially the dynamic and joyful nature of educational work and concentration" (Scocchera 2000, XXXIX).

The Method, later *The Discovery of the Child*, is best characterized by being both a bridge and a watershed. A bridge because the educational system of the Casa dei Bambini is nourished by Montessori's work in 1896–1907: her scientific, pedagogical, and social work with children with intellectual disability; her commitment to civil rights of women; and her teaching at the university. The experience of the Children's Houses of San Lorenzo was an ethical-civil commitment of the young Montessori to construct an inclusive and supportive community and society. *The Method* was a watershed text because of the novel idea of a hard working, independent, and competent child. New light was also shed on fundamental aspects of the learning process and the child's validation of specific materials that support their love of learning and knowledge. The importance of the prepared environment, individualized teaching, the adult-child relationship, and the school-family relationship are aspects of education now understood as commonplace and as an aid to life, but only thanks to pioneers like Montessori. Nobly, within this work, Montessori did not neglect the theme of peace: the environment of the Casa dei Bambini was already defined as peaceful in the book *Pedagogical Anthropology* of 1910 because the laws of life are respected throughout her work. The whole of 1909 to 1950 is held together by the unmistakable eloquence and calm of the author. Her stylistic register uses various tones: scientific, narrative, lyrical, denouncing the denial of childhood and its rights. This register makes reading the book interesting even today.

The Discovery of the Child does not exhaust the Montessori educational proposal. It is the cornerstone of her conviction that "humanity can hope for a solution of its problems, the most urgent of which are those of peace and unity only by turning its attention and energies to the discovery of the child and the development of great potentialities of the human personality in the course of construction" (Montessori 2000, 67). Thus, *The Method* illuminates and animates her future work.

Notes

1. The translation of the quoted passages from *Il metodo della pedagogia scientifica* (2000) is by the author of this chapter. Hereafter, *Il Metodo* is cited as *The Method*. The translation of the quoted passages of *La scoperta del bambino* is taken from *The Discovery of the Child*, Indian edition in English, 1948.
2. As of April 2022, the five Italian editions of the book are available on the following site: www.atlantemontessori.org. The realization of the *Montessori Atlas* is part of the Project of Relevant National Interest on the subject *Maria Montessori from the past to the present: Reception and implementation of her educational method in Italy on the 150th anniversary of her birth*. Four universities are involved in the project: University of Bologna, Milano-Bicocca, LUMSA (Roma), and Valle d'Aosta.
3. Alice Hallgarten Franchetti (1874–1911) belonged to a wealthy German Jewish family. She was born in New York and then moved to Rome where she met Baron Leopoldo Franchetti (1847–1917), whom she married in 1900. Her activities in the field of childhood were linked to social commitment and the international culture in which she grew up. Together with frequent trips abroad, this allowed her to come into contact with the pedagogical movements of the early twentieth century. Leopoldo, first deputy and then senator, engaged in the study of the social and economic problems of the Kingdom of Italy.
4. *The Method* was published in French in 1912; Russian, Polish, German in 1913; Romanian and Japanese in 1914; Spanish in 1915; Dutch in 1916; and Danish in 1917 (Trabalzini 2011).
5. The organizer of the Montessori conference tour was the journalist Samuel McClure, director of "McClure's Magazine." McClure had published some articles by the journalist Josephine Tozier regarding the origin and principles of the pedagogical proposal of Montessori. The success of the articles prompted McClure to go to Rome to visit the Montessori schools. He was impressed by her and organized the pedagogue's first trip to the United States (Montessori 2013).
6. Spiritual research is presented in Montessori under two aspects: the interest in theosophy, a philosophical-religious doctrine, with the enrollment in the Theosophical Society in 1899; and, in the first decade of the twentieth century, the proximity to Modernism, a movement within the Catholic Church that proposed to settle the disagreement between faith and the results of the positive sciences. Pius X condemned Modernism with the encyclical *Pascendi* (1907).
7. The blessing was also published by Montessori in 1948 in the introduction to the Indian edition in English of *The Discovery of the Child*, thus giving testimony to the history of the book.

References

Cives, Giacomo. 2000. "Carattere e Senso delle Varianti di *Il Metodo*." In *Il Metodo della Pedagogia Scientifica Applicato All'educazione Infantile nelle Case dei Bambini. Edizione critica*, edited by Paola Trabalzini, XVII–XXX. Rome: Edizioni Opera Nazionale Montessori.

Fornaca, Remo. 1988. "La Scuola Italiana e il Positivismo." In *Il Positivismo e la Cultura Italiana*, edited by Emilio R. Papa, 335–49. Milan: Franco Angeli.

Kramer, Rita. 1988. *Maria Montessori: A Biography*. Reading, MA: Addison-Wesley.

Maccheroni, Anna Maria. 1956. *Come Conobbi Maria Montessori*. Rome: Vita dell'infanzia Editrice.

Mack Smith, Denis. 1997. *Storia d'Italia dal 1861 al 1997*. Rome-Bari: Giu, Laterza & Figli Spa.

Montessori, Maria. 1912. *The Montessori Method: Scientific Pedagogy as Applied to Child Education in "The Children's Houses" with Additions and Revisions by the Author*. Translated by Anne E. George. New York: Frederick A. Stokes.

Montessori, Maria. 1948. *The Discovery of the Child*. Translated by Mary A. Johnstone. Adyar, Madras: Kalakshetra. https://archive.org/stream/in.ernet.dli.2015.498938/2015.498938.the-discovery_djvu.txt.

Montessori, Maria. 2000. *Il Metodo della Pedagogia Scientifica Applicato All'educazione Infantile nelle Case dei Bambini. Edizione Critica*. Edited by Paola Trabalzini. Rome: Edizioni Opera Nazionale Montessori.

Montessori, Maria. 2013. *Maria Montessori Sails to America: A Private Diary, 1913*. Translated by Carolina Montessori. Amersfoort: Montessori-Pierson Publishing Company.

Ravasi Garzanti, Sofia. 1965. "Ultime Trepide Parole di Maria Montessori." *Vita dell'infanzia* XIV (7–8): 18.

Scocchera, Augusto. 2000. "Da *Il Metodo Della Pedagogia Scientifica* a *La Scoperta del Bambino*: Storie di Nomi, di Titoli e di Illustrazioni." In Maria Montessori *Il Metodo Della Pedagogia Scientifica Applicato all'Educazione Infantile Nelle Case dei Bambini. Edizione Critica*, edited by Paola Trabalzini, XXXI–XLIII. Rome: Edizioni Opera Nazionale Montessori.

Trabalzini, Paola. 2011. "Maria Montessori through the Seasons of the 'Method'." *The NAMTA Journal* 36 (2) (Spring): XI–218.

Chapter 6
School Years: *The Advanced Montessori Method* and *From Childhood to Adolescence*

Clara Tornar
Translation By: Eva-Maria Tebano Ahlquist

Although *The Advanced Montessori Method* and *From Childhood to Adolescence* were published three decades apart, they present some exciting elements of continuity. In both, we find an accurate description of the cognitive processes that the author considers particularly relevant in childhood and adolescence. Moreover, Montessori operationally outlines a school curriculum designed to provide effective educational responses to the psychological needs manifested in these two different stages of development.

The Advanced Montessori Method

After the success of the educational experiment conducted in Via dei Marsi in 1907 and the extraordinary international fame achieved with the publication of *The Montessori Method*,[1] Montessori began to experiment with the application of her pedagogy in elementary schools. Her efforts in this area led to the publication in Italy of her substantial volume, *L'autoeducazione nelle scuole elementari* (1916). The long subtitle, *Continuazione del volume Il Metodo della pedagogia scientifica applicato all'educazione infantile nelle Case dei Bambini (Continuation of the Volume The Method of Scientific Pedagogy Applied to Infant Education in Children's Homes)*, highlights the author's view of the importance of establishing a close continuity between the two school levels. It also highlights, to some extent, the existence of specific themes common to the two works, such as the polemic against traditional education and the defense of the pedagogical principles of autonomy and freedom, which are still often ignored in educational practice.

The publication of the work in the United States took place only one year after the Italian edition, but with a new title and subtitle: *The Advanced Montessori Method: Scientific Pedagogy as Applied to the Education of Children from Seven to Eleven Years* (Montessori 1917). In addition, the two parts of the original edition became the two volumes of *The Advanced Montessori Method* that we know today as *Spontaneous Activity in Education* and *The Montessori Elementary Material*. The first volume provides essential insights into the Montessori approach and its scientific premises; the second provides specific operational elements for developing the didactics in elementary schools.

The Advanced Montessori Method I

The first volume of *The Advanced Montessori Method* is an essentially theoretical treatment. In the first chapters, which can be considered a preface to the whole work, Montessori analyzes with lucidity the educational needs of children, denouncing vehemently the educational errors committed by adults and by the educational system in general. The sociopolitical aspects of her study are particularly interesting since she explicitly speaks of a "social issue" of the child, affirming the need to introduce "Civil rights of the child in the twentieth century" (9). In this way, she became the spokesperson for the demands around child's rights emerging at the time; in 1924, the League of Nations signed a Declaration of the Rights of the Child, the first step toward the one proclaimed by the UN General Assembly in 1959. Montessori considers children and adolescents individuals with fundamental rights that the legislator must recognize. This remains a recurring theme in all her subsequent works. She asserts that despite the growing awareness of children's needs among those involved in education, society is still only concerned with the needs of the adult.

In the following chapters, Montessori addresses issues of great interest for understanding the scientific rationale behind her pedagogical approach. The work highlights her expertise in the field of psychophysiology, her scientific references, and indications for the organization of an optimal learning environment. This is still of considerable interest today, particularly in the light of neuroscientific studies (Oliverio 2006). The observations within the text include the following:

1. First, she establishes the need to observe the first manifestations of "polarization of the child's attention" when interacting with the learning environment, since these interactions represent the beginning of a constructive relationship with the environment itself (Montessori 1917, 53). Montessori devotes an entire chapter to this theme later in the text. Sharing with her contemporary William James the assertion that attention can be considered the intellectual force of individuals (James 1890), this process assumes in her pedagogy a propulsive function since it "offers the means to understand and to dominate," as she would later affirm in other works (Montessori 1946, 27).
2. Secondly, we see in this volume the importance of using external stimuli that are "experimentally determined" because "the child, left at liberty to exercise his activities, ought to find in his surroundings something organized in direct relation to his internal organization" (Montessori 1917, 55). Therefore, Montessori stresses that a process of self-learning is only possible if the environment contains the means to support it and that the discovery of these means "must be the result of an experimental study" (57).
3. Furthermore, Montessori notes the need to establish the quality and "quantity of external stimuli" (58), which are to be determined "[b]y the degree of the psychical reaction shown by the child" (59). Based on her observations in this area, she comes to define the principles of isolation of quality and gradation of each quality, which she had already discussed in *The Montessori Method* when describing the developmental materials she had designed.
4. Finally, she asserts, "The material of development is necessary only as a 'starting-point'" (64). In other words, it is to be regarded only as an initial point of support, necessary to gradually facilitate the subsequent process of abstraction.

Within the first volume, Montessori discusses the four points above extensively. Together these constitute a lucid and precise reference for understanding the scientific requirements underlying the Montessori learning environment and analyzing the criteria necessary to create the materials it contains. For example, the environment must contain only "what is necessary and sufficient" (61); in other words, she states the importance of guaranteeing the gradualness and appropriateness of the stimuli concerning the children's different ages and psychic needs. Finally, Montessori argues the importance of allowing error control—that is, the triggering of a feedback process between the environment and the child. Through this process, children can verify the correctness of their performance and remedy any errors by themselves.

More generally, Montessori's treatment of the theme of evaluation in the learning environment provides important insights into this work. Given the more recent debate on the theme of assessment and evaluation, this is especially prudent at the present time (Anderson 2003). According to her conception, assessment is, first and foremost, a process self-directed by the child; it is also a process that allows the teacher to analyze the way the child learns rather than focusing on the product of learning. In fact, Montessori states that, to study and understand child behavior scientifically, it is necessary "to divest oneself completely of the old scholastic conception according to which the progress of the child is assessed according to his proficiency in the various subject of study" (Montessori 1917, 67). This explains her preference for evaluation methodologies centered on direct observation of behavior without detracting from the correctness of the observation method, which seems to anticipate an ecological type of assessment schema. She dwells at length, in fact, on the need to observe children by leaving them free to act in their environment—in other words, while they are engaged in carrying out authentic tasks—rather than subjecting them to decontextualized tests, as is the case with most traditional assessments. In this respect, Montessori provides precise indications for setting up observation grids for school guidance (96–97).

Interesting and illuminating for understanding the Montessori approach is her subsequent discussion on volition and imagination into the work. As far as the volitional process is concerned, Montessori speaks of the "formation of the will," emphasizing the importance of acquiring habits and the need for appropriate exercise for their acquisition. For Montessori, the final goal must be the conquest of character, the development of which is closely linked to that of the ability to express one's own will. The training ground for these processes should be the action itself, through which she says that one learns the right balance between impulses and inhibitions. According to her, there is only one way to achieve this: "the child should act together with other children, and practice the gymnastic of the will in the daily habits of life" (134).

Imagination and related educational problems are also the subjects of careful consideration in the text. Montessori's position in this regard is that "[t]he true basis of imagination is reality" (196). As such, creative imagination is only possible when the mind has been progressively structured through a learning environment rich in multiple experiences conducted in contact with reality. This position agrees on many points with Vygotsky (1992) regarding productive imagination. Therefore, while imagination should be stimulated in childhood because, in this phase of development, the mind can go beyond the immediately perceived, learning should be strictly anchored to reality in the first years of life. This concept is often misconstrued in contemporary Montessori critiques as Montessori being opposed to play rather than stating a pedagogical understanding of the value of tasks situated in real-life contexts in service of the development of the child.

The Advanced Montessori Method II

The contents of the second volume, *The Montessori Elementary Material*, are very different from the first. As the English title promises, this volume deals in an operational way with the theme of the elementary school curriculum, presenting systematically its constituent basic disciplines: grammar, reading, arithmetic, geometry, drawing, music, and metrics. The teaching of these disciplines is carefully analyzed. The general criteria are defined, which, in continuity with the Casa dei Bambini, must always be based on a principle of operability and active involvement of the pupil. Also analytically described are the learning materials, specifically created to ensure a teaching-learning process based on concrete experience, which Montessori calls the first step toward the subsequent process of abstraction. The resulting commentary in the volume is a vision of the teaching-learning process in which various school disciplines are considered proper tools for intellectual development rather than opportunities for acquiring content and knowledge. This distinction is critical in understanding Montessori's work as she puts forth a new vision of scholastic learning, which she would develop further in the following years by focusing on three key disciplines: arithmetic, geometry, and grammar, which she called Psychoarithmetic, Psychogeometry, and Psychogrammar.

However, the programmatic framework of the elementary school outlined in the work is not a complete vision of the pedagogy related to this age child. Although it remains an indispensable reference for the knowledge of Montessori's thought and the application of the approach in the elementary schools, it lacks indications and insights for a broader renewal of school life, such as opening the school to the surrounding social and geographical environment. Moreover, the teaching-learning process is not yet placed within the broader cosmic vision that the author will develop in the following years. It is probable that Montessori herself later had perceived these shortcomings. In *From Childhood to Adolescence* (1948), which is dedicated to illustrating the approach in the secondary school, she took up the problem of education and instruction in the elementary school. In this, she indicated the exploration of the environment and nature, placed within a cosmic vision of education, as the most suitable forms to complete the school activity.

From Childhood to Adolescence

After the publication of *The Advanced Montessori Method*, Montessori, who had until that time concentrated her research activities on observing childhood between the ages of three and twelve, began to turn her attention to the study of other important phases of development. Around the second half of the 1930s, she dealt with adolescence and the psychological, social, and educational problems connected with this developmental period. Within this framework, she published the book *De l'enfant à l'adolescent* (From Childhood to Adolescence) (1948) in Belgium. The text is based mainly on lectures given in the preceding decade. The lectures on this subject were given at the Fifth International Montessori Congress at Oxford University (1936–1939) and immediately afterward in Utrecht, Amsterdam, and London. The last two initially were published by the Montessori Association Internationale (AMI) (Montessori

1939a, 1939b) and later were included in the 1948 volume. Inexplicably, the English translation of the book was published three decades after the original French edition (Montessori 1973).

Among Montessori's texts, *From Childhood to Adolescence* is one of the most interesting and original, above all from a psychological point of view. It effectively expresses the idea of a process of development whose stages must be analyzed vis-à-vis their interconnections. It is no coincidence that we find it re-proposed in the publications of other scholars in the second half of the twentieth century, most notably by Jean Piaget in *De la logique de l'enfant à la logique de l'adolescent* (The Growth of Logical Thinking from Childhood to Adolescence) (Inhelder and Piaget 1955).

The description of development, conceived by Montessori as a succession of levels from childhood to maturity, considers the thread of continuity that links the different stages, illustrating that (a) the changes that occur in the transition from one developmental level to another are qualitative and (b) each developmental level descends from the previous one and in turn prepares the next. In particular, the changes analyzed in the text occur in the second and third levels of development, corresponding to childhood and adolescence, up to the threshold of adulthood.

From Childhood to Adolescence is also an interesting text from a pedagogical point of view. Firstly, it translates psychological observations into precise educational, didactic, and practical indications. Secondly, it can be considered the first translation into didactic terms of the cosmic education, which Montessori was beginning to develop in the years in which she was exploring the issues of adolescence and of which she had spoken in a 1935 lecture in London (Montessori 1989). The operational aspects of her philosophy of cosmic education occupy the central part of *From Childhood to Adolescence* and are based on an analysis of the psychological characteristics of childhood. Montessori dwells on the new capacity of the child to ask questions, seek answers, and formulate and verify hypotheses, hence the necessity of encouraging the children to explore reality in contact with nature (the "Going Out") and the importance of offering them elements for an overall representation of the universe grasped in its interconnections. The capability of activating the imagination is considered the incredible power of this age (Montessori 1948, 33–40). To this end, Montessori asserts, providing children with the possibility of discovering the relationship between the parts, rather than the details, offers them the keys to knowledge and the motivation to learn more.

Cosmic education is a particular choice, organization, and presentation of cultural content to offer relevant answers to cognitive needs at this stage of development. Moreover, this explains the importance given to this theme in the text; the pages dedicated to water and chemistry (43–90) offer us didactic demonstrations that are genuinely exemplary both for the freshness of the psychological observations that accompany them and for their extraordinary capacity to adhere to the psychological world of the child with intelligence and acuity.

Equally interesting in the text is the analysis of psychological and educational issues in adolescence. When Montessori began to deal with these issues, the scientific literature did not yet show any specific attention to this subject. Apart from Stanley Hall's 1904 study, *Adolescence*, from which Montessori certainly draws inspiration when she speaks of adolescence as a "new birth," absolute attention to this theme will occur above all from the middle of the century.

The analysis that Montessori presents to us in *From Childhood to Adolescence* highlights the characteristics that distinguish this evolutionary period, wanting above all to place it in the overall framework of human development. She grasps the character of crisis and of substantial ambiguity, aspects that have also been highlighted within psychological and social studies conducted more recently (Vegetti Finzi and Battistin 2000; Zuanazzi 1995). It also underlines how the process of transformation for adolescents concerns both biological and psychic life. She asserts that adolescents exist in a state of weakness on the physical level and an actual "regression" on the intellectual level (Montessori 1948, 101). Winnicott (1965) and others have since confirmed this assertion. Completely new social and ethical needs dominate the attention of adolescents, Montessori notes; adolescents feel the need to strengthen their self-confidence and construct a new individual identity, but they appear emotionally defenseless and fragile. They open up to social life, presenting themselves as "social infant[s]" with an overwhelming need to live and produce socially. Adolescence is also the "sensitive period" for developing feelings of justice and personal dignity (Montessori 1948, 101).

Montessori begins from this premise to motivate the need to identify environmental conditions that can create an alternative to the adolescent's dependence and subordination generally underlying his relationship with the adult. She believes that many behavioral problems found in this development period are deviations attributable to the inadequate environment that channels, controls, and represses many of their manifestations.

However, she notes adolescence is also the period in which human energy is manifested. This phase of development is a precious resource for the future of humanity, introducing an original dimension to the contemporary debate. In fact, she refers to an adolescent placed in the condition of manifesting their creative characteristics, which can only emerge within an environment that meets their needs. Also, for the adolescent age, the educational process is configured as a process of normalization—or more precisely of "valorization" of the personality (103); adolescents can recognize and employ their own resources in the service of the greater community's needs. Starting from this psychological and sociological analysis, Montessori defines what functions should be assigned to the educational process and what structure the secondary school should assume.

Montessori begins her reflection by considering what she believes to be the main limitations of secondary school. She argues that "they do not correspond to the social conditions of our time" (100). She condemns their approach, in which students are forced to work out of duty and necessity, not by interest (100), and therefore waste the best of their individual energies. She also identifies the primary limits of traditional schooling as the absence of connection between culture and real life. She does not share the objectives of traditional schooling, which she argued do not consider in any way those psychological, sociological, and historical elements that she places at the center of her analysis. Therefore, she claims that reforming the secondary school entails a reformulation of programs and methods and requires moving forward with a new social organization of studies and work. Montessori argues that since we are facing a radical change in the adolescent person, we must realize that a radical change in their education is necessary. The task of the education process in the general sense—and the education agencies in a more specific sense—must first and foremost be to give young people the opportunity to become the main character in their development.

Through critical sociohistorical analysis, Montessori glimpsed the signs of the epochal changes that would occur in the last years of the twentieth century. This enabled her to anticipate with extraordinary timeliness what turned out many decades later, to identify the school's strength as a vital force for adapting to rapidly changing circumstances and for the ability to orient oneself (99).

To begin with the above considerations, Montessori draws an outline for the reform of the secondary school, which considers two fundamental factors: the vital needs of the adolescent and the new needs emerging from a changing society. It is based on certain indispensable assumptions:

1. The needs of the adolescent period are the construction of one's social identity and the strengthening of one's self-confidence.
2. The adolescent must be provided a clear awareness of the social reality in which they must operate, which must go as far as to make young people aware of the reality of life lived, including its economic aspects. Hence the overall sense of the secondary school should be that of a real "school of experience in the social life" (102).
3. Making "culture" in the broadest and most profound sense of the term is important, since, as Montessori argues, "education must be wide and very thorough, and not only in the case of the professional intellectuals, but for all men who are living at a time that is characterized by the progress of science and its technical applications" (99).
4. There is a need to build transversal competencies capable of putting individuals in a position to operate concretely even in unpredictable situations. The pedagogue will point to the ability to adapt as the essential quality of the modern person because, while social progress constantly opens new possibilities of work and career, it simultaneously closes or overturns traditional types of work and employment.

Within this scheme, the secondary school is seen as a "Plan of Studies and Work" (111) a true, self-managed community based on alternating phases of study and work, marked by rhythms established by the children themselves. Montessori believed that the ideal location for this type of community should be away from the family, in a quiet place in the countryside—perhaps a farm—where ample space can be given to activities in contact with nature. She called it *Erdkinder* (see Chapter 16: "Erdkinder: An Educational Approach for Adolescents Ages 12–15"). This expression was most likely suggested to her during a stay in Germany (Barker 2001), where some interesting secondary school projects, such as the *Landerziehungsheime* (country education homes) founded by Hermann Lietz in 1898, were centered on rural life and the formative importance of work.

From Childhood to Adolescence goes on to outline and describe Montessori's project of a unified, non-vocational, full-time school, where cultural activities, mainly oriented toward a historical and scientific dimension, can be carried out in close synergy with activities centered on productive work. Montessori outlines the program based on three fundamental aims: (1) to provide opportunities for self-expression, leaving the adolescent with a full choice of activities within three areas: music education, language education, and art education; (2) to meet the fundamental needs in relation to the adolescent's psychological development through three fundamental subjects: moral education, mathematics, and languages; and (3) to provide a *general culture* that can place adolescents in relation to the civilization of their time through theoretical teachings and practical activities.

The result is a school model that focuses on the needs of the adolescent, a subject on which the future of humanity depends and whose education therefore requires radical change. Montessori's reflections and pedagogical assertions remain relevant today and offer stimulating ideas and indications for a different consideration of the psychological and educational needs in this delicate phase of human development.

Note

1. The two volumes are today known as *The Advanced Montessori Method I* and *II* in English editions.

References

Anderson, Lorin W. 2003. *Classroom Assessment: Enhancing the Quality of Teacher Decision Making*. Mahwah, NJ: Lawrence Erlbaum Associates.
Barker, Devan. 2001. "A Historical Look at Montessori's Erdkinder." *The NAMTA Journal* 26 (3): 283–315.
Hall, G. Stanley. 1904. *Adolescence: Its Psychology and Its Relations to Physiology, Anthropology, Sociology, Sex, Crime, Religion, and Education*. 2 vols. New York: D. Appleton & Co.
James, William. 1890. *The Principles of Psychology*. New York: Henry Holt & Company.
Montessori, Maria. 1916. *L'autoeducazione nelle scuole elementari: Continuazione del volume il metodo della pedagogia scientifica applicato all'educazione infantile nelle Case dei Bambini*. Rome: Maglione & Strini.
Montessori, Maria. 1917. *The Advanced Montessori Method: Scientific Pedagogy as Applied to the Education of Children from Seven to Eleven Years*. 2 vols. Translated by Florence Simmonds and Arthur Livingston. New York: Stokes.
Montessori, Maria. 1939a. "The 'Erdkinder': A Scheme for a Reform of Secondary Education." *Halfyearly Bulletin of the Association Montessori Internationale* 2 (1): 5–23.
Montessori, Maria. 1939b. "The Functions of the University." *Halfyearly Bulletin of the Association Montessori Internationale* 2 (1): 27–36.
Montessori, Maria. 1946. *Education for a New World*. Madras, Adyar: Kalakshetra.
Montessori, Maria. 1948. *De l'enfant à l'adolescent*. Translated by Georgette Jean-Jacques Bernard. Paris: Desclée De Brouwer.
Montessori, Maria. 1973. *From Childhood to Adolescence, Including Erdkinder and the Function of the University*. Translated by The Montessori Educational Research Center. New York: Schocken Books.
Montessori, Maria. 1989. *The Child, Society and the World: Unpublished Speeches and Writings*. Translated by Caroline Juler and Heather Yesson. Oxford: ABC-Clio Press.
Oliverio, Alberto. 2006. *Come nasce un'idea: Intelligenza, creatività, genio nell'era della distrazione*. Milan: Rizzoli.
Inhelder, Bärbel, and Jean Piaget. 1955. *De la logique de l'enfant à la logique de l'adolescent*. Paris: Presses Universitaires de France.
Vegetti Finzi, Silvia, and Anna Maria Battistin. 2000. *L'età incerta: I nuovi adolescenti*. Milan: Mondadori.
Vygotsky, Lev S. (1926) 1992. *Educational Psychology*. Translated by Robert Silverman. Florida: St. Lucie Press.
Winnicott, Donald W. 1965. *The Family and Individual Development*. London: Tavistock Publications.
Zuanazzi, Gianfrancesco. 1995. *L'età ambigua: paradossi, risorse e turbamenti dell'adolescenza*. Brescia: La Scuola.

Chapter 7
What Is Childhood? *The Child in the Family*, *The Secret of Childhood*, and *The Absorbent Mind*

Carmela Franzese
Translation By: Ariel Rothman

There is the profound belief within the writing of Maria Montessori that education must begin at birth. Among the elements that constitute the scope of Montessori's contributions, we find first the recognition of the learning potential of the small child, to whom she argues physical and intellectual stimuli must be offered. For Montessori, a child's education must embody the building blocks for life, meaning children should be encouraged to learn and act autonomously and respect their own interests and timelines.

The three writings discussed here are linked by recurring foundational themes, discussed to different degrees of depth within each of the works. It is impossible to exhaustively discuss every aspect of Montessori pedagogy in the limited space of a short chapter such as this. As such, the goal is simply to highlight for each text the most defining aspects of the works at hand in chronological order. To begin we examine the contributions of Montessori in 1923 included in *The Child in the Family*, published in Italy in 1936. From there we move on to explore *The Secret of Childhood* (1936) where Montessori elucidates her philosophy and pedagogy for a child's education until age 6. Finally, there is an analysis of *The Absorbent Mind* (1949), focusing primarily on a child's psychological development.

The Child in the Family

The Child in the Family (1991) is a collection of texts from conferences held by Montessori in Brussels in 1923, published first in Vienna and subsequently in Italy. Here we see the conceptual foundations of an innovative pedagogical vision, as well as the practices that emerge from the vision. Focusing on the child from birth in a new way, Montessori asserts the need for educators and caregivers to rethink the relationship between adults and children, both in family and school environments. She notes that difficulties, conflicts, and unrealistic expectations toward children are often, in fact, the result of mistaken conceptions and expectations of childhood. She argues that these conceptions originate from the failure of adults to recognize the needs and learning potentials (motor, sensory, exploratory) of children, producing educational practices inadequate for meeting the developmental needs of children. When this happens, the adult is called upon to remediate this problem, which then becomes an issue of social and moral order.

Montessori argues that adults must be the architects of the changes to learning environments necessary to guarantee that subsequent generations have not only adequate learning opportunities but also conditions of psychological serenity and functional relationships with caregivers at both home and school. Importantly, this collection of texts stresses the home as the primary educational environment. Montessori understood the home setting to be one where her educational practices could be applied in perfect continuity with the school environment.

Family Life: Preconceptions and Learning Opportunities

According to Montessori, punishments and disagreements originate from the belief that a child should adapt to the adult's environment and way of thinking—a clear premise of educational and relational errors. Her discussion of the underrated theme of childhood tantrums within the text presents revolutionary ideas within the world of pedagogical discourse. Montessori affirms that tantrums can actually originate from the young child's need for order, which she asserts is a necessary condition for them to "build their own mind" (20). The task of self-regulation allows for the developmental process of categorization. In these moments, children interpret their reality, and systematization of knowledge begins. Moreover, Montessori notes, tantrums are a manifestation of the child's need for attention and involvement. She states, "If one wanted to establish a principle, we would say that the child's participation in our life is necessary, because in the period in which they are to learn to navigate through life, they would not be able to grasp how to do it well if they do not see it modeled" (49). Offering this hospitality is certainly difficult, since it entails, first and foremost, the restructuring of patterns of thought and ingrained cultural representations about family roles and organization, including the responsibilities of each member. It is important to highlight the relevance of these considerations, especially contextually in the historical time she was writing. Its current day impact is equally notable as the quality of life around the globe is impacted by the constant drive toward hyper-productivity, digital hyper-connection, and growing job insecurity, which challenges adults' time and emotional availability.

Montessori argues that while everyday life offers children numerous exploratory and learning opportunities, parents, and sometimes even teachers, are not in the right position to understand the potential offered by these opportunities. She stresses the importance of shedding mistaken parenting and educational beliefs so that, liberated from such obstacles, adults can facilitate a child's full development. By giving their children an active role along their developmental journey, adults avoid imposing their own will on them. She also notes the importance of observation to understand each child's needs and their learning opportunities and to develop a respect for their personality. This allows the creation of environments that stimulate the potential of their absorbent minds.

What Is Childhood?

The Role of Concentration

Montessori's pedagogy is rooted in her discovery of children's ability to focus their attention for long periods of time on appropriate stimuli and activities suitable to their developmental needs. In fact, Montessori reports of having observed a 4-year-old child who "displayed the maximum attention" (63) while repeating the correct manipulation of solid wooden joints over forty times without losing concentration, even when Montessori began playing the piano and gathering the other children in song. Only after the child finished did the toddler begin to show interest in what was happening around her while appearing calm and rested.

Montessori notes that in addition to developing the "work instinct" (261) during these years, activities that stimulate concentration also have a beneficial effect on a child's mood. Concentration-oriented tasks, characterized by the prolonged repetition of specific actions, are conducted with pleasure as they satisfy exploratory needs at different levels: refining motor skills, spatial awareness, and hand-eye coordination (see Figure 7.1). This is a prime example of

Figure 7.1 Child with cylinder blocks. Photo courtesy of Carmela Franzese.

what Montessori calls "the great work" (73). Additionally, Montessori argues that the toddler's satisfaction resulting from manual work prepares them for social relationships and prosocial behavior. This work is evidence refuting the common critique of Montessori pedagogy as emphasizing the individual to the detriment of socialization and community. In light of these new understandings, Montessori designed materials and space with deep intentionality to ensure children have "the most favorable external conditions" (64–5) to promote concentration. Montessori affirmed that the domestic environment also offers opportunities of deep concentration as long as it is organized to meet the needs of childhood development.

The Domestic Environment

Montessori saw the fact that children are born into home environments designed for adults as a challenge. Still today, this is not an oft-discussed conundrum even as new parents prepare for an infant's arrival. Her work communicated the challenges of living in an environment built for adults, arguing that this takes away a child's learning and developmental opportunities. When toddlers are unable to suitably use objects and furniture which are too large or valuable, they have fewer opportunities to understand cause-and-effect relationships between elements in the environment and the environment and themselves. *The Domestic Environment* describes at length the preparation of an adequate child-centered environment in terms of dimensions, practicality, and usability to respond to the psychomotor and exploratory needs of the toddler.

For Montessori, a child's needs are met by equipping the home with small sinks, small arm chairs, low beds, and furniture that is light in color (so that dirt is evident), lightweight, and small in size (so that it can be easily moved). Such a space allows for the toddler to take charge of the area, independently carry out activities, and enjoy a sense of satisfaction from feeling like the protagonist. Additionally, autonomy is favored by giving the child time to experiment with different activities of everyday life, such as eating and washing independently. "Toddlers should be able to use everything around them that is required to keep a house in order, and they should be able to complete all the activities of daily life, such as sweeping, brushing the carpets, washing themselves, dressing themselves, etc." (83). This starts them on tasks that have a real-life application from a young age.

This Children's House classroom or, relatedly a home environment, is absent from dangers and obstacles. It is equipped with everything a child needs, allowing the adult to intervene as little as possible. The parents would need "to observe them from a certain distance," without, obviously, "abandoning them" (87).

The Adult

Montessori also reminds us that a well-organized environment allows the adult to maintain discreet control, avoiding ill-timed invasiveness during the process of independent learning. Nonetheless, the importance of adult guidance is not in dispute. The presence of the adult willing to meet the child's developmental needs is a guarantee of a relational exchange that is divided into various arenas, including the development of language, concentration, reasoning, analysis of reality, and co-construction of shared meaning. The preparation of the environment supports the scaffolding of young people to support their development related to specific tasks not yet mastered (Bruner et al. 1976). Thus, the role of the parent or caregiver proves to be a particularly delicate one; it requires an effort of awareness in order to embrace the fight necessary for the universal rights of a child. This is an authentic social matter, a fundamental topic addressed in the introduction of *The Secret of Childhood*.

The Secret of Childhood

Published in France in 1936, *The Secret of Childhood* (1989) presents a deeper look into the educational method developed for preschool-aged children.[1] Moving from a strong critique of the traditional view of childhood, calling for social reform, Montessori analyzes children's psychological qualities as the basis of learning; from there, she describes the essential components in children's learning: environment, materials, and the adult's role.

Sensitive Periods

Montessori spends a great deal of time discussing the concept of the sensitive periods of childhood. Here she argues that children's interests reflect their developmental phase and must be understood and encouraged. Children educate themselves by exploring their environment and hold within themselves the secret of human nature, hence the title of this work. For this reason, Montessori argues that the child should be the adult's teacher. The adult has the task of promoting the development of delicate psychic constructions, identifying the signs of the sensitive periods or "special awarenesses" (52). For Montessori, sensitive periods are transitional phases characterized by the presence of developmental needs and a powerful desire for learning particular skills or dispositions. The periods prompt children to search for activities aligning with their emergent developmental needs. For Montessori, finding the tools to allow the child to practice emergent cognitive, sensory, and motor skills is critical. Here one also sees the child repeat tasks until they feel intrinsically satisfied and understands the activity undertaken. Eventually, these conditions allow the child to move forward to other activities.

Corresponding to each of the sensitive periods is the child's inclination to perform specific tasks, that is to say, activities with a goal. The teacher's job then, Montessori notes, is to make sure that the child works with materials suitable to that sensitive period. This is made possible through the appropriate learning environment.

The Method: Learning Environment, Materials, and the Adult's Role

Montessori highlights the necessity for the educator to carry out precise observation and analyses of children's behavior to inform the creation and maintenance of educational environments suitable for children. Observation and analysis allow teachers to offer successful learning opportunities through the preparation of an appropriate environment, equipped with materials that allow the child to develop an independent learning process. The learning environment as conceived and implemented by Montessori is safe and free from physical barriers including those that limit autonomous choice, free movement, and sensory experiences. Furthermore, it is organized in such a way that the child is invited to complete tasks and to make these choices, all of which should have a scientific basis.

Autonomy and choice lead to the elimination of psychological barriers to learning, such as boredom, frustration, or overstimulation. In this way, Montessori shares children find themselves working in an environment that they perceive as their own, where they do not have to wear themselves out or ask for help from an adult to meet a need or reach an objective. In the Children's House environment, each child can be independent. The environment inspires the child to improve via self-correction of errors and materials that allow for this type of self-reflective behavior. Attention to the aesthetics of the objects also plays an important role as they entice use and render the place welcoming and pleasant. Montessori emphasizes that the materials should also be presented in the appropriate manner. These are the critical tasks of the teacher, who, using discretion in their role, will need to try to understand if the child has taken the right path in using the material correctly. From this perspective, rewards and punishments are stripped of their traditional connotations as Montessori understood them to be inappropriate means in the pursuit of a pedagogical purpose.

The elements that determine the normalization of children—a state of calm purposeful independence—include the following: choice of activity, the possibility to operate in a functional environment and manipulate materials capable of responding to children's needs, being in control of one's own learning, and concentration promoted by the aforementioned conditions. The resulting silence during work fosters concentration. And, Montessori adds, the outcome is the feeling of satisfaction deriving from all the above. Normalization can also be described as a state of serenity where motivation to carry out work without fear, aggressiveness, or shyness is present. This state describes the experiences of the child whose development needs are adequately met. Normalization allows children to self-regulate, experiencing active self-discipline and allowing them to give their movements order and meaning. Furthermore, Montessori argues, "Like moral defects, many diseases and unhealthy states can disappear in children ... with normalizing activities" (254). Thus, she compares her schools to "Houses of Health" where children can find healing (254).

The Absorbent Mind

Published in India in 1949, where in the mid-twentieth century Montessori pedagogy garnered immediate and considerable success, *The Absorbent Mind* (1999)[2] is Montessori's final work on the evolutionary path of the first six years of life. In it, she introduces new themes of great importance, such as the absorbent mind of a child and the periods of growth from birth to young adulthood. Most importantly, this volume bequeaths a social and moral legacy of Montessori, since therein education is attributed an indispensable, life-supporting role that plays a fundamental part in building a conflict-free society.

From Education for Life to Reflection on Embryology: A New Direction

In Montessori's perspective, education is therefore a tool for life development and therefore must be anchored to concrete existence: "The world of education is a type of island where individuals, isolated from the world, prepare themselves for life ahead while remaining strangers from it ... Education should no longer be based on a pre-existing curriculum, but rather on the understanding of human life" (Montessori 1999, 9, 12). A successful education, therefore, cannot overlook a deep appreciation of the learning potentials that are typical of the different periods of life. Montessori proposes an education plan that extends from birth to young adulthood, dedicating particular attention to the first six years. These first years are a delicate period and fundamental for development. Nevertheless, Montessori's interest is also focused on the prenatal period, especially embryology. This offers an opportunity to comment on the child's psychic life through the use of a metaphor: if the child goes through an embryonic phase during the course of gestation (physical embryo), then once born, it becomes a spiritual embryo.

The Spiritual Embryo

A reference to the notion of a spiritual embryo already appears in *The Child in the Family* and is then proposed again in *The Secret of Childhood*. Later on, this concept is analyzed further in depth in *The Absorbent Mind*. Contrary to the then-current understanding, which only recognized a newborn's physiological needs, Montessori's notion of the spiritual embryo identifies the potential of an individual as possessing both physical and intellectual predispositions. These can easily develop and be adequately expressed only if the adult is able to promote a healthy psycho-motor development. In this way, the innate personological structure of the child can find fertile ground for its own expression, "culminating" in the adult they will become. However, it is essential that this intervention be timely. We witness here a reappearance of the notion of sensitive periods: the child's absorbent mind is particularly sensitive to specific learnings.

Recognizing the Absorbent Mind

> [W]e can say that we are born with one vital stimulus (horme) already organized in the general structure of the absorbent mind. Its specialization and differentiation are prefigured in the nebulae. [...] These structures guide psychic growth and development. They are constituted by the absorbent mind, the nebulae, and the sensitive periods, whose mechanisms are hereditary and characteristic of the human species. However, their development can only happen when the child can freely act upon the environment.
>
> *(99)*

The nebula is the creative energy which steers the child in the process of absorbing environmental stimuli. Montessori conceived the nebulae as germinative cells specific to each function of an individual. The mental organism is a dynamic unit, whose structure is transformed through the active experiences completed in the environment. These experiences are guided by *horme*, an energy "of which the nebulae are differentiated and specialized modes or levels" (82–83). The nebulae—that is to mean, the infant potentialities stimulated by the *horme*—are developed over the course of specific sensitive periods, giving rise to psychic functions. Under the right conditions, the subconscious worker (the child through about the age of three) can transform themselves into a conscious worker (from three years onward). The child gradually acquires and refines oral language as long as they actively participate in the adult's life, an essential prerequisite of linguistic development.

Language and Movement

The theory of linguistic development proposed by Montessori is the fruit of observations carried out over many years with a great number of children. Within this text, Montessori underlines the importance of understanding processing in order to acquire the tools best suited to assist the child in the mastery of language. Linguistic development is articulated in a series of nonlinear achievements, characterized by the presence of explosive growth. Additionally, Montessori emphasizes the centrality of a child's motor skills for the development of language and more broadly in child education. Nowadays, it is understood that the brain needs tactile and motor experiences to develop the sensory-motor areas that are the starting point for the maturation of the parts of the brain designated to language and complex thought (Oliverio 2007). In fact, Montessori affirms, "Movement should be considered from a new point of view. Due to errors and misunderstandings, movement has always been considered as something less noble than what it actually is" (140). Education is called to respect this principle. Indeed, Montessori devotes great consideration to the argument that intelligence is refined and also manifest through manual explorations.

In this work, Montessori reminds the reader that tactile exploration and perfecting fine motor skills offer irreplaceable opportunities for intellectual development. This calls for reflection on today's use of technological devices by children, a trend that has significantly deprived children of opportunities for manual exploration of their environment (Sadeghi 2019). Montessori understood that integrated learning and the development of complex and multisensory visions of reality are essential to flourishing. Presently, the function of technology for the purpose of entertaining children interferes with their natural tendency toward motor exploration. Research has suggested that this tendency may result in the onset of problems in their physical development, such as musculoskeletal deficiencies, obesity, irregular sleep patterns, and difficulties with concentration (Mustafaoglu et al. 2018). Thus, Montessori's work is important for the reminder it provides that the first six years of a child's life are a crucial period. Indeed, she argues, "[N]othing can be accomplished exclusively with time and patience if one has not taken advantage of the opportunities presented during the creative period" (208). The learning experiences that happen during this phase constitute the foundation of later developments.

Conclusion

The strong relevance of these three volumes is especially relevant in an age in which, next to a clear interest in valuing childhood potential (European Commission 2019), we often find a general tendency to entertain children—even very young ones—with technology for long periods of time (Erikson Institute 2016; Sadeghi 2019). This then translates to a deprivation of sensory-motor experiences, which may generate very negative consequences for the development of cognitive, emotional, and social functions (Bruzzone 2018; European Commission 2020). Research suggests the need to integrate the visual data offered by screens with complex experiences capable of offering sensory stimulation as well as opportunities able to enhance the relational dimension of growth (Peper 2014).

Montessori's model of education and caregiving (observation, analysis, and personalized learning practice/environments) indicates a need for constant awareness and purposeful action. The goal, as she states ever so eloquently in these three texts, is to encourage the manifestation of individual natural tendencies. Montessori educators today are also paying special attention to cultural and social disadvantages of differently abled children and their individual learning needs (Multidisciplinary University Research Initiative [MURI] 2018). Finally, Montessori's writing invites reflection on the limited space that daily life grants to concentration, due to hectic rhythms and a general tendency toward hyper-connection. Thus, she might demand that attentiveness is essential and that the delicate mind of a child is intentionally educated to foster concentration with appropriate materials. It is crucial to urge adults to consider childhood in light of the benefits that optimal educational practice can have. "The child is gifted with unknown abilities, which can lead to a bright future. If one truly aims to rebuild, the primary goal of education must be the development of human potential" (Montessori 1999, 2). Such testimony is just as current and meaningful today.

Notes

1. The Garzanti edition of the work includes new writings with which the author enriched in a recent Portuguese edition.
2. The original version of the text contains twenty-eight chapters which assemble Montessori's contributions during a series of conferences held at Ahmedabad, following her internment in India, which lasted until the end of the Second World War. The Italian version of the text, to which this chapter refers, includes additional sections.

References

Bruzzone, Sara Luna. 2018. "Bambini col Digitale, Più Danni o Più Yantaggi?" Agenda Digitale. Last modified January 12, 2018. https://www.agendadigitale.eu/cultura-digitale/bambini-col-digitale-piu-danni-o-piu-vantaggi-che-fare/.

Erikson Institute. 2016. "Technology and Young Children in the Digital Age: A Report from the Erikson Institute." https://www.erikson.edu/wp-content/uploads/2018/07/Erikson-Institute-Technology-and-Young-Children-Survey.pdf

European Commission. 2019. "Cifre Chiave sull'educazione e Cura della Prima Infanzia in Europa, Edizione 2019." *Rapporto Eurydice*. Luxembourg: Publications Office of the European Union. http://publications.europa.eu/resource/cellar/5816a817-b72a-11e9-9d01-01aa75ed71a1.0006.01/DOC_1

European Commission. 2020. "Shaping Europe's Digital Future." Luxembourg: Publications Office of the European Union. https://ec.europa.eu/info/sites/default/files/communication-shaping-europes-digital-future-feb2020_en_4.pdf

Montessori, Maria. 1989. *Il Segreto dell'Infanzia*. Milan: Garzanti Editore.

Montessori, Maria. 1991. *Il Bambino in Famiglia*. Milan: Garzanti Editore.

Montessori, Maria. 1999. *La Mmente del Bambino. Mente Assorbente*. Milan: Garzanti Editore.

Multidisciplinary University Research Initiative. 2018. "Altri Bisogni Educativi Speciali (BES)." Rome: Ministero dell'Istruzione. https://www.miur.gov.it/altri-bisogni-educativi-speciali-bes-

Mustafaoglu, Rüstem, Zirik Emrah, Zeynal Yasacı, and Aruz Razak Özdinçler. 2018. "The Negative Effects of Digital Technology Usage on Children's Development and Health." *Addicta* 5: 227–47. https://doi.org/10.15805/addicta.2018.5.2.0051

Oliverio, Alberto. 2007. "La Mente in Azione. Il Ruolo Della Motricità nei Processi di Rappresentazione Mentale." *Vita dell'Infanzia* 56: 27–34.

Peper, Erik. 2014. "Support Healthy Brain Development: Implications for Attention Deficit/Hyperactivity Disorder." *Psychophysiology Today* 9 (1): 4–15.

Percy, Thomas Nunn. 1920. *Education: Its Data and First Principles*. London: Longmans, Green and Company.

Sadeghi, Saeid, Hamid Reza Pouretemad, Reza Khosrowabadi, Jalil Fathabad, and Sedighei Nikbakht. 2019. "Effects of Parent–Child Interaction Training on Children Who Are Excessively Exposed to Digital Devices: A Pilot Study." *The International Journal of Psychiatry in Medicine* 54 (6): 408–23.

Wood, David, Jerome S. Bruner, and Gail Ross. 1976. "The Role of Tutoring in Problem Solving." *Journal of Child Psychology and Psychiatry* 17: 89–100. https://doi.org/10.1111/j.1469-7610.1976.tb00381.x.

Chapter 8
Math and Grammar: *Psychoarithmetic, Psychogeometry,* and *Psychogrammar*

Benedetto Scoppola and Clara Tornar
Translation By: Ariel Rothman

Montessori mathematical and linguistic thinking was first introduced in three celebrated books concerning the education of young children, *The Montessori Method: Scientific Pedagogy as Applied to Child's Education in the Children's House* (1912);[1] *Dr. Montessori's Own Handbook* (1914); and her work concerning education for elementary age children, *The Advanced Montessori Method* (1917). After the success of these publications and her educational program for elementary school children, Montessori devoted herself to the completion of a curriculum geared toward that level of education.

During this phase of her research, she focused her attention on three key curricular areas: Psychogeometry, Psychoarithmetic, and Psychogrammar, as she intentionally called them. These names followed her observations about how cognitive needs arise during the different phases of psychic development. With their common prefix, "psycho," Montessori's intent was to highlight her way of understanding geometry, arithmetic, and grammar not only as disciplines to be taught but also as instruments to promote a child's cognitive development. Thus, *Psychogeometry, Psychoarithmetic,* and *Psychogrammar* were the chosen titles of a trilogy that she would write about those very disciplines (Montessori 1934a, 1934b, 2017). The first two were both published in Barcelona, Spain, where she was living, during a particularly turbulent historical period. *Psychogrammar*, on the other hand, remained incomplete and was only published many decades later.

Psychogeometry and *Psychoarithmetic*

Mathematical importance may be summarized in a single sentence, one with which Montessori likely wholeheartedly agreed: mathematics is a privileged way to construct abstract thought based on active experiences. With this respect, Montessori's final pedagogical plans around math, especially seen in the light of modern cognitive neuroscience, are incredibly suitable for our times. In this section, we briefly describe the features of her disciplinary proposal in two often under-noticed Montessori publications, *Psychoarithmetic* and *Psychogeometry*. Using the lens of modern neuroscience, we analyze her design of mathematical thinking and pedagogy.

In *Psychoarithmetic* and *Psychogeometry*, Montessori describes an environment which surrounds children with opportunities to learn mathematics. These are represented by many different materials which a teacher prepares and presents to the children, allowing for the children to explore them and use them freely. From there, each child is unique in their engagement, discovering for themselves the mathematical content hidden in the chosen material. This freedom of choice, Montessori notes, guarantees work guided by interest. The final reward for the child is the pleasure of the discovery hidden in every material.

For Montessori, all activities—and by extension, all materials—have several critical common features. First, the materials are each an accurate and concrete representation of abstract objects. The perception of a (well-made) wooden equilateral triangle, for instance, comes much earlier than its rigorous definition. Second, the design of the material isolates what is meant to be learned; Montessori understood the isolation of quality as a key aspect of the function of any material (Ahlquist and Gynther 2019). Third, Montessori reminded us, the material can be completely understood through manipulation, moving the hands (but sometimes the whole body) to "discover the secret" hidden in it.

Montessori calls this way of understanding the object's "driving idea" (Montessori 2011, 11). She believed the driving ideas are much more natural than the abstract definition usually presented in school settings. Finally, each material is coupled to a more abstract representation of words, symbols, or drawings after the material manipulations mentioned above. For example, the first ten numbers, presented to very young children, are accompanied by cards in which the digits are represented in relief by sandpaper. The basic geometric shapes, also presented to very young children, are paired to cards with the name of each shape. The learning of a specific vocabulary is then integrated within the materials. Montessori reminds her readers that arithmetic and geometry have a profound link in all the activities presented throughout the two volumes.

Before describing the relationship between the latest neuroscience and some of the characteristics listed above, one must consider the development of Montessori's treatment of mathematics. Prior to her medical training, Montessori studied mathematics and physics at the Istituto Tecnico ad Indirizzo Fisico Matematico Leonardo da Vinci (Leonardo da Vinci Technical Institute for Physics and Mathematics). Montessori valued this part of her education, as shown by the high grades she obtained and in her subsequent work to create, explain, and use mathematical materials that engaged children and supported intrinsic motivation around mathematical thinking and application. Her coursework was primarily focused on the study of Euclidean geometry and the theory of relations developed in *Euclid's Elements*. Since the *Elements* were a profound treatise of mathematics in terms of geometric description, we can say that the link between arithmetic and geometry was built into Montessori's writing and the development of her mathematical pedagogy. Moreover, the *Elements'* careful presentation of the proofs of its propositions may have been one of the main drivers of Montessori's idea of self-discovery in math learning.

It is worth taking the time to consider a few concrete examples. In the fifth book of Euclid's *Elements* (Joyce 1998), the idea of natural numbers is not explicitly defined. However, natural numbers are presented implicitly in the first definition, which reads, "A magnitude is a *part* of a magnitude, the less of the greater, when it measures the greater" (n.p.). According to this definition, the natural numbers are the result of a measure when the unit (one) divides exactly into the quantity to be measured without a remainder. This definition is highly concrete and applicative. While the *language* of Euclid is not suitable for children, the *concept* appears to

Math and Grammar

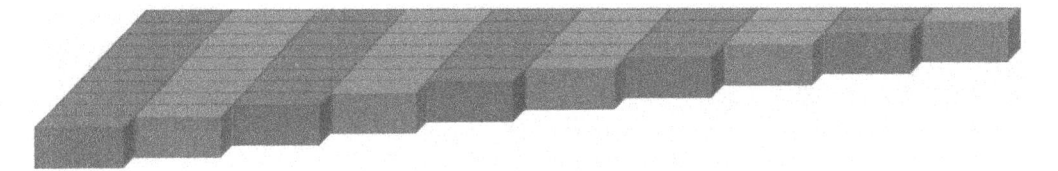

Figure 8.1 Number rods. Illustration by Eva-Maria Tebano Ahlquist.

have been very useful to Montessori. Montessori's solution, presented in the first pages of *Psychoarithmetic*, is the translation of this idea into materials: the concept of integer numbers is first understood through Number Rods (see Figure 8.1), which are nothing but length exactly measured by the first unit.

The material must be manipulated carefully and slowly by the children; the hand must move along each rod, counting the number of different sections composing it. In such a way, the extremely abstract idea of natural numbers becomes "driving": the number comes out from the movement and by comparing different rods. The counting (and hence the sequence of the names of the digits) is also given by the same movement of the hand.

Another example related to discovery is one of the last subjects presented in *Psychogeometry*: Pythagoras's theorem. In *Elements*, it corresponds to Book 1, Proposition 47, which reads, "In right-angled triangles, the square on the side opposite the right angle equals the sum of the squares on the sides containing the right angle." The proof for this construct is quite difficult. And while we do not delve into it here, it is worth noting that the material in Figure 8.2 represents this same construct within a Montessori framework.

The geometrical shapes are colored and can be moved inside the green inset. The principle is that of conservation of the area: if the same region can be formed by the white triangle and a rectangle or a rhomboid, the rectangle and the rhomboid have the same area. This conservation principle is not explicitly stated, but, as with all of Montessori's materials, she considered it easy to perceive and thus interesting and engaging for the child. The sequence of the three movements presented above is proof of Pythagoras's theorem.

Since this Euclidean inspiration is never mentioned throughout *Psychogeometry*, we surmise that either she followed it consciously or that it was an unconscious outcome of her college studies. Fortunately, we have the transcription of many Montessori lessons where the question finds a complete answer. During her International Montessori course, in lesson 31 on May 5, 1931, she said, "First arithmetic and geometry were united, then it became necessary to divide

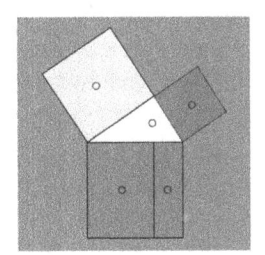

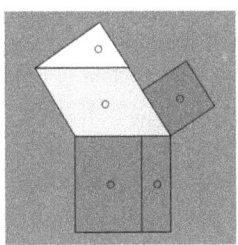

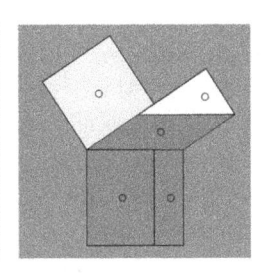

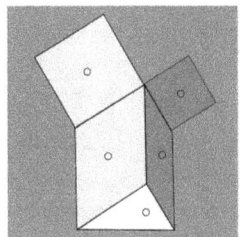

Figure 8.2 The proof of Pythagoras's theorem. Illustration by Eva-Maria Tebano Ahlquist.

them. But the origin of things is most natural and simple. As I always repeat, the child has to have the origin of things, since it is most natural and clear for his mind. We just have to find a material to make the origin accessible." Here, another principle of these texts emerges: the original way certain ideas were understood is an ideal way to present them to children. In other words, if the ancient mathematicians introduced an idea in a particular way, perhaps that was the way most natural for our brain. Guided by this idea, recent results in cognitive neuroscience can be compared to Montessori's pedagogy.

A Neuroscientific Point of View on *Psychogeometry* and *Psychoarithmetic*

The problem of mathematics perception is one of the most intriguing in cognitive neuroscience. From an evolutionary perspective, the modern study of mathematics has taken place over a very short period. Hence, we cannot think that our brain is naturally selected to perform mathematics. It is, perhaps, more reasonable to assume that some neural circuits have been recycled for use with arithmetic and geometry (Leron 2004). Such neural circuits, located in about the same area for all human beings, work according to some general rules imposed by natural selection.

Dehaene's (1997) book *The Number Sense* is instructive for consideration of these Montessori texts. Dehaene argues that through various techniques we understand something more about the rules of our brain concerning math perception. For instance, we understand that the natural representation of the numbers in our brain is to put them, one after the other, on a line. Moreover, we intuit that numbers are farther apart when they are small and closer when they are large. So, in our brain, the spontaneous distance between one and two is more significant than the distance between ninety-one and ninety-two. The construction of the so-called Cartesian line of the number, with equal space between numbers, is a product of culture. Note that this cultural construction coincides precisely with the definition of integers presented in the *Elements* mentioned above and, therefore, with the very first mathematical material Montessori proposed, the Number Rods. After a long period in which humans intuitively used geometry, the necessity of proofs emerged and corresponded to an enormous development of science during the Hellenistic period. Montessori observed the same explosion of understanding and use in children before the elementary level.

Another relevant discovery of neuroscience is that we must use both hemispheres of the brain to do mathematics well. This is not an easy task for children of ages 6 and 7 because the part of the brain that connects the different hemispheres is not yet mature (Dehaene 2011). However, it is necessary to propose mathematics to children in such a way that both hemispheres are used. Pragmatically, this is exactly what Montessori does, for instance, when the Number Rods are presented with the Sandpaper Numerals and when the various classifications of figures are made by means of the of the Geometric Insets material and the corresponding Geometric Form Cards presented in *Psychogeometry* (9–16). Learning through multiple modes in this way supports students leveraging diverse encoding pathways which neuroscience now recognizes is beneficial in the learning process (Shin et al. 2022). Such multiple modes are a constant of Montessori Math pedagogy.

Montessori reminds us that tactile experience and movement are essential to learning, especially for children. The fundamental idea of movement in learning has been supported over time by the scientific community and specifically emergent neuroscience. One essential reference for this line of research is Rizzolatti and Sinigaglia's (2008) *Mirror in the Brain*. Consider the classical model of the brain: the senses give input to the cognitive spaces, which then send a signal to our motor functions controlled by the brain to answer to the inputs of the senses. This simplified model is wrong. In most brains, especially in some species like primates and birds, there is a tremendous exchange in both directions between motor and cognitive functions. Thus, we can say simply that our brain learns most of all by movement(s), first seen and then performed. From an evolutionary point of view, this seems to be quite natural; our ancestors learned complex movements to survive, and imitation was of great help to this process.

Montessori asserted that our schools do not devote significant attention to learning with and through movement. While in the modern-day context we must learn sport and physical education, movement is not used extensively when considering more academic disciplines. Even in the texts we highlight here from almost a century ago, Montessori understood the importance of movement and the profound link between movement and abstract thought as described by Regni and Fogassi (2019). Neuroscientists are often surprised that the concrete Montessori prescription is often correct from a neuroscientific point of view. One notable example is that, in a Montessori environment, the material at hand is always presented side by side with the children, never in front. This is extremely important to show the movement that the children must repeat correctly; a hand moving from right to left is seen moving, by an observer in front, from left to right, and vice versa.

Psychogrammar

Psychogrammar (2017), unlike the previous volumes in the trilogy, is a text with quite a complex publishing story. Written between 1924 and 1936, Montessori never completed it herself, presumably because of her intense work obligations and the complex events of her life during that time; she had relocated several times during the upheavals of early twentieth-century Europe, living in Spain, Italy, and the Netherlands. The text remained unedited for many years and was ultimately published in Italy in 2017.

Montessori had already devoted 122 pages of the second volume of *The Advanced Montessori Method* (1917) to grammar, as well as twenty tables that illustrated materials and showed pictures of children learning through action. *Psychogrammar* is largely based on the information that was already included in the 1917 book but is enriched by original in-depth analysis. The work presents an innovative conception of the grammar teaching-learning process. Montessori posits an idea that is consistent with the theory Noam Chomsky (1957) later proposed that children possess a certain *implicit* grammar spontaneously acquired during their linguistic development. She maintains that a grammatical reflection "is certainly not the way to 'learn' the language"; at the same time, she underlines the value of reflection as "a wonderful means to perform a gymnastics of the mind, and to understand oneself," and as a "way of 'perfecting' and 'establishing' language forms … that is extremely useful to the child when they are organizing the language on its own" (Montessori 2017, 27).

In this respect, Montessori asserted that the teaching-learning process, like mathematical thinking, must be directed toward the discovery of the functional elements of the language that the child is already using. To achieve this goal, Montessori applies to grammar the hands-on learning modalities typical of childhood development rooted in sensorimotor experiences, action, and movement conducted within an organized environment: "Our grammar is not a book" (1973, 10), she stated in *Volume II of the Advanced Montessori Method*; and, as she would later explain in *Psychogrammar*, "To understand the nuances of language there is but action" (XIV).

Psychogrammar begins with a brief history of written language founded on Edward Clodd's (1900) discovery of the first alphabets. Montessori's work in *Psychogrammar* is an excursus on the origins of human language and its fascination for children. Following the brief history comes an interesting exploration of the different parts of speech (a total of nine in the Italian language), each assigned a specific color and a geometric symbol. With regard to nouns, for instance, the author writes, "To indicate a noun, we will use a black equilateral triangle symbol, well planted on its base, stable, and fixed" (Montessori 1917, 45). When describing verbs, she states, "A verb is well represented by a red circle, which, like the sun, never stops moving and radiates its strength, giving life to matter" (121).

Grammatical functions are presented to a child in groups of three, which is particularly interesting as it is in line with structural linguistics (de Saussure 1916) and with the later generative linguistics (Chomsky 1957). The three grammatical groups are as follows: the noun family, represented by a noun, adjective, and article; the verb family, composed of a verb, adverb, and pronoun; and the three "helpers," made up of preposition, conjunction, and interjection. Montessori turns to classifications that are accessible to children ("family" and "helper") and close to their affective world. For example, in describing the noun family, she explains, "The noun is like a mother that on one side, holds the younger boy (the article) in that arm, and with the other hand, leads the older daughter (the adjective)" (Montessori 2017, 68) (see Figure 8.3).

Montessori understood the centrality of nouns as symbols of objects and verbs as symbols of actions. She makes a clear distinction between them on the morphological level (inflection) and the syntactic level (ability of verbs to "enliven" nouns). This understanding represents an insight now confirmed by studies on linguistic typology, which considers these two parts of speech to be linguistic universals (Greenberg 1966), and by the findings of neuroscience, which have identified different areas of the brain designated to the processing of nouns and verbs (Caruana and Borghi 2016).

In fact, *Psychogrammar* addresses children even before they start elementary school through the encounter with nouns, starting with concrete nouns since their interest in words is particularly pronounced at this stage. However, the actual, proper reflection on the rules of written language takes place at the elementary level. At this stage of development, children show the ability to recognize and appreciate the rules that allow them to construct sentences. To this end, as with mathematics, various materials are used to create a tangible form of *lived grammar*. Moveable Alphabets are utilized to combine word roots. Grammatical Boxes, composed of sections with words written on different colored poster boards, are employed to study the parts of speech. Through the commands written on note cards, children are asked to perform the action that is at the center of the sentence. Various activities, including word repositioning, let children reflect on the order of the words,

Figure 8.3 The noun family: Article noun adjective. Sketch by Maria Montessori. Courtesy of the Maria Montessori Archives, photo section, Amsterdam.

explore how a word can be changed or replaced within a sentence, and understand how meaning changes based on said manipulation.

One specific aspect of *Psychogrammar* is that it uses pictures and cartoons depicting everyday situations to highlight the different parts of speech. For example, the picture of an action *underway* or the same action *completed* is used to explain the differences in the *present* and *past* tenses of a verb. Throughout, *Psychogrammar* is a masterclass both in the practical use of materials to teach the form and function of language but also the theory and philosophy behind the pedagogy.

Conclusions: A Guide to Reading Psychological Disciplines

Given the discussion above, Montessori's *Psychoarithmetic*, *Psychogeometry*, and *Pscyhogrammar* are instructive in the work of thinking about *how* to teach mathematical and linguistic thinking. These writings, not simply manuals to be used straightforwardly, can be used to explore the complex cognitive frameworks children have to motivate their own learning and understanding. This teaching and learning approach is largely built upon children's direct and unique activities and is based on exercises fundamentally tied to action, objects, and experimentation. In this regard, the trilogy presents interesting elements of modernity that are specifically attributable to the Montessori's insights and are also expressed in some of her later writings (Montessori 1949). Today, Montessori's intuition about the deep interconnections between the mind and body is upheld by the findings of neuroscience. Her pedagogy can therefore be defined in some circles as neuropedagogy. This approach, which is a recurrent theme throughout all of Montessori's works, promotes and values the child's learning processes, making these texts especially interesting considering recent key studies conducted on verbal learning in neuroscience (Dehaene 2009).

Montessori reminds us it is easier to prepare a compelling lesson on a particular topic than to create an environment where children are free to choose their work and develop an intrinsic interest and understanding of the work at hand. Her work also consistently reminds us that the adult who can put children at the center of an educational activity must have an intimate knowledge of the origins of thought in each discipline and its specific technical lexicon. As such, the reading and complete understanding of this trilogy is quite demanding. Even small details can only be understood by readers who are knowledgeable in modern educational theories, neuroscience, and disciplinary and historical issues and who do not underestimate their importance. However, these texts deserve such an effort because Montessori's work is powerful in light of current understanding of learning processes even though it is almost a century old.

Note

1. The dates refer to the first English edition.

References

Ahlquist, Eva-Maria Tebano, and Per Gynther. 2019. "Variation Theory and Montessori Education." *Journal of Montessori Research & Education* 2 (1): 13–23. http://doi.org/10.16993/jmre.12.
Caruana, Fausto, and Anna M. Borghi. 2016. *Il Cervello in Azione: Introduzione alle nuove scienze della mente*. Bologna: Il Mulino.
Chomsky, Noam. 1957. *Syntactic Structures*. The Hague: Mouton.
Clodd, Edward. 1900. *The Story of the Alphabet*. New York: D. Appleton and Company.
Dehaene, Stanislas. 1997. *The Number Sense: How the Mind Creates Mathematics*. Oxford: Oxford University Press.
Dehaene, Stanislas. 2009. *Reading in the Brain: The New Science of How We Read*. New York: Penguin.
Dehaene, Stanislas. 2011. *The Number Sense: How the Mind Creates Mathematics*, 2nd ed. New York, NY: Oxford University Press.
de Saussure, Ferdinand. 1916. *Cours de Linguistique Générale*. Paris: Lausanne.
Friederici, Angela, and Michael Skeide. 2015. "Neurocognition of Language Development." In *The Cambridge Handbook of Child Language*, edited by Edith L. Bavin and Letitia R. Naigles, 61–88. Cambridge: Cambridge University Press.
Greenberg, Joseph H., ed. 1966. *Universals of Language*. Cambridge: MIT Press.
Joyce, David E. 1998. *Euclid's Elements*. http://aleph0.clarku.edu/~djoyce/java/elements/.
Leron, Uri. 2004. "Mathematical Thinking and Human Nature: Consonance and Conflict." International Group for the Psychology of Mathematics Education. Proceedings of the Annual Meeting of the

International Group for the Psychology of Mathematics Education (PME) (28th, Bergen, Norway, July 14–18, 2004). Volume 3. 217–24.

Montessori, Maria. 1914. *Dr. Montessori's Own Handbook.* New York: Frederick A. Stokes Company.

Montessori, Maria. 1917. *The Advanced Montessori Method: Scientific Pedagogy as Applied to the Education of Children from Seven to Eleven Years.* 2 vols. Translated by Florence Simmonds and Arthur Livingston. New York: Stokes.

Montessori, Maria. 1934a. *Psicogeometría: El Estudio de la Geometría Basado en la Psicología Infantil.* Barcelona: Araluce.

Montessori, Maria. 1934b. *Psicoaritmética: La Aritmética Desarrollada con Arreglo a las Directrices Señaladas por la Psicología Infantil, Durante Veinticinco Años de Experiencia.* Barcelona: Araluce.

Montessori, Maria. 1949. *The Absorbent Mind.* Translated by C. A. Claremont. Adyar, Madras: The Theosophical Publishing House.

Montessori, Maria. 1973. *Volume 2 of the Advanced Montessori Method.* New York: Schocken Books.

Montessori, Maria. 2011. *The Montessori Series.* Vol. 16, *Psychogeometry.* Amsterdam: Montessori-Pierson Publishing Company.

Montessori, Maria. 2016. *The Montessori Series.* Vol. 20, *Psychoarithmetic.* Amsterdam: Montessori-Pierson Publishing Company.

Montessori, Maria. 2017. *Psicogrammatica: Dattiloscritto Inedito, Revisionato, Annotato e Introdotto da Clara Tornar e Grazia Honegger Fresco.* Milano: Franco Angeli.

Regni, Raniero, and Leonardo Fogassi. 2019. *Maria Montessori e le Neuroscience: Cervello, Mente, Educazione.* Rome: Fefè Editore.

Rizzolatti, Giacomo, and Corrado Sinigaglia. 2008. *Mirrors in the Brain: How Our Minds Share Actions, Emotions, and Experience.* Translated by Frances Anderson. Oxford: Oxford University Press.

Shin, Dajung Diane, Minhye Lee, and Mimi Bong. 2022. "Beyond Left and Right: Learning Is a Whole-Brain Process." *Theory into Practice* 61 (July): 1–11. https://doi.org/10.1080/00405841.2022.2096386.

Chapter 9
Peace Education: *Education and Peace*

Stephanie Van Hook

Purpose is a driving force for action, though when action takes over, the purpose can easily be buried or forgotten. Throughout our lives, we must question and reestablish our purpose. Maria Montessori understood this undertaking and its relevance in the fields of education and peace. Consider questions like these: What is the purpose of education? What kind of world are we building? What or whom does education serve? Similarly, as we consider peace, we must ask: Does it have a purpose unto itself? Is the purpose of peace to ease fighting among ourselves or to help us evolve, to realize our true nature? How do we go about these tasks? The practical nature of these questions and the conveyance of a higher order of purpose to both endeavors are foundations of Maria Montessori's text, *Education and Peace* (2007).

First published in 1949 in Italian, the book is a series of speeches that Montessori gave throughout Europe during the interwar period of 1932–1939. Part I of the volume provides an overview of Montessori's understanding of peace. The second part of the text collects the lectures from the Sixth International Montessori Congress in Copenhagen, 1937, while part three focuses on the lecture, "The Importance of Education in Bringing about Peace," from an address to the International School of Philosophy in Amersfoort, 1937. The final section contains Montessori's "Address to the World Fellowship of Faiths" in London, 1939.

Always the scientist, Montessori approached her subject through observation. In the case of this text, she observes that something has gone terribly wrong with humanity; instead of advancing toward peace, we are de-evolving into greater forms of violence. From there, she is always constructive, believing that humans can concretely address this problem. Montessori's work assumes a worldview where peace is the most natural state of consciousness. She begins from this perspective while developing what she calls a "science of peace" (Montessori 2007, 3). Her views in these lectures are complex and her vision powerful, so the text requires some background knowledge and the occasional interpretation.

Taken together, these speeches present a "crash course" in peace theory, reimagining who we are as human beings. Her work is a breathtaking endeavor, and yet there's more than one message that one needs to disentangle to fully appreciate and participate in her vision. The themes and nuances to explore in greater depth include the nature of Montessori's religious or mystical experiences, the concepts of negative versus positive peace, and her call for a renewed image of who we are and, therefore, what our relationship with the child should be.

Religious Experience and Montessori's Vision of Peace

Instructive here is a Hindu story about Lord Krishna when he was just a child. It goes roughly like this: Lord Krishna's (adopted) mother, Yaśodā, did not know that Krishna was the Lord of the Cosmos; to her, he was just her little boy—mischievous, playful, and darling. One day Krishna put dirt into his mouth. When his mother found him and asked him if he had been eating dirt, he kept his mouth closed and shook his head no, a smile on his face. Frustrated, Yaśodā asks Krishna to open his mouth. With the playfulness of the child, Krishna obliges and opens his mouth to reveal the entire cosmos inside it. In that moment, his mother sees him as he really is—according to Hindu tradition—the Lord of All because through his grace, as the story goes, he revealed his true nature to her. When he closed his mouth, he was again her very own sweet child ("Yashoda" n.d.).

In a lecture to the 1939 World Fellowship of Faiths in London, Montessori describes a similar experience in precise detail. She understands Christ, the embodied Savior of Humanity, to be in the child. Montessori describes the circumstances of her brief vision, her spiritual breakthrough, much like Yaśodā in Hindu lore. Through this experience, Montessori took "almost a vow" to see the child as a spiritual teacher and to become a "follower of the child"; for her, this meant devoting herself fully to the development of children and using service and love as a path to unfolding spiritual self-knowledge (Montessori 2007, 113).

One might wonder if this experience is anything more than the pious imagining of a devoted Catholic. For some readers, her vibrant religious descriptions about Christ and the child, which are not limited to this text, may be quietly passed over or perhaps interpreted with caution, carefully balancing her religious language with her upbringing and the function of culture, time, and history or a question of Montessori's personality. Yet, for those familiar with seminal writings about religious experience, such as those of Montessori's contemporary Evelyn Underhill (1914) or much later Huston Smith (1976), Montessori's description of the child as Christ incarnated goes beyond mere devotional emotionalism. It becomes something more fundamental and even scientific—religion and faith as part of a search for self-realization, also known as mysticism. The often-misunderstood term describes the lived expression of what may be called religious experience, a silent knowing that fills our awareness of life around us. It is derived from the Greek root *mu*, meaning silent or mute—literally, "close," as in closing the eyes, as mystics might when absorbed in a vision. It's an inward search that, much like Montessori's approach to learning, prioritizes self-awareness and experience over dogma and ritual.

Either way, to fully appreciate her vision of peace and education in this text, Montessori asks us to at least unfold and take account of our spiritual life; this, as evidenced by violence around us, has been severely overlooked as a human endeavor. Her work points us beyond a merely pedagogical renewal toward something much greater, a "spiritual reconstruction." She warns us that humanity is threatened, not by war or even weapons, but by our spiritual hunger, "the emptiness in men's souls." The rest, she says, "is merely a consequence of this emptiness" (Montessori 2007, 42).

What Is Peace?

Montessori's writings indicate that she believes humanity is using much of its energy against itself. Although the human spirit longs for a state of peace, she argues, we do not conduct investigations and experiments to understand it and achieve it. Instead, we have created a world full of destructive machines and broken relationships; these threaten not just our own continuation as a species but all life on the planet. Something has gone off course. Because of this, she is gravely concerned about humanity, which dedicates so little time and energy into the question of peace that might help us to flourish. She calls our experience a kind of "moral chaos" where we cannot collectively distinguish between what helps us and what hinders us (6).

Montessori concerned herself with the question of peace because of its effect on the development of children and the possibility for the development and evolution of humanity. Throughout the lectures, she gives four key arguments on education and peace: educational pedagogy is a science, education must be constructive and positive, peace through education is achievable, and education has a purpose beyond the discrete learning of facts, ideas, or skills.

Montessori contrasts two conceptions of peace: negative peace, which is the absence of something, and positive peace, the presence of something. Negative peace, she asserts, is the kind of peace called for in the political realm, where one power dominates over another and fighting ends because one side has lost. "What is generally meant by the word *peace* is the cessation of war. But this negative concept is not an adequate description of genuine peace. Most important, if we observe the primary aim of a war, peace in this sense represents, rather, the ultimate and permanent triumph of war" (4).

Positive peace, or true peace as Montessori sees it, is something that reaches much further. It is the presence of an awareness of unity in diversity, a state of freedom, and an active force of love. While she is almost never recognized as such in the field of Peace Studies today, she is very likely the first person to coin this distinction. Achieving positive peace to save us from violence will require an immense effort of reimagining who we are, Montessori argues. We will need a new conception of humanity itself—a "new man" (18)—and an environment that allows people to thrive in the highest ways possible through the realization of our freedom and our collective responsibility to life.

Here Montessori turns to the role of the child in peacemaking endeavors. The child must be the center of our endeavor, Montessori asserts, just as they are in the classroom. It is important to take note of how Montessori depicts the relationship between the child and the adult; education, she argues, has been misused, and the relationship is out of balance. Children need to be seen as fully endowed human beings worthy of dignity and respect; more than any other factor, the way children are taught to ignore their inner development and disregard the silent call of the spirit will lead to violence. Relevant to the geopolitical context of the 1930s, she implies that she can understand the causes that lead us into the politics of violent dictators. She goes on to hypothesize that we can become peaceful as adults because of how we were raised and educated, the place we were told we occupied in the hierarchies of the world, and whether our deepest needs were met or not. Montessori thus places great promise in the child and great responsibility on the adult.

According to Montessori, the relationship between adult and child can easily slide into a microcosm of dictatorship and domination when adults deny children their nature and their social and emotional needs, instead layering forced obedience and other violence upon the child's psyche. For Montessori, the political and the personal are connected; if we are to end dictatorship and violence, we need to stop our own tendencies toward domination and self-will regarding the child. She acknowledges that this is tall order, but it is not impossible if we tell ourselves a different story about who and what we are and what our relationships can and ought to be.

To this end, Montessori argues that an education that helps us know our true nature must be the education par excellence for all of humanity. Here, she treats education in the true sense of the Latin word *educere*, to draw out, or perhaps even more closely of the Greek *anakalýpto*, to dig out, uncover, or discover. Through education, we discover our own nature and a more conscious vision of which actions hinder us in our collective and individual development. The key concept is consciousness. Education must lead us to become conscious of who we are, the workings of social life, and the results of our actions (20).

A New Understanding of the Child and of Humanity

Montessori's conception of peace and education in this text asks the reader to envision a paradigmatic shift from a negative worldview to a positive one. Her positive view, rooted in the world's wisdom traditions and having, today, the backing of modern science, runs contrary to the Hobbesian notions that perpetuated the industrial age and continue to influence everything from our economic systems to our political. Montessori argues that human beings are not selfish, isolated, material beings who care only about themselves at the expense of everyone else; rather, they are naturally connected and loving, desiring the well-being of all.

We do not need long studies to show us this, Montessori implies; just look at the child. She bases her conviction on observation rather than unquestioning faith. Through her observations of children with developmental delays, she notes that the child has a natural proclivity toward connection and love. The children love their environment, and the environment provokes and urges love from them. This love is the most natural state for us, a pull toward harmonious connection. It is when this love does not develop that we can safely say that there's been hindrance in that person's development.

Once humans have reimagined themselves, not only will this "new man" have a new (or renewed) relationship to all of life, but they will live in an entirely new world without national borders (18, 23). We will see ourselves as one humanity, entirely interconnected and interdependent in our larger evolutionary task in the cosmos. Montessori is thinking big in these lectures and doesn't try to hide it.

Without understanding the implications of this positive understanding of humanity, it's quite hard to grasp Montessori's plan for peace as anything but a naive, idealistic vision. However, Montessori denies this interpretation throughout the text. She repeatedly reinforces her stance with demands that her work and warnings be taken seriously:

> A new world for a new man—this is our most urgent need. If this were a utopia or some kind of joke, it would be a sacrilege to speak of it at this moment when

humanity is living at the edge of an abyss, threatened by total catastrophe. But we have had blindingly vivid glimpses of a world of miracles since the beginning of this century.

(18–19)

From War to Climate Disruption: Will We Awaken?

As Maria Montessori developed her philosophy and system of education, she tapped into truths about human nature that could establish a lasting peace on earth. What she found when observing children in the microcosm of the classroom lends itself to the understanding that human relationships, if properly ordered, could easily provide the framework for the policy and conduct of nations. She believed that when children are placed at the center of human relationships, leaders will see their actions as part of a larger system rather than separate fragments. Montessori's clarity of vision for a well-ordered, child-centered system that worked when it was properly implemented was prescient.

In *Education and Peace,* Montessori worked to expand her circles of influence to establish a long-lasting peace. Notably, it remains a challenge that her writing is studied mostly within education and therein can be dismissed or unnoticed. Yet in her lectures in *Education and Peace* she clearly notes that peace, a spiritual reconstruction of humanity, is the job of everyone: educators, politicians, parents, bakers, nonprofit directors, caregivers, doctors, bankers, etc. It is not enough, Montessori argued, to teach about peace in schools. We must reflect it in our structures or systems; we must recognize it and help it grow around us. Based on these lectures, it is reasonable to say that it is irresponsible, if not impractical, to believe that peace is only the job of educators or for the public to conceive it as a mere intellectual endeavor.

At the time of this writing, we have not yet overcome the scourge of war. However, as Montessori argued, peace and its active expression as nonviolence are long-term games. Consider Montessori's work in *Education and Peace* in the context of climate disruption as a global concern. We can take heart that the major movement led to address climate change, to hold power to accountability, and to make the future livable is led by children dedicated to nonviolence. A future that Montessori helped make possible is coming to life more than ever before, but there's still work to do. Will we finally awaken?

References

Montessori, Maria. 2007. *Education and Peace*. Translated by Helen R. Lane. Amsterdam, Netherlands: Montessori-Pierson Publishing Company.

Smith, Huston. 1976. *Forgotten Truth: The Primordial Tradition*. New York, NY: Harper & Row Publishers, Inc.

Underhill, Evelyn. 1914. *Practical Mysticism: A Little Book for Normal People*. New York, NY: Dent.

"Yashoda." n.d. Wikipedia. Accessed December 20, 2021. https://en.wikipedia.org/wiki/Yashoda.

Chapter 10
Philosophical Writings: *Education for a New World*, *To Educate the Human Potential*, and *The Formation of Man*

Raniero Regni
Translation By: Ariel Rothman

Montessori's three books *Education for a New World* (1946), *To Educate the Human Potential* (1948), and *The Formation of Man* (1955),[1] which were published first in India, are among her last and most evolved texts. Published in English with the assistance of the Theosophical Society of Adyar and written during and after the tragic disruptions caused by the Second World War, the texts coincide with her consequent stay in India and the time directly following. A member of the Theosophical Society since 1899, Montessori was invited to its headquarters in India by its president, George Sydney Arundale. She shared the universalist spiritual inspiration of the theosophical vision: the idea of brotherhood of humanity and the search for common threads among all religions. After the destruction of the Second World War, Montessori felt the need for a global reconstruction. She realized that this reconstruction must necessarily start from one's childhood and upbringing.

Like many of Montessori's texts, the works included in this chapter are based on transcriptions of conferences or lessons held in various teacher training courses. In fact, the primary inspiration of Montessori's written work is almost always her various lectures. These three texts are arguably some of her most famous after *Il Metodo*. To convey her discoveries, as all the great masters do, she relies on both the spoken and written word. Words, while simple and ordinary, are subjected to semantic twists with unknown results; they acquire an often-unfathomable depth, which directs the attentive reader toward reflection. An element of her spoken lectures permeates her writing. As Wittgenstein (2009) explains, the child is like the mystic, who cannot be told but only shown. This is deeply true for Montessori in her approach to education and her instruction for educators. Montessori's work is a radical commentary on conventional child-rearing and education. In fact, one might argue that in these writings (and related lectures), she asserts an unprecedented and emancipatory view of educational pedagogy.

To bring this emancipatory view of education forward, Montessori invented a new language and lexicon uncompromised by historical norms. Going against millennia of traditional education, armed only with her own strength, she worked to share a new type of radical pedagogy—a form of anti-pedagogy, if you will, similar to how in some contexts one speaks of "anti-philosophy" (Badiou 2011). Indeed, she tried to imagine and act in ways no one had before, something one can feel when reading her work.

Education for a New World

In *Education for a New World* (1970a), taken from lectures at three different conferences, Montessori writes about the natural order and obstacles to this order in child development. She explains biases toward children in science, education, and the world. In this text, there are echoes of an acute spirituality and the fascination and influence of Indian culture, and she observes the behavior of children of different ethnicities and cultures.

As her starting point, Montessori focuses on the power of childhood. She asserts that a child's psychology is different from an adult's and the notion that children are simply small adults is the origin of every evil. Montessori understood that a person's first two years are the most crucial in their life. Today, neuroscience supports the critical function of synaptogenesis in the decisive first thousand days and the malleability of the brain. This period marks the formation of the most important neural networks, which form the basis of the origins of the adult's brain. As such, Montessori writes about the importance of the creative actions of children in early childhood. She insists that the purpose of education is to provide the building blocks to help prepare a new human for life. In this text, Montessori also returns to her original work with children in San Lorenzo; she reminds the reader that the basis of her work is her own observations of children's explosive, independent learning, which she saw as paving the way for learning literacy and math with joy.

Montessori believed that the method, materials, and prepared environment are simply instruments, tools to see the invisible—that is, the secret power of the child's mind. Montessori argues that, from birth, the child's mind is the most capable learning machine that one can imagine. The child is not, in fact, an empty soul, but rather a being full of innate developmental stages that Montessori called sensitive periods. The absorbent mind is guided by these internal teachers, which push it to search and prioritize certain environmental stimuli over others. For school-aged children, there are also other specific guiding instincts that today we can call timed evolutionary windows.

The act of a small child learning a language is a real and true creation that compels Montessori to conclude "language develops, it is not learned" (72). The human language is not a catalog of words but a system made up of interconnected structures. For example, a child a few months old can handle the complex systems that constitute language. Montessori argues that the child can experiment with language by the absorption of the uses and the rules implicit to that usage. Psycholinguistic and neuroscientific research, which Montessori anticipates down to the details, reveals that a newborn in the lallation phase can discern and produce more than 600 phonemes. Montessori notes that "babbling"—a newborn's cute play with different sounds—is the enactment of an exceptional speaker who has the potential to speak all human languages. As they grow, the child will select the sounds from the linguistic environment in which they are immersed, and these 600 phonemes slowly are reduced to approximately 46. Here we see the child's entire potential and superiority in respect to the adult. While adults could indeed learn many languages, they would always do so with the imprinting of their mother tongue.

According to Montessori, movement, like language, is also a child's creation; it is not the adults who teach children to talk or walk, as society would have us believe. In all the Eastern thought that she discusses here, Montessori finds confirmation of the significance of movement to cognition. Movement requires thought; the discovery of mirror neurons and of the innate motor repertoires in children today represents a resounding confirmation of this. The mind and hand, like the mind and movement, are part of the same bio-psychic cycle. Children's activities are not simply play; rather, these activities represent productive work, which is later reflected in an adult's humanity. This very imitation is an active recreation that comes from within. A child's interests are attracted to real things; they scorn everything that is childish and want to grow up. Their incessant activity is carefree like play time but serious and focused like work. We should create a new word, *play-work*, to avoid falling into biases associated with these two terms in adult society, which separate and alienate that which a child unites.

Montessori then discusses the role of the teacher and training, one of the two core tenets of the entirety of Montessori's work. Trained educators, then and now, often want to control a classroom with their teaching, which runs counter to the free, autonomous learning capabilities of children. Montessori tells us of epistemological obstacles, which include erroneous scientific theories that represent hard-to-handle biases and push an adult to interfere more than necessary with a child's learning. Montessori argues that educators must learn to be humble and follow a model of non-interference—observing more, interfering less, and leaving the child free to act in a meticulously prepared, organized, and inviting environment. To do this, Montessori understands that educators undergo a true transformation in their preparation—a liberation from pedagogical biases and a faith that children will reveal themselves within that environment.

To Educate the Human Potential

To Educate the Human Potential (1992) is a comprehensive curriculum for a Montessori elementary school, covering topics from the natural history of the universe to the history of humans. It addresses the second phase of human development and the respective sensitive periods that characterize the child at the elementary level (ages 6 through 12). These characteristics include a sense of justice and sociability and a need for abstraction, imagination, and culture.

Cosmic education is a central theme in this work. Montessori began to espouse this idea in England in 1935. However, it was her experience in India that opened the idea of a relationship between the micro- and macrocosms of the world, the psychic and corporeal life of the individual child, and the entire universe. For Montessori, the direct contact with Indian culture represented a confirmation of her whole scientific curriculum as well as her ethical and spiritual understandings of the world. "The problems of education need to be resolved by the laws of cosmic order. These laws range from the eternal ones influencing the makeup of human life to changeable ones that set society on the path towards evolution on earth" (17). The term *cosmic* derives from the ancient Greek *kòsmos*, a word that has a rich multitude of meanings. Montessori believed that "cosmos" encompasses the world, universe, and ideas such as order, beauty, and holiness. In each instance, we see these terms as antonyms of chaos, indistinction, and monstrousness. In the text, Montessori uses cosmic as an adjective, placing it next to four nouns: cosmic plan, cosmic education, cosmic agent, and cosmic vision.

Understanding of Montessori's cosmic vision requires us to understand that this was also her philosophy on life, developed within the context of her quest to understand childhood. Her vision becomes a core influence of her psycho-pedagogy. Montessori's pedagogical epistemology rests on her singular vision of a universal order—that is to say, the universe tends toward the one and toward the unification of humanity into one global nation. This vision also holds Montessori's personal religious, philosophical, and scientific concepts of life and the world within it. Though she did not often write philosophically, much of her work is interwoven with a philosophy of the cosmos. In fact, it is impossible to understand Montessori without this philosophical construct. Science looks for causes that can explain phenomena; religion seeks to find the meaning and purpose of human existence. Montessori presents her work as an act of scientific research imbued with acts of faith, and she links scientific discoveries to mystic elements and religion to science.

Montessori writes on the knowledge of Earth's creation, the birth of life on our planet, and the appearance of humans. She believed each of these instances represents a stage of learning that is of interest to the elementary-level child. Montessori lays out a cosmic vision of life that is finalistic but not deterministic because of the great variable represented by human freedom. Human freedom, Montessori argues, is affected by education. An essential feature of this work is expressing the value of freedom and autonomy in how one walks through the world while agreeing that there exists a "Cosmic Plan in which all, consciously or subconsciously, respond to the great Aim of Life" (10).

According to Montessori, life follows cosmic law. Everything is evolving and related. Nature is governed by an ordered relationship, and a higher purpose connects each of these categories. If nature does not have a purpose, our lives are devoid of meaning. She is clear that she does not believe in either chance or intelligent design, fortuitism or determinism; rather, she believes in a nondeterministic finalism. Grazzini (2013) identified a mystical dimension of unity and higher purpose in Montessori's ideas; however, Montessori does not concern herself with abstract discourse. She includes this mystical dimension in a coherent structure of cosmic education where each element always ties back to the universal dimension, each microscopic detail relates to the macroscopic sphere, and the microcosm of education finds meaning and scope in the most expansive and comprehensive realm of the macrocosm.

Within Montessori's vision for education, children learn astronomy, cosmology, and culture early in their schooling career, a radical reversal from traditional education. Children at the elementary level, she reminds us, are attracted to scientific knowledge and the study of a world that is teaming with plant and animal life. These scientific introductions form the foundation of a crucial ecological awareness, which, in the Anthropocene and our climate crisis, is more imperative than ever. Montessori also argues that the child is ripe for the presentation of cultural topics. By focusing on culture here, Montessori is responding to the evolving needs of the child in a new plane of development. Cosmic education thus becomes a foundation and a guide for the rest of a child's education. It prevents one from getting lost in the notional specificities of the multiple disciplines because, Montessori reminds us, everything is connected to those larger stories of the world.

The cosmic plan is the highest plane of education, not only because of its inclusivity and the range of content that encompasses the entirety of nature and history, but also because the child finds clear answers to explicit questions that they ask themselves. Her cosmic vision is neither a discipline nor a cosmic course or curriculum. It does not exist on paper or in any text specifically. Rather, cosmic vision is the all-encompassing focus of Montessori's philosophy of education. It is worth noting that Montessori is not simply advocating for interdisciplinary practice, even if such a practice could be consistent with her philosophy; instead, her cosmic vision is based on complex systems made up of connections, relations, and contexts. Throughout her life, Montessori wrote, taught, and developed materials within this paradigm of scientific understanding.

Cosmic education is indeed exploration: the study and understanding of the universe considered in its totality and complexity. It is the discovery of the existing interdependencies in all that is living. It is the creative experimentation of a comprehensive ecological model that exposes children to the powerful and fragile miracle of life, a miracle that needs observing, studying, and respecting. Montessori sees the potential for a cosmic vision to unveil nature's greatness and inspire admiration for beauty, rather than threatening her destruction. For Montessori, it is out of this knowledge that love and respect will grow. The admiration and sense of wonder for the universe grow through the study of biology, physics, and geography; out of these develops an awareness that is necessary considering the environmental threats we face. As Montessori writes, "the child who is guided through several of the more exciting eras of the history of the world realizes that humanity has lived through an embryonic stage, and it is only now emerging from a true birth, capable of becoming aware of its true function and unity" (Montessori 1992, 11). Her work offers several concrete and extraordinary examples of passionate study of the history of the cosmos, earth, and life on our planet, all corresponding to young people's sensitive periods of culture and imagination.

An important contribution of *To Educate the Human Potential* are Montessori's assertions that wonder and mystery strike a chord with one's imagination and that children need to be exposed to both at the elementary level. Montessori's approach in the text connects what Bruner (1986) calls the two dimensions of the mind: the narrative and paradigmatic. The latter explains the world as science through cause-and-effect relationships, whereas the former explains the world by telling a story. The combination of these two fundamental modes of the human brain is represented in her cosmic fables, which scientifically explain the world through fascinating stories.

Montessori argues that the elementary school environment should be vast like the world. The calm phase of uniform growth that characterizes a child at the elementary level is the ideal period to learn the keys to the world and the seeds of culture. If, as Montessori shares with us, toddlers think with their hands, then elementary-level children think with their feet. She advocates a pedagogy of travel, adventure, and going out that can satisfy the child's need to leave the closed environment of the classroom or home. Going out into the world, she writes, is a necessary part of the life of a child in the second plane of development. In this plane, the child searches for the causes of phenomena and needs invisible theories to explain visible realities. Children need to see the world around them to reduce the contrast between sensory-motor education and symbolic knowledge. In this manner, schools become "institutions that aid beauty" (Montessori 1992, 169). For Montessori, to educate means to collaborate on the cosmic plan; satisfying the needs of childhood requires participating in the creation of a new world. One can posit that, if the great contribution of the Children's House is normalization, the elementary school's is cosmic education.

Finally, in *To Educate the Human Potential*, Montessori repeatedly reminds the reader that the focus is always the child. With their long and mysterious childhood, children are the most powerful cosmic agents of change. Montessori explains that we are all—from the smallest unicellular beings, like the corals of the Indian Ocean, to the complex organisms like human beings—involved in furthering the evolution of the cosmos. She believed deeply that the world needs a generation of children educated for this task; they must discover solidarity with other life, and they must develop an awareness of their agency and capacity for facilitating collaboration. Only then can they bring together people, nations, and other living beings.

The Formation of Man

With the 1912 English translation of her first major book, *The Montessori Method* had come significant critiques of her work; in the first chapter of *The Formation of Man* (1970b), Montessori defended the development of her pedagogy. Montessori wrote that she would like not only the name, but also the common concept of method be abolished (translated paraphrase). The Montessorian message was not focused on a method for teaching early literacy, however efficient that might have been. She argued that her work was a manner of understanding children, child development, and pedagogy, and the salvation of humanity was at stake. Further, she argues that she did not discover a method but rather focused on the power of childhood, which had been consistently ignored in scholarship and practice with rare exceptions. For Montessori, the critiques were worrisome and reminded her of the dismissal of educational pedagogues Pestalozzi and Tolstoy.

Montessori also addressed why she did not join the New Education Fellowship, with which she had a contentious relationship. She writes, "[T]he method seems to be selfish. It appears to be following its own path without intermingling with anyone else; and yet, no other method continuously takes advantage of every opportunity to preach as much about unity and world peace!" (8). This disclosure resulted in Montessori being accused of individualism, elitism, and defending the spread of Montessori across the globe. Montessori's work is now often considered a precursor to the work of the New Education Fellowship. However, despite her desire to separate herself from the New Education Fellowship's active education movement, her work was inserted within the movement after the fact.

Thus, despite Montessori's defense in the opening chapter, *The Formation of Man* led to Montessori becoming more isolated and misunderstood. To complicate matters, Montessori did not have a standing relationship with the Italian university system. She was often criticized by academics of the time, including followers of Piagetian psychology and others (see Dehaene 2009). Only much later was her reputation restored to a degree, thanks to Bruner's (1986) criticism of Piaget's theories regarding childhood egocentrism. Not only was Montessori reestablished as a classical pedagogue, but some of her theories were confirmed, in part, by prominent neuroscientists like Dehaene (2009). Take, for example, her anticipatory idea of the creative potential of children regarding who they will grow up to be as adults; this is a concept that can only be explained today by science, specifically neuroscience.

Returning to the text, *The Formation of Man* (1970b) discusses themes specifically related to early childhood education. Montessori shares her belief that the discovery of childhood involves an uprooting of secular biases and the end of the senseless, ancient wars that pit children against adult society. She contends that one fundamental element of educational biases is related to discipline. Montessori discusses this topic at length, arguing that correcting children must involve expanding their world so they can find a suitable environment for their developmental needs. Prizes and punishments compromise the critical trust of children who are fragile beings, which adult society has always overpowered. Montessori asserts that children are easy to love, hard to understand, and even harder still to respect. However, she argues that the experiences of childhood are of the utmost importance because the children of today will be the parents of tomorrow.

Within these three works, readers are presented with Montessori's scientific understandings sprinkled with ancient knowledge and wisdom. Contemporary society faces gargantuan challenges: climate change, economic inequality, overpopulation, the gap between the immense technical capabilities and actual use, all of which are compounded with the challenge of peaceful coexistence between nations. With these three texts, Montessori argues that a positive and peaceful response to these issues will only be possible if we make peace with children. As Montessori says, "When biases will be ruled out by knowledge, then the 'superior child' will appear in the world with their wonderful powers that are still hidden today, then the child that is destined to form a humanity capable of understanding and supervising civilization of the present will appear" (99).

Note

1. Hereafter, this article will refer to the Italian editions: *Educazione per un mondo nuovo* (1970a), *Come educare il potenziale umano* (1992), and *Formazione dell'uomo: Preguidizi e nebule* (1970b), respectively.

References

Badiou, Alain. 2011. *Wittgenstein's Antiphilosophy*. Translated by Bruno Bosteels. London and New York: Verso Books.
Bruner, Jerome. 1986. *Actual Minds, Possible World*. Cambridge, MA: Harvard University Press.
Dehaene, Stanislas. 2009. *Reading in the Brain: The New Science of How We Read*. New York: Penguin.
Grazzini, Camillo. 2013. "Maria's Cosmic Vision, Cosmic Plan, and Cosmic Education." *NAMTA Journal* 38 (1) (Winter): 155–76.
Honegger Fresco, Grazia. 2007. *Maria Montessori, Una Storia Attuale: La Vita, il Pensiero, le Testimonianze*. Naples: L'Ancora del Mediterraneo.
Montessori, Maria. 1946. *Education for a New World*. Madras, India: Kalakshetra Publications.
Montessori, Maria. 1948. *To Educate the Human Potential*. Madras, India: Kalakshetra Publications.
Montessori, Maria. 1955. *The Formation of Man*. Translated by A. M. Joosten. Madras, India: Kalakshetra.
Montessori, Maria. 1970a. *Educazione per un Mondo Nuovo*. Milan: Garzanti Editore.
Montessori, Maria. 1970b. *Formazione dell'uomo: Preguidizi e Nebule*. Milan: Garzanti Editore.
Montessori, Maria. 1992. *Come Educare il Potenziale Umano*. Translated by Letizia Berrini. Milan: Garzanti Editore.

Regni, Raniero. 2007. *Infanzia e Società in Maria Montessori: Il Bambino Padre dell'uomo*. Rome: Armando.
Regni, Raniero, and Leonardo Fogassi. 2019. *Maria Montessori e le Neuroscience: Cervello, Mente, Educazione*. Rome: Fefè Editore.
Wittgenstein, Ludwig. 2009. *Tractatus Logicus-Philosophicus e Quaderni 1914–1916*. Translated by Amedeo G. Conte. Torino: Einaudi.

Chapter 11
Societal Responsibility and the Child:
The Child, Society and the World: Unpublished Speeches and Writings

Per Gynther

The Child, Society and the World: Unpublished Speeches and Writings was first published in a German translation in 1979. As the English title notes, the text is a collection based on notes transcribed by different individuals along with unedited notes from lectures to teachers or other speeches. Almost all the lectures within this text were translated from Italian to English because Maria Montessori preferred to lecture in Italian. These circumstances are important context for the reader, as it is vital to understand that the exact words and their meanings may have been altered to some extent in transcription notes and translations. Yet the text at hand is still valuable given that it allows readers to learn various aspects of Montessori's pedagogy. Readers will come to see the directness of Montessori's lectures between 1930 and 1951 and her descriptions of widely differing topics related to the pedagogy. For some, this means that the content of the text can seem fragmented and loosely related. This effect is partly mitigated by the work of the first volume's editor, Günter Schulz-Benesch who worked to create a logical structure by arranging the texts into six different sections addressed below.

"To Parents" and "To Teachers"

The first two sections, "To Parents" and "To Teachers," include two pieces from 1930 in which Montessori speaks directly to parents, one very short appended extract from a radio interview in 1950[1] and two course lectures to teachers. In the 1930 texts, Montessori urges parents to respect children's interests and occupations, during which they build concentration and develop self-discipline. Montessori's insistence on respect for the child is repeated often in her writings, underlining what Montessori saw as a necessary condition for children's successful development. However, when Montessori pointed out that a child's chosen activities should be respected as long as the child is not harmed, readers should remember that children today have access to very different types of materials from children in the 1930s, such as digital technology. These circumstances mean that concepts such as *active* and *harm* must be interpreted and discussed. Otherwise, the more modern applications of her writing may risk being incompatible with her intentions.

In the two course lectures given to teachers, readers learn how Montessori describes the role of the early childhood teacher from a perspective later in her life. Her thoughts on teaching and the role of the teacher is a topic that is often discussed among Montessori teachers. In these lectures, the same message from the 1930 texts is given to teachers: they too must respect children's activities as they concentrate on a piece of work. As Montessori declares in the first sentence of her 1946 lecture, "[c]oncentration is a part of life. It is not the consequence of a method of education" (12).[2] Thus, when children concentrate and work for themselves, not because of the will of the teacher, they act normally, or as Montessori expressed it, they "become normalized" (15). This phenomenon, described as "creative energy" (12), was of utmost importance to Montessori. She believed when this energy is set free, a state of construction and development of the individual occurs during which "all deviations cease" (12).[3] Therefore, she notes, teachers must create conditions for this energy to arise within the child, which Montessori describes in this lecture as providing freedom. Montessori understood freedom as a construct very different than most when the idea is applied to children. Freedom for Montessori is about children's intrinsic agency and ability to make choices about their needs and learning. In practice, this means that the teacher must be able to recognize when a child is deep in concentration and not interfere with his work in any way. To do so, however, "the eyes of the teacher must be trained" (13), like the biologists train their eyes to see with a microscope. Otherwise, the teacher will not always understand when this energy emerges. At the same time, she asserts, the teacher must be a guide who defends "the honest citizens from the disturbers" (16); in other words, the teacher must make sure that children who are concentrating on a piece of work are not disturbed by other children. To support normalization, Montessori highlights the need for an attractive, ordered environment that is prepared for children's needs. She notes how important this aspect of the role of the teacher is for learning. These aspects of her writing reflect Montessori's emphasis on an educational environment that is *entirely* prepared, including the teacher. When children in such an environment eventually become normalized, Montessori notes the teacher has been successful and is "no longer necessary, because all the children are normal" (15). Over time, this belief has been misconstrued as advocating an entirely passive role for the teacher, which may be why some people have said that Montessori teachers abdicate their role to the materials (e.g., Kilpatrick 1914; Quarfood 2005). Even if some of her writing seems to support this conclusion, it omits Montessori's nuance which, in her 1933 lecture, describes twelve discrete duties for teachers in preschools. In those duties, a more complex and active approach to teaching emerges, not a passive one. For example, the teacher must "be 'active' when putting the child in rapport with the environment, and be 'passive' when this rapport is achieved" (18) and "tireless in trying to offer objects to those who have rejected them; and in teaching those who still haven't learnt and who make mistakes" (19). The learning process described in this lecture can therefore be interpreted as one that is led by the teacher, who, along with the environment, inspires and challenges children.[4] In short, the misconception of the passive role of the teacher is challenged carefully in this section.

Additionally, the interest in Montessori's concept of normalization has not diminished making this work still timely for consideration. For example, the National Agency for Education in Sweden reported that staff in schools, including preschools, had experienced an increased number of children with concentration difficulties and need increased support to deal with this challenge (National Agency for Education 2015). Montessori's message to parents and teachers may be an important contribution to facing the challenge.

"On Recurring Themes"

The next section of the text, "On Recurring Themes," considers diverse topics including social education, religious education, fantasy and fairy tales, and Montessori's lesson on silence. In the course lecture on social education that is included, Montessori makes clear that children develop sociability in a natural way within the prepared environment. Montessori believes in the development of "society by cohesion" (22), which she understands to be a characteristic of young children who are normalized through concentrated work. In this writing, Montessori also observes that children have a "social sense as a gift" and "show respect for and interest in each other" (22). She emphasizes that her concept of social education is not just an indirect effect of normalization. It is also a result of abundant experience and practice in social life. Consequently, Montessori asserts in her writing that the learning environment must provide opportunities to develop characteristics such as respecting each other, being patient, and working together. By describing how children in this environment are part of a mini society in which all individuals are responsible for each other, Montessori responded to critiques that her work did not acknowledge the social aspects of education.[5] In his introduction to this section, Schulz-Benesch addresses the incompleteness of this critique since it is only based almost entirely on Montessori's writings and does not "take into account the rest of the work and its practical applications" (20). In fact, one value of this text is that the lectures within it are added evidence of Montessori's interest in developing not just the individual but wider society as well.

The lecture "Lesson of Silence," mentioned only briefly in other writings, is an example of the social education described above. This lecture solidifies that part of social education in a Montessori environment is embedded in the community as children often work together, in groups, with a common aim. This need for cooperation is exemplified in the "lesson of silence" because "you cannot achieve silence in a crowd unless every individual within the crowd wants to achieve it for a moment" (55). Cooperation is therefore necessary for silence to be experienced. The result of such lessons is not only that children's ability to cooperate is strengthened, but also that children become highly sensitive to noise, which, according to Montessori, contributes to a "superior discipline, which you could not achieve with an order" (56–57). Readers may wonder why Montessori devotes an entire lecture to this lesson. However, Montessori clearly sees the need for silence in human development declaring: "All those people who are on a higher spiritual plane, all those who achieve greatness have felt the *need for silence*" (57). However, in her view, silence "is missing in human life" (57). After explaining the intellectual significance of silence, Montessori admits that, in the beginning of her career as a pedagogue, she did not associate silence with such meaning: "At that time, however, I was materialistic enough not to appreciate this: I was very much a doctor and psychologist, that's to say an experimental and clinical psychologist, and therefore superficial" (57). This statement is particularly interesting given her strictly medical and scientific perspectives on children's sensibilities to silence at the beginning of her career. It is only later, based on a great deal of observation, that she develops a deeper understanding of the phenomenon. Again, we look to Schultz-Benesch in the introduction to this section for clarity; this lecture "thus describes how Montessori's original positivist, clinical method changed to one based on the loving observation of phenomena, followed by committed pedagogic action" (51). However, as Ludwig (2008) reminds us, Montessori's appreciation of observation did not mean that she completely rejected medical and scientific research. Instead, she concluded that scientific work and observation must be supplemented with other forms of knowledge acquisition, such as interpretation and philosophical reflection.

"On Recurring Themes" also includes two lectures on religious education. The editor's introduction mentions that Montessori's opinion on this matter "always provoked a lively debate" (28). This is a very reasonable conclusion as different cultures reflect different beliefs about whether religious education should be included at all in educational programs. Montessori states her view on this question clearly in these lectures though it is important to remind readers of the Catholic context in which she was raised both religiously and culturally. In her 1937 lecture to Catholic nuns, she declares that religious education, just as for all education, must "correspond to what we might call the psychological needs of development belonging to various ages" (30). For instance, the child from birth shows "love for the environment, and for what is in it, he obeys an inner urge" (31). Therefore, "from the first year of age, place religious objects and pictures in the child's room" (32). Between the ages of two and four, "there is a sensory and, at the same time, intellectual stage which represents a step forward in comparison with the previous period" (32). This sensory period will, according to Montessori, "allow him to take in religion by his senses" (34). Preschool teachers should therefore let children sensorially experience what happens in religious settings. Furthermore, the preschool child also has "the need to feel himself protected" (34); therefore, any religious education "ought to make the child feel that there is supernatural protection" (34). To fulfill this end, Montessori continues, a certain amount of instruction should also be given by telling stories with "vivacity and with great simplicity" (34), including the Christian story of the Nativity and later the story of creation.

However, in her 1946 London lecture, Montessori clarifies that the telling of stories does not mean that religion, what some would define as faith in a modern context, is something adults give to children. Rather, faith is something children already have within themselves, which develops over time. She then declares that "language and religion are the two characteristics of every group of men" (36). Therefore, in addition to describing how religious education may be conducted,[6] Montessori also discusses some of her anthropological views of religion, which are also subject to current controversy. Notably, compared with the beginning of the twentieth century when Montessori sought to bring religion into children's lives, contemporary society is more multicultural and aware of the pluralistic nature of religion.[7] Many people question whether the religious teaching that Montessori suggests in these writings prepares children for a diverse world and often push this aspect of her work to the side.

In the last lecture of this section, Montessori addresses imagination and fairy tales, topics that are widely discussed in contemporary conversations because of the common misperception that Montessori viewed fairy tales as dangerous to children's development during their first years. This perception was supported by the fact that, according to Schulz-Benesch, she "occasionally spoke out too crossly and aggressively on" the subject (43). Montessori challenged this perception later in her life, making this lecture a valuable contribution on the subject. Instead of arguing against fairy tales—which she notes are sometimes "beautiful little stories for children, but not in place of this concentration of work" (46)—Montessori reports that children in her schools were "very interested in things in the external world" (45). During work, when they concentrated with their hands and were "normalized," their interest in fairy tales disappeared: "If they are free to choose, they choose something which is more important for their development" (46). Montessori did believe, however, that we should give stories rooted in science and society to children that are "like fairy tales and give knowledge under the guide of these stories" (47). For example, she notes history should be presented with the characteristics of a fairy tale: "The story must be short, with a few well-drawn characters, the environment must be limited, unusual and very clear. They must all be built around something fantastic" (47). Montessori continues that the child's mind is nourished with these stories, not bored or tired, because knowledge is "taken in with imagination and not through memorizing" (49).

Montessori's "Alternative Comprehensive School"

This section includes just one course lecture, in which Montessori outlines important principles that must be present in a Montessori school. The lecture highlights the need for education based on a child's free choice, a classroom and school organization in which children of different ages cooperate, and an environment that acknowledges the child's "need of a place which is his home, a fixed point" (67). Montessori discusses these principles in many of her writings, but in this lecture she goes farther distinguishing her understanding of free choice with other contemporary proposals for education, such as the Decroly Method[8] and the "method of individual work."[9] According to Montessori, the teacher in the Decroly Method does not base himself upon the child's center of interest but upon "what he chooses to be the [center] of interest." This is a decided different for Montessori (62). Her "method of individual work," on the other hand, offers "complete freedom for the children who may even bring any material from home" (63). Montessori notes that the problem with Decroly's understanding is the lack of "continuity in the material" (63) the children work with. She emphasizes the necessity of a practice based on the child's interest that also is nestled in a systematic, sequential presentation of materials and the curriculum, for learning to be successful.

Montessori also gives detailed recommendations for class size and age differences in class. According to Montessori, the class should be between thirty and forty children; fewer than twenty-five children is not recommended because the "really profitable[10] results come when the number grows; twenty-five is a sufficient number, and forty is the best number that has been found" (65). Regarding ages, Montessori continues there "must be a difference of at least three years" in age (65) because the presence of children of different ages "has a great influence on the cultural development of the child" (68). Communication between groups of children in different ages is also arranged with open doors between classes that provide children with free choice of work, but also "free circulation" (67) in the classrooms. At the same time she writes, the environment is arranged so that each child has a personal, fixed place for a cupboard or cabinet and personal belongings; "each man will feel this need of a place which is his home, a fixed point" (67). These recommendations are often controversial in contemporary school design despite the benefits Montessori argues are embedded in each aspect of the environment.

"Child and Society"

The section "Child and Society" consists of three lectures given by Montessori. The common denominator in the three talks is the discussion of the triad formed by the adult, the child, and the environment. Here she puts forth a discourse dedicated to explaining the development of "errors in the children's behavior" (73). As Montessori points out in one lecture, "it is not a question of the morality in the children, of something wrong inside individual children" (75) and, accordingly, children should not be treated in clinics by "doctors of psychology" (73). Rather, she argues, the source of a child's challenges is an environment in which the child is oppressed because they are prevented from creating meaningful learning experiences for themselves. Such experiences, labeled "work" by Montessori, need to come "from an inner source" (85) and are about more than just skill development. Consequently, in one of these lectures, Montessori criticizes the reality of education of adolescents at that time in which "the formation of man evolves in a way that is anything but democratic" (87) because in her view young people have no choices nor influence on their education.

Montessori's lecture certainly illustrates a powerful, almost terrifying image of traditional schools for adolescents at that time. However, in practice she was much more reserved about her own reforms for that age saying only that adolescent education should be "based on a hitherto undiscovered passion which comes from the children's own desire to study without force or direction" (89). She describes her educational reforms for that age in much greater detail in *From Childhood to Adolescence*, published three years before this "Child and Society" lecture was given.

"Man's Place in the Cosmos"

In the last section of the book, "Man's Place in the Cosmos," Montessori's ultimate pedagogical aim becomes evident: a new and better world achieved through the child. Montessori was strongly convinced that "the child has within himself the capacity to develop into a being that is far superior to us" (101). Consequently, she asserts that education has a vital role to play if society is to be changed in such an indirect way.

An essential part of such education is what Montessori describes as "cosmic education," whose essence, meaning, and underlying theory Montessori describes in the final lecture in this text. This lecture is particularly interesting because this concept is very little discussed by Montessori in her previous books. She writes that cosmic education is an educational approach whose aim is to develop children's awareness of humanity's "essential functions which contribute to the upkeep and development of the earth" (107). According to Montessori, cosmic education must be understood in relation to her cosmic task theory, which is based on the belief that all animals' behavior has a specific aim, "the purpose not only to maintain themselves, but above all, of carrying a specific item in the complex task of the upkeep of the earth and of maintaining harmony on it" (107). Her cosmic task theory also includes humans.

However, according to Montessori, humans do not always obey the laws of creation included in the theory and are therefore "not 'prepared' to dominate the environment which is composed of a 'supra-nature' created upon the earth by himself" (110). Consequently, cosmic education therefore seeks to connect children with the laws of creation so that they can someday confront environmental challenges better than previous generations have. Montessori emphasizes the ethical dimensions of cosmic education by building up her philosophy centered around the premise that "upon the work of each depends the possibility of the life of the whole" (107) and that "humanity is effectively united" (109), while also stressing human awareness of such conditions is lacking and therefore must be developed. She also responds to critical questions regarding sustainable development, such as "whom we ought to take into account in our strivings for a sustainable future and to what extent; whether we are only responsible for sustainable development in our part of the world or throughout the whole world" (Öhman 2008, 17). These questions seem even more relevant today than they were in 1946 when Montessori delivered the lecture and remind us of the importance of this collection of works in profound ways.

Notes

1. In this interview, Montessori stated that the first six years of children's lives have been neglected in the field of education.
2. Independent page numbers refer to the text under discussion, *The Child, Society and the World*.
3. In *The Absorbent Mind*, published in 1949, Montessori describes that what she conceptualized as "normalization" is the most important result of her work.
4. This interpretation was supported in other lectures too. In a 1942 course lecture in India, Montessori talked about children finding interest in reading, saying "it is this interest which the teacher must be able to inspire in the child, and then know how to educate it" (61).
5. See, for example, Kilpatrick who describes a child in a Montessori environment as "an isolated worker" (Kilpatrick 1914, 14).
6. Montessori reported in this lecture that she gave "a course on religion to people of many different religions, Hindus, Moslems, Catholics, and others" in India (41). However, in her book *The Discovery of the Child*, first published in 1949, Montessori reported that "the experiment in religious education was eventually abolished in our Children's Houses because it was aimed exclusively at instruction in Catholicism which lends itself to exercises in moving about and preparing various objects, whereas there is no place for such activities in religions that are almost entirely abstract" (Montessori 1967, 300).
7. Further reading about this topic can be found in *The Child in the Church*, first published in 1929.
8. Ovide Decroly (1871–1932) was a Belgian educationalist and professor of child psychology.
9. This method probably refers to Helen Parkhurst, a former student of Montessori who also administered Montessori schools for some years and later developed her own teaching method, *The Dalton Plan*.
10. Here Montessori is implying the value of larger groups of children to socialize with not monetary gain.

References

Kilpatrick, William Heard. 1914. *The Montessori System Examined*. New York: Houghton Mifflin.
Ludwig, Harald. 2008. "Elevprestationer i Montessoriskolor och Traditionella Skolor [Student Performances in Montessori Schools and Traditional Schools]." In *MER om Montessori. 7 professorer om montessoripedagogik [MORE about Montessori: 7 Professors on Montessori Education]*, edited by Eva-Maria Ahlquist, 67–77. Stockholm: 08 tryck.

Montessori, Maria. 1949. *The Absorbent Mind*. Madras (Chennai): Theosophical Publishing House.
Montessori, Maria. 1967. *The Discovery of the Child*. New York: Ballantine Books.
Montessori, Maria. 1989. *The Child, Society and the World: Unpublished Speeches and Writings*. Santa Barbara: Clio.
Öhman, Johan. 2008. "Environmental Ethics and Democratic Responsibility: A Pluralistic Approach to ESD." In *Values and Democracy in Education for Sustainable Development: Contributions from Swedish Research*, edited by Johan Öhman, 17–32. Malmö, Sweden: Liber.
Quarfood, Christine. 2005. *Positivism med Mänskligt Ansikte. Montessoripedagogikens Idéhistoriska Grunder. [Positivism with a Human Face: The Historical Foundations of Montessori Education]*. Eslöv, Sweden: Östlings Bokförlag Symposion.
Skolverket [National Agency for Education]. 2015. *Att Planera för Barn och Elever Med Funktionsnedsättning. En Sammanställning av Forskning, Utvärdering och Inspektion 1994–2014. [Planning for Children and Students with Disabilities: A Compilation of Research, Evaluation and Inspection 1994–2014]*. Stockholm: Elanders Sverige AB.

PART III

Montessori Pedagogy across the Lifespan

Introduction: Montessori Pedagogy across the Lifespan

Eva-Maria Tebano Ahlquist

Maria Montessori's background in medicine and anthropology, and her study of children in an environment where their needs for activity were accommodated, formed the basis of her theory of development. On multiple occasions, she presented graphic designs to illustrate this theory and link it to her vision for how education should address the needs of children at each developmental phase. She also compared her vision to traditional schooling and highlighted the deficiencies she perceived. The pedagogy Montessori developed is based on the four phases of development, which she theorized consisted of a series of four 6-year periods beginning at birth (Montessori 1971). Montessori stressed that children in each phase had unique needs and that the transition to a new phase of psychological development is dramatic and can be compared to a rebirth. Therefore, the phases are divided into sub-periods to represent the calm periods of growth that follow the dramatic transformation indicative of the transition into a new phase. The core of Part III is organized around these phases, or what Montessori termed "planes," of development.

While Montessori's early diagrams depicted the planes as triangles, she later reworked the design into a plant-based metaphor using a bulb to illustrate "life as energy" (Grazzini 2004, 44). The diagram raises awareness that these planes represent developmental phases rather than biological age and reinforces the importance of the early years. In this revised illustration, the first years (ages 0–6) are represented as the plant's bulb with conditions to satisfy growth. It depicts the stem growing steadily during middle childhood (ages 6–12) and thickening to represent the crucial stage of adolescence (12–18). The growth trajectory of the plant in the diagram plateaus at the age of 24. Along with the diagram, Montessori contrasts the traditional school with its inverse emphasis on adolescence and young adulthood with little attention to the early years, demonstrating less of a focus on the developmental needs of the child and more on society's orientation.

Before outlining the structure of Part III, we first provide context around the term "didactic," which is integral to Montessori pedagogy. Usage of the term differs between German- and English-speaking cultures. In English today the term is sometimes viewed as a pejorative, indicating rigid and teacher-directed instruction. In contrast, Montessori followed the German tradition that refers to didactics in terms of the classical questions of the content of teaching and how it should be presented. Here, some of the central questions exemplified by Jank and Meyer (2018) are: *Who* should participate in learning? *What* should be learned? *Why* should someone learn something intended. By and *with whom* and *with or through what* should someone learn? *How* will it be made available? *When and where* will the learning take place? These are fundamental questions about education that Montessori sought to answer in developing her pedagogy.

The first chapter in Part III, which is an overview of the Montessori learning environment, naturally incorporates the concept of didactics and addresses the principle of movement placing the human being in relation to the world as a foundation of Montessori education (Montessori 1973). The next chapters outline Montessori pedagogy as it is designed to meet the needs of children at each stage of development. The first plane is divided into two chapters reflecting what is crucial for the young child beginning with the newborn's needs to around three years of age with the crucial importance of a safe and calm environment allowing the child to make discoveries little by little. The chapters then give the reader an idea of preschool, elementary school, and adolescent education and how didactic activities are carried out in Montessori classrooms. The final chapter is about the transformation of the teacher. We see it as an essential conclusion for this part since the Montessori teacher must be given space and opportunity for continuous development to become an "intellectual; a person committed to transforming society and perceiving their professional activity as a contribution to a better, non-oppressive humanity" (from Chapter 17: "Adult Formation and Transformation").

References

Grazzini, Camillo. 2004. "The Four Planes of Development." *NAMTA Journal* 29 (1) (Winter): 27–61.
Jank, Werner, and Hilbert Meyer. 2002. *Didaktische Modelle*. Berlin: Cornelsen Scriptor.
Montessori, Maria. 1971. "The Four Planes of Education." *AMI Communications* (4): 4–10.
Montessori, Maria. 1973. *The Absorbent Mind*. Madras: Kalakshetra Publications Press.

Chapter 12
Learning in the Montessori School Environment

Eva-Maria Tebano Ahlquist

The main principle of Montessori pedagogy is the active child. This chapter discusses what is required to implement the idea in terms of the design of the environment, didactics, and the teacher's role, according to Maria Montessori. To begin, there is a brief history of how Montessori's own experiences became crucial in shaping her pedagogy.

Montessori's Educational Vision

When the socially and politically conscious student Maria Montessori pursued her studies and scientific career, Italy was a young nation undergoing rapid industrial and economic development. Still, the country was divided, poverty prevailed, and widespread illiteracy existed. Social conditions for marginalized children from economically and socially deprived homes were difficult. These circumstances concerned Montessori so much that after receiving her medical training she pursued further university studies to deepen her knowledge in pedagogy and anthropology to assist children on the margins. In 1903 she initiated anthropological field studies at elementary schools. A year later, in an article, she pointed at the impact of family circumstances on students' intellectual level (Tornar 2007).

Through her studies, Montessori was acquainted with the history of education as well as emerging developments in the field. On a theoretical level, these developments advocated for student-centered learning, collaboration, didactic principles through sensory training, and experiences from the world outside the school premises. However, Montessori stated that the implementation of scientific research on education had, thus far, failed because of the constraints of a traditional school environment. She referred to her former teacher, Sergi, who believed that a science of education requires knowledge of human beings, precise observations of human behavior and especially of children, to build the foundations of education and culture (Montessori 1964). Using the metaphor of how the scientist could not observe the lives of butterflies by studying them chained to boxes, she illustrates that the teacher cannot make scientific observations of children confined to their school desks. To see the true nature of children, she believed, they must be able to move freely (Montessori 1964), which implied that her pedagogical research had to take place in an authentic setting in which students would be free to move.

Her studies provided a basis, yet she continued her experimental research throughout her life (Montessori 1964) for preschool children and gradually for older children. Over time, her research gradually expanded into the philosophy of education (Schulz-Benesch 1980).

The Montessori Early Childhood Environment

During the beginning of the twentieth century, Rome faced significant social and economic problems, such as housing shortages, poverty, and crime. Montessori was known for her commitment and defense of the potential of children if they received a proper education. In 1906, while head of the Education Department at the Milan International Exposition, Montessori received an offer from the director and creator of a real estate institute in Rome to set up a school in a working-class housing complex in San Lorenzo. She accepted, and in January 1907, the school was inaugurated (Montessori 1964).

Montessori's intention led to a modest start. The classroom was set up with long tables facing the teacher. She replaced screwed-in benches with lightweight chairs, so children were able to move. The Sensorial materials from her earlier experiments with cognitively delayed children were modified or discarded (Montessori 1964). Upon noting their willingness to work, Montessori gave the children small tables and chairs and access to didactic materials and permission to engage with these materials. Now, Montessori was prepared for studying the child in a setting that "permits the child's free natural manifestations" (Montessori 1964, 15).

At the suggestion of a friend, Montessori named her school Casa dei Bambini (Children's House). This name has since been adopted by many Montessori schools worldwide and is the hallmark of Montessori preschools. Unfortunately, the English translation emphasizes the building structure itself. However, Regni clarifies "La Casa dei Bambini ... è la 'loro' Casa" (2007, 75). That is, "The Children's House ... it is their home." In an unpublished letter found in the 1920s, Montessori wrote:

> The children's "home" is what the title says: a "home," a place where we live, where peace and happiness make us feel good: where we know that we are met by a sanctuary "that we have created" and where we are the "owners," the "owners" who have designed harmony between us and the environment. The "home" belongs to all who live here, and each of us finds everything necessary to gain strength and rest.
>
> *(as cited in Honegger Fresco 2000, 83)*

Bachelard compares the home with a snail shell, a secure place where you "inhabit with intensity" (2000, 39). It can be likened to Montessori's idea as she adds that this home "is more than walls that create security. 'It lives!'" (Montessori 1964, 68). In this home, everything is well organized, and children can find what they are looking for. However, Montessori makes it clear that the school should not be a copy of an ordinary home, nor "simply a place where the children are kept" (1964, 62). Rather, it is an "inhabited space" (Bachelard 2000, 43), a "true school for their education ... inspired by the rational principles of scientific pedagogy" (Montessori 1964, 62).

Figure 12.1 Girl working with bells, Holliday Montessori School, Kansas City, Missouri, USA. Courtesy of Jennifer Baker Powers.

Montessori's (1965) guidelines for her school represented an ideal middle-class European home. Considering the circumstances in which the children of San Lorenzo grew up, Montessori's focus on hygiene, peace, and order was forefront. A "home" is culturally and socially conditioned, but the underlying values in the Montessori environment cannot be overlooked. Montessori designed the Casa dei Bambini to resemble a miniature home made up of different spaces such as a hall, kitchen, study, and bathroom, along with space for recreation and socializing. Since the children are the protagonists of this pedagogical home, they have access to master it. Therefore, it is furnished with low cupboards and light tables and chairs that the children can easily move around. In this environment, the children can, and do, perform adult tasks (Montessori 2019), such as sweeping the floor, dusting the shelves, tending the flowers, setting the table and serving food, and clearing the table after lunch with all that this entails. Other aspects of a home, such as personal care and caring for family members and friends, are also found in this school. Just as an ideal home satisfies the senses, emotions, creativity, and intellect, the same is true at this school.

The classroom provides materials that encourage independence; prepare the child to experience through the senses; encourage literacy and mathematics; and give experiences through culture, art, music, and nature (see Figure 12.1).

Nature is a recurring theme of Montessori (1972), and she saw danger in the modern tendency to distance oneself from nature. Therefore, for example, a garden is present in the school environment, where the child can be close to life-giving forces by cultivating and tending it. There may also be animals to take care of (Montessori 1964). To cherish nature can only be done by interacting with it firsthand. Even if children are given opportunities to participate in descriptions of nature, however educational they may be, Montessori writes, no deep connections with nature can occur in a classroom. Instead, children should be brought up to have an intimate relationship with the outdoors. Montessori (1972) writes about the young child's relationship with nature in an almost poetic passage.

> Let the children be free; encourage them; let them run outside when it is raining; let them remove their shoes when they find a puddle of water; and, when the grass of the meadows is damp with dew, let them run on it and trample it with their bare feet; let them rest peacefully when a tree invites them to sleep beneath its shade.
>
> *(68)*

The Design of the School

In Austria in the 1920s, Lili Roubiczek (McFarland et al. 2020) wrote an article about Montessori preschools and the basic principle of architecture, where space has a dominating influence on the child. She described an ideal design as having an octagonal shape, with a center that would always attract the child back when the work was completed. The architects Schuster, Singer, and Dicker designed a Montessori school in Vienna, where pedagogy, psychology, and architecture interacted. Furniture, door handles, and windowsills were designed in size for the child. The boundary between the outdoor and indoor environment was blurred, creating the freedom to work outside in the garden where trees provided shade. In the Netherlands in 1926, Brinkman and Van der Vlugt designed a Montessori school using the idea of a central space, surrounded by four more minor extensions reminiscent of Palladio's villa, La Rotonda (Hertzberger 2008). During the 1960s, the Dutch architect Hertzberger (1991) designed Montessori schools with a central place to meet and socialize. The Montessori environment offers the child a range of artifacts: Montessori materials, books, plants, lab materials, and displays of the children's collected work. The teacher facilitates, supports, and challenges the children both in classroom and outside the school building (see Figure 12.2). Cold (2002) talks about school as a bazaar, where one acquires knowledge and skills, develops thoughts and ideas, experiences and participates in creative activities, explores, discusses, collaborates, meets friends, and gets to know others. This meaning-making environment considers children's activity and experience as a prerequisite for learning and, thus, transcends the physical environment. It is a lived space, which symbolizes freedom, embodied learning, and social relationships as part of the space itself (Tebano Ahlquist 2012).

Montessori Environment and Its Material

The Montessori environment is filled with motion: children get materials, someone sweeps the floor, another waters the flowers. The children are concentrating on their tasks, which fulfill a specific meaning. The environment requires them to know how to move calmly and with poise, which may be a challenge. The phenomenologist Buytendijk (1932, 5) expresses that a Montessori child connects to the environment because of the fragility of the objects. They develop an individual structure by "uniting the soul with one's own future oncoming world." The external structure of the environment and the didactic function of the material are aimed at organizing the child's inner life (Montessori 1917). Since the material in a Montessori school is a learning material rather than a material used for free play, it is "gender-neutral" (Gustafsson 2020, 1110) and makes every child "an actor in a living scene" (Montessori 1965, 47), opening up opportunities for children to work together regardless of gender (Montessori 1965, 47). Whether factory-made or teacher-made, the materials are designed to attract children's attention. Color-coded Mathematical materials, shiny Geometric Solids, cut-out Sandpaper Letters, and Puzzle Maps with continents and countries in different colors are just some of many materials that invite the child by calling: "Take me!" (Montessori 1972, 83). This call opens new learning possibilities, for "[o]nce a direction is given to them, the child's movements are made towards a definite end, so that he himself grows quiet and contented, and becomes an active worker, a being calm and full of joy" (Montessori 1965, 53). The materials offer themselves as possible actions. Montessori's quote echoes Merleau-Ponty when he describes man's relationship with the environment: "In the action of the hand which is raised towards an object is contained to a reference to the object, not as an object represented, but as that highly specific thing towards which we project ourselves, near which we are, in anticipation, and which we haunt" (2004, 159).

Play is an often-discussed topic in Montessori education. Montessori (1966) was not against play. In fact, she often uses play and work synonymously when describing children's work with the materials (Montessori 1965). However, by referring to the children's work, the activity gets respected. One does not interrupt a person who is working. Montessori shows examples of playfulness when she presents the number zero and asks children to come to her zero times or send zero kisses (1964). Although this is an example of a game to reinforce the understanding of zero, it is a demonstration of what can be perceived as play. Still, Montessori points out that children want to be involved in meaningful chores; free play is a pastime, and for this purpose, the school should offer a "club-room" (Montessori 1965) for socializing or resting.

In addition, and quite important, play should not be confused with imagination. According to Montessori, imagination leads to the ability to make associations; without it, children cannot understand things they have not experienced (Montessori 1973). The activities that children experience in the Montessori school through systematic training of the senses and the environment's practical work create these conditions. Montessori (1973) rejects the idea that fairy tales support imagination. Fairy tales were once used as intimidation to make children obey adults. That is why she believed children need to reach a certain level of maturity to distinguish between fairy tales and reality (Tebano Ahlquist 2012, 2020).

Didactic Requirements: Embodiment and Variation Theory

The design of didactic materials is grounded in Montessori's theoretical-philosophical framework. Montessori disagrees with Descartes's (2008) proposition that body and mind are separate entities. Instead, she suggests from a biological perspective that the sensorimotor system led to human abilities such as reason and understanding. Montessori (1989a) gives examples from early human development. The free thumb that meets each finger was essential for using the hand for precision work, and consequently, the early human brain developed. Montessori's recurring reference to the importance of the hand cannot be overemphasized (see Chapter 18: "Revisiting the Foundations of Montessori Education from a Modern Neuroscience Perspective").

Research shows that what we do with our hands affects the organization of our brains (Lundborg 2011). This is in alignment with Montessori, who states, "The hand is the delicate and structurally complicated organ that allows the mind not only to manifest itself but to enter into special relations, with his environment" (2019, 85). Learning requires exploration not limited to visual or auditory reception. Cognition and movement intertwine, leading to abstract understanding as well as mastery of movement, each activity generating much more learning than the observer might notice (Gettman 1987). For example, when children work with the Sandpaper Letters, they do not just trace the shape of a letter and make the phonetic sound; they incorporate the experience of shape and the sound of the letter. When the child's fingers are following the sides of the Geometric Figures, they identify contours of the shape represented; they "involve the hand moving ... and the movement gives a driving idea" (Montessori 2011, 11), while the visual image of the shapes enhances the experience. As Johnson (2017, 99) states, "[t]his is not merely the obvious claim that we need bodies and brains in order to think. It is the much-stronger claim that the nature of conceptualization and even reason itself are shaped by ways our bodies work and by the nature of our bodily encounters with our environments." The German word "*begreifen*" means to grasp, which has its sensorimotor domain in object manipulation (Lakoff and Johnson 1999).

Montessori materials are designed to provide a limited number of characteristics of a particular phenomenon that the child will pay full attention to at any given time. Montessori talks about a "technique of isolation" (1917, 44), which is consistent with variation theory (Marton 2015; Tebano Ahlquist and Gynther 2020). By contrast, the materials help the child discern what is intended to be learned. When the child is about to learn colors, we cannot show them things in the same color. The Color Tablets exemplify this. Different colors are depicted on small boards (tablets) of the same shape and size to isolate the color feature. In the same way, in other materials, language acquisition exercises are carried out, where the teacher starts with the extremes and gives the nomenclature by comparing (e.g., the largest with the smallest, the longest with the shortest, the thickest with the thinnest) and then gives words of the different gradations in between (Gettman 1987; Montessori 1965). To learn geometric shapes, a square is contrasted with a circle while keeping the color and size invariant. If the shape, size, and color were to vary, it would confuse the child in distinguishing the specific quality. Montessori writes: "[I]t is necessary to eliminate as far as possible all other perceptions ... and so to polarize attention on them that all other images shall be obscured in the field of consciousness" (1917, 42). The materials sharpen the child's senses, enabling them to make observations, comparisons, and judgments, which clarifies its inner aim (Montessori 1965). What is highlighted in the examples is a combination of variation theory and embodiment in Montessori pedagogy.

The Elementary and Middle School Environments

The skills, values, and knowledge that the child acquires during early childhood provide a platform for subsequent school years. However, Montessori environments, regardless of age, invite students to engage in active learning. For example, students can be inspired by observing classmates working on a task that is facilitated by the mixed-age classes. Student-centered learning evolves into collaborative inquiry-based learning. Elementary and middle school children work together on large projects in an environment that is a mixture of a creative workplace, a studio, a library, and a laboratory. Didactic Montessori materials are still available in subjects like Mathematics, Geometry, and Language as a continuation of early childhood materials. Although the seeds of cosmic education were planted during early childhood (Honegger Fresco 2000; Tebano Ahlquist 2020), the concept evolves to demonstrate interconnectedness and interdependence, illustrating symbiosis between ecological and human culture (Tebano Ahlquist 2012). Montessori (1971) argues that such studies suit the elementary students' stage in life, since they are interested in cultural topics. The classroom environment, therefore, contains materials such as timelines presenting the existence of the Earth and the epoch of modern humans in a chronological, holistic, and systematic way during the course of history. There are classification materials in biodiversity, scientific literature, laboratory experiments, and aesthetic activities. The environment continues to challenge children's creativity and intellectual potential. Although the outdoor environment with its garden is part of early childhood, the boundaries of the classroom for older children extend to include society, nature, and cultural institutions providing broader experiences and satisfying children's curiosity and needs through an activity Montessori called "Going Out" (1976, 17–23).

Older students still perform Practical Life activities at school, but now they have an actual purpose and are not done for the activity itself, as in early childhood (Montessori 1966). For example, students can oversee the school library or store; they can run a school cafe or they can chair or act as secretary to class councils.

The passage from elementary to middle school reflects the child moving from simply being in the family to a child on its way to society—a physically and psychologically dramatic transition. Montessori proposed a very different school environment for older students, arguing that education must become "a school for the experience of the elements of social life," requiring experiences similar to those of an adult member of society. Montessori called this school model "Erdkinder" (1976, 97). Literally translated as "children of the Earth," the Erdkinder model is a combination of practical and intellectual work in which the management of agriculture and commerce, among other things, is part of the school's direction. These were almost utopian ideas that were not realized during Montessori's lifetime. Today there are a few examples, but there are many urban compromises.

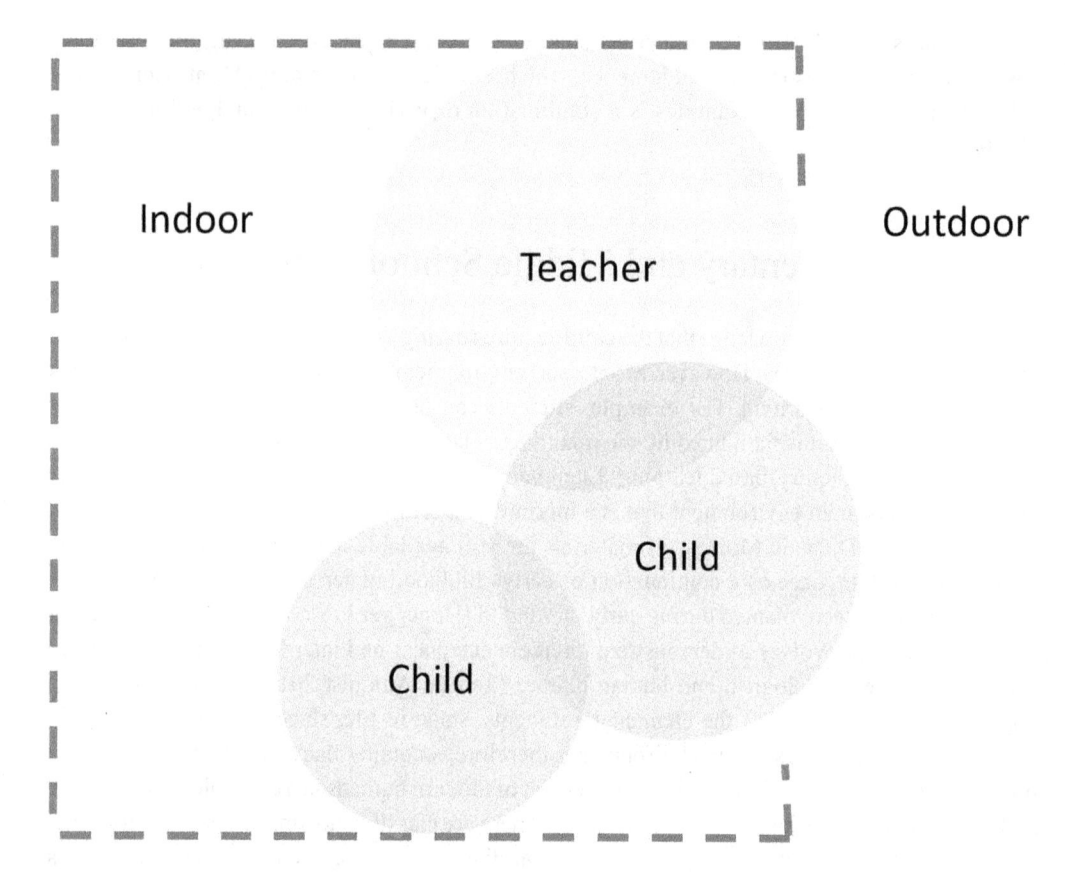

Figure 12.2 The Montessori Lived Environment. Illustration by the author.

At all stages of childhood, learning in Montessori environments takes place through meaningful and reciprocal relationships between children and the school environment with its artifacts. "Help me to do it by myself" is a famous quote by Maria Montessori (2019, 224) associated with the preschool age. Montessori (1976) reiterates this as valid for adolescents as well, which illustrates this connection. One of the Montessori teacher's responsibilities is to prepare an environment that offers a continuum from early childhood to elementary and middle school, where developmental psychology, didactics, and philosophy form a unifying thread in a strikingly systematic way (Tebano Ahlquist 2012).

Freedom to Learn

"Spontaneous manifestation" is a term Montessori (1964, 143) used to describe a child's true nature emerging when provided the freedom to develop. Allowing children the freedom to meet their authentic needs on the path to independence is a key tenet of Montessori education. Creating an environment that allows for a child's liberty requires strict organization. The teacher's task is to prepare the classroom environment to function as a workplace so that everyone can work undisturbed in a socially harmonious manner. The child will discover that freedom does not mean that one can always do what one wishes. There are rules to follow, such as always putting back a material in the same place and in the same condition as they found it and never taking material from another child (Montessori 1972). Materials are provided in one copy, which means that sometimes children must stand back and wait for their turn. At the same time, it can provide opportunities to work together. Learning how to behave toward another person is not always easy, and conflicts can arise. Through the practical activities of Grace and Courtesy exercises, issues of moral dilemmas relating to the good of the individual and the school are raised.

Montessori education encourages children's participation and influence over their own daily lives and learning. With increasing age, the child can participate when lessons are planned and choose topics, themes, and activities, thus exercising influence and responsibility, a prerequisite for democracy in school and in society. As Montessori writes, "Everything that concerns education assumes today an importance of a general kind, and must represent a protection and a practical aid to the development of man; it must aim at improving the individual in order to improve society" (1976, 59).

The Montessori Teacher's Role

The Montessori teacher is sometimes described as passive, with the materials replacing the teacher. However, according to Ludwig (2017), such general objections neither apply to Montessori theory nor do justice to the practice of Montessori education. The demands on a Montessori teacher are high with a basis in terms of theoretical and philosophical knowledge. Through anthropological studies, Montessori (1989b) developed an ability to make careful observations and, like Gadamer, argued that we see the world through our preconceptions. Gadamer (1983) discusses the concept of theory based on the Greek etymological meaning "to look closely." Teachers should not be satisfied with a ready-made system but be critical and, for example, review material that may not work or be scientifically appropriate today.

Developing education in the spirit of Montessori requires in-depth knowledge through study, evidence-based teaching, and sharing of experiences to benefit children's learning. Just like scientists, they will then be able to move Montessori pedagogy forward in a positive direction through careful considerations (Montessori 1989b). However, Montessori argues that although teachers are scientifically trained, the heart must also be present as they study "the awakening of [the children's] intellectual life" (1964, 12), which signifies the "intimate relationship" with the child being observed (1964, 12). As Langeveld describes, "encounter does not mean that we meet 'others,' but it means that we meet 'each other': that is, in a human and undeniably creative social reality; in a complex but never completely understood network of circumstances and problems to which human thinking and acting responsibly must be responsive" (Langeveld 1983, 5). Montessori speaks of the child as the "father of man" (1966, 17), which dissolves the dichotomy between teacher and child; the child is also the teacher's teacher in the Montessori environment.

Montessori recognized early on that children grow up in different circumstances and not all children are equal. However, all children have the potential to learn if given the right conditions. Montessori's solution was a new school environment with all that it implies, and her holistic solution makes Montessori pedagogy unique. Although education should evolve with the times, children's activity in accordance with Montessori's fundamental pedagogical principles addresses needs that remain relevant today. In other words, in a Montessori environment, butterflies are free.

References

Bachelard, Gaston. 2000. *Rummets Poetik*. Lund: Novapress.
Buytendijk, Frederick. 1932. *Bildung der Jugend Durch Lebendiges Tun*. Berlin: Der Neue Verlag.
Cold, Birgit. 2002. *Skolemiljø: Fire Fortellinger*. Oslo: Kommuneforlaget.
Descartes, René. 2008. *A Discourse on the Method*. Oxford: Oxford University Press.
Gadamer, Hans-Georg. 1983. *Lob der Theorie: Reden und Aufsätze*. (1. Aufl.) Frankfurt am Main: Suhrkamp.
Gettman, David. 1987. *Basic Montessori Learning Activities for under Fives*. New York: St. Martin Griffin.
Gustafsson, Christina. 2020. "Maria Montessori." In *The SAGE Encyclopedia of Children and Childhood Studies*, edited by Daniel Thomas Cook, 1108–11. Thousand Oaks: Sage Publications.
Hertzberger, Herman. 1991. *Lessons for Students in Architecture*. Rotterdam: 010 Publishers.
Hertzberger, Herman. 2008. *Space and Learning, Lessons in Architecture 3*. Rotterdam: 010 Publishers.
Honegger Fresco, Grazia. 2000. *Montessori: Perché no? Una Pedagogia per la Crecita*. Milano: FrancoAngeli.
Johnson, Mark. 2017. *Embodied Mind, Meaning, and Reason: How Our Bodies Give Rise to Understanding*. Chicago: The University of Chicago Press.
Lakoff, George and Mark Johnson. 1999. *Philosophy in the Flesh: The Embodied Mind and Its Challenge to Western Thought*. New York: Basic Books.
Langeveld, Martinus Jan. 1983. "Reflections on Phenomenology and Pedagogy." *Phenomenology & Pedagogy* 1 (1): 5–7.
Ludwig, Harald. 2017. "Grundgedanken der Montessori Pädagogik." In *Kritik und Metakritik der Pädagogik Maria Montessoris*, edited by Harald Ludwig. Freiburg: Herder.
Lundborg, Göran. 2011. *Handen och Hjärnan. Från Lucys Tumme till den Tankestyrda Robothanden*. Stockholm: Atlantis.
Marton, Ference. 2015. *Necessary Conditions of Learning*. London: Routledge.
McFarland, Rob, Georg Spitaler, and Ingo Zechner. 2020. *Das Rote Wien*. Oldenburg: De Gruyter.
Merleau-Ponty, Maurice. 2004. *Phenomenology of Perception*. London: Routledge.
Montessori, Maria. 1917. *Spontaneous Activity in Education*. New York: Frederick A. Stokes Company Publishers.
Montessori, Maria. 1964. *The Montessori Method*. New York: Schocken Books.
Montessori, Maria. 1965. *Dr. Montessori's Own Handbook*. New York: Schocken Books.
Montessori, Maria. 1966. *What You Should Know about Your Child*. Madras: Kalakshetra Publications.
Montessori, Maria. 1971. "The Four Planes of Education." *AMI Communications* nr 4: s. 4–10.
Montessori, Maria. 1972. *The Discovery of the Child*. New York: Ballentine Books.
Montessori, Maria. 1973. *The Absorbent Mind*. Madras: Kalakshetra Publications Press.
Montessori, Maria. 1976. *From Childhood to Adolescence*. New York: Schocken Books.
Montessori, Maria. 1989a. *Education for a New World*. Oxford: Clio.
Montessori, Maria. 1989b. *The Formation of Man*. Oxford: Clio.

Montessori, Maria. 2011. *Psychogeometry*. Amsterdam: Montessori Pierson Publishing Company.
Montessori, Maria. 2019. *The Secret of Childhood*. Eastford: Martino Fine Books.
Regni, Raniero. 2007. *Infanzia e Società in Maria Montessori. Il Bambino Padre dell'Uomo*. Rom: Armando Editore.
Schulz-Benesch, Günter. 1980. *Montessori*. Darmstadt: Wissenschaftliche Buchgesellschaft.
Tebano Ahlquist, Eva-Maria. 2012. *Skolans Levda Rum och Lärandets Villkor: Meningsskapande i Montessoriskolans Fysiska Miljö*. Diss. Stockholm: Stockholms Universitet.
Tebano Ahlquist, Eva-Maria. 2020. "Educazione Cosmica e Immaginazione." In *Sensi Immaginazione Intelletto in Maria Montessori*, edited by Paola Trabalzini. Rome: Fede Editore.
Tebano Ahlquist, Eva-Maria, and Per Gynther. 2020. "Teaching in the Montessori Classroom." *Journal of Montessori Research* 6 (1): 33–45. https://doi.org/10.17161/jomr.v6i1.12051.
Tornar, Clara. 2007. *La Pedagogia di Maria Montessori tra Teoria e Azione*. Milan: FrancoAngeli.

Chapter 13

The Montessori Approach to Children 0–3 Years Based on Grazia Honegger Fresco's Studies

Sara Honegger
Translation By: Ariel Rothman

This chapter was written by Sara Honegger, Grazia Honegger Fresco's daughter, based on several texts her mother left to her. Honegger Fresco (b. Rome, 1929, d. Castellanza, province of Varese, 2020) was one of Maria Montessori's students. In 2008, having dedicated her whole life to children, founding schools, and reforming nurseries through careful training of educational personnel, she was given an award by UNICEF. She authored more than thirty books and edited the magazine Il Quaderno Montessori *for 30 years.*[1] *Honegger Fresco performed her research with Centro Nascita Montessori di Roma (Montessori Center for Newborns in Rome), which is still in operation today. In Northern Italy, her work was organized in the cooperative Percorsi per Crescere. The author thanks Sabrina Ricci, one of Honegger Fresco's students and coordinator of the nursery at Cardano al Campo (Varese, Italy), and Carlo Alberti, Honegger Fresco's collaborator in Percorsi per Crescere.*

Even at the age of 90, Grazia Honegger Fresco (1929–2020) would jot down her observations of Laila, her great-granddaughter. She prepared little gifts for her. They were never toys with an intended purpose. They were objects of everyday use, found around the house, which she would prepare with care: a box with various buttons inside, some metal chains, different types of containers, curtain rings, and balls of different-colored threads braided together. Before her great-granddaughter arrived, she would put these objects around the room without ever giving them to her directly, much less showing her their possible uses. Where did this manner of interaction with a 2-year-old child come from?

Child-Rearing Starts from Birth

Honegger Fresco was one of Maria Montessori's pupils. She dedicated a seminal biography to Montessori (Honegger Fresco 2018b) and completed lengthy studies about her. In these studies, Honegger Fresco demonstrates how deeply Montessori investigated newborn children from the beginning of her research on human infancy and how Montessori underlined the importance of holistic and precise care, even in 1915 (Honegger Fresco 2018a). Montessori was one of the first researchers who shone a new light on how to view newborns (Montessori 1998, 2021); that is, they are individuals who are separate from their mothers, and yet, inextricably tied to them, requiring special and "delicate attention" (Honegger Fresco 2018a, 34). In 1916, Montessori also pondered how newborns are cared for (Montessori 1916). Then, in 1920, while living in Barcelona, Spain, she tackled the psychology of newborns, having been encouraged by the Catalan government to build a children's institute devoted to the in-depth study of the first years of life:

> I have for many years interested myself in the study of children from three years upwards. Many have urged me to continue my studies on the same lines with older children. But what I have felt to be most vital is the need for more careful and particularized study of the tiny child. In the first three years of life the foundations of physical and also psychological health are laid. In these years the child not only increases in size but passes through great transformations. This is the age in which language and movement develop. The child must be safeguarded so that these activities may develop freely.
>
> *(Montessori in Radice 1920, 67–72)*

Adele Costa Gnocchi, a collaborator of Montessori who implemented the Montessori approach in a variety of settings (Honegger Fresco 2001), spearheaded the study of the first three years of life, as well as the training of new parents and young women to care for newborns. Under Montessori's aegis she established the first experimental class of the future Montessori Infants' Assistants (AIM) school in Rome in 1947. One of her first students was 18-year-old Grazia Honegger Fresco. The school was research focused—based on the same scientific rigor in pedagogy applied by Montessori—observation, observation, and more observation. Students would undertake long internships in hospitals—in the birthing and maternity wings—and with some families. Observations were also performed in Rome's orphanage, which housed many children left orphaned in the wake of the Second World War. During this period, recordings filmed in the United States by René Spitz (1965) detailed the psychological and physical deaths of institutionalized children who were deprived of significant relationships in their development. Concurrently, John Bowlby (1950), upon request by the World Health Organization, investigated how a lack of strong bonds in the first phases of life harmed human beings. At the same time, in Rome, Adele Costa Gnocchi started the AIM school based on Montessori's instructions to develop the child's potential in a different way. Within her training she developed the ability to observe newborns in an empathetic fashion so as not to take anything for granted but rather to grasp the innate skills and needs of newborns and toddlers through their signs of pain and pleasure. Specifically, Costa Gnocchi paid special attention to the ways in which newborns react to changes—in people, places, and habits—and to changes in their caregivers' behaviors, how the caregivers handle newborns, and how they change and wash the newborns.

The first results of this exciting work presented at the 8th International Montessori Congress in San Remo in 1949 (Opera Montessori 1950) highlighted the ways in which newborns differ from one another, how they are sensitive to their environment, and how they need protection.

The presentation also detailed how newborns are active and unique from the moment they are born. The observations presented were conducted by two Montessorians focusing on the individual care provided to two newborns: one born at home and the other born in a clinic. They demonstrated how the home environment is ideal to guarantee the calmness, intimacy, and bond that the mother and child need; however, they noted that with simple adjustments even a hospital ward can protect a budding mother-child bond and the newborn, who, although fragile, is full of potential (Montessori 1997, 241–7). These changes include reducing the coming and going of hospital personnel, avoiding separations and unnecessary interferences between the mother and child, dimming the lights and muting noises, bathing and dressing the newborn with care and without sudden movements, and protecting the baby from the cold and from unnecessarily invasive practices, especially in the moments immediately following birth. Examples of such changes, revolutionary at the time, were to use a small, enameled tub with water at 98.6°F (instead of running water) for the newborn's first bath; bathing the newborn in a dimly lit area using soft towels heated on radiators to dry them; and advising the mothers to always breastfeed in the same spot, seated in the same chair. The results from the study presented were notable: In addition to the absence of crying at the moment of birth and the calm immediately found when bathing them in warm water, both children were able to find their regular rhythms. They seldom cried, and in the span of several weeks, their cries were replaced with soft cooing. Smiles quickly appeared, and their sleep patterns regulated themselves starting the second week. This phenomenon continues to present itself at every new assisted birth and showcases how the *achievement of independence*, greatly underlined by Montessori, already exists in the newborn in the form of their *self-regulatory abilities*. These, if not stifled, last their whole life. Such theory is backed by the actual studies found in *Infant Research and Adult Treatment: Constructing Interactions* (Beebe and Lachmann 2015).

The fundamental role of this caregiver-child relationship is confirmed by the observations conducted in Rome's orphanage. Honegger Fresco writes,

> It is difficult to imagine today the conditions of these toddlers who would spend their days in bed or in large, wooden enclosures, without doing anything, without loving relationships with an adult. An exception are those toddlers who were housed in the ward with their mother, who, in exchange for food and board, would see to house-cleaning tasks and breastfeeding not only her child, but two others. The difference between the children who had their mothers with them, and the others was significant.
>
> *(Honegger Fresco 2001, 122–3)*

Thus, Honegger Fresco observed newborns to investigate how those who spent a long time in institutions could develop a relationship with other adults. This practice, later labeled by psychoanalysis as infant observations in the 1960s, viewed these relationships as fundamental for the structuring of the mind because the relationality offers an experience that satisfies all the senses, which are already so active and demanding in a newborn. Honegger Fresco would devote the rest of her life to researching how to safeguard these essential encounters in the first year of life (later highlighted in the 1980s by Daniel Stern [2018]) by offering children the Montessori educational environment.

The Sensitive Period for Order

In 1960, Honegger Fresco moved to the outskirts of Milan, opening a school that operated from nursery through elementary school. She logged the results of her extended work on newborns at the AIM school in one of her first books (Honegger Fresco 1970). The text of those results soon became a reference point for the training of educational personnel in many nurseries in Northern Italy. She was subsequently elected President of the Montessori Center for Newborns, which managed the Bank of Italy's nurseries in Rome. In this role, she had the opportunity to compare educational experiences that took place across different Italian regions. The cardinal principle of Montessori's pedagogy consistently guided her work: *observe and follow the child*. Her work with the educators confirmed the existence of several sensitive periods, starting with the sensitive period for order (see Chapter 18: "Revisiting the Foundations of Montessori Education from a Modern Neuroscience Perspective"). Montessori (1998) wrote about this period in *The Secret of Childhood*, reframing so-called tantrums as signs of protest in the face of sudden changes. The sensitive period for order, often narrowly interpreted as a need for order in their environment and traditionally thought of as emerging at a later phase of their development, is manifested from birth as the need for stability and continuity, starting with the relationship with the mother or caregiver. The importance of this first bond cannot be emphasized enough, as it is fundamental to the child's subsequent development of independence. Honegger Fresco was aware that every child sees their own reflection in the eyes of the adult, and she paid special attention to the moment the child transitions from the mother's arms—the child's first environment—to the care of the nursery. She carefully chooses the phrase *familiarization with their environment*[2] to describe this delicate moment to underline that this relationship begins with the educator's welcoming gaze and is supported by an educational environment intentionally prepared for the newborn.

Creating a Non-anticipatory Environment

Montessori was one of the first to understand that a child's development cannot flourish without an adequate physical and emotional environment, conducive to the different developmental stages. Through interacting with the environment, children are exposed to experiences essential to the emerging architecture of their mind. At the same time, the child must be able to feel that they can respond to their physical and emotional environment, experiencing a feeling of *reciprocity*. This stage is especially important because a child's brain continues to grow after birth and in the first 18 months, during which the right orbital frontal lobe specifically plays an important part in social-emotional development.

According to Montessori, the educational environment of nurseries should be designed according to a newborn's ability to respond to the different phases of life that are articulated by sensitive periods, keeping in mind that their ways of understanding the world are unique to this time and will not appear again. Beginning in the first year, children start exploring on the floor, with objects at their disposal on thin rugs, which allows them to develop their autonomous motor skills (Honegger Fresco 2019). Each spontaneous achievement of every position, once steady and secure, becomes a preface to the next position. These observations were confirmed by Emmi

Pikler's studies (1969) happening in parallel. Much attention is placed on the individual child-educator relationship and ratio (1:3) in moments of care—changing clothes and diapers, eating, and sleeping. This relational security permits the child to activate their exploratory attitude, which starts a few months after birth through the exploration of their own body, and subsequently the exploration of their environment, objects, and the relationship between these. When the sensitive period of movement begins, provided that it is not interrupted or disturbed unnecessarily by an adult, the child experiences the pleasure of discovery and reveals their surprising ability to concentrate on their own body. The experimentation continues with finding balance via repetitive and repeating motions without ever being stimulated, but rather being allowed to execute their personal discoveries, at their own pace, free of the adult's expectations. If infants spontaneously manage to sit down at a small table, passing from one place of play (the floor) to another (the table), the child will have done it at the right time in their evolutionary stage, not a moment too soon or too late, without restlessness or discomfort, which are emotional states that are often the result of experiences outside of their limits.

When the child has completely tested their own body and come to understand their autonomy and agency, they become deeply aware of their potential and feel ready and curious to face new situations. Spurred by the pleasure of success, the child will engage in difficult and sometimes frustrating situations, but with a steady base capable of supporting them.

Exploratory Wandering

Over the course of the years, Honegger Fresco (2016) continued to hone her research on the specific objects that best resonate with the exploratory nature of children. Together with the other educators who were trained by her, she observed how predetermined games are at first appreciated by children but then are quickly abandoned. She concluded that objects with a prescribed use did not hold children's attention for very long because they limited further exploration.

During the same years, Elinor Goldschmied's (2003) pedagogical proposals began to be adopted by Italian nurseries. For instance, the *treasure chest* was meant for newborns who managed a seated position and grabbed objects, which they brought to their mouths; for those already steady on their feet, there was the *heuristic game*, in which objects easy to recover were stored in a special room where an educator took turns accompanying two or three toddlers at a time. The experience with the treasure chest aligns perfectly to Montessori's criteria. The heuristic game, on the other hand, does not fully allow for freedom of choice because the educator imposes time limits and decides on the group formations. Montessori would suggest to always leave objects, divided in boxes, at the toddlers' disposal: wooden boards and cubes, various types of rope, fabrics, cubes, cardboard, cardboard boxes of various sizes and shapes, little metal chains, coffee filters, jars with plastic tops with one or several holes, colanders, strainers, bottles, small bowls, curtain rings, bottle tops, shells, and pinecones.

The pivotal moment happens when toddlers become sensitive to *the voices of things*, as Montessori would say. They immerse themselves in spontaneous, fruitful, and creative activities and conduct their own search in an individual, inexhaustible manner. So begins what Honegger Fresco called exploratory wandering: toddlers begin wandering, looking around at their surroundings, seemingly without direction, all the while preparing themselves to make a choice. Their process of touching, moving, and scattering things around is the root of continuously renewed discoveries accompanied by intense concentration. Toddlers can occupy themselves for up to 40 minutes threading a chain in a jar, box, or through the tubes of a radiator. Similar to scientists, toddlers proceed by trial and error, experimenting with the same action in different ways—Montessori likened their method to that of a mathematical mind. These actions comprise putting in/taking out, threading/removing, throwing/fetching, climbing up/getting down, opening/closing, and filling/emptying. Toddlers are not aware why they go through these actions, but they complete them in all latitudes, following these unconscious motivations. They do not perform them just once or twice, but ten, twenty, thirty times. This is how the *need for repetition* manifests itself and where the joy of discovery is found. Montessori observed this process and summarized it in three stages: the choice of one or more objects; spontaneous action and repetition; and prolonged action accompanied by deep concentration (Montessori 1916). Owing to neuroscience (Schore 2003), we now know that these psychological events correspond with biochemical transformations in the brain (natural endorphins), which induce a sense of well-being.

The adult follows the child through the first three years and understands when and how new objects or activities should be introduced but avoids the tendency to anticipate or assist. As Montessori argued, any unnecessary help given is an obstacle to development (Montessori 1969). This means not weaning children until they show interest in food, not helping them to sit still or to stand up until they can achieve the position on their own, and not intervening when they are oriented towards symbolic (or pretend) play. The child's observations of the environment and the inspiration the child draws from objects are authentic. The play that the child then performs is a result of what they have learned and is revealed, for example, by a leaf becoming a plate and a stick becoming a piece of cutlery. Protected by the educator's trusting gaze and a specifically designed environment, the child can fully experience the achievements in line with their age. This exemplifies their capabilities to choose freely, even at a very young age, representing a natural shift toward satisfying two primary needs: first, independence from adults and second, spontaneous socialization.

The Alphabet of Human Work

The binary scheme previously described (putting in/taking out, opening/closing, etc.) is of the child's utmost interest as soon as they begin to move. It is a critical phase of development, foundational to all the complex actions that our species is capable of processing: a true *alphabet of human work*.[3] Often, adults do not recognize the value of these freely chosen actions nor their limitless repetitions; instead they interrupt toddlers by diverting their interests toward activities or games that the adults determine to be more intelligent or by soliciting them to use sensory materials before they are ready for them. However, as Honegger Fresco often mentioned, the nursery cannot be an adulterated version of a Casa dei Bambini (Children's House) (Honegger Fresco 2016).[4] Toddlers are indeed able to interest themselves in solid joints (inside/outside) or the Pink Tower (over/under). Montessori created these materials to allow children to discover the differences between shapes and sizes and equivalences and similarities, which are rather complex concepts meant for children who are interested in grouping, dividing, and classifying. Could this behavior already be observed in a toddler's last period at a nursery? Sometimes. Here too, the educator's gaze and observational skill is of the utmost importance because it can identify a child's new interests. Through careful demonstrations where the educator moves and uses objects at the Children's House, they can gauge the child's level of motor maturity. Before this maturity is seen in the mind and body, a child absorbs information from their environment, reciprocating this understanding onto objects and people, from what they have experienced and seen.

Child-Rearing Is a Delicate Process

Honegger Fresco often advised the educators she trained to put their hands in their pockets, highlighting the importance of limiting direct intervention with toddlers, except in the case of safety (Honegger Fresco 2018b). She would say that the child knows, so educators should adequately prepare the environment to allow them to explore and experiment while protected from external interference. They do not need external stimulation to develop their innate ability to move from supine to erect position or acquire their native language. They instead need responses from educators trained in observation to allow children the freedom of exploring and experiencing in the first three years of life. In this way, Montessori's vision for a culture of peace can be constructed from early infancy.

Honegger Fresco learned from Montessori that certain children's reactions, which can be dismissed by adults as personality traits, uncontrolled vivacity, challenges, and demanding behavior, in reality hide thoughtful, motivated reasons for various behaviors. Honegger Fresco never relented in inviting educators to observe carefully, to listen deeply and empathetically to children, and to continue to research with pedagogical humility so that *every child could be an answer*. If the nursery corresponds with this vision, it is translated into an experience of well-being for the toddler where they can develop a healthy sense of *agency*. Working toward this vision, Honegger Fresco's work allowed the Montessorian idea of the competent and active child to be realized in the 0–3-year phase as well. Thanks to Honegger Fresco's work, many educators today continue the spirit of research that originated with Montessori, and was continued by Costa Gnocchi and herself, to help every child be a completely unique being.

Notes

1. Find more information in English here at www.graziahoneggerfresco.it.
2. In Italian, the word "*ambientamento*" unites familiarization with the external environment (*environment*), the atmosphere of the house (*house-room*), and the process through which a human being (but also a plant or animal) slowly adapts to what surrounds them (*to acclimatize*) and modifies it through their presence.
3. As the individual letters are combined in infinite ways giving life to words, so too, these first actions, repeated countless times, constitute the base of all the complex actions that we complete during our lives (see Honegger Fresco 2016).

4. Among many educators working with children between the ages of 0 and 3, there is an idea that they should be preparing them for the next step (ages 3 to 6). Because the young ones are not yet ready for the complex activities that will be offered, they are convinced that they must be trained in advance to be prepared to respond to the challenges that will come. Montessori always stressed the need to observe and respond moment by moment to the silent requests of the children (Honegger Fresco 2019).

References

Beebe, Beatrice, and Franck M. Lachmann. 2015. *Infant Research and Adult Treatment: Constructing Interactions*. New York: Taylor & Francis.
Bowlby, John. 1950. *Maternal Care and Mental Health*. Geneva: World Health Organization.
Eibl-Eibesfeldt, I. 1975. *Ethology: The Biology of Behavior*, 2nd ed. New York: Holt, Rinehart, and Winston.
Goldschmied, Elinor, and Sonia Jackson. 2003. *People under Three: Young Children in Day Care*, 2nd ed. London: Routledge.
Honegger Fresco, Grazia. 1970. *Il Neonato con amore*. Milano: Ferro.
Honegger Fresco, Grazia. 2001. *Radici nel Futuro*. Molfetta: La Meridiana.
Honegger Fresco, Grazia. 2016. "Observations on Sara's First Eight Months by Her Mother." *NAMTA Journal* 41, no. 3 (Summer): 50–7. https://eric.ed.gov/?q=grazia±honegger±fresco&id=EJ1125320.
Honegger Fresco, Grazia. 2018a. *Da Solo, Io! Il Progetto Pedagogico di Maria Montessori da 0 a 3 Anni*. Molfetta: Edizioni La Meridiana.
Honegger Fresco, Grazia. 2018b. *Maria Montessori: Una Storia Attuale*. Torino: Il leone Verde.
Honegger Fresco, Grazia. 2019. "The 'Cosmic' Task of the Youngest Children—Direct, Anticipate or Respect? Experiences Working with Small Children." *Journal of Montessori Research & Education* 2 (1): 1–12. http://doi.org/10.16993/jmre.10.
Montessori, Maria. 1916. *L'Autoeducazione Nelle Scuole Elementari*. Roma: Loescher.
Montessori, Maria. 1969. *The Absormnent Mind*. New York: Buccaneer Books.
Montessori, Maria. 1997. *The California Lectures*. Santa Barbara, CA: ABC Clio Publishing.
Montessori, Maria. 1998. *The Secret of Childhood*. London: Sangam.
Montessori, Maria. 2021. *Lezioni da Londra 1946*. Torino: Il Leone Verde.
Opera Nazionale Montessori. 1950. "Proceedings of the 8th International Montessori Congress." 159–85. Atti dell'VIII Congresso internazionale Montessori, S. Remo, 22-29 agosto 1949, Ente Opera Montessori, Roma, Translated Act from the VIII International Montessori Congress, San Remo, August 22–29, Opera Montessori Rome.
Pickler, Emmi. 1969. *Per una Crescita Libera*. Milano: Emme edizioni.
Radice, Sheila. 1920. *The New Children: Talks with Dr. Maria Montessori*. London: Hodder and Stoughton.
Schore, Allan N. 2003. *Affect Regulation and the Repair on the Self*. New York: Norton.
Spitz, Rene. 1965. *The First Year of Life*. Preface by Anna Freud. New York: International University Press.
Stern, Daniel. 2018. *The Interpersonal Work of the Infant. A View from Psychoanalysis and Developmental Psychology*. London and New York: Routledge.

Chapter 14
The Children's House for Children Ages 3–6

Uma Ramani

The foundations of Montessori pedagogy can be traced to Maria Montessori's experiences in the first Casa dei Bambini in the San Lorenzo quarter of Rome. Her work with children ages 2.5–6 led to the understanding that "education is not something which the teacher does, but that it is a natural process which develops spontaneously in the human being" (Montessori 2007, 5). The work of education is the creation of environments that support this natural process. For the child ages 3 through 6, this environment is "a house for children, rather than a real school" (Montessori 2007, 4). This reframing of educational practice is best understood in the context of Montessori pedagogical principles. The following concepts provide the foundations for practice.

Planes of Development

Montessori offers us a perspective of human development as an active process of creative self-construction wherein a child's innate potential is realized through their interaction with the environment. Based on her observations of the physical, social, psychological, and cognitive characteristics of the child and young adult, she identified four sequential planes of development. Each lasts about six years, making the first twenty-four years of life foundational to self-construction (Montessori 1971).

The work of the child in the first plane of development (ages 0–6) is to realize the innate potential for characteristically human functions: biped locomotion, the use of the hands, language, a reasoning mind, the capacity to choose. This tremendous task of creative self-construction is made possible through two characteristics identified by Montessori (2007) as specific to this plane: sensitive periods and the absorbent mind.

Sensitive Periods

Montessori observed that young children around the world were attracted to certain activities during certain periods of development. However, nothing in the developmental psychology literature of her time could explain this, nor why the children were engaged with such deep focus and concentration.

Based on the studies of two biologists, she postulated the presence of sensitive periods of human development. The botanist Hugo de Vries first named and described sensitive periods in the development of poppy plants (De Vries 1904). The biologist Jacques Loeb described sensitivity to light in the larvae of the Porthesia butterfly for a period after hatching, which impelled activity that was essential to its survival (Loeb 1900, 188). Montessori saw a parallel to the observed behavior of children and in 1936 described sensitive periods in human development.

> These periods correspond to special sensibilities to be found in creatures in process of development; they are transitory and confined to the acquisition of a determined characteristic. Once this characteristic has evolved, the corresponding sensibility disappears. Thus every characteristic is established by the help of an impulse, of a transient sensibility which lasts over a limited period of growth, that is, during the corresponding sensitive period.
>
> *(2017b, 28)*

In her writings, Montessori described the sensitive periods in the first plane as being for order, movement, language, and the development and refinement of sensory perception.

The Absorbent Mind

In 1949, Montessori coined the term "the absorbent mind" to describe the mind of the young child and how it functions in a fundamentally different way in this first plane. She says, "[T]he child absorbs knowledge directly into his psychic life … the child undergoes a transformation. Impressions do not merely enter his mind; they form it. They incarnate themselves in him" (Montessori 2007, 21). She writes that the absorbent mind is supported by the sensitive periods of development. Today, neuroscience confirms that environmental experience determines the architecture of the brain, and its function and sensitive periods guide this development (for example, see Eliot 1999).

Montessori (2007) asserted that it is by virtue of these two powers that children around the globe complete the work of laying the foundations of their personality during the first plane, according to a universal timetable. Most of the work of creation is done in the first three years of life, the first sub-plane. In the second sub-plane, ages 3–6, the work of consolidating and refining movement, language, will, and the cognitive processes is central. Integrating these in daily life to become a functionally independent individual participating in and contributing to the life of the community is the primary goal. The understanding of sensitive periods and the absorbent mind is fundamental to the pedagogy for this period.

Education as an Aid to Life for Ages 3–6

The Montessori method of education offers conditions to support the natural processes of creative self-construction. Essential to the practice of education as an aid to life are three factors: *a prepared adult* (that is, an educator who understands that it is the learner who is central to education and who has the knowledge and skills to prepare the other two factors); *a prepared environment* (which offers a physical, social, and psychological space that is appropriate to the needs of the plane of development); and *means of development* (the materials and activities appropriate to the plane). Here we see that Montessori's concept of education redefines the role of the adult. The work of the adult is not the teaching of a predetermined curriculum in developmentally appropriate ways. Rather it is the creation of environments for the optimal realization of the human potential. It is a work of collaboration with nature in the context of the observed needs of development (Montessori 1912).

The Prepared Adult

An integrated spiritual, intellectual, and technical preparation *of the teacher* helps to develop the attitudes, knowledge, and skills necessary to practice education as an aid to life. The preparation of the educator, often called a guide or simply the adult, into someone who can approach education from this perspective is critical for Montessori pedagogy. The teacher for 3–6 year old children has a deep understanding of the functioning of the absorbent mind and sensitive periods and the lifelong impact of the work of this period of development. They are an integral part of the environment, as children absorb the attitudes, values, and behavior patterns of the adults around them. Consequently, the guide (adult) must be engaged in an ongoing process of self-reflection and continued preparation of self. The adult must also have the knowledge and interest to "diffuse culture" (Montessori 2007, 4) that the young children can assimilate. And the adult must have the technical skills to prepare the environment and be the dynamic link to the environment.

The Prepared Environment

The Montessori prepared environment for children ages 3–6 is often called the Children's House. It is a space for living life in a community in which each child continues their work of creative self-construction. Careful attention is given to the physical, social, and psychological space that will offer the child the conditions for natural development.

The physical environment of the Children's House is unique and includes the built environment and furniture as well as the outdoor environment. Fixtures and furniture must be physically proportionate to the young child. Thus, for example, careful attention is given to the placement of door handles, the height of steps and counters, and the size of the toilet. There is also emphasis on the careful preparation of the outdoor environment as an integral part of the child's space. Every object in the Children's House is mindfully chosen to support the child's development, and order and beauty are evident throughout.

The social environment consists of a mixed-age group of children ages 3–6. Since the classroom has a three-year cycle, every year a new group of 3-year-olds moves in and a group of 6-year-olds leaves, giving the children new experiences.

The psychological environment is set by routines that offer a framework for harmonious community living. Within this framework, children find a safe, caring community and the conditions of freedom to work at their individual development. There is a culture of respect, of maximum effort, and an acceptance that error is part of learning. The rhythm and pace of the classroom are appropriate to the young child. There are no set places or workstations. The child is free to choose from the shelves an activity that responds to their needs. There is a clear understanding of the work cycle by both the child and the adult in the room. The work cycle begins with the child choosing an activity and organizing the work area, continues with the child working purposefully with the material, and ends with the child returning the material to the shelf in its proper place and in proper condition. The schedule of the day allows at least one three-hour uninterrupted work period so that the child can follow their natural rhythms. The adult is central to the psychological environment as their attitudes, behaviors, and biases are implicitly manifested in its ethos and incarnated by the absorbent mind of the young child. The ongoing preparation of the adult ensures that every child finds the conditions of freedom to follow the natural path to development (Montessori 2013).

The Means of Development

The means of development in a Montessori environment are carefully chosen materials and activities that serve the specific developmental needs of this plane of development:

a. to consolidate, refine, and develop movement so as to become functionally independent;
b. to consolidate, refine, and develop speech and language to support abstraction and communication;
c. to consolidate, refine, and develop sensory perception and lay the foundation for cognition, intelligence, abstraction, and a reasoning mind; and
d. to incarnate the culture of the time and place and create deep connections with the environment and community.

The activities in the Children's House can be broadly classified as the exercises of Practical Life, Sensorial Exercises, Language Exercises, Mathematics Exercises, and Cultural Exercises. The materials and activities in all areas appeal to the sensitive periods for order, movement, language, and refinement of sensory perception (Montessori 2007).

The Exercises of Practical Life

Young children find the activities of daily life—also known as exercises of Practical Life—to be irresistible. They want to participate in the care of the environment, the care of their person, and the social interactions that they have been observing from birth. The movements and the order intrinsic to each activity appeal to the sensitive periods of the first plane and serve to refine and consolidate fine- and gross-motor skills, as well as equilibrium, leading to functional independence.

Even the simplest of daily life activities is a complex of series of movements. For example, to get a drink of water from the tap, it is necessary to be able to lift and carry a glass, open and close a faucet, take the glass to one's lips, and tilt it just enough to allow for a sip. To demonstrate this to the child, Montessori writes, "Every complex action is analysed into its formative elements. Each element is detached and isolated. An exercise is formed around each element and attached to the corresponding sensitive period. Thus, each item becomes a motive of pleasure for the child, a stone by which he can build up the edifice of his intelligence, under the guidance of the urge to grow" (2020, 172). Thus the child is shown aspects of handling everyday objects such as cups, glasses, trays, doors, and faucets to lift, carry, set down, open, and close. Thus, for example, consider the Dressing Frame. This Montessori learning material consists of a wooden frame that has two panels of fabric attached to opposite sides with a means for the child close them where they meet in the middle (buttons, zipper, laces, etc.). Learning how to manipulate the fasteners helps the child develop skills they will need when getting dressed. Similarly, every movement in hand-washing is clearly demonstrated through a setup that enables the child to practice the sequence (e.g., Gettman 1987). Regardless of culture, the materials are child-sized and functional.

The presentation of a given Montessori work, offered with exactitude and precision, gives the child the keys necessary for activity and stimulates spontaneous repetition, resulting in the refinement of movement and sensory perception and the development of the intellect and the will. The activities are presented with analysis of movements. By slowing down the action and observing a minimal pause between each movement, the child is shown that every activity is a chain of movements done in a particular sequence. At the end of a presentation, the desired result is clearly demonstrated so that the child is aware of the criteria to judge their work; e.g., when pouring, there should be no spills.

The exercises of Practical Life result in functional independence by supporting the coordination of movement. This coordination requires the integration of thought, will, and movements and results in their harmonious functioning. Montessori uses the term "normalization" to describe this phenomenon and says that normalization is "the most important single result" (2007, 181–6) of the work of this plane. The result is the formation of an individual adapted to their time and place who can function with agency within the context of a community, making appropriate choices and adapting their actions in context—which today we call executive functioning.

The Sensorial Exercises

At this stage of development, the child, having developed the basics of sensory perception, now has the task of consolidation of the ability to perceive the qualities of matter and better appreciate their environment. The Sensorial exercises of Montessori support the development and refinement of sensory perception and offer the tools for classification and categorization of the material world. The Sensorial materials give form to the abstract qualities of matter such as color, shape, dimension, pitch, volume, texture, weight, and smell, and so are "*materialized abstractions*" (Montessori 2020, 80). Each material consists of a series of objects that are identical in all respects except for one quality, which becomes isolated (Tebano Ahlquist and Gynther 2019). For example, a set of small tablets are identical in size, shape, texture, weight, smell, and taste and only differ in color—this then becomes the only quality perceived. Furthermore, the tablets are in pairs (by color), which makes it possible to match them. By observing the child match the tablets, the adult can determine if a perception has been built. At this point language is offered. Naming the quality helps to crystallize the perception, freeing the child from the material (Montessori 2020). The child can now identify the quality in the world around them and express their perception. The child is then offered material to grade objects according to degree of a quality, leading to refinement of sensory perception.

The Sensorial activities offer the child the keys to the world, helping them classify, categorize, and find patterns in their environment.

The Language Exercises

The child has absorbed the language of their environment and laid the foundations of speech. Now the work is to build on these spoken language acquisitions to consolidate speech and language and lay the foundations for writing and reading.

Several spoken language exercises isolate each aspect of communication to support adaptation to place and the development of expressive and receptive language skills. Stories and planned conversations build on daily life experiences and interactions with plants, animals, people, places, and all aspects of human culture, including history, art, music, and literature. Vocabulary is offered in the context of these experiences. Expression is guided through a series of questions that facilitates the building of a coherent narrative. Receptive language skills are built through commands that the child acts on. The adult is a key material for these spoken language exercises.

Other spoken language exercises focus on the exploration of language. Sound games explore sounds in known words and lay the foundation of phonemic awareness. The letters of the alphabet are offered as symbols for the sounds of spoken language in the form of Sandpaper Letters that invite children to trace the letter as they look at the shapes and say the sound. The children are then introduced to a box of cutout wooden letters, known as the Moveable Alphabet, which allows them to set out symbols as they listen to the sounds in a word in sequence—for example, p-l-a-n-t. This leads to the discovery that symbols can make thoughts visible. Montessori calls this writing "freed from mechanics" (2017a, 232). Preparation of the hand for writing follows the principle of isolation of difficulties. While the Sandpaper Letters prepare the hand for the formation of letters, Sensorial activities and the exercises of Practical Life aid the development of the tripod pencil grip, lightness of touch, flexibility of the wrist, and muscular memory for shapes. The child is now offered a set of geometric shapes (Metal Insets) to use for drawing outlines on paper and filling in with light, vertical pencil strokes. This enables the child to gain mastery over the writing instrument. These preparations converge in a spontaneous explosion into writing as a form of expression of thoughts. Spoken language exercises for vocabulary and communication have laid the foundations for strong written expression.

Literacy activities also follow the principle of isolation of difficulties. A group of materials and activities focus on the mechanics of reading to prepare the child for fluent decoding. Materials for reading practice offer known vocabulary in print and children gain confidence in their ability to read and interpret. Other reading exercises help the child use syntax and sentence structure to interpret meaning. The reading materials offer words, phrases, and sentences in a sequence. This foundation in the elements of reading enables the child to become an independent reader with a lifelong love of reading—someone with the capacity to understand ideas and appreciate the feelings implicit in written words. Writing and reading become a tool for communication with embedded purpose and meaning.

The Mathematics Exercises

Mathematical thinking is a human trait and mathematical processes help to quantify and express patterns. All the activities in the Children's House support the development of mathematical thinking by offering tools to find patterns, classify, and categorize. The mathematics exercises focus on mathematical processes and introduce the child to the concepts of number, counting, and calculation. Materials and activities are organized in the following groups: numbers one to ten, the decimal system, calculation, number syntax beyond ten, mental arithmetic, and fractions. In each group, concepts are introduced following the principle of isolation of difficulty, using concrete materials. Numbers are then associated with the concrete materials and finally, the child works only with numbers.

This introduction of numbers one to ten is illustrative of this process (Tebano Ahlquist and Gynther 2019). The first activity in this group connects these number words to Number Rods, a material that represents the linear progression of numbers one to ten. The shortest rod represents the number one and is 10 centimeters long. The longest rod is 100 centimeters and represents the number ten. Each successive rod is a multiple of the first rod and alternate segments are colored red and blue. The child counts each rod using number words to tag segments in order. In a parallel activity, Sandpaper Numerals are used to introduce the number symbols. Finally, number cards from one to ten are matched to the number rods. This set of activities lays the foundation for understanding the linear progression represented by the number words and symbols and introduces the principles of counting.

The child is then introduced to counting in sets through the Spindle Box, which has ten compartments—one for each of the numbers 0–9—and forty-five wooden rods for counting. This material also introduces the number zero, which here illustrates an absence of quantity. The next material in this series, the Cards and Counters, consists of cards for numbers one through ten with fifty-five counters to match. Here the child sets out the numerals in order before matching the counters, consolidating the understanding of the order of numerals. In the final activity in this group, the memory game of numbers, the child picks from a set of eleven cards with numbers 0 to 10, identifies the numeral, and creates sets of objects from the environment to match, discovering that they can count anything.

With this foundation in number and counting, the child is introduced to the decimal system: names of categories are introduced with the Golden Beads, which are concrete representations of the decimal categories; symbols for the categories are introduced with the Decimal System Cards; and then quantities and symbols are associated. Parallel to this work, children are introduced to the conventional number syntax for their own language, often combinations of units and sets of ten, first with concrete materials and then symbols, and finally associating quantities and symbols. Further exploration of the decimal system continues through counting and calculation with large numbers, exploring the play of hierarchies in the decimal system. Through this work, the young child is introduced to the nature of the four basic operations. A series of materials, both concrete and symbolic, leads the child to discover the basics of mathematical algorithms. Through the playful exploration with these materials, children begin to internalize math facts, which they then combine with the understanding of the dynamics of the decimal system and place value to begin mental arithmetic and calculation on paper. By offering abstract mathematical concepts to the absorbent mind of the child in the first plane, these mathematics exercises lay the foundations of numeracy (Montessori 2007).

The Cultural Exercises

Culture is diffused throughout the Children's House. Language, Sensorial exploration, and exercises of Practical Life connect the child to the world of plants, animals, people, music, art, and literature, through stories, activities, and explorations. This exposure lays the foundation for further exploration using concrete materials. Introduction of concepts follows the principle of isolation of difficulties. Reading, writing, music, and art become tools for this exploration and expression. For example, in geography, picture cards, stories, and experiences introduce children to places around the world, including their flora and fauna and how people have met their fundamental needs in different places. The study of the Earth continues with a globe that introduces the Earth as land and water and then continues with the introduction of continents and Puzzle Maps for each continent. This approach communicates to the young child that they are a part of an interdependent whole that includes the Earth, plants, animals, and people around the globe and that they have a role to play in the harmony of this interdependent whole.

The Role of the Adult

Once the environment and materials are prepared, it is the ongoing work of the adult to observe each child and connect them, as necessary, to the appropriate materials in the environment. Continuous observation of children, the environment, and the materials as well as self-reflection helps the adult to practice education as an aid to life and not as the delivery of a curriculum. "We had prepared a place for children where a diffuse culture could be assimilated from the environment, without any need for direct instruction" (Montessori 2007, 4).

Conclusion

The Children's House is a harmonious environment designed to support the physical, social, and intellectual development of children ages 3–6. By the end of the three-year cycle, the child has laid the foundations of executive functioning, a reasoning mind, and imagination. They have also laid the foundations of social cohesion, with a sense of belonging that is the basis of social organization. They are now ready to enter the second plane of development, study the different areas of human culture, and explore the mechanics of functioning in organized society.

References

De Vries, Hugo. 1904. *Species and Varieties: Their Origin by Mutation*. Chicago: The Open Court Publishing Company.
Eliot, Lise. 1999. *What's Going on in There? How the Brain and Mind Develop in the First Five Years of Life*. New York: Bantam Books.

Gettman, David. 1987. *Basic Montessori Learning Activities for Under Fives*. New York: St. Martin Griffin.
Loeb, Jacques. 1900. *Comparative Physiology of the Brain and Comparative Psychology*. New York: G.P. Putnam's Sons.
Montessori, Maria. 1912. *The 1946 London Lectures*. Amsterdam: Montessori-Pierson Publishing.
Montessori, Maria. 1971. "The Four Planes of Development." *Communication, Association Montessori Internationale* (4): 4–10.
Montessori, Maria. 2007. *The Absorbent Mind*. Amsterdam: Montessori-Pierson Publishing Company.
Montessori, Maria. 2013. *The 1913 Rome Lectures*. Amsterdam: Montessori-Pierson Publishing.
Montessori, Maria. 2017a. *The Discovery of the Child*. Amsterdam: Montessori-Pierson Publishing Company.
Montessori, Maria. 2017b. *The Secret of Childhood*. Amsterdam: Montessori-Pierson Publishing Company.
Montessori, Maria. 2020. *Creative Development in the Child: The Montessori Approach*. Amsterdam: Montessori-Pierson Publishing Company.
Tebano Ahlquist, Eva-Maria, and Per Gynther. 2019. "Variation Theory and Montessori Education." *Journal of Montessori Research & Education* 2 (1): 13–23. http://doi.org/10.16993/jmre.12

Chapter 15
The Montessori Elementary School for Children Ages 6–12

William (Biff) Maier

As discussed previously in this handbook, Montessori described four planes of development, from birth through age 24, each with its own physical, psychological, and pedagogical characteristics. She also outlined methods for optimizing children's development during each plane by responding to the special characteristics of the age group. This chapter introduces the reader to Montessori education at the elementary level, which responds to the unique needs of the child in the second plane (ages 6–12), while holding essential elements of the pedagogy consistent with other levels.

The fundamental goal of Montessori education is to promote social, psychological, and emotional well-being by empowering children to fully express their authentic personalities. Montessori defined her method as "Means offered to deliver the human personality from the oppression of age-old prejudices regarding education" (1978, 5). The entire organization of a Montessori classroom or school is based on the theory that children are internally motivated and that they will progress naturally toward their potential unless detoured by "deviations." Montessori education is "the basic process by which the human being is spiritually regenerated, by which the deviations of growing up fall away and what emerges is a truly 'normal' life" (Montessori 1997, 8). Montessori wrote, "Normalization is the single most important result of our work" (1963, 8). Normalization is Montessori's term for the natural state of young children when they are quietly focused and engaged in their work.

In the Children's House, a prepared environment normalizes young children through what Montessori called constant activity and effort. As children enter elementary school in Montessori's second plane of development, they begin to think more abstractly. The names of things no longer intrigue them as they did previously; they want reasons for how things work and fit together. They are urgently concerned about fairness. Newly aware of the human limitations of parents and caregivers, they are attracted by heroic visions of justice and good. What, one might ask, is the catalyst for spiritual regeneration and return to normalcy for this age? Montessori argued, "If the human personality is one at all stages of its development, we must conceive of a principle of education which has regard to all stages" (1978, 6).

For over a century, Montessori educators have worked to specify the list of educational elements that support children's optimal development. These include multiage communities, specialized didactic materials, student choice, the role of the teacher as guide, and engagement of the developmental characteristics of the age group. Although these elements are present at all developmental planes, they are applied in distinct ways at the elementary level.

Multiage Classrooms

Researchers have documented how multiage classrooms enhance attitudes toward school, self-esteem, and leadership skills (Lillard 2017). Montessori classrooms take special advantage of these opportunities. The three-year relationship between the teacher and the child and family permits patient focus on a student's natural unfolding. The three age levels within a classroom take on a birth-order-type pattern, with leadership and caring expressed by the students in the third year of the cycle (the *elders*), vulnerable enthusiasm shown by students in the first year of the cycle, and benign neglect experienced by students in the middle year, who know the routines and go about their business. Elementary elders facilitate democratic class meetings and inspire their younger friends by modeling leadership and responsibility. In this family-style mix, learning differences are natural, so students work collaboratively, and peer teaching abounds. Classroom elders are quick to offer help to younger classmates, and the young students seek the elder's experience and guidance with materials and routines. In response to an increase in anxiety being observed in children, today's educational journals repeatedly emphasize the importance of school-based social-emotional learning. As such, Montessori's model of the family-style classroom may be more applicable than ever. Extended relationships with caring teachers and the wise guidance of classroom elders promise calm and comfort for children navigating difficult times (Lillard 2017).

Didactic Materials

Carefully chosen didactic materials—that is, learning materials that facilitate choice and purposeful decision-making—play a central role in Montessori classrooms. The materials in the elementary classroom are still manipulative, as in the Children's House, but on a different level. Montessori argues that the young children's work with Sensorial materials orders and focuses their minds. The manipulative work with materials for older children supports their construction of concepts, appealing to their intellect and imagination as well as their ability to collaborate and share understanding. What follows are several examples based on my forty years of experience as an elementary Montessori teacher educator of how didactic materials support the characteristics of the elementary plane of development.

Children at the early childhood level begin learning with materials that help form the basis for an understanding of how our decimal system works. The iconic Montessori Golden Beads help them see that a ten-bar is formed by connecting ten discrete unit beads, a hundred-square is formed by connecting ten ten-bars, and a thousand-cube is formed by connecting ten hundred-squares. Thus, when they hold a thousand-cube, it has literally one thousand times the heft. Color-coded numerals are used to represent these quantities: green for units, blue for tens, and red for hundreds. The thousand-cube is again represented by green, identifying it as a unit of the next hierarchical level. These activities support the children's understanding of how and why we perform and record mathematical operations.

To continue with the example, the multiplication sequence begins along two strands when children skip-count the color-coded bead bars on chains (e.g., 5, 10, 15, 20 …); they also combine identical addends with Golden Bead materials (2321 + 2321 + 2321). Skip-counting leads to many activities with charts and bead bars where students explore and discover patterns, including the associative, commutative, and distributive properties. Golden Bead operations also teach a hierarchical color-coding system through the use of numbers with green units, blue tens, red hundreds, and green units of thousands.

Tactile cues are then removed when the elementary student uses the Stamp Game material, where the green, blue, and red stamps (small square tiles) that denote units, tens, and hundreds are the same size, and value depends on place. Both Golden Bead materials and stamps accumulate during the multiplication, so the child counts and exchanges groups of ten for items of the next hierarchy. The next step employs Bead Frames, where strands of ten hierarchically colored beads are used. The child must now do the regrouping mentally to work the problem, since there is no way to accumulate beads.

Elementary Math materials combine several color-coding systems that continually reinforce number patterns. The Multiplication Checkerboard, for instance, shows the repetitive pattern of hierarchies with green, blue, and red squares. See Figure 15.1 for an example of children using the more advanced Decimal Checkerboard. By placing color-coded beads on the squares, the child builds rectangular configurations of multiplication. There are no ten-bars included in this work, reminding them that they must regroup in the next hierarchy. Forming these patterns with their hands gives them multisensory information that helps them remember the procedure and the concepts. The Checkerboard material patterns provide the final step to mental multiplication. Methodical progress through this system provides a firm grasp of underlying concepts as children construct understanding of the algorithm (Montessori 1964, 2011).

Figure 15.1 Elementary students at Lexington Montessori School practice multiplication with the decimal Checkerboard, 2019. Courtesy of Biff Maier.

In similar fashion, the elementary grammar exercises build up children's ability to compose rich sentences as they isolate, one at a time, the functions of words to create meaningful expressions. Teachers use stories, metaphors, and games to introduce the "jobs" words do, and each function is represented with an iconic grammar symbol. The teacher introduces the noun, for instance, by describing how black charcoal from a forest fire may have been the earliest writing instrument of prehistoric people. They then tell how the Great Pyramid of Giza in Egypt has kept its shape for more than 4,000 years! The pyramid is, in turn, represented by a large, two-dimensional black triangle, then used to symbolize nouns they find in sentences. Each of the functions of words is introduced in this way, with follow-up exercises reinforcing the concept.

Again, for example, a child takes a Sorting Tray for the study of the adverb, along with a box containing sentences that highlight the function of the adverb. The box also contains individual word cards that make up the sentences. The task is to select a sentence, find the appropriate individual cards, and identify the function of each of the words in the sentence—for example, "Shut the door slowly." They repeat the process for a second sentence that is identical except for the adverb—"Shut the door silently"—noticing the significance of the descriptors. The choosing of the activity, the organization and movement of the materials, and the isolated focus on the work of the adverb are all part of the learning process. The cycle concludes when the student disassembles all materials and puts them back, ready for the next person. These structured steps make the activity non-linear and engaging (Montessori 1964).

All subject areas and materials in Montessori elementary classrooms have a cumulative structure supporting understanding how things work and are connected to one another. Often, the structure is interdisciplinary. To explore the subject of history, students must understand the concept of time and how it is represented by units of length in timelines (Montessori 1973). Timelines continue to be used for many purposes: to celebrate students' growth, to show verb tenses, to display prehistoric times, to study the evolution of humans, to compare and contrast historic cultures. Children create timelines alongside dioramas, charts, drawings, models, and booklets to demonstrate learning.

Observing an elementary classroom, one sees students choose their work, collect the needed materials from assigned locations, and take them to a workspace. They make meaning by assembling the disparate pieces of materials according to the task at hand, often recording the process in a notebook. For example, the sequence of materials for the study of mathematics proceeds step by step, utilizing consistent coding systems, toward abstract calculations. Each material represents a single advance along this path, building on previous work while introducing and isolating a new challenge. Montessori believed that these sequences should be constructively analytical. She wrote, "Analysis is involved quite as much in building as in taking to pieces" (Montessori 1964, 10).

The use of manipulative, didactic materials scaffolds the thinking and slows the abstract processing so that students make sense of equations, formulas, grammar patterns, and cultural concepts for themselves, rather than just accepting their validity without understanding why. Nonlinear sorting, categorizing, and researching stimulate creative projects and make endless connections among topics and subjects. Teachers observe the students' use of materials and interact with them individually and in groups to get information about where children are in terms of knowledge and skills. In this way, they also challenge students' work and provoke more and deeper learning (Montessori 1974).

Student Choice

Research indicates that when people feel they have control of their environment and choices, they feel and perform better (e.g., Lillard 2017). They are more motivated, interested, resilient, and creative. Autonomy fosters confidence and a sense of well-being. Montessori elementary teachers carefully define the objectives of the work they introduce so that students understand which parts of the learning are mandatory. Students then choose when, how, where, and with whom they will work toward the defined outcomes. In this way they are empowered to maximize their strengths and interests as they collaborate with peers.

Children experience *flow* (Csikszentmihalyi 1990), or fully energized involvement and do their best learning when work offers just-right challenges and high interest. Montessori learning environments encourage students to make powerful learning choices. The teacher observes each student's work and converses with them to gauge their understanding. Together they set goals in various subjects. Around the world in Montessori classrooms, elementary students typically arrive at school, check a posted schedule of events for the day, and make a personal plan for their learning. This plan includes follow-up practice activities of various types from smaller lessons (often called presentations) offered by the teacher that they are expected to complete by a designated time and personal projects of interest. The latter may include research work, compositions, artistic expressions, and extended studies. Students learn to balance their spontaneous interests with other responsibilities. As students grow into autonomous learners, they identify their own challenges and preferences, and they leverage their agency to regulate their behavior and to find "just-right" academic matches.

The Role of the Teacher and Time in Montessori Classrooms

Long before popular culture education writers urged teachers to be a "guide on the side" (Morrison 2014, 1), Montessori described the role of the "new type of teacher," saying they should observe children, "aflame with interest" in their development (1964, 125–41). She sought to professionalize teaching by making it scientific. Montessori educators aim to be coaches, leaders, and role models. Their interest is the child's holistic development, so they observe student work and behavior to understand and guide their academic growth, social-emotional development, and the acquisition of executive functioning skills. The curriculum and the classroom community are the means through which they support this growth.

At the heart of every Montessori program is the profoundly respectful environment fostered and maintained by teachers. Aiming to promote autonomy, the teacher prepares an optimal environment with clearly defined and consistently maintained systems for self-management. Systems and routines enable students to maintain momentum without frequent interruptions and announcements. The teacher's goal is to create an active, collaborative workspace, into which they inject stimulating seeds of interest as they demonstrate their own curiosity and disciplined thinking. The teacher also coaches the community in democratic decision-making, inclusive problem-solving, responsibility, conflict resolution, and self-regulation. The Montessori teacher plays a subtle leadership role, guiding by example and advice rather than power.

Montessori early childhood teachers employ what is known as the three-period lesson which Montessori borrowed from Édouard Séguin, who named them "identity, recognition, and recall" (Séguin 1907). At the elementary level, Montessori's three periods of engagement resemble Whitehead's stages of "romance, precision, and generalization" (Whitehead 1967, 35). The elementary lesson begins with what Whitehead called "romance," provoking interest and emotional engagement in the topic of study. During the elementary years, children are infinitely curious about space, dinosaurs, and fantastic creatures. Montessori encouraged elementary teachers to take advantage of this age of the imagination, saying, "Not only can imagination travel through infinite space, but also through infinite time" (1973, 10). Teachers use metaphors, whimsical hand-drawn graphics, and stories to engage the minds of children and to make complex concepts understandable and memorable. Montessori believed that narratives and storytelling create interest. As such, many teachers build their curriculum around a dramatic telling of what are called the Great Lessons: (1) the creation of the universe, (2) the evolution of life, (3) the evolution of human beings, (4) the development of language, and (5) the development of numbers (Lillard 2017) (see Chapter 3: "Cosmic Education: The Vital Center of the Montessori Perspective"). In fact, the Montessori teacher enlivens all manner of topics through dramatic narrative and joyful exercises (Montessori 1973). Once again, examples illustrate this best. A Robinson Crusoe shipwreck scenario inspires children to brainstorm the things that are necessary for survival. They go on to discover the diverse ways that people meet these needs and the materials needed to do so. Similarly, a teacher might take students traveling through time to visit Babylonian astronomers to set the scene for learning why we measure angles as parts of a 360° circle. They use a specially designed protractor to measure the angles of the geometric shapes in the room.

Once intrigued, the student begins Whitehead's second period, "precision." Montessori elementary students spend the bulk of their time in this sort of work, practicing and organizing in order to integrate the learning. As they manipulate materials and complete projects, they come to recognize and seek accuracy. Sometimes this involves repeating procedures that have been demonstrated by the teacher. Often, it involves the collaborative work of groups. To illustrate, upper elementary students create a timeline to exhibit what they have learned about groups of early humans. A few students create illustrations and compose explanations to show the tool-making, shelters, and use of fire by *Homo erectus*. Others display what they have learned about habilines and other early *Homo sapiens*. Collaborators proudly check the accuracy and carefulness of each other's work. The assembled timeline will be unveiled and presented to the community. Groups like this investigate animals and plants that are of interest, human body systems, simple machines, electrical circuits, coding and robotics, and so much more.

Frequently the second period of "precision" spontaneously transitions into the third period, which Whitehead calls "generalization." The knowledge illustrated by the students' calculations, compositions, problem-solving, and artwork demonstrates their understanding. The teachers use formative, real-time assessment to support students with their work along the way. Throughout the three periods of learning, teachers protect students' dignity by maximizing success. Information is generously offered, wrapped in clarity and interest. Students are asked to demonstrate learning only when they have shown the readiness to do so. This culture of success is a key factor in producing the enthusiasm and intrinsic motivation that characterizes Montessori classrooms.

While some Montessori teachers resist any divergence from the curriculum content and scripts that they received in their training, most take a more liberal approach. Innovative teachers are prepared to apply core elements of the method: three-period lesson, open-ended exploration, cross-discipline learning, peer teaching, student choice, etc., as they adapt new studies to fit the pedagogy. For example, many teachers seamlessly integrate reading and writing workshops, robotics, engineering, and other topics.

Engaging Developmental Characteristics

How do teachers prepare the environment for the second plane of development? Montessori described the idea of cosmic education (Montessori 1973). Elementary children yearn to know where they fit in the scheme of things. Whereas the younger child's absorbent mind, as Montessori often refers to it, enables them to acquire vast stores of vocabulary and sensory information, the elementary child's imaginative mind empowers them to travel through time and space, to witness the beginnings of things, to occupy the bodies of beasts. Montessori explained, "Imaginative vision is quite different from mere perception of an object, for it has no limits" (1973, 14). It transcends knowledge and understanding; it creates enthusiasm.

Elementary teachers help students focus their minds by appealing to the deep sensitivities that are unique to that age. "[The child's] consciousness is thrown outwards with special direction," Montessori wrote. She continues, "Intelligence is extroverted, and there is an unusual demand on the part of the child to know the reasons for things" (1973, 4). They like group work, organizing and negotiating with each other. Children deliberate over right and wrong, good and bad. They have boundless curiosity about origins of things and connections among things. They feel kinship and empathy for all living things.

Montessori teachers open lessons with big picture concepts that show interrelatedness of parts to whole. They teach grammar by showing how word types contribute meaning to sentences. Each type of word has a job to do, and together the words make meaningful language. Similarly, in biology, the significance of a part of the body of a fish is the role it plays in the functioning of the animal. Some fins propel the animal forward; others steer it from side to side. Some keep the oxygenated water moving over the gills. Together they keep the fish alive. In geography, Montessori elementary teachers compare the planet to an exquisitely complex organism, with systems that keep it vital, whereby the movement of winds and water continually change the surface. Children come to realize that the choices they make can enhance or degrade their planetary home.

Students learn to view the planet as an organism, to understand the interplay of solar radiation, winds, and rains and how they all relate to Earth's atmosphere. They study networks of goods and services, so they appreciate how upstream and downstream decisions impact sustainability. Most important, the medium of this curriculum is emotion. Teachers weave information through dramatic stories that tell of service, inventiveness, community, interdependence, and love. As children learn about the context within which players make contributions, they develop both gratitude and a sense of responsibility.

Elementary-age children want to expand their experiences beyond the boundaries of their home and school. To this end, Montessori teachers arrange various Going Out opportunities (Lillard 2017). Older elementary classes frequently travel together to give students opportunities to practice care for themselves and others as they learn about the area they visit. Closer to home, teachers plan outings that deepen subject learning by exposing children to experts and specialized settings. Students, too, plan outings. When feasible, teachers support them to identify sites related to projects, and the students take charge of the planning and communications necessary to carry out the excursion.

Children at the elementary level also yearn to know where they fit in the scheme of things. Montessori's construct of cosmic education merges the study of context with the wonder of the universe. Learning is meaningful because it focuses on constructive forces in nature's functioning: appreciating origins, adapting to change, overcoming challenges with inventiveness, seeking to serve. Feelings of awe, gratitude, and interdependency center the student's mind so they can commit to the good that is in nature and in themselves. The idea of the universe "helps the mind of the child to become fixed, to stop wandering. ... [They] begin to ask, 'What am I? What is the task of humans in this wonderful universe? Do we merely live here for ourselves, or is there something more for us to do?'" (Montessori 1973, 8–10). This is the curative power of work at the elementary level. Montessori called this a kind of "psychic hygiene" (Montessori 1978, 39), which helps a person to grow up in good mental health, with a positive identity. Ideally, Montessori elementary classrooms celebrate diversity in learning, cultural background, and thought, so students learn to listen respectfully and speak boldly. The community governs itself democratically, with elders learning to lead and to guide.

Montessori envisioned schools that would foster the holistic health needed to repair broken society, "The movement ... aims at the simple realization of human values, that is what is of primary interest over and above all political and national differences. ... This ideal is universal in its scope. It aims at the deliverance of the whole of humanity" (1978, 9–15). Hers was a vision of reconstructing the world by raising conscientious children. The elementary cosmic education curriculum invites autonomy, motivation, and hope in students as it engenders their commitment to participate in making the world ever better.

References

Csikszentmihalyi, Mihaly. 1990. *Flow: The Psychology of Optimal Experience*. New York, NY: Harper.
Lillard, Angeline Stoll. 2017. *Montessori: The Science behind the Genius*, 3rd ed. New York, NY: Oxford University Press.
Montessori, Maria. 1963. *The Absorbent Mind*. Chennai, India: Theosophical Publishing House.
Montessori, Maria. 1964. *The Advanced Montessori Method: The Montessori Elementary Material*. Cambridge, MA: Robert Bentley.
Montessori, Maria. 1973. *To Educate the Human Potential*. Chennai, India: Kalakshetra Publications.
Montessori, Maria. 1974. *The Advanced Montessori Method: Spontaneous Activity in Education*. New York, NY: Schocken Books.
Montessori, Maria. 1978. *The Formation of Man*. Chennai, India: Kalakshetra Publications.
Montessori, Maria. 1997. "The Spiritual Regeneration of Man." *NAMTA Journal* 22 (2): 58–66.

Montessori, Maria. 2011. *Psychoarithmetic vol.20a*. Amsterdam: Montessori-Pierson Publishing Company.

Morrison, Charles D. 2014. "From 'Sage on the Stage' to 'Guide on the Side': A Good Start." *International Journal for the Scholarship of Teaching and Learning* 8 (1), Article 4. Available at: https://doi.org/10.20429/ijsotl.2014.080104.

Séguin, Édouard. 1907. *Idiocy: And Its Treatment by the Physiological Method*. New York, NY: Teachers College, Columbia University.

Whitehead, Alfred North. 1967. *The Aims of Education and Other Essays*. New York, NY: Macmillan Information.

Chapter 16
Erdkinder: An Educational Approach for Adolescents Ages 12–15

Ela Eckert

Maria Montessori detailed the period of transition from child to adult as a phase of comprehensive crisis and challenge with physical, psychological, and social instability. She described her primary concern in studying this age group, "We want to grasp these needs better, want to understand them better, but above all we want to meet these needs better" (Montessori 2015, 422).[1]

In addition to the physical changes of puberty, hormonal shifts, and restructuring of the brain, Montessori (2007) observed a particular susceptibility to illness as well as an increased risk of suicide. So much so that she recommended regular monitoring of adolescents by a physician specializing in endocrinology. To support healthy development during these years, she advocated for adolescents to spend additional time outside, engage in physical activities to strengthen the body without overexertion, including working outdoors, walking, biking, and swimming as well as focusing on a healthy diet of locally grown food and by abstaining from tobacco and alcohol. In addition, she pointed out young people's need for rest and contemplation should also be considered.

Montessori characterized younger adolescents as being emotionally fragile and having vulnerabilities to their self-esteem, with an enormous need for respect and dignity. She noted the lack of adult consideration for this fact, especially the indifference of many secondary school teachers, focusing on teaching whole groups of students through only textbook approaches. Montessori believed wholeheartedly that the first priority of any educational measure, but particularly with adolescents, should not be instruction of academic content, but the promotion of personal development. She saw it as a matter of "opening up of ways of expression, which through exercises and external aids will help the difficult development of the personality" (Montessori 2007, 75).

Additionally, Montessori recognized the unpredictability of the future and what future societies might look like. As such, she believed the strengthening of the adolescent personality was the very best preparation for meeting future challenges (Montessori 1939). Montessori saw the difficulty in engaging adolescents in learning extensive curricular content, which was often incoherently conveyed. She understood that this was not caused by students' lack of goodwill but by a temporary reduction of their intellectual capacity caused by the rapid restructuring of the brain during puberty. However, she did not see this change as a problem; in her experience, children of this age had already acquired a great deal of the content traditionally taught in secondary school because of their magnificent capacity for learning before puberty, between ages 6 and 12 (Montessori 2015, 521).

With regard to their social needs, Montessori recognized that adolescents were attracted to great tasks and challenges, which they wanted to tackle purposefully with their peers and teachers within an age-appropriate, safe, and thoughtfully dependable community. In this way, young people could gradually prepare themselves for society and its complex mechanisms and functioning. According to Montessori, however, most families showed little understanding of these needs and still others disregarded her belief that "the essential reform is this: to put the adolescent on the road to achieving economic independence" (Montessori 2007, 64). She was convinced that adolescents longed for real adult work—work that should be paid, combine practical *and* theoretical elements, and be selected from a wide range of choices. Montessori understood that monetary compensation and participation in the world of economic exchange are both means by which adults are viewed, valued, and classified though it should be noted this was only one aspect of adulthood focused on in her work (Montessori 2007).

Montessori (2007) argued that civilization is based on divisions and collective outcomes of human labor, with each generation building on the previous work of individuals and humanity as a whole. In this respect, work unites humans across generations and is a centerpiece of the development of civilization. Young people who are starting to work enter the world of adults in their *own* society and within their *own* era. At the same time, though, they become part of the evolution and history of human civilization as a whole. Work processes that shape civilization are therefore important for the adolescent to consciously become a responsible and creative cocreator of future development.

These ideas were significant factors in Montessori's concept of a learning arrangement for adolescents (i.e., between ages 12 and 18) that she called a "school of experience in the elements of social life" (Montessori 2007, 64). In her vision for this setting, adolescents would spend time in nature working with agriculture and then use or sell the products of their work. Students would have access to a variety of practical work experiences connected by an overarching plan of development. Student agency and choice was central to the model that supports the development of practical skills but also more complex understandings of systems and structures in the world. Montessori understood solving real-life questions and problems allowed for interdisciplinary thinking and working. This, in short, is her ideal for the developing adolescent. Montessori also understood the importance that all learning be up to date, grounded in sound scientific thinking and discovery, and involve art, culture, and community. She also saw the work of adolescents as an important inroad to their understanding of the value of sustainability and responsibility toward the future of our planet.

Like her earlier work, Montessori's observations of adolescents undergird her educational plan, with a consistent focus on their developmental needs. Her work is supported by contemporary neuroscience and our most advanced understanding of the adolescent brain. Empirical work confirms Montessori's findings (e.g., Konrad et al. 2013). Developmental psychologists and educational scientists today all support, as Montessori did in her day, adolescents being given greater responsibility to participate in decision-making, to prove themselves in society, and to demonstrate the great potential of adolescence (Csikzentmihalyi 2011; Fend 2003; Largo and Czernin 2017; Rathunde and Csikzentmihalyi 2005).

Center for Study and Work on the Land: A Learning Environment for Adolescents

Montessori's concept for ages 12 through 18, typically referred to as adolescence, builds on her notion of cosmic education. Her understanding of the child included the idea that by about the age of 12 children stand on a firm foundation of interdisciplinary knowledge and skills gathered in their elementary years. During the years that follow, adolescents question their contributions as future adults in the context of nature and society. This requires a different type of work and study with opportunities to tackle big, real-world challenges and express their understandings of justice and equity.

Montessori developed her recommendations for adolescents over several decades, beginning around 1920. Important sources of inspiration included various European boarding schools, especially the Abbotsholme School in England. Early on, she was in contact with the New Education Fellowship, founded in England in 1921. There, she met education reformers from various countries and familiarized herself with German reform pedagogues including Peter Petersen's Jena Plan School, Hermann Lietz's Landerziehungsheime (country education homes), and others. According to Ludwig (2015), during her visits to Berlin Montessori may even have been in contact with educators at Wilhelm Blume's Schulfarm Insel Scharfenberg. In each case, these schools offered adolescents learning environments outside of cities providing a healthy life in inspiring surroundings, manual labor, a rich choice of activities, and promotion of holistic personality development (Barker 2011; Ludwig 2015, 91).

Montessori published her entire plan for educating adolescents in 1939 in a compact but powerful document of just over twenty pages. For many years, her ideas were considered difficult to execute in their entirety. As a result, Montessori schools around the world, if they offered a concept for their older students at all, often practiced just select facets of the original concept. In the mid-1990s, however, a working group, under the leadership of American Montessori expert David Kahn, was formed with the goal of launching an authentic implementation of her work for adolescents. Hershey Montessori Farm School opened in Huntsburg, Ohio, in 2000 as the first authentic model worldwide for adolescents ages 12 to 15 and expanded to become Hershey Montessori High School in 2008 (Kahn 2015). Hershey's success quickly attracted a great deal of attention. The work of Hershey also ushered in a new era for training for educators in adolescent curriculum and philosophy.

Montessori named her program for adolescents Erdkinder (Children of the Earth), writing "The stage of adolescence we call 'Erdkinder'. ... For the earth may be said to be the origin of society, and it represents man's first real field of labor" (Montessori 2015, 373).[2] For her adolescents learning how to engage in work related to the functions of society, especially through agriculture, allowed for social and relevant economic experiences, including the production, marketing, and selling of goods such as produce or other handmade items and managing the related proceeds and processes. Montessori believed that this type of hands-on work also allowed learning about resource allocation, scarcity, conflict, technology, and human impact on the world to be done in context. In this way, history, geography, and hard sciences could come to life. As she notes, "[t]herefore work on the land is an introduction both to nature and civilization and gives a limitless field for scientific and historic studies" (Montessori 2007, 68).

The Center for Study and Work on the Land includes the following components and represents, according to Montessori, the adequate prepared environment for educating adolescents (especially for ages 12–15):

- Residential House for Adolescents (community living in a manageable setting)
- Farm Production (work with land, plants, and animals)
- Shop and Exchange of Goods (sales, communication, investment)
- Guesthouse
- Museum of Machinery (learning about equipment, machines, and technology)
- Adolescents
- Adults

Montessori believed that this type of learning environment reproduces basic social structures of production, trade, and services in a manageable and protected framework for young people where a variety of real work, product sales, and experience with services can be learned and practiced. Guided by adults with specialized knowledge and a particular interest in working with adolescents, the students are introduced to various types of work, assume real responsibility for specific processes and areas, learn the theoretical background individually and in teams, and achieve increasing economic independence.

In addition to shared daily living and working, self-expression, preparation for adult life, and psychic development (moral and cognitive development) form the basis of what is often referred to as Montessori's education syllabus for adolescents. Her first priority of self-expression includes a call for opportunities of personal expression through visual art, music, literature, poetry, and drama as a manner of strengthening character development. Moral education, mathematics, and languages are Montessori's second priority allowing for continued cognitive and personal growth through modeling and differentiation. Finally, Montessori believed in allowing young people time and space to connect these skills to further, more complex academic study related to the scientific, cultural, and natural world. She understood preparation for adult life to include the study of earth and natural sciences as interdisciplinary sets of topics, with varied perspectives and contexts. Likewise, the study of human progress, the building of civilization, and a comprehensive survey of the history of humankind are critical to this final piece of Montessori's outline for adolescents.

Regarding the pedagogy related to working with adolescents, Montessori notes, "[T]he best methods are those which arouse in the pupil a maximum of interest, which give him the opportunity of working alone, of making his own experiences, and which allow studies to alternate with practical life" (Montessori 2015, 133). She spoke of work-theory-linked subject areas or occupations. Later, the term "Work and Study" was used to describe and organize the learning processes of Montessori adolescents. Montessori (2007) understood active learning for adolescents as important for continuing to prioritize freedom of choice, cooperation, and the development of both individual and group working skills.

Staffing a Center for Study and Work on the Land requires on-site house parents; an on-site farm manager to guide the practical work; qualified, adaptable teachers, some of whom live on-site, and others who come from outside to teach within the model of Erdkinder; and craftspeople and experts to advise and support the young people with specialized knowledge when needed.

The adults assisting with all aspects of Montessori's (2007) educational syllabus for adolescents are an important part of the prepared environment. Their roles vary according to the needs of the youth and community.

Work and Study in Practice: Three Examples of Implementation

"It is impossible to fix a priori a detailed program for study and work. We can only give the general plan. This is because a program should only be drawn up gradually under the guidance of experience." (Montessori 2007, 71).

Montessori was clear in her writing about adolescence that this work would need to evolve over time. Over the past twenty years, a considerable number of Erdkinder implementations have emerged in several countries. They look very different, as Montessori intended, depending on their setting, and not all include a farm setting.

The next section describes three Erdkinder applications especially for adolescents from 12 to 15. At this age, Montessori's insistence on practical, hands-on work as a starting point is particularly significant. While the implementation of Montessori's vision is different in each of these examples there are consistencies among them; student decision-making and responsibility supported by adults and older student mentors are central (Eckert 2020).

Farm School La Granja: The Abba's Orchard in the Philippines

The Abba's Orchard,[3] founded in 1998 by Maria Angelica Paez-Barrameda and Christopher Barrameda, offers Montessori education for children and youth on several islands in the Philippines. Their work includes rural and urban farm-school arrangements in four locations. Approximately 120 adolescents attend La Granja on Northern Mindanao, where they implement all of the components of Montessori's vision except boarding. Students in mixed-age groups in grades seven through nine follow a farm-school approach. Beyond age 15, students then move to focus on preparing for college or work post-graduation. Work and Study in the farm schools of Abba's Orchard emanates from the conditions found in the environment, including their focus on aquaponics.

The term "aquaponics" originates from the words *aquaculture* (the growing of fish in a closed environment) and *hydroponics* (the growing of plants in a soil-free environment). Students farm tilapia, which grow quickly and are not very demanding. The system of aquaponics is one that uses all elements of the process to their fullest extent, including the fish waste. Fish waste contains ammonia which bacteria convert into nitrites. Nitrites are then cultivated into plant food which is composted and fed to the vegetable beds nearby. Water from the process is also recaptured, purified, and reused in the fish-farming process. One student expressed that they want to offer their organically farmed fish and organic vegetables at an affordable price.

The theoretical studies in this Work and Study concern:

- anatomy and lifestyle of fish and the water quality needed to breed and farm them;
- fish species suitable for farming;
- the aquaponics process and conditions of biological water purification;
- the hydroponic conditions needed for plants to thrive.

Students are able to explain the business plan of their Work and Study in detail and with great confidence. Because profits and losses are integral to any business, students also keep precise financial accounts and determine how to use profits. Teachers, visitors, and parents to the school note students are very knowledgeable and professional in their presentations. Students also are committed to achieving sustainable operations for their products and demonstrate a cooperative attitude toward team members. In a recent case study on the efficacy of the Abba Orchard Schools, graduates of La Granja's high school described their experiences in the farm school. Students appreciate working with others and many note the value of learning to collaborate with peers, even after finding it initially difficult to cooperate with them. They were also grateful for the opportunities to work hard because it inspired them to persevere in their work. One adolescent said, "Work and Studies were a highlight of my junior high years. They led me to become confident and [learn] how to guide others" (Paez-Barrameda 2017, 284).

Montessori Campus Vienna: Smooth Transition from City to Countryside

The Montessori Campus in Vienna,[4] founded in 1995, began an adolescent program in 2008 for children ages 12 to 15. Since 2013, older adolescents can also earn the International Baccalaureate diploma and enter university. About fifty adolescents attend this Center for Work and Study on the outskirts of Vienna. The campus offers access to nature but also enables students to independently visit museums and historical places in and around Vienna.

Work and Study here occurs in two locations, one center where there are chickens, bees, herbs, vegetables, and fruits and another site, which is a larger farm about 30 kilometers away where the possibility of larger agricultural operations, timber farming, and landscape conservation are all possible. In these spaces, all components of Montessori's vision for a Center for Work and Study are present except boarding. Montessori cautioned early on that the development of such a center would be ongoing and evolve over time. In the instance of this particular school there was no electricity on the farm. As a result, a student group undertook the development of a solar and/or wind power system to provide electricity. After exploring the topics of climate change and energy transition, students' focus moved to technical implementation and the logistics behind constructing alternative power sources.

Across the learning landscapes students also focused on the real-time work of the land and its possibilities with varied small groups of students focusing on different aspects of community life and living. For example, one group focused on the development of products for market. This group cultivated herbs and beeswax for use in the production of cosmetics. These student-developed cosmetic products sell so well that students are now also producing soap. Another

Figure 16.1 Preparing a meal. Courtesy of Roman Klune.

group of students worked on photography and public relations related to these products and publicizing the center's bed and breakfast offerings (Klune 2020, 126–7). In all of the work of the students at the Montessori Campus Vienna, the focus on integrating classroom learning and practical applications of that learning and vice versa is at the center of the prepared environment (see Figure 16.1).

In high school, the time and intellectual commitments of the adolescents move away from the farm and farm-like activities in preparation for their move toward becoming adults in the world. To meet this need, the Vienna campus offers opportunities for students to develop outward-facing work and projects aimed at bettering something in the world or working to solve a particular problem that is relevant to their specific time and context. For example, the Montessori Campus, Vienna, created a program called Make a Difference (MAD) Projects. The issues related to these projects are decided upon by students in community at the beginning of a school year. These projects could include serving the local community in a variety of ways from assisting individuals in poverty, to raising awareness about drug use, to collecting school supplies for those in need. Projects may also include other types of activism.

While the school is not a traditional one in the most common sense and embodies Montessori's principles and goals, it is still an educational environment full of rigor and application. The director of the Vienna Erdkinder model summarized the results of the program in this way, "It has been shown that Montessori children, who have experienced neither learning pressure nor grades at school, can very well manage an international graduation diploma. De facto, all (!) young people coming from our Montessori campus have received the [International Baccalaureate] diploma so far" (Klune 2020, 144).

An Urban Compromise: Montessori's Erdkinder Concept in Göttingen

The Montessori School in Göttingen is another example of Erdkinder in action in a contemporary setting. Former head of school Wiebe Möller[5] describes how Montessori's concept for adolescents can be successfully implemented in an exclusively urban school in a recent publication around adolescent education (Möller 2020, 146–60). Founded in 1999, the school consists of mixed-age classes for elementary school children as well as a group of sixty-three adolescents in grades seven through ten. The school is located in a traditional school building but one that is used quite differently than one might think when seeing it from the outside.

In the four-story building, the adolescents have an entire floor to themselves. They are completely responsible for this separate area and accomplish much of Montessori's Study and Work Plans here. For example, they built their own kitchen, including furnishings, under the guidance of a carpenter.

To gain important experience with agriculture, the school leases a thousand-square-meter garden area with an apple orchard on the outskirts of Göttingen. Here the students take care of the site, harvest apples, make apple cider and jam, and later sell their goods. There are also bee colonies on the property, tended by a group of students. Moreover, in cooperation with the city forestry office, the young people have access to a city forest. Guided by a forestry scientist from the University of Göttingen, they conduct practical, interdisciplinary research on the forest ecosystem, learn to recognize stress-related imbalances in the forest, and understand the resulting consequences, while also acknowledging human responsibility for the forest ecosystem.

The adolescents at the Göttingen school also participate in the Montessori Model United Nations (MMUN). After a full year of preparation, a student delegation travels to Rome every summer for an MMUN conference replicating the United Nations General Assembly. While the Model UN program is not unique to Montessori, this is yet another way that Göttingen has found ways to honor Montessori's intent for young people to move into the work of preparation for adult life. Participation in this international meeting of students allows for dialogue and collaboration on a new scale. Young people learn to imagine themselves in other countries, talk with Montessori students from all over the world, and negotiate compromises on contemporary issues. The MMUN experience promotes Montessori's most important goal: striving for solidarity and peace across borders and cultures. Adolescents begin to see themselves as citizens of the world.

Conclusion

Maria Montessori systematically analyzed the developmental needs of adolescents and understood the value of space to strengthen their personality, expand social contacts with peers, and strive for economic independence while participating in real work. This formed the foundation of her recommendations for educating adolescents. She designed a comprehensive concept that reproduces the basic social structures of economic, social, and cultural functions of a community including production and exchange, communal living and governance, and care for one another and the planet. Her Erdkinder model does this in a manageable, transparent, and protected framework that is responsive to the needs of adolescents and prepares them for further life as citizens, family and community members, and economic agents. In this context, young people learn and practice real adult work, economic independence, community building, and cultural and artistic production.

Contemporary studies in neuroscience and developmental psychology confirm Montessori's observations and support the structure of the learning environment Montessori envisioned where student agency is central and decision-making, responsibility, and natural consequences are integral parts of the work (Fend 2003; Konrad et al. 2013; Rathunde and Csikzentmihalyi 2005). Montessori's concept for adolescents is a model of great potential and relevance, especially in the twenty-first century. The opportunity to gain extensive interdisciplinary experiences prepares adolescents for their future lives as citizens of the world, capable of becoming agents of change for the best of the planet and its inhabitants.

Notes

1. All quotes have been translated by the author from each text's original language to English.
2. A number of Montessori's lectures from 1939 to 1951 clarify and differentiate aspects of the 1939 original text and provide better understanding of it. Many of these are published in *Von der Kindheit zur Jugend* (Montessori 2015).
3. To learn more about Abba's Orchard in the Philippines, visit: https://www.theabbasorchard.com/campuses.
4. To learn more about the Montessori Campus in Vienna, visit: https://www.montessoricampus.at.
5. To learn more about the Montessori School in Göttingen, visit: www.montessori-schule-goettingen.de.

References

Barker, Devan. 2011. "A Historical Look at Montessori's Erdkinder." *Communications, Journal of the AMI* (1–2): 96–112.

Csikzentmihalyi, Mihaly. 2011. "Becoming an Adult: Pathways to Maturity." *The NAMTA Journal* 36 (3): 159–77.

Eckert, Ela. 2020. *Erdkinderplan: Maria Montessoris Erziehungs—und Bildungskonzept für Jugendliche*. Freiburg: Verlag Herder.

Fend, Helmut. 2003. *Entwicklungspsychologie des Jugendalters*. Wiesbaden: Verlag für Sozialwissenschaften.

Kahn, David. 2015. "Geleitwort Eines von den 'Erdkindern' Inspirierten Praktikers." In *Von der Kindheit zur Jugend*, edited by Michael Klein-Landeck and Harald Ludwig, XVII–XXXI. *Maria Montessori—Gesammelte Werke* (14). Freiburg: Verlag Herder.

Klune, Roman. 2020. "Das Wiener Modell: Fließender Übergang von Stadt und Land." In *Erdkinderplan: Maria Montessoris Erziehungs—und Bildungskonzept für Jugendliche*, edited by Ela Eckert, 123–45. Freiburg: Verlag Herder.

Konrad, Kerstin, Christine Firk, and Peter J. Uhlhaas. 2013. "Hirnentwicklung in der Adoleszenz—Neurowissenschaftliche Befunde zum Verständnis dieser Entwicklungsphase." *Deutsches Ärzteblatt* 110 (25): 425–31.

Largo, Remo H., and Monika Czernin. 2017. *Jugendjahre: Kinder durch die Pubertät Begleiten*. Munich: Piper Verlag.

Ludwig, Harald. 2015. "Die Entwicklung der Sekundarschulkonzeption bei Maria Montessori." In *Von der Kindheit zur Jugend*, edited by Michael Klein-Landeck and Harald Ludwig, 83–97. *Maria Montessori—Gesammelte Werke* (14). Freiburg: Verlag Herder.

Möller, Wiebe. 2020. "Ein Urbaner Kompromiss: Der Erdkinderplan in der Montessori-Schule Göttingen." In *Erdkinderplan: Maria Montessoris Erziehungs—und Bildungskonzept für Jugendliche*, edited by Ela Eckert, 146–60. Freiburg: Verlag Herder.

Montessori, Maria. 1939. "The 'Erdkinder': A Scheme for a Reform of Secondary Education." *Halfyearly Bulletin of the Association Montessori Internationale* 2 (1): 5–23.

Montessori, Maria. 2007. *From Childhood to Adolescence*. Amsterdam: Montessori-Pierson Publishing Company.

Montessori, Maria. 2015. "Von der Kindheit zur Jugend." In *Maria Montessori—Gesammelte Werke*, edited by Michael Klein-Landeck and Harald Ludwig, 14. Freiburg: Verlag Herder.

Paez-Barrameda, Maria Angelica. 2017. "The Montessori Education Program: Its Impact on Cognitive Achievement." PhD diss., Xavier University, Cagayan de Oro City, Philippines.

Rathunde, Kevin, and Mihaly Csikzentmihalyi. 2005. "Middle School Students' Motivation and Quality of Experience: A Comparison of Montessori and Traditional School Environments." *American Journal of Education* 111 (3): 341–71. https://doi.org/10.1086/428885

Chapter 17
Adult Formation to Transformation

Jaroslaw Jendza

The Montessori approach is oriented to the child. Nonetheless, Montessori was also very clear about the role of adults in education. This aspect, the preparation of the adult, is one of the most radical ideas of Montessori's work, demanding never-ending development. Adults construct, prepare, and modify the educational environment for children. Thus, the issue of adult (trans)formation is a matter of utmost importance in providing children with the educational opportunities described and proposed by Maria Montessori. Policymakers, teacher educators, and parents are the adults Montessori addressed in her work. Most of the theories Montessori formulated toward these three groups are identical; however, several specific characteristics can be attributed to each of the roles separately. The development of teachers, especially their attitude toward the pedagogical conventions that they implement in their everyday practices, is essential to consider alongside the development of particular competencies. Finally, we consider both teachers and parents and the aspects of transformation Montessori understood as critical around "what a Montessori teacher needs to be" (Montessori 2007, 65–7).

Teachers' Transformation

Let's consider Montessori teachers as an example of a community of practice: a group of people who work in one domain and make continuous attempts to develop and learn (Wenger 1998). Without going deeper in the critique of this concept (Contu and Willmott 2003), we could say that they ascribe to a certain educational convention and may adopt various cognitive and moral strategies toward it.

The notion of convention is usually attributed to traditional schooling and therefore is at times used in a pejorative sense by those who advocate for alternative or progressive approaches. On the other hand, the Latin origin of this term (*conventionem*) shows that it can be treated as an assembly, meeting, or agreement. If people come together and agree to do something in a specific way, they form and maintain a certain convention. From such a perspective, the Montessori approach, as with any other intersubjectively shared idea of practices, is a convention. The concept of shared responsibility and cohesion among a group played an important role in Kohlberg's (1981, 1984) idea of the stages of moral and cognitive development. Although his analysis was initially based on the research of adolescent boys and later young adults, and despite the criticism it received (Gilligan 2016), moral development is an intriguing interpretative frame in which the adult Montessori practitioners and their (trans)formation can be characterized for a better understanding of the holistic nature of Montessori education.

With this framework of moral development in place, we see how Montessori adults can also go through stages of development in relation to Montessori education conventions. In fact, it is even useful to apply Kohlberg's (1981) terminology to their development and assert that they move through the preconventional, conventional, and postconventional stages as educators, policymakers, and parents. This is not to say that Kohlberg's is the only framework to examine adult formation related to Montessori pedagogy but simply that the process Kohlberg describes can also be applied in this context.

In Kohlberg's model, cognition and morality are externally controlled during the preconventional stage, and people primarily accept the rules of authority figures. When the second or conventional stage is achieved, the rules of authority figures are still accepted, but people tend to act in order to achieve social acceptance of the group they belong to. Later, development in the postconventional stage involves individual choices and leads to the questioning of the rules of a convention and, if necessary, changing or eliminating some of them (Kohlberg 1981).

Applying this framework to Montessori education, teachers and other adults begin in the conventional stage relying on teacher educators or experts in the field as authority figures. Newer Montessori teachers are familiarized with the approach while taking part in various teacher preparation programs. They spend the majority of the time being instructed on giving presentations in a very specific manner, working with particular materials properly, and analyzing selected Montessori writings and quotes. It is not a coincidence that this form of teachers' education is called training. The most important questions that may arise during this stage are the *how:* how to present material properly, how to manage a group of children, how to behave in the classroom, and so on. This indispensable stage gives teacher trainees orientation in a new convention, allowing them to find order in this unique, still-unknown educational environment and build their feeling of certainty. However, to fully complete their transformation as educators, teachers need to go to the second and then the third stages of development, taking practice into action.

In the second or conventional stage, Montessori adults could be conceived as behaving in ways that enhance acceptance among their fellow teachers, parents, or other community members. Practitioners working in various educational institutions belong to communities of practice where there is a consensus that Montessori works. Nonetheless, everyday experiences initiate questions, bring dilemmas, and provoke temporary doubts. These are all helpful feelings. Teacher assistants, apprentices, and novices seek mentors who can assure them they have chosen a good path as they search for acceptance and answers. From the psychological perspective, for educators at this stage, conformity seems to be the most efficient strategy. Time, money, and the outlay of effort along with a need to understand their place in the Montessori context, and the fear of group exclusion often prevent new educators from asking too many questions.

Finally, in the postconventional stage, Montessori adults would be seen expressing their own personal authorship and critical attitudes toward Montessori pedagogy. Kohlberg (1984) was of the opinion that only 10 to 15 percent of people reach the third (postconventional) level of development in the domain of morality, and additional research suggests that achieving the third stage of his model is not universal (Bergling 1981; Edwards 1981). While we do not know if this is the case when applying this theory of development to Montessori adults, the postconventional stage can be seen as a moment of transformation or, to use the idea of psychologist Dąbrowski, can become a process of positive disintegration leading to autonomous personality (Dąbrowski 1964). Here he made a clear division between individuality and personality, which he defined as "a self-aware, self-chosen, self-affirmed, and self-determined unity of essential individual psychic qualities" (Dąbrowski 1964, 301). In this sense, we may be individuals but without fully formed, unique personalities. Postconventional development in the Montessori context means experiencing transcendence through difficult, painful, and repeatable acts of breaking with well-established patterns of thinking and behaving. Montessori teachers in the postconventional stage constantly question, make autonomous choices, and try to be heretical toward any orthodoxies (Holmes 1913, 24). This is true of all conventions, perhaps especially those formulated by authority figures, including Montessori herself. Only then can we say they are autonomous and self-guiding educators in the way that Montessori envisioned.

Communities like Montessori education have developed and conserve precise ways of professional functioning, which can make moving to a stage of fully integrated and used understanding more difficult. The more closed such a group, the tougher it is to positively disintegrate and later integrate again in a different form. On the other hand, openness, minimalizing bureaucracy, collaboration, sharing knowledge, and reaching new agreements with other communities of practice can help practitioners to reach this third stage of development. Thus, the first two stages of adult development in a Montessori educator formation context can be treated as a process of routine adult formation, while the third one might be understood as transformation. Turning to a specific group of Montessori teachers' competencies is illustrative of adult transformation and the related emergent themes.

Montessori Educator Development

There is no consensus on one operational definition of teachers' competencies (Kouwenhoven 2009), and there is constant debate on how and why such sets of competencies are being developed by policymakers. Bearing that in mind, three metaphorical figures would be useful to consider here: the artisan, the reflective practitioner, and the transformative intellectual to discern what it might mean to be a competent Montessori teacher. These three metaphors can be treated as a conceptual triad (vertices of a triangle) in which the Montessori teacher's transformation may take place.

Consider an artisan, one who has professional knowledge in a craft and effectively uses this knowledge in everyday practices. In the context of Montessori education, it is the teacher who knows the approach so well that it brings about optimal educational opportunities for children. This, obviously, includes a thorough knowledge of the material, class management, and ability to engage children in independent work. Elite artisans know not only their craft but also how to deal with conflicts and ambiguity, enhance cooperation, and engage ethically in freedom within limits. To use Montessori terminology, they initiate the normalization processes, leading to love of work, concentration, sociability, and self-discipline (Montessori 1995). Similarly, we could say that being a competent teacher in the sense of an artisan denotes possessing a "skill of making things well" (Sennett 2008, 8) and "the sense of understanding things, experiencing them, learning how to do them, and getting tangible results" (Frayling 2011, 16).

A second metaphor, the reflective practitioner, coined by Donald Schön, has for many decades dominated in the discourse of teachers' competencies. Here we see a clear shift in pedagogical thought moving away from technical rationality toward reflection in action and over action (Schön 1991). The two pillars within the metaphor about adult transformation are the development and use of tacit knowledge (Polanyi 1967) and the experience of dilemma (Schön 1991). Tacit rather than articulated knowledge refers to deeply rooted internal beliefs, opinions, and judgments developed since childhood that an adult uses in professional practices. These procedural, self-explanatory individual conceptions, including uninformed ideas around being a Montessori teacher, may be radically different from, or even contrary to, the realities and declarative knowledge of the craft (Kagan 1992; Taylor 1999). An individual with the ability to recognize, question, and modify this foundational knowledge would characterize a teacher who wishes to transform themselves as the reflective practitioner example notes. Experiencing dilemmas is possible when a person accepts uncertainty and ambiguity and lives their (professional) life as inquiry (Gearty and Marshal 2021). A reflective practitioner is also a humble observer and investigator rather than the main protagonist while accompanying children on their journey of development. In this way, the teacher presents subject matter and "brings it to the table" for collaborative or individual study (Masschelein and Simons 2013, 62). From there the teacher withdraws and patiently observes, maintaining the researcher spirit within the prepared environment (Montessori 1997).

Critical pedagogist Henry Giroux (1988) noted the construct of a transformative intellectual, which also fits the Montessori paradigm and completes the triad. By focusing on additional competencies Montessori teachers are asked to develop in the processes of transformation, we see there is more to being a Montessori educator than passive acceptance of ideas. A transformative intellectual refers to an educator taking responsibility for influencing the broader sociocultural and economic order, being aware of power relations, and deconstructing interests of various social agents involved in education. Montessori educators are presented with the opportunity to do exactly this within the framework of Montessori philosophy, pedagogy, and materials. In this sense, Montessori schools are not neutral places where simply the declared values and objective knowledge are constructed. By extension, teachers are not simply adults who are apolitical companions in children's development. For Montessori educators, the moral character of their professional activity exceeds the technical skills or even reflection over practice. A moral intellectual is one whose horizons let them perceive every action in terms of reconstructing a given social order, discourse patterns, intersubjective relations, and social justice. Here we understand the preparation of the Montessori educator as radical transformation in ways that differ from other education programs and pedagogies.

A Montessori teacher willing to transform in this direction of the triad of examples must sever the ties of the myth of the apolitical character of schooling, deconstruct their own personal position in the social order, and embrace reconstruction focusing on building socially just, unbiased, and peaceful humanity. In other words, the Montessori teacher is ideally a transformative intellectual, a person committed to transforming society and perceiving their professional activity as a contribution to a better, nonoppressive humanity. Given this, the knowledge of pedagogical technique or even the competency of careful observation is not sufficient. Individual educators and the body collective must be aware of macroscale consequences of their microscale actions taking place every single day spent with children and parents. The three examples illustrate the need to be in constant movement within this conceptual triangle of developmental patterns if one is thoroughly committed to transformative adult education, especially in a Montessori context. The multitude of competencies and the variety of teacher roles and responsibilities should prevent inertia and lead to the consistent evaluation and reevaluation of practice.

Parent and Caregiver Transformation

For many adults there is an assumption that time and experience offer a perspective that cannot be questioned. Life experiences, including those of school and social life, often lead us to demand that people not question experts' authority on a given subject idea. And to be fair, isn't it rational to think that because I have a PhD, I have the right to tell my university students how to work? Isn't it natural for the parents to direct their offspring from the very first day of their lives? Such questions must be asked and explored critically if one wishes to transform parent and caregiver modes of thinking and child-rearing.

More than fifty years ago, an American cultural anthropologist as well as one of the pioneers in childhood research, Margaret Mead (1901–1978), characterized three possible intergenerational relations and called them pre-, co-, and postfigurative (Mead 1970).

Despite some critical opinions of her contemporaries (Furstenberg 1970) as well as later, mostly conservative, commentators questioning her schema (Bloom 1987; Freeman 1998), these conceptual frames, based on three lectures given in March 1969, can be thought-provoking in the context of Montessori caregiving and the transformation that might be needed or occur as a result of this mindset.

Mead (1970) suggests that various cultures might be past, present, or future oriented. In postfigurative cultures, the sources of knowledge, wisdom, authority, and values are the older generation of adults. Children learn from the adults, and students learn from professors. Cofigurative cultures are temporary and present oriented; here people gain knowledge from their peers in an ongoing and circular manner. In prefigurative cultures "it will be the child—not the parent and the grandparent that represents what is to come" (Mead 1970, 88). Here we see Mead reflecting Montessori's worldviews in her representation. When referring to children, Mead added, "[o]ut of their new knowledge—new to the world and new to us—must come the questions to those already equipped by education and experience to search for answers" (1970, 94). It is essential to note how children may be the source of questions and can teach adults on the way to creating a better world, learning from them, and keeping the world peaceful (Gribble 2010).

For those who have been enculturated and socialized in postfigurative cultures, the idea of a child leading adults is difficult to understand and even more difficult to accept. The assumption that the adults know better is, at least for some, a tacit parenting ideology, the air we breathe, as Allen Cunningham put it in a slightly different context, "we breathe it into our tools" (2014, 47). One of most important tools is family and the attendant parenting styles (Smetana 2017).

Apart from the most popular distinction of parenting styles (authoritarian, authoritative, permissive, uninvolved), researchers and popular media alike have also paid a great deal of attention to the style referred to as "helicopter parenting" (Ginott 1988). In these instances, parents and caregivers hover over every aspect of their child's development, tend to be overprotective, and work ostensibly to keep their children safe and free of any stress (Padilla-Walker and Nelson 2012). This parenting style is a modified and more modern form of the older, well-known parent model of conservatism (postfiguratism). This parenting style builds from the discourse of ubiquitous evil and dangers waiting just around the corner, and it excuses parents and caregivers for keeping a domineering position over submissive children while at the same time diminishing their moral dilemmas connected with constant surveillance (Segrin et al. 2013). This form of "suppressive love" is closely related with the need for parental control and unfettered, constant visibility. Numerous educational institutions, including Montessori in some instances, support the demand of surveillance under the veil of safety with the implementation of video monitoring as well as software systems following every move of the child and eliminating the secrets of educational phenomena (Foucault 1980; Sobe 2004).

In an essay to parents and titled "When Your Child Knows Better Than You," Montessori (2017, 44) noted, "The greatest help you can give your children is the freedom to go about their own work in their own way, for in this matter your child knows better than you." In this sense, the transformation of the parent or caregiver may mean investigation and self-analysis of tacit parental ideologies much like educators must explore their own biases and preconceived notions. Once explored, they can be questioned and modified. In some instances, this may demand deep reconstruction of the modes of thinking and behavior of the caregivers because, as Montessori reminds us, trust needs to substitute fear, humility needs to eliminate arrogant confidence, and appreciative inquiry needs to win over unquestionable answers and top-down surveillance. This is a long, challenging, and sometimes even unsuccessful process, yet worth trying nonetheless as we consider adult preparation in life, since the future of humanity is in the child.

Conclusion

In one of her essays discussing the issue of the teacher's desired characteristics, Montessori (2007, 65) pointed to the necessary steps of transformation. Having examined and eliminated "pedagogical prejudices," the adult must work on their imagination and their faith in the child's capacities. While accompanying children on their journeys of learning, they are then able to focus on the interventions and activities that bring difficulties so they can see the child that is not yet there and yet squarely on a path to learning what needs to be learned. In this future-oriented, prefigurative mode of thinking, the teachers, parents, and other caregivers pay attention to, create, and take care of the optimal, prodevelopmental environment, having faith that children will unveil their potentials in purposeful, spontaneous, and meaningful work.

The ability to humbly "withdraw into the background" (Montessori 2007, 66) for adults and, in a nod to a disposition of constant learning, to constantly study the child is the central characteristic of the transformed adult whether it be the educator, parent, or caregiver. Instead of being the main protagonist who controls the life of younger generations, adults offer and put educational things on the table and intervene only when asked. They become true researchers of the phenomenon of development and maintain a scientific attitude formed on unconditional love, trust, and hope.

References

Bergling, Kurt. 1981. *Moral Development: The Validity of Kohlberg's Theory*. Stockholm: Almqvist and Wiksell.

Bloom, Alan. 1987. *The Closing of the American Mind: How Higher Education Has Failed Democracy and Impoverished the Souls of Today's Students*. New York: Simon and Schuster.

Contu, Alessia, and Hugh Willmott. 2003. "Re-embedding Situatedness: The Importance of Power Relations in Learning Theory." *Organization Science* 14 (3): 283–96. https://doi.org/10.1287/orsc.14.3.283.15167.

Cunningham, Allen M. 2014. *The Flickering Page: The Reading Experience in Digital Times*. Portland, OR: Atelier26 Books.

Dąbrowski, Kazimierz. 1964. *Positive Disintegration*. Boston: Little, Brown.

Edwards, Carolyn P. 1981. "The Comparative Study of the Development of Moral Judgment and Reasoning." In *Handbook of Cross-cultural Human Development*, edited by Robert L. Munroe, Ruth H. Munroe, and Beatrice B. Whiting, 501–27. New York: Garland STPM Press.

Foucault, Michael. 1980. "The Eye of Power." In *Power/Knowledge: Selected Interviews and Other Writings, 1972–1977*, edited by Colin Gordon, 146–65. New York: Pantheon Books.

Frayling, Christopher. 2011. *On Craftsmanship: Towards a New Bauhaus*. London: Oberon Books.

Freeman, Derek. 1998. *The Fateful Hoaxing of Margaret Mead: A Historical Analysis of Her Samoan Research*. Boulder, CO: Westview Press.

Furstenberg, Frank F. 1970. "Book Department: Margaret Mead." Review of *Culture and Commitment: A Study of the Generation Gap*, by Margaret Mead. *Annals of the American Academy of Political and Social Science* 391: 243–4.

Gearty, Margaret R., and Judi Marshall. 2021. "Living Life as Inquiry—A Systemic Practice for Change Agents." *Systemic Practice and Action Research* 34: 441–62. https://doi.org/10.1007/s11213-020-09539-4.

Gilligan, Carol. 2016. *In a Different Voice: Psychological Theory and Women's Development*. Cambridge, MA: Harvard University Press.

Ginott, Haim G. 1988. *Between Parent and Teenager*. New York: Avon.

Giroux, Henry A. 1988. "Teachers as Transformative Intellectuals." In *Teachers as Intellectuals: Toward a Critical Pedagogy of Learning*, edited by Henry A. Giroux, 121–8. New York: Bergin and Garvey.

Gribble, David. 2010. *Children Don't Start Wars*. London: Peace News.

Holmes, Edmond. 1913. "Introduction." In *A Montessori Mother*, edited by Dorothy Fisher, xvii–xlviii. London: Constable and Company.

Kagan, Dona M. 1992. "Implication of Research on Teacher Belief." *Educational Psychologist* 27 (1): 65–90. https://doi.org/10.1207/s15326985ep2701_6.

Kohlberg, Lawrence. 1981. *Essays on Moral Development, Vol. I: The Philosophy of Moral Development*. San Francisco: Harper and Row.

Kohlberg, Lawrence. 1984. *Essays on Moral Development, Vol. II: The Psychology of Moral Development: The Nature and Validity of Moral Stages*. San Francisco: Harper and Row.

Kouwenhoven, Wim. 2009. "Competence-Based Curriculum Development In Higher Education: A Globalised Concept?" In *Technology, Education and Development/Monograph*, edited by Aleksandar Lazinica and Carlos Calafate, 1–22. Rijeka, Croatia: InTech.

Masschelein, Jan, and Maarten Simons. 2013. *In Defence of the School: A Public Issue*. Loeven, Belgium: E-ducation, Culture & Society.

Mead, Margaret. 1970. *Culture and Commitment: A Study of the Generation Gap*. Garden City, NY: American Museum of Natural History Press.

Montessori, Maria. 1995. *The Absorbent Mind*. New York: Holt.

Montessori, Maria. 1997. *The 1915 California Lectures: Collected Speeches and Writings*. Amsterdam: Montessori-Pierson.

Montessori, Maria. 2007. *Education for a New World*. Amsterdam: Montessori-Pierson.
Montessori, Maria. 2017. "When Your Child Knows Better Than You." In *Maria Montessori Speaks to Parents: A Selection of Articles*, 25–8. Amsterdam: Montessori-Pierson.
Padilla-Walker, Laura M., and Larry J. Nelson. 2012. "Black Hawk Down?: Establishing Helicopter Parenting as a Distinct Construct from Other Forms of Parental Control during Emerging Adulthood." *Journal of Adolescence* 35 (5): 1177–90. https://doi.org/10.1016/j.adolescence.2012.03.007.
Polanyi, Michael. 1967. *The Tacit Dimension*. London: Routledge.
Schön, Donald A. 1991. *The Reflective Practitioner*. Aldershot, England: Basic Books.
Segrin, Chris, Michelle Givertz, Paulina Swiatkowski, and Neil Mongomery. 2013. "Overparenting Is Associated with Child Problems and a Critical Family Environment." *Journal of Child and Family Studies* 24: 470–9. https://doi.org/10.1007/s10826-013-9858-3.
Sennett, Richard. 2008. *The Craftsman*. London: Penguin.
Smetana, Judith G. 2017. "Current Research on Parenting Styles. Dimensions and Beliefs." *Current Opinion in Psychology* 15: 19–25. https://doi.org/10.1016/j.copsyc.2017.02.012.
Sobe, Noah W. 2004. "Challenging the Gaze: The Subject of Attention and a 1915 Montessori Demonstration Classroom." *Educational Theory* 54 (3): 281–97.
Taylor, Edward W. 1999. "A Critical Review of Teaching Belief Research: Implications for Adult Education." In *Proceedings of the 18th Annual Midwest Research-to-Practice Conference in Adult, Continuing and Community Education*, edited by Ann Austin, Geraldine E. Hynes, and Roxanne T. Miller, 257–64. St. Louis, Missouri.
Wenger, Etienne. 1998. *Communities of Practice: Learning, Meaning, and Identity*. New York: Cambridge University Press.

PART IV

The Science of Montessori Education

Introduction: The Science of Montessori Education

Angela K. Murray

Part IV: The Science of Montessori Education in the *Bloomsbury Handbook of Montessori Education* connects the sections on the history, philosophy, and pedagogy of Maria Montessori with modern issues related to Montessori schooling in the field of education. From the chapters examining the science of Montessori education, the handbook continues with a collection of country profiles that illustrates the proliferation of Montessori education around the globe. The text closes with chapters relating a number of important contemporary issues in the field to Montessori education.

We have chosen to include Part IV on the science of Montessori education in the handbook because Maria Montessori was first and foremost a scientist. Her research on child development, learning, and pedagogy is rooted in her training in medicine, psychiatry, educational anthropology, and pedagogy (Bobbio 2021). As one of the twentieth century's most prolific transdisciplinary scholars, she exemplifies the value of bringing diverse branches of knowledge together when studying education. This "pluridisciplinary" (Bobbio 2021, 24) aspect of the educational sciences is represented in Part IV. Here, we see authors from multiple fields of psychology (e.g., educational, cognitive, developmental), as well as human development, evaluation and assessment, teaching and learning, and neuroscience.

A common refrain among Montessori scholars is that now is an exciting time to be involved in Montessori research. The long history of Montessori education is bearing fruit, attracting global interest in its potential to address educational challenges in a complex and ever-changing world. This enthusiasm is buoyed by expanding empirical evidence related to Montessori pedagogy. Meanwhile, the future of Montessori research is strong; the community of scholars is growing, and research is becoming more sophisticated. Evidence of this growth is seen in the 2021 creation of the Montessori Education Special Interest Group (SIG) within the American Educational Research Association (AERA). AERA is international in scope and growing global networks of scholars focused on Montessori education are emerging.

New research continues to offer insights and identify challenges for the future of the field, and Part IV of the handbook provides a direct connection to Parts I, II, and III with an examination of Montessori's theories in light of current neuroscience. Chapters on a logic model for Montessori research and on issues of fidelity in Montessori education set the foundation for the remaining chapters. These chapters introduce overviews of Montessori research in a range of areas, including efficacy, assessment, neuroscience of error monitoring, optimal experience, executive functions, and motivation. We recognize that these authors represent just some of the scholars around the globe who are studying these topics. We intend for the works here to lead readers to additional researchers and source material in the field. Most importantly, we hope these contributions spark readers' interest in continuing to develop, conduct, and participate in high-quality research related to Montessori education.

Reference

Bobbio, Andrea. 2021. "Maria Montessori between Medicine and Pedagogy. Roots, Actuality and Educational Perspectives." *Ricerche di Pedagogia e Didattica. Journal of Theories and Research in Education* 16 (2): 23–39. https://doi.org/10.6092/issn.1970-2221/12161

Chapter 18
Revisiting the Foundations of Montessori Education from a Modern Neuroscience Perspective

Mara Fabri

The educational philosophy of Maria Montessori was rooted in her lifelong observation of children, which resulted in several strikingly accurate hypotheses on child development that predated related neuroscientific discoveries by decades (Babini and Lama 2016; Gazzaniga 2004). Montessori's unique training and background (See Chapter 1: "Maria Montessori: Life and Historical Context") provided the foundation for her theories, which integrated biological notions of development and the effects of the environment, with particular attention to physiological and animal behavior studies (Montessori 1949). Based on her observations, Montessori refined her theories by studying the existing scientific work of her contemporaries and exchanging ideas with other scholars within the cultural context of that time. Some of Montessori's hypotheses were already in discussion while she was developing her pedagogy (e.g., importance of touch and parental stimuli, existence of critical periods, and language structures), but other hypotheses were confirmed during the middle of the twentieth century, which was a critical period for language and vision ability development. Other hypotheses were confirmed more recently and continue to be supported by emerging research (e.g., importance of movement for brain development, working with the hands for thinking and language development). The result of Montessori's efforts was a revolutionary theory of education, which is still influencing modern pedagogical methods (Regni and Fogassi 2019).

Montessori's most significant pioneering ideas related to current neuroscience evidence are listed. The remainder of this chapter elaborates on the ideas, presenting fundamental neuroscience findings, which, since the second half of the twentieth century, provide support for the Montessori pedagogy and confirm Montessori's foresight (Fabri and Fortuna 2020).

Critical Periods during Psychobiological Development

> ...one of the special characteristics that we have discovered in the child: a power of such intense sensitivity that the things which surround him in the environment awaken in him an intense interest and such a great enthusiasm that they seem to penetrate into his very life.
>
> *(Montessori 1949, 21)*

Montessori described the child as a "spiritual embryo" in that, at birth, the psychological life has yet to be developed, being indeed in an embryonic phase. From this point psychological development proceeds along with biological development (Montessori 1949, 63). During sensitive periods, the child develops particular abilities, is specifically interested in certain experiences, and is especially receptive to these experiences. Montessori's theories about critical periods were inspired by Dutch biologist de Vries's theory about sensitive periods in the early development of organisms, the same source of inspiration that would guide Konrad Lorenz's experiments on animal imprinting (Montessori 1952). It is important to note that, although related, sensitive and critical periods are different, with sensitive periods indicating the limited time window in which particular experiences have the greatest impact. When these experiences are essential for normal development and lead to permanent changes in brain performance, they are termed "critical periods" (Knudsen 2004).

In agreement with early childhood psychologists during Montessori's time (Bühler 1931; Jones 1922; Montessori 1952; Stern 1930), Montessori divided children's development into three main periods—birth to 6 years of age, 6 to 12 years of age, and 12 to 18 years of age—detailed in subsequent sections of this chapter (Montessori 1949). The temporal borders between these periods are seen in evident physical changes: at the end of the first period, children lose their first set of teeth and start growing the second set; between the second and the third period, puberty occurs. Montessori's unique contribution was building on these ideas by using the concept of critical periods as the foundation for an educational model.

Birth to 6 Years of Age

Montessori (1949) described this first phase as containing two distinct subphases, characterized by large transformations, particularly during the first subphase (birth to 3 years of age). More recent neuroscience findings have supported this theory by showing that during the first period of life, the human brain is highly plastic and can be influenced by the environment. Research during the 1960s by David Hubel and Torsten Wiesel (1962) was groundbreaking in providing empirical evidence for a critical period for visual development. Specifically, their studies on animal models demonstrated how vision impairment during the critical period can affect the future development of neurological vision pathways. In contrast, they found that similar sensory deprivation in adults elicits only a general diminution of cortical sensitivity to peripheral stimulation rather than the drastic neurological impact experienced when such loss occurs during the critical period in early childhood (Hubel and Wiesel 1970). Wiesel and Hubel's work earned them the 1981 Nobel Prize in Physiology or Medicine. Later, other research has demonstrated that critical periods are present in other systems, such as neural circuits underpinning the acquisition of language (Hensch 2004).

6 to 12 Years of Age

Montessori described the elementary years as a period of calm, serenity, and physical growth, so critical periods were not emphasized during this time (Montessori 1949). Nevertheless, researchers today recognize early adolescence as the end of the cumulative critical period for language with implications for the cortical representation of grammatical processes and the brain regions employed in second-language learning for this age group (Hensch 2004).

12 to 18 Years of Age

Montessori proposed that the teen years are a period of major transformation, similar to the first period and also having two distinct subphases (Montessori 1949). During this period the body achieves maturity, and physical development can be considered completed at its conclusion. Neuroscience studies are confirming that the brain undergoes profound reorganization, mainly in terms of connectivity rather than neural growth, until 18 to 20 years of age, when the structure and functions typical of adulthood are reached (Giorgio et al. 2008). An example of such reorganization is directly related to emotional development, and particularly to emotional reactivity and regulation, as revealed with modern imaging studies that contributed to greater understanding of the complex nature of this developmental trajectory (Casey et al. 2019).

Effect of the Stimulating Environment

> If he (the child) is to acquire any ability or faculties he must be among people who habitually use those abilities and faculties.
>
> *(Montessori 1949, 86)*

Another important intuition of Montessori was that a rich and stimulating environment is necessary to allow adequate neural/cerebral development and to promote the learning process (Montessori 1949, 80). This concept is now well established, but at that time it was groundbreaking. Today, scientific studies confirm that when a child's physical and human environment is rich and varied, changes within the cerebral internal environment are induced (Maharjan et al. 2020). Enriched environments provide complex sensorimotor stimulation that promotes cerebral development, which reinforces the connections and information exchanges between different cortical areas (Di Garbo et al. 2011). Other studies demonstrate that exposure to a rich environment provokes neuronal changes, resulting in improved cognitive ability and increased synaptic plasticity of the adult visual cortex (Sale et al. 2009).

Importance of Sensory Affective Stimulation

> If the child is kept in nurseries … with as his sole companion a nurse who obstructs more or less the development of the child, because no expression of truly maternal sentiment or feeling are shown to the child, there are serious obstacles to normal growth and development.
>
> *(Montessori 1949, 87)*

Montessori espoused the idea that sensory affective stimulation is necessary for normal psychological maturation. She stressed the importance of the relationship of children with their primary caregivers, considering affective stimulation as part of an enriched environment (Montessori 1949). This concept has been confirmed by neuroscientific research, although it was already recognized by scientists contemporary to Montessori. In particular, in 1945 the description of Spitz syndrome, which is caused by sensory affective deprivation, eventually led to the identification of hospitalism or analytical depression in children separated from their caregivers, with all symptoms disappearing when the child was reunited with the mother or caregiver (Barker Schaerer and Cramer 2000; Spitz 1945). John Bowlby (Partis 2000) developed an attachment theory suggesting that mental health and behavior problems could be related to early childhood experiences. He was influenced by ethological theory, especially by Konrad Lorenz's study of animal behavior (Montessori 1952). In 1935, Lorenz showed that attachment to a parental figure was innate in ducklings, suggesting a survival value. More recent work examining the neural mechanism for the beneficial effects of affective stimulation includes a seminal study showing that rat pups raised by a "good mother"—one that spends time licking and grooming them—will be healthier and more resistant to stress as adults (Meaney and Szyf 2005). Because of a higher expression of hormone receptors that mediate stress response induced by affective sensory stimulation (McGowan et al. 2011; Zhang et al. 2010), the young animals were found to be less anxious in novel situations and more positively oriented in dealing with new experiences.

Human Capacity for Acquiring Language from the Environment

> The child remains mute for a fairly long time, after which he speaks the language he finds being spoken about him. So will it happen that a Dutch child growing up among Italians will speak Italian and not Dutch, despite the long Dutch lineage of his parents. It is therefore clear that the child does not inherit a pre-established language model, but the possibility of building one through an unconscious absorption activity.
>
> *(Montessori 1995, 79)*

Through her studies, Montessori understood that human beings possess specific neural structures that allow the acquisition of language, the peculiarity of which is defined by the environment. During Montessori's time, it was known that different regions of the brain served different functions (Phillips et al. 1984) and that the effect of specific brain lesions, particularly in the left hemisphere, affected language functions in humans (Montessori 1949). Studies by Noam Chomsky provided further support. In 1957, Chomsky formulated a theory according to which the uniquely human ability to speak arises from cortical structures present in the human brain from birth but not present in animals (Chomsky 1981); those cortical structures possess a specific computational ability that allows humans to generate any sentence in any language. This ability has identifiable correlates in the brain and is unchanged since the origin of language

(Berwick et al. 2013). Although some animal languages, such as in songbirds, seem to share with humans a vocal imitation learning ability and a similar neural organization, language is exclusively human.

Role of Movement

Perhaps one of Montessori's most striking insights is the critical role of body movement for optimal development of the brain and nervous system. Starting from a rather banal observation—that muscles amount to about 30% of a person's body weight—Montessori suspected that movement must have a priority beyond preserving healthy breathing and circulatory functions (Montessori 1949). For this reason, Montessori included two types of movement as fundamental activities in her educational programs: movement of the whole body to support development of the brain (Montessori 1949, 118) and performance of fine manual activity, in the firm belief that "the hand is the organ of the brain" (Montessori 1949, 23).

Importance of Body Movement for Learning

> One of the mistakes of modern times is to consider movement separately from the higher functions. People think that the muscles are merely there and have to be used in order to keep better bodily health. ... This mistake is penetrating education. This is, physiologically speaking, as though a great prince had been made use of to serve a shepherd. This great prince, the muscular system has become a handle to turn in order to stimulate the vegetative system.
>
> *(Montessori 1949, 117)*

Montessori (1949) argued that motor activity is necessary for children to explore the environment, gain awareness of their bodies in space, and acquire sensory information about the physical space around them. This idea represents an early insight on the cognitive role of the motor system, now finally recognized. Since 1990, many studies have demonstrated that physical activity stimulates neurogenesis in healthy subjects, even in adults and elderly people, and improves fiber myelination (Chaddock-Heyman et al. 2018; Erickson et al. 2013; Ruotsalainen et al. 2020). Specifically, physical exercise has been shown to increase the number of neurons and capillary vessels in the brain, although the effect is not uniform over the whole brain and some regions are more sensitive to the healthy influence of exercise (Erickson et al. 2013; van Praag et al. 2005). Regular moderate physical activity generally enhances cerebral functions, which increase cognitive ability, memory, general plasticity, and the volume of gray matter; physical activity also improves mood and may convey positive consequences on all brain functions by increasing neural connectivity and stimulating the production of specific growth factors (Gons et al. 2013; Pedersen 2019). A growing body of evidence from the past three decades has led to the motor system finally being considered as part of the cognitive system based on its involvement in cognitive abilities across many areas in the brain (Battaglia-Mayer and Caminiti 2019; Di Cesare et al. 2020; Rizzolatti and Sinigaglia 2016).

Hand as Organ of the Brain

> [The child] becomes a man by means of his hands, by means of his experience ... The hands are the instrument of human intelligence. And by means of this experience he becomes a man, he takes a definite form and becomes limited because consciousness is always more limited than unconsciousness or subconsciousness.
>
> *(Montessori 1949, 23)*

Montessori (1949, 23) described the hand as an organ of the brain—a notion that is being confirmed today in human brain-mapping studies, mainly of the cerebral cortex. In humans, the area of the motor and sensory cortex devoted to the hand is large relative to the actual ratio of the dimensions of the hand compared with the rest of the body. The first evidence of this cortical organization in the human brain emerged in Penfield's work, published in 1937 (Gandhoke et al. 2019; Penfield and Boldrey 1937). By recording the electrical activity of the brain during neurosurgical operations, Penfield showed that cortical areas activated by hand movement or sensory stimulation are much larger than those activated by movement or sensory stimulation of other body parts (Penfield and Boldrey 1937). This means that a large number of neurons are involved in the control of hand movements, which, consequently, can be highly precise because many neurons analyze information coming from the tactile receptors of the hand with high sensory resolution; it is the fingertip sensitivity that makes Braille reading possible. Furthermore, intense use of the hand in simultaneous motor and sensory activity will expand the cortical area and the number of neurons resulting in neural plasticity. This plasticity has been described in string musicians for whom the left-hand representation within the sensorimotor cortex is much larger than in nonmusicians (Elbert et al. 1995; Wilson 2010). Finally, research has demonstrated that hand activity may improve cognitive processing and problem-solving (Vallée-Tourangeau et al. 2016b). For example, in mathematical and problem-solving tasks, manual activity during mental performance augmented overall or systemic working memory resources (Vallée-Tourangeau et al. 2016a). Conversely, the prevention of extensive and complete practice of hand movements in childhood could have dramatic effects, such as a delay in language development (Radesky and Christakis 2016), reinforcing once more the direct relationship between hand activity and language (Corballis 2002).

Conclusion

This chapter provides an overview of the ways in which Montessori's theories are being confirmed through technological advances in neuroscience that she could only have dreamed of so many years ago. As a scientist and educational innovator, her unique perspective on children's development formed the basis of an educational approach that has endured over a century. Many insights on which her child-centered educational method rests predated major neuroscientific discoveries, often by decades. The foundations of Montessori education can now be reexamined with modern tools that provide empirical evidence to support the practices that are demonstrating effectiveness for a broad range of learners, as discussed in other chapters in this part. The challenge for the educator is to be knowledgeable about the scientific basis on which Montessori education rests and to be familiar with how this foundation impacts current practice.

Acknowledgments

The author acknowledges profound gratitude to Professor Stefania Fortuna, colleague and friend, who, in spite of the myriad of her appointments, found the time to critically read the manuscript and gave her valuable suggestions.

References

Babini, Valeria Paola, and Luisa Lama. 2016. *Una Donna Nuova: Il Femminismo Scientifico di Maria Montessori*. Milano: Franco Angeli.

Barker Schaerer, Mandy, and Bertrand Cramer. 2000. "Les Dépressions Chez l'Enfant." *Archives de Pédiatrie* 7 (8): 883–7. https://doi.org/10.1016/S0929-693X(00)80200-6.

Battaglia-Mayer, Alexandra, and Roberto Caminiti. 2019. "Corticocortical Systems Underlying High-Order Motor Control." *Journal of Neuroscience* 39 (23): 4404–21. https://doi.org/10.1523/JNEUROSCI.2094-18.2019.

Berwick, Robert C., Angela D. Friederici, Noam Chomsky, and Johan J. Bolhuis. 2013. "Evolution, Brain, and the Nature of Language." *Trends in Cognitive Sciences* 17 (2): 89–98. https://doi.org/10.1016/j.tics.2012.12.002.

Bühler, Charlotte. 1931. *Kindheit un Jungend: Genese des Bewußtseins*. Leipzig: S. Hirzel.

Casey, B. J., Aaron S. Heller, Dylan G. Gee, and Alexandra O. Cohen. 2019. "Development of the Emotional Brain." *Neuroscience Letters* 693: 29–34. https://doi.org/10.1016/j.neulet.2017.11.055.

Chaddock-Heyman, Laura, Kirk I. Erickson, Caitlin Kienzler, Eric S. Drollette, Lauren B. Raine, Shih-Chun Kao, Jeanine Bensken et al. 2018. "Physical Activity Increases White Matter Microstructure in Children." *Frontiers in Neuroscience* 12: 950. https://doi.org/10.3389/fnins.2018.00950.

Chomsky, Noam. 1981. "Knowledge of Language: Its Elements and Origins." *Philosophical Transactions of the Royal Society B* 295 (1077): 223–34. https://doi.org/10.1098/rstb.1981.0135.

Corballis, Michael C. 2002. *From Hand to Mouth: The Origins of Language*. Princeton, NJ: Princeton University Press.

Di Cesare, Giuseppe, Marzio Gerbella, and Giacomo Rizzolatti. 2020. "The Neural Bases of Vitality Forms." *National Science Review* 7 (1): 202–13. https://doi.org/10.1093/nsr/nwz187.

Di Garbo, Angelo, Marco Mainardi, Santi Chillemi, Lamberto Maffei, and Matteo Caleo. 2011. "Environmental Enrichment Modulates Cortico-Cortical Interactions in the Mouse." *PLoS One* 6 (9): e25285. https://doi.org/10.1371/journal.pone.0025285.

Elbert, Thomas, Christo Pantev, Christian Wienbruch, Brigitte Rockstroh, and Edward Taub. 1995. "Increased Cortical Representation of the Fingers of the Left Hand in String Players." *Science* 270 (5234): 305–7. https://doi.org/10.1126/science.270.5234.305.

Erickson, Kirk I., Ariel G. Gildengers, and Meryl A. Butters. 2013. "Physical Activity and Brain Plasticity in Late Adulthood." *Dialogues in Clinical Neuroscience* 15 (1): 99–108. https://doi.org/10.31887/DCNS.2013.15.1/kerickson.

Fabri, Mara, and Stefania Fortuna. 2020. "Maria Montessori and Neuroscience: The Trailblazing Insights of an Exceptional Mind." *The Neuroscientist* 26 (5–6): 394–401. https://doi.org/10.1177/1073858420902677.

Gandhoke, Gurpreet S., Evgenii Belykh, Xiaochun Zhao, Richard Leblanc, and Mark C. Preul. 2019. "Edwin Boldrey and Wilder Penfield's Homunculus: A Life Given by Mrs. Cantlie (In and Out of Realism)." *World Neurosurgery* 132: 377–88. https://doi.org/10.1016/j.wneu.2019.08.116.

Gazzaniga, Valentina. 2004. "Unperfect, Handicapped Persons: For a History of Didactics of Neuro and Psychomotor Rehabilitation of Children in Italy." *Medicina nei Secoli* 16 (3): 627–50. [In Italian].

Giorgio, Antonio, Kate E. Watkins, Gwenaëlle Douaud, A. C. James, S. James, Nicola De Stefano, Paul M. Matthews et al. 2008. "Changes in White Matter Microstructure during Adolescence." *NeuroImage* 39 (1): 52–61. https://doi.org/10.1016/j.neuroimage.2007.07.043.

Gons, Rob A. R., Anil M. Tuladhar, Karlijn F. de Laat, Anouk G. W. van Norden, Ewoud J. van Dijk, David G. Norris, Marcel P. Zwiers et al. 2013. "Physical Activity Is Related to the Structural Integrity of Cerebral White Matter." *Neurology* 81 (11): 971–6. https://doi.org/10.1212/WNL.0b013e3182a43e33.

Hensch, Takao K. 2004. "Critical Period Regulation." *Annual Review of Neuroscience* 27: 549–79. https://doi.org/10.1146/annurev.neuro.27.070203.144327.

Hubel, David H., and Torsten N. Wiesel. 1962. "Receptive Fields, Binocular Interaction and Functional Architecture in the Cat's Visual Cortex." *Journal of Physiology* 160 (1): 106–54. https://dx.doi.org/10.1113%2Fjphysiol.1962.sp006837.

Hubel, David H., and Torsten N. Wiesel. 1970. "The Period of Susceptibility to the Physiological Effects of Unilateral Eye Closure in Kittens." *Journal of Physiology* 206 (2): 419–36. https://doi.org/10.1113/jphysiol.1970.sp009022.

Jones, Ernest. 1922. "Some Problems of Adolescence." *British Journal of Psychology* 13 (1): 31–47. https://doi.org/10.1111/j.2044-8295.1922.tb00075.x.

Knudsen, Eric I. 2004. "Sensitive Periods in the Development of the Brain and Behavior." *Journal of Cognitive Neuroscience* 16 (8): 1412–25. https://doi.org/10.1162/0898929042304796.

Maharjan, Reeju, Liliana Diaz Bustamante, Kyrillos N. Ghattas, Shahbakht Ilyas, Reham Al-Refai, and Safeera Khan. 2020. "Role of Lifestyle in Neuroplasticity and Neurogenesis in an Aging Brain." *Cureus* 12 (9): e10639. https://doi.org/10.7759/cureus.10639.

McGowan, Patrick O., Matthew Suderman, Aya Sasaki, Tony C. T. Huang, Michael Hallett, Michael J. Meaney, and Moshe Szyf. 2011. "Broad Epigenetic Signature of Maternal Care in the Brain of Adult Rats." *PloS One* 6 (2): e14739. https://doi.org/10.1371/journal.pone.0014739.

Meaney, Michael J., and Moshe Szyf. 2005. "Maternal Care as a Model for Experience-Dependent Chromatin Plasticity?" *Trends in Neurosciences* 28 (9): 456–63. https://doi.org/10.1016/j.tins.2005.07.006.

Montessori, Maria. 1949. *The Absorbent Mind*. Madras, India: Theosophical Publishing House.

Montessori, Maria. 1952. *La Mente del Bambino: Mente Assorbente*. Milano: Garzanti.

Montessori, Maria. 1995. *The Absorbent Mind*. New York: Henry Holt.

Partis, Mary. 2000. "Bowlby's Attachment Theory: Implications for Health Visiting." *British Journal of Community Nursing* 5 (10): 499–503. https://doi.org/10.12968/bjcn.2000.5.10.12988.

Pedersen, Bente Klarlund. 2019. "Physical Activity and Muscle–Brain Crosstalk." *Nature Reviews Endocrinology* 15 (7): 383–92. https://doi.org/10.1038/s41574-019-0174-x.

Penfield, Wilder, and Edwin Boldrey. 1937. "Somatic Motor and Sensory Representation in the Cerebral Cortex of Man as Studied by Electrical Stimulation." *Brain* 60 (4): 389–443. https://doi.org/10.1093/brain/60.4.389.

Phillips, C. G., S. Zeki, and H. B. Barlow. 1984. "Localization of Function in the Cerebral Cortex: Past, Present and Future." *Brain* 107 (1): 328–61. https://doi.org/10.1093/brain/107.1.328.

Radesky, Jenny S., and Dimitri A. Christakis. 2016. "Increased Screen Time: Implications for Early Childhood Development and Behavior." *Pediatric Clinics of North America* 63 (5): 827–39. https://doi.org/10.1016/j.pcl.2016.06.006.

Regni, Raniero, and Leonardo Fogassi. 2019. *Maria Montessori e le Neuroscienze*. Roma: Fefè.

Rizzolatti, Giacomo, and Corrado Sinigaglia. 2016. "The Mirror Mechanism: A Basic Principle of Brain Function." *Nature Reviews Neuroscience* 17 (12): 757–65. https://doi.org/10.1038/nrn.2016.135.

Ruotsalainen, Ilona, Tetiana Gorbach, Jaana Perkola, Ville Renvall, Heidi J. Syväoja, Tuija H. Tammelin, Juha Karvanen et al. 2020. "Physical Activity, Aerobic Fitness, and Brain White Matter: Their Role for Executive Functions in Adolescence." *Developmental Cognitive Neuroscience* 42: 100765. https://doi.org/10.1016/j.dcn.2020.100765.

Sale, Alessandro, Nicoletta Berardi, and Lamberto Maffei. 2009. "Enrich the Environment to Empower the Brain." *Trends in Neurosciences* 32 (4): 233–9. https://doi.org/10.1016/j.tins.2008.12.004.

Spitz, René. 1945. "Hospitalism: An Inquiry into the Genesis of Psychiatric Conditions in Early Childhood." *Psychoanalytical Study of the Child* 1: 53–74. https://doi.org/10.1080/00797308.1945.11823126.

Stern, William. 1930. *Psychology of Early Childhood: Up to the Sixth Year of Age*. London: Routledge.

Vallée-Tourangeau, Frédéric, Miroslav Sirota, and Gaëlle Vallée-Tourangeau. 2016a. "Interactivity Mitigates the Impact of Working Memory Depletion on Mental Arithmetic Performance." *Cognitive Research: Principles and Implications* 1 (1): 26. http://dx.doi.org/10.1186/s41235-016-0027-2.

Vallée-Tourangeau, Frédéric, Sune Vork Steffensen, Gaëlle Vallée-Tourangeau, and Miroslav Sirota. 2016b. "Insight with Hands and Things." *Acta Psychologica* 170: 195–205. https://doi.org/10.1016/j.actpsy.2016.08.006.

van Praag, Henriette, Tiffany Shubert, Chunmei Zhao, and Fred H. Gage. 2005. "Exercise Enhances Learning and Hippocampal Neurogenesis in Aged Mice." *Journal of Neuroscience* 25 (38): 8680–5. https://doi.org/10.1523/JNEUROSCI.1731-05.2005.

Wilson, Frank R. 2010. *The Hand: How Its Use Shapes the Brain, Language, and Human Culture*. New York: Random House.

Zhang, Tie-Yuan, Ian C. Hellstrom, Rosemary C. Bagot, Xianglan Wen, Josie Diorio, and Michael J. Meaney. 2010. "Maternal Care and DNA Methylation of a Glutamic Acid Decarboxylase 1 Promoter in Rat Hippocampus." *Journal of Neuroscience* 30 (39): 13130–7. https://doi.org/10.1523/JNEUROSCI.1039-10.2010.

Chapter 19
A Logic Model for Informing Montessori Research

Brooke Culclasure and Sally Morris Cote

Researchers regularly use logic models to inform designing aspects when conducting a research study. A logic model uses a graphic format to depict core components and activities, underlying assumptions, and intended outcomes of a program. The model strives to create a widely shared and accepted understanding of an intervention or curriculum and the intended effect.

Montessori researchers in the United States have recently begun to increasingly use logic models, striving to align language to create a shared understanding of the core components of Montessori pedagogy and to focus on assessing the outcomes of Montessori experiences. With these goals in mind, while recognizing the need for a common frame of reference for the larger Montessori research community, a group of US researchers developed and published the Logic Model for Montessori Education (Culclasure et al. 2019).

This chapter describes the common uses and potential benefits of using a logic model in research, outlines the potential benefits of a logic model for Montessori research, summarizes the components of the Logic Model for Montessori Education, and discusses the logic model's ability to lay a foundation across disciplines for future research that is rigorous and systematic in its measurement of Montessori processes and outcomes. We first outline the common uses and potential benefits of using logic models in a variety of research contexts.

Use of Logic Models in Research

Originating in the field of evaluation research (Centers for Disease Control and Prevention 1999; United Way of America 1996; Weiss 1997; W. K. Kellogg Foundation 2004), logic models represent a powerful way to succinctly and clearly communicate the core components of a program or approach to communities of practitioners, researchers, and other stakeholders. Used in research in the United States and internationally (Battjes-Fries 2016; Coldwell and Maxwell 2018; Morgan-Trimmer et al. 2018; Rickinson et al. 2016), logic models can act as a collective reference point to reconcile conversations across different disciplines and audiences, providing a common language and starting point for understanding best practices and the ways variations in implementation can lead to differences in results (Knowlton and Phillips 2012; McLaughlin and Jordan 2015). Additionally, by reducing complex narratives and theories to a relatively simple and intuitive flow diagram, these models can increase access to information in audiences that do not have expertise in an area (Knowlton and Phillips 2012). Logic models can help individuals see both the forest and the trees, providing an overall picture of what a multifaceted approach, such as Montessori education, aims to do, while simultaneously considering the way in which each part of the approach affects the whole.

Logic models have been developed in several scholarly disciplines and for a variety of research paradigms in many countries, in part because of the practical applications detailed in this chapter. Instances where scholars have designed logic models for specific approaches and practices can be found throughout the literature. Lafferty and Mahoney (2003) created a logic model for use in studies of US-based health community initiatives. Similarly, Ebenso et al. (2019) constructed a logic model to support an evaluation of a community health worker program for promoting access to maternity services in Nigeria.

An increasing number of examples detailing the use and integration of logic models exists in education research (Byun et al. 2018; Coldwell and Maxwell 2018; Culclasure et al. 2019; Fuller and Templeton 2019; Moore et al. 2015; Stegemann and Jaciw 2018). For example, LaForett and De Marco (2020) published a logic model for practices that is used to reduce racial disparities in student suspension and expulsion in the United States. Several studies from the UK, including England, Wales, and Northern Ireland, leveraged logic models to support evaluations of educational programs ranging from educating children in the early years, educating children with visual impairments, supporting students with disabilities, and evaluating endowment-funded educational programs (Coldwell and Maxwell 2018; Maynard et al. 2013; Scott et al. 2018; Yeşilkaya 2021). In Australia, Rickinson et al. (2016) used a logic model to structure an evaluation of a sustainable schools program; in Norway, Larsen and Holsen (2021) used a logic model to evaluate peer-mentoring roles in a youth development program in upper secondary schools.

Framework for a Montessori Logic Model

The logic modeling process, widely used in program evaluation and design, is a systematic process of documenting how a program or intervention works. Logic modeling results in a visual plan that outlines the connections among a program or intervention's inputs/resources, activities/actions, outputs, short-term outcomes, and long-term impacts. When read from left to right, logic models display how a program works over a specific time—from the acquisition of resources and funding to the implementation of core activities intended to result in desired changes (W. K. Kellogg Foundation 2004). An overview of the components of a logic model, with examples specific to Montessori contexts, is presented in this chapter.

Inputs/Resources

According to the W. K. Kellogg's *Logic Model Development Guide* (2004, 2), inputs/resources are the "human, financial, organizational, and community resources a program has available to direct toward doing the work." This comprises funding and staff to office space, technology, curriculum, and professional development. Didactic materials designed to promote students' concentration, independence, and self-correction are input-specific to Montessori education (Culclasure et al. 2019). Researchers may elect to study nontraditional instructional materials designed to support a child's learning and development across multiple domains. Additionally, the actions and dispositions of teachers and their interactions with students are key areas of research to better understand student outcomes within a Montessori context.

Activities/Actions

Activities/actions are the actual processes and events used to produce intended results of a program or intervention. One action specified in the Logic Model for Montessori Education is individualized learning within an ordered environment (Culclasure et al. 2019). Researchers could examine the processes embedded within Montessori classrooms that are designed to facilitate individualized learning.

Outputs

Typically described numerically, outputs in a logic model reflect the measurable products of activities/actions. Examples in Montessori education include the number of children participating in Montessori programs who are ready to move to the next level of education. Note that outputs do not provide information about the quality of an activity or action.

Short-Term Outcomes

These outcomes refer to the changes in "behavior, knowledge, skills, status, and level of functioning" (W. K. Kellogg Foundation 2004, 2). Outcomes also can be examined at the system level, for example, changes in organizational culture or policy. In Montessori education, expected outcomes specified in the logic model presented in this chapter are participant oriented, focusing on cultivating student behaviors, beliefs, and attitudes (Culclasure et al. 2019). Examples of student outcomes that researchers can examine include increased executive function, creativity, and academic achievement. Studies on these and other outcomes related to Montessori education are detailed in another chapter in this volume (Chapter 21: "Evaluating the Efficacy of Montessori Education").

Long-Term Impacts

Long-term impacts (seven to ten years) are expected to be consistent over a sustained period (W. K. Kellogg Foundation 2004). In the logic model presented in this chapter, we propose that children who participate in authentic Montessori programs over a long period will develop into young adults who are physically healthy, mentally and psychologically fulfilled, highly educated, and active participants in their communities (Culclasure et al. 2019). These constructs are broad and often difficult for researchers to operationalize and measure; thus, research and evaluation typically focus on outcomes rather than impacts.

Benefits of Using a Logic Model for Montessori Research

From a research perspective, increasing understanding of core Montessori components and processes may lead to additional, intentional research collaboration. Establishing a shared understanding of the intended outcomes of Montessori education can facilitate a conversation among researchers about how to standardize outcome operationalization and measurement (Centers for Disease Control and Prevention 1999; Knowlton and Phillips 2012; W. K. Kellogg Foundation 2017). One of the main limitations of prior research on Montessori education is the lack of comparability between study methodologies and results. Currently, Montessori studies exist in isolation because variations in contexts make comparison across studies difficult. Data gathered using the same input and outcome definitions and measurement tools developed from a common logic model could be synthesized to create a foundation on which future studies can build, thus enabling researchers to more easily and accurately identify and attribute data inconsistencies to program implementation rather than to outcome measurement (McLaughlin and Jordan 2015; Newton et al. 2013).

Modeling the Montessori process also opens the door to multiple research opportunities and pathways. Logic modeling explicates core program components and processes that clearly articulate the relationships among program activities, outputs, and outcomes in ways that can inform research questions for process and impact studies (W. K. Kellogg Foundation 2017). Process evaluations examine the fidelity of program implementation regarding the original program model, whereas impact (summative) evaluations assess whether the program had the intended effect on program participants (Bamberger and Mabry 2019). A Montessori logic model serves as an invaluable resource because it establishes the standard aspects of an authentic Montessori program and process. Researchers, particularly those less familiar with Montessori education, can use this model when designing research studies, allowing them to have a consistent understanding of authentic Montessori education and thereby avoiding potentially flawed research designs. Moreover, by connecting the key components of a Montessori education with expected student outcomes, a logic model can help researchers answer questions about the (in)effectiveness of a Montessori program with more precision, preventing the drawing of faulty conclusions (Centers for Disease Control and Prevention 1999; Newton et al. 2013).

Logic models provide researchers a common vocabulary, a shared understanding of activities and expected outcomes, and ideas for valid measurement tools for the outcomes of interest; logic models also have other practical uses that make them important for researchers to consider. At the beginning of the research process, having a solid logic model is an important tool for helping a researcher design a study, whether the study is qualitative, quantitative, or mixed method (Knowlton and Phillips 2012; W. K. Kellogg Foundation 2017). The logic model acts similarly to a hypothesis, illustrating how a program or approach is designed to work to achieve intended results (McLaughlin and Jordan 1999). For researchers, designing a study—from identification of relevant research questions to selection of data collection methods and measurement instruments—is significantly easier with a clear hypothesis in hand. Some logic models, such as the Logic Model for Montessori Education, also include suggested measurement instruments outlined in a clear and organized way with corresponding references; this can help significantly when determining the best methodology to address a given research question. Moreover, a logic model can be extremely helpful to researchers when they are charged with designing measurement instruments from scratch. For example, having clearly defined activities is helpful when designing a survey to measure program implementation and to model fidelity (Holliday 2014).

In addition, logic models frequently are used to help frame studies, particularly the theory of change and literature review sections. The theory of change and literature review sections of a scholarly article are often overwhelming and time-consuming, especially for researchers new to a field. Logic models make the theory of change behind a program or approach transparent, depicting the key elements that, together, should lead to expected outcomes (Knowlton and Phillips 2012; McLaughlin and Jordan 2015; Newton et al. 2013). With an obvious clear theory of change, researchers can more efficiently identify and present literature that points directly to the mechanism of change a study is intending to test. In addition, unlike many logic models, the Logic Model for Montessori Education provides vetted references to help future researchers in this field sort through the myriad sources that typically should be read and synthesized to develop a proper literature review.

Finally, logic models are often required when researchers seek financial support through grant applications for research activities because organizations and government entities expect a researcher to visually illustrate the program or initiative being investigated (Gugiu and Rodríguez-Campos 2007; McLaughlin and Jordan 1999; Scheirer 2000; W. K. Kellogg Foundation 2017). Having a common and peer-reviewed logic model to reference can give Montessori researchers an advantage in the funding process, bringing clarity to the subject for those outside the field and lending legitimacy to theoretical claims about the ways in which a Montessori education leads to specific outcomes (e.g., improved academic performance, greater social fluency, and emotional flexibility).

Using the Logic Model for Montessori Education

Figure 19.1 presents a graphic display of critical components of the Logic Model for Montessori Education (Culclasure et al. 2019). The elements of the Logic Model for Montessori Education were developed by a broad coalition of researchers participating from 2015 to 2019 in the Montessori Research Working Group, which was based on in-depth knowledge of Montessori practices and the appropriate uses of logic models. More details about the development of the Logic Model for Montessori Education are available in Culclasure et al.'s article, *Designing a Logic Model to Inform Montessori Research* (2019).

The Logic Model for Montessori Education is organized in a way that frames the overall influence of Montessori education as facilitating the development of teachers who "model kindness, restraint, humility, enthusiasm, consistency, appreciation, trust, patience, respect, and hope" and of children who are "physically, mentally, and psychologically fulfilled, spiritually nurtured and aware, and highly educated" (Culclasure et al. 2019, 45). Following the description of the overall effect, the contributions of Montessori education are detailed, which include the critical components of authentic implementation such as specific age groupings, requisite

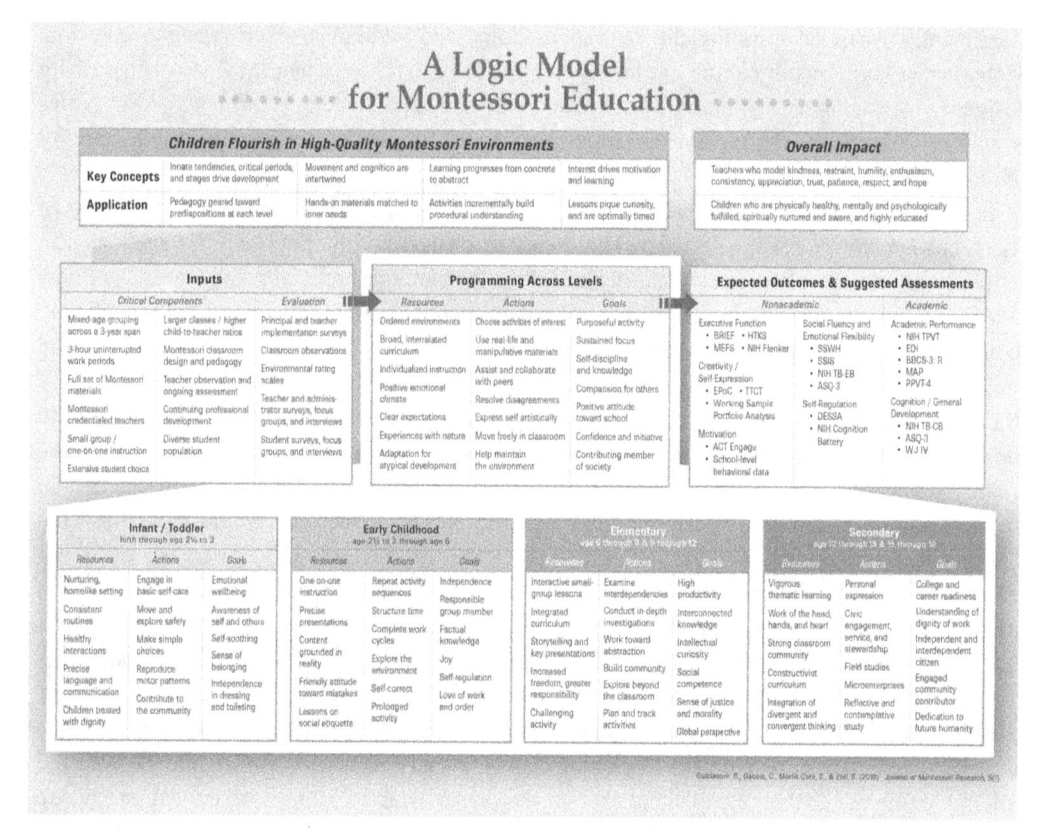

Figure 19.1 Montessori logic model. Image courtesy of the author.

materials, and uninterrupted work periods. Programming resources, actions, and goals are further expanded across the four broad Montessori age groupings—infant/toddler, early childhood, elementary, and secondary—to make the logic model as specific as possible for different age groups. The input and programming sections of the logic model are followed by a description of the expected outcomes of Montessori education and suggested tools to assess them. These outcomes include nonacademic domains such as increased executive functioning, social fluency, and emotional flexibility as well as academic performance and cognitive development.

It is essential to note that this logic model is a living document (Knowlton and Phillips 2012; W. K. Kellogg Foundation 2017), and it is expected that subsequent versions of the logic model, supported by the most current research, will be published in the future. The original article releasing this logic model discusses in detail each section of the model and provides specific references on how content for each section was determined. The article also provides a full listing of suggested validated assessments for the measurement of the outcomes listed in the logic model.

Although the Logic Model for Montessori Education presented in this chapter is the first of its kind for the Montessori research community and is relatively new—published spring 2019—Montessori researchers have already begun to use the model in their work. For example, in 2019, an article published about measurement of Montessori instructional practices was organized around the logic mode's inputs (Murray et al. 2019). Researchers also used the logic model in two articles published in 2021, examining the ways in which Montessori educators responded to the COVID-19 global pandemic to effectively frame the study and to describe the theoretical and philosophical foundations of their inquiry (Murray et al. 2021a, 2021b). The logic model was also referenced in a 2021 article exploring the association between Montessori education in early childhood and adult well-being (Lillard et al. 2021). It is expected that a larger number of researchers will use the logic model in their work as scholars across the world become increasingly aware of its availability and utility.

Conclusion

Logic models are tools that are commonly used in research across the social sciences. The logic model presented in this chapter is a valuable tool for researchers seeking to study Montessori education because the model has the potential to lay a foundation across disciplines for research that is rigorous and systematic in its measurement of Montessori processes and outcomes. The accessible, visual nature of the Montessori logic model displays the core components and activities, underlying assumptions, and intended outcomes of the approach to create a shared understanding that is valuable for researchers, funders, and practitioners. The model facilitates a common understanding of Montessori pedagogy and appropriate assessment of the outcomes of Montessori experiences. Practical applications of logic models make them valuable for helping facilitate research, particularly among scholars that are new to the field, and for increasing the number of rigorous research studies related to Montessori education.

References

Bamberger, J. Michael, and Linda S. Mabry. 2019. *RealWorld Evaluation: Working under Budget, Time, Data, and Political Constraints*, 3rd ed. Los Angeles: SAGE.

Battjes-Fries, Marieke. 2016. "Effectiveness of Nutrition Education in Dutch Primary Schools," PhD diss., Wageningen University, Wageningen, Netherlands.

Byun, Wonwoo, Erica Y. Lau, and Timothy A. Brusseau. 2018. "Feasibility and Effectiveness of a Wearable Technology-Based Physical Activity Intervention in Preschoolers: A Pilot Study," *International Journal of Environmental Research and Public Health* 15 (9): 1821–34. https://doi.org/10.3390/ijerph15091821.

Centers for Disease Control and Prevention. 1999. "Framework for Program Evaluation in Public Health." *Morbidity and Mortality Weekly Report* 48 (RR–11): 1–40.

Coldwell, Mike, and Bronwen Maxwell. 2018. "Using Evidence-Informed Logic Models to Bridge Methods in Educational Evaluation." *Review of Education* 6 (3): 267–300. https://doi.org/10.1002/rev3.3151.

Culclasure, Brooke T., Carolyn J. Daoust, Sally Morris Cote, and Susan Zoll. 2019. "Designing a Logic Model to Inform Montessori Research." *Journal of Montessori Research* 5 (1): 35–49. https://doi.org/10.17161/jomr.v5i1.9788.

Culclasure, Brooke T., Kyle C. Longest, and Troy M. Terry. 2019. "Project-Based Learning (PjBL) in Three Southeastern Public Schools: Academic, Behavioral, and Social-Emotional Outcomes." *Interdisciplinary Journal of Problem-Based Learning* 13 (2). https://doi.org/10.7771/1541-5015.1842.

Ebenso, Bassey, Ana Manzano, Benjamin Uzochukwu, Enyi Etiaba, Reinhard Huss, Tim Ensor, James Newell et al. 2019. "Dealing with Context in Logic Model Development: Reflections from a Realist Evaluation of a Community Health Worker Programme in Nigeria." *Evaluation and Program Planning* 73: 97–110. https://doi.org/10.1016/j.evalprogplan.2018.12.002.

Fuller, Molly J., and Nathan R. Templeton. 2019. "Principal as Servant-Leader: An Embedded-Descriptive Single-Case Study of One Prekindergarten School's Efforts to Build Teacher Capacity in Foundational Skills." *ICPEL Education Leadership Review* 20 (1): 190–204.

Gugiu, P. Cristian, and Liliana Rodríguez-Campos. 2007. "Semi-structured Interview Protocol for Constructing Logic Models." *Evaluation and Program Planning* 30 (4): 339–50. https://doi.org/10.1016/j.evalprogplan.2007.08.004.

Holliday, Lisa R. 2014. "Using Logic Model Mapping to Evaluate Program Fidelity." *Studies in Educational Evaluation* 42: 109–17. https://doi.org/10.1016/j.stueduc.2014.04.001.

Knowlton, Lisa Wyatt, and Cynthia C. Phillips. 2012. *The Logic Model Guidebook: Better Strategies for Great Results*, 2nd ed. Los Angeles: SAGE.

Lafferty, Carolyn K. and Colleen A. Mahoney. 2003. "A Framework for Evaluating Comprehensive Community Initiatives." *Health Promotion Practice* 4 (1): 31–44. https://doi.org/10.1177/1524839902238289.

LaForett, Doré R., and Allison De Marco. 2020. "A Logic Model for Educator-Level Intervention Research to Reduce Racial Disparities in Student Suspension and Expulsion." *Cultural Diversity and Ethnic Minority Psychology* 26 (3): 295–305. https://doi.org/10.1037/cdp0000303.

Larsen, Torill Bogsnes, and Ingrid Holsen. 2021. "Youth Participation in the Dream School Program in Norway: An Application of a Logic Model of the Six Cs of Positive Youth Development." In *Handbook of Positive Youth Development,* edited by R. Dimitrova and N. Wiium, 387–98. Springer: Cham. https://doi.org/10.1007/978-3-030-70262-5_26.

Lillard, Angela S., M. Joseph Meyer, Dermina Vasc, and Eren Fukuda. 2021. "An Association between Montessori Education in Childhood and Adult Wellbeing." *Frontiers in Psychology* 12: 721943. https://doi:10.3389/fpsyg.2021.721943.

Maynard, Trisha, Christopher Matthew Taylor, Samuel Waldron, Mirain Rhys, Robin Smith, Sally Power, and Jennifer Clement. 2013. *Evaluating the Foundation Phase: Policy Logic Model and Programme Theory*. Welsh Government, 37.

McLaughlin, John A., and Gretchen B. Jordan. 1999. "Logic Models: A Tool for Telling Your Programs Performance Story." *Evaluation and Program Planning* 22 (1): 65–72. https://doi.org/10.1016/S0149-7189(98)00042-1.

McLaughlin, John A. and Gretchen B. Jordan. 2015. "Using Logic Models." In *Handbook of Practical Program Evaluation,* 4th ed., edited by Kathryn E. Newcomer, Harry P. Hatry, and Joseph S. Wholey, 62–87. San Francisco: Jossey-Bass.

Moore, Julia E., Brittany Rhoades Cooper, Celene E. Domitrovich, Nicole R. Morgan, Michael J. Cleveland, Harshini Shah, Linda Jacobson, and Mark T. Greenberg. 2015. "The Effects of Exposure to an Enhanced Preschool Program on the Social-Emotional Functioning of At-Risk Children." *Early Childhood Research Quarterly* 32 (3rd Quarter): 127–38. https://doi.org/10.1016/j.ecresq.2015.03.004.

Morgan-Trimmer, Sarah, Jane Smith, Krystal Warmoth, and Charles Abraham. 2018. *Creating a logic model for an intervention: evaluation in health and wellbeing*. England: Public Health.

Murray, Angela K., Jie Chen, and Carolyn J. Daoust. 2019. "Developing Instruments to Measure Montessori Instructional Practices." *Journal of Montessori Research* 5 (1): 75–87. https://doi.org/10.17161/jomr.v5i1.9797.

Murray, Angela K., Katie E. Brown, and Patricia Barton. 2021a. "Montessori Education at a Distance, Part 1: A Survey of Montessori Educators' Response to a Global Pandemic." *Journal of Montessori Research* 7 (1): 1–29. https://doi.org/10.17161/jomr.v7i1.15122.

Murray, Angela K., Katie E. Brown, and Patricia Barton. 2021b. "Montessori Education at a Distance, Part 2: A Mixed Methods Examination of Montessori Educators' Response to a Global Pandemic." *Journal of Montessori Research* 7 (1): 31–50. https://doi.org/10.17161/jomr.v7i1.15123.

Newton, Xiaoxia A., Rebecca C. Poon, Nicole L. Nunes, and Elisa M. Stone. 2013. "Research on Teacher Education Programs: Logic Model Approach." *Evaluation and Program Planning* 36 (1): 88–96. https://doi.org/10.1016/j.evalprogplan.2012.08.001.

Rickinson, Mark, Matthew Hall, and Alan Reid. 2016. "Sustainable Schools Programmes: What Influence on Schools and How Do We Know?" *Environmental Education Research* 22 (3): 360–89. https://doi.org/10.1080/13504622.2015.1077505.

Scheirer, Mary Ann. 2000. "Getting More 'Bang' for Your Performance Measures 'Buck.'" *American Journal of Evaluation* 21 (2): 139–49. https://doi.org/10.1177/109821400002100202.

Scott, Suzi J., Louise D. Denne, and Richard P. Hastings. 2018. "Developing a Logic Model to Guide Evaluation of Impact for Learning Disability Projects: The Case of the Positive Behavioural Support (PBS) Academy." *Tizard Learning Disability Review* 23 (3): 125–32. https://doi.org/10.1108/TLDR-10-2017-0038.

Stegemann, Kim Calder, and Andrew P Jaciw. 2018. "Making It Logical: Implementation of Inclusive Education Using a Logic Model Framework." *Learning Disabilities: A Contemporary Journal* 16 (1): 3–18.

United Way of America. 1996. "Measuring Program Outcomes: A Practical Approach." *Evaluation/Reflection* 47.

Weiss, Carol H. 1997. "Theory-Based Evaluation: Past, Present, and Future." *New Directions for Evaluation* (76): 41–55. https://doi.org/10.1002/ev.1086.

W. K. Kellogg Foundation. 2004. *Using Logic Models to Bring Together Planning, Evaluation, and Action: Logic Model Development Guide*. United States: W.K. Kellogg Foundation.

W. K. Kellogg Foundation. 2017. *The Step-by-Step Guide to Evaluation: How to Become Savvy Evaluation Consumers*. Battle Creek, MI: W. K. Kellogg Foundation.

Yeşilkaya, Eda. 2021. "Using the Medical Research Council Framework for Developing a Logic Model to Support Children with Visual Impairments in Their Learning Environments." *British Journal of Special Education* 48 (1): 7–25. https://doi.org/10.1111/1467-8578.12336.

Chapter 20
Fidelity Issues in Montessori Research

Angela K. Murray and Carolyn Daoust

Program fidelity is an important consideration for researchers studying any type of educational intervention, and unique aspects of Montessori education make the topic of assessing the model's authenticity even more critical and complex. This chapter has two goals: discuss early efforts to ensure the integrity of educational programs using the Montessori name[1] and examine the range of approaches researchers now employ to account for implementation fidelity in their studies. We focus on fidelity issues as they relate to research in this chapter; however, debates about what constitutes authentic Montessori programs also have practical implications linked to efficacy and access.

Today, many authors use the terms "integrity" and "fidelity" interchangeably (Carroll et al. 2007; Durlak and DuPre 2008). In this chapter we use "integrity" when referring to historical efforts to ensure Montessori practices remained true to Maria Montessori's vision and "fidelity" when referring to modern efforts to account for variability in Montessori practices in research studies. Because Montessori's most comprehensive program was designed for the early childhood level (ages 3 to 6), that is our focus for this chapter. A larger volume of research exists for this age group than for older or younger children, so measuring implementation fidelity is even less well developed for other age groups.

Montessori's focus on authenticity in the application of her method predates the scientific study of implementation fidelity, which traces its history to the field of psychiatry in the 1960s (Bond et al. 2000). Put simply, fidelity measurement represents the degree to which a program or intervention follows the original model. Although rigorous examination of fidelity is relatively new to the field, information on implementation fidelity is now expected in high-quality clinical research, education research, and program evaluation. For claims regarding effectiveness to be valid, evidence must show that a study involves a well-defined and replicable program and that the findings represent the results of the program itself rather than an alternative factor (Feely et al. 2018; Mowbray et al. 2003). In the first section, we discuss how issues of program integrity are woven throughout the history of Montessori education and provide important context for researchers today.

History of Efforts to Maintain Montessori Integrity

Issues of maintaining integrity emerged as soon as interest in Montessori's ideas began to grow. As she became a popular public figure, efforts to replicate her success in the first Children's House gained momentum well beyond what she could effectively monitor. Fervent enthusiasm around the world coupled with the limitations of one person's resources resulted in often well-intentioned but still unauthorized efforts that invoked the Montessori name. Although quality control was likely a primary objective, the fact that Montessori operated independently and outside the context of established university institutions required her to consider the practical financial implications of protecting her intellectual property as well (Kramer 1988).

Early Efforts to Maintain Control

In the decade following Montessori's introduction of her educational method in 1907, public interest grew exponentially around the world (see Part V: "Global Montessori Education"). Schools were appearing in countries across western Europe and the United States and also in India, China, Mexico, Japan, Australia, New Zealand, and Argentina; government support for Montessori schools was found in London, Rome, New Zealand, Australia, and the United States. Montessori was concerned about this explosive growth because she believed that failure to implement her method exactly as she intended would result in "distortion and exploitation" (Kramer 1988, 224).

Despite increasing demand for trained teachers around the world—the 1919 training course received 2,000 applicants for 250 places—Montessori initially insisted that she alone was qualified to conduct training courses (Kramer 1988). In fact, training program diplomas included language that authorized the holders to open Montessori schools but not to train others (Standing 1998). Surging interest in Montessori education coupled with a lack of trained teachers led to growth in schools created by individuals who had learned about the approach through books and periodicals but who had not trained through sanctioned courses. It is difficult to discern the degree to which these efforts were well intentioned or simply exploiting Montessori's popularity, but a combination of these sources of inspiration seems likely (Kramer 1988).

Examples of Montessori's early commitment to retaining tight control over teacher training affected the spread and expansion of the movement (see Part V "Introduction: Global Montessori Education"). Although many advocates wished to expand access to Montessori training, the reluctance of Montessori—and later of her son—to permit others to conduct training courses led to conflicts, rescinded teaching credentials, organizational excommunications, and schisms with key proponents in several early supporting countries, including the United States, Germany, and India (Gutek and Gutek 2020; O'Donnell 2014; Wilson 1987). Montessori's efforts to maintain the integrity of her method extended beyond teacher training programs to the distribution of her materials as well. Although the Montessori name was not a legally protected trademark until 1939, the didactic materials were patented by Maria Montessori and were generally distributed under license from her directly.[2] One example of this licensing arrangement is the relationship with the House of Childhood, Inc., in the United States. Montessori herself conducted quality assurance checks to ensure precision and durability. American and British materials manufacturers disclaimed that the "apparatus is not a set of separable toys ... [and] should not be purchased by anyone who does not intend a careful, intelligent use according to the principles of the Montessori method" (Boyd 1914, 14). In the United States, they further stated that "infringers and imitators will be vigorously prosecuted" (Boyd 1914, 14).

Montessori authorized locally organized societies to help spread the word about her educational method across the globe. She envisioned activities of these societies to include newspaper articles, public lectures, fundraising benefits, popular meetings, and regularly scheduled days for visits to schools. However, the growth of these societies prompted concern about unauthorized activities, so Montessori issued the General Regulations for the Formation of an Authorized Montessori Society in 1915 (Gutek and Gutek 2020). This memorandum suggested that, in addition to journalists, businesspeople, and prominent authorities who could support the growth of Montessori education, societies should recruit lawyers as members so they could focus on "'the legal defense of the Method [and] of the name Montessori' so that no school or society could use her name without her authorization" (Kramer 1988, 224).

Montessori had strong reactions to those who engaged in activities related to her educational method without her permission. Upon learning about lectures delivered by her trainees, Montessori wrote a letter to the *New York Times* in 1913 in which she publicly stated that only the training courses she conducted in Rome were authorized (Kramer 1988). In response to an American author's manual outlining the method for teachers and parents, Montessori wrote a letter in 1914 to the *Times Educational Supplement* in London to renounce the book and state she would not be responsible for the lack of success from relying on the book (Kramer 1988). Even when she began to authorize others to train teachers in her method, after initially insisting that she was the only person qualified to do so, Montessori implemented strategies to retain control over dissemination.

Strategies for Growth

During the First World War, Montessori began to designate representatives to give training courses, which made availability more consistent. The Netherlands was one of the first countries where she allowed the establishment of a local teacher training system because the war made it impossible for her to personally conduct courses there (Kramer 1988). Shortly thereafter, she appointed Helen Parkhurst to conduct teacher training and to represent her in all aspects of Montessori education in the United States, although the arrangement was brief and ended when Parkhurst left to develop her own educational ideas into the Dalton method (Gutek and Gutek 2020). By personally selecting trainers to continue her work, Montessori expanded the pool of qualified teachers significantly while maintaining a direct role in ensuring consistency in the method's implementation. In subsequent years, Montessori representatives brought teacher training to Calgary, Berlin, London, Santiago, Dublin, and around India with Montessori's blessing (Kahn and Barnett 2007; Wilson 1987).

In 1929, the Association Montessori Internationale (AMI) was created to counteract the fragmentation of Montessori education and to consolidate efforts under the direction of Montessori along with her son, Mario Montessori (Kramer 1988). The organization's primary purpose was to internationally sustain the quality of Montessori schools, societies, and training. In addition, the organization would control rights to the publication of Montessori's books and the sale of the materials she designed. Upon her death, Mario was appointed her successor in directing and continuing the work of AMI. He also embraced his mother's legacy of attempting to maintain the integrity of the Montessori name around the world. Examples of these efforts are evident in the United States and in India. In the United States, the rift with Nancy McCormick Rambusch over the establishment of an American version of Montessori education resulted in the creation of the American Montessori Society (AMS; see Chapter 46: "Montessori Education in the United States"; Kramer 1988). In fact, a trademark battle occurred during the 1960s between AMS and AMI over exclusive rights to use the Montessori name. The US courts ultimately ruled that the term "Montessori" was not protected because of its generic usage and could thus be used by any organization (Povell 2010). Similarly, Mario threatened members of AMI in India with legal action in the 1960s and 1970s in response to unauthorized use of the Montessori name, which he claimed resulted in poor outcomes and damage to the Montessori reputation (Association Montessori Internationale/India 1963, 1971). Although Montessori education is widespread in the United States and India today, these conflicts around maintaining the integrity of Montessori practices have grown into organizational schisms that slowed Montessori growth and accessibility (see Chapter 40: "Montessori Education in India" and Chapter 46: "Montessori Education in the United States").

Current Trends

Despite Montessori's efforts during her lifetime—and the efforts of others in the years after her death—to limit what she saw as the dilution of a complete and coherent educational program, practical realities continue to exert pressure for modifications to the method as originally introduced. In fact, even beyond Montessori education, the field of implementation science discusses adaptation as sometimes necessary or desirable to address diverse local needs and to allow new ideas to spread more broadly (Durlak and DuPre 2008). The tension between growth and fidelity in Montessori education continues today largely because of its expansion in more diverse geographic regions; in broader socioeconomic, racial, ethnic, and diverse abilities contexts; and in government-funded programs (Debs 2019).

Although differences are found in global definitions of what constitutes authentic Montessori practice, broad agreement exists on fundamental criteria, which include mixed age groupings, teachers with Montessori training, emphasis on Montessori materials, children's freedom of choice, and blocks of uninterrupted work time (Murray et al. 2022). Within each of these criteria, however, debate remains about how much variability from Montessori's original model is acceptable. As efforts to define authentic Montessori practice emerge, the field must consider the effect of cultural context as well as local resources on implementation (see Part V "Introduction: Global Montessori Education").

Although Montessori argued that her approach is universal and many authors suggest that cultural responsiveness is embedded within the model, particularly in Practical Life activities, educators often modify the approach to better suit the cultural and political priorities of national and local communities (Chen and Guo 2021; Kai 2009; Lillard 2019; Schonleber 2011; Shuker 2004). In addition, limited access to teacher training and manufactured materials affect how Montessori is implemented in some areas of the world, particularly the Global South (see Part V "Introduction: Global Montessori Education").

As government-funded Montessori programs proliferate, they are subject to evaluation based on traditional education system criteria, including narrow definitions of academic achievement.

Even though the unique character of Montessori education is the basis for its popularity, performance pressure leads some parents, administrators, and policymakers to demand the inclusion, in both public and private Montessori contexts, of more traditional practices that align with required assessments (Lillard 2019). Without administrative support and high-quality training that provide a deep understanding of underlying theory, teachers may modify their classroom practices and revert to more traditional strategies (Lillard 2019).

In this section we traced the path from early efforts to maintain the integrity of the Montessori method to present-day pressures for adaptation. Understanding the challenges in defining and sustaining authentic Montessori programs provides important context for examining the issue of fidelity in Montessori research. Inconsistency in implementation complicates efforts to gauge Montessori education's effectiveness, so researchers' efforts to systematically account for the variation in Montessori practices are discussed in the next section.

Implementation Fidelity in Montessori Research

Despite Montessori and Mario's efforts to ensure the integrity of her method, variety in implementation today continues to create challenges and opportunities for researchers who study Montessori education. Empirical evidence across the field of education consistently demonstrates that studies of higher-fidelity programs tend to show more positive results and lower fidelity can be used to explain negative or null findings (Durlak and DuPre 2008). However, positive results in less authentic environments also raise questions about possible alternative explanations.

Researchers must provide evidence about the Montessori settings they study, but no widely accepted tool exists for assessing Montessori fidelity. Some authors simply state that study sites employ the Montessori method or use Montessori materials (Ahmadpour and Mujembari 2015; Chisnall and Maher 2007; Güven et al. 2020; Tobin et al. 2015). However, while not exhaustive, this section provides an overview of the range of approaches employed, which can be broadly categorized as descriptions of implementation in schools being studied, organizational criteria, assessment tools, or some combination of these.

Descriptions of Implementation in Schools Being Studied

The simplest method researchers use for addressing variation in Montessori practices is describing the structure of the programs being studied. Even when authors provide substantial detail about the schools in their research, readers unfamiliar with Montessori education struggle to determine the degree of fidelity those practices represent. However, study site descriptions often include insufficient information to assess the quality of Montessori implementation. The following examples show two ways researchers describe their research sites. In a study where children were randomly assigned to a Montessori treatment group or a control group, Kayılı found that the treatment group, described as "educated through the Montessori Method by certificated Montessori educators in a classroom arranged in accordance with the Montessori Method" (2018, 4), was more reflective and less impulsive than the control group. In a favorable comparison of math and science test scores of US high school students who had or had not attended urban public Montessori preschool and elementary programs, Dohrmann et al. described the schools as "well-established and considered to have good Montessori implementation," with rigorously trained teachers, multiage groupings of students, and offering participating students eight to nine years of Montessori education (2007, 209–10).

In other situations, limited details are a direct result of the study design, as in the case of secondary analysis similar to that conducted by Ansari and Winsler (2014). The authors found that Latinx Montessori students in a large urban public school district in the United States had more positive outcomes on preacademic skills assessments at the end of preschool than students in a separate preschool program, but they acknowledged that information was lacking about how the Montessori programs were implemented. As a result, conclusions of Montessori's effectiveness, or lack thereof, are significantly impacted by the confounding variable of Montessori implementation.

Montessori Organizational Criteria

Several more recent studies rely on criteria from Montessori organizations as evidence that study sites implement Montessori programs with fidelity. Organizations around the world that work to support and expand Montessori education have established standards, with varying levels of specificity, to ensure program quality (Debs et al. 2022). Lillard et al. (2017) and Denervaud et al. (2019) leveraged criteria from AMI and its affiliated organization, AMI/USA, in their studies. Consistency across AMI training programs and accreditation requirements make AMI an attractive quality proxy for research purposes. In the United States, Lillard et al. (2017) found superior outcomes for Montessori preschoolers on academic and socioemotional outcomes based on randomized lottery-based admission designs. Similarly, in Switzerland, Denervaud et al. (2019) used AMI criteria for teacher training, Montessori materials, use of work time, and use of mixed ages to provide evidence of the quality of the five schools in which Montessori students outperformed children from traditional schools on academics, creativity, and self-reported well-being.

Assessment Tools

Some researchers have developed assessment tools to evaluate the fidelity of individual Montessori classrooms. These tools have taken the form of teacher questionnaires and observation instruments. The authors of this chapter developed the Teacher Questionnaire of Montessori Practices based on the Logic Model for Montessori Education (see Chapter 19: "A Logic Model Informing Montessori Research") along with standards from international Montessori organizations, prior implementation research, and the writings of Montessori and other respected Montessori experts (Murray et al. 2019). Although the questionnaire has not yet been used in research to examine Montessori outcomes, a pilot study in the United States supported three hypothesized dimensions of Montessori implementation, including program structure, curriculum, and freedom. A research team in the Netherlands has adapted the Teacher Questionnaire of Montessori Practices for the Dutch context and has published a paper along with a spreadsheet, allowing schools to evaluate their own implementation (de Brouwer 2020).

In other studies, researchers have developed observation tools to gather information about what occurs in classrooms. In a study in the United States, Lillard (2012) employed an observation checklist of materials students were engaged with to study the impact of children exclusively using Montessori materials rather than supplemental materials. Trained observers used a list to record what each child was doing during 5-minute snapshots. In the classrooms she labeled as "classic," 95 percent to 100 percent of children were engaged with Montessori materials. In classrooms termed "supplemented," only 38 percent to 56 percent were doing so (Lillard 2012, 389). "Conventional" classrooms, which offered no Montessori materials, were included for comparison (Lillard 2012, 389). Relative to children in the supplemented and the conventional classrooms, children in classic Montessori settings experienced superior school-year gains on executive function, reading, math, vocabulary, and social problem-solving outcomes.

In an Italian setting, researchers designed a checklist for teachers to use as a self-evaluation tool for monitoring the gap between actual implementation and Montessori theory (Caprara 2018). The checklist applied to four areas—the classroom environment, the child, the material, and the teacher—and included dichotomous items representing presence or absence of a characteristic and items gauging intensity or frequency using a five-point Likert scale. Although the article does not provide citations for each item and outcomes were not measured, the checklist content aligns with other tools discussed in this chapter.

A recent 2021 randomized-controlled study in the French public school system examined the effects of Montessori education on academic, cognitive, and social development of economically disadvantaged preschoolers (Courtier et al. 2021). Researchers compared adapted public Montessori programs to high-fidelity AMI programs and conventional programs in the same city. To address programmatic variability, the authors developed a scale to assess fidelity of Montessori implementation based on three subscales: proportion of Montessori materials present; number of characteristics of Montessori education present based on Montessori's writings and the Lillard (2012) study, which required teacher input and observations; and proportion of children engaged in Montessori activities at a particular point in time, also based on Lillard's (2012) study. Findings suggested relatively high scores for both public and private Montessori classrooms on the activities and characteristics scales, but fidelity scores for public programs were lower than private schools. The study concluded that the adapted Montessori curriculum produced results comparable to the conventional program in math, executive functions, and social skills, whereas children from the Montessori public school in the economically disadvantage neighborhood surpassed their peers on reading, with their performance comparable to children who attended private school. Outcomes for the children in the private school surpassed those of students in conventional and adapted-Montessori classrooms overall, but confounding factors cannot be ruled out as a contributing factor.

Conclusion

The conflicting goals of expanding Montessori education and maintaining authenticity were issues for Montessori, beginning in the earliest days of growing interest in her method, and they are issues that continue in Montessori research today. In this chapter we discussed the history of efforts to sustain program integrity woven throughout the history of Montessori education, and we outlined the various approaches that researchers take to assess fidelity today. Future research on the effects of Montessori education will require authors to address fidelity considerations. Our goal here is to provide a broad understanding of the unique fidelity issues related to the growing body of scientific knowledge about Montessori education. Increased interest in accounting for variation in Montessori implementation is leading to more robust tools for measuring fidelity, which will strengthen understanding and evaluation of Montessori efficacy over the long term.

Notes

1. The name "Montessori" was formally registered as an international trademark in 1939, renewed in 1959, and then in 2003 it was ruled that the mark/brand had degenerated (https://www3.wipo.int/madrid/monitor/en/showData.jsp?ID=ROM.220723).
2. From 1909–32, Maria Montessori had at least eighteen international patents to her name that concerned materials related to her method of educational instruction (https://patents.google.com and https://www.epo.org/).

References

Ahmadpour, Nooshin, and Adis Kraskian Mujembari. 2015. "The Impact of Montessori Teaching Method on IQ Levels of 5-Year Old Children." *Procedia—Social and Behavioral Sciences* 205 (May): 122–7. https://doi.org/10.1016/j.sbspro.2015.09.037.

Ansari, Arya, and Adam Winsler. 2014. "Montessori Public School Pre-K Programs and the School Readiness of Low-Income Black and Latino Children." *Journal of Educational Psychology* 106 (4): 1066–79. https://doi.org/10.1037/a0036799.

Association Montessori Internationale/India. 1963. "News of the Montessori Movement." *Around the Child* 8: 84–94.

Association Montessori Internationale/India. 1971. "News of the Montessori Movement." *Around the Child* 14: 92–104.

Bond, Gary R., Lisa Evans, Michelle P. Salyers, Jane Williams, and Hea-Won Kim. 2000. "Measurement of Fidelity in Psychiatric Rehabilitation." *Mental Health Services Research* 2 (2) (June): 75–87. https://doi.org/10.1023/A:1010153020697.

Boyd, William. 1914. *From Locke to Montessori: A Critical Account of the Montessori Point of View*. London: G.G. Harrap.

Caprara, Barbara. 2018. "Between Action and Theory: A Check List for Teachers Self-Evaluation in Montessori Contexts." *Form@re—Open Journal Per La Formazione in Rete* 18 (3): 322–31. https://doi.org/10.13128/formare-23930.

Carroll, Christopher, Malcolm Patterson, Stephen Wood, Andrew Booth, Jo Rick, and Shashi Balain. 2007. "A Conceptual Framework for Implementation Fidelity." *Implementation Science* 2 (40) (November): 315–40. https://doi.org/10.1186/1748-5908-2-40.

Chen, Amber, and Shu Lin Guo. 2021. "The Spread of Montessori Education in Mainland China." *Journal of Montessori Research & Education* 3 (1): 1–8. http://doi.org/10.16993/jmre.17.

Chisnall, Nicola, and Marguerite Maher. 2007. "Montessori Mathematics in Early Childhood Education." *Curriculum Matters* 3: 6+. https://link.gale.com/apps/doc/A180749120/AONE?u=anon~e9784490&sid=googleScholar&xid=6fafb6f6.

Courtier, Philippine, Marie-Line Gardes, Jean-Baptiste Van der Henst, Ira A. Noveck, Marie-Caroline Croset, Justine Epinat-Duclos, Jessica Léone et al. 2021. "Effects of Montessori Education on the Academic, Cognitive, and Social Development of Disadvantaged Preschoolers: A Randomized Controlled Study in the French Public-School System." *Child Development* 92 (5) (September/October): 2069–88. https://doi.org/10.1111/cdev.13575.

De Brouwer, Jaap. 2020. "Vragenlijst Montessori Implementatie." Saxion University of Applied Sciences. www.saxion.nl/onderzoek/meer-onderzoek/vernieuwingsonderwijs/montessori-nl.

Debs, Mira. 2019. *Diverse Families, Desirable Schools: Public Montessori in the Era of School Choice.* Cambridge, MA: Harvard Education Press.

Debs, Mira, Jaap de Brouwer, Angela K. Murray, Lynne Lawrence, Megan Tyne, and Candice von der Wehl. 2022. "Global Diffusion of Montessori Schools: A Report From the 2022 Global Montessori Census." *Journal of Montessori Research* 8 (2): 1–15. https://doi.org/10.17161/jomr.v8i2.18675.

Denervaud, Solange, Jean-François Knebel, Patric Hagmann, and Edouard Gentaz. 2019. "Beyond Executive Functions, Creativity Skills Benefit Academic Outcomes: Insights from Montessori Education." *PLOS ONE* 14 (11): 1–13. https://doi.org/10.1371/journal.pone.0225319.

Dohrmann, Kathryn Rindskopf, Tracy K. Nishida, Alan Gartner, Dorothy Kerzner Lipsky, and Kevin J. Grimm. 2007. "High School Outcomes for Students in a Public Montessori Program." *Journal of Research in Childhood Education* 22 (2) (November): 205–17. https://doi.org/10.1080/02568540709594622.

Durlak, Joseph A., and Emily P. DuPre. 2008. "Implementation Matters: A Review of Research on the Influence of Implementation on Program Outcomes and the Factors Affecting Implementation." *American Journal of Community Psychology* 41 (3–4): 327–50. https://doi.org/10.1007/s10464-008-9165-0.

Feely, Megan, Kristen D. Seay, Paul Lanier, Wendy Auslander, and Patricia L. Kohl. 2018. "Measuring Fidelity in Research Studies: A Field Guide to Developing a Comprehensive Fidelity Measurement System." *Child and Adolescent Social Work Journal* 35 (2): 139–52. http://dx.doi.org/10.1007/s10560-017-0512-6.

Gutek, Gerald L., and Patricia A. Gutek. 2020. *America's Early Montessorians: Anne George, Margaret Naumburg, Helen Parkhurst, and Adelia Pyle.* Cham, Switzerland: Palgrave.

Güven, Yıldız, Cihat Gültekin, and A. Beyzanur Dedeoğlu. 2020. "Comparison of Sudoku Solving Skills of Preschool Children Enrolled in the Montessori Approach and the National Education Programs." *Journal of Education and Training Studies* 8 (3) (March): 32–47. http://redfame.com/journal/index.php/jets/article/view/4620/4873.

Kahn, David, and Elise B. Barnett. 2007. "A Montessori Journey, 1907–2007: The NAMTA Centenary Exhibit." *NAMTA Journal* 32 (3): 1–195.

Kai, Kimiko. 2009. "The Modification and Adaptation of Montessori Education in Japan." *International Journal of Learning Annual Review* 16 (7): 667–76. https://doi.org/10.18848/1447-9494/CGP/v16i07/46431.

Kayılı, Gökhan. 2018. "The Effect of Montessori Method on Cognitive Tempo of Kindergarten Children." *Early Child Development and Care* 188 (3): 327–35. https://doi.org/10.1080/03004430.2016.1217849.

Kramer, Rita. 1988. *Maria Montessori: A Biography.* New York: Diversion Books.

Lillard, Angeline S. 2012. "Preschool Children's Development in Classic Montessori, Supplemented Montessori, and Conventional Programs." *Journal of School Psychology* 50 (3): 379–401. https://doi.org/10.1016/j.jsp.2012.01.001.

Lillard, Angeline S. 2019. "Shunned and Admired: Montessori, Self-Determination, and a Case for Radical School Reform." *Educational Psychology Review* 31 (April): 939–65. https://doi.org/10.1007/s10648-019-09483-3.

Lillard, Angeline S., Megan J. Heise, Eve M. Richey, Xin Tong, Alyssa Hart, and Paige M. Bray. 2017. "Montessori Preschool Elevates and Equalizes Child Outcomes: A Longitudinal Study." *Frontiers in Psychology* 8: 1783. https://doi.org/10.3389/fpsyg.2017.01783.

Mowbray, Carol T., Mark C. Holter, Gregory B. Teague, and Deborah Bybee. 2003. "Fidelity Criteria: Development, Measurement, and Validation." *American Journal of Evaluation* 24 (3) (September): 315–40. https://doi.org/10.1177/109821400302400303.

Murray, Angela K., Jie Chen, and Carolyn J. Daoust. 2019. "Developing Instruments to Measure Montessori Instructional Practices." *Journal of Montessori Research* 5 (1) (Spring): 75–87. https://doi.org/10.17161/jomr.v5i1.9797.

O'Donnell, Marion. 2014. *Maria Montessori*. London: Bloomsbury.

Povell, Phyllis. 2010. *Montessori Comes to America: The Leadership of Maria Montessori and Nancy McCormick Rambusch*. Lanham, MD: University Press of America.

Schonleber, Nanette S. 2011. "Hawaiian Culture-Based Education and the Montessori Approach: Overlapping Teaching Practices, Values, and Worldview." *Journal of American Indian Education* 50 (3): 5–25.

Shuker, Mary Jane. 2004. "The Historical Evolution and Contemporary Status of Montessori Schooling in New Zealand, as an Example of the Adaptation of an Alternative Educational Ideal to a Particular National Context." PhD diss., Massey University, Palmerston North, New Zealand. http://hdl.handle.net/10179/2117.

Standing, E. M. 1998. *Maria Montessori: Her Life and Work*. New York: Plume.

Tobin, Tierney, Prairie Boulmier, Wenyi Zhu, Paul Hancock, Peter Muennig. 2015. "Improving Outcomes for Refugee Children: A Case Study on the Impact of Montessori Education along the Thai-Burma Border." *International Education Journal: Comparative Perspectives* 14 (3): 138–49.

Wilson, Carolie Elizabeth. 1987. *Montessori in India: A Study of the Application of Her Method in a Developing Country*. PhD diss., University of Sydney. http://hdl.handle.net/2123/12044.

Chapter 21
Evaluating the Efficacy of Montessori Education

Karen Manship

Montessori schools can be found in 148 countries, with a 2022 census estimating nearly 15,800 Montessori schools worldwide (AMI 2020; Debs et al. 2022). The popularity and widespread use of Montessori education is bolstered by a limited but growing body of evidence showing that it can support students' academic skills, executive functions, and social problem-solving skills. Evidence is most consistent on its effectiveness in supporting language arts skills; research regarding its impact on math skills is more mixed. This chapter considers the challenges of evaluating the efficacy of Montessori education and surveys the existing literature. I summarize findings by academic and nonacademic outcomes, identifying those with the strongest research designs and evidence. Most research available in English has been conducted in the United States, but I also summarize studies conducted elsewhere. Despite individual studies' acknowledged limitations, the preponderance of research suggests that Montessori schools can support students' academic skills, executive functions, and social problem-solving skills.

Challenges

Researchers encounter several challenges in evaluating the efficacy of Montessori education, including defining fidelity and establishing what "Montessori" means; determining appropriate student outcomes to measure; and implementing strong controls in study designs. I turn to each in turn.

Fidelity

Understanding Montessori implementation fidelity is a common challenge (see Chapter 20: "Fidelity Issues in Montessori Research"). The Montessori name does not ensure a fully implemented Montessori system because there is no copyrighted or otherwise refereed definition (Marshall 2017). In studies conducted in the 1970s and 1980s with Head Start Montessori preschools, fidelity to Montessori implementation was quite low, with 0.5 to 2 hours per day spent with the specially designed didactic materials rather than three uninterrupted hours, only 4-year-olds in the classroom rather than a mixed-age group, and a minimally trained teacher (Karnes et al. 1983; Miller and Bizzell 1984; Miller et al. 1975). This variability within the

United States is mirrored by its equally high variability internationally, for reasons including resource constraints, profit motives, philosophical orientation, national curricular directives, and cultural contexts (Chen 2021) (see Part III: "Montessori Pedagogy across the Lifespan" for a detailed discussion of Montessori practices and Part V: "Global Montessori Education").

Even among accrediting organizations, criteria defining an accredited Montessori program differ greatly. Association Montessori Internationale standards for early childhood classrooms include three-hour work periods, class sizes of twenty-four to thirty-five, one trained teacher, and Montessori materials but no extraneous learning materials (AMI n.d.). American Montessori Society accreditation standards permit supplemental materials "that meet the needs of the student, … provided that they do not replace the primary use of the Montessori materials" (AMS 2022, 5), allow lower student-to-teacher ratios, and have no work-period requirements. Although many Montessori organizations in specific countries worldwide endorse the same broad principles and structures, details are scarce and varied (Debs et al. 2022).

Diverse Outcomes

Montessori programming, with its whole-child focus, incorporates unique instructional practices to help children achieve optimal development. Research evaluating Montessori programs has thus examined a diverse array of outcomes using a variety of tools (Marshall 2017). Outcomes investigated have included academic skills as well as skills that support learning, including executive functions, theory of mind, social skills, learning behaviors, and creativity (Marshall 2017). Selecting appropriate measures for research that permit comparison can also be hard because Montessori education individualizes the timing of content coverage, so the whole class may not be on the same schedule.

Research Design

Evidence on Montessori programming's efficacy is limited by the rigor of the research designs and by the challenge of comparing children who choose Montessori schools with those who do not, leading to questions about generalizability and alternative explanations for results. The early childhood education pages on the Institute of Education Sciences' What Works Clearinghouse website—an initiative of the U.S. Department of Education that reviews and summarizes studies according to strength of evidence—lack information on Montessori programming because of an insufficient number of studies meeting their criteria (WWC 2005).

Some studies of the Montessori method's effectiveness use inadequate sample sizes or controls to be able to draw confident conclusions about effectiveness. In some cases, students were not randomly assigned or otherwise matched to account for baseline differences between groups (Marshall 2017). Only a few randomized-controlled trials (RCTs), which provide the strongest research evidence, have been conducted. RCTs randomly assign students to receive an intervention, or they use a natural experiment like an enrollment lottery, and then compare students who are admitted with those who are not in order to generate the strongest research evidence.

Studies that use quasi-experimental designs do not use random assignment but still implement controls to avoid drawing faulty conclusions due to preexisting differences in groups or selection bias due to unmeasured systematic differences in students whose families choose Montessori schooling. Some quasi-experimental studies use matching techniques to compare Montessori students to a similar group. Findings from other less rigorous studies are also summarized in this chapter with the caveat that their more limited samples or fewer controls generate weaker evidence. Also included are meta-analyses and other reviews, which account for the strength of the studies they include.

Research Findings on Montessori Efficacy

Evidence from Montessori research is most consistent on its effectiveness in supporting language arts skills; research on the model's impact on math skills is more mixed, with Montessori students performing better primarily when given more conceptual assessments (Basargekar and Lillard 2021). Emerging evidence also indicates that Montessori students may show less anxiety and greater well-being as adults (Lillard et al. in press, 2021). Studies have found particular effectiveness of the Montessori experience for children of color (Brown and Lewis 2017) and low-income students (Lillard et al. 2017). Furthermore, research suggests that greater fidelity to Montessori's original principles may moderate the effects detected, with greater fidelity typically yielding more positive effects (Lillard 2012; Marshall 2017).

The next section provides more details about findings from individual studies of Montessori effectiveness conducted around the world and across grade levels, organized by student outcomes in academic skills and other skills that support learning.

Academic Skills

Many studies have examined the effectiveness of Montessori education in supporting students' academic skills. The strongest evidence comes from studies that used random assignment, with the first of such studies taking place in the United States in the late 1960s and early 1970s. At least two studies randomly assigned preschoolers from low-income families to attend one of several programs, including Montessori schools (Karnes et al. 1983; Miller and Bizzell 1984; Miller et al. 1975). These early RCTs reported stronger cognitive performance for boys in Montessori programs, even though the dosage of the model was notably low and fidelity was less than ideal, as classrooms were not mixed age.

More recent studies have taken advantage of the fact that many public Montessori schools select students through admission lotteries, resulting in a natural experiment with comparison groups. Lillard and Else-Quest (2006), in a study conducted in Milwaukee, Wisconsin, found that 5-year-olds who had attended high-fidelity Montessori programs since age 3 obtained higher scores on assessments of letter and word identification, phonological decoding, and math than children who were wait-listed. A randomized study using public school lotteries in Hartford, Connecticut, found similar effects (Lillard et al. 2017). Equal at their entry at age 3, children in these high-fidelity Montessori programs—particularly those from lower-income families—showed greater growth on measures of academic achievement than their non-Montessori peers three years later. Statistically, three years in a Montessori program virtually eliminated the difference in scores between higher- and lower-income students. A study conducted in France randomized students from low-income neighborhoods to attend either public prekindergarten or an adapted Montessori program. Results showed comparable math performance in both groups; however, the adapted Montessori program had shorter work periods, fewer materials, and less teacher training in Montessori methods than AMI standards require (Courtier et al. 2021). The results of studies with the strongest, randomized designs suggest that early childhood Montessori programs in high-fidelity settings consistently yield advantages for participating students on early academic skills.

Evidence from quasi-experimental studies is more mixed. In a study of public Montessori programs in South Carolina, Culclasure et al. (2018) compared standardized test outcomes for over 7,000 students in early childhood, elementary, and middle school Montessori classrooms with a demographically matched group, controlling for various characteristics. Only students who attended schools that met a minimum level of fidelity to the Montessori model were included in the analysis. Across the state, Montessori students scored significantly higher on English/language arts standardized tests than their peers in all three years examined and higher on mathematics and social studies tests in two of the three years; however, results were mixed in science, with students scoring lower than the comparison group in one year and higher in a later year. Another study in a large urban US district found higher scores in reading for African American third-grade Montessori students compared to their matched peers in traditional schools, but there were no differences on math scores (Brown and Lewis 2017).

Mixed results were also found in a study of students in Milwaukee (Wisconsin) Public Schools that compared high school outcomes for demographically matched Montessori and non-Montessori students who participated in programs from preschool through fifth grade. Students who had participated in Montessori programs showed significantly stronger mathematics and science skills, but no significant group differences were found on English or social studies composite measures (Dohrmann et al. 2007).

Nonrandom studies with fewer controls paint a more varied picture. A comparison of Montessori standardized test scores with overall public district scores in the ten US states with the most public Montessori schools found consistently higher scores for Montessori students in English/language arts in third and eighth grades but mixed results for math, with Montessori schools posting less proficient average scores in third grade but trending toward greater proficiency in eighth grade. Achievement gaps by racial groups were also generally smaller in Montessori schools (Snyder et al. 2022). Three other large but nonrandom studies using US administrative assessment data found that at least some groups of Montessori students scored higher on academic assessments than their non-Montessori peers in pre-K and early elementary grades (Ansari and Winsler 2014, 2022; Rodriguez et al. 2005). One of these studies focused specifically on the Montessori method's effectiveness with Black and Latinx students and found different effects for those two groups; Latinx students attending single-age (i.e., lower fidelity) Montessori programs at age 4 showed larger gains and ended the year scoring above national averages, but Black children showed slightly greater gains when attending traditional pre-K. Ansari and Winsler (2022) looked at students' identification as gifted and talented and at their grade point averages in third grade but found no Montessori advantage. Two other large-scale studies in US districts, also examining administrative data with standardized assessment scores, found mixed effects (Mallett and Schroeder 2015) or no effects (Lopata et al. 2005) for Montessori education. However, many of the public school classrooms studied were low fidelity, and these studies were unable to look at variation in implementation fidelity, given their reliance on administrative data.

Smaller nonrandom studies conducted outside the United States have also produced varied evidence. Several studies have found associations between Montessori education and language skills (Denervaud et al. 2021; Franc and Subotić 2015; Musa and Adeyinka 2021; Peng and Md-Yunus 2014). However, a team in Zurich found that although Montessori students showed an advantage in alphabet knowledge at entry to first grade, this advantage later faded (Elben and Nicholson 2017). A study in Taiwan found no association between Montessori participation and social studies scores in elementary school (Peng and Md-Yunus 2014), and this study as well as at least two others in different countries found an inconsistent relationships between Montessori participation and math skills in preschool and elementary school students (Chisnall and Maher 2007; Chytrý et al. 2020). Importantly, these studies were unable to provide critical information about the nature and fidelity of the Montessori intervention.

Although Montessori schools exist that enroll students up to age 18, few published studies address Montessori secondary education (Marshall 2017). The results of the few studies examining the efficacy of Montessori education in both elementary and secondary grades are more mixed and typically have fewer rigorous controls. In a study comparing multiple comprehensive school reform models, Montessori schools had one of the largest effects on achievement of all the programs reviewed (Borman et al. 2003). However, not all studies have found Montessori programs to be consistently better at producing positive academic outcomes for elementary and secondary students. Mixed results across studies, as well as studies' weak designs, suggest that more research is needed to understand the effect of the Montessori model on both literacy and math skills beyond preschool and kindergarten.

Although the body of research as a whole provides mixed evidence regarding the efficacy of Montessori schooling on students' academic skills, studies with the strongest research designs have found consistent advantages for students attending high-fidelity Montessori programs compared to their peers, particularly in early childhood.

Other Skills Supportive of Learning

Because the Montessori approach aims to support the development of the whole child, it is also critical to look at the evidence for the model's effectiveness in advancing other skills supportive of learning, including executive functions, creativity, response to challenges, and approaches to learning. Mastery orientation—a tendency to pursue a task for complete understanding rather than choosing simpler tasks to experience easier success—and theory of mind—the ability to understand others' perspectives—are linked to long-term success (Dweck and Sorich 1999; Kloo and Perner 2008). Executive functions, which are comprised of skills incorporating self-regulation, working memory, and cognitive flexibility, are also thought to be critical to school success (Meltzer 2018; Zelazo et al. 2016) (see Chapter 25: "Executive Functions in Montessori Education"). Montessori programs are thought to promote these skills in young children through child-selected activities and classroom organization (Bagby and Sulak 2018). Two lottery-based studies in the United States (Lillard and Else-Quest 2006; Lillard et al. 2017) found consistently positive effects of the Montessori method on theory of mind and executive functions compared to wait-listed children. Lillard and Else-Quest (2006) found that 5-year-old Montessori students scored higher on a social problem-solving task and exhibited more positive playground behaviors, and Lillard et al. (2017) found stronger mastery orientation in Montessori students compared to their wait-listed peers. Even a modified Montessori program may provide benefits in social and behavioral skills; the randomized study of Courtier et al. (2021) in France found benefits for preschoolers who attended an adapted Montessori program on executive functions and social skills.

As with academic outcomes, quasi-experimental studies examining other outcomes supportive of learning have shown more varied results. In the study of South Carolina's Montessori program, mixed results were noted for measures of executive functions, and no group differences were found in work habits or social skills. Montessori students did show somewhat greater creativity, with the difference especially notable in boys (Fleming et al. 2019).

Nonrandom studies examining social-emotional outcomes and creativity have also typically found positive associations with Montessori attendance, consistent with studies with stronger designs. Two small studies in Iran describe a positive association of the use of Montessori materials (though limited) and self-directed instruction with reduced anxiety in elementary students (Dhiksha and Suresh 2016; Hajjar 2021). Other small studies have found advantages for Montessori students in social maturity (5-year-olds in Iran; Ahmadpour and Mujembari 2015), emotional recognition (elementary students in Switzerland; Denervaud et al. 2020), and creativity (Besançon and Lubart 2007). Overall, the evidence that the Montessori method is effective at supporting social-emotional and other outcomes supportive of learning is notably consistent.

Future Directions

Research efforts on many aspects of Montessori education are accelerating globally, leading to a rapidly growing body of knowledge. For example, a meta-analysis of research on Montessori early childhood programs in Turkey included twenty-two studies and summarized findings from both qualitative and quantitative analyses (Kiran et al. 2021). Because research is being conducted in many different countries, access to the broad range of published studies is limited by both database coverage and language. Efforts to create an international database of resources and to share translated work would expand our knowledge of the efficacy of Montessori education globally (see Chapter 52: "Future Directions in Global Montessori Research").

With the continued expansion of Montessori programs in US public schools, especially in states with lotteries, more rigorous research is likely in the next decades. At the time of this writing, a study funded by the U.S. Department of Education's Institute of Education Sciences is underway that will take advantage of admission lotteries nationwide to rigorously test the efficacy of the Montessori early childhood model. The study aims to address research gaps by taking advantage of existing lotteries in several school districts; notably, there has never been a large-scale US national study of the Montessori early childhood model that uses a rigorous random design.

Importantly, the studies with the greatest demonstrated efficacy of the Montessori method are those studying programs with high dosage and high fidelity to Montessori's original principles. Research must clearly document the implementation characteristics of the Montessori model, including practices, materials, and timing and duration, so that researchers, policymakers, and practitioners can understand which aspects of the approach are crucial to its efficacy. Investments in research with strong research designs such as random assignment will provide the strongest evidence for future policy and practice decisions.

References

Ahmadpour, Nooshin, and Adis Kraskian Mujembari. 2015. "The Impact of Montessori Teaching Method on IQ Levels of 5-Year Old Children." *Procedia—Social and Behavioral Sciences* 205: 122–7. https://doi.org/10.1016/j.sbspro.2015.09.037.

AMI (Association Montessori Internationale). 2020. "Montessori Schools in 2020." 2020 AMI annual general meeting.

AMI (Association Montessori Internationale). n.d. "Standards for AMI Montessori Classrooms." https://amiusa.org/schools/standards-for-ami-montessori-classrooms/. Accessed April 26, 2022.

AMS (American Montessori Society). 2022. "AMS School Accreditation Standards and Criteria." https://amshq.org/-/media/Files/AMSHQ/Educators/Montessori-Schools/Accreditation/AMS-School-Accreditation-Standards-and-Criteria—Updated-March-2022.ashx?la=en. Accessed April 26, 2022.

Ansari, Arya, and Adam Winsler. 2014. "Montessori Public School Pre-K Programs and the School Readiness of Low-Income Black and Latino Children." *Journal of Educational Psychology* 106 (4): 1066–79. https://doi.org/10.1037/a0036799.

Ansari, Arya, and Adam Winsler. 2022. "The Long-Term Benefits of Montessori Pre-K for Latinx Children from Low-Income Families." *Applied Developmental Science* 26 (2): 252–66. https://doi.org/10.1080/10888691.2020.1781632.

Bagby, Janet, and Tracy Sulak. 2018. "Montessori and Executive Function." *Montessori Life* 30 (1): 15.

Basargekar, Abha, and Angeline S. Lillard. 2021. "Math Achievement Outcomes Associated with Montessori Education." *Early Child Development and Care* 191: 1207–18. https://doi.org/10.1080/03004430.2020.1860955.

Besançon, Maud, and Todd Lubart. 2007. "Differences in the Development of Creative Competencies in Children Schooled in Diverse Learning Environments." *Learning and Individual Differences* 18 (4): 381–9. https://doi.org/10.1016/j.lindif.2007.11.009.

Borman, Geoffrey D., Gina M. Hewes, Laura T. Overman, and Shelly Brown. 2003. "Comprehensive School Reform and Achievement: A Meta-analysis." *Review of Educational Research* 73 (2): 125–230. https://doi.org/10.3102%2F00346543073002125.

Brown, Katie, and Chance W. Lewis. 2017. "A Comparison of Reading and Math Achievement for African American Third Grade Students in Montessori and Other Magnet Schools." *Journal of Negro Education* 86 (4): 439–48.

Chen, Amber. 2021. "Exploration of Implementation Practices of Montessori Education in Mainland China." *Nature Humanities and Social Sciences Communications* 8: 250. https://doi.org/10.1057/s41599-021-00934-3.

Chisnall, Nicola, and Marguerite Maher. 2007. "Montessori Mathematics in Early Childhood Education." *Curriculum Matters* 3: 6–28.

Chytrý, Vlastimil, Janka Medová, Jaroslav Říčan, and Jiří Škoda. 2020. "Relation between Pupils' Mathematical Self-Efficacy and Mathematical Problem Solving in the Context of the Teachers' Preferred Pedagogies." *Sustainability* 12 (23): 10215. https://doi.org/10.3390/su122310215.

Courtier, Philippine, Marie-line Gardes, Jean-Baptiste Van der Henst, Ira A. Noveck, Marie-Caroline Croset, Justine Epinat-Duclos, Jessica Léone, and Jérôme Prado. 2021. "Effects of Montessori Education on the Academic, Cognitive, and Social Development of Disadvantaged Preschoolers: A Randomized Controlled Study in the French Public School System." *Child Development* 92 (5): 2069–88. https://doi.org/10.1111/cdev.13575.

Culclasure, Brooke, David J. Fleming, Ginny Riga, and Alexis Sprogis. 2018. "An Evaluation of Montessori Education in South Carolina's Public Schools." Riley Institute, Furman University.

Debs, Mira, Jaap de Brouwer, Angela K. Murray, Lynne Lawrence, Megan Tyne, and Candice von der Wehl. 2022. "Global Diffusion of Montessori Schools: A Report From the 2022 Global Montessori Census." *Journal of Montessori Research* 8 (2): 1–15. https://doi.org/10.17161/jomr.v8i2.18675.

Denervaud, Solange, Christian Mumenthaler, Edouard Gentaz, and David Sander. 2020. "Emotion Recognition Development: Preliminary Evidence for an Effect of School Pedagogical Practices." *Learning and Instruction* 69: 101353. https://doi.org/10.1016/j.learninstruc.2020.101353.

Denervaud, Solange, Alexander P. Christensen, Yoed N. Kenett, and Roger E. Beaty. 2021. "Education Shapes the Structure of Semantic Memory and Impacts Creative Thinking." *npj Science of Learning* 6 (1): 1–7. https://doi.org/10.1038/s41539-021-00113-8.

Dhiksha, J., and A. Suresh. 2016. "Self-Esteem and Academic Anxiety of High School Students with Montessori and Traditional Method of Education." *Indian Journal of Health and Wellbeing* 7 (5): 543–5.

Dohrmann, Kathryn R., Tracy K. Nishida, Alan Gartner, Dorothy K. Lipsky, and Kevin J. Grimm. 2007. "High School Outcomes for Students in a Public Montessori Program." *Journal of Research in Childhood Education* 22 (2): 205–17.

Dweck, Carol S., and Lisa Sorich. 1999. "Mastery-Oriented Thinking." In *Coping: The Psychology of What Works*, edited by C. R. Snyder, 232–51. Oxford: Oxford University Press.

Elben, Judy, and Tom Nicholson. 2017. "Does Learning the Alphabet in Kindergarten Give Children a Head Start in the First Year of School? A Comparison of Children's Reading Progress in Two First Grade Classes in State and Montessori Schools in Switzerland." *Australian Journal of Learning Difficulties* 22 (2): 95–108. https://doi.org/10.1080/19404158.2017.1399913.

Fleming, David J., Brooke Culclasure, and Daniel Zhang. 2019. "The Montessori Model and Creativity." *Journal of Montessori Research* 5 (2): 1–14. https://doi.org/10.17161/jomr.v5i2.7695.

Franc, Vendi, and S. Subotić. 2015. "Differences in Phonological Awareness of Five-Year-Olds from Montessori and Regular Program Preschool Institutions." In *Dječji jezik i kultura*, edited by Lidija Cvikić, 12–21. Zagreb: Učiteljski fakultet Sveučilišta u Zagrebu.

Hajjar, Nahid. 2021. "The Effect of Montessori's Educational Approach on Anxiety and Self-Efficacy in Elementary Students' Interpersonal Relationships." *Journal of Advanced Pharmacy Education and Research* 11 (suppl 1): 48–55.

Karnes, Merle B., Allan M. Shwedel, and Mark B. Williams. 1983. "A Comparison of Five Approaches for Educating Young Children from Low-Income Homes." In *As the Twig Is Bent: Lasting Effects of Preschool Programs*, edited by the Consortium for Longitudinal Studies, 133–70. Hillsdale, NJ: Erlbaum.

Kiran, Işıl, Bilal Macun, Yusuf Argin, and İlkay Ulutaş. 2021. "Montessori Method in Early Childhood Education: A Systematic Review." *Cukurova University Faculty of Education Journal* 50 (2): 1154–83.

Kloo, Daniela, and Josef Perner. 2008. "Training Theory of Mind and Executive Control: A Tool for Improving School Achievement?" *Mind, Brain, and Education* 2 (3): 122–7. https://doi.org/10.1111/j.1751-228X.2008.00042.x.

Lillard, Angeline S. 2012. "Preschool Children's Development in Classic Montessori, Supplemented Montessori, and Conventional Programs." *Journal of School Psychology* 50 (3): 379–401. https://doi.org/10.1016/j.jsp.2012.01.001.

Lillard, Angeline, and Nicole Else-Quest. 2006. "Evaluating Montessori Education." *Science* 313 (5795): 1893–4. https://doi.org/10.1126/science.1132362.

Lillard, Angeline S., Megan J. Heise, Eve M. Richey, Xin Tong, Alyssa Hart, and Paige M. Bray. 2017. "Montessori Preschool Elevates and Equalizes Child Outcomes: A Longitudinal Study." *Frontiers in Psychology* 8: 1783. https://doi.org/10.3389/fpsyg.2017.01783.

Lillard, Angeline S., M. Joseph Meyer, Dermina Vasc, and Eren Fukuda. 2021. "An Association between Montessori Education in Childhood and Adult Wellbeing." *Frontiers in Psychology* 12: 721943. https://doi.org/10.3389/fpsyg.2021.721943.

Lillard, Angeline S., Jessica Taggart, Daniel Yonas, and Mary N. Seale. in press. "An Alternative to 'No Excuses': Considering Montessori as a Culturally Responsive Pedagogy." *Journal of Negro Education*.

Lopata, Christopher, Nancy V. Wallace, and Kristin V. Finn. 2005. "Comparison of Academic Achievement between Montessori and Traditional Education Programs." *Journal of Research in Childhood Education* 20 (1): 5–13. http://dx.doi.org/10.1080/02568540509594546.

Mallett, Jan Davis, and Jennifer L. Schroeder. 2015. "Academic Achievement Outcomes: A Comparison of Montessori and Non-Montessori Public Elementary School Students." *Journal of Elementary Education* 25 (1): 39–53.

Marshall, Chloe. 2017. "Montessori Education: A Review of the Evidence Base." *npj Science of Learning* 2: 11. https://dx.doi.org/10.1038%2Fs41539-017-0012-7.

Meltzer, Lynn, ed. 2018. *Executive Function in Education: From Theory to Practice*. New York: Guilford.

Miller, Louise B., and Rondeall P. Bizzell. 1984. "Long-Term Effects of Four Preschool Programs: Ninth- and Tenth-Grade Results." *Child Development* 55 (4): 1570–87.

Miller, Louise B., Jean L. Dyer, Harold Stevenson, and Sheldon H. White. 1975. "Four Preschool Programs: Their Dimensions and Effects." *Monographs of the Society for Research in Child Development* 40 (5/6): 1–170.

Musa, Rose Jummai, and Adeyemi Abiodun Adeyinka. 2021. "School Environment and Methods of Teaching as Correlates of Language Skills Achievement of Pre-Primary School Pupils in Edo State Nigeria." *Education Quarterly Reviews* 4 (3): 243–51. http://dx.doi.org/10.31014/aior.1993.04.03.335.

Peng, Hsin-Hui, and Sham'ah Md-Yunus. 2014. "Do Children in Montessori Schools Perform Better in the Achievement Test? A Taiwanese Perspective." *International Journal of Early Childhood* 46 (2): 299–311. http://dx.doi.org/10.1007/s13158-014-0108-7.

Rodriguez, L., B. J. Irby, G. Brown, R. Lara-Alecio, and M. M. Galloway. 2005. "An Analysis of Second Grade Reading Achievement Related to Pre-kindergarten Montessori and Transitional Bilingual Education." In *NABE Review of Research and Practice*, Vol. 3, edited by Virginia Gonzalez and Josefina Tinajero. New York: Routledge.

Snyder, Allyson L., Xin Tong, and Angeline S. Lillard. 2022. "Standardized Test Proficiency in Public Montessori Schools." *Journal of School Choice* 16 (1): 105–35. https://doi.org/10.1080/15582159.2021.1958058.

WWC (What Works Clearinghouse). 2005. "*WWC Summary of Evidence: Montessori Method.*" Washington, DC: U.S. Department of Education, Institute of Education Sciences.

Zelazo, Philip David, Clancy B. Blair, and Michael T. Willoughby. 2016. "Executive Function: Implications for Education." *Institute of Education Sciences (IES), National Center for Education Research (NCER)*. https://ies.ed.gov/ncer/pubs/20172000/. Accessed April 17, 2022.

Chapter 22
Assessment in Montessori Education

Susan Zoll, Laura Saylor, and Arya Ansari

Educational researchers are increasingly focused on evidence-based and holistic classroom assessment practices that encompass the teacher's understanding of clear purposes and targets for assessment, as well as appropriate methodologies to yield accurate results and improve outcomes for all children (Andrade 2010; Brookhart et al. 2019). However, a significant research-to-practice gap still exists with much emphasis from the public, politicians, and policymakers on high-stakes, standardized assessments (Au 2011).

Even though standardized assessments receive significant public attention, classroom assessment—the activities that teachers engage in to understand and document student learning—plays a substantial role in the day-to-day educational interactions of teachers and students around the world (Cumming 2010).

Although Montessori teachers do not usually think of themselves as focused on assessment practices except when required by outside mandates, in reality, assessment strategies are continually employed in a Montessori classroom. These Montessori practices and assessment strategies are aligned with formative-assessment practices, which are assessments that take place throughout the learning process and which researchers are showing yield strong benefits to student learning. To provide context for understanding assessment in Montessori education, we begin this chapter with an overview of assessment in education. We then discuss observation as the integral assessment strategy in Montessori education and provide specific examples of the practical assessment strategies used in Montessori classrooms. Finally, we close with current directions in Montessori assessment.

Overview of Educational Assessment

Assessment tools are generally thought of as fulfilling either formative or summative purposes, as described below, although the distinction can sometimes be blurry (Andrade 2010; Dixson and Worrell 2016). Although high-stakes, large-scale assessments that are so prevalent in the field generally only address summative evaluation questions, classroom assessments can be used for formative or summative purposes.

Formative assessment is a means of providing teachers and programs with information about student understanding during the instructional process, while learning is taking place (Andrade 2010; Bennett 2011; Black and Wiliam 1998; Harlen and James 1997). Teachers use this type of assessment to give students feedback on their learning, inform the next steps in the instructional process, and improve their instruction.

Summative assessment takes place at the end of a lesson, semester, or school year, providing teachers and programs with information and feedback summarizing student learning and achievement. It is often used to identify the degree to which learning objectives were met (Andrade 2010; Bennett 2011; Black and Wiliam 1998; Harlen and James 1997).

Although summative assessment data are typically used in many studies, a growing body of research is beginning to focus on the instructional benefits of formative assessment (Andrade 2010; McManus 2008; Shute 2008). Interest in formative assessment spans multiple countries as evidenced by efforts of the global Organization for Economic Co-Operation and Development (OECD), which has hosted conferences and published reports stressing the potential of formative assessment to improve student learning (OECD 2008). Themes emerging from formative-assessment research suggest the importance of (1) identifying what will be learned and what success looks like, (2) using dialogical learning, (3) offering forward-looking feedback, (4) empowering students with ownership of their learning, and (5) entrusting students to instruct one another (Wiliam 2010).

Overview of Assessment in Montessori Education

Montessori schools serve students from infancy through 18 years of age. However, because of the prevalence of early childhood and elementary Montessori classrooms, this chapter will most specifically speak to these younger ages, especially as assessment practices for Montessori adolescents often mirror those found in many more-traditional junior and senior high school settings.

Not surprisingly, summative standardized tests are implemented in Montessori environments when required by predominantly publicly funded educational settings. In a 2019 survey conducted by the American Montessori Society, Montessori school administrators identified standardized summative assessments used in their schools to report and translate student achievement and learning outcomes including the Stanford Achievement Test, the Dynamic Indicators of Basic Early Literacy Skills, AIMSweb, and the Measures of Academic Progress (MAP).

Although Montessori schools, especially those situated in the public sector, must follow government testing mandates, the use of student-focused, formative, classroom assessment practices are more congruent with the Montessori philosophy and have more practical implications for the instructional process. Therefore, the remainder of this chapter will explicitly focus on classroom assessment strategies in Montessori settings.

Observation at the Core of Montessori Assessment Practices

As a physician and a scientist, Montessori valued careful observation and insisted that her teachers be trained and well practiced in using observation to understand the needs of children (Montessori 1965); from the outset of her career, Montessori valued forms of assessment that differed from those that were used in typical school settings (Standing 1984). Montessori equated systematic and rigorous observation with a primary type of diagnostic or formative assessment so a teacher may understand what a child had understood, where the child was struggling, and then adjust the environment as necessary (Montessori 2012). She explained, "If you do not possess this capacity (to observe), especially this sensitiveness, which allows you to learn the intimate facts, which the children reveal without warning anyone as to which is an important thing or which is worthy of claiming attention, then this sensitiveness, this capacity for observation is the labor you must accomplish in yourselves" (Montessori 2013, 20). For Montessori, observation was assessment, and it was central to the method.

Although two educators may observe the same child at the same time, the more expert observer will likely identify patterns in behavior and, through reflection, make more meaning from what they observe (Ruiz-Primo and Brookhart 2018; Schon 1983, 130). Montessori also recognized how observational data could be influenced by the observer's own biases, an idea that has been supported by decades of educational research (Gilliam et al. 2016; McGrady and Reynolds 2013). To minimize bias, she developed a systematic methodology of observing and assessing students that promotes greater objectivity by asking teachers to separate observations from inferences. This methodology is a significant part of training and daily teacher practice in a Montessori classroom. Further, unlike more typical classrooms in which teachers are expected to spend most of their time engaging with children, Montessori teachers are expected to spend time observing their students at work and meticulously recording those observations.

The ability of a trained Montessori teacher to rigorously observe is seen in the extensive records the teacher keeps regarding lessons given, a child's activity and work, and a child's progress. Further, Montessori called for educators to use these records to inform their work in understanding the development and learning of their students, as well as in planning future learning activities (Montessori 2012). Montessori referred to this as "following the child" (Montessori 2012, 29). This ubiquitous phrase embraced by Montessorians is often misunderstood to mean allowing children the freedom to do whatever they like. What Montessori intended, however, was for teachers who are knowledgeable about children's development to use their thoughtful observations of each child to plan lessons and learning activities that align with the child's location on the developmental and educational continuum as the child moves from simple concepts to more complex ones and from concrete representations to more abstract types of classroom work. As she stated, "[m]y method is founded on the child himself. Our study has its origins in the child. The method has been achieved by following the child and his psychology" (Montessori 2012, 29). Accordingly, "following the child" indicates a teacher using knowledge of children's development and observations of a child and then applying them in planning of formal and informal lessons.

Classroom Assessment in Montessori Education

Montessori teachers today implement a variety of student-centered classroom assessment activities, most of which revolve around observation. Much assessment occurs during the instructional process as teachers offer lessons guiding children to directly interact with Montessori didactic learning materials. Montessori intended for instruction and assessment to be intertwined and inseparable so that children may learn by correcting their own work and making their own discoveries, while the teacher carefully observes and documents the learning process. As an example, the Cylinder Blocks, a series of cylinders varying by width and depth that fit puzzle-like into a wooden block, have a built-in control of error that offers one spot along the wooden block in which a given cylinder properly fits. While observing the child interacting with the material, the teacher notes the degree to which the child has mastered the activity or whether they might benefit from additional similar experiences. Thus, the teacher's assessment documentation includes formal record keeping (identifying which materials were used and when), anecdotal teacher reflections (brief qualitative notes), as well as student work plans and portfolios of student work (Roemer 1999; Thorne 2014).

Teacher-Directed Assessment

Because Montessori teachers deliver lessons primarily to individuals or small groups of children, direct interaction provides an immediate opportunity to gauge understanding. Especially in younger age groups, the three-period lesson is a procedure for assessing understanding as the instructional process is underway (Becker et al. 2022). The assessment strategy was developed by Edouard Séguin, a physician who worked with children with special needs and who influenced Montessori's work and the use of this strategy along with others in her method (Montessori 2017). For example, a teacher providing instruction on letter sounds and symbols might work with a young child on Montessori's Sandpaper Letters, which are individually formed letter shapes made with fine sandpaper, mounted on a small board. What follows is a brief description of the three-period lesson in using Sandpaper Letters to teach a child letter-sound correspondence for the letter sounds /m/, /s/, and /a/.

The teacher places the *m* Sandpaper Letter directly in front of the student and slowly traces the letter. The teacher says the letter sound aloud to the child—/m-m-m/—and then repeats the sequence with the remaining two letters. Next, the teacher invites the child to trace the letter, saying the letter sound aloud as the student traces. This same sequence is followed for all three Sandpaper Letters in the lesson. This process is referred to as the first, or naming, period.

If the child successfully completes this portion of the activity and remains interested, the teacher can now move to the second period, in which they lay out the three Sandpaper Letters on the table in front of them and asks the child (allowing the child to respond to each question):

"Which letter makes the sound /m/?"
"Point to the letter that makes the sound /s/."
"Show me the letter that makes the sound /a/."

This portion of the activity serves as a scaffolded learning opportunity with repetition as the teacher says the sounds and the child simply points to the correct letter (recognition).

After a few rounds of playful inquiry, if the child continues to be successful and interested, the third period of the lesson can begin. In this period, the teacher asks the child to name each letter sound as they point to them (recall).

As highlighted in the example and as implemented in many lessons in the Montessori classroom, during the first period, the educator models the language (naming) as they demonstrate each step of the lesson to the student. Then, during the second period, the teacher assesses learning by asking the student to point to a correct response (recognition). Last, in the third period, the teacher asks the student to respond with the correct name when asked (recall). Simultaneous with conducting the lesson, the teacher notes the student's level of success at each stage and makes in-the-moment decisions regarding the progression of the lesson. This authentic assessment practice formatively guides the teacher's work with each child. Rather than completing a lesson that is not yet understood, the teachers can conclude the lesson at any stage when they determine the child has experienced an appropriate level of challenge while not yet demonstrating mastery (Lillard and McHugh 2019).

Assessment Embedded in Learning Materials

Embedded assessment occurs as a natural part of the learning process (Becker et al. 2022). Montessori learning materials are designed to give evaluative feedback directly to the student. Montessori referred to this as "the control of error," and she designed her materials to not only attract students to learning but also provide direction for that learning (Montessori and Montessori 1988, 26). This direction of learning not only indicates correctness but also reveals the child's understanding to both the child and the teacher, making way for what Montessori referred to as auto-education, during which the learning materials are self-corrective (Lillard 2011). This type of embedded formative assessment—leading to the outcomes of auto-education such as independence, decision-making, confidence, and thoughtful problem-solving—can be observed in materials such as the Pink Tower and the wooden cylinders in early childhood classrooms as well as in the use of control charts (i.e., answer keys) in elementary programs (Murray et al. 2017). As a means of illustration, the classic Pink Tower consists of ten pink, stackable wooden cubes. The smallest cube is 1 cm^3, and the remaining cubes progressively get larger, with the largest one being 10 cm^3. When a young child stacks these cubes, there is a control of error in that if the cubes are out of place, there may be a leftover cube, or they will not stack properly and possibly fall over. Therefore, the child can work independently of the teacher and self-assess whether the activity (in this exercise, the Pink Tower) has been completed accurately.

Observation

Montessori developed a record-keeping document that she referred to as the biographical chart, which provides a framework for teachers' classroom observations using indicators that are relevant even in modern-day classrooms. The tool guided teachers' observations, documenting children's self-selected work and the time the child remained on task, as well as noting behavioral responses to invitations to classroom work. The biographical charts also cataloged information about a child's background, noting the professions of the adults in the home, the number of family members, and information pertaining to the child's physical development and health, among other things (Montessori 2013, 52–3).

In her work, Montessori also prescribed a repeated-measures methodology, widely used in current educational research designs, by collecting student data throughout the academic year. In collecting data at two or more points and analyzing differences, Montessori could assess students' growth over time, which she viewed as critical because "the life of the child is nothing but rapid transformation" (Montessori 2013, 62). Similar to video analysis used to improve teacher practices in classrooms today (Baecher 2019), Montessori was greatly influenced by advancements in technology in the early 1900s; she used and advocated for using photography and early cinematography to showcase teachers' work with children (Montessori 2013, 44). Therefore, it is likely that she would be in favor of continued contextualized and varied assessment methods today.

To further organize teachers' observations, Montessori also provided the diary of individual psychology, a simple notebook that included observations to be filed in the child's individual biographical chart at the end of each day. She anticipated these observations would be analyzed to understand students' learning, much like the assessment cycles described in the previous section (Montessori 2013, 43).

Over time, classroom observations became more systematic and were represented in a format called work curves (Patell 2016, 255; O'Shaughnessy 2016, 61). For example (see Figure 22.1), while observing students during a three-hour work cycle, observations were graphed along three horizontal lines representing (1) a child's restful state of inactivity, recorded along the state of

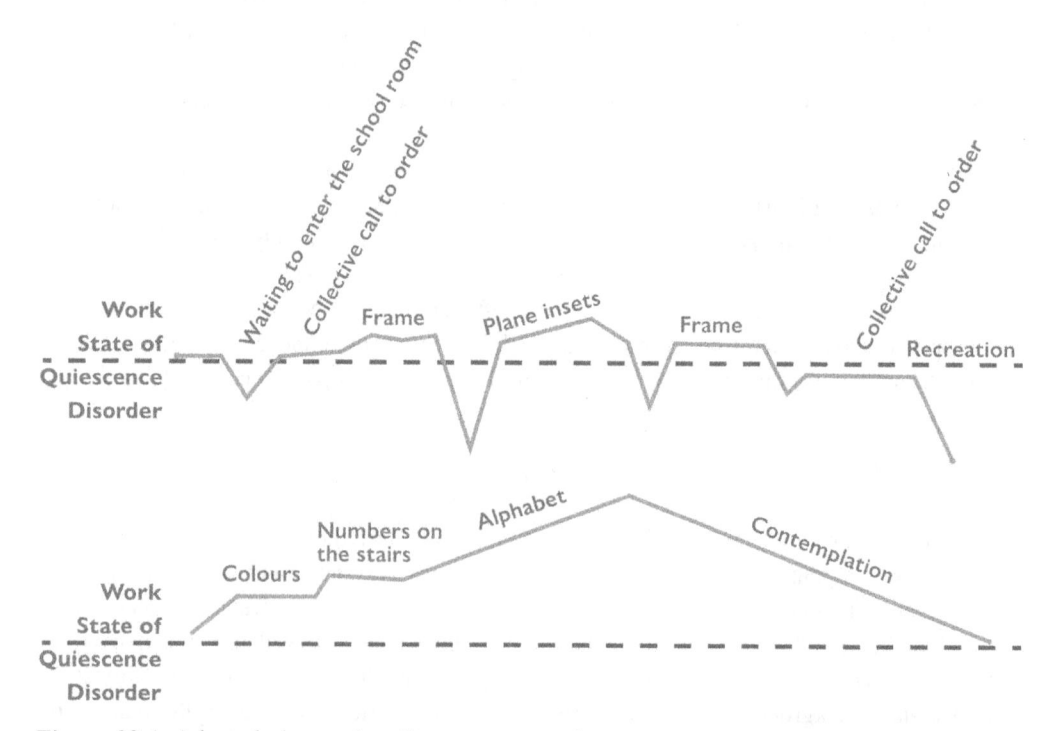

Figure 22.1 Adapted observation diagrams, or work curves, representing the three-hour work cycles of two students. Courtesy of the National Center for Montessori in the Public Sector (NCMPS), adapted from *Spontaneous Activity in Education*, Maria Montessori, 1917.

quiescence (or inactivity) and represented by the dotted line in the middle of the graph; (2) any periods of disorganized activity in the classroom, represented below the quiescent line; and (3) a child's engagement with classroom material, represented above the quiescent line.

The two work curves documented in Figure 22.1 represent Montessori's assessment of two children's engagement during a three-hour morning work period. The first student moves between focused work and periods of inactivity and distraction, while the second student shows periods of deep engagement in several tasks throughout the work cycle, followed by a sustained period of contemplation of their own work and that of other students. A modern reader may be startled by this period of contemplation, but Montessori's inclusion of this time as an exemplar highlights understanding and respect for children's internal mental processes, even if their learning process is not immediately evident. These work curves are still used by Montessori teachers today to document a child's development and progress, resulting in customized lessons for each child.

Record Keeping: Anecdotal and Running Records

Montessori teachers often develop varied record-keeping tools to track sequential lessons that are progressively more complex and given to each student over time (Montessori 1967, 44). For example, a teacher may develop a checklist to record which Sandpaper Letters have been introduced and then mastered by each child. Checklists are often an important tool, as instruction is highly personalized in Montessori classrooms. Record keeping in the early childhood classroom is primarily teacher-directed, whereas early childhood and elementary age students often incrementally assume ownership of their educational records as a self-assessment strategy. Similar checklists are used in all areas of the Montessori classroom (e.g., Math, Cultural Subjects, Practical Life) to systematically document students' learning throughout the curriculum.

Currently, in Montessori environments with more resources, there is a shift to documenting student learning on tablets or smartphones through electronic applications specifically designed for use in Montessori classrooms, such as Montessori Compass, Transparent Classroom, and brightwheel in the United States, and Cfolio in Europe. Teachers use these tools to electronically capture observation data, photographs, work samples, and anecdotal notes. These records guide teachers as they offer feedback to students, prepare individualized lesson plans, provide information to share with families about students' learning, and communicate program data to school administrators to inform future professional development needs.

Montessori's approach to observation highlights the need for educators to develop observation skills that allow them to accurately assess and respond to children's learning. Montessori teacher education programs provide comprehensive training on the attributes needed to be an effective observer, including the ability to observe a child and remain aware of the needs of the rest of the group and to be patient, objective, and understanding of children's development (Patell 2016, 252). Preservice Montessori teachers are also trained to identify each child's areas of interest and development, which Montessori referred to as *sensitive periods*, by observing how students interact with materials in the classroom environment (L'Ecuyer et al. 2020, 325). Further training includes writing anecdotal records that capture snapshots of children's interactions in the classroom, objective and subjective notes, as well as later reflections on how the observation data may inform a future lesson. "Such reporting is individualized, highly detailed, and focused on the strengths of the child as well as areas where further development is needed" (Montessori Australia 2010, 1). It is important that this reporting illustrate student progression through the curriculum to ensure that all students are progressing.

Work Plans and Portfolios

Checklists are often maintained by the early childhood classroom teacher, but students in Montessori elementary classrooms can learn to take ownership of the documentation process of their own work in the classroom. This process includes the use of work plans that are jointly created by the student and teacher and guide students to perform learning activities each week. Elementary students also typically create portfolios that curate completed work samples, reflections, and activities that are still in progress. The use of portfolios in Montessori upper elementary classrooms has been illustrated in Thorne's (2014) action research in which the researcher found that her students' engagement and intrinsic motivation increased with the use of portfolios (7). Portfolios also provide students with opportunities to review their work during weekly one-on-one meetings with their teacher or peers, and they can be shared with families during student-led parent conferences. These opportunities lead to students' increased sense of pride and accountability (Thorne 2014, 27).

The assessment practices described in this section align with pedagogical principles of Montessori education, as well as with embedded formative-assessment principles issued by national and international educational assessment organizations. These practices activate students as owners of their learning and have been shown to produce improvements in motivation and achievement (Black and Wiliam 1998; National Association for the Education of Young Children 2003). Formative-assessment practices, whereby teachers guide students to consider their own progress, provide supportive feedback that suggests growth and give students control of their own learning, supporting all students in becoming autonomous and independent learners (Wiliam 2018).

Current Directions in Montessori Assessment

Montessori teachers may not think of their daily instructional practices as assessment, but assessment is at the very core of who a Montessori educator is. New guidance for Montessori education is beginning to articulate this classroom assessment process in ways that help Montessori teachers align their language with the broader field of education and provide school leaders with tools to highlight to policymakers how assessment is an integral part of Montessori practice. Recognizing the complexity of developing comprehensive assessment systems that document children's learning, the US-based National Center for Montessori in the Public Sector (2019) developed a playbook to demonstrate ways in which to assess "children, classrooms, and schools in ways that are constructive, equitable, and rigorous, and that also advance the overarching goal of human flourishing" (3). Montessori Australia recently (2022) published a report on assessment and reporting that recognizes observation and record keeping as appropriate assessment practices in Montessori classrooms. This report lays the groundwork for future research to provide empirical evidence about formative assessment in Montessori classrooms that can inform both Montessori and non-Montessori educational practices.

Conclusion

A child-centered approach to observing and documenting children's learning is a universal principle of Montessori pedagogy. Therefore, documented observation by the teacher is required as the teacher formatively utilizes their anecdotal and running records to gently direct students' activities and to determine the next lessons they should present to their students or, in Montessori's words, to "follow the child." At the elementary level, these activities are sometimes formalized through collaboratively developed work plans in which students are highly involved in reflecting on their work as collected in their self-created learning portfolios. These Montessori practices and assessment strategies significantly align with formative-assessment practices. Collecting classroom data and analyzing the data to then inform next steps in classroom instruction are necessary components of effective assessment practices that influence teachers' work with their students. Unequivocally, if Montessori educators look carefully enough, they will see that many of the current trends in educational assessment share commonalities with their Montessori training, preparation, and practices that feature the teacher as a scientist, diagnostician, and a well-trained observer focused on the growth and learning of the whole child (Becker et al. 2022). Further study of Montessori formative-assessment practices may lead to improved teaching and learning in both Montessori and non-Montessori settings.

References

Andrade, Heidi L. 2010. "An Introduction to Formative Assessment." In *Handbook of Formative Assessment*, edited by Heidi Andrade and Gregory J. Cizek, 3–17. New York: Routledge.
Au, Wayne. 2011. "Teaching under the New Taylorism: High-Stakes Testing and the Standardization of the 21st Century Curriculum." *Journal of Curriculum Studies* 43 (1): 25–45. https://doi.org/10.1080/00220272.2010.521261.
Baecher, Laura. 2019. *Video in Teacher Learning: Through Their Own Eyes*. Thousand Oaks, CA: Corwin.
Becker, Ian, Vanessa M. Rigaud, and Ann Epstein. 2022. "Getting to Know Young Children: Alternative Assessments in Early Childhood Education." *Early Childhood Education Journal*. https://doi.org/10.1007/s10643-022-01353-y.
Bennett, Randy Elliot. 2011. "Formative Assessment: A Critical Review." *Assessment in Education: Principles, Policy & Practice* 18 (1): 5–25.
Black, Paul, and Dylan Wiliam. 1998. "Assessment and Classroom Learning." *Assessment in Education: Principles, Policy & Practice* 5 (1): 7–74.
Brookhart, Susan, Rick Stiggins, Jay McTighe, and Dylan Wiliam. 2019. *National Panel on the future of Assesment Practices: Comprehensive and Balanced Assessment Systems*. Blairsville, PA: Learning Sciences International.
Cumming, Joy. 2010. "Classroom Assessment in Policy Context (Australia)." In *International Encyclopedia of Education*, edited by Gary McCulloch and David Crook, 417–24. London: Routledge.

Dixson, Dante D., and Frank C. Worrell. 2016. "Formative and Summative Assessment in the Classroom." *Theory into Practice* 55 (2): 153–9. https://doi.org/10.1080/00405841.2016.1148989.

Every Student Succeeds Act of 2015. Pub. L. No. 114-95. Title VIII—Sec. 8002. Definitions.

Gilliam, Walter S., Angela N. Maupin, Chin R. Reyes, Maria Accavitti, and Frederick Shic. 2016. *Do Early Educators' Implicit Biases Regarding Sex and Race Relate to Behavior Expectations and Recommendations of Preschool Expulsions and Suspensions?* New Haven, CT: Yale University Child Study Center. no. 28: 1–16.

Harlen, Wynne, and Mary James. 1997. "Assessment and Learning: Differences and Relationships between Formative and Summative Assessment." *Assessment in Education: Principles, Policy & Practice* 4 (3): 365–79.

L'Ecuyer, Catherine, Bernacer Javier, and Güeli Francisco. 2020. "Four Pillars of the Montessori Method and Their Support by Current Neuroscience, Mind, Brain, and Education." *Institute for Culture and Society, University of Navarra, Spain* 14 (4): 322–34. https://doi.org/10.1111/mbe.12262.

Lillard, Angeline S., and Virginia McHugh. 2019. "Authentic Montessori: The Dottoressa's View at the End of Her Life Part II: The Teacher and the Child." *Journal of Montessori Research* 5 (1): 19–34. https://doi.org/10.17161/jomr.v5i1.9753.

Lillard, Paula Polk. 2011. *Montessori, a Modern Approach*. New York: Schocken Books.

McGrady, Patrick B., and John R. Reynolds. 2013. "Racial Mismatch in the Classroom: Beyond Black-White Differences." *Sociology of Education* 86 (1): 3–17.

McManus, Sarah. 2008. "Attributes of Effective Formative Assessment." https://www.ccsso.org/sites/default/files/2017-12/Attributes_of_Effective_2008.pdf.

Montessori Australia. 2010. "Montessori Approach to Assessment and Reporting." *Montessori Australia Foundation* 1: 1. https://barrenjoeymontessori.com.au/wp-content/uploads/2021/01/MAF-Montessori-approach-to-assessment-and-reporting.pdf.

Montessori Australia. 2022. "What Is the Montessori Approach to Assessment and Reporting." Accessed February 5, 2022. https://montessori.org.au/what-montessori-approach-assessment-and-reporting.

Montessori, Maria. 1965. *Spontaneous Activity in Education*. New York: Schocken.

Montessori, Maria. 1967. *The Discovery of the Child.* Translated by M. J. Costelloe. New York: Ballantine Books.

Montessori, Maria. 2012. *The 1946 London Lectures*. Vol. 17. Amsterdam: Montessori-Pierson Publishing Company.

Montessori, Maria. 2013. *The 1913 Rome Lectures: First International Training Course*. Edited by Susan Feez, Larry Quade, Carolina Montessori, and Joke Verheul. The Montessori Series, 18. Amsterdam: Montessori-Pierson Publishing Company.

Montessori, Maria. 2017. *The Discovery of the Child.* Edited by Joseph Costello and Fred Kelpin. The Montessori Series, 2. Amsterdam: Montessori-Pierson Publishing Company.

Montessori, Maria, and Mario M. J. Montessori. 1988. *The Clio Montessori Series*. Oxford: Clio Press.

Murray, Angela K., Jade C. Lee, J. Baker-Powers, D. Dryer, L. Hosek, E. P. Holtzclaw, and K. Klocke. 2017. "The Montessori Approach to Classroom Assessment." Paper presented at the NCME 2017 Special Conference, Lawrence, KS, September 2017.

National Association for the Education of Young Children. 2003. *Early Childhood Curriculum, Assessment, and Program Evaluation: Building an Effective, Accountable System in Programs for Children Birth through Age 8*. Washington, DC: ERIC Clearinghouse. https://www.naeyc.org/sites/default/files/globally-shared/downloads/PDFs/resources/position-statements/pscape.pdf.

National Center for Montessori in the Public Sector. 2019. *Montessori Assessment Playbook*. West Hartford, CT: National Center for Montessori in the Public Sector Press.

Organization for Economic Co-Operation and Development (OECD). 2008. "Assessment for Learning: Formative Assessment." International Conference, Learning in the 21st Century: Research, Innovation and Policy. https://www.oecd.org/site/educeri21st/40600533.pdf.

O'Shaughnessy, Molly. 2016. "The Observation Scientist." *The NAMTA Journal* 41 (3): 57–99.

Patell, Hilla. 2016. "Observation." *The NAMTA Journal* 41 (3): 249–57.

Roemer, Kathy L. 1999. "Assessment Practices Used by Montessori Teachers of Kindergarten through Sixth-Grade Students in the United States." PhD diss., University of Memphis.
Ruiz-Primo, Maria Araceli, and Susan M. Brookhart. 2018. *Using Feedback to Improve Learning*. London: Taylor and Francis.
Schön, Donald. 1983. *The Reflective Practitioner: How Professionals Think in Action*. New York: Basic Books.
Shute, Valerie J. 2008. "Focus on Formative Feedback." *Review of Educational Research* 78: 153–89. https://doi.org/10.3102/0034654307313795.
Standing, E. M. 1984. *Maria Montessori: Her Life and Work*. New York: Plume.
Thorne, Suzanne C. 2014. "The Effects of Creating Self-Assessed Work Portfolios on Student Learning Engagement in an Upper Elementary Montessori Classroom." Master's thesis, St. Catherine University.
Wiliam, Dylan. 2010. "An Integrative Summary of the Research Literature and Implications for a New Theory of Formative Assessment." In *Handbook of Formative Assessment*, edited by Heidi Andrade and Gregory J. Cizek, 18–40. New York: Routledge.
Wiliam, Dylan. 2018. *Embedded Formative Assessment*. Bloomington, IN: Solution Tree Press.

Chapter 23

Neuroscience of Error Monitoring in the Montessori Context

Solange Denervaud

Life is full of mistakes—or at least events that do not go as planned. Systematically, when unforeseen events are encountered, we slow down. This moment of pause directs our attention to important information, allowing us to integrate it in order to adjust behavior and thoughts. We can then adapt. This mechanism is called error monitoring, and because of it, we have an intrinsic ability to correct ourselves and not make the same mistakes again. We thus learn and evolve (Ullsperger et al. 2014).

The mechanism of error monitoring is more or less flexible, depending on the individual. For most adults, making a mistake is an unpleasant event resulting in a negative affective reaction; it may also be linked to social shame (Koban and Pourtois 2014). Most adults thus try to avoid risky situations so as to not make mistakes. In addition, most adults tend to repeat or imitate known answers, to the detriment of their thinking. Conversely, flexible error monitoring is reflected by an excellent ability to handle the unexpected by leveraging adversity, along with access to individual creative ideas to deal with it. But why are some adults more flexible than others when they make a mistake or face an unexpected event? There is probably a genetic component; not everyone is equipped in the same way to deal with stress or fear of the unknown. Still, there is also a variable component that results from experience with mistakes during childhood.

The brain regions involved in error detection and monitoring undergo significant changes in plasticity and permeability between ages 5 and 12 (Kelly et al. 2009). For children in this age range, what they experience will greatly influence how their brains create connections; these connections may explain some of the habitual behaviors observed in adulthood. Thus, students' experience with their mistakes during this time may have more consequences than at other ages.

Error Monitoring in Traditional and Montessori Classrooms

In a school with traditional practices, students learn primarily from adults. The teacher first chooses and prepares the lesson's topic and then passes it on to the students, who listen. The students repeat this new knowledge with exercises during a defined time. These exercises are corrected by the teacher for students to review. Students are asked to memorize this new knowledge for a test. The test will evaluate what each student has learned, which will be quantified by a grade.

The social environment for these students is artificially created so that the children are the same age and perform similar activities simultaneously, which creates a competitive climate (Hayek et al. 2015, 2017).

In Montessori schools, both the learning process and the social dimension differ. Students learn with the help of didactic materials that appeal to their senses and understanding. They are called on to seek and find the correct answers by and for themselves. New concepts are introduced to children when the teacher decides the time is right. The curriculum's progression follows the child's learning pace, not a predefined schedule. Knowledge is taught individually (especially to 3- to 6-year-olds), or it may be taught in small groups (6- to 12-year-olds) when several children are ready at the same time. Students are free to practice as they wish, without interruption or judgment regarding the repetition required. Because the material is primarily self-correcting, students do not rely on social evaluation of their work (see Figure 23.1). There is no formal test, quantitative knowledge measurement, or work-speed or memorization-capacity assessment. This ensures that concepts are not learned but understood. At the social level, students learn in a multiage environment, reinforcing peer-to-peer learning and tutoring habits. Students observe older peers and know that they are a resource when needed (Lillard 2017; Marshall 2017; Montessori [1936] 1981).

These differences are fundamental to how errors are experienced and perceived at ages when the mechanism of error monitoring may be amended by experience. We studied the development of error monitoring in students in Switzerland aged 4 to 15 years experiencing traditional classroom practices compared to Montessori practices (Denervaud et al. 2019, 2020a, 2020c, 2020d, 2020e, 2021; Denervaud et al., unpublished data; Décaillet et al., pers. comm.). Montessori schools in Switzerland are private whereas traditional schools are public, so multiple

Figure 23.1 Peer learning in a Montessori classroom, using self-correcting materials. Courtesy of Ecole Montessori Vevey.

group variables were collected. Children were matched for socioeconomic background and intelligence level. For some studies, we even controlled for parental habits with their children as well as children's physical home environment. We then measured children's behavior in the face of errors using standardized computerized and paper-based lab tasks. We also assessed how their brains reacted and changed in response to errors using advanced neuroimaging techniques, such as magnetic resonance imaging (MRI), to record brain activity and structure. Combining different types of measures shows how children develop and how pedagogy could optimally support children's monitoring of mistakes.

Research Outcomes

Error Monitoring

We measured error monitoring at the behavioral level in 234 students aged 4 to 15 years (Denervaud et al. 2020b). First, we noticed that young children need time after making a mistake to correct themselves. The more time they take, the less they will be slowed down by their mistakes as they grow up. However, at around age 8 to 10, a change occurs. The young adolescents who slow down the least after a mistake are the ones who correct themselves the best. This change occurs in learners at a younger age in a Montessori environment than in a traditional setting. This fact may reflect that when they enter the Children's House at age 3, learners have didactic material at their disposal that will educate and train their senses. As a result, they develop their sensory tools, which are the basis of their ability to perceive their environment and thus detect differences quickly (Denervaud et al. 2020b). Moreover, these children work with self-correcting material from a very young age. Such exercises undoubtedly modulate their discrimination and error-detection abilities.

In contrast, children from traditional schools began to detect errors (as reflected by a slowdown in routine reaction times) later, after the age of 6. This observation may be explained by the fact that in Switzerland, where this study was conducted, children start actual academic work when they are about 6 years old. Error detection is a fundamental step in the error-monitoring process. Therefore, it is likely that sensory training and self-correcting materials from age 3 support this first step. Indeed, at these ages, brain plasticity is optimal for sensory development—what Maria Montessori refers to as sensitive periods. Children who develop and train their perceptions will be quicker and better at detecting the unexpected; further, they are probably less frightened or surprised by it. The second stage of error monitoring is the ability to self-correct. Unsurprisingly, Montessori students who use self-correcting materials daily grow in their ability to bounce back from mistakes; they are not surprised to be wrong from time to time. This is reflected by a stable reaction time and a good capacity to self-correct after erroneous responses.

Second, we found that Montessori students were more willing to take risks and make mistakes. Research shows that most adults fear making a mistake and automatically show a negative affective response when they make an error (Aarts et al. 2012, 2013). This affective bias is easily measured with a priming task; after any incorrect responses, adults are faster at categorizing negative words (war) than positive ones (sun). However, we found Montessori students' school experience prevents the emergence of affective bias. We explored whether the affective reactions observed in adults were the same in students and whether they were modulated by school experience. In a study involving 101 children and 46 adults, we found that although adults showed a negative affective bias after a mistake, children did not (Denervaud et al. 2020c). Instead, children show the opposite pattern: an attraction for correct answers. However, we observed affective bias in students from traditional schools. For them, doing right becomes associated with a positive bias or positive response—for example, "It is good to do right," which reflects an affective response to an action. In contrast, for students from Montessori schools, there is no such affective bias. Responding correctly or incorrectly was perceived as neither good nor bad. Montessori students are thus less sensitive to making mistakes, in part as a result of Montessori teachers' providing less strongly worded positive or negative feedback. When teachers make value judgments about student work, even positive ones, students begin to strongly associate these external affects with their actions.

We might think that positive reinforcement is a good thing, but let's extend this scenario over time. Young children who strongly associate doing right with good will inevitably later feel that doing wrong is bad. They will have learned that doing right is externally rewarded, so they will have a feeling of losing something when they do wrong, which is experienced as unfavorable. Montessori students, however, are freed from these external value judgments because teachers mainly provide observational feedback and do not quantify outcomes. These students are free to explore because doing right or wrong will not be linked to a feeling of gain or loss; rather, students' desire to do things by and for themselves will be reinforced as they grow up. Our studies suggested that when the error-monitoring system is sensitive to experience, it can be hijacked by any value-based judgment, even a positive one. Therefore, adults must educate themselves to give the child only observational feedback, not value-based or judgmental feedback.

We also see differences between students attending traditional schools and Montessori schools in terms of how children's brains work with errors. A study of thirty-two 8- to 12-year-olds performing a math task while being assessed by MRI, thus allowing us to capture children's brain reactions while they were performing the task, showed that Montessori school students were more engaged overall, as measured by brain activity (Denervaud et al. 2020a). The brain regions involved in mathematical processes, primary visual attention, and executive control were more active than in traditional-school students. When we looked at the differences in brain activity when students got problems right or wrong, we found, unlike in adults, a more significant response to correct answers. Usually adults tend to react more to errors because errors are less frequent. The fact that children's brain activity is stronger for correct responses could be because children with a still-maturing error-monitoring system are initially more oriented and learn more from their successes than from their mistakes; indeed, across the time course of the learning process, successes are less frequent. This result is not isolated; it joins other studies in showing a particular sensitivity for correct actions or feedback (van Duijvenvoorde et al. 2008; van den Bos et al. 2009). Children would consequently benefit from adults directing their attention to what children do right rather than what they do wrong.

Functional brain imaging studies reveal that students construct connections in the face of errors, and correct responses reflect their experience in school. Indeed, students in traditional schools seem to connect their brains in a way that memorizes correct answers; they show greater connectivity between the error-monitoring system and the memory system (the hippocampus).

However, students in Montessori schools connect their brains in a way that solves errors; they show greater connectivity between the error-monitoring system and the reasoning region (the prefrontal cortex). Throughout development, these connectivity patterns can influence students' thinking toward being solely outcome oriented (the correct answer) or process oriented (working toward the correct answer). Knowing as we do that we will experience significant changes at the societal, climatic, and professional levels, where no correct answer is currently known, it seems dangerous to orient young people's minds toward a static, outcome-based way of thinking.

The Social Dimension of Error

Social context plays an important role in how we learn from our mistakes. A competitive context interferes with the ability to learn from the other; conversely, a cooperative climate allows for learning from the other (Koban et al. 2010). There is good reason to believe that Montessori pedagogy promotes a collaborative social context. Indeed, individualized work, mixed-age classes, and peer-to-peer learning, along with an absence of grades, are all factors that promote mutual aid. Conversely, it is recognized that a traditional approach enables a competitive social context. Because students are all about the same age, they will naturally compare themselves, especially because they are usually doing the same work and being graded on it. We therefore assessed emotion-recognition abilities in fifty-seven students aged 8 to 12 through two different experiments (Denervaud et al. 2020e).

We first showed that traditional-school students showed a high sensitivity to fear, even in emotionally neutral contexts; when neutral faces were displayed in contexts, children classified the target faces as afraid. Conversely, students from Montessori schools were better at correctly discriminating emotions; when neutral faces were displayed in contexts, children classified the target faces as surprised. The second experiment measured attentional bias to either positive or negative emotional stimuli. Montessori students had a preference for positive stimuli; they looked longer at faces expressing joy. In contrast, students from traditional schools were biased toward negative stimuli; they looked longer at faces expressing anger. Thus, these fundamental emotional recognition skills appear to be sensitive to school experience. These results, which are the foundation of social skills, are essential. For example, students who cope with social diversity in a cooperative atmosphere are more likely to later interact and work with others. This is probably the result of a ripple effect: the more diverse and varied social situations children experience in a calm atmosphere, the better socially prepared they will become.

A Possible Sensitive Period for Error Monitoring

Given the differences observed between children experiencing Montessori and traditional pedagogy, we wondered whether some experience-dependent plasticity occurs. Is there an optimal period to learn to detect and self-correct after error responses? Advanced neuroimaging techniques make it possible to explore this question. Such techniques have revealed that when we make a mistake, the brain reacts quickly to signal the error. The first reaction is easily measured with electroencephalogram electrodes placed on the scalp, permitting rapid detection of changes in brain signals. We measured this first reaction in a cohort of twenty-six Montessori and traditionally schooled students aged 6 to 12 as well as their brain anatomy using MRI. We found that the magnitude of the error response is closely related to the degree of maturation of the brain region involved in error detection (Denervaud et al., unpublished data). However, other studies have shown that this is not the case in adolescents. It could be that learning to manage mistakes is based on a sensitive period, like those described by Maria Montessori for young children. Therefore, there is a specific age during which children's brains have particular plasticity as well as an attraction to making and regulating mistakes. Their experience will significantly influence their later reflexes and habits.

Consequences on Creative Thinking, Flexibility, and Autonomy

Why is it important to construct a flexible error-monitoring system, knowing that errors inevitably occur? Why is it useful for orientation toward self-correction for success? The short answer is that it may affect creative thinking abilities. It may be that if children learn in a flexible way, they train their error-monitoring system while building creativity. In traditional classes, children memorize concepts brought in by the teacher mainly through books, paper-based activities, and stories. On the basis of the observation that concepts and knowledge are attained in an interdisciplinary and concrete way within a Montessori environment, we measured semantic memory organization in Montessori-schooled versus traditionally schooled children (Denervaud et al. 2021). We measured in sixty-seven students aged 5 to 14 the network of their learned concepts: children had to name as many animals as possible within 1 minute. This simple task reveals how the names of the animals are stored in memory; for example, "cat" and "dog" stand close to each other, whereas "cat" and "reindeer" stand farther apart. How concepts are organized may reflect experience. We observed that the Montessori students had a more enriched and denser (i.e., more interconnected) animal vocabulary than their peers studying at traditional schools. We also observed that children attending Montessori schools organized concepts more flexibly while also scoring higher on measures of creative thinking. These two aspects are undoubtedly linked. Children immersed in social diversity with interrelated and real life-based knowledge develop more flexibility because they learn to face more extraordinary events, be it an unexpected event or an error. Students who are able to deal with the unexpected can in turn create the unexpected and thereby innovate.

It is undoubtedly because children tame the unknown that they can free themselves if necessary to access their creative potential. Thus, as our study of 201 students aged 4 to 15 shows, children from Montessori schools do not develop better execution skills but rather more significant creative thinking abilities (Denervaud et al. 2019). We should note that if we did not measure any differences in executive functions, it is perhaps because our students all came from relatively wealthy family backgrounds, with easier access to music or sports lessons. These activities are known factors of training executive functions. However, as a result of this highly homogeneous population, we found that Montessori pedagogy does not promote self-control but rather supports the development of self-management and monitoring of errors or unexpected events. Students who develop executive skills in the service of their regulation will not only be more autonomous and flexible but will also grow innovative minds, as they are not used to simply learning but rather understanding. Conversely, students who develop executive skills in the service of external demands may become excellent performers. In the short term, academic outcomes may not differ between these two types of students. However, concerns about identity and life satisfaction may emerge in the long term.

Children who have the skill to deal with the unexpected, such as errors, therefore grow autonomy (Posner and Rothbart 2007). However, autonomy does not imply that these children will become individualists. They have learned that peers and other social beings are essential resources for success. They have also experienced processes, not outcomes, and are thus more inclined to learn from others and create by integrating others' ideas. We found that Montessori-schooled children do not imitate adults' demonstrations but rather identified the goal and targeted helpful information to be reproduced. Conversely, students in traditional schools tended to imitate what adults showed, even unnecessary actions (Décaillet et al., pers. comm.).

Conclusion

Quantitative measures of behavior, brain structures, and neural responses reveal that students who learn at Montessori schools develop an ability to detect errors early and learn to self-correct, whereas students from traditional schools tend to be response oriented. Between the ages of 6 and 12, the way children learn how to learn at both the individual level and the social or peer level greatly affects their error-monitoring development. Many sensitive periods have been described for young children; thus, the same logic suggests that a sensitive period may exist for children facing errors. Cerebral maturation is such that during development, children can learn to face different forms of unexpected events, including those of the physical world (sensory and motor), those of thought (error), and those of society (social group). Interests and sensitivities are thus created that are defined over time, permitting children to learn how to regulate themselves to gradually acquire autonomy. This autonomy confers an intrinsic capacity to handle the self without depending on external feedback. However, if children's self-regulatory capacity fails to be created during this optimal period, then needs and expectations, including reward and recognition, interfere with the capacity for exploration as well as for intrinsic curiosity and individual creative potential.

Several different factors characteristic of Montessori pedagogy could have a direct impact on error monitoring, including multiage classrooms, the peer-to-peer learning process, the absence of grades and rewards, few adults to many students (resulting in less intervention by the adult and less possibility of direct judgment), self-correcting materials, and even interrupted working hours. More research is still needed to understand how these factors affect children's development as well as their learning from both errors and correct responses. Although each factor sheds some light on this process, it is likely that the union of many or all of these factors is required to permit students the freedom to construct a healthy relationship to error.

Adults are primarily the result of a traditional education, so it is essential to remember that most of us fear the unexpected, which can take many forms, including social, cultural, and religious. We were likely not trained well enough as children to face them today. As Antoine de Saint-Exupéry has noted, we cannot love what we have not given ourselves time to tame. It therefore seems urgent that adults identify this aspect of their functioning and give themselves the time and the means to work on it. We may be able to train our own error-monitoring abilities to recover flexibility and access to our unique creative potentials.

References

Aarts, Kristien, Jan De Houwer, and Gilles Pourtois. 2012. "Evidence for the Automatic Evaluation of Self-Generated Actions." *Cognition* 124 (2): 117–27. https://doi.org/10.1016/j.cognition.2012.05.009.

Aarts, Kristien, Jan De Houwer, and Gilles Pourtois. 2013. "Erroneous and Correct Actions Have a Different Affective Valence: Evidence from ERPs." *Emotion* 13 (5): 960–73. https://doi.org/10.1037/a0032808.

Denervaud, Solange, Jean-François Knebel, Patric Hagmann, and Edouard Gentaz. 2019. "Beyond Executive Functions, Creativity Skills Benefit Academic Outcomes: Insights from Montessori Education." *PLoS One* 14 (11): e0225319. https://doi.org/10.1371/journal.pone.0225319.

Denervaud, Solange, Eleonora Fornari, Xiao-Fei Yang, Patric Hagmann, Mary Helen Immordino-Yang, and David Sander. 2020a. "An fMRI Study of Error Monitoring in Montessori and Traditionally-Schooled Children." *npj Science of Learning* 5: 11. https://doi.org/10.1038/s41539-020-0069-6.

Denervaud, Solange, Edouard Gentaz, Pawel J. Matusz, and Micah M. Murray. 2020b. "Multisensory Gains in Simple Detection Predict Global Cognition in Schoolchildren." *Scientific Reports* 10 (1): 1394. https://doi.org/10.1038/s41598-020-58329-4.

Denervaud, Solange, Adrian Hess, David Sander, and Gilles Pourtois. 2020c. "Children's Automatic Evaluation of Self-Generated Actions Is Different from Adults." *Developmental Science* 24 (3): e13045. https://doi.org/10.1111/desc.13045.

Denervaud, Solange, Jean-François Knebel, Mary Helen Immordino-Yang, and Patric Hagmann. 2020d. "Effects of Traditional versus Montessori Schooling on 4- to 15-Year Old Children's Performance Monitoring." *Mind, Brain, and Education* 14 (2): 167–75. https://doi.org/10.1111/mbe.12233.

Denervaud, Solange, Christian Mumenthaler, Edouard Gentaz, and David Sander. 2020e. "Emotion Recognition Development: Preliminary Evidence for an Effect of School Pedagogical Practices." *Learning and Instruction* 69: 101353. https://doi.org/10.1016/j.learninstruc.2020.101353.

Denervaud, Solange, Alexander P. Christensen, Yoed N. Kenett, and Roger E. Beaty. 2021. "Education Shapes the Structure of Semantic Memory and Impacts Creative Thinking." *npj Science of Learning* 6 (1): 35. https://doi.org/10.1038/s41539-021-00113-8.

Hayek, Anne-Sophie, Claudia Toma, Dominique Oberlé, and Fabrizio Butera. 2015. "Grading Hampers Cooperative Information Sharing in Group Problem Solving." *Social Psychology* 46 (3): 121–31. https://doi.org/10.1027/1864-9335/a000232.

Hayek, Anne-Sophie, Claudia Toma, Sofia Guidotti, Dominique Oberlé, and Fabrizio Butera. 2017. "Grades Degrade Group Coordination: Deteriorated Interactions and Performance in a Cooperative Motor Task." *European Journal of Psychology of Education* 32 (1): 97–112. https://doi.org/10.1007/s10212-016-0286-9.

Kelly, A. M. Clare, Adriana Di Martino, Lucina Q. Uddin, Zarrar Shehzad, Dylan G. Gee, Philip T. Reiss, Daniel S. Margulies, F. Xavier Castellanos, and Michael P. Milham. 2009. "Development of Anterior Cingulate Functional Connectivity from Late Childhood to Early Adulthood." *Cerebral Cortex* 19 (3): 640–57. https://doi.org/10.1093/cercor/bhn117.

Koban, Leonie, and Gilles Pourtois. 2014. "Brain Systems Underlying the Affective and Social Monitoring of Actions: An Integrative Review." *Neuroscience and Biobehavioral Reviews* 46 (pt 1): 71–84. https://doi.org/10.1016/j.neubiorev.2014.02.014.

Koban, Leonie, Gilles Pourtois, Roland Vocat, and Patrik Vuilleumier. 2010. "When Your Errors Make Me Lose or Win: Event-Related Potentials to Observed Errors of Cooperators and Competitors." *Social Neuroscience* 5 (4): 360–74. https://doi.org/10.1080/17470911003651547.

Lillard, Angeline Stoll. 2017. *Montessori: The Science behind the Genius*, 3rd ed. New York, NY: Oxford University Press.

Marshall, Chloë. 2017. "Montessori Education: A Review of the Evidence Base." *npj Science of Learning* 2: 11. https://doi.org/10.1038/s41539-017-0012-7.

Montessori, Maria. (1936) 1981. *The Secret of Childhood*. New York: Ballantine.

Posner, Michael I., and Mary K. Rothbart. 2007. *Educating the Human Brain*. Washington DC: American Psychological Association.

Ullsperger, Markus, Claudia Danielmeier, and Gerhard Jocham. 2014. "Neurophysiology of Performance Monitoring and Adaptive Behavior." *Physiological Reviews* 94 (1): 35–79. https://doi.org/10.1152/physrev.00041.2012.

van den Bos, Wouter, Berna Güroğlu, Bianca G. van den Bulk, Serge A. R. B. Rombouts, and Eveline A. Crone. 2009. "Better Than Expected or as Bad as You Thought? The Neurocognitive Development of Probabilistic Feedback Processing." *Frontiers in Human Neuroscience* 3: 52. https://doi.org/10.3389/neuro.09.052.2009.

van Duijvenvoorde, Anna C. K., Kiki Zanolie, Serge A. R. B. Rombouts, Maartje E. J. Raijmakers, and Eveline A. Crone. 2008. "Evaluating the Negative or Valuing the Positive? Neural Mechanisms Supporting Feedback-Based Learning across Development." *Journal of Neuroscience* 28 (38): 9495–503. https://doi.org/10.1523/JNEUROSCI.1485-08.2008.

Chapter 24

A Critical Consideration of Montessori Education in Its Relation to Cognitive Science and Concrete-to-Abstract Thinking

Elida V. Laski and Muanjing Julia Wang

The title of this chapter should be familiar: it alludes to the title of the first chapter of *The Montessori Method*, by Maria Montessori (1912), "A Critical Consideration of the New Pedagogy in Its Relation to Modern Science." The fact that Montessori strove to situate her ideas in relation to science demonstrates her understanding of the value of science in informing pedagogical approaches. In this spirit, we aim here to provide some research basis that supports the alignment between Montessori education and modern cognitive science. Although many cognitive science research areas apply to Montessori education (Lillard 2008), here we will specifically discuss three of them: the current understanding of young children's ability to engage in abstract thinking and the relation between concrete and abstract thinking; the ways in which the design and presentation of concrete materials can facilitate abstract representations; and the relation between movement and thought. The discussion and examples provided will focus primarily on mathematics instruction, an area in which the concrete-to-abstract tenet is particularly prominent in the Montessori method.

Concrete-to-Abstract Development and Learning

The idea that learning and development proceeds from concrete to abstract is deeply entrenched in Montessori philosophy and teaching. It is rooted in Montessori's (1912) idea of the absorbent mind: from birth through about age 6, young children absorb learning through interactions with the environment that prepare them for a gradual transition to the reasoning mind of adulthood. This notion manifests in the sequence of lessons and materials used in Montessori classrooms. Concrete materials are designed to instantiate abstract concepts such as color, size, and number. Hands-on experiences with these materials are thought to allow children's minds to grasp the concept inherent in the material, so the children will gradually be able to abstract and understand the concept symbolically with development (Chattin-McNichols 1998; Standing and Havis 1998). The sequence of lessons from early childhood to upper elementary school is thus built on the inherent assumption that developmentally appropriate instruction should proceed from concrete experiences early in childhood to increasingly abstract ones as children get older.

The idea that thought develops from concrete toward greater abstraction has been expressed by many foundational developmental psychologists (Bruner 1966; Inhelder and Piaget 1958; Vygotsky 1962). Piaget (1936) famously identifies four progressive stages of cognitive development: sensorimotor, operational, concrete operational, and formal operations. Piagetian theory suggests that only at the final operational stage can children start thinking abstractly, with reasoning executed using pure symbols without perceptive cues. Like Piaget, many traditional theorists believe that children's learning and adults' learning underpin two opposite ends of various dichotomies, such as perception to concept (Bruner 1966) or similarity to theory (Quine 1977).

However, the current developmental and cognitive literature challenges this view as either wrong or too simplistic (Keil and Wilson 2000; Mandler 2004). It may also underestimate the abilities of the youngest learners (Eggen and Kauchak 2000), suggesting that even very young children can understand both concrete and abstract ideas. The most prominent challenge to this view has emerged from research on infants indicating that they possess abstract concepts that direct and facilitate their learning (Baillargeon 2004; Spelke and Kinzler 2007). Further, the dominant model of language acquisition is that children rely on an abstract expectation of grammatical structure that guides their learning of more concrete language-specific details, such as tense marking and subject-verb agreement (Chomsky 1988; Seidenberg and MacDonald 1999; Yang 2004).

Core knowledge theory, a prominent contemporary theory of cognitive development, proposes that young children possess an abstract understanding of fundamental aspects of the world, such as the properties of objects and people (Gelman and Noles 2011; Gopnik and Wellman 2012). These naive theories, apparent as early as infancy, have two characteristics that highlight their abstract nature: they explain events in terms of unobservable causes, and they are widely applied to situations including those that the child may have never encountered. For example, 1-year-old children already demonstrate an understanding of the abstract concept of "living." Both 9- and 12-month-olds show surprise when they see an inanimate object like a robot, but not a person, move on its own, suggesting they have formed the abstract understanding that self-locomotion is a distinctive characteristic of people (Poulin-Dubois 1999). Core knowledge theorists also emphasize that these early abstract concepts grow more sophisticated with age and experience.

Other work has shown that number is a natural domain of cognition, with a foundation of its own. Infants are endowed with a general all-purpose ability to learn, but in particular, they possess the capabilities to form representations in this domain, with sensitivity to arithmetic operations such as addition and subtraction appearing as early as 5 months. Research that examined infants' looking time reveals that infants are able to understand that a single object added to a second hidden object results in two objects instead of one or three objects. Infants also look longer when a single object is removed from a hidden two-object display resulting in two objects instead of one (Wynn 1992). Of course, children's knowledge will undergo development; nevertheless, basic principles of domain-specific knowledge are discernible early in life, even before the emergence of language and the cultural socialization.

Theoretical and empirical advances in developmental science indicate a complex interplay between concrete and abstract thinking during development (Goldstone et al. 2000). Although very young children can reason abstractly about some concepts and domains, they are also more bound to perceptual information for learning than older children (Sloutsky 2010). The perceptual cues young children attend to for learning is directed by their abstract concepts; in turn, processing these concrete cues improves their abstract understanding (Goldstone et al. 2000; McNeil and Alibali 2004; Stahl and Feigenson 2019). As early as infancy, an iterative relation exists between abstract and concrete reasoning.

Although the general idea that children's learning progresses from concrete to abstract still applies, new evidence showing that children's abstract thinking emerges early suggests that it may happen at different times in different subjects for different children. This is particularly pertinent to Montessori education because the classrooms' individualization allows tailoring of progression from concrete to abstract to each child's individual needs in each area of study. To illustrate this process, we use the Math curriculum in Montessori classrooms to show how the materials facilitate learning abstract mathematical concepts.

Learning from Concrete Materials

A central aspect of Montessori pedagogy is the use of concrete, physical materials to introduce children to abstract concepts. This aspect is most apparent in the mathematics curriculum, which centers around materials explicitly designed to help children understand Math concepts like place value and multiplication (Chattin-McNichols 1998; Lillard 2008). With few exceptions, cognitive science research has found that using concrete materials to introduce complex concepts benefits learning (Martin 2009; Sarama and Clements 2009). However, even though manipulatives are concrete objects, understanding their relationship with abstract concepts still requires abstract thinking. It is dangerous to place faith in the power of concrete materials and to assume that the underlying mathematical concept can be read off the manipulatives. Uttal (2003) argues that young children often fail to make the connection between concepts represented by manipulatives and the written representations of the same concepts. Therefore, researchers have identified four principles for using manipulatives in a traditional Math curriculum. We address each, in turn, to demonstrate why the Montessori Math curriculum is effective.

The first principle states that using the same or similar manipulatives repeatedly over a long time to solve problems leads to a deeper understanding of the relation between physical objects and abstract concepts (Martin 2009). Children become better able to interpret the relation between a symbol and its referent with age, but even older children need cumulative experience with a symbol in order to use it for sophisticated reasoning (Liben and Myers 2007). Children are better able to identify the relation between two constructs—in this case, a concept and a manipulative—when they have many opportunities to compare them (Gick and Holyoak 1983; Son et al. 2011).

The Montessori approach allows for long-term use of similar manipulatives through both the program structure (three-year cycle, open-ended three-hour work period) and the design of the manipulatives. Montessori herself also stressed the importance of "repetition" and she suggested that "repetition is the secret to perfection" (Montessori 1986). It is through repetition using the Math manipulatives in the Montessori classroom that the child will be able to grasp the concepts, achieve mastery, and eventually internalize the underlying abstract concepts.

The second principle states that it is beneficial to begin with highly transparent concrete representations and move to more abstract representations over time. Research on the development of symbolic representations and analogic reasoning suggests that children are more likely to understand an abstract concept if the manipulatives physically look like the concept that is being represented (Chen 1996; DeLoache et al. 1991; Gentner and Markman 1997; Goswami 1996; Laski and Siegler 2014).

The Montessori Math materials are not only structured in a logical sequence but also exemplify the progression from highly transparent concrete materials to less-transparent abstract materials. For instance, Golden Beads are used to teach the decimal system, with a single golden bead representing one unit, 10 golden beads connected in a bar representing tens, 10 of the golden 10 bars connected together into a square representing hundreds, and 10 of the 100 squares stacked into a cube representing thousands. After mastering these highly transparent concrete materials to learn about the decimal system, elementary schoolchildren then use highly abstract materials, with the ones, tens, hundreds, and thousands printed on same-size but different-colored tiles (see Figure 24.1). In addition, a transitional material, a Bead Frame, helps make the transition to

Figure 24.1 Elementary student works on Math exercises at Fruitful Orchard School, Lagos, Nigeria. Courtesy of Junnifa Uzodike.

abstraction. Using it to calculate thousands requires more abstract thinking because the individual beads are no longer labeled with their place values.

The third principle for manipulatives to be effective is to avoid using manipulatives that resemble irrelevant everyday objects or that have distracting features. Instructions with manipulatives that represent everyday objects, like teddy bears, are least effective for children aged 3 to 6, with small or even negative effects (Carbonneau et al. 2013; Petersen and McNeil 2013). This result partly stems from the fact that such objects, with their captivating perceptual features, distract children from the underlying mathematical concepts they represent (Sarama and Clements 2009). Current research suggests that manipulatives without irrelevant perceptual features promote the greatest learning in children (McNeil et al. 2009).

Consistent with this research, and as we have indicated in our discussion of the Golden Bead method used to teach decimals, Montessori Math materials are basic representations of mathematical concepts without irrelevant perceptual features, and they do not represent everyday objects. For example, the Spindle Box, which teaches children one-to-one correspondence and the association between quantity and numerals, consists of 45 plain wooden, uncolored spindles and two boxes with compartments that fit 1 to 9 spindles.

The last principle states that instruction needs to be explicit so children can understand the relation between concrete materials and the abstract concepts they represent because the physicality of the manipulatives does not carry the meaning of the mathematical concept. Even with the best-designed manipulatives, it is unreasonable to expect a child to extract the abstract concepts that the concrete materials represent without guidance. Research also demonstrates that children under the age of 5 have trouble abstracting concepts without explicit instruction (DeLoache et al. 1999). Therefore, it is best to provide explicit instruction on the relation between concrete materials and abstract concepts; it helps direct children's attention to the materials' relevant features. Kirschner et al. (2016) found that directing children's attention promoted learning because it allowed children's limited cognitive resources to focus on the mathematical concepts instead of trying to abstract the relation between concrete material and Math concepts. Carbonneau and Marley (2015) found that children who received explicit instruction on how counters corresponded to their numerical symbols outperformed students on measures of procedural and conceptual knowledge transfer compared to students who received no explicit instructions.

In Montessori classrooms, the teachers, in brief presentations known as lessons, use succinct language to introduce mathematical concepts with concrete materials. For example, in the lesson introducing the decimal system with Golden Beads, the teacher first lays down a single golden bead, points to it, and says to the child, "This is a unit." The teacher then puts 9 units down, counts with the child, and asks the child how many units there are when one more is added. After the child counts to 10, the teacher replaces the 10-unit golden beads with one golden 10 bar(s). The teacher points to the golden 10 bar and explicitly tells the child, "This is a 10 bar. Ten unit beads make up a 10 bar." The lesson next introduces the concepts of hundreds and thousands. The simple, precise nature of the lessons stems from Montessori's belief that the teachers should say no more than absolutely necessary. Whatever is added beyond this tends to confuse and distract children from the very mathematical concept that the materials intend to teach (Standing and Havis 1998).

Relation between Movement and Thought

Along with the way that Montessori Math materials align with cognitive science research around effective teaching and learning with manipulatives, a key advantage of concrete, physical materials is that they allow children to interact with them in a manner that facilitates knowledge construction (Glenberg et al. 2004) by prompting physical actions that ease conceptual understanding and retention (Martin and Schwartz 2005). This idea that body movements and cognition are closely intertwined and that physical movement can enhance learning and thinking is called embodied cognition. Contemporary philosophers of embodied cognition, including Lakoff et al. (1999) and Thompson (2007), maintain that "cognitive processes emerge from … continuous sensorimotor interactions involving the brain, body and environment" (Thompson 2007, 11). They assert that the relationship between mind and body is unitary; no cognition would exist without physical, sensory experience of the surrounding environment. Their position of embodied cognition, extrapolated to the field of education, suggests that bodily interaction with the material at hand or with the surrounding environment can facilitate mental processes associated with learning. Further, research shows that cognition is closely tied to the sensorimotor system (Kiefer and Trumpp 2012). For example, when subjects are mentally processing numbers, activation of motor areas associated with finger movements is consistently found (Andres et al. 2007).

Montessori embraces the belief that minds develop through bodily action, stating, "He does it with his hands, by experience, first in play and then through work. The hands are the instruments of man's intelligence" (1995, 150). According to Montessori, any experience is retained as a memory trace known as an engram, which is stored in a child's unconscious mind. Thus, sensory experience may provide a basis for more abstract concepts (Chattin-McNichols 1998). Sandpaper Numerals—iconic in the Montessori Math curriculum—allow tactile experiences to be recruited to introduce children to the names and shapes of the symbols that represent quantity.

Montessori (1995) notes that movement must be "connected with [the] mental activities that are going on" (142). The concept of embodied cognition suggests that knowledge is grounded in sensorimotor routines and experiences by interactions among mind, body, and environment (Lakoff et al. 1999). Montessori suggests that movement facilitates both the physical and intellectual growth of children. In a Montessori curriculum, movement is incorporated into some lessons as sensory activities that directly connect to the developing brain. When we teach children to make 10 back-and-forth trips to get the 1 to 10 number rods to the mat, then 10 more trips to return the material, we are not asking them to do this to keep them busy. Instead, we are helping them form the muscular memory of the concept of 10. Children, with their minds together with their whole bodies, see 10 rods, pick up 10 rods, and physically carry 10 rods, thus learning about counting to 10 as well as about the decimal system and the magnitude of numbers.

Conclusion

Much of the Montessori pedagogical approach is predicated on the view that children's learning benefits from a progression from concrete-to-abstract materials at all ages of development. This idea is consistent with recent cognitive science findings about the value of concrete representations for the acquisition of abstract mental representations of concepts that aid transfer of the idea to novel contexts. Although appreciation in the abstract reasoning that children of all ages are capable of is increasing, substantial evidence indicates that grounded representations help children form abstract concepts and generalization. Montessori Math pedagogy in particular can be understood from a cognitive psychology perspective as introducing Math concepts simply and concretely in the early years, followed by reintroduction several times in the years that follow with increasing abstraction and complexity—a progression both logically and developmentally appropriate.

References

Andres, Michael, Xavier Seron, and Etienne Olivier. 2007. "Contribution of Hand Motor Circuits to Counting." *Journal of Cognitive Neuroscience* 19 (4): 563–76. https://doi.org/10.1162/jocn.2007.19.4.563.
Baillargeon, Renée. 2004. "Infants' Physical World." *Current Directions in Psychological Science* 13 (3): 89–94. https://doi.org/10.1111/j.0963-7214.2004.00281.x.
Bruner, Jerome S. 1966. *Toward a Theory of Instruction*. Vol. 59. Cambridge MA: Harvard University Press.
Carbonneau, Kira J., and Scott C. Marley. 2015. "Instructional Guidance and Realism of Manipulatives Influence Preschool Children's Mathematics Learning." *Journal of Experimental Education* 83 (4): 495–513. https://doi.org/10.1080/00220973.2014.989306.
Carbonneau, Kira J., Scott C. Marley, and James P. Selig. 2013. "A Meta-analysis of the Efficacy of Teaching Mathematics with Concrete Manipulatives." *Journal of Educational Psychology* 105 (2): https://doi.org/10.1037/a0031084.
Chattin-McNichols, John. 1998. *The Montessori Controversy*. New York: Delmar.
Chen, Zhe. 1996. "Children's Analogical Problem Solving: The Effects of Superficial, Structural, and Procedural Similarity." *Journal of Experimental Child Psychology* 62 (3): 410–31. https://doi.org/10.1006/jecp.1996.0037.
Chomsky, Noam. 1988. *Generative Grammar: Its Basis Development and Prospects*. Kyoto: Kyoto University of Foreign Studies.
Chomsky, Noam. 1998. *Language and Problems of Knowledge: The Managua Lectures*. Cambridge MA: MIT Press.
DeLoache, Judy S., Valerie Kolstad, and Kathy N. Anderson. 1991. "Physical Similarity and Young Children's Understanding of Scale Models." *Child Development* 62 (1): 111–26. https://doi.org/10.1111/j.1467-8624.1991.tb01518.x.
DeLoache, Judy S., Olga A. Peralta de Mendoza, and Kathy N. Anderson. 1999. "Multiple Factors in Early Symbol Use: Instructions, Similarity, and Age in Understanding a Symbol–Referent Relation." *Cognitive Development* 14 (2): 299–312. https://doi.org/10.1016/S0885-2014(99)00006-4.
Eggen, Paul D., and Don P. Kauchak. 2000. *Educational Psychology: Windows on Classrooms*. 5th ed. Upper Saddle River, NJ: Prentice-Hall.
Gelman, Susan A., and Nicholaus S. Noles. 2011. "Domains and Naïve Theories." *WIREs Interdisciplinary Reviews: Cognitive Science* 2 (5): 490–502. https://doi.org/10.1002/wcs.124.
Gentner, Dedre, and Arthur B. Markman. 1997. "Structure Mapping in Analogy and Similarity." *American Psychologist* 52 (1): 45–6. https://doi.org/10.1037/0003-066X.52.1.45.
Gick, Mary L., and Keith J. Holyoak. 1983. "Schema Induction and Analogical Transfer." *Cognitive Psychology* 15: 1–38. https://doi.org/10.1016/0010-0285(83)90002-6.
Glenberg, Arthur M., Tatiana Gutierrez, Joel R. Levin, Sandra Japuntich, and Michael P. Kaschak. 2004. "Activity and Imagined Activity Can Enhance Young Children's Reading Comprehension." *Journal of Educational Psychology* 96: 424–36. https://doi.org/10.1037/0022-0663.96.3.424.

Goldstone, Robert, Mark Steyvers, Jesse Spencer-Smith, and Alan Kersten. 2000. "Interactions between Perceptual and Conceptual Learning." In *Cognitive Dynamics: Conceptual Change in Humans and Machines*, edited by Eric Dietrich and Arthur B. Markman, 191–228. New York: Routledge.

Gopnik, Alison, and Henry M. Wellman. 2012. "Reconstructing Constructivism: Causal Models, Bayesian Learning Mechanisms, and the Theory Theory." *Psychological Bulletin* 138 (6): 1085. https://doi.org/10.1037/a0028044.

Goswami, Usha. 1996. "Analogical Reasoning and Cognitive Development." *Advances in Child Development and Behavior* 26: 91–138. https://doi.org/10.1016/s0065-2407(08)60507-8.

Inhelder, Bärbel, and Jean Piaget. 1958. *The Growth of Logical Thinking from Childhood to Adolescence: An Essay on the Construction of Formal Operational Structures*. New York: Psychology Press.

Keil, Frank C., and Robert A. Wilson, eds. 2000. *Explanation and Cognition*. Cambridge, MA: MIT Press.

Kiefer, Markus, and Natalie M. Trumpp. 2012. "Embodiment Theory and Education: The Foundations of Cognition in Perception and Action." *Trends in Neuroscience and Education* 1 (1): 15–20. https://doi.org/10.1016/j.tine.2012.07.002.

Kirschner, Sophie, Andreas Borowski, Hans E. Fischer, Julie Gess-Newsome, and Claudia von Aufschnaiter. 2016. "Developing and Evaluating a Paper-and-Pencil Test to Assess Components of Physics Teachers' Pedagogical Content Knowledge." *International Journal of Science Education* 38 (8): 1343–72. https://doi.org/10.1080/09500693.2016.1190479.

Lakoff, George, Mark Johnson, and John F. Sowa. 1999. "Review of Philosophy in the Flesh: The Embodied Mind and Its Challenge to Western Thought." *Computational Linguistics* 25 (4): 631–4.

Laski, Elida V., and Robert S. Siegler. 2014. "Learning from Number Board Games: You Learn What You Encode." *Developmental Psychology* 50 (3): 853. https://doi.org/10.1037/a0034321.

Liben, Lynn S., and Lauren J. Myers. 2007. "Developmental Changes in Children's Understanding of Maps: What, When, and Why?" In *The Emerging Spatial Mind*, edited by Jodie M. Plumert and John P. Spencer, 193–218. Oxford: Oxford University Press.

Lillard, Angeline Stoll. 2008. *Montessori: The Science behind the Genius*. Oxford: Oxford University Press.

Mandler, Jean M. 2004. *The Foundations of Mind: Origins of Conceptual Thought*. Oxford: Oxford University Press.

Martin, Taylor. 2009. "A Theory of Physically Distributed Learning: How External Environments and Internal States Interact in Mathematics Learning." *Child Development Perspectives* 3 (3): 140–4. https://doi.org/10.1111/j.1750-8606.2009.00094.x.

Martin, Taylor, and Daniel L. Schwartz. 2005. "Physically Distributed Learning: Adapting and Reinterpreting Physical Environments in the Development of Fraction Concepts." *Cognitive Science* 29: 587–625. https://doi.org/10.1207/s15516709cog0000_15.

McNeil, Nicole M., and Martha W. Alibali. 2004. "You'll See What You Mean: Students Encode Equations Based on Their Knowledge of Arithmetic." *Cognitive Science* 28 (3): 451–66. https://doi.org/10.1207/s15516709cog2803_7.

McNeil, Nicole M., David H. Uttal, Linda Jarvin, and Robert J. Sternberg. 2009. "Should You Show Me the Money? Concrete Objects Both Hurt and Help Performance on Mathematics Problems." *Learning and Instruction* 19 (2): 171–84. https://doi.org/10.1016/j.learninstruc.2008.03.005.

Montessori, Maria. 1912. *The Montessori Method*. New York: Stokes.

Montessori, Maria. 1986. *The Discovery of the Child*. New York: Ballantine Books, Azkar Books.

Montessori, Maria. 1995. *The Absorbent Mind*. New York: Holt.

Petersen, Lori A., and Nicole M. McNeil. 2013. "Effects of Perceptually Rich Manipulatives on Preschoolers' Counting Performance: Established Knowledge Counts." *Child Development* 84 (3): 1020–33. https://doi.org/10.1111/cdev.12028.

Piaget, Jean. 1936. *Origins of Intelligence in the Child*. London: Routledge & Kegan Paul.

Poulin-Dubois, Diane. 1999. "Infants' Distinction between Animate and Inanimate Objects: The Origins of Naive Psychology." In *Early Social Cognition: Understanding Others in the First Months of Life*, edited by Philippe Rochat. New York: Routledge.

Quine, Willard V. 1977. "Natural Kinds." In *Naming, Necessity, and Natural Kinds*, edited by Stephen P. Schwartz, 155–75. Ithaca NY: Cornell University Press.

Sarama, Julie, and Douglas H. Clements. 2009. "'Concrete' Computer Manipulatives in Mathematics Education." *Child Development Perspectives* 3 (3): 145–50. https://doi.org/10.1111/j.1750-8606.2009.00095.x.

Seidenberg, Mark S., and Maryellen C. MacDonald. 1999. "A Probabilistic Constraints Approach to Language Acquisition and Processing." *Cognitive Science* 23 (4): 569–88. https://doi.org/10.1016/S0364-0213(99)00016-6.

Sloutsky, Vladimir M. 2010. "From Perceptual Categories to Concepts: What Develops?" *Cognitive Science* 34 (7): 1244–86. https://doi.org/10.1111/j.15516709.2010.01129.x.

Son, Ji Y., Linda B. Smith, and Robert L. Goldstone. 2011. "Connecting Instances to Promote Children's Relational Reasoning." *Journal of Experimental Child Psychology* 108: 260–77. https://doi.org/10.1016/j.jecp.2010.08.011.

Spelke, Elizabeth S., and Katherine D. Kinzler. 2007. "Core Knowledge." *Developmental Science* 10 (1): 89–96. https://doi.org/10.1111/j.1467-7687.2007.00569.x.

Stahl, Aimee E., and Lisa Feigenson. 2019. "Violations of Core Knowledge Shape Early Learning." *Topics in Cognitive Science* 11 (1): 136–53. https://doi.org/10.1111/tops.12389.

Standing, E. M., and Lee Havis. 1998. *Maria Montessori: Her Life and Work*. New York: Plume.

Thompson, Evan. 2007. *Mind in Life: Biology, Phenomenology, and the Sciences of Mind*. Cambridge, MA: Harvard University Press.

Uttal, David H. 2003. "On the Relation between Play and Symbolic Thought: The Case of Mathematics Manipulatives." In *Contemporary Perspectives in Early Childhood*, edited by Olivia N. Saracho and Bernard Spodek, 97–114. Charlotte, NC: Information Age.

Vygotsky, Lev. 1962. *Thought and Language*. Cambridge, MA: MIT Press.

Wynn, Karen. 1992. "Addition and Subtraction by Human Infants." *Nature* 358 (6389): 749–50. https://doi.org/10.1038/358749a0.

Yang, Charles D. 2004. "Universal Grammar, Statistics, or Both?" *Trends in Cognitive Sciences* 8 (10): 451–6. https://doi.org/10.1016/j.tics.2004.08.006.

Chapter 25
Executive Functions in Montessori Education

Jan Mallett

Executive functions, representing the brain's governing and self-regulation, are multifaceted and somewhat malleable. Having strong executive functions can be a predictor of school readiness, literacy skills, and even life success (Berninger et al. 2017; Diamond and Lee 2011; Fitzpatrick 2012; Foy and Mann 2013; Lonigan et al. 2017; Mischel et al. 2011; Weintraub et al. 2013). Research indicates that, although executive functions are influenced by heredity and develop throughout childhood and into young adulthood, they are also affected by environment and experience (Ahmed et al. 2018; Blair 2017; Diamond 2016). Educational settings that foster executive functions have been shown to diminish the risk of academic and social difficulties and to improve academic achievement (Fitzpatrick 2012). Childhood is a critical period for enhancing lifelong executive-function skills that serve an individual throughout their life (Otero et al. 2014). The purpose of this chapter is to examine Montessori education as an effective means of enhancing the development of executive functions by providing an overview of executive functions, connecting Montessori practices to executive functions, and examining empirical evidence related to the effects of Montessori education on executive functions.

Overview of Executive Functions

The Subcomponents of Executive Functions

Neurologists and psychologists generally agree that executive functions consist of several subcomponents; frequently, three in particular are considered: working memory, inhibitory control, and cognitive flexibility (Diamond 2012; Hass et al. 2014; Weintraub et al. 2013). Working memory is the mental space where information is accessed and manipulated, allowing children to keep the steps of basic tasks, such as getting ready for school in the morning or solving a math word problem, at the mental center stage (Diamond 2012). Inhibitory control is the ability to consider and regulate one's own behavioral, cognitive, or emotional responses, that is, to exhibit self-control (Diamond 2012). Cognitive flexibility is the ability to consider more than one idea at a time and adjust responses according to new information (Diamond 2012; Weintraub et al. 2013). For example, one might act on the basis of one rule for a time and then later change one's behavior to adhere to a new rule. Taken together, working memory, inhibitory control, and cognitive flexibility enable an individual to sustain focus, carry out complex tasks, and adapt to the circumstances at hand, critical factors to succeeding in schools, work, and daily life.

The Development of Executive Functions

Executive functions appear to emerge in infancy and develop throughout childhood and adolescence (Anderson 2002; Carlson 2005; Hass et al. 2014; Weintraub et al. 2013; Zelazo et al. 2003). They are believed to be malleable and to be both enhanced with early intervention and disrupted by adverse experiences (McClelland and Wanless 2012). Each subcomponent has a distinct developmental trajectory that varies between individuals (Hass et al. 2014). Furthermore, these three foundational subcomponents appear to be prerequisites for more-complex executive functions such as perseverance, resilience, reasoning, problem-solving, planning, goal setting, strategy selection, self-monitoring, and life management (Blair 2017; Diamond 2016; Hass et al. 2014).

Montessori Education and Executive Functions

Authors discussing interventions that support the development of executive functions highlight curricular approaches that integrate skill-fostering activities into children's daily lives and produce positive outcomes. Features of such interventions include structures that facilitate regular exercise of emerging executive-function skills, a differentiated curriculum with scaffolding to allow for student choice, active rather than passive learning experiences, and a focus on socioemotional development (Blair 2017; Diamond 2010, 2012; Diamond and Lee 2011). Experts suggest that these features work together to foster the development of executive functions (Diamond 2012; Diamond and Lee 2011). Montessori education is consistently described as an approach that includes these features (Diamond and Lee 2011; Takacs and Kassai 2019).

Maria Montessori (1989) was forward-thinking in observing that children develop optimally when provided with a nurturing, carefully prepared environment that focuses on the needs of the whole child, not just academic learning. Many aspects of the Montessori method align with features of programs that enhance the development of executive functions. The next section elaborates on four broad features that characterize model learning environments for enhancing executive functions, linking them to key elements of high-quality Montessori implementation.

Regular Exercise of Executive Functions

Model programs regularly embed opportunities for children to exercise executive-function skills. Montessori designed her method with many features that help children practice self-control and concentration skills (Lillard and McHugh 2019a). Montessori students in high-fidelity classrooms have daily three-hour blocks of uninterrupted work time within which they choose their learning activities, allowing them to work for a sustained period of time on several tasks, thus developing concentration. In contrast, in traditional classrooms, tasks are often divided into small units of time, placing the teacher rather than the student in charge of the schedule. Furthermore, because only one set of each of the Montessori learning materials is available in the classroom, children practice inhibitory control while learning to wait respectfully for their turn (Lillard and McHugh 2019a). Finally, Montessori lessons themselves are designed to foster concentration, having been developed through careful observation of the types of activities that are most engaging for children at each developmental stage (Lillard and McHugh 2019a). For example, the youngest children begin with Practical Life lessons, including scooping, pouring, and preparing food, to draw their deep interest to mastering their immediate environment independently. This practice establishes a pattern of fully concentrating on the work at hand and provides the foundation for children to immerse themselves in more challenging work as they develop (Lillard and McHugh 2019b). Older students become engrossed in long-term, large-scale research projects that they initiate with their classmates, fostering intrinsic motivation and flow experiences (see Chapter 26: "Motivation and Self-Determination in Montessori Education" and Chapter 27: "Montessori Education, Optimal Experience, and Flow").

Differentiation, Scaffolding, and Choice

Model environments offer differentiation according to individual needs, support for emerging skills, and opportunities for children to exercise choice (Center on the Developing Child at Harvard University 2011). In an authentic Montessori classroom, children choose work during long blocks of time, providing ample opportunity for decision-making with support from teachers who know them well (Lillard and McHugh 2019b). Children's choices are supported by observant, responsive adults who scaffold experiences with gradually increasing levels of responsibility, allowing children to practice skills before they are expected to be fully self-directed (Bruner 1978; Diamond 2012). In addition, the scaffolding process builds over an extended time as Montessori students remain with the same teacher in a multiage classroom for three years (Diamond and Lee 2011).

Active Learning Experiences

Model programs incorporate active, hands-on learning experiences (Diamond 2012). Physical activity is a key element of authentic Montessori education as children are often moving about the classroom and manipulating both small and large learning materials (Lillard and McHugh 2019b). In fact, Grissmer et al. (2010) found that attention and fine motor skills in preschool-aged children predicted later academic achievement. The materials that comprise the foundational Montessori curriculum provide what today is referred to as "embodied learning," experiences in which the "mind is integrated into the body's sensorimotor systems" (Macedonia 2019, 2). For example, Montessori preschool students are offered Practical Life exercises that include pouring, tweezing, spooning, cleaning, polishing, and dressing (Marshall 2017). These exercises allow for the systematic development of fine motor control, particularly the pincer grasp, which is necessary for efficient pencil control (Marshall 2017).

Socioemotional Focus

A final feature of model programs is a socioemotional focus, which integrates emotional regulation and social skills while fostering joy, pride, confidence, and a sense of community in a low-stress environment (Diamond 2010, 2012). High-fidelity Montessori classrooms are designed to nurture the intellectual, social, emotional, physical, and spiritual development of each child (Lillard and McHugh 2019b). They tend to be low stress, avoid or de-emphasize traditional grading schemes, and affirm rather than embarrass the child (Diamond 2012). Functioning as a respectful community is a primary goal of Montessori environments and is facilitated with multiage groupings, collaborative work, and specific lessons to help students learn to be respectful members of the group (Diamond 2012). Three-year, multiage Montessori classrooms and infrequent whole-group activities allow children to engage in many types of social interactions on their own, such as self-selected small-group work and peer tutoring (Diamond and Lee 2011). Furthermore, the 3-year age span of children in each class and the intentional avoidance of competition provide students with the opportunity to begin their tenure in a classroom as novices and to leave as mentors of other children (Diamond and Lee 2011). Explicit Grace and Courtesy lessons, such as how to greet one another, offer assistance, and tidy up work areas, are incorporated into the daily life of high-fidelity Montessori classrooms, providing a framework for harmonious community life (Gilder 2012).

As the previous paragraphs illustrate, Montessori environments provide concrete examples of the features present in model executive-function classrooms. Given this alignment of Montessori practices with executive-function principles, not surprisingly, research studies have found evidence of Montessori effectiveness in fostering executive-function outcomes. Before discussing these studies, we first address the challenges of measuring executive functions in children.

Research on Executive Functions

Measurement Tools

Despite considerable attention on determining the best ways to measure executive functions, several factors contribute to the difficulty of assessing this construct in children (Hass et al. 2014; Willoughby et al. 2016). First, executive functions comprise a multifaceted construct that requires consideration of subcomponents rather than a single, unitary measure (Hass et al. 2014). Because no single measure of executive function effectively isolates each subcomponent, assessment tools inherently involve multiple overlapping skills (Willoughby et al. 2016). In fact, Willoughby et al. (2016) concluded that considering executive functions via composite scores was preferable to considering the factors independently. Second, neurological development is not mature until near the end of adolescence, making it difficult to precisely measure neurological function in children (Center on the Developing Child at Harvard University 2011). Third, because many existing measures are simplified versions of scales developed for adults, they fail to account for the unique features of executive functions at earlier developmental stages

(Hass et al. 2014). Although improved measures of executive functions are needed, especially for children, current research provides an initial understanding of the development of executive functions (Ahmed et al. 2018).

Several executive-function measures have been used in Montessori research studies and are discussed later in this chapter. For example, the Head Toes Knees Shoulders (HTKS) task measures inhibitory control and working memory by asking children to perform tasks that are the direct opposite of the administrator's instructions (e.g., touch the toes when instructed to touch the head; McClelland et al. 2014). Lillard et al. (2017) used the Visuospatial Processing section of the NEPSY-II to assess attention, inhibitory control, and working memory through a paper-and-pencil task in which children recreate a presented image (Korkman et al. 2007). The Preschool Self-Regulation Assessment evaluates emotional regulation and attention and impulsivity during direct observation (Smith-Donald et al. 2007). The Kansas Reflection-Impulsivity Scale for Preschool (KRISP)—Form A asks children to match line drawings with duplicate images among a series of choices to measure attentiveness (Wright 1971). The Minnesota Executive Function Scale (MEFS App) is a tablet-based measurement tool of the executive functions of 2-year-olds through adults (Carlson 2017). These tools have varying strengths, yet each addresses executive functions only partially.

The National Institutes of Health Toolbox (NIH Toolbox) significantly improves on efforts to measure executive functions in children by providing easy access to digital, tablet-based applications of tools with strong psychometric properties (Northwestern University 2022). Each assessment may involve multiple subcomponents of executive function, as they are difficult to isolate. The NIH Toolbox includes a Cognitive Battery, with a version for early childhood (ages 3 to 6) and older children (ages 7 and older). Specific examples of some of these assessments follow. The Dimensional Change Card Sort (DCCS) is one tool in the NIH Toolbox that assesses cognitive flexibility and working memory by asking the child to match increasingly complex visual stimuli with the same type of instruction as the DCCS to provide a response that is contrary to the expressed researcher request (Weintraub et al. 2013). The Flanker Inhibitory Control and Attention Test asks children to identify the direction a visual stimulus is pointing when it is surrounded by other competing visual distractions (Weintraub et al. 2013). Finally, the Working Memory Test assesses memory by requiring children to repeat lists of incrementally increasing numbers of related items (Weintraub et al. 2013).

Evidence of Executive Function Development in Montessori Education

Because Montessori education aligns theoretically with practices thought to enhance the development of executive functions, researchers have examined its effects empirically. Two important considerations affect the credibility of these studies. First, research design is an issue, as samples in Montessori studies are often small and nonrandomized, limiting their ability to infer causality (Lillard et al. 2017; Marshall 2017). A second concern is fidelity of implementation; Montessori classrooms vary significantly, and, because of a lack of legal protection for the name, any school can claim to be a Montessori school, regardless of actual educational practices (Lillard and McHugh 2019a; Lillard et al. 2017; Marshall 2017; see Chapter 20: "Fidelity Issues in Montessori Research"). With these considerations in mind, we summarize the evidence of Montessori education's impact on the development of executive functions.

The most rigorous studies incorporate some type of randomization and provide evidence of Montessori fidelity. In investigating a wide range of outcomes in the United States, Lillard and Else-Quest (2016) and Lillard et al. (2017) utilized randomization based on lottery admissions in Montessori public schools to compare cohorts of children who did and did not gain admission to Montessori preschool. In one small study, Montessori 5-year-old children scored higher than their non-Montessori counterparts on cognitive flexibility and working memory as measured by the DCCS; however, no significant difference was evident in inhibitory control between children with Montessori and non-Montessori schooling (Lillard and Else-Quest 2006). The school involved in this study was affiliated with Association Montessori International/USA (AMI/USA), which the authors consider a "relatively strict" interpretation of Montessori education (Lillard and Else-Quest 2006, 1894).

More recently, Lillard et al. (2017) used a random-lottery design for a longitudinal study comparing children from high-fidelity AMI/USA Montessori preschools and non-Montessori preschools on a variety of measures, including executive-function tasks. Researchers found that, although children in Montessori classrooms experienced significant academic gains in comparison to the control group, the growth of the executive functions of Montessori children was actually not greater than in the non-Montessori children. Typically, executive functions predict academic achievement (Ahmed et al. 2018). In this study, however, Montessori children's executive-function scores, whether low or high, did not predict academic achievement. However, executive function scores *were* predictive for the children who did not attend Montessori schools (Lillard et al. 2017). Authors hypothesized that this result could be due to the inclusion of differentiated instruction as a core practice in Montessori education (Lillard et al. 2017).

Another study with random assignment involved a pretest-posttest design with a comparison group that used the KRISP assessment to examine differences between Montessori students and students receiving the national preschool curriculum in Turkey (Kayılı 2016). Results indicated that Montessori students responded less impulsively and made fewer errors than did the national curriculum students. A limitation of this study is the minimal information about the fidelity of implementation, which was limited to a description of Montessori classrooms taught by teachers with Montessori certificates. Similar limitations occurred in a French study in which Courtier et al. (2021) compared the executive functions of disadvantaged preschoolers randomly assigned to public Montessori and non-Montessori classrooms. Although there were no significant differences in executive functions between the groups, the fidelity of Montessori implementation was compromised as the authors noted that Montessori materials, work periods, and teacher training were abbreviated.

A pretest-posttest design comparing an intervention to a control condition without randomization is another, albeit less-rigorous, approach for examining differences in outcomes for children in Montessori classrooms. One such study conducted in Turkey involved an intervention in a newer Montessori program and compared it to a non-Montessori preschool control group with comparable demographic characteristics on the same university campus (Tiryaki et al. 2021). The newly created Montessori program included the purchase of Montessori materials and the creation of a Montessori training program for teachers. The study's focus was on self-regulation, measured with a form of the Preschool Self-Regulation Assessment that was adapted and validated for use with children in Turkey (Findik and Yildiz 2014). The children who attended the Montessori preschool showed significantly more growth over time in self-regulation and impulse control compared to their non-Montessori counterparts (Tiryaki et al. 2021).

A similar pretest-posttest study of eighteen intact classrooms in US private preschools compared the executive functions, among other outcomes, of 3- to 6-year-old children in classic Montessori, supplemented Montessori, and conventional programs (Lillard 2012). Classic Montessori programs were defined as those using only Montessori materials. Supplemented Montessori programs included commercially prepared non-Montessori materials along with more authentic Montessori materials and practices, and conventional programs were highly regarded schools with no Montessori implementation. The researcher found that children in classic Montessori settings fared significantly better than children in either conventional preschool programs or supplemented Montessori programs on many measures, including executive functions as measured by the HTKS, although the delay task showed no difference.

A one-group pretest-posttest design study in a US public Montessori preschool accredited by the American Montessori Society found that growth in inhibitory control and cognitive flexibility among a small group of 3-year-old students increased at a greater pace than expected relative to norm-referenced data from the beginning to the end of the school year on the NIH Toolbox DCCS and the Flanker Test (Phillips-Silver and Daza 2018). Researchers proposed that the inherent control of error in Montessori materials was a contributing factor. A weakness of this study was that, although children were admitted by a lottery, there was no explicit comparison group.

Finally, a Swiss study included kindergarten and elementary-aged children attending existing Montessori and traditional schools at a single point in time, controlling for age, gender, socioeconomic status, and fluid intelligence (Denervaud et al. 2019). The study used a version of the Flanker Test and a number-ordering assessment and found no difference between Montessori and traditional students in selective attention or cognitive flexibility. Only working memory showed significant differences in favor of students attending a Montessori school. The authors suggested that previous research may have overstated the role of executive function in the academic success of Montessori students and called for more research.

Conclusion

Supporting development of children's executive-function skills is a significant opportunity because these skills often predict social and academic outcomes and even life success. Montessori education provides environments that foster executive functions because of aspects of the approach that align with features of programs known to enhance executive functions. First, Montessori environments are structured so that students have regular opportunities to exercise their emerging executive-function skills. Second, Montessori education offers a differentiated curriculum with significant student choice within a supportive framework. Third, Montessori education relies heavily on active rather than passive learning activities. Finally, Montessori education incorporates a focus on students' socioemotional development.

Research on the impact of Montessori education on executive functions has yielded many positive results, as well as conflicting findings in some studies. Children in Montessori schools had stronger working memory than did children in non-Montessori schools (Denervaud et al. 2019; Lillard and Else-Quest 2006), and children in Montessori schools with greater fidelity had stronger working memory than did children in non-Montessori schools and schools with supplemented Montessori practices (Lillard et al. 2012). The cognitive flexibility of Montessori students was greater than in non-Montessori students (Lillard and Else-Quest 2006; Phillips-Silver and Daza 2018); however, Denervaud et al. (2019) found no difference in cognitive flexibility between Montessori and non-Montessori preschool students. Lillard et al. (2017) did not find a significant difference in the growth rate of executive functions of Montessori and non-Montessori students. Several studies indicated that Montessori students have stronger inhibitory control than non-Montessori students (Kayili 2016; Lillard 2012; Phillips-Silver and Daza 2018; Tiryaki et al. 2021).

These results, promising yet in some cases disparate, demonstrate the need for additional robust research to truly understand how Montessori education broadly affects executive functions. Implementation fidelity and inclusion of expanded age ranges will illuminate Montessori impacts over time. Continued improvements in instruments for measuring both executive functions and Montessori fidelity, along with a growing number of well-designed, large-scale studies, will provide enhanced understanding of how Montessori education affects executive functions and how that insight may apply to a wider variety of educational contexts.

References

Ahmed, Sammy, Sandra Tang, Nicholas Waters, and Pamela Davis-Kean. 2018. "Executive Function and Academic Achievement: Longitudinal Relations from Early Childhood to Adolescence." *Journal of Educational Psychology* 111 (3): 446–58. https://doi.org/10.1037/edu0000296.

Anderson, Peter. 2002. "Assessment and Development of Executive Function (EF) during Childhood." *Child Neuropsychology* 8 (2): 71–82. https://doi.org/10.1076/chin.8.2.71.8724.

Berninger, Virginia, Robert Abbott, Clayton Cook, and William Nagy. 2017. "Relationships of Attention and Executive Functions to Oral Language, Reading, and Writing Skills and Systems in Middle Childhood and Early Adolescence." *Journal of Learning Disabilities* 50 (4): 434–49. https://doi.org/10.1177/0022219415617167.

Blair, Clancy. 2017. "Primer Educating Executive Function." *Cognitive Science* 8: e1403. https://doi.org/10.1002/wcs.1403.

Bruner, Jerome S. 1978. "The Role of Dialogue in Language Acquisition." In *The Child's Concept of Language*, edited by A. Sinclair, R., J. Jarvelle, and W. J. M. Levelt. New York: Springer-Verlag.

Carlson, Stephanie. 2005. "Developmentally Sensitive Measures of Executive Function in Preschool Children." *Developmental Neuropsychology* 28 (2): 595–616. https://doi.org/10.1207/s15326942dn2802_3.

Carlson, Stephanie. 2017. *Minnesota Executive Function Scale Technical Report*. St. Paul, MN: Reflection Sciences, Inc.

Center on the Developing Child at Harvard University. 2011. "*Building the Brain's 'Air Traffic Control' System: How Early Experiences Shape the Development of Executive Function: Working Paper No. 1.*" https://developingchild.harvard.edu/resources/building-the-brains-air-traffic-control-system-how-early-experiences-shape-the-development-of-executive-function/

Courtier, Philippine, Marie-Line Gardes, Jean-Baptiste Van der Henst, Ira A. Noveck, Marie-Caroline Cruset, Justine Epinat-Duclos, Jessica Leone, and Jerome Prado. 2021. "Effects of Montessori Education on the Academic, Cognitive, and Social Development of Disadvantaged Preschoolers: A Randomized

Control Study in the French Public School System." *Child Development* 92 (5): 2069–2088. https://doi.org/10.1111/cdev.13575.

Denervaud, Solange, Jean- François Knebel, Patric Hagmann, and Edouard Gentaz. 2019. "Beyond Executive Functions, Creativity Skills Benefit Academic Outcomes: Insights from Montessori Education." *PLoS ONE* 14 (11): e0225319. https://doi.org/10.1371/journal.pone.0225319.

Diamond, Adele. 2010. "The Evidence Base for Improving School Outcomes by Addressing the Whole Child and by Addressing Skills and Attitudes, Not Just Content." *Early Education Development* 21: 780–93. https://doi.org/10.1080%2F10409289.2010.514522.

Diamond, Adele. 2012. "Activities and Programs That Improve Children's Executive Functions." *Current Directions in Psychological Science* 21 (5): 335–41. https://doi.org/10.1177/0963721412453722.

Diamond, Adele. 2016. "Why Improving and Assessing Executive Functions Early in Life Is Critical." In *Executive Functions in Preschool Age Children*, edited by J. Griffin, P. McCardle, and L. Freund. Washington, DC: American Psychological Association).

Diamond, Adele, and Kathleen Lee. 2011. "Interventions Shown to Aid Executive Function Development in Children 4 to 12 Years Old." *Science* 333 (6045): 959–64. https://doi.org/10.1126/science.1204529.

Findik, Ezgi and Tulin Yildiz. 2014. "Preschool Self-Regulation Assessment (PSRA): Adaptation Study for Turkey." *Education and Science* 39 (176): 317–28.

Fitzpatrick, Caroline. 2012. "Ready or Not: Kindergarten Classroom Engagement as an Indicator of Child School Readiness." *South African Journal of Childhood Education* 2 (1): 1–32.

Foy, Judith, and Virginia Mann. 2013. "Executive Function and Early Reading Skills." *Reading and Writing* 26: 453–72. https://doi.org/10.1007/s11145-012-9376-5.

Gilder, Sharon. 2012. "Hands as Companions of the Mind." *Montessori Life* 3: 24–9.

Grissmer, David, Kevin J. Grimm, Sophie M. Aiyer, William M. Murrah, and Joel S. Steele. 2010. "Fine Motor Skills and Early Comprehension of the World: Two New School Readiness Indicators." *Developmental Psychology* 46 (5): 1008. https://doi.org/10.1037/a0020104.

Hass, Michael, Ashley Patterson, Jocelyn Sukraw, and Brianna Sullivan. 2014. "Assessing Executive Functioning: A Pragmatic Review." *Contemporary School Psychology* 18: 91–102. http://dx.doi.org/10.1007/s40688-013-0002-6.

Kayılı, Gökhan. 2016. "The Effect of Montessori Method on Cognitive Tempo of Kindergarten Children." *Early Child Development and Care* 188 (3): 327–35. https://doi.org/10.1080/03004430.2016.1217849.

Korkman, Marit, Ursula Kirk, and Sally Kemp. 2007. NEPSY-II: *Clinical and Interpretive Manual*. San Antonio, TX: The Psychological Corporation.

Lillard, Angeline S. 2012. "Preschool Children's Development in Classic Montessori, Supplemented Montessori, and Conventional Programs." *Journal of School Psychology* 50 (3): 379–401. https://doi.org/10.1016/j.jsp.2012.01.001.

Lillard, Angeline, and Nicole Else-Quest. 2006. "Evaluating Montessori Education." *Science* 313: 1893–4. https://doi.org/10.1126/science.1132362.

Lillard, Angeline S. and Virginia McHugh. 2019a. "Authentic Montessori: The Dottoressa's View at the End of Her Life Part I: The Environment." *Journal of Montessori Research* 5 (1): 1–18. https://doi.org/10.17161/jomr.v5i1.7716.

Lillard, Angeline S. and Virginia McHugh. 2019b. "Authentic Montessori: The Dottoressa's View at the End of Her Life Part II: The Teacher and the Child." *Journal of Montessori Research* 5 (1): 19–34. https://doi.org/10.3389/fpsyg.2017.01783.

Lillard, Angeline S., Megan J. Heise, Eve M. Richey, Xin Tong, Alyssa Hart, and Paige M. Bray. 2017. "Montessori Preschool Elevates and Equalizes Child Outcomes: A Longitudinal Study." *Frontiers in Psychology* 8: 1783. https://doi.org/10.3389/fpsyg.2017.01783.

Lonigan, Christopher, Darcey Allan, and Beth Phillips. 2017. "Examining the Predictive Relations between Two Aspects of Self-Regulation and Growth in Preschool Children's Early Literacy Skills." *Developmental Psychology* 53 (1): 63–76. https://doi.org/10.1037/dev0000247.

Macedonia, Manuela. 2019. "Embodied Learning: Why at School the Mind Needs the Body." *Frontiers in Psychology* 10: 2098. https://doi.org/10.3389/fpsyg.2019.02098.

Marshall, Chloe. 2017. "Montessori Education: A Review of the Evidence Base." *npj Science of Learning* 2: 11. https://doi.org/10.1038/s41539-017-0012-7.

McClelland, Megan, and Shannon Wanless. 2012. "Growing up with Assets and Risks: The Importance of Self-Regulation for Academic Achievement." *Research in Human Development* 9: 278–97. https://doi/10.1080/15427609.2012.729907.

McClelland, Megan, Claire Cameron, Robert Duncan, Ryan Bowles, Alan Acock, Alicia Miao, and Megan Pratt. 2014. "Predictors of Early Growth in Academic Achievement: The Head-Toes-Knees-Shoulders Task." *Frontiers in Psychology*. https://doi.org/10.3389/fpsyg.2014.00599.

Mischel, Walter, Ozlem Ayduk, B. J. Marc Berman Ian Gotlib Casey, John Jonides, Ethan Kross, Theresa Teslovich, Nicole Wilson, and Yuichi Shoda. 2011. "Willpower over the Life Span: Decomposing Self-Regulation." *Social Cognitive and Affective Neuroscience* 6 (2): 252–56. https://doi.org/10.1093/scan/nsq081.

Montessori, Maria. 1989. *To Educate the Human Potential*. Oxford: Clio Press.

Northwestern University. 2022. *NIH Toolbox*. https://www.healthmeasures.net/explore-measurement-systems/nih-toolbox.

Otero, Tulio, Lauren Barker, and Jack Naglieri. 2014. "Executive Function Treatment and Intervention in Schools." *Applied Neuropsychology: Child* 3 (3): 205–14. https://doi.org/10.1080/21622965.2014.897903

Phillips-Silver, Jessica, and María Theresa Daza. 2018. "Cognitive Control at Age 3: Evaluating Executive Functions in an Equitable Montessori Preschool." *Frontiers in Education* 3: 1–8. https://doi.org/10.3389/feduc.2018.00106.

Smith-Donald, Radiah, C. Cybele Raver, Tiffany Hayes, and Breeze Richardson. 2007. "Preliminary Construct and Concurrent Validity of the Preschool Self-Regulation Assessment (PSRA) for Field-Based Research." *Early Childhood Research Quarterly* 22 (2): 173–87. https://doi.org/10.1016/j.ecresq.2007.01.002.

Takacs, Zsofia K., and Reka Kassai. 2019. "The Efficacy of Different Interventions to Foster Children's Executive Function Skills: A Series of Meta-Analyses." *Psychological Bulletin* 145 (7): 653–97. https://doi.org/10.1037/bul0000195.

Tiryaki, Aybuke, Ezgi Findik, Saliha Sultanoglue, Esra Beker, Mudriye Bicakci, Neriman Aral, and Ece Ozbal. 2021. "A Study on the Effect of Montessori Education on Self-Regulation Skills in Preschoolers." *Early Child Development and Care* 191 (7–8): 1219–29. https://doi.org/10.1080/03004430.2021.1928107.

Weintraub, Sandra, Sureyya Dikmen, Robert Heaton, David Tulsky, Philip Zelazo, Patricia Bauer, Noelle Carlozzi et al. 2013. "Cognition Assessment Using the NIH Toolbox." *Neurology* 80 (11–13): S54–S64. https://doi.org/10.1212/WNL.0b013e3182872ded.

Willoughby, Michael, Jolynn Peck, and Clancy B. Blair. 2016. "Measuring Executive Function in Early Childhood." *Psychological Assessment* 28 (3): 319–30. https://doi.org/10.1037/a0031747.

Wright, John C. 1971. "*Kansas Reflection-Impulsivity Scale for Preschoolers (KRISP)*." St. Louis, MO: CEMREL, Inc.

Zelazo, Philip David, Ulrich Müller, Douglas Frye, Stuart Marcovitch, Gina Argitis, Janet Boseovski, Jackie K. Chiang et al. 2003. "The Development of Executive Function in Early Childhood." *Monographs for the Society of Research in Child Development* 68 (3): vii–137. https://doi.org/10.1111/j.0037.976x.2003.00260.x.

Chapter 26
Motivation and Self-Determination in Montessori Education

Abha Basargekar and Angeline S. Lillard

To adults entering a Montessori classroom for the first time, the activities they observe may not seem particularly academic. Depending on the students' ages, children might be found working independently, having spirited discussions in small groups, or working on long-term projects. Inconspicuous teachers observe and take notes or give lessons to small groups. Especially if habituated to classrooms that are teacher led and dominated by whole-group instruction, observers might not notice that learning is happening through a different route. In this method, learning activities are self-determined, initiated, and controlled by students according to their own wishes.

As we describe below, learning in the Montessori system hinges on students' self-determined engagement. Students are given opportunities and encouragement to exercise choice in several aspects of their learning; indeed, psychology research indicates that such engagement is good for students' learning and well-being (Gottfried 1986; Hardre and Reeve 2003; Lepper et al. 2005). We explain how environmental conditions that can enhance engagement are encoded in Montessori classrooms. Finally, we review research on motivational and educational outcomes from Montessori education and conclude with questions for future research.

Self-Determination in Montessori Schools

The child, not the adult, is the center of the Montessori educational system. The optimal learning process for the child takes precedence over the teaching process most convenient for the adult. Montessori (2017a, 2017b) holds that children are naturally interested in learning about the world, and a teacher's primary task is to create an environment where this interest can find its natural and ideal expression. Therefore, intrinsic motivation, or motivation to engage in activities because they are interesting and challenging, is not simply a goal but rather both an assumption and a crucial guiding principle of the Montessori method (Lillard 2019).

Montessori schools are organized to optimally support learners at different developmental stages, so the environment varies accordingly (Montessori 2007). The educational psychology literature calls this stage-environment fit (Eccles et al. 1993). This solves what Hunt (1961, 267) famously called "the problem of the match," wherein the educational environment ideally offers activities that are challenging—but not too challenging—for each child. Montessori schools provide choices suitable for a particular developmental stage within the framework of a comprehensive curriculum including Math, Language, Practical Life, and Sensorial activities. Children work on sequenced lessons presented by a teacher, who subtly monitors work to ensure that children engage with all curricular areas. Montessori classrooms have mixed-age groupings of students based on what Montessori thought were key needs during different developmental stages. Children younger than 3 are in infant or toddler classrooms. Children ages 3 to 6 are enrolled in early childhood classrooms, while children ages 6 to 12 are enrolled in elementary classrooms. When there are enough students to create two classes, the elementary group may be split into lower elementary (ages 6 to 9) and upper elementary (ages 9 to 12) classes. Children older than 12 are in adolescent programs, which may extend to ages 15 or even 18.

At all stages, Montessori education involves creating an environment that enables children to discover and develop their interests. The curriculum is oriented around and springs from these interests—unlike traditional schools, wherein a preestablished body of knowledge is conveyed to the whole class and externally reinforced using grades and extrinsic rewards. Montessori students' self-determination guides them through successive classroom levels that support development at each stage.

Self-Determination and Intrinsic Motivation

Motivation, or the drive to do something, is a strong predictor of positive life outcomes, including good relationships (Gable 2006), high performance at work (Gagné and Forest 2008), and general well-being (Miquelon and Vallerand 2008). Motivation also predicts positive functioning within the educational context (Lepper et al. 2005; Ratelle et al. 2007; Reeve 2002). Indeed, sustaining and bolstering motivation may be critical in education because research in traditional school settings shows that academic motivation declines across the school years (Lepper et al. 2005). One established way to increase motivation is to provide opportunities for self-determination (Ryan and Deci 2000).

Motivation is a broad construct. As portrayed in Figure 26.1, self-determination theory (SDT) postulates a range: amotivation, controlled motivation, then autonomous motivation (Deci and Ryan 2000). Autonomous motivation predicts positive life outcomes better than controlled motivation (Deci and Ryan 2008).

Whereas amotivation refers to an absence of motivation, controlled motivation is externally regulated through rewards and punishments, or it results from a desire to gain approval and avoid shame. Autonomous motivation is composed of: identified regulation, which is observed when individuals have strongly identified with an activity's value and therefore undertake actions because they want to; integrated regulation, when an activity is viewed as being consistent with one's values and goals; and intrinsic motivation, defined as an internal drive to explore new topics and develop knowledge and skills (Ryan and Deci 2000).

Intrinsic motivation is especially important for learning and academic achievement. Intrinsically motivated students persist longer (Hardre and Reeve 2003; Ratelle et al. 2007), experience less anxiety about content (Gottfried 1986), and engage with content at deeper conceptual levels (Grolnick and Ryan 1987). Although the nature of the relation is known to be complex (Cerasoli et al. 2014), research demonstrates the predictive relation of intrinsic

Motivation and Self-Determination

	Amotivation	Controlled Motivation		Autonomous Motivation		
		External Regulation (Extrinsic)	Introjected Regulation (Extrinsic)	Identified Regulation (Extrinsic)	Integrated Regulation (Extrinsic)	Intrinsic Motivation
Definition	No motivation or regulation on activity	External rewards associated with the activity	Avoidance of guilt, anxiety, or shame	Personal valuation of the activity	Activityttjs congruence with the self	Interest and inherent satisfaction from the activity
Examples	Not working on onettjs math problems at all, because one does not feel the need to.	Doing math problems because one expects to get ice-cream after they finish.	Doing math problems to show that one is good at math.	Doing math problems because one believes that math is important for onettjs life goals.	Doing math problems because it is consistent with onettjs identity as a good student.	Doing math problem because one finds it engaging and challenging.

— Nonself-determined ———————————————————— Self-determined —

Adapted from Ryan and Deci (2000: 72)

Figure 26.1 Types of motivation described by the self-determination theory. Image courtesy of the authors.

motivation to academic achievement and performance (Areepattamannil et al. 2011; Lepper et al. 2005; Ratelle et al. 2007). Intrinsic motivation also predicts academic adjustment later in life (Otis et al. 2005). Further, autonomously motivated students have higher self-worth, display positive emotionality, have higher rates of retention, and show greater creativity (Reeve 2002).

According to SDT, individuals' intrinsic motivation in any context is supported through the fulfillment of three fundamental psychological needs: perceiving oneself as competent, feeling a sense of autonomy, and feeling interrelated with others (Ryan and Deci 2000). Such individuals experience high intrinsic motivation, enabling them to exercise control over aspects of their lives. They feel capable of doing something that is important to them. They also feel strong social connections with others. Thwarting of all three needs is associated with amotivation. The levels of motivation between amotivation and intrinsic motivation manifest when the needs of competence and relatedness are met to some extent, but the need for autonomy is thwarted.

Different school situations can support those needs, and therefore affect student motivation, through their principles and practices. Figure 26.2 illustrates the relationship between these three SDT needs, intrinsic motivation, and key features of the Montessori environment.

Need for Autonomy

Within educational contexts, substantial evidence indicates that intrinsic motivation is enhanced when students' autonomy is supported, like when they are offered choices (Patall et al. 2010). Compared to controlling teachers, autonomy-supportive teachers, who listen more to their students, spend less time holding instructional materials, give students time for independent

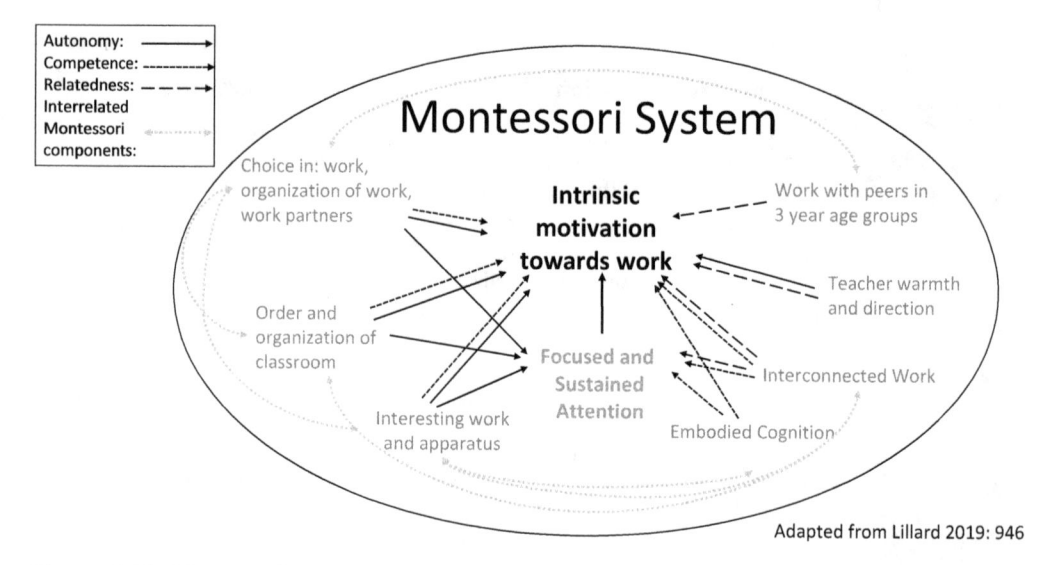

Figure 26.2 Montessori system's support for intrinsic motivation through the fulfillment of the three self-determination needs. Image courtesy of the authors.

work, and provide fewer answers are more likely to have students who thrive (Reeve 2002). When learning goals are presented in an autonomy-supportive rather than a controlling manner, depth of processing, test performance, and persistence are enhanced (Vansteenkiste et al. 2004). Conversely, external controls, such as reward and punishment, detract from the sense of self-determination, thereby undermining intrinsic motivation (Deci et al. 1999). In educational contexts, external regulators include high-stakes assessments, grades, or rewards, including approval and praise.

The clearest way Montessori schools support student autonomy is by providing choice in learning activities within the limits defined by a structured environment and the teacher's discernment. Students choose activities from the ones available and introduced by their teacher, and they work on them for long, uninterrupted periods of time. Whereas younger children work independently most of the time, elementary-age children often make their activities collaborative, learning in self-chosen groups. Yet all Montessori schoolchildren set their own schedules and follow their interests. For instance, a child especially interested in art may take the lead on creating illustrations for a team project; elementary and older children may organize small-group field trips to an external location they choose. Adolescent programs support independence by emphasizing real-world applications of academic material and engagement in meaningful work in the school and/or community (Montessori 2007). As children get older, opportunities to become autonomous within their communities multiply.

Learning driven through students' autonomous choices is possible in Montessori classrooms because the materials are inherently interesting and because the classroom processes are orderly and organized (Figure 26.2). Choice also fosters focused and sustained attention—another manifestation of intrinsic motivation. Yet the Montessori system limits choices to be commensurate with children's current abilities because "to let the child do as he likes when he has not yet developed any powers of control is to betray the idea of freedom" (Montessori

2007, 204). Teachers limit children's choices to work that children are capable of performing and then expand options as children mature. Finally, features that can deplete one's sense of self-control, such as grades, are absent from the Montessori system (Montessori 2017a, 2017b).

Need for Perceived Competence

Intrinsic motivation is enhanced when people work within what Vygotsky (1978) calls their zone of proximal development, the theoretical learning space containing tasks that a child may not be able to accomplish independently but can complete with support. Even infants seek out stimuli slightly more complex than what they have already mastered, thereby driving their own development (Kidd et al. 2012, 2014). Problems that are too hard diminish motivation, likely because they deplete the sense of competence; in contrast, problems that can be solved with effort and attention increase the sense of competence.

In Montessori schools, offering choice within limits may contribute to a sense of competence, and thus intrinsic motivation, because students can decide to engage in work that is in their zone of proximal development (Figure 26.2). Children only take out work that they have been shown how to do, and teachers only present materials that they perceive children are ready to engage with. Even in cases when children might errantly attempt too-difficult work, the classroom's support of their autonomy allows them to recognize this and choose alternative optimally challenging work. Hands-on activities allow students to see what they have accomplished, thus supporting perceived competence. Extrinsic motivators are absent, so no external source tells children they are underperforming; instead, children can keep trying until they master the material. Finally, the interrelated curriculum and orderly classrooms allow children to build on what they know. All these elements work together to promote competence.

Need for Relatedness

In line with SDT predictions, intrinsic motivation is enhanced in situations that impart a sense of security and interpersonal relatedness (Grolnick and Ryan 1987). In school research, this is likely why a warm, responsive relationship with a teacher is one of the best predictors of children's success (Cash et al. 2019). Humans function best when they are part of a social network while also perceiving themselves to have autonomy within that network. Montessori classrooms foster a sense of relatedness through mixed-age groupings, which give students a consistent company of peers and teachers across multiple years (Figure 26.2). Children may freely interact with their peers. They need not keep quiet while listening to the teacher for long periods of time; they can converse and collaborate with friends, thereby building relationships. In addition, relatedness to the teacher is fostered through the lack of grades (a form of judgment) and through the ways Montessori instructed teachers to interact with students: to behold them with love and trust and to see misbehavior as a fault of the environment rather than the child. Children help care for their classrooms and their curricular materials, which may also foster relatedness to the shared environment.

Substantial research thus supports the SDT prediction that situations fostering individual autonomy, a sense of competence, and a sense of social connectedness are conducive to students' intrinsic motivation, which in turn supports good academic outcomes. Montessori schools, which are made up of features and practices that support these three needs, are well poised to foster students' intrinsic motivation to learn.

Motivation in Academic Activities

The limited research on young children's motivation in Montessori schools suggests that the environment encourages motivation compared to traditional school models. One lottery-controlled study based in the Northeastern United States examined 3- to 5-year-old students' mastery orientation—that is, the belief that through effort, abilities can be increased and challenging tasks mastered (Lillard et al. 2017). Students who are mastery oriented choose challenging work in order to learn (Dweck 2017). Because the propensity to approach relatively unfamiliar and challenging content is a hallmark of intrinsic motivation, mastery orientation encompasses intrinsic motivation; indeed, it may even promote it by making work rewarding. Compared to their traditional preschool peers, 4- and 5-year-old Montessori students are significantly more likely to choose a task they previously found challenging, indicating their mastery orientation. In contrast, their peers in conventional preschools were more likely to choose a task they found easy, or no task at all.

Other studies have looked at older children. Rathunde and Csikszentmihalyi (2005a) found that compared to students in traditional middle schools in the US Midwest, their peers in demographically matched Montessori schools reported higher levels of flow and intrinsic motivation while engaged in schoolwork. Further, the Montessori students had a more positive perception of the social environment of their schools: they found their teachers to be more supportive, experienced their classrooms as less disruptive, and experienced greater emotional safety in the classrooms (Rathunde and Csikszentmihalyi 2005b). However, the study's almost nine-year gap between data collection confounded results; further, four of the study's five Montessori schools were private, whereas the traditional schools were all public.

Ruijs (2017), comparing Montessori and non-Montessori students, provided an experimental control by using school-admission lotteries in the Netherlands. Lottery-winning adolescent students reported slightly but not significantly higher school enjoyment and better relationships with their teachers than their peers in traditional schools. No differences were found in motivation or independence. Besides the lottery preferences rendering the groups unequal at the outset, insufficient information about characteristics of the Montessori schools in this study raises questions about implementation fidelity. Because Montessori adolescent programs were the last to develop, advancing primarily after Montessori's death, they vary in their conceptualization and implementation, including the extent to which they adhere to core Montessori principles. Even assuming that secondary schools implement the Montessori method faithfully, any advantage may be more strongly evident in some educational systems than others. Montessori and typical secondary schooling experiences in the Netherlands may both afford students substantial autonomy (Ruijs 2017), given the widespread general movement toward self-regulated learning and individual time (Veugelers 2004). Motivational differences may be more accentuated in systems where traditional school students' activities are highly externally regulated.

Qualitative research on Montessori students' self-determination has also attempted to elucidate the ways that student motivation is supported. Classroom observations and teacher interviews in one Montessori elementary classroom showed that teachers espoused beliefs and demonstrated practices upholding students' autonomy (Koh and Frick 2010). Students in a Montessori adolescent program in Indonesia had positive perceptions of the motivating qualities of their school environment (Setiawan and Ena 2019). In another study, when asked about their experiences, adolescent Montessori students addressed autonomy, relatedness, and competence, suggesting that all three SDT psychological needs were being met (Johnson 2016). Although these studies hint at intriguing findings across different country contexts, most included only a small number of participants, and several lacked a comparison group—reasons why we cannot draw strong conclusions. Overall, however, the theoretical features of Montessori schooling support intrinsic motivation, with some research supporting this finding.

Implications for Future Research

Students are optimally motivated in educational contexts when their needs for autonomy, competence, and relatedness are supported. In line with this principle, Montessori schools, which are organized to support students' stage-specific needs, have been generally associated with positive motivational outcomes. However, these studies have raised many questions for future research to address. One study found associations between Montessori education and long-term well-being; a possible reason for the association (if causal) is the high degree of self-determination in Montessori contexts (Lillard et al. 2021, Ryan & Deci 2000). Well-being often coexists with intrinsic motivation.

Much of the research investigating self-determination and motivation in Montessori schools has involved students from early to late adolescence. This emphasis may be well-placed because motivation to learn in school declines across middle and high school (Lepper et al. 2005); adolescents may be particularly vulnerable to a drop in intrinsic motivation. Further, the most prevalent research methods involve self-report, which may be less reliable at younger ages. Nevertheless, studying motivation among younger children, potentially using behavioral observations or experience sampling, can contribute to our understanding of developmental outcomes. While we know that Montessori education prepares students to develop a mastery orientation from an early age (Lillard et al. 2017), longitudinally studying the effects of such self-determination support at younger ages may help us examine its long-term benefits.

Future studies might also investigate the effects of the Montessori system's stage-specific approach for sustaining motivation. Developmental research supports some aspects of this approach; adolescents have a higher need for autonomy, for contributing to society, and for closer peer interactions (Eccles et al. 1993; Fuligni 2019). The Montessori curriculum for adolescents may provide an appropriate stage-environment fit. However, we know relatively little about how independent and collaborative approaches work together to support motivation to learn at the early childhood and elementary levels.

Research could also investigate the interactions between Montessori schooling and the broader sociocultural contexts that shape motivational outcomes. Teachers in more collectivistic societies are more likely to adopt a controlling motivating style; those in more individualistic societies are more likely to adopt an autonomy-supportive style (Reeve et al. 2014). Indeed, such cultural variations exist within Montessori implementations. Montessori classrooms in China depart from strict Montessori implementation by having shorter work cycles and lower student-teacher ratios (Chen 2021). We still have much to learn about the adaptiveness of these variations within their sociocultural contexts; evidence suggests that the universal need for autonomy may have different thresholds in different cultural contexts. Iyengar and Lepper (1999) show that in contrast to European American children, who showed the highest intrinsic motivation when they were allowed to choose their activities, Asian American children were the most intrinsically motivated when activities were chosen by their parents. What constitutes optimal autonomy may vary according to one's socialization in specific cultural contexts, with implications for motivation and schooling. Research should therefore investigate whether Montessori schools in individualistic and collectivistic cultures differ in their approach for supporting students' self-determination, and how these practices support student engagement.

Conclusion

Students' engagement and learning in Montessori schools is predicated on sustained support for self-determination, which leads to good motivational outcomes for individuals at different ages and in different contexts. Accordingly, Montessori schools have been associated with positive outcomes related to students' intrinsic motivation, academic engagement, and social cohesion. However, studies have not always reported details related to the quality of the Montessori schools or the comparison samples, or the schools' broader cultural contexts. Many questions related to students' motivation and engagement in Montessori schools await investigation. However, available research-based knowledge on Montessori schools' impact on student motivation is promising, with strong theoretical grounds for such a relation.

References

Areepattamannil, Shaljan, John G. Freeman, and Don A. Klinger. 2011. "Intrinsic Motivation, Extrinsic Motivation, and Academic Achievement among Indian Adolescents in Canada and India." *Social Psychology of Education* 14 (3): 427–39. https://doi.org/10.1007/s11218-011-9155-1.
Cash, Anne H., Arya Ansari, Kevin J. Grimm, and Robert C. Pianta. 2019. "Power of Two: The Impact of 2 Years of High Quality Teacher–Child Interactions." *Early Education and Development* 30 (1): 60–81. https://doi.org/10.1080/10409289.2018.1535153.
Cerasoli, Christopher P., Jessica M. Nicklin, and Michael T. Ford. 2014. "Intrinsic Motivation and Extrinsic Incentives Jointly Predict Performance: A 40-Year Meta-Analysis." *Psychological Bulletin* 140 (4): 980–1008. https://doi.org/10.1037/a0035661.
Chen, Amber. 2021. "Exploration of Montessori Practices of Montessori Education in Mainland China." *Humanities and Social Sciences Communications* 8 (250): 250. https://doi.org/10.1057/s41599-021-00934-3.
Deci, Edward L., and Richard M. Ryan. 2000. "The 'What' and 'Why' of Goal Pursuits: Human Needs and The Self-determination of Behavior." *Psychological Inquiry* 11 (4): 227–68.

Deci, Edward L., and Richard M. Ryan. 2008. "Self-Determination Theory: A Macrotheory of Human Motivation, Development, and Health." *Canadian Psychology* 49 (3): 182–5. https://doi.org/10.1037/a0012801.

Deci, Edward L., Richard Koestner, and Richard M. Ryan. 1999. "A Meta-analytic Review of Experiments Examining the Effects of Extrinsic Rewards on Intrinsic Motivation." *Psychological Bulletin* 125 (6): 627–68. https://doi.org/10.1037/0033-2909.125.6.627.

Dweck, Carol S. 2017. "The Journey to Children's Mindsets—And Beyond." *Child Dev Perspectives* 11 (2): 139–44. https://doi.org/10.1111/cdep.12225.

Eccles, Jacquelynne S., Carol Midgley, Allan Wigfield, Christy Miller Buchanan, David Reuman, Constance Flanagan, and Douglas Mac Iver. 1993. "Development during Adolescence: The Impact of Stage-Environment Fit on Young Adolescents' Experiences in Schools and in Families." *American Psychologist* 48 (2): 90–101.

Fuligni, Andrew J. 2019. "The Need to Contribute During Adolescence." *Perspectives on Psychological Science* 14 (3): 331–43. https://doi.org/10.1177/1745691618805437.

Gable, Shelly L. 2006. "Approach and Avoidance Social Motives and Goals." *Journal of Personality* 74 (1): 175–222. https://doi.org/10.1111/j.1467-6494.2005.00373.x.

Gagné, Marylène, and Jacques Forest. 2008. "The Study of Compensation Systems through the Lens of Self-Determination Theory: Reconciling 35 Years of Debate." *Canadian Psychology* 49 (3): 225–32. https://doi.org/10.1037/a0012757.

Gottfried, Adele E. 1986. "Academic Intrinsic Motivation in Elementary and Junior High School Students." *Journal of Educational Psychology* 77 (6): 631–45. https://doi.org/10.1037/0022-0663.77.6.631.

Grolnick, Wendy S., and Richard M. Ryan. 1987. "Autonomy in Children's Learning: An Experimental and Individual Difference Investigation." *Journal of Personality and Social Psychology* 52 (5): 890–8. https://doi.org/10.1037/0022-3514.52.5.890.

Hardre, Patricia L., and Johnmarshall Reeve. 2003. "A Motivational Model of Rural Students' Intentions to Persist in, versus Drop Out of, High School." *Journal of Educational Psychology* 95 (2): 347–56. https://doi.org/10.1037/0022-0663.95.2.347.

Hunt, J. McVicker. 1961. *Intelligence and Experience*. New York: Ronald Press.

Iyengar, Sheena S., and Mark R. Lepper. 1999. "Rethinking the Value of Choice: A Cultural Perspective on Intrinsic Motivation." *Journal of Personality and Social Psychology* 76 (3): 349–66. https://doi.org/10.1037/0022-3514.76.3.349.

Johnston, Luz Marie Casquejo. 2016. "Examining a Montessori Adolescent Program through a Self-Determination Theory Lens: A Study of the Lived Experiences of Adolescents." *Journal of Montessori Research* 2 (1): 27–42. https://doi.org/10.17161/jomr.v2i1.4994.

Kidd, Celeste, Steven T. Piantadosi, and Richard N. Aslin. 2012. "The Goldilocks Effect: Human Infants Allocate Attention to Visual Sequences That Are Neither Too Simple nor Too Complex." *PLoS One* 7 (5): e36399. https://doi.org/10.1371/journal.pone.0036399.

Kidd, Celeste, Steven T. Piantadosi, and Richard N. Aslin. 2014. "The Goldilocks Effect in Infant Auditory Attention." *Child Development* 85 (5): 1795–804. https://doi.org/10.1111/cdev.12263.

Koh, Joyce H. L., and Theodore W. Frick. 2010. "Implementing Autonomy Support: Insights from a Montessori Classroom." *International Journal of Education* 1 (2): 1–15. https://doi.org/10.5296/ije.v2i2.511.

Lepper, Mark R., Jennifer Henderlong Corpus, and Sheena S. Iyengar. 2005. "Intrinsic and Extrinsic Motivational Orientations in the Classroom: Age Differences and Academic Correlates." *Journal of Educational Psychology* 97 (2): 184–96. https://doi.org/10.1037/0022-0663.97.2.184.

Lillard, Angeline S. 2019. "Shunned and Admired: Montessori, Self-Determination, and a Case for Radical School Reform." *Educational Psychology Review* 31 (April): 939–65. https://doi.org/10.1007/s10648-019-09483-3.

Lillard, Angeline S., Megan J. Heise, Eve M. Richey, Xin Tong, Alyssa Hart, and Paige M. Bray. 2017. "Montessori Preschool Elevates and Equalizes Child Outcomes: A Longitudinal Study." *Frontiers in Psychology* 8: 1783. https://doi.org/10.3389/fpsyg.2017.01783.

Lillard, Angeline S., M. Joseph Meyer, Dermina Vasc, and Eren Fukuda. 2021. "An Association between Montessori Education in Childhood and Adult Wellbeing." *Frontiers in Psychology* 12: 721943. https://doi.org/10.3389/fpsyg.2021.721943.

Miquelon, Paule, and Robert J. Vallerand. 2008. "Goal Motives, Well-Being, and Physical Health: An Integrative Model." *Canadian Psychology* 49 (3): 241–9. https://doi.org/10.1037/a0012759.

Montessori, Maria. 2007. *The Absorbent Mind*. Amsterdam: Montessori-Pierson.

Montessori, Maria. 2017a. *The Discovery of the Child*. Amsterdam: Montessori-Pierson.

Montessori, Maria. 2017b. *From Childhood to Adolescence*. Amsterdam: Montessori-Pierson.

Otis, Nancy, Frederick M. E. Grouzet, and Luc G. Pelletier. 2005. "Latent Motivational Change in an Academic Setting: A 3-Year Longitudinal Study." *Journal of Educational Psychology* 97 (2): 170–83. https://doi.org/10.1037/0022-0663.97.2.170.

Patall, Erika A., Harris Cooper, and Susan R. Wynn. 2010. "The Effectiveness and Relative Importance of Choice in the Classroom." *Journal of Educational Psychology* 102 (4): 896–915. https://doi.org/10.1037/a0019545.

Ratelle, Catherine F., Robert J. Frédéric Guay Simon Larose Vallerand, and Caroline Senécal. 2007. "Autonomous, Controlled, and Amotivated Types of Academic Motivation: A Person-Oriented Analysis." *Journal of Educational Psychology* 99 (4): 734–46. https://doi.org/10.1037/0022-0663.99.4.734.

Rathunde, Kevin, and Mihaly Csikszentmihalyi. 2005a. "Middle School Students' Motivation and Quality of Experience: A Comparison of Montessori and Traditional School Environments." *American Journal of Education* 111 (3): 341–71. https://doi.org/10.1086/428885.

Rathunde, Kevin, and Mihaly Csikszentmihalyi. 2005b. "The Social Context of Middle School: Teachers, Friends, and Activities in Montessori and Traditional School Environments." *Elementary School Journal* 106 (1): 59–79. https://doi.org/10.1086/496907.

Reeve, Johnmarshall. 2002. "Self-Determination Theory Applied to Educational Settings." In *A Handbook of Self-Determination Research*, edited by Edward L. Deci and Richard M. Ryan, 183–203. Rochester, NY: University of Rochester Press.

Reeve, Johnmarshall, Maarten Vansteenkiste, Avi Assor, Ikhlas Ahmad, Sung Hyeon Cheon, Hyungshim Jang, Haya Kaplan, Jennifer D. Moss, Bodil Stokke Olaussen, and C. K. John Wang. 2014. "The Beliefs That Underlie Autonomy-Supportive and Controlling Teaching: A Multinational Investigation." *Motivation and Emotion* 38 (1): 93–110. https://doi.org/10.1007/s11031-013-9367-0.

Ruijs, Nienke. 2017. "The Effects of Montessori Education: Evidence from Admission Lotteries." *Economics of Education Review* 61 (December): 19–34. https://doi.org/10.1016/j.econedurev.2017.09.001.

Ryan, Richard M., and Edward L. Deci. 2000. "Self-Determination Theory and the Facilitation of Intrinsic Motivation, Social Development, and Well-Being." *American Psychologist* 55 (1): 68. https://doi.org/10.1037/0003-066X.55.1.68.

Setiawan, Niko Albert, and Ouda Teda Ena. 2019. "Junior High School Students' Perceptions on the Implementation of Montessori Approach in Vocabulary Learning." *Journal of English Teaching and Research* 4 (2): 75–92.

Vansteenkiste, Maarten, Joke Simons, Willy Lens, Kennon M. Sheldon, and Edward L. Deci. 2004. "Motivating Learning, Performance, and Persistence: The Synergistic Effects of Intrinsic Goal Contents and Autonomy-Supportive Contexts." *Journal of Personality and Social Psychology* 87 (2): 246–60. https://doi.org/10.1037/0022-3514.87.2.246.

Veugelers, Wiel. 2004. "Between Control and Autonomy: Restructuring Secondary Education in the Netherlands." *Journal of Educational Change* 5 (2): 141–60. https://doi.org/10.1023/B:JEDU.0000033070.80545.01.

Vygotsky, Lev S. 1978. *Mind in Society*. Cambridge MA: Harvard University Press.

Chapter 27
Montessori Education, Optimal Experience, and Flow

Kevin Rathunde

Montessori education has flourished in many cultures for over a hundred years and continues to thrive today. Given this longevity, it is important to ask why this approach has been able to connect with generations of students across disparate cultural contexts. One reason is the central emphasis placed on enhancing students' quality of experience and deep focus. Such an emphasis was rare when Maria Montessori established her method, but it has garnered increasing theoretical and empirical attention in contemporary research on education, especially through concepts such as optimal experience, intrinsic motivation, interest, and flow experience (Csikszentmihalyi et al. 1997; Renninger et al. 1992; Ryan and Deci 2000). These concepts highlight the importance of heightened states of concentration and focus for optimal learning and are consistent with an increased emphasis in the field of human development on the importance of the quality of subjective experience for healthy development and lifelong learning (Rathunde and Csikszentmihalyi 2006).

I begin by comparing the conceptual frameworks of Montessori education and optimal experience or flow theory. The latter perspective is based on extensive, cross-cultural research of the flow experience (Csikszentmihalyi 1990). The word "flow" describes an experiential episode when someone is fully concentrated on the task at hand, relatively oblivious to the passage of time, feeling clear about what needs to be done from one moment to the next, and intrinsically motivated by the enjoyment of the activity. Over the last few decades, flow research has been broadly applied to educational contexts. First, I will highlight the significant similarities between Montessori philosophy and flow theory in characterizing optimal development and learning. Second, I will build on the theoretical connections I have articulated and consider how school contexts facilitate students' optimal experience and positive learning outcomes. Third, I will summarize research that I conducted suggesting that students in Montessori middle schools report more flow and optimal experiences than their peers in traditional middle schools. Finally, I will discuss the implications of these theoretical connections and empirical findings for the continuing relevance of Montessori education and the stimulation of future research.

Exploring Connections between Montessori Education and Flow Theory

Montessori's anticipation of current trends in education has been well documented (Lillard 2005). Her practices were child centered before it was standard practice, and like Piaget, she understood the importance of sensory and motor activities as a foundation for knowledge. However, the extent to which Montessori anticipated an experiential perspective on education, one that places the quality of moment-to-moment attention at the center of learning, has been far less explored, but it is an essential facet of the pedagogy. This becomes evident when we compare Montessori education and flow theory, a contemporary motivational/developmental perspective that explicitly highlights focused attention as the dynamic, self-propelling motor of lifelong learning.

Montessori education and flow theory both highlight the developmental and educational importance of deeply engaged states of concentration. It is fair to say that such immersive states lie at the center of both perspectives. Montessori (1946, 83–4) thought deep concentration was a natural state for children and was essential for education: "It has been revealed that children not only work seriously but they have great powers of concentration ... Action can absorb the whole attention and energy of a person. It valorizes all the psychic energies so that the child completely ignored all that is happening around him."

This description of concentration as being so deep that one becomes unaware of surroundings immediately calls to mind almost fifty years of research on flow (Csikszentmihalyi 1990). In addition to flow's being oblivious to distraction, studies show that it is associated with the merging of action and awareness, a change in the awareness of time (e.g., time passing quickly), feelings of clarity and control, a lack of self-consciousness, and feelings of intrinsic enjoyment. According to the theory, flow is triggered by a good fit between a person's skills in an activity and the challenges afforded by the environment. Flow therefore refers to a bidirectional relationship to the environment wherein someone is fully engaged with a challenging task. Flow promotes learning because such immersive experiences are inherently enjoyable and motivate repetition of the activity that produces them. As habituation sets in, however, repeating the same activity at the same level of challenge and skill will not produce as enjoyable an experience. In terms of education, then, to recapture flow, students must continually raise their level of challenge and/or skill. Students become motivated to learn not just because the teacher expects it but also in order to again experience the thrill of engagement.

This dynamic of continual differentiation and integration underlying human development and learning has held a prominent place in psychology throughout the twentieth century (Baldwin 1906; Piaget 1962; Werner 1958), but it has seldom been viewed so fully through an experiential lens. What distinguishes flow theory is the prominent focus on subjective experience. In other words, while past approaches described the integration and differentiation of knowledge from the outside, a flow perspective reorients the discussion to how the person is connecting with a task at the moment, as revealed by the quality of attention and experience. In addition to Montessori's prescience about child-centered and hands-on learning, she also anticipated this modern turn toward the importance of subjective experience and the inherent motivation that results when children are completely immersed in what they are doing.

Montessori began building her method around the notion of deep concentration during an appointment as director of an "orthophrenic" school in Italy that served children with developmental challenges. Her observations convinced her of the significance of concentration. Famously, a turning point is said to have occurred when Montessori saw a young child occupying herself by trying to fit wooden cylinders into a wooden block (Standing 1984). The child demonstrated unwavering focus, even after Montessori asked the other children to intentionally cause distractions. Witnessing this episode evolved into a main theme of the Montessori method: to create school conditions and teaching practices that make episodes of intrinsically motivated concentration more likely to occur. Such episodes were seen as the key to education because they were directed by "inner sensibilities intrinsic to life" rather than external forces (Montessori 1981, 252). Today these sensibilities might be conceptualized in terms of the central nervous system's drive for optimal arousal, which is manifested from birth by an infant's unlearned attempts to avoid too much or too little stimulation (Berlyne 1960; Field 1985).

Creating a School Context for Optimal Student Experience

When adopting an experiential perspective and highlighting deep concentration or flow as a centerpiece for education, traditional questions about how to create an effective school context may be reimagined. Instead of asking what dimensions of a school context facilitate children's achievement, an experiential perspective starts by asking what aspects of a school context facilitate concentration, interest, and flow. Instead of asking what student attributes are associated with school success, an experience-first perspective is curious about the qualities of students that help them sustain focus. Before jumping straight to outcomes, an experiential perspective reinterprets important questions about education and places a greater emphasis on the process of student engagement. The assumption is that once a dynamic person-environment relationship is established, one that sustains interest and flow, continued learning and achievement will follow naturally. Once an educational environment is set up to facilitate an optimal experience, positive learning outcomes are more likely to occur (Csikszentmihalyi et al. 1997; Shernoff and Schmidt 2008; Shernoff et al. 2021).

Exploring Connections

Montessori put into practice a reorientation toward education. Once she prioritized a student's quality of experience, she set out to create school contexts and teaching practices that facilitated intrinsically motivated concentration. She referred to such contexts as prepared school environments, by which she meant being prepared to enhance deep student engagement. A fundamental aspect of a prepared environment was the balance of skills and challenges encountered by students—a balance that is also at the heart of flow theory. Montessori paid close attention to observing students and selecting activities that were deeply engaging and suitably challenging for children at different stages of development. A great deal of a Montessori teacher's time was spent organizing learning materials that provided progressive challenges and demonstrating their use. Because an educator's purpose was to protect and facilitate a child's intrinsically motivated concentration, keeping an environment free of distractions was an essential part of authentic Montessori education (see Chapter 26: "Motivation and Self-Determination in Montessori Education").

Intrinsic Rewards

Another primary goal of Montessori teachers was to be astute observers of a child's subjective experience so they could ascertain when to help and when to let students work independently. Montessori anticipated contemporary research that revealed how adult praise and extrinsic rewards can undermine intrinsic motivation (Ryan and Deci 2000). She warned that even a simple comment like "how nicely you are doing that" could be enough to disrupt concentration (Standing 1984, 314). The general rule was not to interrupt children when they were engaged in some activity that was orderly and creative.

Zone of Proximal Development

Montessori's views of teaching were also in line with current perspectives on scaffolding or guided participation to help students reach an optimally arousing zone of proximal development—that is, a level where challenges slightly outpace skills and learning is most likely to occur (Rogoff 1990; Vygotsky 1962). She believed in what has been called a golden mean, whereby a teacher, perhaps through a demonstration, provided the "perfect dose" or the "indispensable minimum" amount of instruction to get an activity started, then observed the child to see when to retreat, and let the child continue working independently (Standing 1984, 311). Such give-and-take paid attention to challenging children at the edge of their skills. From an experiential perspective, it is in the zone of proximal development that a student is more likely to find flow (Shernoff et al. 2021).

Freedom and Discipline

For Montessori (1989), a crucial consideration when preparing a learning environment for deep focus was the balance of freedom and discipline. Montessori education is widely recognized as providing students with the freedom to choose activities that interest them; what is sometimes overlooked, however, is that discipline and rule-based order are also considered essential to a prepared school environment, dispelling the notion that Montessori education is anything goes. Montessori was clear on this point: "On this question of liberty ... we must not be frightened if we find ourselves coming up against contradictions at every step. You must not imagine that liberty is something without rule or law" (Standing 1984, 286). Freedom and discipline were seen as interdependent in a classroom where children are free to make appropriate educational choices, not any choice whatsoever.

A parallel is clearly evident between Montessori education and flow theory. Previous research on the family context of flow (Rathunde 1996, 2001) has suggested that a supportive family context that allows children the freedom to be themselves and pursue their interests, combined with a challenging context that expects them to be disciplined and to respect the views of others, is associated with their flow experience at school. The benefits of such a balance are bolstered by a large body of research emanating from Baumrind's (1989) notion of authoritative parents and its extension to teachers in schools (Wentzel 2002) as well as instructors in outdoor recreation courses (Sibthorp et al. 2015). New insights may be gained when magnifying this commonsense wisdom through the experiential lens of flow theory or Montessori philosophy. The combination of freedom and discipline is ideal for regulating the optimal arousal of children. Further, when teachers allow children freedom, children can raise their own arousal by pursuing self-chosen interests; when teachers provide structure and discipline, it helps children channel and modulate their arousal by following rules and respecting the interests of others.

In addition to its benefits for helping to negotiate arousal, the combination of freedom and discipline in a school context serves another critical purpose: promoting children's affective and cognitive involvement (Rathunde and Csikszentmihalyi 2006). Studies using the experiential sampling method (ESM) have shown that flow experience is associated with a distinct set of affective and cognitive elements merging together in flow (Csikszentmihalyi et al. 1997). Likewise, Dewey's ([1910] 1997, 218) conception of an optimal mental state for learning combines affective and cognitive elements, or "being playful and serious at the same time"; and Maslow's (1968) qualitative studies of self-actualization document an emotional and intellectual synchrony in moments of peak experience. A context with support/freedom and challenge/discipline is ideal for stimulating affective and cognitive processes that contribute jointly to flow. Support/freedom is empirically associated with children's positive moods, whereas challenge/discipline is associated with a stronger cognitive focus and goal orientation (Rathunde 1996, 2001). A school context with this combination of characteristics is thus one that simultaneously activates affective and cognitive processes, making it more likely that both kinds of engagement can co-occur in some learning activity and trigger an optimal experience.

The Inspirational Role of Teachers

Teachers are the most important influence on creating a school context for flow, and Montessori's view of teacher preparation and the individual characteristics needed for success were consistent with her overall perspective on deeply engaging experiences. She said the following about students in *From Childhood to Adolescence:* "What he learns must be interesting, must be fascinating. We must give him grandeur." A few pages later, she added of teachers: "Would that the teacher allowed herself to be imbued by the grandeur of this whole to be able to transmit it to the child" (Montessori 1973, 37, 40). In other words, a teacher's own engagement and optimal experience are required to facilitate the same in students. Montessori addressed the same idea about teacher preparation in other writings: "[A teacher] must be filled with wonder; and when you have acquired that you are prepared ... It is not enough for you to love the child. You must first love and understand the universe. You must prepare yourself and truly work at it" (Standing 1984, 309).

Preparation to be a Montessori teacher involves teachers' own intrinsically motivated paths of immersive experiences where they can gain an insider's perspective on optimal experience

(Rathunde 2015). Such a path is described in flow theory as being autotelic or having a flow personality (Csikszentmihalyi 1990). In Maslow's (1968) terminology, it is a path of self-actualization. Waterman (1990) refers to the same orientation as personal expressiveness or an authentic self. Growth-oriented people with these characteristics have more frequent episodes of flow and are therefore more likely to have the kind of experiences Montessori recommends for preparation to be an inspiring teacher. Such people would also be better guides for students because they would have fewer personal limitations that interfere with their ability to recognize and appreciate a child's optimal experiences (Rathunde 2015). Moreover, teachers who inspire—those seen as passionate and interesting people by students—have been found to be more likely to elicit student engagement (Csikszentmihalyi et al. 1997). Whether talking about children or adults, therefore, Montessori thought that experiencing flow and deep concentration was essential for personal growth. For adults preparing to be teachers, it was essential for their ability to appropriately guide the attention of children.

Research on Montessori Education, the Student Experience, and Flow

Given the similarities in the importance placed on optimal experience in Montessori education and flow theory, an in-depth study was designed to assess whether Montessori students would indeed report a higher quality of experience and more flow in school compared to a matched sample. Data were collected from five Montessori middle schools, and comparisons were made using existing data from six traditional public schools. Although data collection at the traditional schools occurred approximately ten years before data collection at the Montessori schools, and some of the Montessori schools were private, the samples were carefully matched on the bases of numerous school and family background variables, following the matching procedures of Rathunde and Csikszentmihalyi (2005a, 2005b).

The Montessori and traditional schools compared were relatively advantageous in that parents had above-average educational levels, the schools had ample resources, and teacher-student ratios were good, with approximately fifteen students per teacher. The Montessori schools, however, differed in ways that reflected the philosophy of education that I describe here. A focus was placed on students' intrinsic motivation and optimal experiences; an appropriate balance of challenges and skills was cultivated by allowing student-directed interests and uninterrupted time for solitary or group work; grades were not mandatory; and teachers adopted a background, observational role and tried to facilitate students' concentration by providing free choice and clear rules and expectations. The term "traditional" was applied to schools that minimized these qualities—for example, the schools did not explicitly emphasize intrinsic motivation, they followed block schedules of 45–50 minutes per class period, they did not provide structured time for student self-direction, and they relied on grades and standardized tests to provide students with feedback.

The study compared the responses of sixth- and eighth-grade Montessori and traditional students using the ESM. The ESM used watches programmed to signal students several times a school day (Csikszentmihalyi et al. 1997). Upon receipt of a signal, they took out response booklets and answered questions about where they were, what they were doing, and especially what they were feeling and experiencing. Students in both samples also completed detailed background questionnaires that provided the information used to match the samples and to control for other individual differences.

The main ESM measures used in the study were as follows: affect (i.e., general mood), potency (energy level), salience (feeling that an activity was challenging and involved important goals), intrinsic motivation (sense of enjoyment and interest), and flow (a heightened state of focus). Interest quadrants were created by combining the intrinsic motivation and salience variables as follows: undivided interest (the combination of above-average intrinsic motivation and above-average salience); disinterest (the opposite of undivided interest, or times when intrinsic motivation and salience were both below average); fooling (above-average intrinsic motivation with below-average salience); and drudgery (above-average salience and below-average intrinsic motivation). Students in Montessori middle schools were hypothesized to report more flow, intrinsic motivation, and undivided interest while doing academic activities. In nonacademic activities outside the mission of the school, and thus less influenced by pedagogical differences, students in both school contexts were expected to report a similar quality of experience.

Multivariate analysis of covariance was used to examine the approximately 4,000 signals collected from the Montessori and traditional students while they were at school doing academic and nonacademic activities. Overall, the set of experiential findings strongly supported the hypothesis that Montessori students had a better quality of experience while doing academic work but not while doing nonacademic work (Rathunde and Csikszentmihalyi 2005a, 2005b). Montessori students reported feeling more positive affect and energy doing academic work, but not while doing nonacademic activities like eating lunch, hanging out in the halls, or chatting with friends. They also enjoyed themselves more while doing academic work, were more interested, and wanted to be doing the work more than the traditional students. In terms of the interest quadrants created, Montessori students reported more undivided interest (high motivation and high salience at the same time) for a significantly higher percentage of time (40 percent) than traditional students, who reported this combination only 24 percent of the time. Most importantly, Montessori students reported a significantly higher percentage of flow experience while working on school activities (37 percent) than did traditional students (30 percent).

Some studies have found no motivational differences between students from Montessori and non-Montessori schools; one such economic study, for example, used a random lottery of applicants to Dutch public Montessori secondary schools and academic data and survey responses on motivation to compare both groups (Ruijs 2017). In contrast, the comparison of Montessori and traditional schools that I just summarized is one of the only comprehensive investigations of Montessori students' motivation and quality of experience using in-context experiential measures (Rathunde and Csikszentmihalyi 2005a, 2005b) rather than retrospective, self-reported survey data. Although Rathunde and Csikszentmihalyi (2005a, 2005b) used no objective measures of student achievement, the higher quality of experience reported by Montessori students strongly implies that they were maximizing their potential for learning.

Montessori Education and the Optimal Student Experience

A great deal of research on intrinsic motivation and flow suggests their connection to outcomes of achievement, talent development, creativity, and lifelong learning (Csikszentmihalyi 1996; Renninger et al. 1992; Ryan and Deci 2000). One pertinent example comes from a study of talented teenagers that utilized the same measures described in this chapter and found a strong link between flow experiences and talent development. Students talented in math, science, music, athletics, and art were more likely to develop their talents; they progressed further in the curriculum, received higher teacher ratings, and made college plans to pursue their talent when their ESM reports indicated more flow experiences and undivided interest while doing talent-related work (Csikszentmihalyi et al. 1997).

Csikszentmihalyi's (1996) study of creativity, and related work on lifelong learning that relied on the same in-depth interviews (Rathunde 1995), revealed numerous links between flow states and creative insight and peak performance. For example, MacArthur fellow and Pulitzer Prize-winning poet Mark Strand described how he felt "right in the work" when writing his best poetry (Csikszentmihalyi 1996, 121): "You lose your sense of time ... The idea is to be so saturated with it that there's no future or past, it's just an extended present in which you're making meaning and dismantling meaning." Compare this with Montessori's (1965, 218) remarks on adult geniuses: "The paths the child follows in the active construction of his individuality are indeed identical with those followed by the genius. His characteristics are absorbed attention, a profound concentration which isolates him from all the stimuli of his environment."

The longevity of Montessori education and its ability to connect with generations of students are partly explained by Montessori's attunement to students' optimal experience. Instead of tying her method to short-lived fads or performance goals that change rapidly from one decade to the next, she based her pedagogy on enduring qualities of human nature and the innate need to negotiate optimal arousal. By tying her pedagogical approach to aspects of human nature that affect the process and experience of learning, Montessori's method has been able to thrive for a century. If nurturing a lifelong learner is the most important outcome of education, then Montessori believed that children needed opportunities to regulate their arousal, experience interest and flow, and successfully repeat the entire process often enough for it to become habitual. In order to maintain and build the relevance of Montessori education for the future, its experiential orientation should be celebrated and highlighted to parents, students, and young adults considering the profession of teaching.

References

Baldwin, James Mark. 1906. *Thought and Things: A Study of the Development and Meaning of Thought.* Vol. 1. New York: Macmillan.

Baumrind, Diana. 1989. "Rearing Competent Children." In *Child Development Today and Tomorrow*, edited by William Damon, 349–78. San Francisco CA: Jossey-Bass.

Berlyne, Daniel Ellis. 1960. *Conflict, Arousal, and Curiosity.* New York: McGraw-Hill.

Csikszentmihalyi, Mihaly. 1990. *Flow*. New York: Harper & Row.

Csikszentmihalyi, Mihaly. 1996. *Creativity: Flow and the Psychology of Discovery and Invention*. New York: HarperCollins.

Csikszentmihalyi, Mihaly, Kevin Rathunde, and Samuel Whalen. 1997. *Talented Teenagers: The Roots of Success and Failure*. Cambridge: Cambridge University Press.

Dewey, John. (1910) 1997. *How We Think*. Mineola NY: Dover.

Field, Tiffany. 1985. "Attachment as Psychobiological Attunement: Being on the Same Wave Length." In *Psychobiology of Attachment and Separation*, edited by Martin Reite and Tiffany Field, 415–54. New York: Academic Press.

Lillard, Angeline Stoll. 2005. *Montessori: The Science behind the Genius*. Oxford: Oxford University Press.

Maslow, Abraham H. 1968. *Toward a Psychology of Being*. New York: Van Nostrand.

Montessori, Maria. 1946. *Unpublished Lectures*. London: AMI.

Montessori, Maria. 1965. *Spontaneous Activity in Education*. New York: Schocken.

Montessori, Maria. 1973. *From Childhood to Adolescence*. Madras: Kalakshetra.

Montessori, Maria. 1981. *The Secret of Childhood*. New York: Ballantine.

Montessori, Maria. 1989. *To Educate the Human Potential*. Oxford: Clio.

Piaget, Jean. 1962. *Play, Dreams, and Imitation in Childhood*. New York: Norton.

Rathunde, Kevin. 1995. "Wisdom and Abiding Interest: Interviews with Three Noted Historians in Later Life." *Journal of Adult Development* 2 (3): 159–72.

Rathunde, Kevin. 1996. "Family Context and Talented Adolescents' Optimal Experience in School-Related Activities." *Journal of Research on Adolescence* 6 (4): 603–26.

Rathunde, Kevin. 2001. "Family Context and the Development of Undivided Interest: A Longitudinal Study of Family Support and Challenge and Adolescents' Quality of Experience." *Applied Developmental Science* 5: 158–71.

Rathunde, Kevin, and Mihaly Csikszentmihalyi. 2005a. "Middle School Students' Motivation and Quality of Experience: A Comparison of Montessori and Traditional School Environments." *American Journal of Education* 111: 341–71.

Rathunde, Kevin, and Mihaly Csikszentmihalyi. 2005b. "The Social Context of Middle School: Teachers, Friends, and Activities in Montessori and Traditional School Environments." *Elementary School Journal* 106: 59–79.

Rathunde, Kevin, and Mihaly Csikszentmihalyi. 2006. "The Developing Person: An Experiential Perspective." In *Handbook of Child Psychology, Vol. 1: Theoretical Models of Human Development*, 6th ed., edited by Richard M. Lerner and William Damon, 465–515. New York: Wiley.

Renninger, K. Ann, Susan Hidi, and Andreas Krapp, eds. 1992. *The Role of Interest in Learning and Development*. Hillsdale NJ: Erlbaum.

Rogoff, Barbara. 1990. *Apprenticeship in Thinking: Cognitive Development in Social Context*. Oxford: Oxford University Press.

Ruijs, Nienke. 2017. "The Effects of Montessori Education: Evidence from Admission Lotteries." *Economics of Education Review* 61: 19–34. https://doi.org/10.1016/j.econedurev.2017.09.001.

Ryan, Richard, and Edward Deci. 2000. "Intrinsic and Extrinsic Motivations: Classic Definitions and New Directions." *Contemporary Educational Psychology* 25 (1): 54–67. https://dx.doi.org/10.1006/ceps.1999.1020.

Shernoff, David, and Jennifer Schmidt. 2008. "Further Evidence of an Engagement–Achievement Paradox among U.S. High School Students." *Journal of Youth and Adolescence* 37 (5): 564–80. https://doi.org/10.1007/s109640079241z.

Shernoff, David, Behesteh Abdi, Brett Anderson, and Mihaly Csikszentmihalyi. 2021. "Flow in Schools Revisited: Cultivating Engaged Learners and Optimal Learning Environments." In *Handbook of Positive Psychology in Schools*, 2nd ed., edited by Michael J. Furlong, Rich Gilman, and E. Scott Huebner, 211–26. New York: Routledge.

Sibthorp, Jim, Rachel Collins, Kevin Rathunde, Karen Paisley, Scott Schumann, Mandy Phoja, John Gookin, and Sheila Baynes. 2015. "Fostering Experiential Self-Regulation through Outdoor Adventure Education." *Journal of Experiential Education* 38 (1): 26–40.

Standing, Edwin M. 1984. *Maria Montessori: Her Life and Work*. New York: Penguin.

Vygotsky, Lev. 1962. *Thought and Language*. New York: Wiley.

Waterman, Alan S. 1990. "Personal Expressiveness: Philosophical and Psychological Foundations." *Journal of Mind and Behavior* 11: 47–74.

Wentzel, Kathryn. 2002. "Are Effective Teachers Like Good Parents? Teaching Styles and Student Adjustment in Early Adolescence." *Child Development* 73: 287–301.

Werner, Heinz. 1958. *Comparative Psychology of Mental Development*. New York: International Universities Press.

PART V
Global Montessori Education

Introduction: Global Montessori Education

Mira Debs

The Montessori method has been a global phenomenon almost from its inception in Rome in 1907. Within several years, Montessori schools were established around Europe and in Russia, Brazil, India, Australia, and the United States (Kahn 2007). Students from around the world came to Rome to train with Maria Montessori. Daily newspapers reported on the Montessori method, sparking interest even in regions where there was initially no access to Maria Montessori's writings or learning materials.

In recent years, Montessori education has continued to expand its global influence. Today, one Montessori organization, the Association Montessori Internationale (AMI), documents Montessori schools in 148 countries with an estimated 15,763 schools according to a recent global census (Debs et al. 2022). The number of Montessori schools globally underscores the relevance of the approach as we continue to grapple with educational access and the fundamental purposes of schooling (AMI 2020; Debs et al. 2022; Whitescarver and Cossentino 2008). This global reach makes Montessori education the largest alternative pedagogy in the world, significantly larger and more widespread than International Baccalaureate (IB) and Waldorf, although in contrast to IB, Montessori education is decentralized with many organizations and independently run schools each defining the quality and components of Montessori education (IB 2020; Waldorf 2020) (see Chapter 20: "Fidelity Issues in Montessori Research").

Although prior work has documented the origins of Montessori education in countries around the globe (see Cohen 1974; Chen and Guo 2021; Kai 2009; Kahn 2007; O'Donnell 2014; Tschurenev 2021), Part V of this handbook marks a renewed effort to compile Montessori organizational histories from countries around the world.

The chapters that follow demonstrate the Montessori method's diverse appeal to a wide array of constituents who have embraced and reframed the method to address their community's educational needs in a series of "adapted, contested and competing framings" (Debs 2022). Over the last century, Montessori education has appealed to wealthy, middle-class, and poor families across borders; educators and education researchers; social reformers; independence leaders; Christians, Jews, Muslims, Hindus, and Buddhists; socialists and fascists; Indigenous educators; and profit-minded and grassroots educators alike. Across these different constituencies, educators, children, and families have been inspired by a model that celebrates and pushes each child to their fullest potential.

Viewing so many countries' Montessori organizational histories together enables us to identify some common themes. First, a number of the chapters show how Montessori education spread in several waves throughout the twentieth century (Whitescarver and Cossentino 2008). The first wave occurred in the 1910s and 1920s with the establishment of the method alongside a global interest in progressive or "new education" (Haenggeli-Jenni 2020). After declining in

Africa
Algeria, Angola, Benin, Botswana, Burkina Faso, Cameroon, Cote D'Ivoire, Congo, Egypt, Eritrea, Ethiopia, Ghana, Kenya, Lesotho, Malawi, Mauritius, Morocco, Mozambique, Namibia, Nigeria, Réunion, Rwanda, Senegal, Sierra Leone, South Africa, Swaziland, Tanzania, The Gambia, Tunisia, Uganda, Zambia, Zimbabwe

Central America
Belize, Costa Rica, El Salvador, Guatemala, Honduras, Nicaragua, Panama

South America
Argentina, Aruba, Bolivia, Brazil, Chile, Colombia, Ecuador, Paraguay, Peru, Trinidad &Tobago, Uruguay, Venezuela

Middle East
Afghanistan, Bahrain, Iran, Israel, Jordan, Kuwait, Lebanon, Oman, Qatar, Saudi Arabia, United Arab Emirates

Australasia
Australia, Indonesia, New Zealand, Tonga, East Timor, French Polynesia

North America
Bahamas, Barbados, Bermuda, Canada, Cayman Islands, Dominican Republic, Haiti, Martinique, Puerto Rico, Mexico, USA, Virgin Islands

Europe
Albania, Andorra, Armenia, Austria, Belarus, Belgium, Bosnia & Herzegovina, Bulgaria, Denmark, Croatia, Czech Republic, Cyprus, Estonia, Finland, France, Germany, Greece, Hungary, Ireland, Italy, Kosovo, Latvia, Liechtenstein, Lithuania, Luxemburg, Malta, Monaco, Montenegro, Netherlands, North Macedonia, Norway, Poland, Portugal, Romania, Russia, Serbia, Slovakia, Slovenia, Spain, Sweden, Switzerland, Ukraine, UK

Asia
Bangladesh, Bhutan, Cambodia, China, India, Japan, Laos, Malaysia, Mongolia, Myanmar, Nepal, Pakistan, Philippines, Singapore, South Korea, Sri Lanka, Thailand, Vietnam

Eurasia
Armenia, Azerbaijan, Georgia, Kazakhstan, Turkey, Uzbekistan

148

Figure V.1 A total of 148 countries in 2020 with Montessori schools. Courtesy of Association Montessori Internationale.

a number of countries, Montessori education increased in the postwar period and in the 1960s and 1970s, again mapped on to a resurgent interest in progressive education. Finally, from the 1990s to the present day, an increase in Montessori education has often risen in connection with growing school choice in both the public and private sector, increased public funding for early childhood education, a rising interest in "international" methods of education in the Global South and a global movement away from strict accountability systems to more holistic, student-directed learning, particularly in early childhood education. In recent years, a growing number of countries are moving to develop national Montessori organizations to maintain the quality of Montessori schools and training programs, coordinate public policy, and expand access to Montessori education.

Alongside these waves, there are also several factors that hindered Montessori expansion globally, such as conflicts like the Second World War, which suspended international collaboration and travel. Fascist, communist, and dictatorial regimes often perceived a threat in a model that emphasized children's independence and free will. Despite her initial collaboration with Italian fascist leader Benito Mussolini to spread Montessori education in Italy (see Chapter 1: "Maria Montessori: Life and Historical Context" and Chapter 28: "Montessori Education in Italy"), Maria Montessori was eventually expelled by fascist regimes in Spain and Italy in the 1920s and

Figure V.2 A student at Fruitful Orchard Montessori, Lagos, Nigeria, completes the Pink Tower Brown Stair extension, with some help from a teacher, while her classmates cheer her on. Photo courtesy of Junnifa Uzodike.

1930s. Subsequently, in the 1930s to 1950s, governments closed Montessori schools in Japan, Germany and Austria, Brazil, and throughout Eastern Europe.

Second, the reliance on "charismatic leadership" (Weber 1978) through a training lineage of Montessori educators has preserved the coherence of Montessori's pedagogy but also limited its spread. Montessori training is largely separate from university-based and government-recognized teacher preparation and has led to many organizational splits within the Montessori movement. As an educational philosophy that sometimes functioned like a social movement and other times resembled a religion, Maria Montessori's role as a charismatic leader and her demands of obedience from her students had benefits and limitations. She attracted a devoted following of highly educated and socially progressive women from around the world who spread her method widely, but she, and later her son Mario Montessori, frequently sparred with her most ardent supporters, often over control of the training and disputes over adapting Montessori practice. Examples include Helen Parkhurst and later Nancy McCormick Rambusch in the United States, Margaret Homfray and Phoebe Child in the UK, Gijubhai Badheka and Tarabai Modak in India, and Clara Grunwald in Germany. These fallings-out created schisms, leadership voids, and shutdowns for the Montessori movement in a number of countries until the next revival. Today in a number of countries including India, the United States, Australia, Ireland, and Canada there are multiple Montessori organizations working in separate and sometimes parallel tracks to advance Montessori education. Finally, the insistence on using Montessori materials and Montessori-approved training has maintained the vital core of a Montessori classroom but has also repeatedly limited the spread of Montessori education, particularly in areas far from Montessori's European base.

Considering who has been educated in Montessori schools, Montessori education occurs primarily in private schools around the globe, although there are notable examples of educators past and present developing models to bring Montessori education to poor, rural, and Indigenous communities including Indigenous Montessori educators around the globe, religious organizations, Red Montessori Solidario in Argentina, groups affiliated with AMI's Educateurs Sans Frontierès, the large public Montessori movement in the United States and Puerto Rico, the Netherlands, Thailand, and in parts of South India.

Alongside government-funded Montessori schools, in some countries, Montessori educators have worked closely with the government for official recognition and in some cases access to public funding. In Kenya and Australia, Montessori organizations have successfully lobbied and collaborated to create a recognized national Montessori curriculum. In the United States, Montessori advocacy organizations in roughly a dozen states have gained recognition of Montessori training for state teacher certification in public schools. In other places like Ireland, an expansion of public funding for early childhood recognition has resulted in systems of regulation that are incompatible with Montessori education and have resulted in a number of school closures.

Another common theme in the following chapters is efforts to adapt and align the Montessori method to a variety of cultures. In a number of national cases, Montessori education has been brought by Western missionaries, both religious and secular, who see Montessori education as an empowering vehicle for postcolonial and Indigenous subjects. In other cases, Indigenous people, such as Tibetans living in exile in India and Inuits in Canada's Nunavut province, have themselves embraced Montessori education as a vehicle for cultural and linguistic survival. In other cases, like China, there is ongoing tension between a model focused on individual freedom and cultural and political traditions that emphasize obedience and communal solidarity (Chen and Guo 2021). Questions of how Montessori education can be brought to communities without denigrating their existing systems of education, finding compatibility with traditional models of education, suggest promising avenues for both further research and practice.

Methods and Global Authorship

When selecting countries for case studies, we purposely worked to bring together a diverse set of contrasting cases: places with long histories of Montessori implementation like Brazil and Germany, places where Montessori education is only beginning to be established like in Saudi Arabia, places where Montessori education is rapidly expanding like Thailand and Puerto Rico, or places where growth has stalled or is declining as in Ireland and the UK. What initially began as eight chapters quickly expanded to twenty-five. However, due to length restrictions for the handbook, the country profiles are brief and do not cover all of the countries where Montessori schools exist. We regret disappointing those whose countries were omitted or only covered briefly.

Whenever possible, we sought out scholars in relevant countries who were conducting research on Montessori education. We also enlisted the help of AMI Educateurs Sans Frontierès,[1] heads of regional and national Montessori associations to author, collaborate, or contribute insights on relevant chapters, and undergraduate research assistants from Yale University, University of Notre Dame, and the University of Oklahoma to help us compile several regional chapters, seeking to bring together a range of voices to inform the diversity of Montessori education around the globe. We worked to ensure that each chapter was authored in part by someone from the country or region. Some of these authors are Montessori-trained in a variety of traditions; some are not. We fully acknowledge that others in these countries might write completely different country narratives. We hope that the diversity of perspectives supports a research tradition that allows for expansive engagement in Montessori education for both experts and non-experts, insiders and outsiders.

Given that much of this history has not been previously recorded, the chapters bring together a range of evidence including academic research, newspaper accounts, published accounts, school and association websites, social media pages, and personal communications and oral history interviews with Montessori educators. While it would have been ideal to have researchers on the ground collecting information and observing Montessori schools in the relevant countries, this wasn't possible during the COVID-19 pandemic. Some data collection about contemporary Montessori schools was done at a distance, via websites, social media photos, and videos, which admittedly could not substitute for the experience of being in classrooms but still gave us a window into the variations and continuity of practice around the world.

Considering Montessori Fidelity across Countries

As we compiled these chapters, we also grappled with the perennial question of defining the sufficient implementation of Montessori education in order for schools and institutions to use the label "Montessori," recognizing that the designation has been contested throughout Montessori's life, has created fragmented Montessori movements within countries and globally, and also represents significant resource differences and cultural priorities in local contexts. Several patterns around Montessori fidelity are worth noting: in a number of national contexts, schools that started off with small pieces of Montessori practice were often inspired to deepen their engagement with the pedagogy following a positive initial experience. Private schools and schools in the Global North often have more resources to pursue greater fidelity, although some of these schools combine Montessori education with other methods. We also repeatedly encountered schools and franchises around the globe using the Montessori name as a signifier for early childhood education or for marketing purposes representing prestigious international education without using the Montessori practice (Debs 2022). And finally, parents have difficulty gauging a program's adherence to Montessori standards of practice (Kishore 2015). As we examined schools, especially in the Global South, we used a "wide tent" consideration of Montessori schools, consistent with the AMI 2006 global census.

Directions for Future Research

In aiming to provide a series of snapshots of a range of countries to highlight the cultural dynamism, adaptation, and range of settings of global Montessori education worldwide, we know that Part V of the handbook represents only the tip of the iceberg of global Montessori research. We hope that Part V will be a starting point to encourage additional research about Montessori education's application in countries around the world. The chapters suggest potential future research directions examining comparative studies of Montessori pedagogy in the public sector; Montessori education's relation to neoliberal education reform including school choice; the relationship of Montessori education to philanthropy, especially in the Global South; the comparative experience of Montessori students and parents; and Montessori education's alignment with local cultural, religious, and educational traditions (see Chapter 52: "Future directions in Global Montessori Research").

What emerges in the following chapters is a portrait of the dynamic application of Montessori education around the world for many audiences and varying purposes, but with the consistency in methods, materials, and training across language, location, and community. As parents, educators, and policymakers around the globe continue to seek out learning opportunities that are child-centered, empowering and develop children's independence from an early age, the Montessori method has continued relevance around the globe.

Note

1. We are grateful to Fay Hendricksen of AMI for facilitating many of these connections.

References

Association Montessori Internationale (AMI). 2006. "Montessori Census." *Montessori Centenary*. Accessed August 19, 2021. http://montessoricentenary.org/
Association Montessori Internationale (AMI). 2020. "Montessori Schools in 2020." Annual General Meeting.

Chen, Amber, and Shu Lin Guo. 2021. "The Spread of Montessori Education in Mainland China." *Journal of Montessori Research & Education* 3 (1): 1–8. http://doi.org/10.16993/jmre.17.

Cohen, Sol. 1974. "The Montessori Movement in England, 1911–1952." *History of Education* 3 (1): 51–67.

Debs, Mira. 2019. *Diverse Families, Desirable Schools: Public Montessori in the Era of School Choice.* Cambridge, MA: Harvard Education Press.

Debs, Mira. 2022. "Montessori in India: Adapted, Competing and Contested Framings: 1915–2021." *History of Education Quarterly:* 1–31. https://doi.org/10.1017/heq.2022.25.

Debs, Mira, Jaap de Brouwer, Angela K. Murray, Lynne Lawrence, Megan Tyne, and Candice von der Wehl. 2022. "Global Diffusion of Montessori Schools: A Report From the 2022 Global Montessori Census." *Journal of Montessori Research* 8 (2): 1–15. https://doi.org/10.17161/jomr.v8i2.18675.

Haenggeli-Jenni, Béatrice. 2020. "New Education." *Encyclopédie d'histoire numérique de l'Europe [online].* Accessed July 25, 2021. https://ehne.fr/en/node/12270.

International Baccalaureate. 2020. "Facts and Figures." https://www.ibo.org/about-the-ib/facts-and-figures/

Kahn, David. 2007. *NAMTA Journal.* Special Issue: A Montessori Journey: 1907–2007 32 (3) (Summer).

Kai, Kimiko. 2009. "The Modification and Adaptation of Montessori Education in Japan." *The International Journal of Learning* 16 (7): 667–76.

Kishore, Kavita. 2015. "Montessori Education: Do Your Research First, Say Experts." *The Hindu*, May 16, 2015. https://www.thehindu.com/news/cities/chennai/montessori-education-do-your-research-first-say-experts/article7212389.ece.

O'Donnell, Marion. 2014. *Maria Montessori.* London: Bloomsbury Publishing.

Tschurenev, Jana. 2021. "Montessori for All? Indian Experiments in 'Child Education,' 1920s–1970s." *Comparative Education* 57 (3): 1–19. https://doi.org/10.1080/03050068.2021.1888408.

Weber, Max. 1978. *Economy and Society: An Outline of Interpretive Sociology.* Berkeley, CA: University of California Press.

"Waldorf World List." Freunde der Erziehungskunst Rudolf Steiners, 2020. Accessed August 19, 2021. https://www.freunde-waldorf.de/en/waldorf-worldwide/waldorf-education/waldorf-world-list/

Whitescarver, Keith, and Jacqueline Cossentino. 2008. "Montessori and the Mainstream: A Century of Reform on the Margins." *Teachers College Record* 110 (12): 2571–600.

Chapter 28
Montessori Education in Italy

Erica Moretti

One must pay special attention to Maria Montessori's relationship with Italy, her homeland, to fully appreciate the foundations of her pedagogy. These influences encompass the educator's personal history, particularly her ambition to be recognized in her native country; her relationships with her mentors; her collaboration with the Italian intelligentsia; and her Catholic faith, among other elements. Montessori's eclectic upbringing, her education, her interest in social medicine, her feminism, and her commitment to the betterment of humanity through activism both informed and were informed by her numerous collaborations with artists, social workers, intellectuals, and pedagogues in Rome (Moretti 2021).

Early Beginnings

To study the inception of the educator's work requires delving into the multidirectional currents that shaped Rome during Montessori's formative years. The opening of the first Casa dei Bambini (Children's House) on January 6, 1907, in the run-down district of San Lorenzo, is an ideal case in point. At the turn of the twentieth century, this neighborhood became the target of a series of urban and architectural renovations by the Istituto Romano dei Beni Stabili (IRBS; Roman Association of Real Estate) in 1905. These efforts were designed to respond to the needs of a peripheral neighborhood. They consisted of street-clearance schemes, the construction of model dwellings, and the establishment of new sanitary laws. The IRBS manager, Edoardo Talamo, put Montessori, already a well-known activist at the time, in charge of an empty room meant to serve as a school and a group of undisciplined children.

Per Montessori's vision, the school was part of a vast project of societal renewal, one that addressed each child's development through a rethinking of all family relationships. Working parents could leave their children for the day without worry. A pleasant and sanitary environment could provide solace and comfort to the entire family. Montessori's engagement with this project was the result of her grassroots militancy, which had brought her to volunteer on the streets of Rome in institutions such as the Asdrubali maternity ward in the Esquilino district and to canvass in favor of reforming juvenile detention centers. She conceived a new form of assistance for those living at the social margins, one that entailed creating a public system of support for and passing social legislation in favor of the lower classes, women, and children. From the roots of her first pedagogical experiment in the district of San Lorenzo, other schools sprung up throughout the city of Rome. Most notably, the third Children's House opened in

Figure 28.1 Children's House in a popular building on via delle Rottole run by Umanitaria, Milan, 1913. Courtesy of Biblioteca dell'Opera Nazionale Montessori.

Milan in 1908. Hosted within the socialist organization Società Umanitaria (Humanitarian Society) and administered by Anna Maria Maccheroni, the institution existed to cater to the city's disadvantaged (see Figure 28.1).

In subsequent years, Montessori worked to systematize her pedagogical approach. Her program would be laid out in her book *Il Metodo della Pedagogia Scientifica applicato all'educazione infantile nelle Case dei Bambini* (The Montessori Method. Scientific Pedagogy as Applied to Child Education in "The Children's House"), written while Montessori was in

Città di Castello, Umbria, in 1909 hosted by Leopoldo and Alice Franchetti. During this period of training courses in Città di Castello and Rome, Montessori resigned from her teaching position at La Sapienza University of Rome and gave up her private medical practice in order to concentrate on the development of her pedagogy. Thanks to this newfound focus, the educator's work would take on an international dimension, beginning with the first international training course held in Rome in 1913.

As Montessori's work gradually achieved global recognition and her travel became more frequent, the Italian state began investigating viable strategies to better educate its youngest citizens. The transnational interest in early education that was sweeping the Western world reached its climax in Italy with a state initiative aimed at establishing a national pedagogy for Italian preschools. In 1914, minister of public instruction Luigi Credaro convened a royal commission charged with evaluating pedagogical methods in use throughout Italy. Over the course of this investigation, the educational theories of Maria Montessori and pedagogues Carolina and Rosa Agazzi came under intense public scrutiny. Broadly, whereas the Agazzi sisters' approach encouraged unstructured play for children, Montessori focused on children at work through concrete learning materials and Practical Life exercises. The commission's inquiry called for a curricular orientation essentially in line with the pedagogy of the Agazzi sisters. Probably disappointed by this result, Montessori slowly began to disengage from collaborations with Italian institutions and organizations, moving the bulk of her activities in 1915 to Barcelona, where the municipality promised the educator new facilities.

It would be a few years before the Italian educator tried again to promote her approach in Italy. By the 1920s, however, Montessori was pursuing recognition for her work in her homeland, to "bequeath her spiritual legacy to Italy" (Montessori 1931). This desire to return to her native soil and to obtain financial support from the Italian government occurred in the context of the establishment of the Fascist regime. Montessori and her son, Mario, corresponded with and met Prime Minister Benito Mussolini (who had come to power in 1922) to request financial and institutional support for her methodology in the country. This led to official recognition and extensive establishment of Montessori schools by the Italian government. Despite this official support, at the time only 4.5 percent of Italian preschools adopted Montessori's approach (Leenders 2018). While seeking support for spreading her methodology, she engaged with all of the major pedagogical forces at play in Italian society. These included philosophical idealists and Catholic intellectuals, whose influence was deeply embedded in Fascist educational programming. In 1927, the government supported the opening of a Montessori school for training teachers. It also financed the magazine *L'idea Montessori*, an official part of the organization Opera Nazionale Montessori (National Montessori Organization) (ONM), which Montessori herself had created to preserve and disseminate her thought and work. At the end of 1927, Mussolini presented to the council of ministers a decree for the establishment of another center for training teachers in the Monte Mario neighborhood of Rome, to be opened in January 1929. But the support would be short-lived. The fundamental differences between the principles of Montessori's work and the warmongering rhetoric of the Fascist regime brought the relationship to a predictable halt. Montessori began public peace advocacy throughout Europe. The Fascist police followed her to track her work, and her method progressively lost ground in Italy because nobody would promote teacher training courses and the establishment of new schools.

Montessori, Italy, and the Postwar Period

The relationship between Montessori and Italy resumed upon her return from India in 1946. In the aftermath of the Second World War, the Italian educator was eager to begin the work of reconstruction, propelled by the belief that each child's hidden capacities would contribute to rebuilding humanity. The starting point for this work could be Italy, she felt, writing in a 1947 letter that she could not miss "the call of her own country that awaits her, that needs her" (Montessori 2002). As she wrote from Kodaikanal:

> Italy! Help Italy with all my strength. I did not invent my method of education—the children of San Lorenzo, forty years ago, planted the seed of this pedagogical endeavor. Roman children!! [...] I have tirelessly dedicated myself to them. I traveled the world like a pilgrim—a missionary—who spoke to the wind ... Still consolidating my work: putting roots in Italy.
>
> *(Montessori 2002, 274)*

In 1949, Montessori returned to Europe and attended the eighth International Montessori Congress in Sanremo, where scholars and trainers from twenty countries presented. A model classroom was set up.

Yet, in spite of Montessori's desire to work for her country, she did not find material support for her approach. The Italian government's proposed restructuring of the educational system in 1951—especially nursery schools, pre-kindergarten, and kindergarten—disavowed the principles of the Fascist regime, but, from a pedagogical standpoint, the discourse around childhood and reconstruction remained fundamentally unaltered (Bonetta 1990). The foundational principles of the Montessori method—that is, the placement of children at the center of the learning process and the emphasis on giving them freedom to choose their path of development—were once again ignored.

The second half of the twentieth century witnessed a general lack of interest in the Montessori approach in Italy. The lasting success of the Agazzi method and the mistrust of Marxist educators in Montessori's work led to a stall, while her methodology flourished internationally. In a moment of radical disavowal of Italy's Fascist past, left-wing intellectuals could probably not forgive her attempts to promote her approach during the regime (Cives 1987, 191).

Contemporary Landscape

In spite of these challenges, Montessori nonprofit organizations in the postwar period continued to offer training courses, becoming a beacon for pedagogical experimentation and dialogue among Montessori trainers. The Fondazione Centro Internazionale Studi Montessoriani (International Foundation for Montessori Studies) in Bergamo, founded by Mario Montessori in 1961, was the first permanent Association Montessori Internationale center to prepare teachers for elementary school. Mario himself lectured extensively there throughout the 1960s and 1970s. Organizations like the ONM, and many of the scholars revolving around it, have maintained a lively scholarly agenda and offered a vast array of training courses for Montessori teachers.

ONM also offers training courses together with Libera Università Maria SS. Assunta LUMSA University, Università degli Studi di Verona, Università degli Studi di Foggia, and the *Centro Nascita Montessori* (Montessori Birth Center). AMI's training courses are offered in Bergamo and Perugia through the Distretto Montessori Perugia (Montessori Perugia District), and they normally cater to an international audience. Currently there are approximately 250 Montessori schools in Italy, most of which are private and exist around a few cities like Perugia and Rome (ONM 2018).

The spread of the Montessori curriculum has halted in Italy due to a general lack of investment from national governments in early childhood education and child care. A 2021 study from the Italian National Institute of Statistics (ISTAT) highlights how the number of nurseries and preschools in Italy is significantly below the European average, with further discrepancies between the North and the South. This lack of support for families, especially mothers, has created a feedback loop that has over time prevented wider female employment. Alongside the larger lack of investment in nurseries and preschools is a general perception that the Montessori approach is expensive; it is often considered too costly and out of reach for public schools.

In 2020, the 150th anniversary of Maria Montessori's birth sparked a new intellectual conversation about the Italian educator, one that will lead, one hopes, to the opening of more public schools bearing her name.

Note

Joke Verheul contributed notes and feedback on an earlier version of this chapter.

References

Bonetta, Gaetano. 1990. "La Scuola dell'Infanzia." In *La Scuola Italiana dall'Unità ai Giorni Nostri*, edited by Giacomo Cives, 36–9. Florence: La Nuova Italia.

Cives, Giacomo. 1987. "Il Giudizio sulla Montessori in Italia dopo la Seconda Guerra Mondiale." In *La Pedagogia Italiana nel Secondo Dopoguerra*, edited by Tassinari Gaetano, 187–94. Florence: Le Monnier.

ISTAT. 1926. *Annuario Statistico Italiano*. Cited in Hélène Leenders. 2018. "A Special Meaning of 'Health:' Towards a Theory-Immanent Explanation for the Use of Montessori Pedagogy in Fascist Italy (1926–1934)." *Annali di Storia dell'Educazione e delle Istituzioni Scolastiche* 25: 202.

ISTAT. 2021. *Nidi e Servizi Integrativi per la Prima Infanzia: Anno Educativo 2019–2020*. https://www.istat.it/it/files//2021/11/REPORT_ASILI-NIDO-2019-2020.pdf.

Montessori, Maria. 1931. Letter to Emilio Bodrero, May 16, 1931. Archivio Centrale di Stato, Presidenza del Consiglio dei Ministri 1934–36 f. 5, n. 2069.

Montessori, Maria. 2002. Letter to Luigia Tincani (1947). In *Il Metodo del Bambino e la Formazione dell'Uomo: Scritti e Documenti Inediti e Rari*, edited by Maria Montessori and Augusto Scocchera, 274. Rome: Opera Nazionale Montessori.

Moretti, Erica. 2021. *The Best Weapon for Peace: Maria Montessori, Education, and Children's Rights*. Madison, WI: University of Wisconsin Press.

Opera Nazionale Montessori (ONM). 2018. Nidi e Scuole Montessori. https://www.operanazionalemontessori.it/nidi-e-scuole-montessori/nidi-e-scuole-montessori-in-italia.

Chapter 29
Montessori Education in the Netherlands

Jaap de Brouwer, Hélène Leenders, and Patrick Sins

From the early twentieth century onward, Montessori pedagogy was very successful in the Netherlands in part because Dutch society was ready for school reform. Due to the "Freedom of Education Act" in the 1917 Dutch Constitution, different denominational and social groups including Roman Catholics, Protestants, Liberals, and Socialists were permitted to establish their own schools with funding from the national government. This context, together with Maria Montessori's concept of "freedom," provided the fertile ground for realizing her call for school reform in the Netherlands.

Early Beginnings

Montessori pedagogy was initially introduced in the Netherlands by psychologists associated with the Paedological Society of Amsterdam and the Foundation for Paedological Lectures in the Hague, who monitored international developments on child research and invited Montessori to give a lecture there in 1914. Jo Prins-Werker, the alleged first Dutch Montessori teacher and a socialist-inspired pioneer, attended the first Montessori training course in Rome in 1914. When she returned to the Netherlands, she started a Montessori class in 1914, founded a Montessori school in The Hague in 1916, and translated Montessori's main work, *Il Metodo* (The Method), into Dutch in 1916 (Leenders 2018).

The great success of the Montessori movement in the Netherlands can be explained by the individualizing and liberal approach toward the education of children, and the receptiveness of so many Dutch educators and parents to a new and progressive method of education. Working with the Montessori method involved a radical rupture from traditional lockstep teaching that was claimed to be rigid, authoritarian, and narrowly focused on students' cognitive development (Imelman and Meijer 1986).

This inspiration soon translated into schools, many of them public. Another group of highly educated, socially progressive women from rich families were inspired to apply Dorothy Canfield Fisher's 1912 book, *A Montessori Mother*, in improving child-rearing practices in the Netherlands. A Dutch translation published in 1915 immediately sold out. The fact that working-class children were educated in the Casa dei Bambini complemented the focus on the social uplift of poor families, which was a central theme in the book, and inspired the city council of Amsterdam in 1919 to convert many public primary schools into Montessori schools (see Figure 29.1).

Figure 29.1 Class photo from the sixth Montessori school, Amsterdam, 1938, by J. M. Bakels. Anne Frank was also a student at this school. Courtesy of the Jewish Museum, Amsterdam.

In 1918 Cornelia Philippi Sieuwertz van Reesema, another early Montessori pioneer, started a child research-based Montessori training in The Hague, independently from Montessori herself, while numerous other educators incorporated the Montessori method into existing schools (Leenders 2001). The Dutch Montessori Association was founded in 1917 by representatives of both the Amsterdam and The Hague pedagogical societies.

Montessori-Froebel synthesis

Teachers from several Froebel preschools in the Netherlands employed Montessori's ideas to improve their standard classroom instruction in favor of a more child-centered approach. Their spokesman was Johannes Herman Gunning, the first university professor of pedagogy in the Netherlands. In 1914 and 1915, he published a series of articles on Montessori pedagogy in which he suggested combining Montessori's ideas on self-education with Froebel's emphasis on free play and fantasy. As a result, all Froebel Kindergartens in the Netherlands were transformed into a "Montessori-Froebel synthesis" in a process supervised by the Dutch Montessori Association. In this era in Europe, this combination of pedagogies was unique. Educational practice consisted of classroom instruction in the morning followed by free Froebel play, and in the afternoon, Montessori work and activity (Eyssen 1919).

Part of the drive of this early growth, experimentation, and collaboration was the fact that, until 1920, Montessori's ideas were freely interpreted and used in the Netherlands without interference from Montessori herself. This status quo changed when she delivered a series of lectures in Amsterdam. Reclaiming her influence, Montessori emphasized that her specific materials should be used exclusively in the way she prescribed, and she reasserted control over personally authorized courses and diplomas (Montessori 1920).

Soon after, the Dutch Montessori Association split into two factions. From 1920, the original Socialist-oriented Amsterdam division continued to further develop the Montessori method following Montessori's direct guidance. In contrast, the scientific, child-research oriented division in The Hague continued to adapt and combine Montessori's pedagogy with ideas taken from Decroly, Ferrière, and Froebel. In 1929, Maria Montessori founded the Association Montessori Internationale (AMI) to protect her method from being combined with other education concepts. In 1935, the head office of AMI was transferred to Amsterdam, where it remains today. Montessori education has continued to grow steadily ever since in the Netherlands.

Montessori Continuity to Today

"The Freedom of Education Act" in the Dutch Constitution ensures that all schools are funded by the government. This situation is internationally unique and made it possible to incorporate alternative education that might elsewhere be found in the private sector as a substantial part of primary and secondary education in the Netherlands. About 10 percent of all Dutch schools implement an alternative educational model, such as Dalton, Montessori, Freinet, Jenaplan, or Waldorf. Many Montessori schools that were founded in the early twentieth century still exist today. For example, the first Montessori school in The Hague and the first Montessori high school worldwide, founded in 1930, in Amsterdam, remain open today.

According to the Dutch Montessori Association, there are currently 219 Montessori schools in the Netherlands: 162 Montessori primary schools, 19 secondary schools, and 38 preschools, all of which are publicly funded. Even though Dutch Montessori schools are accessible for all children, research has shown that nationally, students in Montessori schools often have parents with higher levels of education compared to students in traditional schools (Karsten et al. 2006). In addition, there are more students with non-immigrant backgrounds in Montessori schools than in traditional schools (Inspectorate of Education of the Netherlands 2019). This is a trend that can also be seen in other alternative schools in the Netherlands (e.g., Sins et al. 2021). Students at Montessori secondary schools achieve the same academic results as in other schools, but they report liking school more compared to pupils attending traditional schools (Ruijs 2017).

The Dutch Montessori Association is still the driving force behind Montessori schools in the Netherlands. They play a key role in the certification of Montessori teachers. Once trainee teachers receive their teaching degrees from a regular teacher training institute, they can start working as Montessori teachers and then subsequently follow a two-year part-time Montessori training. With eleven Montessori training centers in the Netherlands, teachers have plenty of opportunities to receive their Montessori teacher training. The Dutch Montessori Association has its own training program for Montessori teachers, which involves a mixture of Montessori theory and contemporary educational insights. To capitalize on the latest educational insights, the Dutch Montessori Association is affiliated with the research group for Alternative Education at Saxion and Thomas More University of Applied Sciences, conducting practice-oriented research together with Dutch Montessori schools.

Montessori Implementation

The Montessori method has historically been applied flexibly in Dutch Montessori schools, with one survey of 449 Montessori teachers demonstrating that there is a great deal of variation in the implementation of the Montessori method across classrooms, with no single teacher implementing a strict or "classic" Montessori approach (De Brouwer and Sins 2020; Lillard 2012).

One strength of this flexible approach is a constant balancing between Montessori tradition on one hand and new developments and insights on the other, allowing an ongoing, lively debate between educators, teachers, students, parents, and other stakeholders on how Montessori's ideas can be applied now and in the future. However, this may also create tension with regard to keeping a firm grip on Montessori's original ideas. To broaden the debate, the Saxion research group for Alternative Education published a book examining the long-running debate in the Netherlands between a stricter and a more flexible approach to Montessori (Berends and De Brouwer 2020). In addition, future research aims to contribute to Montessori teachers' professional development, including, for instance, developing an observation tool that enables teachers to collaboratively exchange and co-construct ways to optimize their teaching.

Conclusion

With more than 100 years of history, the Netherlands has a rich tradition in Montessori education. Due to "The Freedom of Education Act," all Montessori schools are government-funded, which made it possible for Montessori schools to become an integral part of the Dutch education system. Nevertheless, historical developments in the Netherlands paved the way for Montessori schools to practice an adapted version of Montessori's theory, giving rise to an ongoing debate on the implementation of the Montessori method across the Netherlands.

References

Berends, Rene, and De Brouwer, Jaap. 2020. *Perspectieven op Montessori*. Deventer: Saxion Progressive Education University Press.

De Brouwer, Jaap, and Sins, Patrick. 2020. *De Implementatie van het Montessoriconcept in Nederland*. Deventer: Saxion Progressive Education University Press.

Eyssen, C. H. 1919. "Iets over de Montessori Gedachten in de Fröbelschool." *Correspondentieblad van den Bond van Onderwijzeressen bij het Fröbelonderwijs* 15: 37–8.

Imelman, Jan Dirk, and Wilna Meijer. 1986. *De Nieuwe School, Gisteren en Vandaag*. Amsterdam, Brussels: Elsevier.

Karsten, Sjoerd, Charles Felix, Guuske Ledoux, Wim Meijnen, Jaap Roeleveld, and Erik Van Schooten. 2006. "Choosing Segregation or Integration? The Extent and Effects of Ethnic Segregation in Dutch Cities." *Education and Urban Society* 38 (2): 228–47. https://doi.org/10.1177%2F0013124505282606.

Inspectorate of Education of the Netherlands. 2019. *De Staat van het Onderwijs. Onderwijsverslag Over 2017/2018*. Utrecht: Inspectorate of Education of the Netherlands.

Leenders, Hélène. 2001. *Der Fall Montessori. Die Geschichte einer Reformpädagogischen Erziehungskonzeption im Italienischen Faschismus*. Bad Heilbrunn: Klinkhardt.

Leenders, Hélène. 2018. "A Special Meaning of Health: Towards a Theory-Immanent Explanation for the Use of the Montessori Pedagogy in Fascist Italy (1926–1934)." In *Annali di Storia dell'Educazione e delle Istituzioni Scolastiche. Maria Montessori e le sue Reti di Relazioni*, edited by Fulvio de Giorgi, 196–208. Brescia: Editrice Morcelliana.

Lillard, Angeline S. 2012. "Preschool Children's Development in Classic Montessori, Supplemented Montessori, and Conventional Programs." *Journal of School Psychology* 50 (3): 379–401. https://doi.org/10.1016/j.jsp.2012.01.001.

Montessori, Maria. 1920. "Opening Lecture by Dr. Maria Montessori at the International Montessori Course in Amsterdam." *Montessori Opvoeding* 3: 25–7.

Ruijs, Nienke. 2017. "The Effects of Montessori Education: Evidence from Admission Lotteries." *Economics of Education Review* 61: 19–34. https://doi.org/10.1016/j.econedurev.2017.09.001.

Sins, Patrick H. M., Symen Van der Zee, and Jaap A. Schuitema 2021. "The Effectiveness of Alternative Education: A Comparison between Primary Dalton Schools and Traditional Schools on Outcomes of Schooling." *School Effectiveness and School Improvement* 33 (2): 167–197. https://doi.org/10.1080/09243453.2021.1987278.

Chapter 30
Montessori Education in the UK

Barbara Isaacs and Hannah Baynham

This chapter focuses on the early interest in Montessori's pedagogy in the United Kingdom (UK). After an initial surge in the early twentieth century and a second wave following the Second World War, from 1946 onward, Montessori teacher training reinvigorated Montessori education in England. Since the 1990s, parental demand, political interest, and funding for preschool have expanded Montessori education in early childhood education (ECE). The fact that Montessori education is delivered primarily in private schools and also in the early childhood sector in the UK places it in the middle of long-standing tensions between private and government-funded education.

Early Beginnings

The long history of Montessori pedagogy in the UK began with Maria Montessori's first visit in 1899, representing Italy at the International Congress of Women in London (Kramer 1976). Between 1912 and 1915, enthusiastic articles about *The Montessori Method* became a frequent feature in the *Times* and the *Times Education Supplement* (Kramer 1976). This interest was enhanced by the first publication of the Montessori method in 1912 with support from Edmond G. A. Holmes, the former chief inspector of schools for the UK Board of Education (Gore 1912). In 1912, the first Montessori school was founded in East Runton, a small fishing village in Norfolk, and a Montessori Society of the UK was established by Bertram Hawker (Kramer 1976). Montessori's works were translated by Lilly Hutchinson and Claude Claremont, the latter of whom trained teachers for four decades in Hertfordshire and Surrey from the 1920s (Kramer 1976).

Not all of the initial discussion about Montessori education was favorable. Charlotte M. Mason, who supported Froebel's approach, critiqued Montessori's practice for being too rigid and authoritarian in several published articles (Mason 1913). Nonetheless, the London County Council sent a dozen teachers to attend the 1913 Rome lectures, and they subsequently introduced Montessori pedagogy in a few private and state schools across England. One notable example was a nursery established in East London by women's suffragist Sylvia Pankhurst serving the children of suffrage movement activists (Oakley 2013). Alongside the creation of a number of Montessori private schools, between 1914 and 1933, seven state elementary schools in the Borough of Acton in West London used the Montessori approach to educate children from diverse migrant communities. This significant investment in government-funded Montessori education in the UK has not since been replicated (Courtney 1995).

British Montessori educators' organizational momentum strengthened the global Montessori movement, although they eventually faced the challenge of defections, external critics, and economic and political challenges (Cohen 1974). Montessori herself delivered the first well-publicized Montessori training course in London in 1919 and continued to visit England biannually to offer training courses until her departure for India twenty years later. The UK hosted the Fifth International Montessori Congress in Oxford in 1936 and the Seventh in Edinburgh in 1938.

The high level of international interest in Montessori's training delivered in London limited access for teachers from across the UK. Scottish teachers negotiated with Montessori to receive transcripts of her 1935 and 1939 London lectures so that a small interested group could follow her training (Newby 1991). Despite this interest, starting in the 1920s, Montessori's growth was slowed by several factors, including renewed criticism by a new generation of progressive educators and several high-profile defections from supporters including G. A. Holmes.

The depression and the outbreak of the Second World War made the operation of Montessori schools even more challenging; between 1930 and 1950 only a few schools remained open (Cohen 1974). Even so, Maria Montessori authorized courses to be offered in Edinburgh and Acton during the wartime ("Montessori Nursery School Courses" 1944).

Montessori Schools and Teacher Training in the UK, 1945–1990

The Second World War disrupted most education in the UK, and in postwar compulsory education, preschool education was not a priority. Despite the lack of government support for preschool, Montessori's training in the UK in 1946 sparked new interest in Montessori education. With classroom space in short supply after the war, Phyllis Wallbank created a Montessori program at the Gatehouse school in the nave and churchyard of St. Bartholomew's church in East London, enrolling a socioeconomically diverse group of students (Phyllis Wallbank Education Trust 2021) (see Figures 30.1 and 30.2).

In 1946, Montessori returned to London to deliver the first International Course following six years in India (Montessori 2012). The visit also demonstrated the need to establish a London training center; in 1947 Maria and Mario strongly supported the establishment of St. Nicholas Training Organization, which achieved charity status in 1951 under the leadership of Margaret Homfray and Phoebe Child. They added a correspondence school in 1953, which had a global impact on training (Newby 1991). From its inception, the distance-learning model created tension. Maria Montessori was initially supportive, but ultimately the Association Montessori Internationale (AMI) withdrew support in 1952, objecting to the lack of hands-on experience offered to students (Montessori 1956). The correspondence course made learning about Montessori accessible to thousands of educators unable to attend courses in person, which contributed to the global spread of Montessori schools as evidenced by the records in MSN diploma book records (Montessori Group 2021).

Figure 30.1 Students at the Gatehouse school use the nave of the St. Bartholomew's church as a classroom. School founder and the rector's wife, Phyllis Wallbank, is in the back of the photo, 1951. Courtesy of Topfoto.

Montessori education in the UK has been strongly linked with several major Montessori organizations. Like St. Nicholas, AMI's Maria Montessori Institute, founded in 1954 and led by Muriel Dwyer, has a long history of international students and outreach projects specifically in Africa, encouraged by Mario M. Montessori. Montessori Centre International (MCI) was created in 1998 by joining forces between Montessori St. Nicholas training college and the London Montessori Centre. The graduates of both colleges hold deep allegiance to these institutions and these relationships have shaped the Montessori landscape in the UK.

The numerous training centers as well as access to the St. Nicholas's correspondence course also facilitated the expansion of Montessori schools around the UK, especially outside of major urban centers. Until the mid-1990s, these schools operated entirely within the private sector and provided an alternative to the 1960s parent-led playgroup movement.

Figure 30.2 Gatehouse Montessori classes are also held outside in the courtyard among the gravestones, 1951. Courtesy of Topfoto.

UK Montessori Today: Landscape and Context

Although there has long been government support for nursery schools, this provided only partial day provisions for young children and was limited to a small number of schools around the country (Pugh 2009). Starting in the early 1990s, growing public interest in early childhood education combined with increased parental demand for childcare has led to renewed growth of Montessori in the UK, especially for early childhood. In 2019, according to the Montessori Schools Association data, there were approximately 850 Montessori early childhood centers (nurseries) operating in the UK (Kristine Largo, pers. comm.). Since 2000, these programs have received financial subsidies from the government in the form of the nursery education grant, for which most 2-year-olds and all 3- and 4-year-olds in the UK are eligible (Gov UK 2021). There are a limited number of Montessori schools serving older children, mostly due to competition from other, well-established private schools.

By accepting government funding, Montessori providers have had to follow regulatory frameworks. In 2008, the Montessori Schools Association, an organization linked to Montessori St. Nicholas, created a guide linking the statutory requirements with Montessori practice (MSA 2008). Alongside the benefit of making Montessori more accessible through subsidized tuition childcare centers, for Montessori providers, keeping abreast with the government requirements and articulating the Montessori approach in the regulatory context became a challenge. Montessori training colleges were prompted to review their qualification and work with universities and awarding bodies to offer further education and higher-degree programs, such as the Foundation Degree Program offered by the Maria Montessori Institute in partnership with East London University. Montessori Centre International's legacy and experience in distance learning via earlier correspondence courses prompted the design of a hybrid face-to-face and online learning platform in 2014, which provided more accessibility for students in the UK and around the world. In the design of the course, students were given a voice in providing feedback on how the course could improve, allowing for more flexibility and an embodiment of Montessori principles when working with adults (Baynham 2021).

The Montessori-focused delivery of the government's early childhood education framework facilitated greater awareness and opened doors for government schools to introduce early-childhood Montessori and apply key Montessori principles for older children. The successful implementation of Montessori in state schools serving children in low-income communities, such as the Rushbrook Primary Academy in Manchester, starting in 2006, prompted interest from several other schools around the UK (Brooker 2006). Montessori St. Nicholas provided financial and pedagogical support for schools interested in implementing Montessori pedagogy, such as Aldersbrook Primary school in Wanstead, London (Aldersbrook 2021). As has been the case elsewhere, Montessori implementation and its ongoing delivery in government schools are directly linked to the leadership team's commitment to Montessori pedagogy, leadership turnover, and professional development of staff.

During 2020, the leadership and trustees of Montessori St. Nicholas significantly reorganized their activities, changing their name to the Montessori Group and closing the London-based teacher training program that had been in operation since 1951, leading to protest from the students. In a new initiative, Montessori Group is partnering with the Carnegie School of Education and Leeds Beckett University to create a BA degree in Montessori education, and a research-based International Montessori Institute (Leeds Beckett 2021). In a separate development, in 2021, Anglia Ruskin University's academic faculty initiated Montessori BA and MA programs leading to Montessori certification and early years license to practice (Anglia Ruskin University 2021).

The current global pandemic has affected both Montessori training colleges and nurseries; however, the Montessori community has pulled together to support parents more effectively, reevaluating the use of technology and the importance of the outdoors, and placing value in personal and professional development. The challenge of establishing a strong Montessori presence and influence within government-funded education remains an aspiration for the UK Montessori community.

Note

Joke Verheul commented on an earlier version of this chapter, and Lynne Lawrence and Sid Mohandas contributed information for the chapter.

References

Aldersbrook Primary School. 2021. Accessed August 28, 2021. https://www.aldersbrook.redbridge.sch.uk/page/?title=Montessori&pid=22.
Anglia Ruskin University. 2021. "Education with Montessori." Accessed August 28, 2021. https://aru.ac.uk/study/postgraduate/education-with-montessori.
Baynham, Hannah. 2021. "Beyond the 3 Period Lesson: Understanding Montessori Teacher Education as Transformation in Teaching and Learning." Master's thesis, London Metropolitan University.
Brooker, Liz. 2006. "Evaluation of the Gorton Mount Primary School Montessori project." University of London Institute of Education. https://discovery.ucl.ac.uk/id/eprint/10003376/1/GM-Montessori-FinalReport.pdf.
Cohen, Sol. 1974. "The Montessori Movement in England, 1911–1952." *History of Education* 3 (1): 51–67.
Courtney, Margaret. 1995. "The Acton Schools in Montessori Education." *Montessori International Magazine* 6 (5) (January 1995): 26–7.
Gov.UK. 2021. "30 Hours Free Childcare." Accessed July 1, 2021. https://www.gov.uk/30-hours-free-childcare
Holmes, Edmond G. A. 1912. "The Montessori System of Education. Educational Pamphlets." *Board of Education*, Great Britain, No. 24, 1–27. London: H. M. Stationery Office. https://archive.org/details/b1680398.
Kramer, Rita. 1976/1992. *Maria Montessori*. London: Montessori International Publishing.
Leeds, Beckett. 2021. "International Montessori Institute." Accessed August 28, 2021. https://www.leedsbeckett.ac.uk/research/the-international-montessori-institute/
Mason, Charlotte M. 1913. "Supplementary Letter: Miss Mason on the Montessori System to the Editor of the Times." In *The Basis of National Strength*, by Charlotte M. Mason, 47–53. London: Middleton. https://hdl.handle.net/2027/uc1.31158008605379?urlappend=%3Bseq=51%3Bownerid=13510798901903217-63
Montessori, Maria. 2012. *The 1946 London Lectures*. Amsterdam: Montessori-Pierson Publishing Co.
Montessori, Mario M. 1956. "Fragment from a Lecture Held by Mr. Mario M. Montessori December 12th, 1939, during an International Training Course in India." *AMI Communications* 3: 3–8.
Montessori, Mario M. 1956. "To Ensure the Continuation of Recognised Montessori Training in England." *AMI Communications* 1956 (1/2): 25.
Montessori Group. 2021. https://montessori-group.com/
Montessori Schools Association (MSA). 2008. "Guide to the Early Years Foundation Stage in Montessori Settings." Accessed September 18, 2021. https://docplayer.net/7856723-Montessori-schools-association-guide-to-the-early-years-foundation-stage-in-montessori-settings.html
Newby, Delta. 1991. *Margaret Homfray: The Spirit of Montessori*. Avila Beach, CA: Multi-task Business Services.
Oakley, Malcom. 2013. "Sylvia Pankhurst and the Suffragette Movement." *East London History*. November 26, 2013. https://www.eastlondonhistory.co.uk/sylvia-pankhurst-suffragette-movement/.
Phyllis Wallbank Education Trust. 2021 "Biography." Accessed September 5, 2021. https://www.pwetrust.org/biography.shtml
Pugh, Gillian. 2009. "Foundations Early Years." In *Children, Their World, Their Education. Final Report and Recommendations of the Cambridge Primary Review*, edited by Robin Alexander, 159–73. Abingdon: Routledge.

Chapter 31
Montessori Education in Ireland

Tia Williams and Kate Stephens

The Republic of Ireland's educational landscape has long been shaped by faith-based schooling and the ongoing tension between reproducing Irish political, social, and religious culture versus developing children as free-thinking citizens. Over the past century, Montessori education has been adopted by the people of Ireland as a viable, independent early childhood and alternative elementary (called primary in Ireland) education option. Despite the lack of government support in a largely centralized education system in a country of just under 5 million, Montessori education persists through local advocates and national institutions.

Montessori Education in Ireland 1920s–1930s

In 1920, Mother de Sales Lowry at the Catholic St. Otteran's School in Waterford incorporated Montessori teachings into her elementary classroom, effectively forming the first Montessori program in Ireland (O'Toole et al. 2021). Though she had only heard about Montessori from a friend who attended the London training course, and initially had neither training, funding, nor support, she was subsequently able to send several teachers to London for Montessori training, and the Montessori program expanded throughout the school. Class sizes averaged 110 students (St. Nicholas Montessori Society 2010). The St. Otteran's Montessori program went on to be officially recognized by the Irish Ministry of Education and was free of charge to children in the area. In 1927, Montessori visited and lauded the school (Cummins and Phelan 1996, 1–12) (see Figure 31.1). Additional early Montessori schools were the Friends School of Newtown, Waterford, which opened in 1920 and the Ursuline Convent, Waterford, in 1925 (St. Nicholas Montessori Society 2010).

In an attempt to increase the number of Montessori programs, the programs' leaders presented the method at the 1924 Irish National Teachers' Organization Conference (Cummins and Phelan 1996, 1–12). After Irish independence in 1922 and the resulting civil war, educational priorities focused on access and the development of a strong, independent Irish cultural identity rather than the adoption of Montessori philosophy (Department of Education (DOE) 1925). Nonetheless, the St. Otteran's Montessori program endured, albeit as an anomaly, until the school was demolished in 1961. It represented one of the first instances of religious and educational leaders investing in Montessori education in Ireland (St. Nicholas Montessori Society 2010).

Figure 31.1 Maria Montessori visits St. Otteran's school, Waterford, 1927. Courtesy of the Maria Montessori Archives, Amsterdam.

One explanation for St. Otteran's success may have been Montessori's own Catholicism and her emphasis on the spiritual formation of the child (Montessori 1912, 372–5), leading to strong Catholic Montessori links in Ireland as well as elsewhere around the globe (see Chapters 36, 37, 43, and 50 on Tanzania, Kenya, Japan, and Brazil, respectively). This attracted other Irish religious supporters into the 1930s, including Quakers and Ursuline and Dominican nuns, who incorporated the method into their own educational strategies as Montessori programs in Ireland grew (O'Toole 2019).

Despite these religious alignments, Montessori's message of child empowerment was controversial during her second Irish visit in 1934. Father Timothy Corcoran, a Jesuit priest and University College of Dublin professor as well as a key educational advisor to the new Irish state, led the charge against her. He asserted that education should focus on controlling children through "the rod of correction" and called her method "an astonishing specimen of braggart blasphemy" (O'Toole 2019). Corcoran's disapproval meant that government-supported Catholic schools in Ireland followed the dominant, authoritarian model of education that sanctioned corporal punishment, antithetical to the Montessori model.

Despite such critiques, Irish educators worked to develop Montessori schools and expand local training. With persistent interest in Ireland, Maria Montessori supported the founding of Montessori AMI College in Dublin in 1934, which operated until 2012 (Casey 2011). After Montessori returned to Europe from India following the Second World War, many Irish educators attended her 1946 London training course and opened their own schools in Ireland, many of them home-based (Montessori World Education Institute). In one notable example, Nancy Jordan, a 1935 graduate of the AMI College, utilized the method to care for children with tuberculosis. The Irish Department of Education granted her funding for a class for disabled children at the Benincasa Special School in Dublin, establishing a program that still stands today. Despite this instance of recognition, overall, Montessori schools were not recognized by the Irish government and therefore had to be private, limiting their accessibility to the broader population.

1940s–1990s

After the Second World War, Irish educators continued training in the Montessori method; they also aided in spreading the tradition. Irishwoman Phoebe Child, who studied with Montessori in London in the 1930s, subsequently split off and, with Margaret Homfray, established St. Nicholas Montessori College in London in 1946. Subsequently, Irish Preschool Playgroups Association parents Sighle Fitzgerald, Patricia Collins, and Anne Geary took part in distance learning and vacation courses there, which inspired them to gather a small group to found the affiliated St. Nicholas Montessori Society of Ireland in 1970; each founding member donated five pounds to make the program a reality (St. Nicholas Montessori Society 2010). In 1980, the society expanded its program to establish St. Nicholas Montessori College in Dun Laoghaire, awarding diplomas through the London center (St. Nicholas Montessori 2020). Though both the AMI College in Dublin and the St. Nicholas College allowed teachers to be trained in the Montessori method in Ireland, the two had different training approaches and remained unaffiliated with one another.

The expansion of these training programs allowed Irish Montessori educators to open additional schools and serve a larger student population. As graduates continued opening small independent schools, they formed their own groups to advocate for Montessori education in Ireland on a larger scale, such as Nancy Jordan's Irish Montessori Association (later, Association of AMI Montessori Teachers of Ireland [AATI]). However, one challenge was that AMI and St. Nicholas, as separate entities, had different Montessori standards, leading to confusion around the country. Thus, in 1997, with encouragement from the government, the organizations joined to form the Irish Montessori Education Board (IMEB), jointly accrediting schools and communicating with the Irish Department of Education (DOE) as a unified entity (Irish Montessori Education Board). This development ensured that independent schools could be officially recognized and that teachers trained under either program would meet minimum requirements for an Irish teacher qualification (Department of Children and Youth Affairs 2016).

While the number of Montessori schools in Ireland remained small, and the schools were private, Montessori exerted significant influence around Ireland on Montessori-based Catholic religious instruction. In 1954, Italian biblical scholar Sofia Cavalletti worked with Montessori educator Gianna Gobbi to develop a Catholic faith formation program they named Catechesis of the Good Shepherd (CGS) (Maresca 2005). They noticed and appreciated children's enthusiasm for learning the Bible and incorporated Montessori's principles of following the child in their fascination, especially in religious contexts, rather than assigning or limiting specific knowledge. Cavalletti provided training at the Dominican Convent at Sacred Heart College, Mount Anville, Dublin, in 1958 (Fox 2009). CGS continues today at the Benincasa Special School in Sion Hill (Catechesis of the Good Shepherd). Since the early 2000s, CGS has experienced some resurgence, and there are Montessori-inspired religious formation programs of this nature in Dublin, Kerry, Sligo, and Galway.

Contemporary Landscape and Perceptions of Montessori

Today, Montessori education still exists on the margins of a large, diversely administered, publicly funded Irish education system where, despite the decline of the Catholic Church in recent years, 88.7 percent of the primary schools are still overseen by the Catholic Church (DOE 2021). The most notable recent shifts are related to policies on early childhood education.

Montessori today occurs primarily in private early childhood education in Ireland. In fact, of the eighty-one Montessori schools accredited by the Irish Montessori Education Board, only one has an elementary program (Irish Montessori Education Board). Efforts to fund and regulate early childhood education have also unintentionally hurt existing Montessori programs. In 2009, the Irish government developed a free-tuition preschool program with its own curriculum, *Aistear* (Journey) (NCCA 2009). Although this scheme allows for public funding for private preschool programs, it requires compliance with the Aistear framework and other regulations. While Aistear and Montessori learning have similar goals, especially the development of the whole child, the Aistear curriculum encourages pretend play, which directly clashes with the Montessori method's focus on natural, applicable skill development. An estimated half of Association of AMI Teachers in Ireland (AATI)-affiliated Montessori schools have closed since 2009. In addition, in 2010, the Department of Children and Youth Affairs required early childhood educators to be certified but declined to recognize the Montessori programs. Although educators have found workarounds, this policy has further complicated the training of Montessori educators.

Montessori advocates continue to work with government agencies to support and certify the training programs through St. Nicholas, but due to the lack of governmental support for Montessori, the remaining Montessori schools are in the private sector, where they can maintain fidelity to the pedagogy but reach fewer children than they would through the Irish public education system.

Conclusion

Montessori education currently faces significant challenges in Ireland. The absence of government approval of Montessori suggests that the number of Montessori schools may continue declining, and the pedagogy will remain restricted to private, tuition-based schools due to the lack of public funding. However, the persistence of Montessori principles within the Irish educational landscape, despite a lack of official support, is a testament to the work of Montessori educators in the national arena. These advocates remain committed to the method in their schools and encourage its adoption, as did their predecessors for nearly a century. The resilience and hope of these educators offer a pathway for Montessori's legacy to continue in Ireland.

Note

Alison Pigot and Joke Verheul commented on an earlier version of this chapter.

References

Casey, Caoilfhionn. 2011. "Association of AMI Teachers, Ireland (AATI)." *Educateurs sans Frontières*. https://montessori-esf.org/sites/default/files/2011Ireland.pdf.

Catechesis of the Good Shepherd. "In Ireland." Accessed June 30, 2021. http://cgs.ie/?page_id=21.

Cummins, Sister M. Redemptoris, and Sister M. Josepha Phelan. 1996. "Maria Montessori—Her Links with Waterford." *The Waterford Archaeological & Historical Society Journal* 52: 1–12.

Department of Children and Youth Affairs (DCYA). 2016. "DCYA Early Years Recognised Qualifications." Accessed June 30, 2021. https://www.kccc.ie/Portals/0/20160422DCYAEarlyyearsQualifications.pdf.

Department of Education (DOE). 1925. "Statistics Relating to National Education in Saorstát for the Year 1922–23." Accessed June 23, 2021. https://www.education.ie/en/Publications/Statistics/stats_statistical_report_1923_1924.pdf.

Department of Education (DOE). 2021. "Statistical Bulletin—July 2021." Accessed July 21, 2021. https://www.education.ie/en/Publications/Statistics/statistical-bulletin-2020-2021.pdf.

Fox, Mary. 2009. *Journals of the Catechesis of the Good Shepherd, 2003–2008*. Chicago: Liturgy Training Publications.

Irish Montessori Education Board. "About Us." Accessed June 10, 2021. http://www.imebtrust.org/About%20Us.htm.

Irish Montessori Education Board. "Our Schools." Accessed June 30, 2021. http://www.imebtrust.org/List%20of%20Schools2.htm.

Maresca, Catherine. 2005. "A Curriculum for Young Children: Catechesis of the Good Shepherd." *Sewanee Theological Review* 48 (4): 387, 457–66.

Montessori, Maria. 1912. *The Montessori Method*. New York, NY: Frederick A. Stokes Company

National Council for Curriculum and Assessment (NCCA). 2009. "Aistear: The Early Childhood Curriculum Framework." Accessed June 30, 2021.

O'Toole, Fintan. 2019. "Ireland's Education System Was Rigid and Violent." *The Irish Times*, February 2. https://www.irishtimes.com/culture/heritage/fintan-o-toole-ireland-s-education-system-was-rigid-and-violent-1.3774797.

O'Toole, Leah, Diane McClelland, Deirdre Forde, Suzanne O'Keeffe, Noel Purdy, Carl Anders Säfström, and Thomas Walsh. 2021. "Contested Childhoods across Borders and Boundaries: Insights from Curriculum Provisions in Northern Ireland and the Irish Free State in the 1920s." *British Educational Research Journal* 47 (4): 1021–38, March 8. https://doi.org/10.1002/berj.3708.

St. Nicholas Montessori Society of Ireland. 2010. *Newsletter*, Spring 2010: 1–2, 7. http://www.montessoriireland.ie/forms/2011/Newsletter%2040th%20Anniversary%20edition%20%202010.pdf

St. Nicholas Montessori Society of Ireland. 2020. "History of St. Nicholas Montessori Society of Ireland." Accessed June 30, 2021. https://smsi.ie/about/.

Chapter 32
Montessori Education in Nordic Countries

Petter Sandgren and Eva-Maria Tebano Ahlquist

The Nordic countries—Sweden, Denmark, Finland, Norway, and Iceland—are often regarded as distinct regarding education politics and policies. The keywords in the Nordic educational model from the postwar years to today have been equality, solidarity, and community, resulting in uniform school systems that significantly influence the diffusion and adaptation of Montessori education.

Despite early enthusiasm in the 1910s and 1920s, the history of Montessori education in Sweden, Denmark, Finland, and Norway has been defined by the struggle to find a place within these uniform school systems as part of the larger welfare state project, and in Iceland, the Montessori method has never taken root (Einarsdottir 2006). More recently, the introduction of school choice and publicly funded but privately controlled so-called free schools have altered the dynamic of the uniform Nordic school systems (except for Finland, which remains predominantly centralized). In this respect, the Nordic countries serve as an illuminating case study of how Montessori education has been implemented in uniform and centralized school systems and how that landscape changes with school choice policies.

Montessori's Early Years and Historical Development

The common theme running through the introduction of Montessori's ideas in the Nordic countries—and across the world—is the central role of women. In Denmark, Marie Helms wrote an article about Montessori's school in Rome in 1911, and in Finland, Oskari Mantere published an article in 1914. In the same year, Ruth Philip, after a visit to the Casa dei Bambini in Rome, wrote in the Swedish Women's Federation magazine, *Hertha*, that the principle of freedom "prevents sadness and fatigue," but that it would be difficult to find teachers capable of applying the educational principles (Ruth 1914, 206). Helms's article was read by Thora Constantin-Hansen, founder of the Montessori Association in Denmark in 1917, who created Montessori classrooms at a school for physically disabled children in 1918 and founded Montessori schools in Southern Jutland, Copenhagen, and Roskilde (Nasgaard 1929). In Stockholm, Montessori classes were incorporated into Anna Schuldhei's school as early as 1914 (Tebano Ahlquist 2012).

Figure 32.1 Children in Ida Sjögren's Montessori school in Norrköping, Sweden, 1924. Courtesy of the Norrköping City Archives.

Other important persons in the diffusion of Montessori's educational ideas were those who had attended Montessori's courses in London in 1919 and 1920, including Elna Marstrand, the first principal of the Montessori kindergarten in Copenhagen; the Swedish educator Anna Pallin, who founded the first full Montessori preschool in Stockholm in 1923; and Maria Moberg and Ida Sjögren, both Froebel teachers in Norrköping (see Figure 32.1).

Montessori education was present among leading Swedish social democrats in the 1930s. Teacher training at the Social Pedagogical Seminary (1939–1945), directed by Alva Myrdal,[1] was influenced by Montessori pedagogy (Gröning 2006). Although Montessori's ideas were frequently discussed in educational circles, the expansion and consolidation of Montessori's ideas in Nordic countries was predominantly a postwar phenomenon (Quarfood 2011).

The Danish Montessori Society was also a locus in spreading Montessori's ideas in the other Nordic countries, arranging popular lecture series in Sweden and Norway. There was also a connection with the scholarly community, where Sigurd Nasgaard and Sofie Rifbjer gave a two-year course in Montessori education in Copenhagen starting in 1928.

Maria Montessori first visited Denmark in 1929, giving a lecture at the New Education Fellowship Fifth World Congress in Helsingør. This was an important venue for the Nordic diffusion of Montessori's ideas, which depended on conferences, networks, and transnational cooperation throughout the interwar period (Kuikka 1996). In 1950, Montessori visited Stockholm and Gothenburg (see Figure 32.2).

Figure 32.2 Maria Montessori visits Sweden, 1950. Courtesy of the Stockholm City Museum.

Montessori Diffusion 1945–1990

From 1945 until about 1970, a comprehensive nine-year compulsory educational system emerged in the Nordic countries as part of the mission of building a new society. The national curricula, with their increased focus on democratic student participation, individualization, and emancipation, made Montessori's work more applicable to the Nordic environment. Many of the key players in the planning of the school system of Sweden, including education scholar Torsten Husén and the social democrat of the 1946 School Commission Stellan Arvidsson, expressed their desire to introduce Montessori's educational ideas into the school system. Arvidsson and Husén would later serve as the first board members of the Swedish Montessori Society, founded in 1960 (Tebano Ahlquist 2012).

This period also brought national Montessori organizing efforts. In addition to the Swedish Montessori Society, the Finnish Montessori Association and the Norwegian Montessori Society were both founded in 1979. In the early 1980s, a proposal from the Nordic Council to create a Nordic Montessori teacher training center was unsuccessful, and as a result, teachers needed to obtain Montessori training abroad (Nordic Council 1988). Montessori education's expansion slowed due to the fact that the pedagogy remained outside the Nordic blueprint, and Montessori training was not integrated into national teacher training programs, receiving only a brief mention at the university level (Larsson and Westberg 2015; SOU 1946, 31).

During the 1980s, when Montessori education was expanding in Finland, the Finnish Montessori Association deemed it unnecessary to start separate Montessori schools; instead, they formed Montessori classes within the regular comprehensive schools. The reasons for this were not solely practical ones; the association feared that separate Montessori schools would create a different sort of pupil group, both socially and with regard to educational training, compared to the youth in the uniform, comprehensive school system (Kuikka 1996). This episode captures much of the thinking of the import and adaptation of Montessori's educational ideas in the Nordic countries; it had to fit in with the rather homogenous educational landscape. Montessori's educational ideas were portrayed as a complement and not a substitute.

Contemporary Landscape, 1990s to 2021

The emergence of school choice, vouchers, and free schools during the early part of the 1990s has influenced the Nordic educational model, creating new opportunities to start Montessori schools in previously centralized educational systems. Although Sweden has gone the furthest with universal school choice for all its pupils and the expansion of free schools, public schools that can be run by for-profit entities akin to charter schools in the United States, market forces, and school choice are also gaining ground in Denmark and Norway, and to a lesser extent in Finland. This leads to the question of whether there still exists a distinctive Nordic model for educational politics and policies. Overall, the private/independent sector, where most Montessori schools are based, is growing across Nordic countries. Since schools in this sector are primarily publicly and not privately funded, they have become a more integrated part of the general educational system. For example, in Norway, the only way to maintain a school in a depopulated area is to convert the school to an alternative pedagogy, which has led to the creation of many publicly funded, privately run Montessori schools.

There is a need, however, for further research on how Montessori schools have been affected by this change: whether they enjoy more institutional independence than before, who enrolls in Montessori schools, and the effects of Montessori schools now more often being part of for-profit educational chains. For example, in Sweden, research has shown that the parents' socioeconomic background tends to be higher in Montessori schools than the municipal average, with differences between urban and rural areas (*Skolverket* 2022). This pattern follows the larger international pattern of social division connected to school choice and is not Montessori-specific (Boterman et al. 2021).

In some of the Nordic countries, Montessori education has a centralized organizational structure and an explicit count of affiliated schools, as exemplified by Norway, which has a national Montessori curriculum that all 131 Montessori schools must follow. In other countries, the organization structure is more diffuse. According to Svenska Montessoriförbundet's (Swedish Montessori Society) website, Montessori preschools and schools number close to 300. With the exception of Norway, across remaining Nordic countries, there is no consensus regarding Montessori curriculum, which schools can use the term "Montessori" and who has the right to call themselves a Montessori teacher. However, courses for Montessori teachers are now offered at the university level, including at Stockholm University and University of South-Eastern Norway. Other private training courses exist, including at the Montessori Centre for Work and Study outside Gothenburg, Sweden, and the Finnish Montessori Training Enterprise in Espoo. The *Journal of Montessori Research & Education* serves as an essential Nordic hub for research. Question of standardization regarding curriculum, professionalization, and research are future challenges for the further consolidation of Montessori education in the Nordic countries.

Conclusion

While Montessori education was enthusiastically brought to Nordic countries in the early twentieth century, much of its influence occurred as ideas were diffused into the standardized, comprehensive government school systems developed after 1945. Montessori education has been regarded as an acceptable pedagogical alternative to the uniform school systems, a complement that has not strayed too far from the values and ideas represented by the national curriculum. Paradoxically, this acceptance has not been fully reflected in the teaching and research at the university level, where the Montessori method is still regarded as a pedagogical outsider searching for recognition.

Note

1. Alva Myrdal received the Nobel Peace Prize in 1982.

References

Boterman, Willem R., Sako Musterd, and Dorien Manting. 2021. "Multiple Dimensions of Residential Segregation: The Case of the Metropolitan Area of Amsterdam." *Urban Geography* 42 (4): 481–506.
Einarsdottir, Johanna. 2006. "Between Two Continents, between Two Traditions." In *Nordic Childhoods and Early Education: Philosophy, Research, Policy and Practice in Denmark, Finland, Iceland, Norway and Sweden*, edited by Einarsdottir and John A. Wagner, 159–82. Charlotte, NC: Information Age Publishing.
Gröning, Lotta. 2006. *Kvinnans Plats: min Bok om Alva Myrdal*. Stockholm: Bonnier.

Kuikka, Martti T. 1996. "Education Policy and Alternative Pedagogies in Finland 1950-1995." *Koulu ja Menneisyys* 34 (January 1996): 17–39.

Larsson, Esbjörn, and Johannes Westberg, editors. 2015. *Utbildningshistoria: en introduktion*. 2nd ed. Lund: Studentlitteratur.

Nasgaard, S. 1929. "The Montessori Movement in Denmark." *The New Era* 10: 61–6.

Nordic Council. 1988. *Nordiska Rådets Verksamhet 1971-1986: Översikt över Rådets Rekommendationer och Yttranden*. Copenhagen: Nordic Council of Ministers.

Philip, Ruth. 1914. "Montessorimetoden." *Hertha, Tidskrift för den Svenskakvinnorörelsen* 1 (10): 205–12.

Quarfood, Christine. 2011. "'Att Rubba det Bestående Skolsystemets Cirklar': Mellankrigstidens svenska Montessoridebatt." In *Förskolans Aktörer: Stat, Kår och Individ i Förskolans Historia*, edited by Johannes Westberg. Stockholm: Historiska institutionen.

Skolverket, National Agency for Education. 2022. https://siris.skolverket.se/siris/f?p=SIRIS:164.

Sverige 1940 års skolutredning. 1946. 1940 års skolutrednings betänkanden och utredningar VI Skolans inre arbete : synpunkter på fostran och undervisning. Stockholm.

Tebano Ahlquist, Eva-Maria. 2012. *Skolans Levda rum och Lärandets Villkor: Meningsskapande i Montessoriskolans Fysiska Miljö*. PhD Diss., Stockholm University.

Chapter 33
Montessori Education in Germany

Jörg Boysen

Montessori education has a long tradition in Germany. It was already widely recognized between the world wars but has substantively grown from the 1950s onward. Today, there are hundreds of Montessori educational institutions in Germany, from early childhood to secondary schools.

German Montessori Beginnings, 1913–1936

Three teachers from Germany, Hilde Hecker, Else Ochs, and Elizabeth Schwarz, participated in Maria Montessori's Second International Course in 1913–1914, inspiring their colleague Clara Grunwald who later trained with Montessori in London. Grunwald helped to run the first German Montessori training in 1923. She established the Montessori-Komitee (Montessori Committee) in 1919, which set up Children's Houses for working-class German families that ultimately developed into the Deutsche Montessori Gesellschaft (German Montessori Society) in 1925, with Grunwald as president (Günnigmann 1979). As early as the 1920s, Montessori education expanded to public elementary schools in Germany. The first Montessori class opened in Berlin-Lankwitz in 1926, and others followed at elementary schools in Lichtenberg and Wedding and at a private Montessori school in the Dahlem district (O'Donnell 2014).

Admiration for Maria Montessori and her ideas was not universal in Germany. Montessori's followers largely came from Catholic and Jewish circles, while socialist circles tended to reject Montessori education. Froebel advocates, who emphasized children's play, opposed Montessori's conception of the child at work. In addition, from about 1929 onward, Maria Montessori and Clara Grunwald argued over control of training courses, paralyzing German Montessori education from within. Maria Montessori formed a competing association, Verein Montessori-Pädagogik Deutschland (German Society of Montessori Pedagogy), excluding Grunwald. By 1934, Montessori's Society had twenty-four Children's Houses and twelve Montessori elementary schools (Günnigmann 1979).

Germany's contribution to the Montessori movement in the late 1920s and early 1930s is also evident from the opening of the office of the Association Montessori Internationale (AMI) in Berlin soon after the organization's founding in 1929. Berlin was to serve as a hub for the Montessori community in Central Europe. AMI's headquarters moved to London in 1934 and to Amsterdam in 1935, where they remain today (O'Donnell 2014). By 1936 at the latest, all Montessori institutions were closed by National Socialist policy directives. Clara Grunwald died in Auschwitz with the children in her care (Holtz 1995).

Renaissance of Montessori Education after 1945

The expansion of the Montessori movement in Germany after the Second World War initially involved several parallel, interdependent initiatives: teacher training, the establishment of Montessori schools, Montessori in academia and finally, a national Montessori organization. For clarity, these four topics are treated sequentially; in practice, of course, the same key institutions and persons were involved in numerous activities as the movement grew.

The German education system differentiates between early childhood education (optional 0–3 daycare and mandatory 3–6 kindergarten); elementary up to grade 4 or 6; lower secondary up to grade 9 or 10, often including selection into three tracks; and then upper secondary school up to graduation in grade 12 or 13. We will refer to all of these as "schools."

Montessori Teacher Training

Shortly before her death, Maria Montessori encouraged her son Mario to reestablish a German affiliate of AMI. With the support of Margarete Aurin and Helene Helming, who had trained with Maria Montessori before the war, and Paul Scheid, they re-founded the Deutsche Montessori Gesellschaft (German Montessori Society) (DMG) in 1952. DMG conducted its first teacher training course for ages 3–7, directed by Mario Montessori, in Frankfurt in 1954. One of the regional groups established within DMG became an independent teacher training association in 1962 and subsequently an AMI affiliate: Deutsche Montessori-Vereinigung (German Montessori Association) (DMV). DMG and DMV conducted teacher training courses that, for a time, were authorized by Mario Montessori and AMI. Now operating separately with their own licensed courses and trainers, both have expanded significantly over the years.

German Montessori also played a significant role in developing Montessori training and schools for disabled children, in what became known as the "Munich Montessori Model." With Margarete Aurin, the Munich-based doctor Theodor Hellbrügge—considered the founder of modern social pediatrics in Germany—launched a Kinderzentrum (Children's Center), kindergarten, and later an elementary school for disabled students, at his medical institute, Aktion Sonnenschein, starting in 1968. Hellbrügge successfully invited Mario Montessori to lead an international teacher training course in Munich in 1970–1971. With Mario Montessori's support, Hellbrügge and Aurin developed an AMI Montessori Special Education Course, the first of which was held in 1976–1977.

Many of Hellbrügge's staff launched schools and teacher training organizations, almost all of which today are members of Montessori Bundesverband Deutschland (German Federal Montessori Association) (see below). Claus Kaul founded the Institut für ganzheitliches Lernen (Institute for Holistic Learning), later merging into Montessori Biberkor, in 1991. Maria Roth set up the AMI Training Center Munich in 1998, at which the AMI trainer Peter Gebhardt-Seele held the first AMI elementary courses in Germany, a pivotal moment for bringing the standards and knowledge of the age group-specific AMI training courses back to Germany. Deutschsprachige AMI-Pädagogen (DAMIP) (Association of German-Speaking AMI Pedagogues) follows this tradition with a course first offered in 2022. Ingeborg Müller-Hohagen and Christa Kaminski founded the Bildungsakademie (Educational Academy) of the Bavarian Regional Montessori

Association in 1998. After German reunification in 1990, Friedemann Schulze founded the association Aktion Sonnenschein Thüringen (Action Sunshine Thuringia), offering Montessori training courses in Erfurt, Thuringia, since 2012. All of these teacher training organizations still conduct Montessori courses with curricula based on or inspired by Aktion Sonnenschein's course. The Heilpädagogische Vereinigung (Therapeutic Education Association) (HPV), which covers similar content but emerged from DMG roots, conducted its first course in 1988–1989; Montessori Labor Berlin emerged from it in 2012.

One challenge posed by the development of so many Montessori training programs in Germany is that curricula and credentials have largely been unregulated. As described, German Montessori training courses were initially based on the curriculum of the AMI courses in the 1950s and 1970s, respectively. These "national" courses became dominant over time, loosening the connection with the ongoing development of AMI courses outside Germany. DMG, DMV, and HPV agreed on the standardization of their national diploma courses in the late 1990s.

Montessori School Growth

As with the training programs, teachers who studied with Maria Montessori in the 1920s and early 1930s led the postwar opening of German Montessori schools. For example, Aurin created a short-lived Montessori school in 1946 in the Soviet sector of Berlin before fleeing to West Berlin. In British-controlled Berlin, Irene Dietrich's school, opened in 1947, was greeted with enthusiasm by the occupying authorities (O'Donnell 2014). Early schools also existed in North-Rhine Westphalia (Günnigmann 1979).

Montessori classrooms or schools starting at the elementary level developed mainly in the state school system in North-Rhein Westphalia and to some extent in Baden-Württemberg and Berlin. Most provinces would not consider Montessori pedagogy for a state-run school, arguing that this would limit parental choice. State schools have substantial leeway in mixing aspects of Montessori education with other pedagogical concepts, spreading Montessori ideas but simultaneously diluting the effectiveness of Montessori pedagogy.

The expanding kindergarten movement in the 1960s and 1970s helped increase the number of German Montessori schools, and since the mid-1980s, parent-led private Montessori schools have grown significantly, comprising a portion of the 10 percent of students attending private schools partially funded by the state. Private Montessori schools can be found in all provinces. Bavaria leads with over 100 schools, most of which span early childhood education up to the lower secondary level and sometimes beyond. Regional Montessori associations covering fourteen provinces have followed, with only Sachsen-Anhalt and Mecklenburg-Vorpommern now without a regional association.

The predominance of Montessori in private schools presents both challenges and opportunities for Montessori education. First, Montessori is not a protected trademark in Germany, so there are no legal restrictions on the labeling of educational institutions as "Montessori-oriented." Depending on the regional development of Montessori education, private Montessori schools can have an elite reputation or are seen, in the other extreme, as schools primarily serving disabled students. Considering the "niche" status it has in practice, the image of Montessori education in Germany is generally positive overall, if somewhat fuzzy.

Montessori teachers typically participate in Montessori training after their state-recognized teacher training. While teachers at state-run schools are typically civil servants with higher pay and job security, tuition costs for students and lower pay for private Montessori teachers put them and their schools at a disadvantage.

Why German families choose Montessori remains a topic for future research. Given Germany's mainly selective secondary school enrollment starting at age 11, parents are often drawn to and have mobilized to create private schools combining children and adolescents in a single school, focusing on individual development and providing a non-selective alternative for secondary education. This system of educational continuity under one roof, from early childhood through secondary, is rarely available elsewhere.

Montessori in Academia

Alongside Montessori growth in training programs and schools, from the 1950s and 1960s, a number of German academics have specialized in Montessori research and practice, starting with Helming at the Pädagogische Akademie (Teachers College) in Essen. Foremost was the Wissenschaftliches Zentrum für Montessori-Pädagogik (Scientific Center for Montessori Pedagogy) at the University of Münster (now the Montessori-Zentrum Münster) (Montessori Center Münster), with successions of Montessori-specialized academics: Günter Schulz-Benesch, Paul Oswald, Hildegard Holtstiege, and Harald Ludwig. Professor Ludwig, in particular, is editing a complete scholarly edition of Maria Montessori's published works and unpublished lectures, in cooperation with the Montessori-Zentrum Münster, the Herder publishing house and AMI (Ludwig 2010).

Contemporary Landscape and National Cooperation

Given the expansion of teacher training and schools, the German Montessori community saw a need for national-level coordination. The Aktionsgemeinschaft deutscher Montessori-Vereine (Action Community of German Montessori Associations) (ADMV) was founded in 1971, bringing together some schools, training organizations, and regional associations (Holtstiege et al. 1996). With improved domestic and international contacts within the last two decades, German training organizations became aware of the increased focus on Cosmic Education in the elementary and the "Erdkinder" adolescent curriculum in the United States and in other parts of Europe. Overall, this has led to modernization of the curricula of German Montessori training courses and an increased focus on age group-specific Montessori teacher qualifications.

In 2004, ADMV became the Montessori Dachverband Deutschland (German Montessori Organization) (MDD). After a failed attempt in 2011 to synchronize national teacher training, MDD and its members developed a Quality Framework with criteria both for Montessori schools and teacher training. MDD became the third German AMI-affiliated society in 2018, with AMI's acknowledgment of the Quality Framework as a key element of affiliation. In 2021, MDD changed its structure to the Montessori Bundesverband Deutschland (German Federal Montessori Association), based in Berlin, with professional staff and direct membership of schools. A recognition program for schools and training courses allows members to display their adherence to a common Quality Framework, thereby helping create a German Montessori "brand."

Conclusion

The German public school system has undergone change over the last decades, especially in early childhood and special education, shifting away from teacher-directed instruction to emphasizing individual, creative learning and written individual assessments instead of grades, at least in elementary school. These developments in public education have affirmed many of the educational principles of Montessori pedagogy even if much is still to be achieved. A newly unified national organization offers opportunities for Montessori to play an even more active role in both public and private education, positioning the pedagogy to significantly benefit more children and adolescents.

Note

Drafts of this chapter were shared with Joke Verheul and all German Montessori training organizations within Montessori Bundesverband Deutschland. Representatives from DMG, DAMIP, Montessori Bavaria, and Montessori Labor Berlin sent feedback, approving the chapter.

References

Günnigmann, Manfred. 1979. *Montessori-Pädagogik in Deutschland: Bericht über die Entwicklung nach 1945*. Freiburg: Herder.
Holtstiege, Hildegard, Gudula Meisterjahn-Knebel, Alexander Nitschke, and Hans Pabst (ed.). 1996. *25 Jahre ADMV—eine Dokumentation* (Pädagogische Schriften Heft 7). Bonn: Aktionsgemeinschaft deutscher Montessori-Vereine.
Holtz, Axel (ed.). 1995. *Clara Grunwald—Das Kind ist der Mittelpunkt*. Münster: Klemm+Oelschläger.
Montessori, Maria and Harald Ludwig (ed.). 2010. *Maria Montessori—Gesammelte Werke*. 21 vols. Freiburg: Herder.
O'Donnell, Marion. 2014. *Maria Montessori*. London: Bloomsbury Publishing.
Waldschmidt, Ingeborg. 2001. *Maria Montessori. Leben und Werk*. Munich: C.H. Beck.

Chapter 34
Montessori Education in Eastern Europe

Jaroslaw Jendza

The attempt to describe Montessori educational practices in Eastern Europe seems to be almost intractable, as defining the very concept of *Eastern Europe* is a topic of ongoing scholarly and political debates (Büscher 2005; Czapliński 2017; Grob 2015). In addition, there are significant differences between these countries in terms of the organization of educational systems, sociocultural and historical conditions, and shared values. For instance, it is quite difficult to find some common denominator for conservative and Catholic Poland, secularized and fairly liberal Czech Republic, and authoritarian Belarus (Wolff 1994).

Therefore, in describing both the history and contemporary trends in Montessori practices in the region, I will rely on the UN Statistical Commission's definition of Eastern Europe as ten countries. According to the Association Montessori Internationale (AMI), in 2020, Montessori education was present in nine of the ten UN-classified Eastern European countries: Belarus, Bulgaria, Czech Republic, Hungary, Poland, Romania, Russia, Slovakia, and Ukraine (that is, all except Moldova) (AMI 2020). Despite the tremendous differences across these countries and their Montessori systems, Montessori education in Eastern Europe is marked by enthusiastic development in the early twentieth century that was halted under communist rule and has reemerged post-1989.

Early Years of Montessori Education in Eastern Europe 1911–1939

During the interwar period (1918–1939), newly independent Eastern European countries embraced independence, modernity, and the global movement of New Education. Montessori's ideas were embraced by educational thinkers and practitioners alike for their connection to these changes in education, politics, and society.

In Russia, Yulia Ivanovna Fausek visited Italy and became acquainted with the Montessori approach in 1908. Soon after, she created the first Montessori group for children ages 3–6 in an existing school in St. Petersburg. In 1914, she attended an international Montessori training course for teachers in Rome and a year later wrote a book describing her experience (Knyazev 2015). Although she remained a prolific researcher and writer for the next few years (1920–24), her initiatives were soon slowed down, and in the early 1930s, Fausek's efforts to promote this model of education came to an end due to Soviet policy opposing all alternative forms of pedagogy (Schnepf 2010).

In Czech Republic and Slovakia, Božena Kožíšková translated *Il metodo* (The Method) in 1926 with a foreword by one of the era's most renowned professors of experimental psychology, František Šeracký. In Romania, Montessori education became well known in the same period thanks to Illie Sulea-Firu, who took Montessori's course in Rome in 1931. Sulea-Firu also maintained correspondence with Maria and Mario Montessori until it was stopped by the Iron Curtain.[1] Assembling some of the most notable Romanian thinkers of that time, he established the Montessori Association of Romania in 1933, opened the first Montessori school in Bucharest, and translated Montessori's writings (Neacşu 2017; Zener Schaefer 1998).

In Lithuania, Montessori was advanced by the Benedictine Sisters of Kaunas (Vasiliauskaitė 2020) and by Marija Kuraitytė-Varnienė, who studied with Maria Montessori in Nice, France, and received permission to conduct Montessori training in Lithuania. Kuraitytė-Varnienė and colleagues founded the Lithuanian Montessori Society in 1934. In addition to promoting Montessori education across Lithuania through magazine articles, several books, and radio programs, she established a Children's House in her home in Kaunas with classroom furniture built by her husband, artist Adomas Varnas (see Figure 34.1). Through photographs, they documented a vibrant Montessori community, soon to be disrupted by war. Kuraitytė-Varnienė later set up a Montessori school in a displaced persons camp in Ravensberg, Germany, and later opened a Montessori school in Chicago (Mackevičiūtė 2017).

Figure 34.1 Two boys collaborating in Kaunas, Lithuania, 1931. Courtesy of the Lithuanian Museum of Educational History.

In Poland, the Montessori approach became well known as early as 1912 through reviews in journals and the translation in 1913 of *Le Case dei Bambini*. From 1925 onward, Polish early education journals frequently published both positive assessments and critiques of Montessori pedagogy, and Polish educators attended Montessori courses, particularly between 1914 and 1933 (Hessen 1931). As a result, the approach was covered, to varying extent, in almost all teacher training programs (Dybiec 2009). This led to many kindergartens implementing a complete or partial form of Montessori elements in practice.

1980–Present

The Second World War and subsequent communist regimes eliminated Montessori education in practice and in scholarly research across much of Eastern Europe. Montessori's emphasis on individuality, creativity, and self-reliance was perceived as being incompatible with the communist vision of the state, and Montessori education was seen as "too close" to Western-initiated progressive education. It was not until the outburst of the Polish Solidarity movement in the 1980s, the collapse of Berlin Wall, and the end of Soviet Bloc that the Montessori approach could flourish again. In Eastern European countries, the democratization of the public sphere resulted in diversity in many areas of life, including education, and led to a renewed interest in a pedagogy focused on independence and peace.

As Montessori education in Eastern Europe expands, Montessori schools and organizations, like other social institutions, are shaped by four diverse cultural codes: totalitarianism, *folwark*[2] (feudal relations), modernization, and neoliberal rationality, each of which may present challenges to Montessori implementation. The totalitarian code seeks unity and eliminates difference, while the folwark code frames hierarchical power relations. The modernization code, largely related to democratic and equal relations between people, is much weaker in Eastern Europe, leading to a rise in neoliberal forces that are also uncritically accepted (Zamojski 2018). Further research might examine how these forces are influencing the expansion of Montessori education across Eastern Europe.

In the context of these four competing forces across Eastern Europe, the net of Montessori institutions has been growing rapidly over the last thirty years. In some countries like Moldova, Bulgaria, or Belarus, Montessori schools in the tens but in others, like Poland, Czech Republic, and Russia, there are more than a hundred schools. Unfortunately, there is no credible database, so the total number and growth demands future research.

Organizationally, Montessori efforts across Eastern Europe are diverse and grassroots, popularizing the Montessori approach and developing local communities of practitioners. In recent years, eight Eastern European countries have created AMI-affiliated national Montessori organizations to attempt to coordinate national Montessori efforts, but these organizations represent only a small fraction of Montessori schools and training programs in many countries. Similarly, while there are AMI-affiliated Montessori training centers in four countries, the vast majority of Montessori training programs across Eastern Europe do not have a national or international organizational affiliation.

In Poland there are two major organizations: Polskie Stowarzyszenie Montessori (Polish Montessori Association) (1994) with approximately 200 institutional and individual members, and Polski Instytut Montessori (Polish Montessori Institute) (2008), which so far has trained more than 2,150 teachers (Polski Instytut Montessori 2019). In the Czech Republic, there are several organizations affiliated with Association Montessori Internationale (AMI) and American Montessori Society (AMS) as well as the independent Společnosti Montessori ČR (Montessori Society Czech Republic) (1998). Magyarországi Montessori Egyesület (Hungarian Montessori Society) (1933) was reestablished in 1992. Major Russian organizations include the AMI-affiliated Montessori Public Fund and Международный институт Монтессори-педагогики (International Montessori Pedagogy Institute). The Romanian Montessori Institute of Bucharest (MIB) is the first national AMI-affiliated training organization, now operating alongside the Association for the Development of Montessori Education, focused on popularizing Montessori pedagogy. In one of the smallest countries of the region, Slovenia, there is Združenja Montessori Slovenje (Slovenian Montessori Association) created in 2008.

Across Eastern Europe, three major types of Montessori schools can be observed. The first and most popular type is private schools designed for well-off middle-class families. With annual fees approaching the national average salary, such institutions are inaccessible for most families. In this context, Montessori education serves as an international brand, and in some cases it has been treated as a profitable business entity, guaranteeing high returns for the entrepreneur. In Poland, Bulgaria, and Russia such schools can be found in or around big cities; examples include Montessori Academy for International Children in Poland and the Montessori School of Moscow in Russia.

The second type is schools led by NGOs or religious associations for students who have not succeeded in traditional educational environments or have some specific educational needs (for instance, Chrześcijańska Szkoła Montessori in Gdańsk, Poland).

The last and smallest in number are state-funded Montessori institutions, which are usually accessible to all children. Such schools can be found in eastern and southern Poland (for instance, Przedszkole Samorządowe nr 36 im. Marii Montessori in Białystok, Poland [Local Kindergarten number 36 in Bialystok, Poland], and government-funded Montessori schools in Belgorod and Vladimir, Russia).

These three global Montessori archetypes can be observed globally, but in Eastern Europe, they function in a unique way due to local factors such as the youth of democracies, the uncritical attitude toward profit-oriented neoliberal rationality, the afore-mentioned lack of trust between various social actors and the attachment to unsymmetrical and conservative power relations.

Conclusion

The resurgence of Montessori education post-1989 across Eastern Europe demonstrates the vitality of this pedagogy and its interest to Eastern European citizens. Given complicated dynamics with past communist rule and the youth and fragility of some country's democracies, Montessori's emancipatory project of cultivating independence has been downplayed in favor of the method's representation as an elite and international brand. Still, the potential of Montessori, not only as an educational model, but as a vehicle for social change, continues to inspire Montessori educators and families across Eastern Europe.

Notes

1. Maria and Mario Montessori trusted Sulea-Firu so much that some of their studies were published in Romanian before they were printed in Italian.
2. A specific kind of Polish agricultural farm based on work conducted by enslaved peasants was exploited by landlords. This form of social organization influenced the relations between citizens for centuries and, according to some thinkers, still affects social mentality (Leder 2014).

References

AMI. 2020. "Montessori Schools in 2020." Annual General Meeting.
Büscher, Wolfgang. 2005. *Berlin—Moscou, un Voyage à Pied*. Paris, France: Paris Esprit des Péninsules.
Czapliński, Przemysław. 2017. *Poruszona Mapa*. Kraków, Poland: Wydawnictwo Literackie.
Dybiec, Julian. 2009. "Recepcja Metody Marii Montessori w Polsce 1912–2008." In *Pedagogika Marii Montessori w Polsce i na świecie*, edited by Barbara Surma, 33–50. Łódź – Kraków, Poland: Palatium & Ignatianum.
Grob, Thomas. 2015. *The Concept of "Eastern Europe" in Past and Present*. UNI NOVA: University of Basel.
Hessen, Sergiusz. 1931. *Podstawy Pedagogiki*. Warsaw, Poland: Nasza Księgarnia.
Knyazev, E. A. 2015. "Julia Fausek and Free Preschool Education." *Preschool Education* 3: 114–19.
Leder, Andrzej. 2014. *Prześniona Rewolucja. Ćwiczenie z Logiki Historycznej*. Warsaw, Poland: Krytyka Polityczna.
Liviu, Chelcea and Druţă Oana. 2016. "Zombie Socialism and the Rise of Neoliberalism in Post-Socialist Central and Eastern Europe." *Eurasian Geography and Economics* 57 (4–5): 521–44. https://doi.org/10.1080/15387216.2016.12662.
Mackevičiūtė, Gabija. 2017. "Marija Kuraitytė-Varnienė—the Pioneer of Montessori Education." *Šiaurės Atėnai*, April 7, 2017. http://www.satenai.lt/2017/04/07/marija-kuraityte-varniene-montesorinio-ugdymo-pradininke/.
Neacşu, Mihaela Gabriela. 2017. "The Contribution of Professor Illie Sulea-Firu to the Development of the Montessori Pedagogy in Romania." In *Alternative Educational Methodologies*, edited by Ion Albuleşcu and Horatiu Catalano, 119–24. Newcastle, England: Cambridge Scholars Publishing.
Polski Instytut Montessori. 2019. "PIM w Liczbach."https://montessori.info.pl/pim-w-liczbach/.
Schnepf, Candy. 2010. *A Comparative Case Study of the Implementation of Montessori Pedagogy in the United Republic of Tanzania and the Russian Federation*. PhD diss., University of Michigan.
Vasiliauskaitė, Aušra. 2020. "Kauno Seserų Benediktinių Ugdomoji Veikla Lietuvoje 1918–1940 m." *SOTER: religijos mokslo žurnalas* 103 (75): 45–60.
Wolff, Larry. 1994. *Inventing Eastern Europe*. Stanford, CA: Stanford University Press.
Zamojski, Piotr. 2018. "Cultural Codes and Education in Poland—a Plea for a New Educational Imaginary." *Policy Futures in Education* 16 (4): 416–33.
Zener, Rita. 1998. "Montessori to Romania: The First Montessori Training Course in Romania." *NAMTA Bulletin* (March): 1–5. https://files.eric.ed.gov/fulltext/ED443565.pdf

Chapter 35

Montessori Education in Africa: Themes and Examples across the Continent

Amelia J. Murray, Hala Aboulela, Aicha Sajid,
Noyenum Emafo, and Mira Debs

Although Maria Montessori passed away in the midst of planning to travel to Ghana, her method has spread throughout the African continent as more attention is paid to early childhood education (ECE) across the region as a critical means of developing early learning skills and persistence in schooling (Mwamwenda 2014). Currently, 12 percent of children in Africa attend ECE, compared with nearly half of children in other regions of the world (Garcia et al. 2008). At the same time, Africans have long had Indigenous methods of family- and community-based early childhood development for their children (Nsamenang 2008).

According to the Association Montessori Internationale, as of 2020, thirty-three African countries have Montessori schools (AMI 2020). Montessori education throughout Africa occurs in a range of spaces: most popularly in early childhood education (ECE), but also in private, philanthropic, or government-funded efforts, as part of what scholars have called "imported" colonial educational projects (Nsamenang 2008) as well as efforts to decolonize education, to make education culturally responsive, and to empower communities, particularly in African rural areas (Murray 2021). Practitioners around Africa have developed innovative, affordable models for expanding Montessori education, including sponsoring training and creating materials locally. In addition, they have demonstrated how key Montessori components can be aligned with aspects of African culture, including respecting the child; building independence; and cultivating peace, community, and a connection with nature.

Given the diversity of the African subcontinent, with fifty-four countries and an estimated 1,500–2,000 languages, this chapter cannot comprehensively convey the diversity of Montessori education in so many countries across a century (Maho 2004). In this short overview, we examine common themes and differences across a number of countries, providing brief summaries of contemporary Montessori education in South Africa, Nigeria, Egypt, and Morocco (see also Chapters 36, 37, and 38 on Tanzania, Kenya, and Educateurs sans Frontières, respectively). As such, this chapter is a starting point that we hope will inspire future research on Montessori practice in the many contexts around Africa.

Montessori Education's Introduction to Africa, 1910s–1990s

As formal early childhood education developed in Africa in the nineteenth and early twentieth century, it was first available for European settlers and second, to indigenous Africans, often as part of efforts to introduce and assimilate them to European ideas of race, religion, and childhood (Prochner and Kabiru 2008). The first documented Montessori school fit into the former category: it was created in South Africa in 1916 when Mrs. Leigh convinced Montessori-trained Constance Marriott to come from England to open a school in her parents' home. The Montessori Home School in Rondebosch, South Africa, located in a house and garden facing Table Mountain by 1924, served forty students, half of whom were orphans or children of single parents who lived in an accompanying hostel. While the pupils comprised an economically diverse group of white South African children, the school was racially segregated and worked to further segregation. Both Leigh and Marriott hoped that their school's trainees would eventually serve as governesses, to "counter the prevailing local custom of employing ill-educated colored and native women and girls as nurses and nursemaids to white children" (*Call of Education* 1924, 258).

By the 1920s, there were also Montessori schools for Black Africans, such as St. Joseph's School for girls up to age 13 at a Catholic convent in Calabar, Nigeria, opened in 1926 by Sister Magdalene (see Figure 35.1). Children were taught in local languages, and Sister Magdalene viewed Montessori education as a step on the way to developing "African teachers who will in the future evolve an African system of education" for an independent Nigeria (Magdalene 1928, 507). The school was valued by parents for offering economic opportunities, visited by educators around Africa and provided Montessori training to generations of African and European sisters preparing for foreign missions (Williams 2021). At the same time, writing about this school in an Italian Montessori periodical, educators used deficit-based and racist language, describing the school as a "redemption of the natives" living in a "very low" level of civilization "depending completely on their parents who often sell them to the highest bidder" (*L'Idea Montessori* 1928). Such documents illustrate that Montessori education was not immune to the racist ideas that pervaded colonial education more broadly (Prochner and Kabiru 2008). Today, the Nigerian order Sister Magdalene founded, Handmaids of the Holy Child Jesus, still operates several Montessori schools in Nigeria as part of their broader school network (Williams 2021).

Second-Wave Montessori Education in Africa

Aside from Sister Magdalene's program in Nigeria, after the 1920s, there are minimal records of Montessori in Africa until the late 1960s, when a global resurgence of Montessori education led to an increase in schools and training courses on the continent. In Tanzania, Muriel Dwyer led several AMI Montessori training courses starting in 1968 with the support of the Aga Khan Foundation, AMI, and England's Maria Montessori Institute. Working initially with Hilda Mwendopole, Khatoon Bapoo, and subsequently with various African nuns including Sister Gaspara Kashamba, they developed a sustainable, low-cost Montessori training model with

Figure 35.1 Children working at a Montessori school in a Catholic convent in Calabar, Nigeria, 1927. Courtesy of the Maria Montessori Archives, photo section, Amsterdam.

trainees sponsored by an organization or village, and materials handmade by each trainee, a model that expanded to parts of Kenya and Ethiopia (Bruh Tesfa n.d.; Dwyer 1969; Lynne Lawrence, pers. comm.) (see Chapter 36: "Montessori Education in Tanzania"). Starting in the 1970s, Sri Lankan Montessorian Lena Wikramaratne led teacher training in South Africa. AMI ran their first affiliated training in South Africa in 1981–1982 and continued its involvement through that decade (Prudence Ramsey, pers. comm. 2021).

As African countries gained independence, many of them prioritized early childhood education, though its availability was limited. Much of the formal ECE infrastructure developed through private organizations including Christian mission schools (Mwamwenda 2014). Similarly, from the 1960s onward, Montessori programs were supported by missions, Montessori organizations, and NGOs, which developed training infrastructure and schools, particularly in rural areas in Nigeria, Ethiopia, the Gambia, Côte d'Ivoire, Senegal, Kenya, and Tanzania (Lynne Lawrence, pers. comm.; Williams 2021). For example, in Ethiopia, Bruh Tesfa Kindergarten Teacher Training Institute was established by the Sisters of Charity and the Ethiopian Catholic Church in 1986 (Bruh Tesfa). In the Gambia, the SOS Children's Villages were established in 1982 by a Canadian NGO,[1] and the Peter Hesse Foundation has trained teachers and assisted them with purchasing materials and establishing Montessori schools in Haiti, Côte d'Ivoire, and Senegal since 1986 (Carol Guy-James Barratt, pers. comm., 2021). More recently, AMI's Educateurs sans Frontières (see Chapter 38: "AMI Educateurs sans Frontières") works in several African locations to develop affordable schools and training models.

Montessori Cultural Responsiveness in an African Context

Another recent change has been African educators emphasizing the alignment of Montessori education's ideas with indigenous African ideas about child development, such as the emphasis on independence from an early age, self-care, learning through participation rather than instruction, and a strong emphasis on community, peer, and sibling support (Nsamenang 2008; Junnifa Uzodike, pers. comm.). For example, Gambian educator Nnaceesay Marenah, founder of Moonflower Montessori and the Nitte Foundation, finds that Montessori and African ideologies parallel one another in reflective living and purposeful roles in a community (pers. comm.) (see Figure 35.2). Moroccan educator Aicha Sajid has connected Berber symbols and Montessori ideas related to patience, hard work, equilibrium with the environment, and each individual's place in the world (Sajid 2019). Additionally, American Montessori educator Koren Clark has linked Montessori education to Kindezi, a Congolese early childhood educational practice, and has suggested Montessori pedagogy may be a vehicle for developing and affirming cultural identity (Bunseki and Lukondo-Wamba 2000; Clark 2017). In this way, practitioners argue that Montessori education can support affirming indigenous child-rearing, mother tongue language instruction, and community practices throughout Africa.

Figure 35.2 Guide Samwel Kuria works with students Junaid Mercier and Bashir Albretch at Moonflower Montessori school in the Gambia, 2021. Courtesy of Nnaceesay Marenah.

There can also be tensions between Montessori and indigenous African early childhood practices. In the Gambia, Marenah acknowledged that initially, she valued Montessori education because of Western and colonial beliefs, but she later shifted toward a decolonized approach as she began to study the causes of educational injustice, seeking to contextualize Montessori education to reflect African culture. The Nitte Foundation is now focused on making Montessori education accessible for lower-income families, encouraging local leadership in Montessori schools and offering Montessori training using the Gambia's four main national languages: Mandinka, Wolof, Fula, and Diola (Nnaceesay Marenah, pers. comm., 2021). Another challenge is finding Montessori materials, such as Language-learning materials and books, which center Black African children and their experiences. For African teachers who have trained abroad and purchased materials overseas, they can sometimes unintentionally "recolonize instead of decolonize our children" (Junnifa Uzodike, pers. comm.). These examples suggest the importance of creating culturally responsive and sustaining Montessori materials and the need for further research into Montessori education and access, language, and cultural identity in African contexts.

Contemporary Landscape: 2000 to Present

In recent years, alongside prior NGO and religious partnerships, local Montessori organizations have developed to expand Montessori schools in a number of countries in private and nonprofit, urban, and rural contexts. In the private sector, for example, researchers in Nigeria have documented an "explosion" of interest and a "proliferation" of Montessori schools, although many use the name without following Montessori practices (Dahunsi 2014). Similarly, research for this chapter on Montessori schools in other African countries found numerous instances of daycares or nurseries adopting the Montessori name for prestige purposes with little to no emphasis on the pedagogy, and accessing high-fidelity training remains a challenge across many countries.[2]

In the last two decades, several countries have created national organizations to coordinate Montessori efforts, including the Montessori Training Association of Tanzania (1997) and the related Montessori Community of Tanzania (2021), South Africa Montessori Association (SAMA) (2003), Association of Montessori Nigeria (AMEN) (1990s) and subsequently the Foundation for Montessori Education in Nigeria (FMEN) (2018), Teach for the Gambia (2020), now the Nitte Foundation (2022), the Association Maria Montessori de Côte d'Ivoire, the Montessori Teachers Association of Kenya (2009), the Association Montessori Morocco (2016), Montessori Foundation of Egypt (2016), and Montessori for Kenya (2019). Responding to national organizing, in 2019, the Kenyan government officially recognized Montessori early childhood curriculum and training, one of the few countries globally to make such recognition (see Chapter 37: "Montessori Education in Kenya"). South Africa, Kenya, and Tanzania have substantial Montessori infrastructure with hundreds of schools and multiple training centers.

The next section provides short capsules of the contemporary landscape in South Africa, Nigeria, Egypt, and Morocco to share examples of countries with long-standing and more recent Montessori programs.

South Africa

In the final years of South Africa's apartheid regime in the 1980s, Montessori educators like Orcillia Oppenheimer, Prudence Ramsay, Clare Collecott, Sally Hall, Jennifer Moore, Eve Annecke, and Norma Rudolph played a crucial role in reestablishing Montessori education in South Africa, with many schools rooted in Black townships and rural areas (Kahn 1995; SAMA 2007). After training in London, Oppenheimer opened Inanda Montessori School and Training Centre. In the mid-1980s, she helped organize an international conference attended by 2,000 South Africans that led to "an explosion of grassroots Montessori training and programs" in the 1980s and 1990s (Oppenheimer 1999, 64). Examples include the Phumelela Community Training Programme, opened by Nomonde Matiso, and the Zama Montessori Center, serving the Black townships of Daveyton and Etwatwa, both of which opened in 1988, as well as Auburn House Trust in Cape Town, Operation Upgrade in the Eastern Cape, Wonderkids Montessori in Kwa Zulu Natal, Woz óbona, and The Learning Project in Gauteng (Kahn 1995; Prudence Ramsay, pers. comm.). The South African Montessori Society (SAMS), affiliated with AMI, was founded in 1981.

The end of Apartheid in 1994 represented a new period of flourishing for South African Montessori, resulting in an estimated 230 Montessori programs, 60 of them serving poor communities, with an additional 420 Montessori-inspired programs in poor and rural communities (Kahn 1995, 7). There was optimism within the Montessori community that the model could be part of efforts to reimagine post-apartheid public education, and SAMS developed a working relationship with the Department of Basic Education as it was developing the new curriculum of outcomes-based education. Unfortunately, SAMS dissolved in the late 1990s, and by the time the South African Montessori Association (SAMA) was founded in 2003, the South African government had moved toward a more prescriptive and traditional national curriculum (Sharon Caldwell, pers. comm.).

SAMA's creation was an effort to bring together all Montessori educators and schools in the Southern African region, unaligned with any organization or training. SAMA documents the existence and activities of roughly 200 schools, offers three levels of membership to include schools with varying levels of Montessori implementation, and is working toward developing a quality assurance process, although there are also a number of unaffiliated schools (SAMA 2019).

In the last twenty years, Montessori education in South Africa has continued to expand through independent schools and training centers. At the same time, educators continue to advocate for investment in quality government early childhood education through organizations like the Indaba Foundation (iAfrica 2021) and to connect Montessori education to sustainable development principles through organizations like the Sustainability Institute (see Figure 35.3). More recently, the Indaba Institute in the Cape Winelands piloted scalable models of low-cost Montessori community-based programs such as the Educateurs sans Frontières (EsF) Community Rooted Education (CoRE) program (EsF).

Although the autonomy of schools and training centers continues to be challenged by ongoing curriculum standardization efforts by the South African government, such as Umalusi accreditation, as well as training discrepancies across centers, Montessori education continues to grow in communities across South Africa (Sharon Caldwell, pers. comm.; Caldwell 2018).

Figure 35.3 Child working with materials at the Lynedoch Children's House, South Africa, 2021. Courtesy of the Indaba Institute.

Nigeria

In the late 1990s, there were only a small number of Montessori schools in Nigeria, and it was difficult for small schools to afford a Montessori-trained teacher. For example, Noyenum Emafo opened what is now Lekki Montessori in 2002 with ten children in her living room. Eventually, several other schools opened in the next few years, including the American Montessori Society-affiliated Discovery House Montessori, also in Lagos. Following the success of some of these schools, in the late 1990s, a group of educators got together to create the Association of Montessori Education in Nigeria (AMEN) with the goal of supporting each other and gaining government Montessori recognition. The activities of AMEN consisted mainly of affordable training for teachers.

In 2018, educators created a second national Montessori group, Foundation for Montessori Education (FMEN), this time affiliated with AMI. Today, there are varying levels of Montessori implementation in schools around Nigeria, with a small and growing number of schools, including Lagos Montessori School, Fruitful Orchard, and Aquila Nidus, among others, offering high-fidelity Montessori as defined by AMI standards. There are two MACTE-recognized training centers, one AMI-affiliated training center, and a number of small indigenous training centers that offer different varieties of Montessori training. Challenges to Montessori expansion in Nigeria include the cost of materials, cost of training, the long and expensive process to becoming a trainer, and the lack of government recognition.

While Montessori has a reputation for being an elitist form of schooling, in Nigeria, Montessori schools can be found in both privileged and underserved communities delivering varying levels of Montessori education given the environmental limitations. FMEN is working with AMI to make Montessori training more affordable and to build and support Montessori awareness in Nigeria among parents and educators.

Egypt

After some Italian-run Montessori schools in Egypt were established in the late 1920s and 1930s, the next Montessori presence began in the 1980s when Marguerite Richardt, an American Montessori teacher who was visiting Egypt, decided to stay in the country and open a Children's House in Cairo. Local teachers who learned from her started their own Children's Houses throughout the 1990s. In 2016, Hala Aboulela created the Montessori Foundation of Egypt (MFE), which became affiliated with AMI the next year (MFE 2017). MFE aims to support schools in the region in maintaining high-quality Montessori and to increase awareness of the method. The organization hosted the first AMI Certificate Course in 2017, and the Montessori Institute in Cairo was established in the following year. As of 2022 there are only two AMI Montessori schools operating in Egypt. Due to the lack of local AMI-trained teachers, many are hesitant to open new schools, which makes the job market for teachers unreliable. Currently, existing Montessori schools with international affiliations are growing and expanding much faster than new, independent (usually unaccredited) schools.

Morocco

The first Montessori school in Morocco, Ecole Montessori Casablanca (EMC), was founded in 2011 by Aicha Sajid. EMC became the first private school employing an alternative educational method to be recognized by the Moroccan government. The organization Association Montessori Morocco (AMM) was founded in association with EMC and became an affiliate of AMI in 2016. There are only a handful of Montessori schools in Morocco, but AMM provides a foundation for quality assurance and supports the dissemination of the method. In Morocco, a key challenge has been aligning Montessori education and parenting practices among affluent families, in which parents sometimes discourage independence by anticipating all of their children's needs. However, Montessori's effectiveness has influenced such parents to be more accepting of developing independence early on and alternative educational methods in general.

Conclusion

As Montessori education has developed in Africa over the last century, it has been attached to a variety of goals: civilizing, social uplift, school preparedness, economic development, and also decolonizing education, community empowerment, and teaching in native languages. Today, though still small in the overall African education sector, Montessori education appears to be expanding across a number of African countries. Its popularity is increasing due to parental and community demand, its international reputation as well as its relevance to local traditions and cultures. While training, materials, and school fees are limiting factors in some locations, in Tanzania, Kenya, and Ethiopia, Montessori trainers have developed an innovative and grassroots model for affordable Montessori training and materials-making. National organizations in several countries are working to develop and sustain Montessori schools and training centers. In some countries like Kenya, government support is enabling this growth, whereas elsewhere, in South Africa, curriculum regulations are creating increasing restrictions for Montessori education in the country.

This chapter has provided an overview examining Montessori education over a century around the African subcontinent, though it omits considerable efforts occurring in numerous countries. It also reflects the limited academic research and organizational documentation of Montessori practices throughout the subcontinent. We hope this chapter can inspire further efforts to chronicle the Montessori landscape.

Notes

Hala Aboulela, Aicha Sajid, Indaba Institute and colleagues contributed detailed country information and commented on drafts. Nnaceesay Marenah, Koren Clark, and Carol Guy-James contributed information and also commented on drafts. Junnifa Uzodike, Fay Hendriksen, Joke Verheul, and Lynne Lawrence made valuable editorial comments on this chapter. Amelia Murray compiled this information into multiple drafts, and Mira Debs added additional research and revised the chapter based on reader feedback.

1. The program still operates but no longer uses Montessori education.
2. Especially in areas where Montessori has a more established presence, like Egypt and South Africa, many schools following traditional teacher-led instruction leverage Montessori's popularity using names such as "Montessori Club," "Play Time Montessori Nursery and Preschool," and "Skills Montessori Academy," even though their websites show little evidence they are following Montessori practices.

References

AMI. 2020. "Montessori Schools in 2020." Annual General Meeting, 2020.
Bruh Tesfa Montessori Kindergarten Teacher Training Institute. N.d. https://bruhtesfamontessoriktti.wordpress.com/
Fu-Kiau, Kimbwandènde Kia Bunseki, and A. M. Lukondo-Wamba. 2000. *Kindezi: the Kôngo Art of Babysitting*. Baltimore, MD: Imprint Editions.
Caldwell, Sharon. 2018. "Position Statement: Umalusi." South African Montessori Association (SAMA). https://samontessori.org.za/wp-content/uploads/bsk-pdf-manager/SAMA_Position_statement_UMALUSI_-_20180917_-_01_266.pdf
The Call of Education. 1924. "The Montessori Home School, Rondebosch, South Africa." *Psycho-pedagogical journal. International organ of the Montessori Movement* 1 (1): 255–8.
Clark, Koren. 2017. "Historical Truths and Montessori Roots: African Pedagogy in Our Montessori World." Presentation at the Montessori for Social Justice Conference, San Antonio, June 2017.

Dahunsi, T. O. 2014. "Montessori Education in Nigeria." *IOSR Journal of Research and Method in Education* 4 (1): 57–60.

Dwyer, Muriel. 1969. "Montessori in Tanzania." *Around the Child* 13: 14–16.

Educateurs Sans Frontieres (EsF). "Community Rooted Education South Africa." Accessed March 29, 2022. https://montessori-esf.org/project/community-rooted-education-south-africa.

Garcia, Marito, Alan Pence, and Judith Evans, eds. 2008. *Africa's Future, Africa's Challenge: Early Childhood Care and Development in Sub-Saharan Africa*. Herndon, VA: World Bank Publications.

iAfrica. 2021. "Thuli Madonsela Calls for a Fair and Equal Start in Life for All SA Children." https://iafrica.com/thuli-madonsela-calls-for-a-fair-and-equal-start-in-life-for-all-sa-children/.

Kahn, David. 1995. *Montessori in South Africa: An Overview of Needs and Development*. Unpublished Report.

L'idea Montessori. 1928. "Notiziario: dall'Italia e dall'estero." *Organo dell'Opera Nazionale Montessori* 2 (2): 11–12.

Magdalene, Sister Mary Charles. 1928. "Education of Girls in Southern Nigeria." *International Review of Mission* XVIII (67): 505–14.

Maho, Jouni Filip. 2004. "How Many Languages Are There in Africa, Really?" In *Globalisation and African Languages*, edited by Katrin Bromber and Birgit Smieja, 279–96. Berlin: De Gruyter Mouton.

Montessori Foundation of Egypt (MFE). "About MFE." Accessed June 25, 2021. https://www.montessori-egypt.org/about.

Murray, Amelia. 2021. "Montessori in Kenya." *The Urge to Help: Resisting Urges, Promoting Reflection.* Accessed August 10, 2021. https://theurgetohelp.com/articles/montessori-in-kenya/.

Mwamwenda, Tuntufye Selemani. 2014. "Early Childhood Education in Africa." *Mediterranean Journal of Social Sciences* 5 (20): 1403–1412.

Nsamenang, A. Bame. 2008. "(Mis)Understanding ECD in Africa: The Forces of Global and Local Motives." In *Africa's Future, Africa's Challenge: Early Childhood Care and Development in Sub-Saharan Africa,* edited by Marito Garcia, Alan Pence, and Judith Evans, 135–49. Herndon, VA: World Bank Publications.

Oppenheimer, Orcillia. 1999. "Montessori in South Africa: The Challenge, the Dream, and the Promise." *NAMTA Journal* 24 (1): 61–8.

Prochner, Larry and Margaret Kabiru. 2008. "ECD in Historical Perspective." In *Africa's Future, Africa's Challenge: Early Childhood Care and Development in Sub-Saharan Africa,* edited by Marito Garcia, Alan Pence, and Judith Evans, 117–33. Herndon, VA: World Bank Publications.

Sajid, Aicha. 2019. "AMI Primary Diploma Graduation Speech." Montessori Institute of Morocco.

South African Montessori Association (SAMA). 2007. "Conversations with Montessorians: Prudence Ramsay." *SAMA Newsletter* (November 2007): 8–11. https://samontessori.org.za/wp-content/uploads/bsk-pdf-manager/SAMA_November_07_Newsletter_141.pdf.

South African Montessori Association (SAMA). 2019. "About Us." December 13, 2019. https://samontessori.org.za/about-us/.

UNICEF. "Education: Middle East and North Africa." September 9, 2020. https://www.unicef.org/mena/education.

Williams, Maria Patricia. 2021. "The Contribution of 'A Sister of Notre Dame' and the 'Nun of Calabar' to Montessori Education in Scotland, Nigeria and Beyond." *Rivista di Storia dell'Educazione* 8 (2): 123–34. https://doi.org/10.36253/rse-10344.

Chapter 36
Montessori Education in Tanzania

Kerstin Forsberg, Hans Forsberg, Joyce Mbuya, and Shose Ngowi

In the shade of a jacaranda tree in Moshi, there is an entrance to a Montessori kindergarten. Bright red shelves in the classroom filled with the didactic Montessori materials made by the teachers catch the eye. The silence of concentration is total. A 5-year-old girl is heading for the world puzzle. A 3-year-old boy is heading for the same material. The girl gets there first, takes the puzzle, and walks back to her mat. The little boy controls himself; it takes all his effort not to grab the puzzle from her hands. The girl takes no notice of the boy as she sits down to do the puzzle. The boy watches her every movement. When finished, the girl puts the puzzle back on the shelf. Now the boy takes the puzzle to his mat with confidence.

The interaction shows two children learning patience, cooperation, and respect, important aspects of Montessori education's long history in Tanzania. From 1967 to today, the Tanzanian Montessori movement is characterized by strong support from Tanzanian families and educators combined with strong connections to Christian organizations, and foreign and local philanthropic support.

Early Years

Montessori education came to Tanzania in 1967, six years after the country's independence. At this time, the country's priority under president and former teacher Julius Nyerere was education for "self-reliance," especially in villages. Recognizing women's centrality to village work accentuated a need for childcare, leading to the development of kindergartens for children ages 2 to 6 (Schnepf 2010). As a result of long-standing rural outreach efforts, the Tanzanian Aga Khan Foundation invited Englishwoman Muriel Dwyer, a representative of Association Montessori Internationale (AMI), to teach a Montessori training course in Dar es Salaam (Dwyer et al. 2001).

Beginning with eight sets of materials imported from Europe and offering a total of four training courses, Dwyer sought to bridge language and cultural barriers with her students as they worked to transform a nursery school of 400 children into a Montessori environment. Working in English and Swahili, Dwyer strove to help her trainees understand what education could look like beyond "sitting still." She shared with her AMI colleagues around the world that "once the children really understood not only that they were permitted to move but that we honestly wanted them to move … they started to run round and round and we thought they would never stop but they did and little by little they settled to free work. … It seemed their desire for new knowledge and abilities was inexhaustible" (Dwyer 1969, 16).

Dwyer worked with Tanzanians including Sister Gaspara Kashamba and Sister Angela Loko to develop a sustainable model for Montessori training in Tanzania. They emphasized educating the poorest students in rural areas, ensuring their trainees could secure jobs in their communities upon completion of their program by arranging sponsorships from a village, mission, or firm. Further, they relied on local rather than imported materials in order to be cost-effective (Dwyer et al. 2001). Dwyer worked with the Swiss Little Sisters of St. Francis of Assisi Msimbazi Mission to open the Montessori Training Centre in a single room in the market in Dar es Salaam in 1967. Dwyer described that "one of the Sisters taught me how to use a fret saw and just using locally available, mostly waste materials (cardboard boxes, bottle tops etc.), we made as much of the apparatus as we could" (Dwyer et al. 2001: 1). The Montessori materials were handmade by teachers in the workshop of the Montessori Training Center, a practice that continues today, helping the schools to be self-reliant and cost-effective (see Figure 36.1).

Figure 36.1 Sister Bertha Kira makes Montessori materials, 2021. Courtesy of Sister Christina Nakey.

Communities of Catholic or Lutheran sisters started six of Tanzania's ten currently operational Montessori training centers, each one supporting a cluster of surrounding Montessori kindergartens. In Moshi, an order of Lutheran sisters called Ushirika wa Neema (Fellowship of Grace) opened a Montessori kindergarten in 1980 and a Montessori Training Centre (MTC) in 1990. Since then, MTC has educated approximately nine hundred Montessori teachers, who now work in Montessori kindergartens all over Tanzania (Arthur Waser Foundation 2021; Church of Sweden 2018). The Northern Diocese of the Evangelical Lutheran Church of Tanzania challenged their parishes to open at least one Montessori kindergarten in every parish. Donor support from parishes in Germany, Switzerland, the United States, and Sweden has supported Tanzanian sisters completing Montessori training in Europe and Tanzania, building schools around Tanzania and subsidizing school fees for students (Church of Sweden 2018; Schnepf 2010; Ushirika Association 2021). In this way religious communities, many of them with European donor support, have been critical to expanding Montessori networks around Tanzania.

Tanzanian families also led the push to expand Montessori schools, often observing a difference in the curiosity and inner discipline of children who attended Montessori programs compared to those who attended other schools or centers. Often, children struggle during the transition to traditional government elementary schools, which leads their parents to request Montessori elementary programs. For example, Sister Denise Mattle, a Swiss nun working in Mwanza, founded a Montessori preschool in 1996. Because of parental requests, she then helped to build a Montessori elementary school and ultimately a secondary school (Sister Denise, pers. comm.; Sister Denise 2021). In Moshi, following long-standing requests from parents to have their children's Montessori education continue past kindergarten, Ushirika wa Neema, together with Nyköping Parish and the Arthur Waser Foundation, built a Montessori elementary school in Moshi. Similarly, separate, secular strands of Tanzanian Montessori schools were started in urban areas by parents seeking to prepare their children for elementary school (Schnepf 2010).

Two Tanzanian Montessori teachers, reflecting on the impact of Montessori education in their communities, have characterized the method as helping children develop "commitment, freedom and social skills … trigger[ing] children to act by themselves and to develop self-confidence" (Joyce Mbuya, pers. comm.; Shose Ngowi, pers. comm.).

Contemporary Landscape

The strong connection between early childcare and Montessori pedagogy persists today in Tanzania. A day care center registration is only issued to owners if they have a trained Montessori teacher (Cosmas Madulu, pers. comm.). As of 2021, there are more than 800 Montessori day care centers serving children 0 to 4, one elementary school and an estimated 5,000 Montessori teachers (Cosmas Madulu, pers. comm.). In one current Montessori school-building project in a remote Maasai area, two Tanzanian architects, Doreen Fred and Dr. Victoria Marwa Heilman, are demonstrating how environmental sustainability, Indigenous design, and Montessori principles can operate harmoniously (Architectural Pioneering Consultants 2019; Fred et al. 2022).

Nine Montessori training centers are located around Tanzania: in Arusha (which has two), Bagamoyo, Bukoba, Lushoto, Moshi, Mtwara, Mwanza, and Dar es Salaam (which offers

Tanzania's only elementary training course). A tenth center is under construction in the southern highlands. The original Montessori training center in Dar es Salaam, which opened in 1967, now has an international collaboration with the Maria Montessori Institute in London and AMI (Montessori Training Centre). While four of the programs have links to religious communities, businessmen started one of the centers in Arusha. The Montessori training centers in Lushoto and Moshi are distinctive for being founded and operated by Tanzanians (Schnepf 2010).

In 2021, the Montessori Community of Tanzania (MCT) was founded as a continuation of the Montessori Training Association of Tanzania (MTAT), founded in 1997. MCT arranges an annual conference, attracting an audience of 200–400 Montessori teachers in rotating locations around the country. The principals of the training centers cooperate on a common curriculum to lessen the variations of Montessori implementation in different schools. One of the current aims of MCT is to develop stronger connections with public teacher training colleges.

As Montessori education grows in Tanzania, several challenges remain, including serving the families who struggle to afford school fees, and maintaining the production of Montessori materials, which are dependent on school fees. COVID-19 has decreased student enrollments at the preschool level, which has impacted teachers' salaries as well (Cosmas Madulu, pers. comm., 2021).

Conclusion

Despite challenges, educators in Tanzania continue to develop and build Montessori education around Tanzania. The social impact of Montessori pedagogy in Tanzania connects the independence of the child to greater social change. "Help me do it myself" is the motto of Montessori education in Tanzania, recurring in images from a Montessori school and orphanage in Bububu, Zanzibar to the Montessori Training Centre in Lushoto. MTC in Moshi proclaims, "We shall change society. Let's work together." Through a long history of collaboration between Tanzanian citizens, educators, and religious communities, as well as domestic and foreign philanthropy, Montessori education in Tanzania continues to thrive throughout the country.

Note

Cosmas Madulu and Joke Verheul commented on an earlier version of this chapter.

References

Architectural Pioneering Consultants. 2019. "Montessori School." https://www.apc-tz.com/work#/montessorischool.
Arthur Waser Foundation. 2021. "Ushirika wa Neema Sisters." https://www.arthur-waser-foundation.ch/en/ushirika-wa-neema-sisters/.

Church of Sweden, Nyköping Parish. 2018. "Nyköping stöttar uppbyggnad av skola i Tanzania." Accessed August 10, 2021. https://www.svenskakyrkan.se/nykoping/projektneema?fbclid=IwAR2jPi2vzHCYXzD4dO0hD-Pnr1B_W-O-gElNqaB5DYNWqsJoHwpIFHLqrTk

Dwyer, Muriel. 1969. "Report from Tanzania." *Around the Child* 13: 14–16.

Dwyer, Muriel, Sister Gaspara Kashamba and Sister Angela Loko. 2001. "Montessori in the Developing World: 33 Years of Excellence." In *Education as an Aid to Life: Conference Proceedings 24th International Montessori Congress [Paris, July 2001]*, 165–8. Association Montessori de France. Reprinted via Montessori Australia https://montessori.org.au/publications/montessori-articles/montessori-developing-world-33-years-experience-africa.

Fred, Doreen, Benjamin Staehli, and Victoria Marwa Heilman. 2022. "Building Schools." *AMI*. January 6, 2022. https://montessori-ami.org/events/ami-talks-building-schools.

Montessori Training Centre Msimbazi Dar Es Salaam. 2016. "About Us." http://www.montessori-africa.com/1/About-us.

Schnepf, Candy. 2010. "Nisaidie nif anye mwenyewe, Помоги мне это сделать самому: A Comparative Case Study of the Implementation of Montessori Pedagogy in the United Republic of Tanzania and the Russian Federation." PhD diss., University of Minnesota.

Sister Denise. 2021. "Montessori School in Mwanza." YouTube. https://www.youtube.com/watch?v=DWZPF3h9FhU

Ushirika Association. 2021. "Scholarships for Montessori Education." http://www.ushirika.se.

Chapter 37
Montessori Education in Kenya

Francescah Kipsoi

Kenya lies on the eastern coast of Africa and has a multiethnic population of 48 million people who speak forty-nine languages. The country's two official languages are English and Kiswahili (2019 Census). Given Kenya's ethnic and linguistic diversity, the long history of Montessori education in the country is linked to delivering culturally relevant education taught in local languages.

Early Years of Montessori Education in Kenya

The first Kenyan Montessori teachers were trained in Dar es Salaam, Tanzania, in 1969 (Dwyer 1970) (see also Chapter 35: "Montessori Education in Africa: Themes and Examples across the Continent" and Chapter 36: "Montessori Education in Tanzania"). Several years later, a conversation between Muriel Dwyer, an AMI trainer from London who had introduced Montessori training in Tanzania, and Father Robert Vujs, a Catholic priest, led to the establishment of the Child Developers Programme, a Montessori teacher training center, in Nairobi in 1974 (Vujs 1974). The first course, taught by Dwyer and Khatoon Murji, included twenty-three Kenyan trainees. Interest in Montessori education grew, and trainees from other African countries including Zambia, Nigeria, Swaziland, and Botswana began traveling to attend the Nairobi training, many sponsored by the Catholic Church and other religious groups. Jericho Nursery School in Nairobi was the first established Montessori early learning education center and remains open today.

Montessori Teacher Training in Kenya

Montessori training in Kenya has grown with the establishment of two more training colleges: St. Irene's Montessori College, established in 2000 by the sisters of St. Joseph in Mombasa, and St. Ann's Montessori College, established in 2009 by the Diocese of Nakuru. After training, the trained teachers automatically become members of Montessori Teachers Association of Kenya (MTAK), an association founded in 2009 for Montessori professionals to network and collaborate.

Figure 37.1 Students at Corner of Hope Montessori. Courtesy of Fay Hendriksen.

Montessori teachers come from different backgrounds and communities across Kenya. Starting with the work of Muriel Dwyer, AMI has focused its effort on supporting the training of teachers from under-resourced areas and hard-to-reach communities. This approach is based on the Educateurs sans Frontières Corner of Hope model (see Figure 37.1), in which internally displaced people (IDPs) in Nakuru are supported in completing Montessori training, which subsequently allows them to serve their own community by providing quality, culturally responsive education for children (see Chapter 38: "AMI Educateurs sans Frontières"). The work in the remote and rural areas of Samburu and Pokot is based on the same model of teacher training.

The colleges in Kenya offer teacher training for students ages 3–6. For many years, AMI has worked closely with the training colleges to provide support and mentorship, collaboratively increasing access to Montessori education while guaranteeing its quality. In 2018, twenty-seven teachers were trained in Kenya at the first Montessori course for students ages 6–12 held in Africa.

A distinctive aspect of training in Kenya is material-making, where each teacher makes a full set of materials by hand during their training. The materials are made with great precision, using locally available materials like grains, cartons, beads, sisal, wool, plywood, and fabric at the workshops that are part of each training college (see Figure 37.2).

Making the materials gives the teachers an excellent understanding of the characteristics and purpose of each material, and it allows the teachers to set up a Montessori classroom wherever

Figure 37.2 A teacher makes Montessori materials at St. Ann's Montessori Teacher Training College in Nakuru, Kenya. Courtesy of Fay Hendriksen.

they go. When materials are damaged or in need of replacement, teachers will be able to repair or replace them independently. This practice, addressing a challenge that has limited the growth of Montessori education elsewhere, has enabled expansion in Kenya.

Contemporary Landscape

After completing their training, teachers join different schools across the country in both urban and rural areas. In the past, most schools were established in wealthy urban areas, which were inaccessible for many families. Currently, most Montessori schools in Kenya offer early childhood education. While the Montessori method is not taught in public schools, it is available in over 200 private schools, including international schools serving foreign residents and workers. Due to issues related to accreditation, most schools offer a blended curriculum incorporating Montessori education at the preschool level and Kenyan or international curriculum at the elementary level. A few schools, including Corner of Hope and Kipepeo School, both in Nakuru, offer the Montessori elementary curriculum.

Official recognition of the Montessori curriculum has represented a persistent challenge to the method's expansion in Kenya. In 2019, through the combined efforts of AMI, the training colleges, the Montessori Teachers Association of Kenya (MTAK), and other stakeholders, the Montessori early childhood curriculum for ages 3–6 was approved by the Kenyan Ministry of Education, making it the only foreign curriculum recognized by the Kenyan government. (Montessori for Kenya 2021).

In 2019, Montessori for Kenya (MfK) was established as a registered nongovernmental organization affiliated with AMI and motivated by the community-based Corner of Hope school model. The organization aims to support Montessori education in Kenya by increasing access to resources that support Montessori education and research and by creating a network to increase access to quality Montessori education in Kenya and beyond. MfK offers support to community-based initiatives across Kenya. Initiatives inspired by the Corner of Hope model are being replicated in Samburu and East Pokot, in the northern region of Kenya, showing how Montessori education can support nomadic tribes and communities across Kenya and Africa, as well as refugee communities across the globe.

Montessori pedagogy is highly regarded in Kenya for supporting the full development of the child, using interactive materials, and instilling cultural values in the child. Moreover, teachers who come from different ethnic groups work to make Montessori education culturally responsive in every community context, meeting the needs of children from different backgrounds without losing their culture and identity. The children are taught in the language they understand, and within a few years, they comfortably learn in multiple languages. During training, teachers make materials sensitive to the community they serve; for example, lessons cover the wild animals that exist in the Kenyan habitat and the traditional practices of Kenyan tribes. In pastoralist communities in the Samburu region, children learn in tented Montessori schools within the community, maintaining their tradition and allowing them to stay connected to their culture.

Additionally, Montessori pedagogy holds promise in the context of Kenyan education reforms, following the grade-level redesign in 2018 that introduced an educational structure of 2-6-3-3 (two years in pre-primary education, six years in primary education, three years in secondary education, and three years in tertiary education), well aligned with Montessori education's planes of development. Moreover, the priorities of Kenya's Sustainable Development Goals and Kenya's Vision 2030 are also aligned with Montessori education (Kaviti 2018).

Conclusion

Montessori education in Kenya continues to provide a strong foundation for children. The approval of the 3–6 curriculum by the Kenya Institute of Curriculum Development sets the ground for the continued growth of Montessori schools in Kenya. It is crucial to support emerging and existing schools through mentorship and other kinds of support from a network of teachers, colleges, and AMI, to strengthen Montessori education in Kenya and to increase access for all children.

Note

Joke Verheul, Fay Hendriksen, and Lynne Lawrence contributed information and commented on an earlier version of this chapter.

References

Dwyer, Muriel. 1970. "Report from Tanzania." *Around the Child* 13: 14–16.
Kaviti, Lillian. 2018. "The New Curriculum of Education in Kenya: A Linguistic and Education Paradigm Shift." *International Journal of Novel Research in Education and Learning* 5 (1): 15–27.
Kenya Census. 2019. "2019 Kenya Population and Housing Census Results." Accessed August 26, 2021. https://www.knbs.or.ke/?p=5621.
Montessori for Kenya. 2021. "Teacher Training." Accessed August 26, 2021. https://www.montessoriforkenya.org/teachers/teacher-training/.
Vujs, Fr. Robert. 1974. "History of Montessori Program at Jericho Catholic Church." *Archives of the Catholic Archdiocese of Nairobi*.
Republic of Kenya, Ministry of Education. 2019. "Basic Education Statistical Booklet." Accessed April 23, 2022. http://dc.sourceafrica.net/documents/120844-Kenya-Basic-Education-Statistical-Booklet-2019.html.

Chapter 38
AMI Educateurs sans Frontières

Fay Hendriksen, Joke Verheul, and Elske Voermans

Maria Montessori's experiences, starting with serving children of the poor in Rome's San Lorenzo district, reinforced her conviction that social progress hinged on the developmental experiences of children as empowered changemakers. When Renilde Montessori, Montessori's youngest granddaughter, became director of Association Montessori Internationale (AMI) in 1995, she called for the Montessori community to strengthen her grandmother's social mission of serving disenfranchised populations and promoting children's rights throughout society to counter the perception of Montessori education as exclusive. Renilde's aspirations were incorporated into the vision and mission of what became Educateurs sans Frontières (EsF), established in 1998 and launched in 1999 (AMI Bylaws). EsF's scope of work can be divided into three areas: a global network of changemakers, advocacy for children's rights, and inspiration and support for global Montessori initiatives.

A Global Network of Changemakers

Initially, the EsF Assemblies were the primary route connecting Montessori educators to develop the vision for EsF. The first EsF Assembly in 1999 brought together twenty-two Montessori educators from twelve countries in Città di Castello, Italy, to study Montessori's works and the social mission of the Montessori movement, working toward a better and more peaceful world (EsF 1999). As ultimately articulated, the focus of EsF is on Montessori "outreach, capacity building, and advocacy in communities, including Indigenous peoples and other vulnerable populations, such as those affected by poverty, displacement, and discrimination, through equitable, inclusive, quality education that respects and celebrates diversity of cultures and languages" (EsF 2021a).

An essential focus of the assemblies, emphasized by AMI Executive Director Lynne Lawrence, is "the need for the community to inform itself from itself. Through the dynamism of the group itself come the ideas, come the connections, comes the network and comes the *permission* to develop something" (Lawrence 2019). During assembly gatherings, individuals exchanged experiences, reflected on their local context and challenges, gained inspiration, and created connections to support their work.

Subsequent multi-week assemblies in Asia, Europe, Africa, and North America inspired new global Montessori initiatives supporting under-resourced communities in various regions (EsF 2021b). Scholarships for attendance supported those working in communities with limited resources. In Hyderabad, India, this led to the development of a new program, Community Rooted Education (CoRE), developing a training model and an affordable set of Montessori materials to introduce the principles of Montessori practice to early childhood educators in rural areas (EsF 2021d).

Over the years, the scope of EsF has expanded to form a network of Montessori practitioners working with multiple partners supporting development from before birth to the end of life. As David Kahn noted, EsF is designed to support "any plane of development, at any time or any place ... beyond Montessori's educational adventure in schools" (Kahn 2004). The open nature of EsF has also allowed for collaborations with those outside of the Montessori network, such as governments, researchers, foundations, and nongovernment organizations (NGO), welcoming anyone with an interest in education for social change, regardless of their Montessori experience.

Advocacy for Children's Rights

Championing the rights of the child and creating an environment that supports these rights are the foundation of AMI's work and at the core of Montessori's mission (Montessori 1947). Ultimately, every Montessori educator contributes to a supportive environment, playing an active part in expanding understanding of the child's developmental needs in society. Montessori's legacy as a champion of children's rights continues through AMI and its EsF work. AMI staffs permanent NGO representatives at both the United Nations Educational, Scientific and Cultural Organization (UNESCO) and the United Nations, collaborating with other NGOs to stress the importance of education and adequately trained teachers, particularly following COVID-19 school closures (Save Our Future 2021). Additionally, EsF promotes children's rights by creating connections between the field of children's rights and Montessori educators through online platforms and presentations (EsF Children's Rights 2021). As part of the online "Voices of EsF" program, participants reach out to their communities, including children, to gain a deeper understanding of the needs and challenges in their local context.

Inspiration and Support for Global Initiatives

EsF has become an important network for initiatives that apply Montessori principles in innovative ways. These examples are recognized for their quality, community-based approach, and sustainability (EsF 2021f). For instance, in the United States, Lumin Education provides support to low-income Latinx families in Houston, offering childcare and parent training through an innovative series of home visits (Lumin 2021). In Haiti, the Peter Hesse Foundation supports a Montessori teacher college and assists graduates in establishing schools. The foundation also supports schools in Cote d'Ivoire, Senegal, and—most recently—in Mali, through training, technical expertise, and financial resources (Peter Hesse 2021).

The following brief profiles of Corner of Hope and Born Inside exemplify the geographical range and broad scope of EsF's work.

Corner of Hope

The community-led Corner of Hope initiative in Kenya presents a model for the potential of Montessori education in refugee and remote communities through accessible training, material making, and community mobilization (see Chapter 37: "Montessori Education in Kenya"). Corner of Hope was initiated by AMI, local partners, the New Canaan community, and a private foundation, as a proof of concept for the establishment of quality Montessori education in the most challenging circumstances.

The first Corner of Hope school was established in 2010, in an Internally Displaced People (IDP) camp in New Canaan, Nakuru, Kenya. The IDP camp emerged after the violence of the 2007 election, which displaced thousands within the country and precipitated a major humanitarian crisis. Initially, eight people from the community attended the training college in Nakuru. As part of their training, the teachers made a complete set of Montessori materials. With support of two mentor teachers, Montessori environments were first set up in tents while classroom buildings were being constructed by volunteers from the community.

Since 2010, over 100 teachers have completed training, and a second school was set up at the request of the community in a nearby location. More than one thousand children have passed through the schools, and additional elementary classrooms were added in 2017. Despite the

Figure 38.1 A Corner of Hope Montessori classroom setup in a tent, Kenya. Courtesy of Fay Hendriksen.

challenging circumstances and limited resources, Corner of Hope provides fully implemented Montessori, embraced by the community as they notice the positive impact on the children. Inspired by the model, and with the support of two Corner of Hope mentor teachers, mobile Montessori schools have been established in Kenya's rural Samburu region, a new cohort of teachers is completing training, and the model is expanding to East Pokot, Kenya, in one of the country's most under-resourced regions (Corner of Hope 2021) (see Figure 38.1).

Born Inside

While Corner of Hope focuses on people living in IDP camps, Born Inside brings Montessori to another community: incarcerated mothers and their children. Born Inside is a UK-based EsF initiative, supported by the Maria Montessori Institute (MMI), London, and coordinated by MMI lecturer Beverley Maragh and psychotherapist Pamela Wyndham-Stewart. It offers a weekly parental support program for the residents of a mother-and-baby unit in a UK detention center. As a pilot initiative, it demonstrates how Montessori principles and training can support infants and mothers while they are held in detention, and it encourages self-reliance and offers a support network along with practical guidance for responsible parenting in a challenging environment (EsF 2021g).

Conclusion and Future Directions

Whereas research in the United States has indicated that Montessori education can bridge the "achievement gap" for children from low-income backgrounds (Lillard et al. 2017), further research is needed to examine the impact and effectiveness of Montessori practices in under-resourced or conflict-affected communities. Further studies of EsF partnerships could study the potential and challenges of such approaches, providing greater support to efforts to scale up successful pilot initiatives. EsF's inclusive and global network of Montessori and non-Montessori practitioners is a platform to expand and demonstrate what Montessori education can look like and who it can serve, taking Montessori principles beyond the classroom, and for all ages.

Note

Abigail Dogbe, Hillary Korir, Victoria Johnson, Jacquie Maughan, and Eder Cuevas commented on chapter drafts.

References

Association Montessori Internationale. 2018. Bylaws. Internal Document.
Corner of Hope. 2021. "Timeline." Accessed July 15, 2021. https://cornerofhope-esf.org/timeline.
Educateurs sans Frontières (EsF). 1999. "1999 EsF Assembly." Accessed September 21, 2022. https://montessori-esf.org/assemblies/1999-esf-assembly

Educateurs sans Frontières (EsF). 2021a. "EsF Sustainable Development Goals Statement." https://montessori-esf.org/what-is-esf/esf-sustainable-development-goals-statement

Educateurs sans Frontières (EsF). 2021b. "Assemblies." Accessed September 3, 2021. https://montessori-esf.org/assemblies.

Educateurs sans Frontières (EsF) 2021c. "Born Inside." Accessed September 3, 2021. https://montessori-esf.org/project/born-inside.

Educateurs sans Frontières (EsF). 2021d. "Community Rooted Education." Accessed September 3, 2021. https://montessori-esf.org/project/community-rooted-education-india.

Educateurs sans Frontières (EsF). 2021e. "What Is EsF." Accessed September 9, 2021. https://www.montessori-esf.org.

Educateurs sans Frontières (EsF). 2021f. "EsF Initiatives." Accessed September 9, 2021. https://montessori-esf.org/esf-initiatives

Educateurs sans Frontières (EsF). 2021g. "Born Inside." Accessed September 9, 2021. https://montessori-esf.org/project/born-inside.

EsF Children's Rights. 2021. Accessed September 28, 2021. https://esfforchildrensrights.com/.

Kahn, David. 2004. "Educateurs sans Frontières: Looking Inward … in Order to Move Outward." https://montessori-esf.org/sites/default/files/downloads/files/2004AssemblyReflections.pdf

Lawrence, Lynne. 2019. Unpublished Interview, AMI Archives.

Lillard, Angeline S., Megan J. Heise, Eve M. Richey, Xin Tong, Alyssa Hart, and Paige M. Bray. 2017. "Montessori Preschool Elevates and Equalizes Child Outcomes: A Longitudinal Study." *Frontiers in Psychology* 8: 1783. https://doi.org/10.3389/fpsyg.2017.01783.

Lumin Education. 2021. Accessed September 21, 2021. https://lumineducation.org/.

Montessori, Maria. 1947. "The Forgotten Citizen." In *Citizen of the World*, 47. Amsterdam: Montessori-Pierson Publishing Company.

Peter Hesse Foundation. 2021. Accessed September 21, 2021. https://www.solidarity.org/.

Save Our Future. Accessed August 26, 2021. https://saveourfuture.world/.

Chapter 39
Montessori Education in Saudi Arabia

Lila A. Alhashim and Ilene Berson

Throughout the Middle East, many early childhood educators have some familiarity with Montessori principles, and there has been a growing demand for certified Montessori teachers throughout the region. There are Montessori teacher training programs in Bahrain and Egypt, and a Montessori Association in the United Arab Emirates. More than eleven countries in the Middle East region offer early childhood programs that have adopted Montessori and Montessori-inspired practices, with globally accredited Montessori schools in Lebanon and Qatar. Through a case study of Saudi Arabia, this chapter explores Montessori as an imported pedagogy and the culturally specific adaptations made for an Islamic educational environment.

Early Years of Montessori in Saudi Arabia

Preschools throughout the Kingdom of Saudi Arabia (SA) have historically used teacher-centered approaches, and Montessori schools originally emerged in the 1960s as an alternative to serve US and UK expatriate families (Almajed 2020). However, starting in the 1990s, as part of the Saudi expansion of early childhood education (ECE), Asrary School was the first Montessori school serving children from high-income Saudi families (Ahlam Albasim, pers. comm.). A few years later, Montessori schools started to expand throughout the urban areas of Saudi Arabia, with lower fees to make them accessible to middle-class families. Reasons for Montessori's success in Saudi Arabia include the fact that Montessori materials are adaptable to many languages, including Arabic (see Figure 39.1), and the flexibility of the Montessori method for educators from diverse contexts to enact the core principles while making adjustments for culturally relevant implementation that supports children's development (Aljabreen 2020). Thus far, all Montessori children's centers and schools in SA are private, serving young children ages 0 to 6 (Habiba Aljad, pers. comm.).

Contemporary Landscape of Montessori in Saudi Arabia

Recently a growing number of preschools in SA have embraced the Montessori curriculum as the Kingdom works toward enacting Saudi Vision 2030, a strategic initiative to diversify the economy through several public-sector improvements, including expanding ECE. Montessori

Figure 39.1 A child works on Arabic vowel letters and matches the words with the objects in a Montessori classroom, Saudi Arabia. Photo courtesy of Sara Aljindan.

principles intersect with national educational aims, which have been refocused on promoting cultural transformation by stimulating creativity and innovation to enhance the critical thinking skills of Saudi students. The Montessori emphasis on self-guided learning is perceived as useful to achieving desired educational outcomes, while the distinctive emphasis on the whole child, including children's spirituality, aligns well with a cultural context in which the Islamic religion is a critical part of the curriculum (Almajed 2020). As a result, the Ministry of Education (MOE) has become more receptive to the establishment of additional Montessori schools throughout the nation as they seek to increase enrolment in kindergarten schools from 17 percent to 95 percent by 2030 (MOE).

Thus far, Saudi Arabia has adopted a single national early childhood curriculum, one that has been characterized as allowing for little autonomy for teachers and children (Rajab 2016). Still, Montessori schools have found ways to flexibly align their approach within the constraints of the curriculum. The plan has motivated private investors to establish additional private Montessori kindergartens and to use Montessori for several "hospitality centers," free programs that support the children of working mothers (Saleha Aljude, pers. comm.). Nonetheless, as private Montessori schools attempt to expand into upper grades, they encounter challenges in the form of the Ministry of Education rules and regulations, which have limited Montessori education to early childhood settings serving children from birth to 6 years of age.

Saudi Montessori teachers have adapted Montessori practices to integrate religious and cultural teachings for Saudi children. Many of the Montessori educational methods, concepts, and principles have "a harmony of values with the principles of Islamic Education Psychology" and Saudi culture, including a central focus on Islam (Gumiandari et al. 2019, 135). For example, both Montessori and Islamic philosophy encourage learning through authentic experiences that promote interaction with the surrounding environment and scaffold children's learning to move from easy to difficult tasks (Gumiandari et al. 2019, 144–5). Further research is needed to study areas where there might be tensions between Montessori education and Saudi religious and cultural teachings. Future study might compare directed parenting practices in contrast to Montessori children's independence in the classroom, and some Saudi teachers using praise and extrinsic rewards as part of Islamic tenets in contrast to Montessori practices of not using extrinsic rewards (Gumiandari et al. 2019, 144–5). Two aspects of the Saudi Montessori curriculum are distinct. The integration of Islamic education is part of the national doctrine, and teachers emphasize religious concepts to ensure that each child has a strong faith in God "Allah" and in the prophet Mohammed (peace be upon him) as a messenger (Rajab 2016). Additionally, the study of Arabic language ensures that children will not only be able to speak the language but also understand the Quran, the holy book of Islam. For example, the Hassan School, a private Montessori kindergarten in SA established by Saleha Aljude, focuses on providing high-quality education by integrating Saudi culture and religion into classroom instruction (Saleha Aljude, pers. comm.). During the morning circle time, teachers present Quranic verses and share guidance from the prophet Mohammed (peace be upon him) throughout the children's daily routine. The children in the Montessori classroom greet each other by saying "*Salam Aliakmon*" (peace be upon you). The children also say daily *duas*, a special prayer, before eating, dressing in their coats, and before and after using the bathroom. In the Practical Life center, students use a *dallah* and *finjan*, a traditional pitcher and cup for coffee, to practice water pouring instead of a jug and a cup. Saudi cultural and religious events, such as *Eid*, the month of *Ramadan*, and the Saudi national day are celebrated with special decorations and activities (Saleha Aljude, pers. comm.). Teacher-made tools supplement official Montessori materials due to the limited availability of licensed Montessori resources that reflect the Arabic cultural context (Aljabreen 2017). The preparation of the environment incorporates these materials to stimulate children's exploration and self-guided learning; however, when engaging in religious instruction, educators often rely on more teacher-directed approaches (Almajed 2020). For example, when children are learning to read the Quran, the Montessori teachers provide teacher-directed guidance to ensure that children learn the correct pronunciation of the letters and follow the Quran recitation rules (Saleha Aljude, pers. comm.).

Given Saudi Arabian Montessori schools' record of blending the Montessori approach with the Islamic view of the child's learning, Montessori's name recognition and reputation have attracted many middle-class Saudi parents who seek both early childhood programs which are both academically rigorous and which support Saudi culture and Islamic values. However, there is considerable variability in how the Montessori method is implemented, suggesting challenges to maintaining fidelity and quality as Montessori-inspired kindergarten programs grow in number. As Montessori expands in SA, not all Montessori schools adhere to Montessori principles in their program delivery and instead may use the Montessori name as a marketing device (Saleha Aljude, pers. comm.).

An additional challenge is a paucity of Montessori-trained teachers in SA. Early childhood teacher preparation programs rarely include Montessori as part of their program of study, and there are still only a limited number of Montessori teacher academies throughout the Middle East. Currently, in Saudi Arabia, there are just a few Montessori teacher training centers, including Daem Training in Riyadh, which offer courses recognized by the SA Ministry of Education. Another example is Ibn Khaldun Schools, which also provide certified Montessori courses (Habiba Aljad, pers. comm.).

Conclusion

Montessori education in Saudi Arabia is in its early stages, but it has already shown promise related to its alignment with Islamic principles, Saudi culture, and the Saudi 2030 vision. Additional research is important to document diverse Montessori practices in Saudi Arabia that align with the Saudi MOE educational policy, greater access to Montessori teacher preparation, and advocacy for extension of Montessori curriculum beyond early childhood. These efforts will be essential to expand Montessori schools in Saudi Arabia.

Note

The authors gratefully thank Sara Aljindan, Haifa Aljabreen, and Amal Albehaijan for contributing information for the chapter. Sara Aljindan read an earlier draft of this chapter.

References

Aljabreen, Haifa Hassan. 2017. "A Comparative Multi-Case Study of Teacher Roles in U.S. Montessori Preschool and Saudi Public Preschool." PhD diss., Kent State University College.
Aljabreen, Haifa. 2020. "Montessori, Waldorf, and Reggio Emilia: A Comparative Analysis of Alternative Models of Early Childhood Education." *International Journal of Early Childhood* 52: 337–53. https://doi.org/10.1007/s13158-020-00277-1.
Almajed, M. A. 2020. "Teachers' Perceptions of Supporting Pre-School Children in Self-Learning in Montessori Classrooms: A Case Study of Three Saudi Pre-Schools." *Multi-Knowledge Electronic Comprehensive Journal for Education and Science Publications* 37: 1–21. https://www.mecsj.com/uplode/images/photo/Teachers_Perceptions_of_Supporting_Pre-School_Children.pdf.
Gumiandari, Septi, Ilman Nafi'a, and Dindin Jamaluddin. 2019. "Criticizing Montessori's Method of Early Childhood Education Using Islamic Psychology Perspective." *Jurnal Pendidikan Islam* 5 (2): 133–48. https://doi.org/10.15575/jpi.v5i2.5835.
Rajab, Adaylah. 2016. "The Idea of Autonomy in Child-Centered Education: The Preschool in Saudi Arabia as a Case Study." Paper presented at the European Conference on Education, Brighton, United Kingdom, 2016. http://papers.iafor.org/wp-content/uploads/papers/ece2016/ECE2016_23242.pdf
The Ministry of Education. n.d. "Early Childhood." وزارة الطفولة | لمبكر ة التعليما (moe.gov.sa).

Chapter 40
Montessori Education in India

Rukmini Ramachandran and Mira Debs

India is one of the few countries with a century-long uninterrupted Montessori tradition, strengthened by Maria Montessori's long stay there in the 1940s. The chapter traces the evolution of Indian Montessori in three phases: an ascendant first wave from 1915 to 1947, in which Montessori's approach was aligned with the Indian independence movement; second, gradual growth between 1947 and 1989 as the method spread slowly in private schools, and rapidly in an adapted form in rural government-funded preschools; and third, as India's expanding middle class since 1989 has fueled private Montessori growth alongside public-private partnerships in South India that have increased the access of poor children to high-fidelity Montessori (Debs 2022).

India currently has the largest youth population in the world, and improving access to early childhood education (currently attended by only half of Indian children) and making education more holistic and project-based are both government priorities and increasingly sought after by Indian families (Donner 2016; Ghosh 2019; UN 2019). Despite these opportunities and strong pockets of Montessori practice around India, a consistent limitation has been division among Montessori organizations, alongside the high cost of materials and training.

First-Wave Montessori, 1915–1939

The first Indian Montessori schools opened in 1915, and the movement grew quickly over the next few decades. Montessori education had special resonance for an Indian audience, which saw colonial education as a tool of British control. Even though Montessori was European, her ideas were embraced by nationalist leaders like Mahatma Gandhi and poet Rabindranath Tagore. Both met Montessori abroad and took inspiration from her in creating education models, which centered Indian art and languages to develop independent future citizens (Wilson 1987). By 1925, nationalist Montessori educators Gijubhai Badheka and Tarabai Modak had established a network of Montessori schools in Gujarat, a teacher training center, a materials manufacturer, Gujarati translations of Montessori's works, a monthly journal *Shiksan Patrika* (Teaching Magazine), published in Gujarati, Hindi, and Marathi and a national Montessori society, the Nutan Bal Shiksan Sangh (NBSS, New Child Education Society). Unfortunately, their inspired efforts were unsanctioned by Montessori, who signaled her disapproval from Europe (Wilson 1987). Other Indian nationalists led parallel expansion efforts. Tagore facilitated the development of a network of Montessori schools in East Bengal. Another cluster emerged in Tamil Nadu, led by the Theosophical Society and the Women's Indian Association in Chennai,

Figure 40.1 Children at the Women's Indian Association Montessori School work outside in the open-air classroom under the banyan trees, Chennai, 1928. Courtesy of the Maria Montessori Archives, Amsterdam.

both pro-Indian independence groups that also created schools, training, materials, and book distribution (Tschurenev 2021; Wilson 1987).

As occurred elsewhere, Montessori also appealed to wealthy families, and a number of elite private schools added Montessori preschool sections. Casa Montessori, created by Dinoo Mehta in Mumbai in 1934 and still operating today, is one of the oldest continuously operating Montessori schools in the world. Between 1915 and 1939, at least fifty Montessori schools opened around India, but only a few served poor students (Debs 2022).

Montessori in India, 1939–1947

Indian Montessori education was boosted by Maria and Mario Montessori's arrival in Chennai in 1939 sponsored by the Theosophical Society. The first course they taught brought together over 200 students from India, Sri Lanka, and Myanmar. As the Second World War broke out, the British limited the movements of the Montessoris along with other Italians, and Mario was briefly interned. Limited in their travel, the Montessoris stayed in Chennai and Kodaikanal, developing the elementary curriculum and cosmic education (Montessori 1942; Moretti 2021; Trudeau

1984; see Chapter 3: "Cosmic Education: The Vital Center of the Montessori Perspective" and Chapter 15: "The Montessori Elementary School for Children Ages 6–12").

In some regards, Montessori's plan to establish an enduring Montessori infrastructure in India was limited: a Montessori university in collaboration with the Theosophical Society was undermined by conflict over the society's financial support of the Montessoris. Montessori was criticized by Gandhi and others for not adapting the model to make it more accessible to poor students (Wilson 1987). Still, in total, the Montessoris and A. M. Joosten taught more than 1,500 students in sixteen courses across the Indian subcontinent (Montessori 1947). When Montessori left India in 1949, the Indian Montessori Training Course (IMTC), led by Joosten and S. R. Swamy, continued the training (Debs 2022; Wilson 1987).

Montessori Post-independence, 1947–1989

After Indian independence, both the federal and regional governments wanted to develop early childhood education, but they had limited funding with which to do so. Montessori expansion shifted to Delhi, Calcutta, Pilani, and Hyderabad, where educators created associations, Montessori journals, and new schools. At a time of limited Montessori activity around the globe, Indian Montessori associations published three journals: *Montessori Magazine* (1946–1950), *Around the Child* (1956–1975), and *Balak* (Child) in Marathi. Newly trained teachers opened schools in the 1950s and 1960s. Momentum was hampered, however, by limited IMTC trainings rotating around India and restrictions in AMI recognition of teachers, schools, training centers, and associations (*Around the Child* 1971). Combined with the expense of materials, many found Montessori requirements too onerous to accommodate rapid expansion, and only a few schools were opened in the 1970s and 1980s (Debs 2022; Wilson 1987).

Even so, Montessori's influence pervaded Indian early childhood education through classroom design, a curricular emphasis on Practical Life, nature, and play as well as manipulative materials, especially for teaching numerical concepts. Montessori educator Tarabai Modak's system of rural preschools, called *balwadis* ("children's garden") and *anganwadis* ("courtyard garden"), adapted Montessori ideas for a wider audience. Developed in 1945 for Dalit and Adivasi tribal communities in Bordhi, Gujarat, Modak's program operated inexpensively using materials found in the village and volunteer teachers. In 1975, the system became a national model as the federal Integrated Child Development Services (ICDS) combined with programs for maternal and child health and nutrition. Today, ICDS operates 1.3 million early childhood centers serving 16 million children as the largest early childhood education system in the world. While the programs follow Montessori's ideas in creating a nurturing, homelike environment, the minimal teacher training limits the implementation of Montessori pedagogy (Tschurenev 2021).

Second-Wave Montessori: 1989 to Today

Since 1989, Montessori education has again been on the rise in India. That year, a 50th anniversary celebration of Montessori education in India brought together multiple generations of Indian Montessori educators, generating national press attention (Srinivasan et al. 2009). Economic reforms increased India's middle class, creating demand for preschool and alternative education (Sridharan 2004).

This demand led to an increase in Indian Montessori teacher training. In 1988, Zarin Malva reestablished AMI training in Mumbai, and today there are AMI-affiliated training centers in four cities with expansion into elementary (since 2007) and infant courses (since 2019). After the death of S. R. Swamy in 1993, the Indian Montessori Centre (IMC) continued under Meenakshi Sivaramakrishnan, an AMI-trained educator and AMI Board member. In 1999, Sivaramakrishnan separated IMC from AMI in an effort to gain autonomy and expand their grassroots work (Shanker 2021). IMC now operates twelve training locations around India. Unaffiliated Montessori training centers have also emerged, especially in Delhi and Kolkata.

Alongside training expansion, Indian Montessori schools have continued to increase from 300 schools in 2006 to an estimated 420 schools today (AMI 2006; Debs 2022). Private Montessori schools range from low-fee, home-based classrooms to elite school campuses. These schools are most concentrated in Bangalore, Hyderabad, and Chennai and appeal to middle class families looking for a pathway to social mobility or elite families seeking a more relaxed, affirming form of education (Debs 2022; Donner 2016). And while preschool remains the most widely available option, in the last decade, elementary programs have expanded in all three cities, and there are now several adolescent farm-based Erdkinder programs around South India (Debs 2022).

Countering this elite focus, educators primarily in South India have in recent years pioneered government and nonprofit models to bring high-fidelity Montessori to poor students. Since 2004, a partnership between Chennai's Corporation schools (government-funded free tuition schools), the Sri Ramacharan Charitable Trust, and IMC Chennai has led to the development of a public Montessori preschool program (Gopalan 2013). The trust and the city support training and materials; all teachers receive an IMC diploma. The program has been popular, significantly increasing enrollment at government schools, with expansion to 100 schools as of 2021 (*DT Next* 2021; Shanker 2021). In Andhra Pradesh, AMI's Educateurs Sans Frontières and the Montessori Training and Research Trust in Hyderabad started Community Rooted Education (CoRE) to develop affordable Montessori training and a low-cost "Montessori in a Box," a partial set of Montessori classroom materials, to support children learning at *anganwadis* (*EsF* 2020). Kerala, Karnataka, Mumbai, and Tamil Nadu are all in the process of expanding Montessori education in government schools and *anganwadis* (Debs 2022). In each of these cases, sustainability is challenged by changing political leadership and developing and maintaining high-level teacher training.

Conclusion

Today, Montessori is growing in both the private and public sectors, with strong alignment to recent government directives like the 2020 National Education policy. While the COVID-19 pandemic has devastated communities and in some cases closed schools, it has also made online teacher training more accessible across India and created opportunities for greater collaborations between schools and training programs. Ongoing challenges include maintaining fidelity, schisms between training programs, and accessing high-quality training and materials, especially for poorer students. Still, despite these challenges, Montessori education's endurance and adaptability in India speaks to its continued salience for the contemporary needs of Indian children.

Note

Uma Shanker, Erica Moretti, Joke Verheul, and Sumathi Ravindranath commented on earlier versions of this chapter.

References

AMI. 2006. "Montessori Census." *Montessori Centenary*. http://montessoricentenary.org/.
Around the Child. 1971. "News of the Montessori Movement." 14: 92–104.
Debs, Mira. 2022. "Montessori in India: Adapted, Competing and Contested Framings, 1915–2021." *History of Education Quarterly* 62 (4): 1–31. https://doi.org/10.1017/heq.2022.25.
Donner, Henrike. 2016. *Domestic Goddesses: Maternity, Globalization and Middle-Class Identity in Contemporary India*. New York, NY: Routledge.
DT Next. 2021. "44 More Corpn Schools to Get Montessori Classes." February 11. https://www.dtnext.in/city/2021/02/11/44-more-corpn-schools-to-get-montessori-classes.
Educateurs sans Frontières (EsF). 2020. "Community Rooted Education in India." https://montessori-esf.org/project/community-rooted-education-india.
Ghosh, Saikat. 2019. "Inequalities in Demand and Access to Early Childhood Education in India." *International Journal of Early Childhood* 51 (2): 145–61.
Gopalan, Pritha. 2013. *PPP Paradox: Promise and Perils of Public-Private Partnerships in Education*. New Delhi: Sage.
Montessori, Mario. 1942. "Dr. Montessori and Her Work in India and Elsewhere during the War." *The Theosophist* 63 (12): 458–60.
Montessori, Maria. 1947. "Interview." *Luce*, uploaded by AMI, August 31, 2020. https://www.montessori-ami.org/news/maria-montessori-interview.
Moretti, Erica. 2021. *The Best Weapon for Peace: Maria Montessori, Education, and Children's Rights*. Madison, WI: University of Wisconsin Press.
Kahn, David. 2013. "Kahn-Wikramaratne Interview. The Kodaikanal Experience. Part 1." *NAMTA Journal* 8 (1): 83–91.
Ramani, Uma. 2016. "Topic: Montessori in India: The Movement and the People." *2016 Educateurs sans Frontières Assembly*. https://montessori-esf.org/sites/default/files/downloads/files/160801UmaRamaniMontessoriIndiaNotes.pdf.
Shanker, Uma. 2021. Interview by Mira Debs, June 22.
Sridharan, Eswaran. 2004. "The Growth and Sectoral Composition of India's Middle Class: Its Impact on the Politics of Economic Liberalization." *India Review* 3 (4): 405–28.
Srinivasan, Prasanna, Rukmini Ramachandran, Vasumathi Srinivasan, Hadrien Roche, and Govind Venkatesan. 2009. *Montessori in India: 70 Years*. Chennai: Indian Montessori Foundation.
Trudeau, Christina Marie. 1984. "A Study of the Development of the Educational Views of Dr. Maria Montessori Based on an Analysis of Her Work and Lectures While in India, 1939–1946." PhD diss., University of Hawai'i at Manoa.

Tschurenev, Jana. 2021. "Montessori for All? Indian Experiments in 'Child Education', 1920s–1970s." *Comparative Education* 57 (3): 1–19. https://doi.org/10.1080/03050068.2021.1888408.
United Nations (UN). 2019. "World Population Prospects." https://population.un.org/wpp/.
Wilson, Carolie. 1987. "Montessori in India: A Study of the Application of Her Method in a Developing Country." PhD diss., University of Sydney.

Chapter 41
Montessori Education in Southeast and East Asia

Saket Malhotra, Kannekar Butt, and Mai P. Nghiêm

In the last forty years, Montessori education has become popular in a number of Southeast and East Asian nations to improve and diversify the education options. According to the Association Montessori Internationale (AMI), in 2020 there were thirteen countries in Southeast and East Asia with Montessori schools: Cambodia, Laos, Malaysia, Myanmar, the Philippines, Singapore, South Korea, Indonesia, Thailand, Vietnam, China, Taiwan, and Japan (AMI 2020). Across the countries, the increase in online information and translated Montessori texts, changes in political leadership, the privatization of the education marketplace, and connections to international organizations have all contributed to the rise of Montessori education in Southeast and East Asia. Challenges in implementation include high costs of teacher training and materials, schools and training centers using the label "Montessori" without engaging the method with fidelity, and compatibility with high stakes state exams. These challenges suggest that continuing to adapt Montessori to the cultural, economic, and social contexts of Southeast and East Asian countries is essential to supporting its further expansion throughout the region. This chapter includes brief case studies of Montessori in Thailand, South Korea, Singapore, and Vietnam (see also Chapters 42 and 43 on China and Japan).

Case Studies of Montessori across Southeast and East Asia

Thailand

In 1939, with a King's Scholarship to study overseas, Chalopchalai Maha Niranon Polangkul studied with Maria and Mario Montessori in England. She returned to Thailand in 1940 to establish the nation's first Montessori school, the Drunothaya School, at Hua Chang Bridge, Bangkok, which remained open until 2006. The Second World War led to many struggles for the fledgling school, including accessing Montessori materials. Forty years later, the expatriate-led Pitisuka School in Chiang Rai opened. The next eight Montessori programs appeared in the 1980s under the leadership of Chulalongkorn University lecturer Jiraphan Poolpat and Khamkaew Kraisorn Pong, who created the Thailand Montessori Association, facilitating a network for schools to more easily share Montessori ideas and materials.

Under the Reform Act of 1999, Thailand moved toward child-centered education; however, this philosophy was unfamiliar to families and educators, and many were unsatisfied with the quality of education provided. A number of Thai officials traveled to observe Montessori schools in Australia, inspiring Kannekar and John Butt to create the Montessori Association of Thailand to improve access to quality Montessori education. The association offered Thailand's first AMI-certified early childhood diploma course in 2006. Kannekar Butt developed and launched a pilot project establishing Montessori in government schools, beginning with six schools in 2004 located in rural areas in Nakorn Pathom, on the outskirts of Bangkok. As of 2020, there were 918 government and private schools around the country after an additional 262 government schools enrolled in a development program to establish new Montessori classrooms.

At its inception, public Montessori in Thailand was supported by public and private partnerships, with the support of KRB Consultant Australia and Australian Thai Montessori (ATM), and schools in Australia, which shared Montessori materials. With the success of the pilot, the Office of Basic Education Commission of Thailand began funding teacher training programs and supporting Montessori's further incorporation into government schools. Montessori in Thailand demonstrates how strong collaboration between Montessori NGOs and the Thai government can provide the funding and resources needed to develop a strong Montessori public sector in a short amount of time.

South Korea

South Korea's Montessori Society was created in 1983, following the growing popularity of the movement among wealthy families in Korea. The demand led to the creation of many new private Montessori schools, although there was a concern about a number of schools using only the Montessori name with no connection to the pedagogy (Jun 1994). Today, training centers include the AMI Korea Montessori Institute, founded in 1994 and offering primary training; the AMI Montessori Center Korea, founded in 2018 and offering infant training; and unaffiliated training centers like Helia.

After Montessori was introduced in the private sphere, public school personnel expressed interest in expanding into early childhood education (Jun 1994). In 1990, the Korean government invested the equivalent of 142 billion USD over ten years into developing curricula for early childhood education (Jun 1994). However only Montessori-influenced "sensory education" was incorporated into the state-mandated early childhood curriculum, demonstrating a potential opportunity for further collaboration between Montessori and Korean public education (Jun 1994).

Singapore

As in South Korea, Montessori education in Singapore has remained a popular option restricted entirely to the private sector; schools like Montessori for Children have been open since the early 1990s (Montessori for Children 2020). In Singapore, families have invested in private preschool in order to make their children academically competitive in their transition to elementary school (Bach and Christensen 2016). Although recent reforms have worked to de-emphasize academic content in Singaporean preschools, parents observe that Montessori schools may still feel pressured to use traditional academic materials such as worksheets in preschools (Bach and Christensen 2016). Even with governmental policy in support of more relaxed, holistic learning, academic pressure and teaching through rote learning remain a challenge even in Montessori schools.

Vietnam

In Vietnam, Montessori was first mentioned in *Giáo Dục Nhi Đồng* (*To Educate the Child*) (1942), a book on children's education by the early-twentieth-century Vietnamese feminist writer and educator Đạm Phương nữ sử (1881–1947) (Trần 2021). Early on, experimental Montessori programs appear to have been operated in Hanoi by Nguyễn Thị Khang (1942–1943) and later by Lê Thị Tuất, and her husband Nguyễn Phúc Vĩnh Bang who, in 1948, joined Jean Piaget's developmental psychology research in Switzerland (Nguyễn 2018; Tường Hân 2019). In Saigon (South Vietnam), before the unification of the country in 1975, there were also a few Montessori kindergartens, namely Anh Vũ Kindergarten (1973–1975) operated by the writer and educator Đỗ Phương Khanh (1936–2020) (Viễn Đông Daily 2020). After the 1954–1975 war, the national education system followed a single curriculum starting with the first grade.

In 1986, in order to be internationally competitive, Vietnam changed course, adopting the *ĐỔI MỚI* (Renovation) policy, which transitioned the country to a socialist-oriented market economy. Plans for education reforms included universal kindergarten and the expected shift toward student-centered learning. These tentative reforms laid the groundwork for alternative pedagogies such as the Montessori approach to gain traction roughly a decade later, with Vietnamese educators training abroad in a variety of traditions and returning to their home country to open schools, training centers, and commercial enterprises.

In 2010, Nghiêm Phương Mai, a Montessori mother and Association Montessori Internationale (AMI)-trained teacher, founded Vietnam Montessori Education Foundation (VMEF), a Canada-based NGO. In 2012, VMEF initiated the first AMI international conference hosted at the University of Social Sciences and Humanities (USSH) in Ho Chi Minh City, leading to an ongoing partnership between USSH and AMI and subsequent training courses bringing in foreign trainers. Another AMI conference was organized in Hanoi in collaboration with Hội Tâm lý Giáo dục học Hà Nội (Association of Psychology in Education) in 2013. A number of Vietnamese Montessori groups and independent Montessori training programs have subsequently arisen from alumni cohorts of the courses.

To make Maria Montessori's works accessible to the broader Vietnamese public, in collaboration with Montessori-Pierson Publishing Company, Nghiêm also worked on the Vietnamese translation of a dozen of Montessori's works, which were first published by Dr. Chu Hảo's Tri Thức Publishing House. In 2016, Nghiêm and a group of Vietnamese Montessori educators created the nonprofit Vietnam AMI Montessori Initiative (VAMI) to serve the Montessori community and to connect Vietnamese teachers and administrators of all training backgrounds in Vietnam. In 2021, the organization also supported the creation of the Do Minh Training Center, which focuses on offering more affordable training to teachers and families in underserved areas.

Although the Montessori approach has been widely accepted with enthusiasm in Vietnam, there has been no official census on the number of Montessori programs in Vietnam, and the fidelity of many of these programs varies widely. One challenge is that without the Ministry of Education recognition of the Montessori curriculum, the early childhood Montessori program must be registered as a private and international program. Otherwise, the Montessori curriculum in Vietnamese schools must be implemented piecemeal, either on a part-time basis or as an after-school activity, losing the full work cycle integral to the Montessori approach. Interestingly, a number of schools, including Mầm Non Khai Tâm and Nebula Children's Home in Saigon (see Figure 41.1), have tried to offer programs according to authentic Montessori principles but do not call themselves Montessori schools because of government regulations. Very recently, a secondary school program apparently applying the Montessori farm school model (see Chapter 16: "Erdkinder: An Educational Approach for Adolescents Ages 12–15") has been started in northern Vietnam (Thanh and Tam 2021). Recognizing the obstacles posed by training and the acquisition of Vietnamese language and culturally relevant materials, VAMI has been working to lower the cost of training, support local providers for Montessori materials, develop culturally responsive Vietnamese Montessori materials, and encourage local AMI graduates to embrace the Montessori trainer pathways.

Figure 41.1 A preschool child in Vietnam peels a carrot as a Practical Life exercise. Courtesy of Vietnam AMI Montessori Initiative (VAMI) and Nebula Children's Home, Vietnam.

Limitations to Montessori Expansion in Southeast and East Asia

Despite considerable Montessori growth around Southeast and East Asia, there have also been consistent economic and cultural roadblocks to expanding Montessori. The high cost of materials and limited well-trained faculty have made Montessori education expensive and often exclusive in the region. As the movement expands to a broader middle-class audience and educational entrepreneurs sense the endeavor can be profitable, schools and training centers have cropped up using Montessori label, sometimes with little resemblance to the method, confusing families as to what Montessori education actually is in practice. Efforts ensuring that countries have their own trainers and training programs and ensuring Montessori schools offer high-quality education are underway in a number of countries.

Thailand is unique in the region for its success with implementing Montessori in government schools. Support for these programs began with a public-private partnership, but more recently the government has stepped up to support quality teacher training and classroom material acquisition. Despite this significant investment, long-term support for Montessori relies on developing and sustaining an affordable training model, as well as providing for ongoing teacher professional development. Similarly, in Vietnam, public-private partnerships combining international Montessori groups and local universities or other educational entities have helped to create pathways for teacher training. This suggests a viable way forward for making Montessori accessible and sustainable in Southeast and East Asian countries.

In addition to the cost barriers, there are a number of social issues hindering Montessori's expansion. In some countries, parents worry that Montessori may be incompatible with existing educational structures. High-stakes national testing requirements in countries such as Singapore and Korea make parents fearful of deviating from traditional education, a track their children will need to rejoin once they age out of the Montessori program. There are also fears that Montessori education will contradict some dominant social norms in Asia. Despite divergence from the mainstream education system, testimony from Thailand suggests that educators emphasize how Montessori builds inner discipline and moral character, valued cultural traits. Building off the Thai cultural focus on community, the multiage classroom becomes a thriving interactive micro-community in which working together and assisting other students are natural and encouraged. This example highlights important lessons about adapting Montessori and communicating its cultural alignment to Southeast and East Asian families.

Conclusion

As this chapter demonstrates, Montessori continues to grow in countries around Southeast and East Asia in both the public and private sector. Buy-in from parents and the government and maintaining high-quality training will be important to its continued success. As high costs pose the greatest barriers to making Montessori accessible, soliciting investment from the government and from international Montessori organizations will be crucial to the success of Montessori.

Further research into Montessori students' long-term prospects will be important in justifying the method's higher costs compared to traditional education, while also alleviating parents' concerns about the unfamiliar method.

References

Association Montessori Internationale (AMI). 2020. "Montessori Schools in 2020." Annual General Meeting, 2020.

Bach, Dil, and Søren Christensen. 2016. "Battling the Tiger Mother: Pre-school Reform and Conflicting Norms of Parenthood in Singapore." *Children & Society* 31 (2): 14–143. https://doi.org/10.1111/chso.12162.

Jun, Young S. 1994. "An Evaluation of the Effectiveness of the Korean Montessori Teacher Training Program as Perceived by Montessori Teachers and Parents of Montessori-Educated Children." Ed.D Diss., Institute for Catholic Educational Leadership, University of San Francisco.

Montessori for Children. 2020. "Welcome to Montessori for Children." https://www.montessori.edu.sg/.

Nguyễn, Thụy Phương. 2018. "Giáo dục Mới tại Việt Nam: Những nhà tiên phong thể nghiệm." http://khoavanhoc-ngonngu.edu.vn/nghien-cuu/giao-duc/7253-giáo-dục-mới-tại-việt-nam-những-nhàtiên-phong-thể-nghiệm.html.

Thanh, Ngoc and Duong Tam. 2021. "Vietnam's First Montessori Secondary School." *Vietnam Express.* January 21. https://e.vnexpress.net/news/travel/places/vietnam-s-first-montessori-secondary-school-4222139.html.

Trần, Đình Ba. 2021. "Đạm Phương nữ sử bàn về giáo dục nhi đồng" https://nld.com.vn/van-nghe/dam-phuong-nu-su-ban-ve-giao-duc-nhi-dong-20210305210803124.htm.

Tường Hân, Theo. 2019. "Hình ảnh trường mẫu giáo theo hướng canh tân đầu tiên ở Việt Nam." *Vietkings.* http://kyluc.vn/tin-tuc/thong-tin/hinh-anh-truong-mau-giao-theo-huong-canh-tan-dau-tien-o-viet-nam.

Viễn Đông, Daily. 2020. "Vĩnh biệt nhà văn, nhà-giáo dục, Đỗ Phương Khanh." http://www.viendongdaily.com/vinh-biet-nha-van-nha-giao-duc-do-phuong-khanh-1936-2020-6ogDLOkd.html.

Chapter 42
Montessori Education in China

Jie Chen and Yu Liu

Montessori education was introduced to China in the early twentieth century and attracted the attention of educational reformers who were committed to establishing a modern education system in China. However, Montessori education failed to take off in this first wave due to economic and social conditions as well as leading educational reformers' divergent perspectives on this education theory. Since the 1980s, along with China's economic reform and increased interest in Western education theories, a second wave of Montessori education has occurred in China. Especially with the market-based economic system reforms of the 1990s, Montessori education, combined with the rapid development of private kindergartens, expanded greatly. This has led to a surge of research and publications as well as teacher training for Montessori education but also provoked criticisms related to elitism and marketization.

Early Dissemination and Development, 1913–1931

In the early twentieth century, as China worked to establish a "new" education system, Chinese educators were eager to emulate Western education methods. Kindergartens, serving 3–6 year-olds, were added to the Chinese education system, replacing informal preschool education, which had taken place in children's homes. As a result, Montessori education was introduced to China in 1913, when three articles on Montessori education were published in the *Journal of Education* and *Chinese Education* (Ding 2021; Tian 2007).[1] Bingqing Fan's *Ms. Montessori and Her New Teaching Method* (1913), published in the first issue of the *Journal of Education*, was written based on his personal experience while visiting Rome. After that, a "short-lived" but keen enthusiasm for the Montessori method emerged in China, which persisted until 1931 (Tian 2007).

The earliest Montessori-related research institution in China, the Montessori Institute of Education, was established in Jiangsu Province in 1914, aiming to explore the adaptation of Montessori in China, called variously sinicization[2] and localization, in consideration of cultural differences and developmental gaps in economics between China and Italy (Chen and Guo, 2021; Wu and Zhang 2015).

The first Montessori school in China appears to have been the Wong Sun Yue Montessori House of Childhood in Beijing, opened in 1916 by two wealthy American sisters, Katherine Clemens Gould and Mrs. Wong Sun Yue Clemens, the latter of whom attended classes with Maria Montessori at the Panama Pacific International Exposition and reportedly received Montessori's blessing for the project (*San Francisco Call* 1915, 1916). Several years later, in 1923, the first Montessori school opened by Chinese educators appeared: a kindergarten affiliated with Beijing Women's Normal High. The director of this kindergarten, Xiuying Lu, graduated from an international Montessori training program in the United States in 1917 (Chen and Guo 2021; Ding 2021; Wu and Zhang 2015). Unfortunately, this trial only lasted for three years due to the expense of Montessori materials and a lack of teachers attributable to the absence of any teacher training program for Montessori in China. By 1931, when Maria Montessori wrote to the Chinese Ministry of Education requesting an update on Montessori education in China, the Ministry's reply echoed these earlier concerns, explaining that Chinese schools had experimented with the Montessori method for ten years, but this method was found to be too "mechanical," "require[d] too many teaching aids," and was not economical (Ding 2021; Tian 2007).

Additionally, according to Chen and Guo (2021), another possible reason why the Montessori method did not flourish in the early days after its introduction to China is the influence exerted by American progressive educators like John Dewey, who were critical of Montessori (see Chapter 1: "Maria Montessori: Life and Historical Context"). Heqin Chen and Xingzhi Tao, leading Chinese reformers of preschool education at that time, were students of Dewey. In fact, Heqin Chen, known as the "father of early childhood education," criticized Montessori materials for being rigid and lacking variation. He believed children should not learn freely without a teacher's guidance (Chen 1927).

Montessori Revival, 1980–2021

Because of the reasons enumerated above, Montessori education stalled in China between the 1930s until the 1980s. After the founding of the People's Republic of China in 1949, alignment with Soviet models of education emphasized teacher-directed learning, a format incompatible with Montessori education. The Great Leap Forward (1958–1960) and the Cultural Revolution (1966–1977) led to the closure of preschools.

With the economic reopening of China in 1978, Chinese educators rekindled their interest in Western pedagogies including alternative pedagogies, leading to a Montessori revival in China (Chen and Guo 2021). Articles introducing Montessori and her teaching methods reappeared in Chinese preschool education journals in the 1980s (Wu and Zhang 2015), and Leshan Lu, a professor from Beijing Normal University (BNU), published a monograph, *Montessori's Early Childhood Education*, in 1985.

In the 1990s, under the influence of market-based economic policy, the Chinese central government cut funding for early childhood education and encouraged the development of private kindergartens. These private kindergartens tended to select Western education models to increase profits and attract parents, who thought educational methods from developed countries were more advanced; Montessori was one of the selected pedagogies (Chen and Guo 2021). Due to relatively weak supervision of private kindergartens, it is difficult to obtain statistics and detailed information about private kindergarten chains created around this time.

This private Montessori growth attracted the interest of researchers and led to the creation of university-affiliated Montessori teacher training. In 1994, Professor Zhishen Liang from BNU founded the first experimental Montessori classrooms in Beijing with the support of Taiwanese Montessori Education Research Foundation, founded by Weiru Shan in 1985 (Chen and Guo 2021; Wu and Zhang 2015). In response to the rapidly increasing demand for Montessori teacher training, BNU partnered with the American Montessori Society (AMS) to develop a Montessori teacher training program in 1998. AMS and Association Montessori Internationale (AMI) both established Montessori teacher training programs in China, launching diploma courses in China in 2005 and 2007, respectively (Chen and Guo 2021). Zhejiang Montessori Institute of Child Development was created as a nonprofit and recognized as an AMI-affiliated national society in 2015, coordinating AMI's training and national conferences as well as providing ongoing support to Montessori alumni.

Despite such extensive development, Montessori education today exists mainly in private kindergartens in China, generating an association of the method with high fees and elitism. This in turn restricts the access of a broader socioeconomic range of children to Montessori education. In addition, after more than ten years of development, private kindergartens in China increasingly favored upper-class families, leading the government to reform education policy in 2010 to more strongly support the development of public kindergartens. This reform challenged the development of Montessori education in China given the method's basis in private kindergartens. As China's Ministry of Education takes additional steps to tackle elitism in China's education system, the question of how to broaden access to Montessori education and integrate it into public kindergartens is essential to the future development of Montessori education in China.

The advancement of Montessori education in China has led to questions about how it has been adapted in China, issues that are discussed in the literature as sinicization and localization. For example, two major challenges include a shortage of Montessori teachers, particularly outside of the main cities, and teachers misunderstanding the essential principles of Montessori education by focusing mainly on teaching children how to use materials (Ji 2017; Yuan 2013). In trying to maintain Montessori fidelity, some teachers rigidly maintain a uniformly prepared environment instead of adapting to the needs of each class of children (Ji 2017; Wang 2018; Yuan 2013). Research has documented Montessori educators in China balance developing individual independence alongside building a collective identity (Chen and Guo 2021). As a result, studies have found that Chinese Montessori classrooms have shorter work blocks and higher teacher ratios in order to have more time for full-group-directed instruction emphasizing a group identity (Chen 2021). Another challenge is many Montessori institutions, schools, etc., use "Montessori" as their "brand" without reflecting Montessori fidelity (Wang 2018). Last but not least, given the cost of Montessori training and materials, Montessori education in China has been perceived as a form of elite education, which contradicts the intention of Montessori's original Children's House in San Lorenzo.

Conclusion

Recent curricular reforms for young Chinese children suggest opportunities for Montessori education in China. The Guidelines for Kindergarten Education (Trial) (MEC 2001) and Guidelines for the Learning and Development of Children ages 3–6 (MEC 2012) issued by the

Ministry of Education of China have advocated the value of child-based and developmentally appropriate education, consistent with Montessori's educational philosophy. This effort suggests alignments with Montessori education and Chinese curricular priorities. Today, as China pays more and more attention to educational equity, how to make Montessori education more affordable and accessible may be the core challenge of its development in China.

Notes

Joke Verheul commented on an earlier version of this chapter.
1. These articles are the earliest Chinese articles about Montessori education discovered so far.
2. Sinicization is a process of taking in something from non-Chinese culture and then changing and making it appropriate for Chinese culture or society.

References

Chen, Amber and Shu Lin Guo. 2021. "The Spread of Montessori Education in Mainland China." *Journal of Montessori Research & Education* 3 (1): 1–8. http://doi.org/10.16993/jmre.17.

Chen, Heqin. 1927. "New Trends in Early Childhood Education." *The Chinese Education Review* 19 (2): 1–9.

Ding, Daoyong. 2021. "Preface." In *The Montessori System Examined*, by William H. Kilpatrick, translated by Daoyong Ding, 1–46. Beijing: Beijing Normal University Publishing Group.

Fan, Bingqing. 1913. "Ms. Montessori and Her New Teaching Method." *The Chinese Education Review* 1: 1–8.

Ji, Kai. 2017. "*A Study on Localization of Montessori Curriculum: A Case Study of D Kindergarten in Xuchang City*." Master's thesis, Xinyang Normal University.

Lu, Leshan. 1985. *Montessori's Early Childhood Education*. Beijing: Beijing Normal University Publishing Group.

Ministry of Education of China. 2001. "Guidelines for Kindergarten Education (Trial)." Accessed October 3, 2021. http://www.moe.gov.cn/srcsite/A06/s3327/200107/t20010702_81984.html.

Ministry of Education of China. 2012. "Guidelines for the Learning and Development of Children Aged 3–6." Accessed October 3, 2021. http://www.moe.gov.cn/srcsite/A06/s3327/201210/t20121009_143254.html.

San Francisco Call. 1915. "Mrs. Gould and Her Sister Mrs. Wong, to Teach in China. Rail Magnate's Wife to Introduce Montessori System in the Orient." November 1, 1915, 1.

San Francisco Call. 1916. "Mrs. Wong in Break with Her Sister Mrs. Gould." June 7, 1916, 1.

Tian, Zhengping. 2007. "Montessori Educational Theory in Modern China: Commemorating the 100th Anniversary of the Montessori 'Children's Home.'" *Journal of Hebei Normal University (Educational Science Edition)* 9 (4): 52–5.

Wang, Xiao. 2018. "*A Study on Sinicization of Montessori Educational Theory*." Master's thesis, Fujian Normal University.

Wu, Hongcheng and Yuanyuan Zhang. 2015. "Montessori Teaching Method in China: Import, Practice, and Reflection." *Journal of Shenyang Normal University (Social Science Edition)* 19 (3): 12–16.

Yuan, Mei. 2013. "*Current Situation of and Reflection on Montessori Early Childhood Education in Inner Mongolia: Based on the Case of Kindergartens X and Y*." Master's thesis, Minzu University of China.

Chapter 43
Montessori Education in Japan

Kimiko Kai

After a long period of isolation, Japan began to modernize in 1858. Since Western civilization was considered a source of modernity, ideas were borrowed in order to create a new state, particularly in the arena of education. The first national Japanese kindergarten, established in 1876, was based on the ideas of Friedrich Froebel. Another key example of Western influence in Japanese early childhood education is Montessori education (Kai 2009).

Early Years of Montessori, 1912–1931

Soon after Montessori's work was shared internationally, Japanese educators, especially those with connections to Europe, brought Montessori's ideas in steady circulation around Japan, although it is unclear how much Montessori's ideas were actually implemented in Japanese schools. According to Tsuyoshi Yoshioka (1993), a 1912 article in the newspaper *Yorozutyoho* introduced Montessori ideas to Japan. Other promoters of the Montessori approach were Sozo Kurahashi, a leading Japanese progressive educator; Tunezou Morioka, who studied pedagogy in Germany, and Nogami Toshio, who studied psychology in Germany, France, and the United States (Kurahashi 1912). Following a visit to a Montessori Children's House in Rome, Yoshizo Imanishi wrote a book in 1914 on Montessori. In the same year, Kiyomaru Kawano, an elementary school principal, published a book about Montessori education. In addition, public lectures were given on the Montessori approach.

Despite Japanese interest in Montessori, there is limited evidence of the extent to which Montessori's ideas were implemented in schools around Japan. The first-trained Montessori teacher was an American, Sophia Arbella Irwin, who had trained with Montessori in Rome and had also studied Froebel's approach in Germany. In 1916, she established a Montessori-Froebelian kindergarten and a teacher training school but was not part of broader Montessori education efforts around the country in Japan (Murayama 1969).

During the politically liberal period between 1912 and 1926, Japanese educators were attracted to the freedom and child-centered ideas reflected in Montessori education. However, by 1931, the change in political climate, growing nationalism, and militarism demonstrated that Montessori's ideas were unwelcome. This was exacerbated by the lack of Montessori teacher training courses. Despite being unfashionable in practice, Montessori ideas persisted through academic research (Yoshioka 1993). For example, as a Tokyo University graduate student, Masunori Hiratsuka introduced Montessori education at a Japanese research study group. The information was then published in a 1932 academic journal (Hiratsuka 1980). Hiratsuka later became a professor at Kyushu University and in 1960 was the first Japanese director of education at the UNESCO Headquarters as well as the head of the National Institute for Educational Policy Research in 1963, all the while maintaining interest in Montessori education.

Revival of Montessori, 1952–2021

Under the American Occupation after the Second World War, American and Japanese educators collaborated to establish a new early childhood education system. Alongside this system, Japanese educators soon began working to establish Montessori education in Japan. Masunori Hiratsuka gave an address on the occasion of Maria Montessori's death in 1952, which was broadcast on national radio. In 1958, he met Mario Montessori (Hiratsuka 1980). Tsuneyoshi Tsuzumi translated Maria Montessori's *The Secret of Childhood* (1936) from German into Japanese. Later revised, this was the first Montessori book published in Japan.

Schools soon followed. In 1964, Tsuzumi began using the Montessori approach in his Kyoto nursery school. He was assisted by Keiko Akabane, the first certified Japanese Montessori teacher who, in 1963, trained in Germany. From 1965 to 1973, she was appointed head of a Children's House in Tokyo (see Figure 43.1). This Children's House was established in 1965 by Rev. Petro Heidrich, a professor at Sophia University, and was affiliated with the university's Social Welfare Vocational School. Using his German connections, Rev. Heidrich secured financial support from German Catholic churches for this program. In 1973, Keiko Akabane established her own teacher training course, and in 1979, she opened a Children's House in Kyoto. Similarly, Hisako Matsumoto, the first Japanese national to complete the Italian AMI training course, opened her own Children's House in Tokyo in 1967. In 1975, Shizuko Matsumoto, in addition to completing AMI training in Italy, opened the Montessori Institute of Tokyo, which was later officially recognized by AMI.

Japanese Catholics contributed to the establishment of Montessori education in Japan. A 1967 study group of teachers at Sophia University, a Jesuit institution, formed the basis of the national Japan Montessori Society in 1968, later renamed the Japan Association Montessori (JAM). Although not officially affiliated with AMI and thus unable to issue AMI certification, JAM has an informal relationship with AMI (JAM 2015; Luhmer 2008, 2009). The connection with Sophia University and Germany continued with JAM's third president, Rev. Klaus Luhmer, a professor at the university. In 1970, a JAM Montessori teacher training course began at Sophia University. In 2006, it became a teacher training course attached to the nonprofit Tokyo Montessori Educational Research Institution.

The increasing interest in Montessori also led to an increased number of training courses, materials manufacturers, and Montessori organizations. Another JAM teacher training center was started in 1976, supported by the Gakken company through sales of Montessori materials from Nienhuis. However, in 1979, this center became independent from JAM. The newly renamed Japan Montessori Research Institute provided a correspondence teacher training course and international exchange program (Hiratsuka 1980). Kimitoshi Matuurai, head of the Montessori practical training course provided by the Japan Montessori Research Institute, has developed

Figure 43.1 Language activity in the early 1980s at the Fukakusa Children's House in Kyoto. Courtesy of Minako Negishi.

activities with the American Montessori Society and in Asian countries. Currently, there are five official JAM-certified teacher training courses, including one at Nagasaki Junshin Catholic University. Matsumoto Kagaku Kogyo, a Montessori materials manufacturer founded in 1957 and officially recognized by AMI in 2006, has started an AMI-recognized teacher training course (Matsumoto Kagaku Kogyo 2021).

In order to promote Montessori educational activities, alongside JAM, several additional Montessori organizations have been founded in recent years. Friends of AMI Nippon was established in 2012. Another AMI affiliate, the International Montessori Training Center in Fukuoka, was founded in 2019.

JAM was formally recognized by the Science Council of Japan as an academic research association in 1996. JAM has over 800 members, organizes an annual conference bringing international Montessori speakers, and certifies training courses.

Montessori Education in the Contemporary Japanese Educational System

Today, Montessori education in Japan is conducted mostly in the private sector, especially at the preschool level (see Figure 43.2). There are 209 JAM member schools and a few additional affiliated schools, a small fraction of the roughly 50,000 early childhood institutions around Japan (Ministry of Education 2021; Ministry of Health 2019). Currently, there are two Montessori elementary schools in Japan from which students may be accepted into public junior high schools.

Government administration of early childhood education and care was radically reformed in 2014. Three government ministries are now responsible for overseeing the standards and guidelines related to educational content, curriculum, and programs in public early childhood

Figure 43.2 Children playing in the bamboo grown at the Fukakusa Children's House in Kyoto. Courtesy of Minako Negishi.

offerings. In contrast, private preschools are much more flexible in developing curricular content and educational principles. Despite efforts by Fumio Takane, who has served as AMI CEO of Japan for twenty years, there remain no public Montessori schools that are officially recognized by the government.

Over the years, the government has revised the standards and guidelines for early childhood education, incorporating new educational trends in child development and offering opportunities for greater alignment with the Montessori approach (Kai 2008a). These include supporting a child-centered approach, the child's individual development, and the child's spontaneous activities through a prepared environment. Historically, government schools have refrained from promoting specific educational approaches, leaving private schools the option to do so. Instead, the government borrows and appropriates aspects of a given pedagogy as it sees fit (Kai 2008b).

Continuing Interest

Moving beyond early childhood education, Japanese researchers have studied Montessori for inclusive education, serving children with special needs, mental and physical disabilities, attention-deficit and hyperactivity disorders, and dementia. Montessori education is featured in various childcare magazines and articles. Several books for parents by Atsuko Sagara have promoted the Montessori approach to the general public. Parents with Montessori qualifications have launched websites on Montessori education. In addition, Montessori materials are available locally and online.

Conclusion

Montessori education was introduced in Japan by educators reading about educational trends abroad. They were joined by scholars returning from their studies in Europe. After the Second World War, Japanese Montessori researchers and advocates undertook a great effort to translate key works of Montessori education into Japanese. At the same time, Catholic educators began promoting Montessori education, disseminating ideas through their schools and universities. Montessori never became a major movement in Japan as it was never officially adopted in the public sector. However, its influence can be seen in the nationwide effort to promote child-centered learning.

References

Hiratsuka, Masunori. 1980. "Relations with Montessori Education and Future Expectation." *Universe* 1: 1–3. Japan Montessori Research Institute.

Japan Association Montessori. 2015. "English Guide Japan Association Montessori: An Academic Research Organization Registered with the Science Council of Japan." Accessed September 8, 2021, from https://japan-montessori.org/pdf/englishguide.pdf.

Kai, Kimiko. 2008a. "The Professional Preparation of Early Childhood Education in Japan." *The International Journal of Learning* 15 (10): 23–30.
Kai, Kimiko. 2008b. "Montessori Education in the Context of Childhood Educational Trends in Japan." *Montessori Education* 41: 51–7.
Kai, Kimiko. 2009. "The Modification and Adaptation of Montessori Education in Japan." *The International Journal of Learning* 16 (7): 667–76.
Kurahashi, Sozo. 1912. "Montessori Education." *Fujin to Kodomo* 12 (4): 155–64.
Luhmer, Klaus. 2008. "Educational Essay Series; 40 Years Montessori in Japan (1)." *Montessori Education* 41: 116–32.
Luhmer, Klaus. 2009. "Educational Essay Series; 40 Years Montessori in Japan (2)." *Montessori Education* 42: 115–32.
Matsumoto Kagaku Kogyo. 2021. Accessed September 8, 2021. http://www.mk-k.com/english/index.html.
Ministry of Education, Culture, Sports, Science and Technology. 2021. "Press Release Basic Survey on August 27, 2021 (Preliminary Figures)." Accessed September 8, 2021, from https://www.mext.go.jp/content/20210824-mxt_chousa01-000017617-1.pdf.
Ministry of Health, Labor and Welfare. 2019. "Summary of the Situation of Nursery Schools." Accessed September 8, 2021, from https://www.mhlw.go.jp/content/11922000/000678692.pdf.
Murayama, Sadao. 1969. "Introduction of Montessori Education and its Criticism." In *The History of Japanese Nursery* Vol. 3, edited by Japan Society of Research on Early Childhood Care and Education, 161–80. Tokyo: Froebel-Kan.
Yoshioka, Tsuyoshi. 1993. "The Way to Montessori Education." In *Montessori & Japan*, edited by Klaus Luhmer, 52–64. Tokyo: Gakuen-shya.

Chapter 44
Montessori Education in Australia

Lesley Payne

Montessori education has been established in Australia for over a century and yet remains marginal in the wider educational landscape. This chapter outlines the progress of Montessori education from its introduction in the early 1900s to the present day. First adopted by social reformers in the early years of the nineteenth century, a second wave in the 1970s and early 1980s was built on parent demand, migration from Europe, and the availability of government grants (Payne 2004). Today, while there is a promising third-wave expansion of Montessori education in the area of childcare, the percentage of Montessori schools in the school sector has not increased. Government accountability, division among Montessori organizations, and the wider provision of schooling for children under 6 in Australia have limited further growth.

Early Years of Montessori Education and the First Wave: 1913–1930

At the beginning of the twentieth century in Australia, many educators embraced education based on the child's natural development. Names like Froebel, Montessori, and Dewey became prominent on the educational scene, and an educational approach based on liberty, independence, and self-reliance resonated in Australia. Philanthropic, educated women saw the need to improve living conditions and education for the underprivileged (Feez 2013).

Martha Simpson, the initial advocate for Montessori education in Australia, established an experimental class at the government Blackfriars Practising School in 1912, making it one of the first government schools in the world to adopt the Montessori approach (Feez 2013; Petersen 1971) (see Figure 44.1).

The success of this early experiment resulted in four Australian teachers attending Montessori's first international training course in Rome in 1913, and thousands of visitors came to observe the classes in Sydney (Feez 2013). Simpson and another advocate, Lydia Longmore from South Australia, were appointed school inspectors for infant schools, enabling them to disseminate the method widely and to exert influence on pedagogy as taught in the early childhood colleges. Montessori principles were integrated in early childhood education across all Australian states from 1913 to 1930 (O'Donnell 1996; Petersen 1983).

Religious orders also had an impact on the introduction of Montessori education in this first wave. A school based on Montessori principles was established by the Sisters of Our Lady of the Missions in 1929, and a kindergarten in the 1930s was operated by the Sisters of Mercy.

Figure 44.1 Children working independently at Blackfriars Practising School, 1914, New South Wales, Australia. Courtesy of the State Library of New South Wales.

However, with Italian nationals forced to leave Australia at the outbreak of the Second World War, schools closed and records were lost, a subject for further research (Feez 2013).

Australian society, deeply affected by the losses of the First World War, retreated from the world, and interest in Montessori education faded. As teachers retired or turned their interests elsewhere, the early programs lost impetus (Feez 2013). The loss of contact with Europe during the Depression and the Second World War and the increasing influence of cognitivists and behaviorists in educational reform movements after the war led to a return to traditional methods and more structured educational programs (Payne 2004).

Montessori Education and the Second Wave: 1970–2000

By the early 1970s, the Australian postwar baby boom generation were now having children and, for many, the severe classrooms of the 1950s and early 1960s had been unhappy places. Liberal, progressive values tapped into the counterculture ideologies of the 1970s and early 1980s and led to growth in alternative, child-centered educational approaches (Dudley and Vidovich 1995). Funding for community initiatives (such as the 1973 federal Choice and Diversity grants),[1] migration of Montessori educators from Europe to Australia, dedicated parents, and a few inspirational Montessori teachers renewed interest in Montessori education (Feez 2013; O'Donnell 1996). Many private or independent Montessori schools—early childhood, elementary, and even secondary—were established during the 1980s and 1990s (Payne 2004).

Trained Montessori teachers were needed to support the rapid growth, but few individuals arrived as immigrants trained in the method or could travel overseas for training (Feez 2013). To meet the demand, the Montessori Institute and the Sydney Montessori Teachers' College[2] were both established in 1983. The Montessori Institute (2021a) had links through Margaret Homfray to the St. Nicholas Training Centre in London and offered studies across Australia (O'Donnell 1996). It still offers nationally accredited graduate and undergraduate courses. The Sydney Montessori Teachers' College utilized Association Montessori Internationale (AMI) trainers to facilitate their training course until 1993 (Feez 2013).

Montessori school growth was supported by the Australian Schools Commission, which operated between 1973 and 1987 supporting government and independent schools through both recurrent funding per capita and targeted grants. The demise of the school commission slowed the growth of new alternative schools including Montessori programs. It became more feasible to add new campuses to existing schools, rather than founding new schools (Angus 2000; Brennan 1994).

During this time, the first-documented use of Montessori pedagogy in Indigenous communities occurred at Weipa State School at the Cape York Peninsula in 1977. In the 1980s, Montessori learning practices were adopted at Strelley Station as part of a Murdoch University study. Other projects involving Indigenous education and the Montessori approach have included Kiwirrkurra and Papulankutja (Western Australia); Gamarada Redfern and Minimbah Armidale (New South Wales); Cairns, Aurukun, Pormpuraaw, Woorabinda, Lockhart River, and Torres Strait Islands (Queensland) (Holmes 2018). These were collaborative projects involving Indigenous leaders and educators, but given their dependence on a few dedicated individuals and the limited availability of ongoing funding, they have been difficult to sustain (Feez 2013).[3]

From the 1990s onward, the largest growth in Montessori education in Australia has been in the area of childcare. Childcare centers are regulated by different authorities than those responsible for schools and are not part of the education sector; they employ less qualified staff and children's attendance can be casual or less than full time. Unlike independent elementary and secondary schools, parents receive direct support for fees according to need. The number of childcare centers identifying with the Montessori method has increased from a few dozen in the 1980s to 262 in 2021 (ACECQA 2021), representing a third expansion of the Australian Montessori landscape (see Figure 44.2).

Montessori Education and the Contemporary Landscape: 2001 to Today

The landscape of Montessori education in Australia over the past two decades is characterized by inertia in the school sector, but promising growth in the area of childcare. The wider educational context is one of regulation and accountability. Montessori schools must fit within the constraints

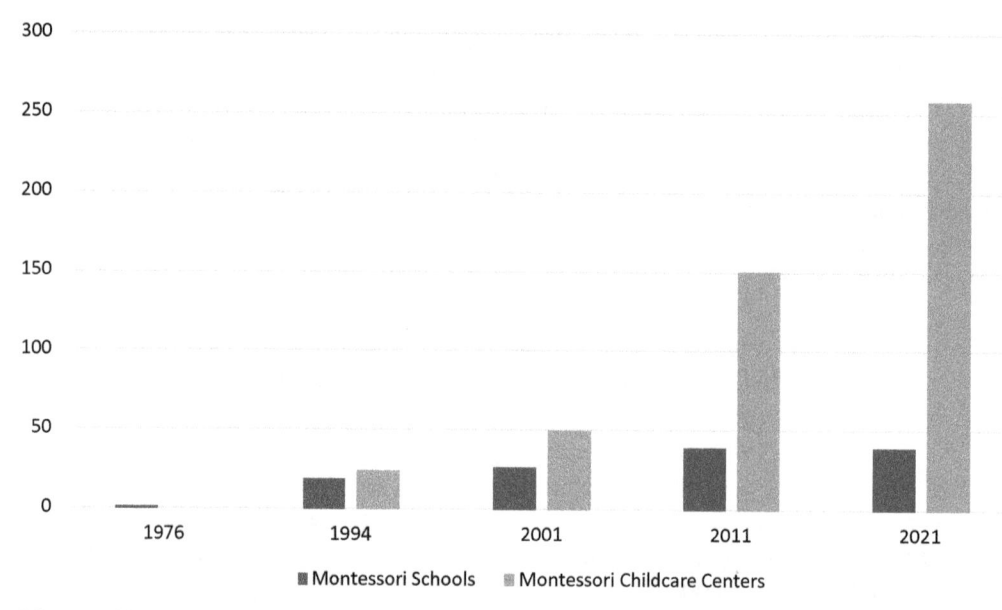

Figure 44.2 Growth of Australian Montessori Schools and Centers 1976–2021. Source: Cleverley 1978; Independent Schools Australia 2011 & 2021; ACECQA. Image courtesy of the author.[4]

of both state and federal government registration, although compliance with these standards grants access to funding (Independent Schools Australia 2021). According to the Australian Bureau of Statistics (2021), government schools have the greatest share of enrollments (65.6 percent), followed by Catholic schools (19.4 percent) and independent schools (15.0 percent). Montessori school enrollments serve 0.8 percent of students in thirty-nine independent schools and thirteen Montessori programs in public schools. The number of students attending Montessori schools has grown from 3,995 in 2011 to 4,871 students in 2021, but there has been no increase in the number of registered Montessori schools (ISA 2011, 2021).

A major opportunity for national recognition came in 2008 when the Australian Parliament required all registered schools receiving government funding to implement the Australian National Curriculum for students ages 5 to 17. Fortuitously, this came at a time when the Australian Montessori community had one national body[5] and was able to coordinate a collaboration between Montessori school heads and representatives of the two established training organizations, AMI's Australian Montessori Teacher Education Foundation (AMTEF) and the Montessori Institute. This culminated in the recognition of Montessori National Curriculum in December 2011 as an alternative curriculum framework by the Australian Curriculum and Reporting Authority (Feez 2013). Childcare centers operate under a different, early years framework and must meet national quality standards (ACECQA 2021).

While government recognition of the curriculum has moved Montessori education forward, an obstacle remains in the recognition of Montessori teacher education. Apart from state teacher colleges in the early 1900s that adopted a Montessori training model, today, the Montessori Institute (2021b) is the only higher education provider with an accredited initial teacher education program. Otherwise, teachers in Montessori schools must complete a mainstream teacher qualification and augment it with a Montessori diploma. The Sydney Montessori Training Centre offers AMI diplomas, and there are independent childcare centers, which offer Montessori training, predominantly for their own staff.

Another significant development during this period has been the application of Montessori principles to support the elderly and those living with dementia. Much of this work was pioneered in Australia, and Montessori for Dementia and Ageing now forms a core component of Montessori work globally.[6]

Conclusion

Despite a long history and significant durability and growth of Montessori around Australia, the unique place that Montessori education occupied in offering formal programs for students ages 3 and up has been eroded by government schools, which now also provide child-centered schooling for children under 6. While the Australian regulatory environment and national testing regime presents challenges to the authentic implementation of Montessori programs, the recognition of the Montessori National Curriculum demonstrates the power of the Montessori community when it is able to organize with a unified voice. The future of Montessori education in Australia will depend upon Montessori principles, their continued relevance, and the community's ability to sustain existing programs, together with the continued growth in the childcare sector.

Notes

1. Choice and Diversity grants encouraged community involvement and "grass roots" initiatives became available to schools and communities under Schools Commission Act 1973 No. 213.23.
2. The Sydney Montessori Teachers College closed in 1993 but AMI continues to offer courses under several other iterations.
3. Lockhart River and Redfern programs continue to support Indigenous students, and the Strait Start initiative has been a sustained and effective program to support early learning across the Torres Strait Islands, https://www.yumi.org.au/strait-start.
4. Childcare numbers estimated before 2011 are based on the authors' personal knowledge. ACECQA (2022) indicates childcare center numbers have risen from 262 in 2021 to 275 services in 2022.
5. Presently there are two competing national organizations, Montessori Australia and Montessori Schools and Centres Australia, contributing to confusion and disunity.
6. For more information, see https://montessoridementia.org.

References

ACECQA. 2021. National Register. https://www.acecqa.gov.au/resources/national-registers.
Angus, Max. 2000. "The Differentiation of Schools and School Sectors." *Unicorn. Journal of the Australian College of Education* 26 (2): 24–9.

Australian Bureau of Statistics. 2021. "Education." https://www.abs.gov.au/statistics/people/education.

Brennan, Deborah. 1994. *The Politics of Australian Child Care: From Philanthropy to Feminism*. Melbourne: Cambridge University Press.

Cleverley, John. 1978. "Non-denominational and Alternative Schools." In *Half a Million Children: Studies of Non-government Education in Australia*, edited by John Cleverley, 250–71. Melbourne: Longman Cheshire.

Dudley, Janice, and Vidovich, Lesley. 1995. *The Politics of Education: Commonwealth Schools' Policy, 1973–95*. Melbourne: Australian Council for Educational Research.

Feez, Susan. 2013. *Montessori: The Australian Story*. Sydney: New South Publishing.

Holmes, Catherine. 2018. "Montessori Education in the Ngaanyatjarra Lands." *Journal of Montessori Research* 4 (2): 33–60. https://doi.org/10.17161/jomr.v4i2.6715.

Independent Schools Australia. 2011. "Snapshots." https://isa.edu.au/wp-content/uploads/2017/04/Snapshot-11.pdf.

Independent Schools Australia. 2021. "Snapshots." https://isa.edu.au/snapshot-2021/

Montessori Institute. 2021a. "About Us." http://www.mwei.edu.au/30th-anniversary-ebook/.

Montessori Institute. 2021b. "Graduate Diploma of Education." http://www.mwei.edu.au/montessori-teacher-training/courses/graduate-diploma-in-education/.

O'Donnell, Dan. 1996. *Montessori Education in Australia and New Zealand*. Sydney: Wild and Woolley.

Payne, Lesley. 2004. *School Governance: Phases, Participation and Paradoxes*. PhD diss., Murdoch University.

Petersen, Robert. 1971. "Montessori in Australia." *Education News* (Commonwealth Department of Education and Science) 13 (3): 16–20.

Petersen, Robert. 1983. "The Montessorians—M. M. Simpson and L. de Lissa." In *Pioneers of Australian Education, Volume 3: Studies of the Development of Education in Australia, 1900–50*, edited by C. Turney, 249–68. Sydney: Sydney University Press.

Chapter 45
Montessori Education in Canada

Margaret Whitley

Geographically, Canada is the world's second largest country, yet it is thirty-ninth largest in population. The country's vastness—with sparsely populated areas, ten provinces, and three territories—contributes to distinct regional characteristics. Each province and territory has its own Ministry of Education guidelines, resulting in separate initiatives and developments. Montessori programs, teacher training centers, and organizations reflect this regionalism with different trajectories around Canada. An added challenge for alternative education, including Montessori, is the widely held belief, supported by Canada's top-ten placement in recent PISA rankings, that the conventional, publicly funded system is good enough (OECD 2018). Despite this complex educational environment, Montessori programs in Canada have slowly grown in numbers and breadth over the years.

Early History

The first Canadian Montessori school, The Children's Laboratory, was established in 1912 at the Nova Scotia summer home of Alexander and Mabel Graham Bell, who became strong supporters of Montessori after meeting her in the United States. They were impressed by her use of developmental materials and focus on the individual needs of children. Twelve students attended, including seven Bell grandchildren (AMI Canada). The next year, 1913, Canadian educator Isa H. Robertson attended the First International Course in Rome.

On the other side of the country in Calgary, Alberta, Margaret Potts opened the second Canadian Montessori school in 1919. She received Dr. Montessori's blessing, even before Potts was able to train with her in London in 1921. Unlike the Bells' classroom, Potts's school proved to be more permanent. Today, Calgary Montessori School is the oldest continuously operating Montessori school in North America. Potts's granddaughter, Alison O'Dwyer, leads the school that she attended as a child (CMS 2018).

There are other stories of small Montessori schools during this time. For instance, in the 1920s, the Southam family, publishers of *The Hamilton Spectator*, operated a small school in their house. In the 1950s, British Columbia had at least one program operating in Victoria, led by Miriam Thomas (*Daily* 1958). In addition, Diana Chalmers of the Discover Montessori Society recalls stories about her family members attending Montessori schools in the 1920s in Edmonton, Alberta, and Tony Evans of Dundas Valley Montessori School in Ontario remembers a great-great aunt who was a Montessori teacher, demonstrating the generational impact of these early Montessori educators (Diana Chalmers, pers. comm.; Tony Evans, pers. comm.).

Aside from these few early programs, Montessori programs in Canada did not gain momentum until the social upheavals of the 1960s, particularly around language rights and political autonomy in the French-Canadian province of Quebec. Education at the time was overseen by a complicated collection of public systems: several provinces funded Roman Catholic as well as secular education, and French First Language (FFL) as well as English First Language (EFL) school systems. The growing demand from French-Canadians for language rights led to the 1965 development of publicly funded French immersion programs in Quebec as well as other provinces (Jezer-Morton 2020). In the same year, the Ontario government commissioned the Hall-Dennis Report, which examined the structure of education throughout the province. The report favored a more child-centered approach, cultivating student autonomy in a way which echoed Montessori (Cole 2021). In short, the complex social and educational landscape of the 1960s, particularly in the two most populous provinces, Quebec and Ontario, created the conditions for more progressive educational options, including the reestablishment of Montessori programs.

At this time Canadians were also influenced by the revival of Montessori in the United States, led by American Montessori Society founder Nancy McCormick Rambusch. To satisfy a growing interest in Montessori education, private schools began to open in Canada, but trained teachers were scarce. (In Canada, most private school teachers do not need to be certified, so Montessori training is sufficient.) Initially, many qualified Montessori educators immigrated from Great Britain, Ireland, Europe, India, and Sri Lanka, which led to a period of flourishing as Montessori schools opened across Canada in the late 1960s and early 1970s. For example, in 1961, Helma Trass from the Netherlands founded the Toronto Montessori School (TMS), hiring staff including Cecile Burg from her homeland (TMS 2022).

As Montessori grew around Canada, in some cases it gained public funding. In 1977 British Columbia passed the Independent School Act, providing partial funding for alternative schools and thus increasing the accessibility of Montessori programs. This opened the door to Montessori throughout many public school districts in British Columbia.

Responding to the demand for teachers, in 1971 Mario Montessori inaugurated the first Association Montessori Internationale (AMI) Teacher Training Centre on the University of Toronto campus, which then moved to the TMS location in 1977. Renilde Montessori, Mario's youngest daughter, was the registrar. In 1989, AMI severed its relationship with TMS, moving again and taking on the name of the Foundation for Montessori Education, with Renilde Montessori as Director of Training. Since then, two other AMI training centers opened, in Vancouver, British Columbia and another one in Quebec, serving French educators. The Quebec location has since closed. Today, at least five other independent training centers exist, primarily focused on infant/toddler and Children's House programs. Most are accredited by the Montessori Accreditation Council for Teacher Education (MACTE).

Over time, various Montessori organizations emerged to support teachers and administrators, such as the Canadian Association of Montessori Teachers (CAMT), founded some time in the 1970s; Montessori au Quebec; and the Canadian Council of Montessori Administrators (CCMA), founded in 1977.

Contemporary Landscape

Today Montessori programs operate in all Canadian provinces and territories, with programs representing every age group from infancy through high school. As in other places, Canadian programs are concentrated in early childhood and decline significantly in number as students get older. Currently, the most significant growth appears to be at the infant/toddler level, filling the need for quality early childcare. CCMA states Canada has over 900 Montessori programs, with the highest concentrations in Ontario (527) and British Columbia (264). Ontario's Montessori schools are entirely private and independently operated, with varied mandates, including bilingualism and religious or cultural affiliations (CCMA). For example, in Toronto, the Montessori Jewish Day School opened its doors over twenty years ago (Andrea Lulka, pers. comm.).

Perhaps the most important and consequential development for Montessori education is the increasing role of public funding and regulation. Public funding of varying degrees is available in five provinces and all three territories. Presently British Columbia offers the most public funding, supporting thirty-one Montessori programs of varying sizes and age levels. In the remaining five provinces, schools are funded entirely through private tuition, and some schools ensure accessibility through scholarships. Currently, discussions are underway regarding a national childcare program, which would subsidize programming in order to increase affordability and equalize resources across provinces (Prime Minister of Canada 2021). This development could subsidize Montessori early childhood programs, making them more accessible to children from diverse cultures and socioeconomic backgrounds. However, additional government regulatory requirements might challenge Montessori practices. Regulation designed to improve the safety of day care and early childhood programs sometimes undermines essential Montessori practices, like mixed-age groups, long uninterrupted work periods, larger classes, and employing Montessori-trained educators (Government of Ontario 2014).

Another important development has been the creation of Canadian Montessori programs in Indigenous communities. In January 2016, the Piruvik Preschool in the territory of Nunavut began "blending Montessori ... and Inuit Qaujimajatuqangit traditional knowledge," utilizing Inuktitut, the most predominant Indigenous language spoken by the Inuit (CBC 2019) (see Figure 45.1).

Similar to Montessori Indigenous efforts in the United States, founders Tessa Lochhead and Karen Nutarak discovered that the Montessori method aligned with aspects of Inuit culture, particularly respect for the child through observation and hands-on learning. Montessori also offered a curricular framework for Indigenous cultural and language preservation. Recognition of their work came in 2018 with a million-dollar Arctic Inspiration Award, funding more student programs across Nunavut as well as virtual teacher training in Inuktitut (Tessa Lochhead, pers. comm.).

Conclusion

The beginnings of Montessori education in Canada and most of its history have been marked by regionality, and while Montessori has grown and developed throughout the country, it has flourished the most in regions that addressed accessibility. For the past fifty years, the availability

Figure 45.1 Child in the Piruvik Preschool doing work learning Inuktitut. Courtesy of Tessa Lochhead, Piruvik Preschool.

of public funding in British Columbia has made it the brightest spot in the Canadian Montessori landscape. Moving forward, a continued focus on accessibility and embracing the multicultural dimension of Canada are essential components of growth. With this in mind, the Piruvik Preschool may provide the most significant contemporary example of Montessori in Canada and perhaps even a model for future growth.

Note

Thank you to Tony Evans, Andy Lulka, Diana Chalmers, and Joke Verheul commented on an earlier version of this chapter.

References

AMI Canada. 2021. "The Early History of the Montessori Movement in North America and the Earliest Montessori Schools in Canada and the U.S.A." Accessed August 16, 2021. https://ami-canada.com/earlyhistory.html

Calgary Montessori School (CMS). 2018. "Calgary Montessori History." Accessed September 3, 2021. https://www.calgarymontessorischool.com/about-us-history.

CBC/Radio Canada. 2017. "La Vie Bilingue: French Immersion Programs in Canada through the Ages." March 12. https://www.cbc.ca/radio/checkup/blog/la-vie-bilingue-french-immersion-programs-in-canada-through-the-ages-1.3630105.

Cole, Josh. 2021. *Hall-Dennis and the Road to Utopia: Education and Modernity in Ontario*. Montreal: McGill-Queen's University Press.

Government of Ontario. 2014. "Child Care and Early Years Act, 2014, S.O. 2014, c. 11, Sched. 1." Ontario.ca. https://www.ontario.ca/laws/statute/14c11.

Jezer-Morton, Kathryn. 2020. "Canada's 'Founding Mothers' of French Immersion." *The Canadian Encyclopedia*. Accessed October 21, 2021. https://www.thecanadianencyclopedia.ca/en/article/canadas-founding-mothers-of-french-immersion-olga-melikoff-murielle-parkes-and-valerie-neale.

OECD. 2018. "Canada: Student Performance (PISA)." Accessed May 5, 2022. https://gpseducation.oecd.org/CountryProfile?primaryCountry=CAN&treshold=10&topic=PI.

OMS Montessori. 2021. "OMS History." Accessed August 16, 2021. https://omsmontessori.com/history/.

Prime Minister of Canada. 2021. "Canada Announces Historic First Early Learning and Child Care Agreement." Prime Minister of Canada. Accessed September 27, 2021. https://pm.gc.ca/en/news/news-releases/2021/07/08/canada-announces-historic-first-early-learning-and-child-care.

Toronto Montessori School (TMS). 2022. "Celebrating 60 Years of TMS." Accessed May 5, 2022. https://www.tmsschool.ca/tms60.

Chapter 46
Montessori Education in the United States

Katie Brown and Richard Ungerer

In this chapter, we trace the century-long history of Montessori in the United States and survey the current status of the movement within the broader education landscape. Due in part to educational decentralization, the Montessori movement in the United States has been propelled by grassroots and Montessori organizational efforts, first in religious and independent schools, and subsequently in the public sector, with over 560 public Montessori schools comprising one of the largest public Montessori programs in the world.

History of the US Montessori Movement

Whitescarver and Cossentino (2008) identify three distinct phases of the American Montessori movement. The first began in 1911, when Montessori became fashionable among urban elites following a glowing profile in *McClure's Magazine*. In short order, however, a scathing critique of the Montessori approach, published by education professor William Heard Kilpatrick, came to dominate the narrative around Montessori. At the same time, Maria Montessori disbanded the burgeoning American Montessori Education Association and halted courses to train American teachers. By the end of the First World War, most of these early Montessori schools had either closed or dropped the name "Montessori," pursuing an eclectic combination of progressive and Montessori education approaches (Debs 2019).

The second phase occurred in the mid-twentieth century, with Nancy McCormick Rambusch's opening of the Whitby School in Greenwich, Connecticut, in 1958 and founding of the American Montessori Society (AMS) in 1960 (see Figure 46.1). This phase was marked by growing support for independent Montessori schools among disparate constituencies, including middle- and upper-class White families, religious orders (especially Catholics), hippies, and Afrocentric educators (Debs 2019).

At the same time, major metropolitan areas like Cincinnati, Ohio; Denver, Colorado; Houston, Texas; Kansas City, Missouri, and New York City (especially in Harlem) leveraged Montessori as a tool in the larger fight to desegregate public schools and serve families eligible for public subsidy (Debs 2019). Nancy McCormick Rambusch worked to make Montessori more compatible with mainstream American education; for example, adapting Montessori teacher training and connecting it to university programs (Povell 2009). These and other differences regarding what constituted "authentic" Montessori education eventually created a schism between Rambusch and Mario Montessori and the Association Montessori Internationale (AMI). This conflict lasted

Figure 46.1 Children working at Nancy McCormick Rambusch's Whitby school, Greenwich, Connecticut, ca. 1959. Courtesy of the American Montessori Society Records, Archives & Special Collections, University of Connecticut Library.

for decades as AMI built a separate training and organizational infrastructure in the United States, including through AMI/USA, founded in 1972, and the North American Montessori Teacher Association (NAMTA), founded in 1970 (Whitescarver and Cossentino 2008).

The third phase, dating from the 1990s to the present day, is marked by the pronounced growth of Montessori programs in the public sector. Many of the public Montessori programs currently operating, especially charter schools (publicly funded but privately run educational institutions), were launched in the context of the school choice movement and amid efforts to provide equitable access to high-quality, developmental learning experiences (Debs 2019). In the years during and after No Child Left Behind, the popularity of these programs reflects a paradigm shift among families and educators away from high-stakes assessment and a narrow focus on discrete academic skills toward more developmentally oriented approaches to education. Many of these programs are the result of families persistently lobbying school boards and collecting signatures to support new or expanded public Montessori schools.

Additional unaffiliated American Montessori organizations were created during this period, including the International Montessori Foundation, created in 1992; Montessori Educational Programs International (MEPI), created in 1995; and the Montessori Accreditation Council for Teacher Education (MACTE), created in 1995. Foundations and social impact funds such as Wend Collective, the Walton Family Foundation, the Hershey Foundation, and the Harold Simmons Foundation have been significant supporters of Montessori education.

Contemporary Landscape

The National Center for Montessori in the Public Sector (NCMPS), a national nonprofit serving public Montessori programs, operates the Montessori Census, the most reliable record of Montessori programs in the United States. As of 2021, the census lists more than 2200 private Montessori schools who self-report following Montessori practice, though we believe this may be an undercount as Montessori schools are decentralized and participation in the census is voluntary. The project has been collecting data since 2012, and it is likely that this number represents the majority of private American Montessori schools. Census data indicate that the number of Montessori schools has increased an estimated 1–2 percent over the past ten years.

These private schools mostly serve the early childhood and elementary levels, though the number of infant/toddler and adolescent programs is growing. Most Montessori private schools are governed as not-for-profit organizations, but some are privately owned. In recent years, several high-profile corporations and organizations (such as Bezos Day One Academies, Endeavor Schools, Higher Ground/Guidepost, Spring Education Group, and Wildflower Schools) have established networks of Montessori schools. The majority of Montessori schools in the United States are secular, but there continue to be a number of faith-based programs, including Catholic, Jewish, Islamic, and Episcopal Montessori schools.

According to the Montessori Census, over 560 American public schools offer a Montessori program, serving an estimated 150,000–200,000 children in what constitutes the largest public Montessori program in the world, though this represents only a small fraction of the 131,000 American public schools (Ayer 2019). South Carolina has more public Montessori schools than any other state or territory, followed by Puerto Rico and California. A plurality of these public Montessori schools (44 percent) are charter schools, while approximately 16 percent are magnet programs, specialized district-based programs designed to attract students from throughout a school district. The remaining 39 percent comprise other district-based programs, including neighborhood schools and school-within-a-school programs, where Montessori classrooms operate alongside traditional classrooms in the same building. In both charter and district Montessori schools, families mainly enroll via a randomized lottery (Debs 2019).

Montessori organizations in the United States have expanded their efforts to promote and sustain quality standards, frequently through a formal accreditation system with a national Montessori organization for their member schools who seek to pursue a rigorous process of self-reflection. This benefits families seeking ways to distinguish between comprehensive "authentic" Montessori schools and the array of "Montessori-inspired" schools. There are also at least thirty-five state and regional organizations supporting local Montessori efforts around the country (Monnier 2019).

Montessori in the Broader Education Landscape

Organizational Collaboration

After nearly fifty years of institutional separation among Montessori organizations, a gradual development in the United States over the past twenty years has been increasing collaboration among the major national Montessori organizations. After a series of intensive meetings between 2011 and 2013, the leaders from the major Montessori associations created the Montessori Leaders Collaborative (MLC) and began to pursue a number of joint activities. MLC founding organizations included AMS, AMI, AMI/USA, Elementary Alumni Association (EAA), International Montessori Council (IMC), MACTE, MEPI, NAMTA, and NCMPS. One tangible outcome was the creation in 2013 of the Montessori Public Policy Initiative (MPPI) as a joint collaboration between AMS and AMI/USA. MPPI's agenda includes uniting the Montessori community, coordinating with state Montessori organizations, and creating an effective advocacy voice at the state as well as national level. One example of the work of MPPI was the creation and dissemination of the "Montessori Essentials," a document outlining the key components of authentic Montessori programs and practice, which facilitate advocacy efforts for equitable access to high-fidelity Montessori education (MPPI 2015).

Teacher Education Programs

Given the number of Montessori schools in the United States, training more Montessori teachers continues to be a high priority for the entire Montessori community, particularly given shortages of public Montessori educators. While most private Montessori schools in the United States only require teachers to have Montessori training and an associate or bachelor's degree, teachers in most public Montessori schools need to be state-certified. The majority of the over 200 US Montessori teacher education programs (TEPs) operate independent of the college and university education programs, which prepare candidates for state teacher certification. Each of the fifty states has a separate certification process, and only nine recognize the Montessori diploma; this means that public Montessori teachers sometimes need to complete two separate teacher preparation programs. To support Montessori teacher recognition, MACTE ensures quality in Montessori TEPs across a number of Montessori organizations through a single accreditation process. Finally, with the dramatic policy interest in expanding early childhood education and universal pre-K, there has been increased federal, state, and district funding as well as innovative workforce development strategies including residencies, apprenticeships, and career pathways designed to support newly trained Montessori teachers.

Research

In recent years, the American Montessori movement has returned to its roots as a scientific pedagogy via a renewed emphasis on research. In 2005, AMS created a Research Committee to advocate for research to expand the knowledge base of Montessori education. One resulting project, the *Journal of Montessori Research*, the first peer-reviewed, scholarly, American journal with a Montessori focus, launched in 2015. Angela K. Murray is the journal's founding editor. The University of Hartford and the University of Kansas founded Montessori research centers in 2017 and 2018, respectively, and the University of Wisconsin River Falls launched the first Doctor of Education (Ed.D.) degree in Montessori Studies in the U.S. in 2022. And, as of 2019, there is a Montessori research section of the American Educational Research Association.

Diversity, Equity, Inclusion, and Social Justice

Like so much of the United States, the Montessori community has, in recent years, turned its attention to questions of marginalization, equity, and inclusion in Montessori schools and institutions. Though Black, Latinx, and Indigenous educators have been instrumental in the US Montessori movement throughout its history (Debs 2019; Murray et al. 2020), the movement has historically been dominated by white, upper- and middle-class voices. Montessori for Social Justice was founded in 2013 to "amplify voices of the Global Majority" and promote Montessori as a force for liberation. In 2020, the Black Montessori Education Fund was created to support Black Montessori teachers and school leaders in training and opening their own schools and supporting all teachers in providing culturally responsive/affirming Montessori environments for Black children. In New Mexico, the Keres Children's Learning Center hosts the Indigenous Montessori Institute and the Indigenous Montessori Network emphasizing decolonizing education, restoring Indigenous knowledge systems and supporting Indigenous language preservation. Other Montessori organizations, large and small, also launched and renewed racial justice and equity initiatives during this period.

Conclusion

From independent preschools in church basements to large public magnet programs, the Montessori movement in the United States has been propelled by local demand from communities, teachers, and families. This growth has been supported by national organizations, supporters, and advocates, but the tenet of local control in American education systems has meant that, to some extent, Montessori programs must reinvent the wheel in every new place they take root. Alongside recent efforts to unify the Montessori community to speak with one policy voice, a significant structural change in public education, such as the advent of universal pre-K, may be necessary for Montessori to exert more influence in the public policy arena over early childhood education and school in the United States.

Note

David Kahn, Virginia McHugh, Keith Whitescarver, Tim Seldin, Maria Gravel, Betsy Coe, and Joke Verheul read and commented on earlier versions of this draft.

References

Ayer, David. 2019. "The Public Montessori Landscape." *MontessoriPublic* 4 (1): 3–16.
Debs, Mira. 2019. *Diverse Families, Desirable Schools: Public Montessori in the Era of School Choice.* Cambridge, MA: Harvard Education Press.
Monnier, Denise. 2019. "Montessori Advocacy Organization." *MontessoriPublic* 3 (2): 10.
Montessori Public Policy Initiative (MPPI). 2015. "Montessori Essentials." https://montessoriadvocacy.org/.
Murray, Angela K., Luz Casquejo Johnston, Ayize Sabater, and Kiara Clark. 2020. "Hidden Black Voices in the History of Montessori Education." *American Educational History Journal* 47 (1/2): 205–21.
Povell, Phyllis. 2009. *Montessori Comes to America: The Leadership of Maria Montessori and Nancy McCormick Rambusch.* Lanham, MD: University Press of America.
Whitescarver, Keith, and Jacqueline Cossentino. 2008. "Montessori and the Mainstream: A Century of Reform on the Margins." *Teachers College Record* 110 (12): 2571–600.

Chapter 47
Montessori Education in Puerto Rico

Ana María García Blanco and Katherine Miranda

Puerto Rico is a Caribbean territory of the United States with 3.2 million inhabitants. Three-quarters of Puerto Rico's school-aged children attend public schools, and 80 percent of them live below the poverty line (DE 2021). Public education in Puerto Rico faces multiple challenges, including dependence on US federal funding, deteriorating school buildings and low student achievement on standardized assessments (Consejo de Educación 2017; Villalón et al. 2017).

While Montessori education has flourished in small private schools in Puerto Rico since the 1950s, in 1994, the island's first public school implemented the pedagogy as a vehicle of social transformation to provide high-quality, student-centered education in which teachers, parents, and community leaders play central roles. The success of Juan Ponce de León school ignited a thirty-year-long public Montessori movement, which established Montessori programs in forty-five public schools (5 percent of Puerto Rico's total), created a local training center, and institutionalized a Montessori Secretariat within the Department of Education (DE). This public movement's achievements in transforming historically marginalized communities through education have influenced debates on public education, democratization, and social justice in Puerto Rico and abroad (López Alicea 2019; Miranda 2019).

Montessori Education in Puerto Rico: 1950–2000

Montessori education arrived in Puerto Rico in the 1950s with the foundation of *Las Nereidas* (The Sea Nymphs), a private school and training center interested in spreading the philosophy. Close to twenty private schools emerged from this effort during the 1980s and 1990s, including Escuela del Pueblo Trabajador, Liceo Montessoriano del Caribe, and Montessori del Sol. The willingness of these pioneers to share their knowledge has been essential for the public-school community.

In the late 1980s, the *barrio* (neighborhood) of Juan Domingo in Guaynabo faced gentrification and school deterioration. Residents were displaced by high-cost development, school buildings were abandoned, 40 percent of students never reached ninth grade, there was little parent participation, and incidents of violence increased (Garcia Blanco 1990). Citing declining enrollment, the DE's response was to close the middle school in 1987. The first Montessori public school, Juan Ponce de León (JPL), eventually opened in the same building out of parental and community resistance to this closure.

Knowing how important school was for their children and for community stability, parents and community leaders organized against the DE's decision and lobbied for three consecutive years. After intense door-to-door organizing, constant visits to the Secretary of Education, and engagement with the media, JPL reopened in 1990 with ninety-nine students and a firm commitment to serve them. Ana María García Blanco, the school's principal, recalls: "The day the gates opened, we made a promise—to 'build' the best school for our community" (García Blanco 2018).

Community organizing methods were part of the reopened school's governance: *mesas redondas* (round tables) provided for the equal participation of community members, teachers, and families in decision-making (García Blanco and Colón Morera 1993, 159). Under the School Community Law (Ley 18), schools were allowed to determine and design their own curricula, and through this collective decision-making structure, JPL chose Montessori pedagogy in 1994 based on the model of the private Liceo Montessori del Caribe located across the street.[1] As a result of intense collective work among teachers and families, the school developed as a stable, peaceful community with strong student academic achievement and family participation. By the late 1990s, school enrollment had tripled to almost 350 students.

During the next ten years, JPL built a team of Montessori educators and academic programming for infants through high schoolers. A study of alumni from 1990 to 2010 demonstrated that 100 percent of JPL students graduated from the ninth grade and went on to high school, and 90 percent went to college (INE 2016).

Public Montessori Movement: 2000–2016

Following the success of JPL, in 2000, four public schools facing closure transitioned to the Montessori method. In response to this increasing interest, the Instituto Nueva Escuela (INE)—a nonprofit organization—was founded by a group of Montessori teachers. It became Puerto Rico's first accredited Montessori training center in 2008, and it was supported by important alliances between public and private school teachers, professors from the Center for Montessori Teacher Education in New York and local universities in Puerto Rico.

INE's model is built on three elements: collective governance, Montessori pedagogy, and family participation. In the collective governance structure, school personnel, families, and students actively participate in decision-making processes and follow a code of honor. Montessori's methodology is inclusive, serves children from 2 months to 18 years of age, and allows for each individual child to experience success (see Figure 47.1). Parents and families are "enrolled" in Montessori public schools: they participate in the school's governance, take part in a Montessori parents' education program, and are invited to be part of the workforce. For example, a mother who starts as a volunteer can become an assistant teacher by taking a Montessori course, which transforms her status socially and economically. She brings a new vision of childhood to the *barrio* and important community issues to the school.

The success of this model attracted other school communities across Puerto Rico. As a result of their advocacy, eight new schools joined the movement in 2012. The DE recognized this network of twelve Montessori schools as "specialized schools" under its traditional academic

Figure 47.1 An assistant teacher with a student in Vieques. Courtesy of the Instituto Nueva Escuela.

program. Although this recognition was an accomplishment in itself, to fully develop authentic Montessori practices, the network would need greater levels of autonomy.

In August 2014, after months of community advocacy by Montessori educators and families, Montessori education was incorporated into the Department of Education through the founding of the *Auxiliary Montessori Education Secretariat* (SAEM by its Spanish acronym). In partnership with INE, which provided certification of new guides and ongoing professional development, the Secretariat would oversee all public Montessori schools, affording them a much greater degree of autonomy than traditional public schools. Between 2014 and 2016, the movement grew to forty-five schools, in both rural and urban areas, all in communities in which a majority of students live below the poverty line.

Sustaining the Movement through Crisis: 2016–2022

Since 2016, Puerto Rico has faced a series of unprecedented crises that the Montessori movement has successfully navigated to ensure the well-being of students and families. In late 2016, an externally appointed fiscal control board was established by the US Congress to control Puerto Rico's indebted finances and began implementing extreme austerity measures. While Hurricanes Irma and María wreaked devastation in 2017, causing thousands of deaths and significant out-migration, the administration of Secretary of Education, Julia Keleher, an American consultant (who was ultimately convicted of federal corruption charges in December 2021), successfully promoted the passage of education Law 85 (2018).

Law 85 gave almost unilateral authority to the Secretary and established charter schools (publicly funded schools run by private entities) and vouchers (public funds for families to pay private school tuition) in Puerto Rico for the first time. These reforms had been resisted by teachers' unions and community groups for decades (Klein 2018). The administration also immediately announced plans to close one-third of all schools by the end of year, one of the largest mass closures in the world (Caraballo Cueto 2020).

In January 2018, Keleher informed INE that Montessori schools would become the first Puerto Rican Charter Management Organization (CMO), that the office of SAEM would be dissolved, and that if INE did not agree to these terms, many Montessori schools would be closed. INE designed a collaborative consultation process in which schools held assemblies with their teacher and family communities to discuss the pros and cons of this ultimatum. Ultimately, the movement rejected conversion to a charter network, believing it would compromise its foundation of collective governance and community participation, and that the competitive nature of charters and its reliance on standardized testing contradicted Montessori philosophy.

Keleher quickly announced the closure of fourteen Montessori schools. The entire network mobilized against this action by organizing protests, social media campaigns, press conferences, and petitions (see Figure 47.2).

Figure 47.2 Teachers from schools across Puerto Rico demonstrate their support for public Montessori education in front of the Capitol, 2020. Courtesy of Instituto Nueva Escuela.

By June 2018, the movement successfully lobbied to keep all fourteen schools open. Senators Migdalia Padilla Alvelo and José Antonio Vargas Vidot proposed a bill to permanently establish SAEM, ensuring it could not be dissolved by any education secretary. Thousands held vigils and lobbied the governor in support of the bill. In December 2018, the governor signed historic Law 277 and legally established the Secretariat within the public system (Ayer 2019).

Although this reform was a huge achievement, the movement continues to face serious challenges. In January 2020, a series of earthquakes closed schools across Puerto Rico, followed by further pandemic-related school closures two months later. While most of the public system struggled to respond to the constraints placed on teaching and learning during the pandemic, the model of collective governance in Montessori schools has supported communities in translating their ideas into concrete actions. The *Montessori en casa* (Montessori at home) platform provided parents and teachers with tools for academic and emotional work at home; each student received a *caja viajera* (traveling box) every two or three weeks that contained materials created by teachers and their assistants, and more than 800 children received materials to start vegetable gardens.

Conclusion

The public Montessori movement in Puerto Rico has introduced a new pedagogical and collective governance model at the school level and within the Puerto Rican Department of Education. Montessori education has built a broad reform movement that humanizes schooling, upholds public education, protects students' rights, and makes its pedagogy accessible to all. The widespread adoption of Montessori education in Puerto Rico advances social justice (Bryan-Silva and Sanders-Smith 2021; García Blanco and Morera 1993; Miranda 2019), as did Maria Montessori a 100 years ago when she founded the first Casa dei Bambini in the marginalized *barrio* of San Lorenzo, Rome, to serve the children no one else saw.

Notes

Members of the INE collective read, commented, and approved this chapter.
1. Renowned Brazilian educator Paulo Freire recognized the democratizing potential of what he termed Montessori methodology crossing the street from the public to the private sector when García Blanco discussed JPL's struggles and reopening with him in the late 1980s.

References

Ayer, David. 2019. "Puerto Rico Recognizes Montessori." *Montessori Public*. April 19, 2019. https://www.montessoripublic.org/2019/04/puerto-rico-recognizes-montessori/.
Bryan-Silva, Kutasha, and Stephanie C. Sanders-Smith. 2021. "H Is for Hurricane, M Is for Maria: Supporting Literacy in Vieques." *Journal of Early Childhood Literacy* 0(0): 1–25. https://doi.org/10.1177/14687984211044196.

Caraballo Cueto, José. 2020. "Estudio #5: Aprovechamiento Académico y el Cierre de Escuelas en Puerto Rico." *Observatorio de la Educación.* https://observatorioeducacionpr.files.wordpress.com/2020/12/caraballo-cueto-aprovechamiento-academico-y-el-cierre-de-escuelas-en-pr.pdf.

Consejo de Educación de Puerto Rico. 2017. *Educación Básica en Puerto Rico del 1980 al 2012: Política Pública y Trasfondo Histórico, Legal y Curricular.* San Juan: Consejo de Educación de Puerto Rico.

Departamento de Educación. 2014. "Plan de Transformación y Reorganización de las Escuelas." https://tribunapr.com/wp-content/uploads/2014/05/20140510-de-presentacion.pdf.

Departamento de Educación. 2019. "Standardized Test Scores." *Perfil Escolar Dashboard.* https://perfilescolar.dde.pr/dashboard/standardizedtest/?schoolcode=State.

Departamento de Educación. 2021. "Certified Enrollment." *Perfil Escolar Dashboard.* https://perfilescolar.dde.pr/dashboard/certifiedenrollment/?schoolcode=State.

García Blanco, Ana Maria. 1990. "Constructing a Ship While at Sea." PhD diss., Harvard University.

García Blanco, Ana Maria. 2018. "La reforma que nació de un pequeño plantel." *El Nuevo Día.* February 21, 2018. www.elnuevodia.com/opinion/columnas/lareformaquenaciodeunpequenoplantel-columna-2400584/.

García Blanco, Ana Maria, and José Javier Colón Morera. 1993. "A Community Based Approach to Educational Reform in Puerto Rico." In *Colonial Dilemmas: Critical Perspectives on Contemporary Puerto Rico*, edited by Edwin Melendez and Edgardo Melendez, 157–72. New York: South End Press.

Instituto de Estadísticas de Puerto Rico. 2016. "Capítulo 6. Una Mirada al Sistema Educativo de Puerto Rico: Una Introducción." In *Informe Sobre Desarrollo Humano en Puerto Rico*, edited by Instituto de Estadísticas de Puerto Rico, 57–185. https://estadisticas.pr/files/Publicaciones/INFORME_DESARROLLO_HUMANO_PUERTO_RICO_1.pdf.

Instituto Nueva Escuela (INE). 2016. *Informe Anual 2015–16.*

Klein, Naomi. 2018. *The Battle for Paradise: Puerto Rico Takes on Disaster Capitalism.* Chicago: Haymarket Books.

López Alicea, Keila. 2019. "Montessori en Puerto Rico Lleva la Delantera Global." *El Nuevo Día.* February 9, 2019. lite.elnuevodia.com/noticias/locales/nota/montessorienpuertoricollevaladelanteraglobal-2475740.

Miranda, Katherine. 2019. "Instituto Nueva Escuela and Montessori Education Reform in Puerto Rico: 'We Count in a Different Way.'" *Sargasso—Transforming Pedagogy: Practice, Policy, and Resistance* 2018–2019 (1/2): 97–122. https://dloc.com/UF00096005/00044.

Villalón Soler, Eva, Orville M. Disdier Flores, and Luis Cruz Soto. 2017. *El Estado del Aprendizaje de la Lectura y la Escritura en los Grados Primarios de la Escuelas Públicas de Puerto Rico 2011–15.* Washington, DC: Flamboyan Foundation.

Chapter 48
Montessori Education in Mexico

Eder Cuevas

Mexico has a strong Montessori tradition dating back to the 1950s, with especially close connections to Association Montessori Internationale (AMI). The country is home to nine AMI-affiliated training centers and a variety of other Montessori organizations.

Introduction and Early Montessori History

Maria Montessori's ideas formally arrived in Mexico in 1952 with the translation of her book *Il segreto dell'infanzia* (The Secret of Childhood) into Spanish. The translation was authorized and printed by the Secretaría de Educación Pública (Secretary of Public Education), the government office for education, and was distributed to 500 Mexican teachers (*Around the Child* 1952, 82).

Although this publishing initiative did not result in the creation of Montessori schools, Montessori education took off eight years later in 1960, when Maria Luisa Ryan de Creel read a magazine article about Montessori. Creel directed teacher Estela Palmieri to visit a Montessori school in Connecticut and take a training course there. Together, in 1962, they founded the first Montessori school in the country, Montessori de Chihuahua, with five students. Two years later, the school opened an elementary classroom headed by teacher Domingo Alba, who had just completed his training in Bergamo, Italy (Colegio Montessori de Chihuahua 2014) (see Figure 48.1).

Mexican families connected with Montessori's emphasis on family, cultural traditions, and spirituality, creating a fusion that supported the rooting of the method across the country. At the end of the 1960s and beginning of the 1970s, families and educators joined together to create Montessori schools in the north of Mexico, including in Juarez, Torreón, Saltillo, and Monterrey. Some schools in Mexico City, including Montessori Kalpilli and Montessori de la Ciudad de México, were founded during this time (see Figure 48.2).

One limitation, however, was that there was no Montessori training center in Mexico limiting the creation and expansion of Montessori schools. Eventually, in 1972, several families and educators from Montessori schools came together to create the Centro de Estudios de Educación Montessori A.C.[1] (Center for Studies of Montessori Education) (CEMAC or *El Centro*), Mexico's first training center, with Dutchwoman Cato "Nan" Hanrath as training director. Hundreds of students at El Centro have gone on to become teachers, trainers, and leaders in the Montessori movement in Mexico (Christian Schjetnan, pers. comm., 2021).

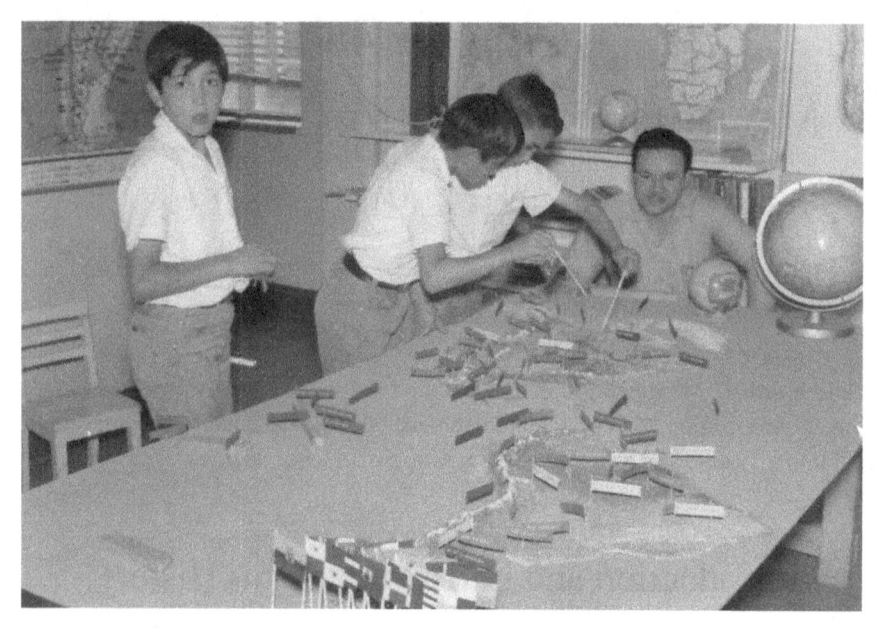

Figure 48.1 Domingo Alba, the first AMI-trained elementary guide in Mexico, working with some of his students, 1980s. Courtesy of Montessori de Chihuahua.

Figure 48.2 A student works with Math materials at Montessori de la Ciudad de México, date unknown. Courtesy of Montessori de la Ciudad de México.

As CEMAC grew and the Montessori method expanded, the Secretary of Education stepped in to offer support by providing a building (Christian Schjetnan, pers. comm., 2019; Pilar Gomez de Ulibarri, pers. comm., 2021). More and more schools were founded around Mexico, and several organizations were created to promote Montessori throughout the country, such as Asociación Montessori de México A.C. (Montessori Association of Mexico) (AMMAC) (n.d.) in 1965 and the Asociación Montessori Mexicana A.C. (Mexican Montessori Association) (AMME) in 1977, the latter of which began holding national conferences in the 1970s. In the 1990s, CEMAC also began organizing national Montessori conferences to strengthen the Mexican Montessori movement and bring together Spanish-speaking Montessori educators across the Americas.

In 2010, Pilar Ulibarri, Christian and Tete Schjetnan and several colleagues founded the AMI-affiliated Sociedad Afiliada México A.C. (Mexican Affiliated Society) (SAMAC), focused on supporting and promoting Montessori education and maintaining the quality standards developed by AMI. Since then, several SAMAC members have been involved in AMI's global organizational efforts and have taught courses in other countries around the world (Christian Schjetnan, pers. comm., 2021).

Contemporary Landscape

Today there are nine AMI-affiliated Montessori training centers in Mexico, located in México City, Morelia, Querétaro, Cuernavaca, Cancún, Puebla, Estado de México, and Tijuana (Montessori México 2021b). There is also a training center associated with the Montessori Sierra Madre School in Monterrey, which was accredited by the American Montessori Society in 2008. Recent efforts have also focused on regional and national coordination. Asociación de Escuelas Montessori de Puebla (Montessori Schools Association of Puebla) (n.d.), a regional organization founded in the early 2000s, coordinates the efforts of the fifteen Montessori schools in the state of Puebla and hosts an annual summit.

In 2018, in order to expand Montessori's presence around Mexico, SAMAC became Montessori Mexico and hired a full-time executive director. Ongoing efforts include strengthening connections across Montessori organizations in Mexico and conducting a census of Mexican Montessori schools. The Sixth Educateurs Sans Frontiers (EsF) Assembly in 2019 in Tepoztlan helped to further strengthen the Montessori community in Mexico as well as build international collaborations around the globe.

Today, it is estimated that there are more than 400 Montessori schools across the nation, as evidenced by an ongoing survey by Montessori Mexico. Nearly all Montessori schools are private, serving children and adolescents from affluent families; approximately 11 percent of Mexican schools in total are private (INEGI).

There are 25 million children under age 15 in Mexico (INEGI 2020). Currently, there are no public Montessori schools in Mexico due to regulations that government schools follow a single curriculum. Little by little, organizations have been incorporating Montessori principles into education in less-advantaged communities, including at orphanages like Otoch Paal in Quintana Roo, which serves Mayan children; Granja Hogar in Chihuahua, which serves Tarahumara children; Montessori Topilhua in Estado de Mexico; and Centro de Aprendizaje Ananda in

Oaxaca. These efforts have received limited governmental support but are supported through other structures including solidarity schools that pair with under resourced schools to share resources, NGOs, and private donations.

Conclusion

Montessori has a substantial organizational structure in Mexico and is a subject of strong interest among families. The main challenge is strengthening networks between the different organizations in order to increase the impact of Montessori education and reach the stated goal of "Montessori for all" in Mexican society.

Notes

Christian Schjetnan and Cecilia Elguero read and commented on an earlier draft of this chapter.
1. A.C. or Association Civile recognizes a nonprofit organization in Mexico.

References

Around the Child. 1952. "News of the Montessori Movement." 2: 79–82.
Asociación de Escuelas de Puebla. n.d. "La Asociación." Accessed May 5, 2022. https://www.montessoripuebla.org/asociacion.html.
Asociación Montessori de México A. C. n.d. "Asociación Montessori de México A.C." Accessed May 5, 2022. https://asociacionmontessori.mx/.
Colegio Montessori de Chihuahua. 2014. "Historia del Colegio Montessori de Chihuahua" Accessed August 22, 2021. https://www.youtube.com/watch?v=BlO0AAtyhoQ.
Instituto Nacional de Estadística y Geografía (INEGI). 2020. "Matrícula escolar por entidad federativa según nivel educativo, ciclos escolares seleccionados de 2000/2001 a 2019/2020." Accessed August 22, 2021. https://www.inegi.org.mx/app/tabulados/interactivos/?pxq=ac13059d-e874-4962-93bb-74f2c58a3cb9.
Montessori, Maria. 2015. *Educación y Paz*. Laren: Montessori-Pierson Publishing Company.
Montessori México. 2021a. "Centros de Entrenamiento." Accessed August 22, 2021. https://montessori-sociedad-afiliada.org.mx/.
Montessori México. 2021b. Accessed August 22, 2021. https://www.montessorimx.com/.
Montessori México. 2021c. "Centros." Accessed August 22, 2021. https://www.montessorimx.com/centros.
Montessori Sierra Madre. 2021. "AMS Training Center." https://www.msm.edu.mx/colegio/.

Chapter 49
Montessori Education in Latin America

Joel Parham, Maria K. McKenna, and Lesli Romero

This chapter provides an overview of Montessori education in Latin America, organized around three "waves" of interest in the method of Montessori in the region, seemingly linked to economic and political factors (Whitescarver and Cossentino 2008). These are (1) the early emergence of Montessori education across Latin America led by government policymakers and social reformers from the 1910s through the 1930s; (2) a second wave of Montessori education from the 1950s to the 1970s, often introduced by foreign volunteers; and (3) the contemporary context of Montessori (from the 1980s onward), largely connected to private preschools, localized community undertakings, or charity and religious schools, particularly in rural areas. Alongside the thematic profiles, this chapter also briefly highlights the development of Montessori in a few national contexts.

The histories of Montessori in various Latin American communities were (and are) often documented locally, such as newsletters, trade publications, and local press coverage, but not often captured in academic sources.[1] Montessori activity has been more extensively documented in Chile, Colombia, Peru, Costa Rica, Nicaragua, and Panama than many of the other Latin American nations (see also Chapters 47, 50, and 51 on Puerto Rico, Brazil, and Argentina, respectively). As such, this chapter acts as a springboard for future research on Montessori in Latin America.

Emergence of Montessori Education

Montessori education in Latin America generally dates to the 1910s or 1920s and has its roots in Argentina, Brazil, Chile, Colombia, Costa Rica, Nicaragua, and Panama. In this section, we will look at two ways Montessori education was adopted across Latin America: through national governments eager to support early childhood education and through social reformers who implemented Montessori education at the grassroots level influenced by the global progressive education movement commonly known as "New Education" (Harding 1982).

Local Governments in Support of Early Childhood Education

One of the earliest instances of government support for Montessori education was in El Salvador in 1916 when Montessori orientations were given under the direction of Don José Laínez, Minister of Public Instruction, to kindergarten programs established in large cities

(Kilgo 1966). Similarly, Guatemala's Montessori roots appear to go back to 1924 when the federal government established new primary education policies ("Public Instruction and Education; Guatemala" 1924).

Later, and more substantially, academics and educational policymakers in Chile took an interest in Montessori pedagogy in the late 1920s during discussions regarding national reforms for the public education system ("Education and Fine Arts; Chile" 1929; "Public Instruction and Education; Chile" 1928). The University of Chile, a public university with close ties to the government, established a lab school to examine Montessori education. Simultaneously, one of the university's education professors, Dr. Darío Salás, attended the Fifth World Conference of the New Education Fellowship[2] where he reported on the method (Boyd 1930, 93–5). Shortly thereafter, a national Montessori society for Chile was established, and one of Salás's colleagues, Arturo Piga, was sponsored by the Chilean government to attend the sixteenth International Montessori Training Course in London in 1931 ("Notiziario montessoriano" 1932, 56).

As outlined above, government interest and support for Montessori education was evident, but funding seems to have been unreliable and unsustainable. Specific reasons for this are not particularly clear, though one can assume that geopolitical strife and economic pressures were factors. Further investigation, possibly through a more thorough analysis of Spanish-language content and a review of government documents and proceedings, is necessary.

Adoption of Montessori Education by Social Reformers

Alongside government efforts, social reformers also brought Montessori education to parts of Latin America. Montessori education appears to have been introduced to Panama around 1913, as evidenced by news related to the establishment of "Mrs. W. S. Harrison's school for little children" in the Canal Zone ("Social Life of the Zone; Mrs. Harrison's School" 1913).

Josefa Toledo de Aguerrí, a social activist and reformer, introduced Montessori education in Nicaragua in 1912 when she established Kindergarten Modelo at the Colegio de Señoritas de Managua (Women's College of Managua). This was, however, short-lived; later that same year, the Nicaraguan government formally dissolved all kindergartens across the country. In 1924, Aguerrí reestablished the program when Montessori kindergartens were implemented nationally by a government-mandated program, Kindergarten Nacional. Shortly after its launch, the program was transferred to the auspices of Aguerrí's Colegio, due to changes in political and economic priorities (López Miranda 1988, 49–50). Under the aegis of the Colegio, the program maintained its Montessori foundations but was no longer directly run by the national government.

Further south in Colombia, Montessori education was implemented at the Gimnasio Moderno, a private boys school in Bogotá established in 1914 under the direction of Agustín Nieto Caballero, who had studied progressive education in the United States and Europe (Brainerd 1928). Montessori methods were used for children 3 to 6, while Decroly methods were used for children 6 and older.

Separately, in Costa Rica, Carmen Lyra established the first Montessori preschool, Escuela Maternal, for children in poor communities along the banks of the Torres River in 1926. She was aided in this project by fellow revolutionary feminists Luisa González, Margarita Castro, and Matilda Caranza (Beam 2016). Costa Rica was a site of struggle between educators and the state over pedagogical reform; though teachers advocated for Montessori education and other progressive education models, the country lacked the economic and political stability to enact long-standing educational reform (Beam 2016).

Nations with Mercurial Montessori Beginnings

Documentation of Montessori activities in several nations—Peru, Ecuador, Uruguay, and Suriname—has been identified but is minimal in substance. A brief mention concerning Montessori education in Peru appears in 1927, and more evidence of Montessori in this nation is captured in a photograph from 1948 ("Public Instruction and Education; Peru" 1927; see Figure 49.1).

Montessori education in Uruguay appears to have been limited to philosophical discussions within academia, as exemplified by the publication of a descriptive overview of the Montessori method as well as a report on a teacher's conference hosted there (Samonati 1912; "Public Instruction and Education; Uruguay" 1928). Given the Dutch colonial influence in Suriname, some newspapers made brief mentions of Montessori-related news, but a substantial presence of the method has not been identified. Further research is necessary to determine to what extent Montessori education was actually implemented in these countries during this era.

Figure 49.1 Rural Montessori school in Muquiyauyo, Peru, ca. 1948. Photo courtesy of the Gabriela Mistral Legacy Writer's Archive, National Library of Chile.

Second-Wave Montessori Education in Latin America

A second wave of Montessori activity in Latin America emerged in the late 1950s and continued through the 1970s. Evidence of interest in Montessori education in Uruguay is evident in the 1950s and early 1960s in the pages of the Uruguayan education journals *Anales de Instrucción Primaria* and *Revista Ecuatoriana de Educación* (e.g., Larraguibel de Parodi 1955; Casa de la Cultura Ecuatoriana 1952). However, despite this interest, evidence of Montessori schools in Uruguay during this second wave have eluded research efforts.

Meanwhile, on the other side of South America, Chile was experiencing a resurgence of interest in Montessori education. The Chilean Montessori Society was "reconstituted" in 1963 with Arturo Alessandri Rodriguez (son of a former Chilean president) as honorary president and Arturo Piga as president. Further research is necessary in order to identify more details concerning implementations of Montessori education across the nation.

Nearby Peru seems to have experienced renewed interest in Montessori education in the late 1960s and into the 1970s. A 1967 issue of *The Green Revolution* (a publication of the School of Living) includes a letter to the editor by Barney and Pat McCaffrey regarding their upcoming travels to Peru, where they planned to work "in a nursery school and Montessori preschool for children from broken families" in the village of Ñaña, approximately "14 miles outside of Lima" (McCaffrey and McCaffrey 1967: 3). Additional evidence of Montessori education in Peru can be found in the work of educator Susan Mayclin Stephenson at Colegio San Silvestre in Lima in 1973 and again in the late 1970s (Stephenson 1973, 2007).

Central America also experienced a second wave of interest in Montessori education. In 1967 a Montessori school was established in Santiago Atitlán, Guatemala, by Reverend Tomas Stafford of the Oklahoma Mission with the assistance of two Montessori-trained guides—Penny Gerbich and Rita Weill—from Cincinnati, Ohio (Bellak 1969). This school provided bilingual education for Indigenous children but, once again, further details regarding this school have not been found. Nearby Honduras also experimented with alternative education methods, including Montessori education, to improve and expand public education ("News of the Montessori Movement" 1963, 91; McTaggert 1979).

Instances of Montessori education are clearly evident across Latin America during the second wave, and additional research can help develop a fuller account of the spread and persistence across a range of countries.

Modern Context of Montessori Education in Latin America

Since the 1980s, Montessori method has grown sporadically around Latin America in the early childhood sector through private preschools, localized community undertakings, or charity and religiously affiliated schools, particularly in rural areas. (Most compulsory education begins at age 6.) This decentralized growth is in contrast to governmental interventions in the earlier part of the twentieth century. As previously mentioned, regional actors were more closely aligned with the American Montessori movement rather than the earlier European influence, mirroring geopolitical shifts of the time. As modern technology, including air travel, electronic communication, and easier access to materials and resources, developed, the footprint of Montessori education across the region grew.

Another important force for Montessori education in Latin America was the creation in 1978 of a regional association, the Comité Hispano Montessori (Hispanic Montessori Committee),[3] spearheaded by Marjorie "Marge" Farmer, an American Montessori educator and peace activist, to identify, connect, and collaborate across Montessori organizations and schools throughout the region. The organization's records and newsletter, *El Boletín*, which was published from 1983 to 2010,[4] document the continued existence and activities of Montessori education. The records indicate a disjointed, but robust, presence of Montessori education across the region along with documented efforts to partner with the American Montessori Society (AMS) for continued longevity (Farmer 1992b). The following section examines nations in which the reintroduction of Montessori education in the 1980s and 1990s was well documented in *El Boletín*.

Nicaragua

Farmer documents the reintroduction of Montessori to Nicaragua through "Project Nicaragua," which consisted of a series of workshops that led to the establishment of small Montessori preschools. Geraldine O'Leary de Macias, with support from the Council of Protestant Churches of Nicaragua (CEPAD), began the Montessori movement anew in Nicaragua at the end of the Nicaraguan Revolution. Beginning in 1981, the Comité Hispano Montessori offered Montessori training courses on the philosophy of Montessori and construction of materials from local resources, as had been done a few years prior in Panama ("News of the Regions" 2000). Following the workshops, several participants established small preschools in their homes. Unfortunately, because of continued conflict in the country, resources and focus shifted away from education, and many of these schools ceased to exist.

Peru

Additional evidence of Montessori training and work is found in brief summaries presented in *El Boletín* in 1992 (Farmer 1992a). This source indicates Sister Brigid O'Connell carried on the work of Dora (Tina) Maldano to bring training accredited by the National Center for Montessori Education (NCME) to Peru, along with Montessori education for orphanages and rural areas. The work of Sister Brigid also included the establishment of a cooperative of orphaned adolescent boys, who worked at creating affordable Montessori materials for the region (Farmer 1992a).

Bolivia

A similar story emerges in Bolivia—*El Boletín* reported on at least two Montessori schools operating in La Paz in the 1980s alongside references to the training courses offered by Sister Brigid O'Connell in the country ("News from the Regions" 1990). *El Boletín* also noted Dr. Jose

Antonio Muñoz's desire for Sister Brigid O'Connell to provide training for educators working with disabled children in Bolivia, indicating perhaps a more robust presence of Montessori education than research currently indicates (1990).

Central America

More generally across Central America, *El Boletín* included numerous announcements and updates about training programs, teacher education, and various Montessori schools, both rural and urban (Farmer 1992a). A national focus on ecological well-being compounded the influence of Montessori at the time. Various volumes of *El Boletín* indicate both the desire for Montessori education in the region and the successful implementation of the method in the late 2000s. However, widespread use of the Montessori method past the mid-1990s is not well documented around Central America.

Contemporary Montessori Landscape

Contemporary interest in Montessori education is evident in Bolivia, Brazil, Chile, Honduras, Peru, Mexico, Puerto Rico, and El Salvador (Apaza Herrera 2017; Mella Donoso 2011; Moncada-Davidson 2012). In recent years, several Latin American countries have created national Montessori organizations. These include Fundación Eco-Educativa Montessori Colombia (FEMCO) (1996), Organização Montessori do Brasil (1996), Fundación Argentina María Montessori (FAMM) (2007), Montessori Mexico (2018), Aruba and Region International Montessori Association, Asociación Montessori de Chile, and Montessori Association Perú. Argentina, Columbia, Mexico, and Peru's groups are also affiliated with the Association Montessori Internationale (AMI). More recently, with the emergence of virtual training, it is conceivable that Montessori education will continue to grow.

Through modern-day programs such as Educación con Participación de la Comunidad (EDUCO) in El Salvador (McConnell-Farmer et al. 2012) and Programa Hondureño de Educación Comunitaria (PROHECO) in Honduras (Di Gropello and Marshall 2011), Latin American governments have aimed to improve early childhood education by providing funding to rural communities and authorizing community councils authority to carry out administrative responsibilities. Additionally, through recent support from NGOs and local grassroots efforts to improve early childhood education in El Salvador, there has been an increase in the use of the Montessori method in schools and orphanages in vulnerable communities. Private Montessori schools also exist in the milieu. The Hilda Rothschild Foundation recognized the neglect of early childhood education in El Salvador and supports the use of the Montessori method to ensure El Salvadoran children receive high-quality early education (Moncada-Davidson 2012). Though there is more freedom to incorporate local culture under the Montessori method, these schools still face the challenge of balancing cultural responsiveness and the integrity of the Montessori method, since many educational systems trend toward structured, colonial models of education (Williams 2002).

Conclusion

Montessori implementation in early childhood spaces in Central and South American countries has undergone ebbs and flows, seemingly due to economic and political factors. A modest beginning in many nations at the start of the twentieth century coincides with the newfound popularity of Montessori education in Europe and the United States, the far-reaching impact of the New Education Fellowship and the Theosophical Society, social and political desire for improved education, and the emergence of more commonplace compulsory education globally. From there, the paths diverge with regard to the implementation, structure, and longevity of interest in the Montessori model. Still, throughout the years, some independent and NGO-related efforts kept Montessori programs going across various regions of Latin America. With the work of Marjorie Farmer and others in the 1980s to establish a network for Montessori practice, a new era of Montessori education emerged, including in marginalized spaces such as rural communities and those focused on serving the urban poor. Still, political strife, stretched budgets, and the neoliberalization of education created impediments for many Montessori programs to firmly take hold in any of these nations in a widespread manner due to a lack of consistent government support for its implementation and persistent fiscal challenges regarding education.

Still, the dogged work of individuals in a variety of spaces, often connected to religious or nonprofit groups, and with ties to earlier connections to Montessori in Europe and later in the United States, continued to allow Montessori to serve rural and urban poor, linguistically diverse, and disabled children in some spaces. At times some of these programs have promoted or perpetuated colonialist perspectives of foreign, rural, indigent, and Indigenous populations. Over the past twenty years a number of tuition-based, private, elite Montessori schools have also emerged. Thus, interest in Montessori education in the region continues to persist on a few parallel tracks.

In recent decades, in places like Guatemala and Costa Rica, the notion that Montessori schools are designed only for communities with high socioeconomic statuses has gradually been shifting (Solares Bolaños 2018). Finally, it is worth noting the connections between various waves of feminist peacemakers and Montessori education. The two are never far apart in Latin America, serving as a reminder that there is still work to do to uncover even more of the rich histories behind the brief and admittedly incomplete highlights of this chapter. To this end, further investigation, possibly through a more thorough analysis of Spanish-language content and a review of government documents and proceedings, is necessary.

Notes

1. The Montessori Bibliography Online (MBO) makes information about Montessori education and the Montessori movement more accessible through an online interface. The MBO is hosted by the University of Kansas Center for Montessori Research at: https://montessoribib.ku.edu.
2. This conference was held August 8–21, 1929, in Helsingør, Denmark where, simultaneously, the first International Montessori Congress was also held.
3. In 1998 Comité Hispano Montessori changed its name to Consejo Interamericano Montessori (Inter-American Montessori Council).

4. Beginning in 2000 *El Boletín* was incorporated into *Public School Montessorian* beginning with the Fall 2000 issue and continuing through 2010.

References

Apaza Herrera, Maria Elizabeth. 2017. "La Influencia del Método Montessori para el Desarrollo Integral en Niños y Niñas de Educación Inicial del Centro Infantil Virgen del Rosario de la Ciudad de El Alto." Undergraduate Thesis, Universidad Mayor de San Andrés, La Paz, Bolivia.

Beam, Krysta Renee. 2016. "Printing Peace: Cultural and Pedagogical Negotiation through Children's Periodicals in Costa Rica, 1912–1947." Master's thesis, University of Illinois at Urbana-Champaign.

Bellak, Richard. 1969. "Montessori in Guatemala." *Saturday Review* 52 (33): 47–49.

Boyd, William. 1930. "New Education in National Re-Creation." In *Towards a New Education*, edited by William Boyd, 64–99. New York: Knopf.

Brainerd, Heloise. 1928. "Progressive Schools in Latin America." *Bulletin of the Pan American Union* 62 (5): 453–67.

Casa de la Cultura Ecuatoriana. 1952. *Revista Ecuatoriana de Educación* 6 (23): 1–167.

Di Gropello, Emanuela, and Jeffery H. Marshall. 2011. "Decentralization and Educational Performance: Evidence from the PROHECO Community School Program in Rural Honduras." *Education Economics* 19 (2): 161–80. https://doi.org/10.1080/09645290902992816.

"Education and Fine Arts; Chile." 1929. *Bulletin of the Pan American Union* 63 (4): 415–16. https://archive.org/details/bulletinofpaname6329pana/page/414/mode/2up.

Farmer, Marjorie. 1992a. *El Boletín* (October). Omaha, Nebraska: Comité Hispano Montessori.

Farmer, Marjorie. 1992b. *Comité Hispano Montessori*. Omaha, Nebraska: Comité Hispano Montessori.

Harding, Faith A. B. 1982. "Identification of Competencies for the Professor Component of a Program for Training Nursery School Teachers in Guyana." EdD diss., Teachers College, Columbia University, New York.

Kilgo, Reese D. 1966. "The Development of Education in El Salvador." PhD diss., University of Texas at Austin.

Larraguibel de Parodi, Aida. 1955. "El concepto de libertad en la educación Montessori." *Anales de Instrucción Primaria* (Uruguay) 18 (1–3): 162–66.

López Miranda, Margarita. 1988. *Josefa Toledo de Aguerri: Una Chontaleña en la Educación Nacional*. Juigalpa, Nicaragua: Asociación de Ganaderos de Chontales.

McCaffrey, Barney, and Pat McCaffrey. 1967. "McCaffreys to Peru." *The Green Revolution* 5 (4): 3, 4.

McConnell-Farmer, Judith Lynne, Pamela R. Cook, and M. W. Farmer. 2012. "Perspectives in Early Childhood Education: Belize, Brazil, Mexico, El Salvador and Peru." *Forum on Public Policy Online* 2012 (1): 1–27.

McTaggert, James F. 1979. "Community and Nonformal Education in the Republic of Honduras." In *International Perspectives on Nonformal Education* (conference proceedings), 119–26. May 3, 1979. Amherst, MA: Comparative and International Education Society.

Mella Donoso, Marcela. 2011. "Método Montessori: Estudio Cualitativo de la Implementación del Método Montessori, en las Niñas y Niños de la Sala de Clases Heterogénea de la Sala Cuna y Jardín Infantil El Roble de la Comuna de La Pintana." Undergraduate Thesis, Santiago, Chile: Universidad Academia de Humanismo Cristiano.

Moncada-Davidson, Lillian. 2012. "Educambio: Transformando las Opciones de Vida de Todos los Niños y Niñas en El Salvador." *Revista de Humanidades y Ciencias Sociales* 3: 47–63.

"News from the Regions." 1990. *El Boletín* 1990: 1–6. https://collections.ctdigitalarchive.org/islandora/object/20002:860564870#page/20/mode/2up.

"News of the Montessori Movement." 1963. *Around the Child* 8: 84–94.

"Notiziario montessoriano." 1932. *Montessori: Rivista Bimestrale dell'Opera Montessori* 1 (1): 55–59.

"Public Instruction and Education; Chile." 1928. *Bulletin of the Pan American Union* 62 (2): 204–5. https://archive.org/details/bulletinofpaname6228pana/page/204/mode/2up.

"Public Instruction and Education; Guatemala." 1924. Bulletin of the Pan American Union 58 (6): 630–31. https://hdl.handle.net/2027/uma.ark:/13960/t9g458w58?urlappend=%3Bseq=728.

"Public Instruction and Education; Peru." 1927. *Bulletin of the Pan American Union* 61 (12): 1257–58. https://archive.org/details/bulletinofpaname6127pana/page/1257/mode/2up.

"Public Instruction and Education; Uruguay." 1928. *Bulletin of the Pan American Union* 62 (1): 104–5. https://archive.org/details/bulletinofpaname6228pana/page/104/mode/2up.

Samonati, Alfredo. 1912. "La Doctora Montessori y su Sistema de Enseñanza." *Anales de Instrucción Primaria* (Uruguay) 11: 97–224.

"Social Life of the Zone; Mrs. Harrison's School." 1913. *Canal Record* (Panama), June 25.

Solares Bolaños, Elfriede Aida María. 2018. "Actitud de las Maestras de Pre-Primaria y Primaria Baja de un Colegio con Sedes en Zona 15 y Carretera a El Salvador Sobre la Metodología Montessori." Undergraduate Thesis, Universidad Rafael Landívar, Guatemala City, Guatemala.

Stephenson, Susan M. 1973. "Lowering the Noise Level in an Open Classroom." Michael Olaf Montessori Company. http://www.michaelolaf.net/susanperu.pdf.

Stephenson, Susan M. 2007. "Notes from the Field." Michael Olaf Montessori Company. http://www.michaelolaf.net/ESF1-08part1.pdf.

Whitescarver, Keith, and Jacqueline Cossentino. 2008. "Montessori and the Mainstream: A Century of Reform on the Margins." *Teachers College Record* 110 (12): 2571–600.

Williams, Nancy L. S. 2002. "A Hermeneutic Exploration: Designing Grassroots Montessori Teacher Education Courses for Resource Limited Communities." EdD diss., University of San Francisco, California.

Chapter 50
Montessori Education in Brazil

Marion Wallis and Paige Geiger

The history of Montessori education in Brazil dates back to 1910 and developed in three waves over the course of the twentieth century. Realities related to social inequality, illiteracy, education of the elite, two world wars, and political interventions affected the trajectory of Montessori education in Brazil, resulting in periods of growth and latency.

Early Years of Brazilian Montessori Education, 1910–45

The first wave of Montessori pedagogy in Brazil was an elite progressive movement, although some educators were interested in Montessori education for mass audiences. Schooling was focused on an abstract liberal arts education. John Dewey greatly influenced the New Education movement, with Montessori education being one of the progressive methods under debate. Some hoped that Montessori education could foster democracy, while others preferred a military-style education (Avelar n.d.; Ballmann 2017; Hamze 2022).

The number of Montessori schools during this period is unknown. However, in 1910, Joana Falce Scalco, a student of the Montessori pedagogy from Europe, developed a public kindergarten program and later introduced Montessori materials to the private Emilia Erichsen Kindergarten in Curitiba in 1924.

Ciridião Buarque and his daughter Mary opened the first private Casa da Infância in São Paulo in 1915 (Ballmann 2017; OMB 2021). In the 1920s, given rising interest in the pedagogy throughout Brazil, Miguel Calmon du Pin e Almeida received Montessori's authorization to translate her book, *Scientific Pedagogy* (1912).

Scalco, corresponding with Montessori between 1925 and 1930, was chosen for training in Italy at Montessori's personal invitation, yet she was unable to travel due to the Brazilian Revolution of 1930 (Avelar n.d.; Ballmann 2017). With dictator Getulio Vargas in power until 1945 and a shift toward traditional schooling, the Montessori method virtually disappeared in Brazil (Braga, pers. comm.). Yet the private Maria Montessori school in São Paulo remained open for forty-four years, from 1935 until 1979, under the direction of Carolina Grossman with Heloisa Marcondes de Faria (Ballmann 2017).

Revival of the Montessori Method, 1945–1975

Following the Vargas era, the Second World War, and the 1948 Declaration of the Rights of the Child, local educational reform focused on meeting the needs of Brazil's diverse populations. Educational philosopher Paulo Freire worked extensively with the illiterate poor from 1946 until the military coup of 1964, and his educational praxis exerted significant influence on emergent liberation theology (Ballmann 2017). Concurrently there was a revival of Montessori education, inspired by its potential to create peace and transform society (Braga, pers. comm.; Salomão, pers. comm.).

Piper de Lacerda and Eny Caldeira founded the Associação Montessori do Brasil (Montessori Association of Brazil) (AMB) in 1950, training preschool educators (Ballmann 2017). Maria Montessori never traveled to Brazil, and only toward the end of her life would de Lacerda and Caldeira meet Montessori when they studied with her in Perugia, Italy.

Around the same time, European and Brazilian missionaries reintroduced Montessori pedagogy to Brazil (Avelar n.d.). The Associação de Educadores Católicos (Association of Catholic Educators) (AEC) drew Jesuit Priest Pierre Faure from Paris, France, in 1955, where he was a Montessori mathematics specialist and director of the Centre d'Études Pédagogiques (Center of Pedagogical Studies), to train teachers at the Colégio Sacré Coeur (Sacred Heart College) in Rio de Janeiro. In 1956, Brazilian Sister Maria Ana (Celma Pinho Perry) came to direct the Montessori-Lubienska program at Our Lady of Sion in São Paulo. She was inspired by Lubienska de Lenval, whose Montessori training in France widely influenced Montessori education in Brazil. It became known as the Escola Experimental, a major center of New Education (Avelar n.d.).

Perry was an assistant and translator for Father Faure's teacher education seminars for seven years, until she fled the country after giving a lecture that was perceived as overly sympathetic to Paulo Freire and communism (Perry 2016). Montessori education declined following the establishment of a military dictatorship in 1964, stifling freedom of speech.

Father Faure's courses led to an experimental class at the Catholic University (PUC) in Sorocaba, directed by Professor Vera Lagoa between 1961 and 1964, and the adoption of the Montessori method at the Escola Irmã Catarina by Edith Dias Menezes de Azevedo (OMB 2021). Additional Montessori schools were established as early as 1960, such as the Montessori-Lubienska Institute at the Colegio Maria Montessori by Irmã Valentina.

There was a resurgence of Montessori education in the 1970s, though Montessori's emphasis on independence caused discomfort among authorities for its incompatibility with the dictatorial regime (Braga, pers. comm.). In July 1974, the first Brazilian Montessori Congress was organized in São Paulo with 600 participants (Colégio Maria Montessori 2015; *Ata da Sessão Solene* 1974).

Two Brazilian organizations held gatherings during the 1970s: the Associação Brasileira de Educação Montessori (Brazilian Association of Montessori Education) (ABEM) founded in 1974 by Talita de Almeida, and the Associação Montessori do Brasil (Montessori Association of Brazil) (AMB) founded in 1950 by Lacerda and Caldeira. Brazilian Montessori programs continued to grow in number during the 1980s and 1990s with the support of partnering schools. During this time, international schools in São Paulo, Rio de Janeiro, and Campinas opened Montessori programs associated with the American Montessori Society (AMS).

Given the growth of Montessori schools during this period, there was a recognized need for a membership-based organization to support professional growth. The Organização Montessori do Brasil (Montessori Organization of Brazil) (OMB), founded in 1996, represented a single national voice for Montessori education, promoting conferences and translations of Montessori's work. The AMB dissolved after the establishment of the OMB. Internationally respected Montessori educators have enhanced national conferences and broadened outreach. Montessori leaders note that the return of Celma Perry to Brazil in 2005 inspired significant growth, providing training for administrators and teachers in a partnership between OMB and Seton Montessori Institute in Chicago (Almeida, pers. comm.; Lima, pers. comm.).

The Contemporary Landscape

Brazil is home to ethnically and economically diverse populations spread across the fifth largest nation in the world in area. Uneven opportunity creates significant disparities in school attendance by income and race. One promising response has been the promotion of national standards for education reform, the National Education Plan (PNE). Strategic priorities have now shifted toward providing universal preschool for 4-year-olds (Todos Pela Educação 2020).

Today, five Montessori teacher education programs are accredited by OMB, which is currently developing a revised accreditation process (Braga, pers. comm.). Most training focuses on early childhood. Most teacher education programs (TEPs) provide extension or postgraduate credit from universities at which Montessori education is a recognized educational alternative. Though traditional university training provides limited Montessori content, Montessori trainers regularly participate as guest lecturers.

As of June 2021, the OMB website listed sixty-eight affiliated schools. An unknown number of additional Montessori schools operate independently (OMB 2021). OMB data indicate that Montessori schools have increased primarily in the South and Southeast, the majority of which are private schools. The total number of public Montessori programs in Brazil is currently unknown, though notable examples serve low-income students in public, NGO, or social business settings. This is a promising moment for Montessori expansion into the public sector in Brazil.

Realities and Challenges to Expansion

Determining quality and fidelity across Montessori schools remains a challenge. The OMB is currently developing standards to guide schools (Braga, pers. comm.; Salomão, pers. comm.). Nationally, the Brazilian Common Curriculum, applicable to both public and private schools, is compatible with Montessori pedagogy, and legislation allows for alternative practices such as Montessori education's multiage grouping (Braga, pers. comm.). Challenges for new schools include few trained teachers and limited materials. Implementing Montessori programs in the public sector is often affected by local elections and political appointments of school directors.

The trajectory of Montessori education in Brazil saw early and enthusiastic implementation in predominantly private schools, followed by politically turbulent times during which the pedagogy faded from view. The Catholic Church played a significant role in bringing the earliest Montessori training and experimental classes to Brazil, and though freedom of speech was curtailed during the military regime (1964–1985), schools continued to seek balance between nationalistic doctrines and the independence promoted in Montessori philosophy. Today Montessori education thrives in public and private settings, supported by a strong national organization.

Note

Sonia Braga and Joke Verheul read and commented on an earlier version of this chapter.

References

Ata da Sessão Solene de Abertura do Primeiro Congresso Brasileiro de Educação Montessoriano. 1974. Minutes from the First Brazilian Montessori Education Conference. July 6.

Avelar, Aracy. n.d. *Educação Montessoriana.* Unpublished booklet. Rio de Janeiro: Associação Montessori do Brasil.

Ballmann de Campos, Simone. 2017. *A Institucionalização do Método Montessori no Campo Educacional Brasileiro (1914–1952).* PhD diss., Universidade Federal de Santa Catarina.

Colégio Maria Montessori. 2015. "Sobre a Escola Visitada." Accessed August 19, 2021. http://metodologiamontessori10.blogspot.com/2015/.

Hamze, Amelia. 2022. "Escola Nova e o Movimento de Renovação do Ensino." Accessed May 5, 2022. https://educador.brasilescola.uol.com.br/gestao-educacional/escola-nova.htm

Organização Montessori do Brasil (OMB). 2021. "Movimento Montessori no Brasil." Accessed June 9, 2021. http://omb.org.br/educacao-montessori/a-classe-agrupada.

Perry, Celma. 2016. *Living, Creating, Sharing: A Montessori Life.* Santa Rosa: Parent Child Press, A Division of Montessori Services.

Todos Pela Educação. 2020. *Anuário Brasileiro da Educação Básica.* São Paulo: Editora Moderna Ltda.

Chapter 51
Montessori Education in Argentina

Astrid Steverlynck

Argentina, a Spanish-speaking nation of 44.3 million people, is home to an Indigenous population and European immigrants and their descendants, mainly from Italy and Spain. For much of the twentieth century, although Montessori's ideas were influential in Argentinian educational, intellectual and political circles, her method was rarely implemented in full. Inhibiting factors include lack of access to Montessori training and the method's separation from Argentina's high-quality, state-regulated education and teacher training system, which was established in the second half of the nineteenth century. In the last fifteen years, a Montessori resurgence is bringing Montessori education to Argentine children in private and public schools and social programs.

Early Years of Montessori Education

The educational foundations for Montessori education in Argentina began with earlier international educational influences, including ideas of free public elementary education, *Escuelas Normales* (teacher training schools), and Froebelian early childhood education, which came from France and the United States during the 1840s through the 1880s (Ponce 2006; Ponce et al. 2017, 25). These projects laid a strong foundation for progressive early childhood education in Argentina, with significant international connections to the United States and Europe. Throughout this period, educators clashed over access to early childhood education, the role of women in education, and the emphasis placed by the kindergarten model, brought to Argentina in the 1890s, on play versus academic work—themes that emerged again in the context of Montessori education (Ponce 2006).

Montessori's educational ideas were first brought to Argentina in 1911, when Argentina's Consejo Nacional de Educación (National Council of Education) reprinted a translated article about the Montessori method from the British Journal of Education (*El Monitor de la Educación Común* 1911). The first school following Montessori principles was opened by Luis Borruat and the Sociedad Amigos de la Infancia in 1915 in the province of Santa Fe to serve vulnerable children (Ponce 2018).

Early enthusiasm for Montessori pedagogy was tempered by criticism. In 1915, Rosario Vera Peñaloza's published lectures, delivered at the Escuela Normal Roque Saenz Peña, argued that Montessori borrowed a significant amount from Froebel without attribution, and her materials did not add anything of value to the pedagogical practices in the Froebelian kindergarten (Peñaloza 1915). Nevertheless, in 1918, Vera Peñaloza carried out an educational experiment in a private school, the Escuela Argentina Modelo, in which she adapted and innovated on Pestalozzi, Froebel, and Montessori to create an interactive pedagogical museum (Ponce 2011, 45).

Although Montessori might have taken off in Argentina in the 1920s, given the strong interest in progressive "New Education" discussed in education journals like *La Obra* (The Work) and in conferences, Montessori's work remained marginal to broader educational efforts, despite her two-month visit to Argentina in 1926. During her trip, Montessori visited schools, delivered several lectures at universities around Argentina, and taught a training course at the Escuela Normal Roque Saenz Peña in Buenos Aires (Kramer 1988, 299). Despite widespread press attention, her method was criticized for being overly structured compared with other New Education models (Todaro 2019, 355). In general, different practices including Montessori were added to the Froebelian kindergarten, producing eclectic programs, which to this day maintain a strong Froebelian influence. During the following decades there seem to have been few private Montessori programs in Buenos Aires serving mostly international families.

The government of Juan Perón, starting in 1946, resulted in an unprecedented experiment in universal, mandatory early childhood education, which lasted until 1951. In these nationalized classrooms, some Montessori materials were incorporated alongside Froebelian ones, potentially due to the influence of first lady Eva Perón, who had been inspired by the Montessori schools she visited in Europe in 1947 (Bulit 2020). Notable during this period was the fact that early education programs were recognized as a fundamental service and were therefore accessible to all. During the dictatorial regimes that followed, many government-run kindergartens were closed as the responsibility for early childhood education was transferred to the private sector and the church, while the state continued to supervise and subsidize such programs (Ponce 2006).

In the 1960s, there was a second wave of progressive education in Argentina, mostly in the private sector. Around this time, Elena Frondizi, the daughter of President Arturo Frondizi, founded a Montessori primary program in the Italian Olivetti company for children of staff. The contemporary resurgence of Montessori education in Argentina began with the opening of Olivos Montessori School, founded by Patricia Moche and Ana Krieger in 1966 in Patricia's home in Olivos (Bulit 2020). The school remains open today, serving 120 children ages 2–6. The advent of democracy in 1982 again opened the door to educational alternatives. Another Montessori primary and elementary school, Colegio del Rosario, was founded in the 1980s by Herminia Wasserzug but closed in 1996 due to facility problems. Wasserzug continued the Fundación del Rosario, creating a Montessori program in collaboration with the Movimiento Los Sin Techo in Alto Verde, a poor neighborhood in the province of Santa Fe. These individual, private efforts did not coalesce into a broader Montessori movement to the wider Argentine public.

Contemporary Landscape

In the early 2000s, there were two Montessori schools (Olivos Montessori School and Colegio Montessori de Luján, founded in 2006 by Guadalupe Cuevas) and a small group of Montessori enthusiasts. A significant challenge at this time was the absence of Montessori training in Argentina, which limited the availability of trained teachers. Interested educators often needed to travel to Chile for the only Spanish-language Montessori training available at the time in

South America. A short-lived Asociación Montessori Argentina (AMA), founded in 2003, was dissolved shortly after, in 2009.

In 2006, several Montessori parents and enthusiasts—Connie Carballo, Marisa Canova, Maria Labanca, and Veronica Monti—began a Montessori study group, which met on Saturdays at Olivos school. The following year, the group founded the *Fundación Argentina María Montessori* (FAMM), with the mission of contributing to the development of children in Argentina and South America through Montessori principles and practices.

FAMM's first step was to bring AMI trainer Dr. Silvia Dubovoy to facilitate the first AMI primary training course in Buenos Aires. This venture led to regular further trainings, generating a supply of teachers for existing schools and the capacity to open new schools, facilitating a strong Montessori revival in Argentina. Since 2006, over 200 Argentine educators have completed Montessori training. Although the development of a permanent FAMM training center in partnership with a collaborating university to certify Montessori AMI courses at the postsecondary level is underway, in the meantime there is an array of independent, unaffiliated training options of varied quality, many of them online and easily accessible.

With an increase in trained Montessori teachers, the number of programs around Argentina has grown significantly. Since 2006, when there were only two Montessori schools, there are now over forty Montessori programs, primarily located in Buenos Aires and the surrounding region, and more in other Latin American countries (FAMM 2020). The Colegio Montessori de Luján became the first Argentine Montessori elementary school in 2009 and in 2015, expanded into the nation's first Montessori high school.

Achieving official government recognition for the Montessori curriculum has posed an additional challenge. Previously, Olivos Montessori School had made compromises with regard to mixed ages and the uninterrupted work cycle in order to exist under the umbrella of the state curricular standards. Colegio Montessori de Luján, run by Guadalupe Cuevas and her team, became the first school with a Montessori curriculum officially recognized by the Argentine government in 2010. An additional challenge, however, is that all teachers, whether at a public or private school, have to be certified in an official state-recognized teacher training program in addition to their Montessori training.

Alongside developing training and seeking state recognition, FAMM is focused on providing quality education to disadvantaged children (see Figure 51.1). This work started in 2008 in partnership with Casa del Niño María de Nazareth, a nongovernment organization (NGO). This program has become a model for FAMM partnerships with other social programs offering Montessori education to low-income communities. These partnerships have developed into a support network of NGOs called Red Montessori Solidario (RMS). Currently, there are twenty-three Montessori programs in sixteen vulnerable communities that participate in RMS, reaching more than 1,200 children and their families (FAMM 2020). FAMM supports the network by offering training scholarships and professional development, providing coaching, organizing an annual conference, and distributing donated materials and resources.

Since 2014, the Argentine government has mandated education for four-year-olds, but only 14 percent of eligible children find a space in public or social programs. To address this deficit, FAMM has collaborated with several municipalities to offer Montessori education in several public schools and government-run early childhood education centers, including two early education centers in the city of Vicente Lopez, a suburb of Buenos Aires. Another

Children reached by Montessori education in Argentina (2020)
By age
Total number of children: 2654

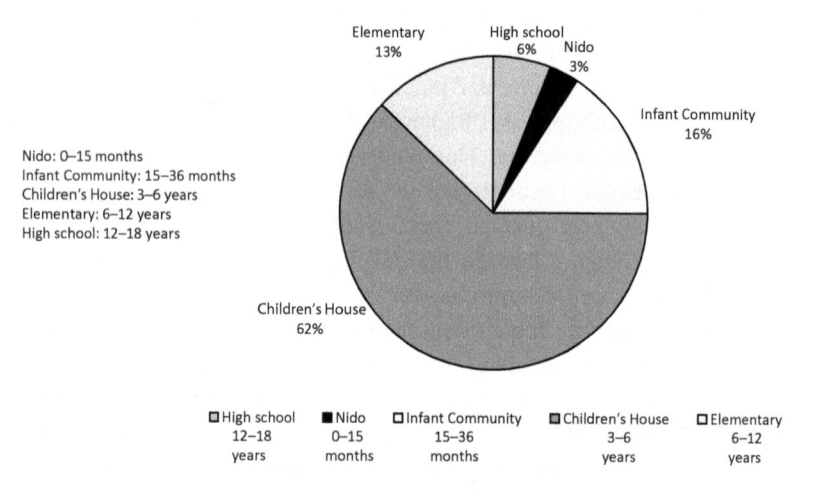

Nido: 0–15 months
Infant Community: 15–36 months
Children's House: 3–6 years
Elementary: 6–12 years
High school: 12–18 years

- Elementary 13%
- High school 6%
- Nido 3%
- Infant Community 16%
- Children's House 62%

Children reached by Montessori education in Argentina (2020)
By context
Total number of children: 2654

- Private 49%
- Public 32%
- RMS 19%

RMS: Red Montessori Solidario, Montessori programs in underserved communities, usually run by NGOs

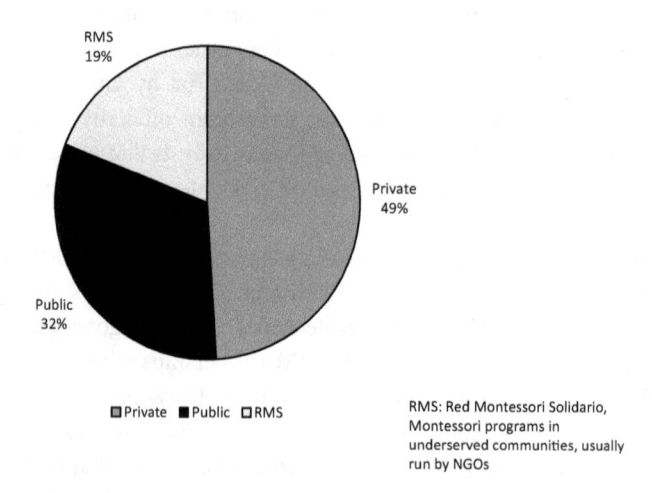

Figure 51.1 Children reached by Montessori education in Argentina in 2020 (N = 2654). Image courtesy of Fundación Argentina María Montessori (FAMM).

project, Crianza Juntos (Parenting Together), undertaken with the province of Buenos Aires, has implemented Montessori education in nine early education centers, with an ongoing evaluation carried out by researchers at the Universidad Torcuato Di Tella. In each of these projects, FAMM follows Educateurs Sans Frontieres' framework for community-rooted programs in underserved communities (see Chapter 38: "AMI Educateurs Sans Frontières").

Today, interest in Argentina might be described as a "Montessori frenzy," with countless mentions of the method in magazines, blogs, and books. Montessori education is also commercialized with Montessori toys, Montessori furniture, Montessori clothes, and Montessori home goods appearing as popular search categories in Argentine online retail platforms. While this increased demand provides greater impetus to families and educators in creating new Montessori schools, there is also the risk of Montessori education being adopted piecemeal rather than as an integrated program.

Conclusion

While Montessori education has been a topic of interest to educators and theorists in Argentina since the early twentieth century, it is only recently that Montessori education has begun rapidly expanding around the country. The founding of FAMM in 2007 made Montessori training widely available and has greatly expanded the number of trained Montessori educators, assistants, and public, private, and social programs. Argentina's Red Montessori Solidario network provides an important model for developing and expanding Montessori programs in low-income communities. With the continued expansion of early childhood education, steady public interest in Montessori education, and efforts to develop a local training pipeline underway, there is potential for Montessori education to continue growing in Argentina.

Note

Milagros Canellada, Silvana Grecco, Marisa Canova, and Constanza Carballo contributed information to this chapter.

References

Bulit, Dolores. 2020. *Montessori en Argentina: Una Historia de Pequeños Pasos desde 1910 Hasta Hoy.* https://alteredu.com.ar/2020/09/14/montessori-en-argentina-una-historia-de-pequenos-pasos-desde-1910-hasta-hoy/.

El Monitor de la Educación Común: Órgano del Consejo Nacional de Educación. 1911. Journal of Education. El Método Montessori 29 (457): 166–71. http://www.bnm.me.gov.ar/giga1/monitor/monitor/457.pdf#page=164.

Fundación Argentina María Montessori (FAMM). 2020. Survey to Schools.

Kramer, Rita. 1988. *Maria Montessori: A Biography*. New York, NY: Addison Wesley Publishing Company.

Ponce, Rosana E. 2006. "Los Debates de la Educación Inicial en la Argentina. Persistencias, Transformaciones y Resignificaciones a lo Largo de la Historia." In *Experiencias y reflexiones sobre la educación inicial: Una mirada latinoamericana*, edited by Ana Malajovich. Buenos Aires: Siglo XXI.

Ponce, Rosana E. 2011. "Herencia y Legado Pedagógico para la Educación Inicial Argentina: Rosario Vera Peñaloza." In *Biografías Maestras*, edited by Silvia Laffranconi, 31–53. Buenos Aires: Ministerio de Educación de la Nación.

Ponce, Rosana E. 2018. "Los Inicios del Jardín de Infantes y de la Formación de Maestras Jardineras en Argentina: Polémicas y Debates Pedagógicos (1884–1944)." In *Cadernos de Pesquisa em Educação*. PPGE/UFES 20 (47): 12–32.

Ponce, Rosana E., Noemí A. Simon and Ana M. Encabo. 2017. *Apuntes de Historia y Política del Nivel Inicial*. Luján: Editorial Universidad de Luján.

Todaro, Letterio. 2019. "Between New Education and Idealistic Vision: Giuseppe Lombardo Radice and the Arduous Path of L'Educazione Nazionale in Italy (1927–1933)." *Schweizerische Zeitschrift für Bildungswissenschaften* 41 (2): 354–68. http://doi.org/10.24452/sjer.41.2.6/.

Vera Peñaloza, Rosario. 1915. *Estudio Comparativo de los Sistemas Montessori y Froebeliano*. Buenos Aires: Sociedad Nacional de Kindergarten.

Chapter 52
Future Directions for Global Montessori Research

Joel Parham

Part V on Global Montessori Education has aggregated over a century's worth of international history and research regarding Montessori education. The field of Montessori research continues to rapidly expand—Google Scholar shows more than 43,000 sources referencing "Montessori" have been created in the last decade. Likewise, global academic research centers devoted to Montessori education are also growing; these include Center for Montessori Research (University of Kansas, USA); Center for Montessori Studies (University of Hartford, USA); Centro di Studi Montessoriani (Roma Tre University, Italy); Montessori-Palau International Research and Training Center (Spain); Montessori-Zentrum Münster (University of Münster, Germany); and Educational Research in Citizenship Competences (Stockholm University, Sweden), among others. Yet there is still more to be uncovered and shared, especially in research across cultures and languages.

This chapter aims to spotlight several future directions for global Montessori research and is arranged into four thematic groupings: (1) supporting displaced communities and cultural preservation through Montessori education; (2) global expansion of public or government-funded Montessori education; (3) efficacy of Montessori education for children around the globe; and (4) histories of Montessori education in other countries and regions omitted from chapter-length country profiles in this section.

The chapter ends with information about the Montessori Bibliography Online, a resource I created as a research archivist to collate Montessori sources spread across libraries, archives, and other repositories around the globe.

Supporting Displaced Communities and Cultural Preservation through Montessori Education

There is a century-long history of Montessori education among refugees or in displaced communities. In 1916, in the midst of the First World War, Montessori education was employed by Mary Cromwell among refugee children in Paris (Cromwell 1919). During the war, Maria Montessori herself was directly involved in supporting war-displaced European children through an attempt to establish a group known as the White Cross (Montessori 1918; Moretti 2021).

In 1960, Tibetan Children's Villages (TCV) was established in Tibetan refugee communities in India, and they decided to use Montessori education to educate their youngest children as part of efforts to retain their language and culture in exile (Eckert 2007). Similarly, Montessori-based educational institutions have been established for refugees along the Thailand-Myanmar border, through the Corner of Hope initiative in Kenya, and for Syrian refugees in Jordan and Turkey (Educateurs sans Frontières 2021; Hadaya Global 2021; Tobin et al. 2015). The recurrence of Montessori education in these settings prompts several questions: what do these programs have in common, how effective are they at providing quality educational experiences while also preserving and transmitting cultural heritage to the next generation, and how might they serve as educational models for displaced persons?

Global Expansion of Public or Government-Funded Montessori Education

Just as Montessori for displaced persons expands traditional audiences for Montessori schools, public or government-supported Montessori education expands the method's reach beyond its predominance in private schools. There is a long history of government-supported Montessori education in a number of nations, including India, Italy, the Netherlands, New Zealand, and Sweden.

For example, the New Zealand Ministry of Education implemented the Montessori method in at least one of their affiliate schools in the early twentieth century (May 2011; Miltich-Conway and Openshaw 1988); a number of European nations historically supported Montessori education through government funding; and, after the collapse of the Soviet Union, the Ukrainian government revisited a pre-Soviet era interest in the Montessori method and ultimately established a public Montessori school in the early 1990s (Zherbovsky 1995). As of 2021, the Montessori Census reports there are 565 public Montessori schools in the USA (National Center for Montessori in the Public Sector 2021).

Much of the recent research pertaining to public Montessori schools has focused on the American context (e.g., Debs 2019; Debs and Brown 2017), alongside some research about Montessori education and school choice in the Netherlands (e.g., Boterman 2013).

Potential avenues for future research include (1) historical analysis of public Montessori on a regional, national, and global scale; (2) analysis of public Montessori schools as a tool for reforming educational programs; (3) studies of who participates in public Montessori programs and how these programs fit into the larger education ecosystems of the regions in which they are located; (4) evaluations of the outcomes of public Montessori students; and (5) ethnographic research into public Montessori families and educators in relation to their perceptions of the pedagogy.

Efficacy of Montessori Education for Children around the Globe

As Montessori education expands to children in diverse cultural, social, and economic contexts around the world, a recurring question is how effective Montessori education is for these diverse groups of children. Thus far, research related to the efficacy of Montessori education has predominantly been focused on the American (Basargekar and Lillard 2021; Fleming et al. 2019; Lillard et al. 2017) and European contexts (Courtier et al. 2021; Ruijs 2017). A few recent studies have explored the efficacy of Montessori education in other contexts: Ecuador (Ascencio et al. 2020), Cyprus (Ender and Ozcan 2019), Indonesia (Budiani 2019), and Turkey (Dereli İman et al. 2017).

Topics for future research could include (1) cross-cultural comparisons of implementations and their outcomes; (2) longitudinal examinations of outcomes in different geographic and cultural contexts; (3) evaluations of implementations and their fidelity to standardized Montessori models; (4) implementation of Montessori education in traditional schools; (5) the impact of Montessori organizations; (6) challenges and possibilities, from a cultural and religious perspective, related to the implementation of Montessori education; or (7) the interpretation and adaptation of Montessori education in different cultures.

Histories of Montessori Education in Other Countries and Regions

A significant amount of Montessori history related to various regions is in local languages or is contained within archival and primary sources that have yet to be the subject of academic study. The following regional subsections highlight relevant research in English and local languages in countries and regions that have not been addressed in this Global section.

Caribbean

In recent years several Caribbean nations have taken particular interest in public Montessori education. Historical accounts of these efforts tend to be cloistered in Montessori organizational publications or only in local-language publications. More recently, there has been some coverage in newspapers regarding Montessori schools in the Caribbean, most notably in Barbados and the US Virgin Islands (Rowe-Forde 2016; Tarta 2008).

Australasia

While the history of Montessori in Australia is well documented, there is less research regarding other countries in this region, specifically New Zealand and Indonesia. New Zealand has a long history with Montessori which stretches back to the early twentieth century (May 2011;

Miltich-Conway and Openshaw 1988). Nicola Chisnall, who died in 2013, left behind a powerful scholarly legacy regarding Montessori education in New Zealand (e.g., Chisnall 2002, 2011). Additionally, the work of Montessori educator Binda Mary Goldsbrough is worthy of scholarly evaluation (Goldsbrough). Indonesia has a history with Montessori education that extends to at least the mid-twentieth century, though many sources are in local languages (e.g., Budiani 2019; Mumtazah and Romah 2018).

South Asia

Montessori's history in South Asia outside of India is generally limited in its documentation. Sri Lanka has a long history with Montessori education which predates the country's independence from India (when it was known as Ceylon) and is connected to the work of pioneers Lena Wikramaratne and Albert Max Joosten as well as the work of the Good Shepherd Training Center in Colombo (Benildus 1994) (see Figure 52.1).

Bhutan's history with Montessori education appears to date to the 1990s and incorporates grassroots and international philanthropic efforts (Global Partnership for Education 2021; Michael

Figure 52.1 Children in Sri Lanka work in a Montessori classroom, date unknown. Courtesy of the Maria Montessori Archives, photo section, Amsterdam.

Olaf Foundation n.d.; Monaghan 1992). These efforts emphasize developing Montessori practice to align with Bhutanese cultural practices; documentation regarding the spread of Montessori and its impact is needed, particularly from the Bhutanese perspective.

Montessori education in Nepal appears to have begun in 1949 (Joshi 1996), but there are limited sources related to the contemporary Montessori education landscape in Nepal.

Maria Montessori offered training in Pakistan pre-partition, though after independence, efforts in Pakistan and later, Bangladesh were separated from the Montessori efforts in India, and contemporary documentation regarding the movement's development is limited (Joosten 1971; Khushi 2008).

Middle East

Outside of Saudi Arabia and Egypt, the history of the Montessori movement in the Middle East has limited documentation—particularly in English publications (e.g., Kotob and Antippa 2020 on Lebanon; Hadaya Global 2021 on Syrian refugees in Jordan and Turkey; Ender and Ozcan 2019; Dereli İman et al. 2017). Research related to this region's history with Montessori education is important, and translation of existing sources in local languages to other languages is valuable for the dissemination of these histories.

Europe

The Montessori movement in Europe is generally well documented, with comparatively more limited documentation of Montessori in Belgium, France, and Spain. The existing literature related to Montessori in France appears to be concentrated in a few sources (Gilsoul 2012, 2014; Huard 2018; Leroy 2020). Belgium has a mixed history with Montessori education due to overlapping influences of Froebel, Decroly, and Montessori (Van Gorp et al. 2017; Thirion 1975). Thirion indicates that from 1927 to 1950 Montessori was particularly important in Belgium (1975, 159), yet little scholarship is devoted to an analysis of Montessori education in Belgium. Further research into this history could be aided by sources which reveal archival and primary sources (e.g., Bonet Abelló 2017; Rubí and García 2012).

Montessori Bibliography Online (MBO)

All of the sources referenced here are listed in the Montessori Bibliography Online (MBO), hosted by the University of Kansas Center for Montessori Research as a resource for future research.[1] The MBO compiles a wide range of citations from library and Montessori indexes and databases around the world to make information about Montessori education and the Montessori movement more accessible. Building on past Montessori print bibliographies and indexes, the MBO's online interface provides direct links to digitized source materials with an intuitive user interface and a robust search capability.

Conclusion

This chapter outlines a number of potential areas for future research related to Montessori in global geographic and cultural contexts, with bibliographical references serving as portals to further research. Cross-cultural comparisons of Montessori education can be facilitated through multilingual scholarship and/or the translation of existing scholarship in order to enable greater visibility of Montessori research. In addition to research about current implementations of Montessori education across the globe, research regarding the history of international Montessori education is similarly vital. As additional research continues to develop this historical picture, so does the understanding of the strengths and weaknesses of the Montessori implementations in various national contexts. This knowledge will empower the Montessori community to become stronger and more resilient, and will also enhance efforts to increase exposure and awareness of Montessori education.

Note

1. The Montessori Bibliography Online (MBO) is accessible at https://montessoribib.ku.edu.

References

Ascencio, Lidia Estrella, Norma Garcés Garcés, and Zila Esteves Fajardo. 2020. "La Aplicación del Método Montessori en la Educación Infantil Ecuatoriana." *Revista SATHIRI: Sembrador* 15 (1): 122–31. https://doi.org/10.32645/13906925.935.

Basargekar, Abha, and Angeline S. Lillard. 2021. "Math Achievement Outcomes Associated with Montessori Education." *Early Child Development and Care* 191 (7–8): 1207–18. https://doi.org/10.1080/03004430.2020.1860955.

Benildus, Sister M. 1994. "50 Years of Montessori in Sri Lanka: 1944–1994." *Communications of the Association Montessori Internationale* (4): 13.

Bonet Abelló, Roser. 2017. "El mètode Montessori a Catalunya a través de revistes i publicacions periòdiques (1911–2014)." Master's thesis, Vic, Spain: University de Vic.

Boterman, Willem R. 2013. "Dealing with Diversity: Middle-Class Family Households and the Issue of 'Black' and 'White' Schools in Amsterdam." *Urban Studies* 50 (6): 1130–47. https://doi.org/10.32645/13906925.935.

Budiani, Yohana Silviani Eka. 2019. "Manajemen Pendidikan Karakter Metode Montessori di Jogjakarta Montessori School." *Media Manajemen Pendidikan* 2 (2): 251–9. https://doi.org/10.30738/mmp.v2i2.5072.g2662.

Chisnall, Nicola. 2002. "On Spinning, Weaving and Darning: Changing Perspectives on Montessori in Aotearoa-New Zealand, 1975–2000." Master's thesis, Wellington: Victoria University of Wellington.

Chisnall, Nicola. 2011. "Montessori Education in Aotearoa-New Zealand: A Framework for Peace and Social Justice." PhD diss., Auckland: Auckland University of Technology.

Courtier, Philippine, Marie-Line Gardes, Jean-Baptiste Van der Henst, Ira A. Noveck, Marie-Caroline Croset, Justine Epinat-Duclos, Jessica Léone, and Jérôme Prado. 2021. "Effects of Montessori Education on the Academic, Cognitive, and Social Development of Disadvantaged Preschoolers: A Randomized Controlled Study in the French Public-School System." *Child Development* 92 (5): 2069–88. https://doi.org/10.1111/cdev.13575.

Cromwell, Mary R. 1919. "Il Metodo Montessori Francia Durante la Guerra." *La Coltura Popolare: Organo dell'Unione Italiana dell'Educazione Popolare* 9 (1): 46–53.

Debs, Mira C. 2019. *Diverse Families, Desirable Schools: Public Montessori in the Era of School Choice*. Cambridge: Harvard Education Press.

Debs, Mira C., and Katie E. Brown. 2017. "Students of Color and Public Montessori Schools: A Review of the Literature." *Journal of Montessori Research* 3 (1): 1–15. https://doi.org/10.17161/jomr.v3i1.5859.

Dereli İman, Esra, Şahin Danişman, Zeynep Akin Demircan, and Dilara Yaya. 2017. "The Effect of the Montessori Education Method on Pre-School Children's Social Competence, Behaviour and Emotion Regulation Skills." *Early Child Development and Care* 189 (9): 1–15. https://doi.org/10.1080/03004430.2017.1392943.

Eckert, Ela. 2007. "Montessori Education in Exiled Tibetan Children's Villages." *NAMTA Journal* 32 (1): 171–95.

Éducateurs sans Frontières. 2021. "Corner of Hope." Éducateurs sans Frontières (EsF) 2021. https://montessori-esf.org/corner-hope.

Ender, Devrim, and Deniz Ozcan. 2019. "Self-Efficacy Perceptions of Teachers on Using the Montessori Method in Special Education in North Cyprus." *Cypriot Journal of Educational Sciences* 14 (4): 652–60. https://doi.org/10.18844/cjes.v11i4.4480.

Fleming, David J., Brooke T. Culclasure, and Daniel Zhang. 2019. "The Montessori Model and Creativity." *Journal of Montessori Research* 5 (2): 1–14. https://doi.org/10.17161/jomr.v5i2.7695.

Gilsoul, Martine. 2012. "Hélène Lubienska de Lenval (1895–1972): Montessori et l'audace de l'intuition." *History of Education and Children's Literature* 7 (2): 221–40.

Gilsoul, Martine. 2014. "Maria Montessori et la France: Genèse d'une histoire." *History of Education and Children's Literature* 9 (2): 379–98.

Global Partnership for Education. 2021. "Bhutan." https://www.globalpartnership.org/where-we-work/bhutan.

Goldsbrough, Binda M. "Goldsbrough, Binda Mary, 1912–2008: Papers Relating to Montessori Method of Education in New Zealand." Wellington, New Zealand. MS-Group-1708. National Library of New Zealand. https://natlib.govt.nz/records/22682372.

Hadaya Global. 2021. "Maha's Montessori Mission." Hadaya Global. https://hadayaglobal.com/mahas-montessori.

Huard, Chrystel. 2018. "L'Essor Actuel de la Pédagogie Montessori dans l'École Maternelle Publique Française." *Tréma* (50): 1–22. https://doi.org/10.4000/trema.4318.

Joosten, Albert M. 1971. "The Expansion of the Montessori Method in India and Neighboring Countries." In *Maria Montessori's Contribution to Educational Thought and Practice*, edited by Albert M. Joosten and Rajendra K. Gupta, 62–70. New Delhi: Association of Delhi Montessorians.

Joshi, Radha Krishna. 1996. "Status of Early Childhood Education in Nepal." *International Journal of Early Childhood* 28 (2): 57–61. https://doi.org/10.1007/BF03174504.

Khushi, Razia. 2008. "The Catechesis of the Good Shepherd Comes to Pakistan." *The Catechesis of the Good Shepherd* 23: 25–6.

Kotob, Mazen, and Venise Antippa. 2020. "Peace Education: A Case Study of a Montessori School in Lebanon." *Millennium Journal of Humanities and Social Sciences* 1 (3): 44–68. https://doi.org/10.47340/mjhss.v1i3.4.2020.

Leroy, Ghislain. 2020. "'Ateliers' et activités montessoriennes à l'école maternelle: quel profit pour les plus faibles?" *Revue Française de Pédagogie* 207 (2): 119–31. https://doi.org/10.4000/rfp.9296.

Lillard, Angeline S., Megan J. Heise, Eve M. Richey, Xin Tong, Alyssa Hart, and Paige M. Bray. 2017. "Montessori Preschool Elevates and Equalizes Child Outcomes: A Longitudinal Study." *Frontiers in Psychology* 8: 1783. https://doi.org/10.3389/fpsyg.2017.01783.

May, Helen. 2011. "Experiments and Expediency, 1910s – 1930s." In *I Am Five and I Go to School: Early Years Schooling in New Zealand, 1900–2010*, edited by Helen May, 75–121. Dunedin: Otago University Press.

Michael Olaf Foundation. n.d. "Montessori Bhutan Project 2006–2013." Accessed December 20, 2021. http://www.michaelolaf.net/bhutan.html.

Miltich-Conway, Betsy, and Roger Openshaw. 1988. "The Montessori Method in the Wanganui Education Board District, 1911–24." *New Zealand Journal of Educational Studies* 23 (2): 189–201.

Monaghan, Janet. 1992. "In the Land of the Peaceful Dragon." *Montessori Courier* 3 (6): 16–17.

Montessori, Maria. 1918. "The White Cross: An Appeal." *The Herald of the Star* 7 (2): 97–8.

Moretti, Erica. 2021. *The Best Weapon for Peace: Maria Montessori, Education, and Children's Rights*. Madison: University of Wisconsin Press.

Mumtazah, Durotun, and Lailatu Romah. 2018. "Implementasi Prinsip-prinsip Montessori dalam Pembelajaran AUD." *Golden Age: Jurnal Ilmiah Tumbuh Kembang Anak Usia Dini* 3 (2): 91–102. https://doi.org/10.14421/jga.2018.32-03.

Pendleton, D. Renee. 2002. *The NAMTA Montessori Bibliography and Research Guide*, 3rd ed. Burton, OH: North American Montessori Teachers' Association. (Published as a special issue of The *NAMTA Journal*, Vol. 27, no. 2).

Rowe-Forde, Peta. 2016. "St. Luke's Academy Opened." *Barbados Advocate*, September 1, 2016.

Rubí, Francesca Comas, and Bernat Sureda García. 2012. "The Photography and Propaganda of the Maria Montessori Method in Spain (1911–1931)." *Paedagogica Historica: International Journal of the History of Education* 48 (4): 571–87. https://doi.org/10.1080/00309230.2011.633924.

Ruijs, Nienke. 2017. "The Effects of Montessori Education: Evidence from Admission Lotteries." *Economics of Education Review* 61: 19–34. https://doi.org/10.1016/j.econedurev.2017.09.001.

Tarta, Katie. 2008. "St. John Montessori School Coming Soon." *St. John Tradewinds*, July 7.

Thirion, Anne-Marie. 1975. "Early Childhood Education in Belgium." *International Journal of Early Childhood* 7 (2): 159. https://doi.org/10.1007/BF03176101.

Tobin, Tierney, Prairie Boulmier, Wenyi Zhu, Paul Hancock, and Peter Muenning. 2015. "Improving Outcomes for Refugee Children: A Case Study on the Impact of Montessori Education Along the Thai-Burma Border." *International Education Journal: Comparative Perspectives* 14 (3): 138–49.

Van Gorp, Angelo, Frank Simon, and Marc Depaepe. 2017. "Frictions and Fractions in the New Education Fellowship, 1920s-1930s: Montessori(ans) vs. Decroly(ans)." *History of Education and Children's Literature* 12 (1): 251–70.

Zherbovsky, Boris. 1995. "Montessori in the Former USSR: Ukraine Government Opens a Montessori School." *Public School Montessorian* 7 (4): 20.

PART VI

Contemporary Considerations Regarding Montessori Education

Introduction: Contemporary Considerations Regarding Montessori Education

Maria K. McKenna

Maria Montessori's vision of education has weathered over a century of scrutiny and adaptation despite not being a part of the traditional canon of educational studies. This unto itself is notable. However, it is common in education circles to only read the work of psychologists Jean Piaget, Lev Vygotsky, and B. F. Skinner alongside philosophers John Dewey, Jean Jacques Rousseau, and Plato; all are considered classical thinkers who laid the foundation of modern education with little regard to female influences, including Montessori. Our educational canon has remained unmoved for much of modern history and within educator training, Montessori seldom gets more than a passing mention or a brief paragraph in a text after intense study of the figures noted above. And yet, Montessori schools, educational programs, and influences have remained a presence in the world of education and continue to gain traction. That Montessori education is both eschewed in traditional educator training and still a relatively significant mode of schooling around the globe is an interesting phenomenon. It is a testament to the tight, though sometimes insular, network of Montessori adherents who have worked to buoy and protect her teachings while also promoting careful and rigorous training. It is simultaneously a testament to the ability of Montessori's work toward peace withstanding the monumental political, technological, and social changes our world has undergone since the beginning of her teachings.

As we learned in previously in the handbook, especially Part V, Montessori's vision was carried across the globe via a number of transnational networks, disciplines, and individuals—networks which continue to expand today. Part IV of the handbook provides insight into the growing body of contemporary psychology and neuroscience supporting many of Montessori's observations and hypotheses about child development, concentration, memory, and motivation. In this way, Montessori education seems to have entered a new and exciting era of its history. Montessori pedagogy is undergoing new and different types of scientific study but also novel, and necessarily more thorough, historical, and cultural scrutiny as well.

Given that contemporary interest in Montessori education remains strong, so, too, does the need to consider the ways Montessori pedagogy must adapt to be more inclusive, thoughtful, and responsive to a changing world. We call on educators and researchers to revisit Montessori's historical and philosophical legacies and understand them differently within cultural and chronological frameworks. Montessori's words, "the cloak of charity and fraternity will be the symbol of a new Humanity" from her work, *The Forgotten Citizen*, are as important now as when she first shared them three quarters of a century ago (Montessori 1951, 3). As ever more inclusive interpretations of cultural influences, language, disability, gender, and economic complexities emerge in the world, this scrutiny is both warranted and important for Montessori's pedagogy. Montessori's writing and teaching are not immune to critique nor should they be in our estimation as editors and writers; in fact, quite the opposite. To this end, our goal is to not only be instructive about Montessori's vast body of writing and teachings and the pedagogical applications of those teachings but also provide space for contemporary questions around her work and its far-reaching implementation to enable it to continue to expand. This section has a strong focus on North America, particularly on topics related to racial and cultural identity, though we understand this content as valuable even outside of their specific contexts. If one believes that Montessori should play a larger role in the educational dialogue then there must also be a willingness to consider Montessori through new lenses and with fresh conversation. We use person-first language honoring varied identities including indigeneity, race, ethnicity, disability, language, gender identity, and age in our writing. Our work also considers the legacy of Montessori's vision of a less anthropocentric view of the world with a focus on all living things. Integral human development is central to her vision and attempts to consider the wider impact of our individual and collective actions on the world. She writes, "[A]n education capable of saving humanity is no small undertaking; it involves the spiritual development of the man, the enhancement of his value as an individual, and the preparation of young people to understand the times in which they live" (Montessori 2007, 30). The section is reflective, illustrative, and forward-looking, as Montessori herself tried to be.

Montessori scholars often write about how she was ahead of her time with the interdisciplinary nature of her observations of children and the combination of her anthropological, medical, and philosophical backgrounds. It is in this interdisciplinary spirit that Part VI is written and presented here.

References

Montessori, Maria. 1951. *The Forgotten Citizen*. Amsterdam: Association Montessori Internationale.
Montessori, Maria. 2007. *Education and Peace*. Amsterdam: Montessori-Pierson.

Chapter 53
Montessori Education in the Digital Age

Elizabeth K. Park and Angela K. Murray

We live in an era where technology and digital media are ubiquitous and have the potential for both positive and negative impacts. As technology permeates much of society, it is naturally incorporated into educational settings and, over the past 20 years, Montessori educators have been asking what Maria Montessori would say about the expansion of technology and digital media in education in general and in Montessori classrooms in particular. Buckleitner (2015), an educational researcher specializing in the design of interactive media, argued that Montessori would have embraced technology. He explained how Montessori spoke positively about emerging technologies of her time such as X-rays and radio. If Montessori were alive today, he believes she would incorporate technology such as iPads as part of her materials because she was a "scientist who was future-centric" (64). However, he also stated that Montessori would be selective about the types of apps she would include on her iPad and that she would recognize sensory limitations of the iPad, using it only to supplement and extend real-life experiences (Buckleitner 2015).

In this chapter, we first describe the foundations of educational technology in Montessori education. Next, we examine the historical background of educational technology in the field of education more broadly. Finally, we outline current perspectives on integrating technology into Montessori environments for the early childhood, elementary, and adolescent age levels as well as Montessori teacher preparation programs.

Foundations of Educational Technology in Montessori Education

To lay out the historical context for understanding educational technology within the Montessori classroom, we begin with examining Montessori's relationship with the technology of her time. Evidence of a positive relationship comes from a 2015 *AMI Journal Treasure Articles* publication. This reprinted an introduction Montessori had written for a publication in India supporting the use of mechanical aids in education (illustrations, maps, models, charts, gramophone, film, slides, photographs, etc.). Montessori wrote,

> I believe, however, that the introduction of mechanical aids will become a general need in the schools of the future. There is no doubt that the schools applying my method, where the cultural development of the children is highly intensified not on account of any pressure exercised by the teacher, but as a natural consequence

of the opportunities given to their individual and social spontaneous activities, will have to avail themselves of these new aids.

(Montessori 2015, 5)

The text accompanying this publication of Montessori's writing emphasized that she was "fascinated by the technology of her time, which absolutely delighted her and where she recognized opportunities to unite our world," and she enjoyed air travel, cinema, and telegram communication from aboard ship (3). In her narrative, Montessori discussed how slides and films provided students with connections to speakers and experts with a depth of knowledge that surpassed that of classroom teachers. In an interview with Buckleitner (2015, 64), former AMI executive director Virginia McHugh stated her belief regarding current technology's fit into Montessori philosophy, saying, "Montessori would appreciate the deep, intuitive connection the iPad fosters between content and user, taking working with knowledge to another level."

However, Montessori's openness to technological advances did not detract from her commitment to the foundational concepts of her philosophy. She continued to emphasize the importance of hands-on activity:

> Children do not learn and do not develop their character by merely listening and looking on. Auditory and visual aids therefore, although very important indeed, are only partial aids. The child learns by means of his own activity and if given an opportunity to learn actively he develops his character and personality too. The child perfects himself even more by means of his hand than by means of the senses.
>
> *(Montessori 2015, 7)*

Montessori also suggested incorporating mechanical aids specifically for elementary children who have mastered reading and writing and who have established a strong cultural foundation (Montessori 2015). Even so, the fact that Montessori embraced the technology of her time is even more relevant when considering the parallels between the agricultural to industrial transition of the 1910s and today's cultural transformation brought about by the Information Age (Buckleitner 2015).

Educational Technology in the Broader Field of Education

The historical context for technology and digital media in Montessori classrooms today also requires understanding the evolution of educational technology more broadly.

Evolution of Language and Guidelines for Incorporating Educational Technology

Several organizations focus on issues in instructional design and technology. Among the oldest and largest is the Association for Educational Communications and Technology (AECT). It was established in 1923 and now has affiliates in twenty-four states and six countries. It is the "national and international voice for improvement of instruction and the most recognized association of information concerning a wide range of instructional and educational technology" (AECT 2022). Today, the organization defines educational technology as "the study and ethical application of theory, research, and best practices to advance knowledge as well as mediate and improve learning and performance through the strategic design, management and implementation of learning and instructional processes and resources" (AECT 2022).

In a book outlining the work of AECT, Januszewski and Persichitte (2008) describe how the definition of educational technology developed over time. As technology changed its form and use over the years, three major conceptual changes occurred, each marked by an accompanying shift in terminology. The first conceptual shift moved understanding technology as a *product* to understanding it as a *process*. This marked the beginning of a paradigm shift as technologists moved their focus from the technologies to the instructional systems that used them (Januszewski and Persichitte 2008). In 1972 came the second change in terminology—from the use of terms "materials" and "machines" to "messages" and "media instrumentation," and from "audiovisual communication" to "educational technology" (Januszewski and Persichitte 2008, 261). These terms reflected a new focus on three central concepts in the field: a broad range of learning resources, individualized and personalized learning, and the use of the systems approach. Finally, in the 1990s, the third major shift introduced the term "instructional technology," further reinforcing the process by incorporating technology into the art of instruction as a field for practitioners and scholars (Januszewski and Persichitte 2008, 271).

The International Society for Technology in Education (ISTE) is another leading organization in instructional technology. ISTE provides standards "for learning, teaching and leading in the digital age, providing a comprehensive roadmap for the effective use of technology in schools worldwide" (ISTE n.d.). Their standards, which have evolved over the organization's twenty-five-year history, no longer focus on technology skills and simply learning with technology; rather, they focus on transforming learning through technology. The focus also shifted from teacher-driven classrooms to student-centered and student-driven classrooms (Crompton 2017).

Of particular interest is the role of educational technology in the early years of education, particularly from birth through age 8. In the United States, the National Association for the Education of Young Children (NAEYC) and the Fred Rogers Center collaborated on writing the first technology joint position statement in 2012. This position statement offers guidance—based on research-based knowledge of how young children grow and learn—on both the opportunities and the challenges of the use of technology and interactive media. The statement focuses on their use in early childhood programs—schools, centers, family childcare—serving children from birth through age 8. The key messages were the following:

> (a) when used intentionally and appropriately, technology and interactive media are effective tools to support learning and development; (b) intentional use requires early childhood teachers and administrators to have information and resources regarding the nature of these tools and the implications of their use with children; (c) limitations on the use of technology and media are important; (d) special considerations must be given to the use of technology with infants and toddlers; (e) attention to digital citizenship and equitable access is essential; and (f) ongoing research and professional development are needed.
>
> *(NAEYC and Fred Rogers Center 2012, 1–15)*

Following the position statement, Donohue and Schomburg (2017, 78) shared what they learned in five years of research:

> Five years ago, NAEYC and the Fred Rogers Center took a bold step in laying out a vision for the critical role technology can play in early learning programs. While the position statement was clearly about technology, it wasn't about which apps to use or how to unlock digital coding. It was directed at early childhood educators and what they, classroom and program leaders, must know and be able to do in order to effectively use technology. Five years later, that is still the most important aspect of our work with technology. Neuroscience and behavioral science point to unparalleled cognitive, physical, and social, and emotional growth in young children. These sciences have also shown us that our lifelong approaches to learning—things like initiative, curiosity, motivation, engagement, problem-solving, and self-regulation—are at their height of development in the early years.

One influence on the changing definition of educational technology in the United States was the National Education Technology Plan (NETP). This set a national vision and plan for learning enabled by technology, building on the work of experts in a variety of fields: leading education researchers; district, school, and higher education leaders; classroom teachers; developers; entrepreneurs; and nonprofit organizations (U.S. Department of Education 2017). Two of the major concerns for NETP were equity and accessibility. Equity in education was defined as "increasing all students' access to educational opportunities with a focus on closing achievement gaps and removing barriers students face based on their race, ethnicity, or national origin; sex; sexual orientation or gender identity or expression; disability; English language ability; religion; socioeconomic status; or geographical location" (U.S. Department of Education 2017, 7). In this context, accessibility referred to "the design of apps, devices, materials, and environments that support and enable access to content and educational activities for all learners" (U.S. Department of Education 2017, 7). NETP's focus on transforming learning with the emphasis on equity and accessibility led to the major shift in ISTE standards.

Despite these organizations' guidance on digital technology in education, rapid development in the field means that these resources are just snapshots of evolving responses as innovation continues. However, the history of how the field arrived at the current state helps illustrate how changes will likely continue to transform the field in the coming years.

Educational Technology in Current Practice

As technology has become more prevalent in the learning environment, the educational technology field began developing models that reflected the integration of technology into learning. These models take a variety of perspectives, some of which include pedagogical and content knowledge, degrees of technology integration, technology in teacher preparation, and even technology acceptance (Kopcha et al. 2020). Now, however, the field is beginning to focus on educators themselves and their decision-making processes for considering technology integration. This new focus brings recommendations that the integration decisions be value-driven, embedded within a dynamic system, and based on the educators' perceptions of the possibilities (Kopcha et al. 2020). Such a systems model of technology decision-making builds on previous technology integration models, which tend to focus on individual aspects of the process, and allows for new ways to understand the process from the perspective of educators making technology decisions for their students.

Educational Technology in Montessori Programs Today

The subject of technology integration in Montessori classrooms today has garnered substantial attention in the field with special journal issues and focused conferences dedicated to the topic (Montessori Europe 2021; NAMTA 2016). Multiple journal articles, conference sessions, and research projects have also addressed the subject. While many of these discussions revolve around how best to integrate technology, many leading voices on the subject also raise potential concerns. Powell (2016, 163) questions how the "new world of cheap, ubiquitous information, and the new ways of relating to one another, which digital technology promotes, change the ways children learn and think?" Jackson (2017, 25) suggests that the tendency for multitasking in today's digital world has jeopardized deep thinking and asks, "In a culture smitten with technology, what does good thinking look like?" She discusses the impact of technology on concentration, which is a primary goal of Montessori education and which she argues requires techniques to foster "slow thinking" (25). McNamara (2020) highlights the fact that current research is providing strong evidence for the mind-body connection while most digital technology is abstract, two-dimensional, and limited to engaging through clicks and swipes (see Chapter 18: "Revisiting the Foundations of Montessori Education from a Modern Neuroscience Perspective").

Despite these areas of concern, McNamara (2020, 224) also acknowledges that "[t]echnology affects every aspect of our life and simply cannot be ignored. In one way or another, new technologies will find their way into Montessori environments. It is our responsibility to screen what comes in according to Montessori principles." Given existing concerns and the inevitability of digital technology's growing influence, there is value in examining the integration of technology within the Montessori context by age level.

Early Childhood (Birth through Age 6)

The American Psychological Association acknowledges that we are still working to understand the research evidence on young children and screens (Pappas 2020). The organization summarized the strongest research to date and concluded that live interactions have a greater impact on learning than screens for children under 2 years of age, co-viewing with adults in the family mitigates many of the negative consequences of screens for young children, and television viewing and obesity are positively correlated in youth (Pappas 2020). Not surprisingly, then, it seems that the greatest debate about the appropriateness of technology in Montessori classrooms is at the 0 to 6 age level (Prozesky and Cifuentes 2014). In discussing digital technology for children in the Children's House (ages 3–6), Sackett (2016, 26) described Montessori educators as "liable to be considered as anti-technology, possibly even scornful of technology, both in our classrooms and in the everyday lives of the children we serve." Even Montessori herself noted that the technology of her day was most appropriate for older children (Montessori 2015).

Today, Montessori educators seem to be largely in agreement that hands-on, real-world interactions in the environment should be prioritized at the early childhood and earlier age levels. Digital devices and screens, which limit the motor and sensory experiences that are so important in the development of young children, should be integrated little (Prozesky and Cifuentes 2014). However, this is not only a Montessori issue; it is an issue for young children regardless of the educational program, as evidenced by the above-mentioned recommendations from NAEYC and the Fred Rogers Center.

Elementary (Ages 6–12)

In contrast to the early childhood and earlier age levels, there are more positive attitudes toward technology integration in Montessori education at the elementary and secondary levels. Technology is commonly accepted as a developmentally appropriate tool for older children. The literature suggests developmentally appropriate use of technology can help elementary students grow and learn, but educators and families must play an active role in keeping materials educationally enriching (Powell 2016). Students are not taught with the devices; rather, devices are used as supplemental tools for their learning. Technology should not replace interactions with peers or teachers but nurture positive relationships and promote engagement with peers.

Part of the challenge is ensuring that any external media used in schools never redirect internal development or interfere with students' intrinsic understanding of the value of work (Powell 2016). MacDonald (2016, 105–6) provides specific insights into the Montessori environment:

> From the elementary years on, we are probably on the safest ground when we treat digital devices as potential tools for self-construction, and when we refrain from introducing them until sensorial avenues have been explored by the children, and exhausted. These devices should be "materials" in the classroom, and they should fully conform to Montessori philosophy and practice. Carefully constructed presentations will be required. Considerations of safety are critical. Access and usage will be moderated by purpose and by the community of the classroom. Access and usage will also likely increase parallel to age, as our elementary children and our adolescents steadily acquire the technological skills and know-how that they need as they take successive steps towards adulthood.

Adolescent (Ages 12–18)

The greatest agreement about digital technology being appropriate for Montessori environments is at the adolescent level. Several presenters at the NAMTA 2016 Conference, titled "A Montessori Integrated Approach to Science, Mathematics, Technology, and the Environment," described the value of technology integration for the older students. They considered, for example, the positive implications of digital technology on adaptability, fostering independence, maintaining community, and connecting students to issues of social justice (Castiglione 2016; McNamara

2016; Moudry 2016; Powell 2016). Even for this age group, however, cautions emerge. Experts are concerned with how to effectively incorporate technology in learning and avoid pitfalls related to students' desire for constant digital connections, which seem at odds with the goals of educating students in any context.

Moudry (2016, 120) recommends an approach that involves embracing technology, saying, "Instead of banning [handheld computers] in the adolescent community, the solution is to work with the technology and guiding adolescents in the process of using the digital technology and applications to connect with each other and society through real and meaningful work." He uses the children of the earth model of a farm school (see Chapter 16: "Erdkinder: An Educational Approach for Adolescents Ages 12–15") as a setting where digital technology can enhance the learning experiences for adolescents in several areas, including modern agriculture, animal care, creative expression, and business ventures. Moudry (2016, 121) also reminds us that digital technology cannot improve upon time and space because, he says,

> Adolescents need time to think and rest their minds, especially these days with all of the continuous input and information people receive. Most young adults will say they love having all of the access, information, and connection their [handheld computers] give them. However … It is all right, and even necessary, for school staff to apply extra restrictions … for students to have direct, in-person social interaction or time for silent reflection.

And, while mastering technical skills is rewarding and necessary preparation for adulthood, employing them in service to the school community or broader society makes the experiences richer and more meaningful as part of the broader goal of Montessori adolescent education.

Teacher Education Programs

Another debate regarding educational technology revolves around Montessori teacher education programs. Although portions of most programs are conducted via distance learning, the Montessori Accreditation Council for Teacher Education (MACTE), an accreditation agency that recognizes programs around the world, continues to require a significant number of in-person training hours across age levels (MACTE 2022). However, especially with so many things shifting to remote formats during the COVID-19 pandemic, online Montessori teacher preparation programs are growing. Recognition of Montessori teacher education programs and accreditation varies substantially with no clear consensus about what constitutes acceptable preparation. Since finding trained Montessori educators is an ongoing challenge in the field, it is likely that new programs will focus on expanding access, both in-person and remote.

The Pandemic and Its Impact

The COVID-19 pandemic that began in 2020 forced teachers to integrate technology and teach at a distance using asynchronous and synchronous online tools. Because so much of the Montessori approach relies on experiences with hands-on materials in a prepared environment within a classroom community, this transition presented unique challenges for Montessori educators (Murray et al. 2021a, 2021b; Scott and Myers 2021). The extended pandemic forced many teachers to consider new ways of teaching by creatively embedding the essence of Montessori principles within new digital tools. While it is yet unclear what the long-term impacts on technology in Montessori classrooms might be, these new experiences are likely to impact how educational technology is viewed in Montessori education and to affect teachers' attitudes about the value of digital tools in their work.

Conclusion

After examining the foundations of educational technology in Montessori education, the historical background of educational technology in the broader field of education, and current perspectives on integrating technology into Montessori environments, it is clear that ideas about the integration of digital technology in a Montessori context are rapidly changing along with the technology itself. While many aspects of Montessori education could be impacted by the introduction of digital technologies in the classroom, McNamara (2020) reminds us that many things remain the same, including an emphasis on stimulating children's interest and imagination, respect for their growing moral awareness, sowing seeds for children's self-discovery, and the importance of the classroom community. With a commitment to the fundamental principles of Montessori education, digital technology is emerging as a valuable tool for educators who see the possibilities for children growing up in the Information Age, just as Montessori herself embraced the profound transformation of society in the Industrial Revolution.

References

AECT (Association for Educational Communications and Technology). 2022. "About Us." Last modified 2022. https://www.aect.org/about_us.php.

Buckleitner, Warren. 2015. "What Would Maria Montessori Say about the iPad? Theoretical Frameworks for Children's Interactive Media." In *Technology and Digital Media in the Early Years: Tools for Teaching and Learning*, edited by Chip Donohue, 54–67. New York: Routledge.

Castiglione, Cynthia. 2016. "Technology and the Prepared Environment for the Third-Plane Child." *The NAMTA Journal* 41 (2) (Spring): 131–50.

Crompton, Helen. 2017. *ISTE Standards for Educators: A Guide for Teachers and Other Professionals*. Eugene, OR: International Society for Technology in Education.

Donohue, Chip, and Roberta Schomburg. 2017. "Technology and Interactive Media in Early Childhood Programs: What We've Learned from Five Years of Research, Policy, and Practice." *Young Children* 72 (4): 72–8.

ISTE (International Society for Technology in Education). n.d. "The ISTE Standards." Accessed July 28, 2021. https://www.iste.org/iste-standards.

Jackson, Maggie. 2017. "A Workmanship of Risk: The Crafting of Thought in an Age of Speed and Distraction." *The NAMTA Journal* 42 (2) (Spring): 25–43.

Januszewski, Alan, and Kay A. Persichitte. 2008. "A History of the AECT's Definitions of Educational Technology." In *Educational Technology: A Definition with Commentary*, edited by Alan Januszewski and Michael Molenda, 259–82. New York: Routledge.

Kopcha, Theodore J., Kalianne L. Neumann, Anne Ottenbreit-Leftwich, and Elizabeth Pitman. 2020. "Process over Product: The Next Evolution of Our Quest for Technology Integration." *Educational Technology Research and Development* 68: 729–49. https://doi.org/10.1007/s11423-020-09735-y.

MacDonald, Greg. 2016. "Technology in the Montessori Classroom: Benefits, Hazards and Preparation for Life." *The NAMTA Journal* 41 (2) (Spring): 99–107.

MACTE (Montessori Accreditation Council for Teacher Education). 2022. "Section H: Online Education Policy." https://www.macte.org/online-learning/online-education-policy/.

McNamara, John. 2016. "How the Montessori Upper Elementary and Adolescent Environment Naturally Integrates Science, Mathematics, Technology, and the Environment." *The NAMTA Journal* 41 (2) (Spring): 83–97.

McNamara, John. 2020. "Technology and Its Use in a Montessori Environment." *AMI Journal* 2020: 224–9.

Montessori, Maria. 2015. "Some Observations on Technology: From an Introduction to a Publication Advocating 'Mechanical Aids' in Education in India." *AMI Journal Treasure Articles* 2015: 1–7.

Montessori Europe. 2021. "Summit: Technology and Montessori?" Virtual Conference, September 25, 2021. https://www.montessori-europe.net/technology-and-sustainable-schools/.

Moudry, Ben. 2016. "Technology, Togetherness, and Adolescents: Creating a Meaningful Adolescent Learning Community in the Digital Age." *The NAMTA Journal* 41 (2) (Spring): 109–29.

Murray, Angela K., Katie E. Brown, and Patricia Barton. 2021a. "Montessori Education at a Distance, Part 1: A Survey of Montessori Educators' Response to a Global Pandemic." *Journal of Montessori Research* 7 (1): 1–29. https://doi.org/10.17161/jomr.v7i1.15122.

Murray, Angela K., Katie E. Brown, and Patricia Barton. 2021b. "Montessori Education at a Distance, Part 2: A Mixed-Methods Examination of Montessori Educators' Response to a Global Pandemic." *Journal of Montessori Research* 7 (1): 31–50. https://doi.org/10.17161/jomr.v7i1.1512.

NAEYC and Fred Rogers Center. 2012. *Technology and Interactive Media as Tools in Early Childhood Programs Serving Children from Birth through Age 8.* Washington, DC: NAEYC; Latrobe, PA: Fred Rogers Center at St. Vincent College. www.naeyc.org/content/technology-and-young-children.

NAMTA (North American Montessori Teachers' Association). 2016. "A Montessori Integrated Approach to Science, Mathematics, Technology, and the Environment." Conference in Portland, OR, March 31–April 3, 2016.

Pappas, Stephanie. 2020. "What Do We Really Know about Kids and Screens?" *American Psychological Association* 51 (3): 42. https://www.apa.org/monitor/2020/04/cover-kids-screens.

Powell, Mark. 2016. "Montessori Practices: Options for a Digital Age." *The NAMTA Journal* 41 (2) (Spring): 153–81.

Prozesky, Kristina, and Lauren Cifuentes. 2014. "The Montessori Approach to Integrating Technology." *Issues in Early Education* 1 (24): 29–38.

Sackett, Ginni. 2016. "The Scientist in the Casa: The Child as Scientist in the Making." *The NAMTA Journal* 41 (2) (Spring): 23–35.

Scott, Catherine M., and Brooke M. Myers. 2021. "Montessori Education: Teacher Perceptions of Challenges in Transitioning to Virtual Instruction." *Journal of Montessori Research* 7 (2): 1–11. https://doi.org/10.17161/jomr.v7i2.15469.

U.S. Department of Education. 2017. *Reimagining the Role of Technology in Education: 2017 National Education Technology Plan Update.* Washington, DC: U.S. Department of Education. https://tech.ed.gov/files/2017/01/NETP17.pdf.

Chapter 54

Interdependent Impact: Contemporary Teacher Education and Montessori Teacher Preparation

Gay C. Ward and Paige M. Bray

Montessori education and teacher preparation exist within a larger framework of teacher education worldwide, and major trends in global teacher education affect Montessori teacher preparation. We also see the intersection of contemporary teacher education and Montessori teacher education in certification programs and policies in the arena of higher education. We begin the chapter with some context.

For the most recent years available (2010 to 2014), we know that more than 5 million additional teachers were added to the education workforce globally (Roser 2017); most of these educators received some type of training in their home countries. Unfortunately, there are no clear data on the number of Montessori educators worldwide or on the addition of Montessori educators to the roster of this same time frame. However, a good faith estimate presented at the American Educational Research Association in 2022 indicates that more than 12,000 Montessori schools exist worldwide (Debs et al. 2022). We also know that the number of Montessori schools, and by extension Montessori educators, continues to grow globally, making an examination of Montessori teacher preparation salient in the context of this book.

In some instances, Montessori education is already on the leading edge of contemporary teacher education, with neuroscience and psychological research regularly noting the value of Montessori principles (see Chapters 18, 23, and 24 for more information on this trend). In other ways, Montessori education is on the receiving end of this work, learning from more traditional programs of teacher education. Specifically, Montessori education leads the work that respects movement, curiosity, interdisciplinarity, observation, and holistic learning. On the other hand, Montessori educator preparation could benefit from new approaches and considerations related to assessment, inclusion, diversity, technology use, and differentiation. This chapter addresses the implications of these observations and the ways in which one might consider the strengths and challenges of Montessori teacher education.[1]

In reviewing the impact of current trends within the wider teacher education landscape on Montessori education, we begin with two assertions. First, Montessori pedagogy is, and always has been, dynamic. Montessori was a scientist who consistently used observation and data collection to adjust her theoretical framework and have these observations reflected back in practice. We support her model and communicate here in that spirit. Second, we assert that students in all planes of development, including adult learners, follow behaviors modeled by their instructors. Thus, effective teacher education provides new educators with significant opportunities to inquire, actively explore, and learn both independently and collaboratively. Adult learners must practice being reflective practitioners, experience a peaceful adult learning community, and have a well-prepared environment to learn their craft.

Montessori Education as a Leader in Teacher Preparation: Hands-on Learning, Curiosity, and Interconnectedness

Montessori teacher education is a model of best practice for teacher education in some areas, including hands-on experiential learning, education informed by curiosity, and a value for the interconnectedness of the world, diverse people, and learning.

Hands-on Learning or Work of the Hands

Montessori pedagogy, and by extension Montessori teacher education, provides a strong foundation for experiential learning in which students construct their knowledge from authentic, frequent hands-on activities and explorations. As Montessori notes, "The human being is a united whole, but this unity has to be built up and formed by active experiences in the real world, to which he is led by the laws of nature" (1989, 184). In contemporary terms, hands-on learning in higher education allows for "the design of creative products to show understanding or communicate ideas" with an emphasis on applying arts, technology, and science to all disciplines (Trust, Maloy, and Edwards 2017, 28). To this end, Montessori teacher education programs often include combined indoor and outdoor classroom designs and extensive practice with pedagogical materials that will be used in classrooms. In fact, a current trend in teacher education around the world, referred to as the *maker movement*, credits its origins to this experiential learning developed by Montessori, Dewey, and Piaget (Hsu, Baldwin, and Ching 2017; Trust, Maloy, and Edwards et al. 2017).

At the secondary level, the Montessori method utilizes the land and surrounding community as pedagogical assets. Montessori expert, David Kahn, describes the essence of secondary education as "cooperation with the land, cooperation in commerce, and cooperation in the cultural life of the rural society" (2016, 1). Because of this focus on real-life activity, Montessori educator preparation includes experiential activities that connect students, teachers, and preservice teachers to organic farming, beekeeping, construction work, and decision-making and problem-solving associated with communal living experiences. Service learning might also be included in the work of educator preparation (Coe 2003). As Montessori educator Marta Donohoe and colleagues write, "Montessori teachers develop skill in creating academic work that fosters a sense of hope and a sense of the progression of the human spirit. This curriculum includes humane action in stewardship of the earth" (2013, 21). Another central aspect of hands-on learning for Montessori educator training is the use of communities of practice. This includes educators using a round table model of professional development and the use of systematic inquiry to support meta-cognition of the educators in training (Bray and Schatz 2013; Dijk et al. in press; La Faille 1996).

Curiosity in Teacher Education

Education informed by curiosity is another arena in which Montessori educator preparation leads the field. Other terms used for this type of work include inquiry learning, project-based learning, and action research. Each is employed as means of acknowledging and honoring curiosity. Montessori was ahead of her time with the value she placed on curiosity for the student and the teacher, and each of these ideas is embedded in Montessori teacher education.

Inquiry-based learning has been a trend in non-Montessori teacher education for decades in the United States (Cochran-Smith and Lytle 2015). There is also evidence that many other countries have highlighted the importance of a similar model of education often referred to as inquiry-based Science Education (though with caveats about being geographically and culturally sensitive) (Rundgren 2018). Inquiry is embedded into every facet of Montessori education whereby students are consistently invited to question, problem-solve, and explore. By the 1940s, Montessori developed her vision of cosmic education, emphasizing big ideas and questions around the purposefulness and interconnectedness of the world (see Chapter 3: "Cosmic Education: The Vital Center of the Montessori Perspective"). Her vision of cosmic education necessitated inquiry and curiosity and she stressed the importance of activity and imagination as tools for children to construct their intelligence (Montessori 1989). As a result, adult learners studying to be Montessori educators learn to create and support frameworks for inquiry learning for their students. Additionally, preservice teachers learn to invite students into individual and collaborative work with long work sessions that encourage independent inquiry. To support the child's curiosity, they also learn to prepare resource-rich environments. Here we see the ways in which Montessori education, which embeds independence, uninterrupted work time, and collaborative work, supports inquiry-based learning (Chaillé 2008). Montessori teacher education benefitted in the mid-twentieth century from curricular and material resources of more mainstream teacher education spaces when inquiry-based learning became more widespread. This trend was especially prevalent in middle and high school social studies and science education and later in elementary settings in the United States (Edwards et al. 1993; Evans 2018; Katz and Chard 1989).

Inquiry learning endures as an important method of authentic education and educator preparation that enhances analytical and social skills (Chandra et al. 2020). However, instructors must understand how to scaffold the investigative process (Zhang 2016). As educational psychologist Geoffrey Scheurman notes, "As educators, we have the enviable and noble calling to construct the archetypal teacher; the person who teaches how to question, who guides students to discovery, and rewards innovation" (2018, 394).

Similar to inquiry-based work, project-based learning and action research are also arenas where Montessori teacher education is leading the way. Educational pedagogue Margaret Rasfeld's (2017) work with secondary students in Germany and Austria suggests collaboration, not competition, is essential to promote responsible and community-minded learning. Her work, though not based in Montessori pedagogy, describes many of the essential elements of a Montessori educational practice and reminds us of the value of Montessori teacher education's lengthy practicum cycles and collaborative nature. Similarly, a study in Portugal by Vasconcelos (2007) notes the value of project-based learning to support comfort in the classroom setting.

Action research is a hallmark of many Montessori educator preparation programs. This is another example of a learning modality for adult learners that promotes curiosity. It is not uncommon for Montessori teacher education programs to ask candidates to design, implement, and analyze an action research project as a part of their credential requirements (Ward et al. 2019). By participating in action research projects, teacher candidates experience phases of inquiry similar to their future students. By way of example, to complete an action research project a person must develop a question; review related literature; develop and implement a research plan; collect, analyze, and reflect on the data; and design a future response (Mertler 2020). Action research within Montessori teacher education (and elsewhere) also supports the development of observation skills for the classroom. In essence, this work prepares the individual to be a reflective practitioner going forward (Ward and Miller 2019). In summary, as a matter of developing curiosity and the skills to promote curiosity, "Montessori teachers are observers and data collectors. Action research offers a focus for these efforts and empowers teachers to make practical, meaningful changes in the classroom" (Bagby and Sulak 2017, 17).

Interconnectedness

Montessori teacher education has a great deal to offer the larger teacher preparation community about interdisciplinary curriculum and practice. Montessori education's use of nature education, service learning, and equity work within the teacher education programs are important examples for others in contemporary teacher education.

Montessori believed sustaining humanity required a respect for human dignity, value for the relationality of the world, and an appreciation for local and global contexts of being a citizen of the world. She worked to impart to her students the absolute importance of the natural world and our human relationship to that world. She also worked to establish routines and procedures in classrooms that were aimed at communal living, peaceful problem-solving, and the need for collaboration in learning (Montessori 1989).

As a result of her beliefs, nature education has always been an integral part of the Montessori curriculum for students and individuals becoming Montessori educators. Hutchinson (2013) notes that nature education is holistic and transdisciplinary because it involves science, history, and geography, and education for citizenship. Montessori understood this idea about learning through the natural world. Engagement with nature can also be seen through the lens of sustainability and place-based learning, which often overlaps with service learning. As researchers Scott and Graham remind us, "[s]ervice-learning must be a collaborative effort in which authentic and articulated learning goals are present, responses to genuine community needs are central, youth decision making occurs, and analytic reflection is used at the end to explore the impact on the self and the community" (2015, 355). This definition is noteworthy because it echoes Montessori's principles of autonomy, intrinsic motivation, care for the earth, and collaborative work. It reminds us not just of the value of service learning for students in the Montessori classroom but for teacher educators as well.

More and more, teacher education programs are coming to value service learning (Resch and Schrittesser 2021; Salam et al. 2019). In this way, non-Montessori teacher education programs are benefiting from Montessori programs where service learning and learning in the natural world have been part of the curriculum for educators since the inception of the Montessori movement. Montessori understood that service learning, though not called this at the time of her teaching, is an effective means of fostering critical thinking skills and connecting the teacher, students, and community. Moreover, similar to many Montessori activities and spaces, service-learning experiences can also be readily adapted for diverse learners (Anderson 2000). Montessori educators must consistently differentiate and collaborate to reach humanitarian commitments.

In contemporary Montessori teacher preparation programs, commitments to understanding and supporting equity and inclusion are necessary, although it is important to note that non-Montessori teacher education is also attending to this work in important and ever-growing ways. The efforts to address and work on equity issues occur at a programmatic level but are most often seen and felt at the level of the course and the instructor. We understand that even with a focus on equity as a mechanism *and* outcome of communal living and learning for our teachers in training and our students, there is work yet to do in this arena. All educator preparation programs must have a more systematic, critical interrogation of the curricula, teaching practices, training modalities, and enrollment to be truly engaged in equity work as a means of teaching interconnectivity (hooks 1994).

Globally, Montessori organizations have taken seriously the need for accountability around equity-based work, modeling institutional reform for teacher education programs. For example, the American Montessori Society and Association Montessori International/USA have full-time staff members to develop and implement diversity, equity, and inclusion goals. Moreover, practitioners and researchers are providing specific recommendations to Montessori education programs around this work. As Montessori education socializes the next generation of educators, modeling and practice in diverse and inclusive settings are essential. Applied, clinical experiences promote enduring teaching practices when embedded over time. It is also essential to have a mentor or coaching component for students with composite feedback from the learners, coach, and cooperating classroom teacher. Researchers Debs and Brown recommend, for example, that Montessori teacher education programs and public school districts collaborate to design teacher education that will prepare educators to work with "racially and socioeconomically diverse students" (2017, 7). Oesting and Speed recommend that "as Montessorians (our work) necessitates that we, the adults, be willing to lean into our own transformation by hearing the personal truths of diverse voices from our community and beyond" (2019, 46). Montessori teacher educators are becoming more aware of the continuum of justice-oriented learning and supportive materials, activities, and opportunities that exist for the classroom and promote culturally sustaining pedagogy. Ultimately, the Montessori framework was one of peace building and care for others. Montessori's insistence that children value themselves, learn to value others, and ultimately learn to value justice in the service of becoming agents for justice is central to her vision (Montessori 1989).

Montessori Educator Programs Making Headway: Differentiated Instruction, Technology Use, and Assessment

Montessori educator preparation programs are working to address the challenges of the historical insularity of Montessori education, the explosion of Montessori education across the globe, and a growing interest, especially in the United States, in accepting Montessori education and Montessori education credentialing as a part of mainstream educational practice. Within these efforts, three areas stand out as key spaces for attention and continued improvement in Montessori teacher education: using and teaching differentiated instruction (DI) to meet the needs of students in a variety of educational settings, using technology effectively with attention to how it impacts the Montessori philosophy, and more effectively using assessment practices to assess teachers in training and to prepare them to use assessment effectively in the classroom setting.

Differentiated Instruction

Preparing Montessori teacher educators to differentiate instruction in classrooms is a priority of all teacher education in the twenty-first century, but especially in Montessori classrooms (see Chapter 56). Although Montessori believed in the capacity of children with a variety of learning needs and understood learning based on assets and growth rather than deficit-minded thinking, more work is yet to be completed. She says,

> The child's development follows a path of successive stages of independence, and our knowledge of this must guide us in our behavior towards him. We have to help the child to act, will and think for himself. This is the art of serving the spirit, an art which can be practiced to perfection only when working among children.
>
> *(1988, 257)*

Montessori pedagogy and teacher education inherently acknowledge key features of DI, while continuing to identify and meet learning needs via Universal Design for Learning and Response to Intervention practices. In Montessori education, DI supports students using a variety of resources, honoring extended work periods, individual goal setting, collaborative work, and flexible grouping. Montessori teacher preparation also values teaching the soon-to-be-educator the value of formative assessment through observation. Researchers understand that child-centered pedagogy, similar to Montessori's, makes DI easier to enact (De Neve and Devos 2016; Hazel and Allen 2013). Nevertheless, DI and interdisciplinary efforts could be better used in many Montessori classrooms, where the multiage classes and frequent revisiting of material are common.

Skilled differentiated instruction is essential for Montessori educators to meet the needs of individual learners in a student-centered, multiage environment. The Montessori teacher needs to know the child's community, interests, readiness, learning profiles, and specific learning goals. Additional mentoring of those studying teacher education is needed to support the growth of their responsiveness to student needs (Bray 2019; Subban and Round 2015). Differentiation occurs on three levels: content, process, and product (Goodnough 2010; Tomlinson and Eldson 2002). Montessori pedagogy supports DI in theory, but teachers need practice and guidance to successfully implement this approach that is consistent with the ways other teacher education programs have enacted its use.

Technology

Technology is also an essential tool for Montessori educators and preservice teachers to consider in contemporary teacher education. Although it can certainly be an aid to differentiation, it is perhaps most importantly a ubiquitous feature of modern society and one that Montessori surely would have had things to say about. More recently, the onset of the global pandemic forced Montessori educators to reevaluate the impact of technology on their methodology and pedagogy and begs us to consider the role of technology in Montessori teacher preparation. We must ask the following question. How can we prepare the adult Montessori learner and their students to navigate the technological world? Are there aspects of technology that have enhanced our teaching that we would retain in a post-COVID-19 world? What assistive technology and virtual experiences can uniquely support learning? Are we effectively modeling the use of digital record keeping that aligns Montessori outcomes to national standards and supports planning, individual and class progress assessment, and communication? Should we teach Montessori educators to support various types of technological engagement as a part of Montessori teacher preparations (Stavredes 2011; see Chapter 53: "Montessori Education in the Digital Age")? Montessori teacher education must lead the way in addressing these questions if we are to remain relevant and engaged with the larger discourse around teacher preparation and education.

Assessment of Teacher Educators

Observation is an integral part of Montessori teacher preparation and the cornerstone of planning, instruction, assessment, and learning at all levels. When observation and other forms of assessment are done consistently and systematically, these tools can inform teacher preparation, the learning environment, instruction, and learning outcomes. Assessment in Montessori education and Montessori teacher preparation is an enduring topic of discussion among Montessori educators and parents. Assessment practices within Montessori schools vary widely; yet, historically Montessori training relied almost exclusively on observation as the one, only, and best method of assessment when working with children (see Chapter 22). Montessori teacher educators and their students would benefit from considering assessment in new ways.

Montessori teacher education programs regularly grapple with how to provide formative assessment to their candidates. Instructors in Montessori teacher education programs understand that traditional assessments are linked to limited academic performances rather than inspiring learning. Most, if not all, would support a more student-centered approach focusing more on helping define learning goals and conferencing with students to achieve their goals as new educators. Although this is common in a Montessori classroom, the parallel is not often experienced by teachers in their course of study.

Researchers and Montessori educators Damore and Rieckhoff (2021) note the emphasis Montessori education places on the role of self-transformation of the teacher via self-reflection and just how important this is. Their findings indicate that school leaders who practiced and modeled self-reflective strategies resulted in more reflective practices being enacted by their classroom teachers. Goodnough (2010) goes so far as to suggest that preservice teachers be encouraged to engage more in pre-assessment and reflection to drive purposeful and responsive instruction. Still other research supports dialogue and response journals as reflective tools for preservice teachers (Lee 2007). This relooking at the importance of reflection is another area where Montessori educators can engage in dialogue and share ideas with non-Montessori educators.

As mentioned previously, observation has always been an integral part of Montessori teacher education. Montessori educator candidates practice varied types of observation using ethnographic, anecdotal, and checklist modalities with individuals and groups. Moreover, most teacher education programs, Montessori and otherwise, recognize the value of observation paired with interpretation, planning, and instruction to lead to more informed decision-making in the classroom. Montessori noted that observation combined with reflection would help teachers understand the miscommunication and misunderstandings that led to challenging behavior and to plan learning experiences for these children responsively (Christensen 2019; Montessori 1988).

Another type of assessment that individuals becoming Montessori educators may benefit from learning and experiencing is performance-based assessment. In this modality, those individuals in training are evaluated on the work that they do with young people. This type of evaluation often leads the teacher candidates to employ a wider variety of strategies for later supporting and assessing student learning. Likewise, teachers who engage in frequent reflection as part of the performance-based assessment gain insight into the importance of self-assessment for the Montessori classroom learner.

To make assessment more of the learning process, many contemporary educators also propose looking at what is termed "ungrading." Grades can be replaced with methods such as individual plans, contracts, portfolios, conferences, discussions, and student-generated rubrics for the sake of the learning process (Blum 2020; Koehler and Meech 2022; Mitchell 2021). The emphasis on observing and guiding improvement, rather than judging, is a fitting model for a student-centered pedagogy (Earl 2021). Often contemporary teacher preparation programs use rubrics to provide formative assessment and guidance for preservice teachers; these rubrics can be designed to show development over time and to help with coaching and goal setting. The Montessori education world is embracing and evolving within this work. To that end, Murray et al. (2021) have developed a rubric particularly designed for elementary educators in Montessori settings.

Evidence also supports that mentoring and coaching for preservice and new in-service teachers in Montessori and non-Montessori environments have the potential to be effective for educators if separate from evaluation (Damore and Rieckhoff 2021; Hobson 2016). Zugelder (2019) suggests that coaching, including co-planning, co-teaching, reviewing lesson plans, reviewing assessments, and observing lessons, can also be effective. Damore and Rieckhoff (2021) add that coaching includes establishing trust, asking open-ended reflective questions and listening and validating.

Deciding how to assess teacher candidates is difficult enough; deciding how to teach assessment is even more difficult. DeLuca et al.'s (2021) research supports the interweaving of assessment concepts through multiple courses along a continuum of study for teacher candidates. By allowing candidates to see assessment practices in action, the teacher in training learns by example. This parallels the spiraling nature of a Montessori curriculum where one revisits concepts at deeper and deeper levels and seems to suggest a best practice that Montessori education programs could ascribe to with planning and coordination. The challenge in implementing gradual learning about assessment is the intensity of Montessori teacher education programs. Continuing further instruction about assessment through student teaching experiences and beyond through professional development is warranted. As Montessori schools work to gain licensure for their teachers in the United States and elsewhere in the world, they are increasingly affected by teacher education trends for assessment, mentoring, and monitoring of preservice and new teachers. Montessori education programs are not exempt from this scrutiny nor are they able to avoid the conversations around these types of assessment. On balance, as indicated here, assessment practices in Montessori education and educator preparation are complex. Assessment will remain a key issue to examine in teacher education in Montessori and non-Montessori settings.

Implications: Further Work for Researchers and Practitioners

The complicated landscape of Montessori teacher education and its intersections with more traditional teacher education programs means that work remains in this arena. We understand that work to improve teacher education will be completed by researchers and practitioners together, aiming to produce data-informed practices that also consider the holistic experience of educational settings. How Montessori educators, including preservice teachers, use scientific observation, data, and a holistic lens in the service of children will continue to be crucial in the changing educational world.

The Montessori community is learning to systematically produce and disseminate research more effectively than ever before. As such, we should continue to look to evidence-based practices, self-assessment, and Montessori's historical work to inform teacher preparation. This is a particular challenge in programs that share accreditation requirements with national-, regional-, and state-level bodies in the United States and elsewhere. As Denervaud describes, Montessori materials allow for self-correction and lead to self-monitoring in younger years. Similarly, preservice and in-service educators should have self-referential feedback cycles to improve their learning and outcomes (2020).

We see considerable benefits to even more inclusive conversations with teacher educators of the global Montessori community. It is crucial that our shared work focuses on the way the next generation of teachers experiences the foundations of Montessori pedagogy but also varied forms of experiential learning (e.g., inquiry learning, nature exploration, service learning), DI, and authentic assessment. We also see the need for curriculum development with new educators that acknowledges scaffolding teaching skills and interweaving inquiry. Finally, teacher preparation programs must be prepared to consider sustainability and social justice in their work. By focusing teacher education this way, opportunities are created for interdisciplinary, holistic learning for our fifth-plane adult learners that parallels a more inclusive, cosmic curriculum, similar to the Montessori model for children and adolescents. To this end, Montessori teacher education programs must focus more intentionally on how contemporary education research and theory inform specific Montessori practices. By always staying vigilant to the process of learning, one can obtain technical accuracy, knowledge development, and a response built on the teaching/learning community.

Note

1. As authors, we use "Montessori," "non-Montessori," and "contemporary" as terms of distinction. We deliberately opt not to use the word "traditional" when referring to schooling and education. We mean to write about teacher education and preparation beyond stand-alone Montessori training and training programs. We draw on extensive professional experience, intersectional knowledge, Montessori experience, and select research literature to identify contemporary trends in teacher education that are impacting Montessori education. Grounded in experience with the first through fourth Montessori planes (and our work across seven continents), our focus over the past two decades has been on what Bray coins "the fifth plane"—the application of Montessori tenets in working with the adult learner. Specific Montessori degree program design at the bachelor, master, and doctoral levels is changing the landscape of sustained Montessori teacher preparation to be global, inclusive, and constantly reimagined.

References

Anderson, Jeffrey B. 2000. "Learning in Deed: Service Learning and Preservice Teacher Education." http://digitalcommons.unomaha.edu/slceslgen/16.

Bagby, Janet, and Tracey Sulak. 2017. "Connecting Montessori Practice with Action Research." *Montessori Life* 29 (1): 17.

Blum, Susan. 2020. *Ungrading: Why Rating Students Undermines Learning (and What To Do Instead)*. Morgantown, WV: West Virginia University Press.

Bray, Paige M. 2019. "Letter to a Future Teacher." *Montessori Collaborative World Review: The Montessori Roots of Social Justice* 1 (1): 208–13.

Bray, Paige M., and Steve Schatz. 2013. "A Model for Developing Meta-Cognitive Tools in Teacher Apprenticeships." *Journal of Teacher Education for Sustainability* 15 (1): 48–56.

Chaillé, Christine. 2008. *Constructivism across the Curriculum in Early Childhood Classrooms: Big Ideas as Inspiration*. Boston: Pearson.

Chandra, Kiky, Nyoman Sudana Degeng, Dedi Kuswandi, and Punaji Setyosari. 2020. "Effect of Guided Inquiry Learning Model and Social Skills to the Improving of Students' Analysis Skills in Social Studies Learning." *Journal for the Education of Gifted Young Scientists* 8 (1): 613–22. https://doi.org/10.17478/jegys.654975.

Christensen, Olivia. 2019. "Montessori Identity in Dialogue: A Selected Review of Literature on Teacher Identity." *Journal of Montessori Research* 5 (2): 46–56.

Cochran-Smith, Marilyn, and Susan L. Lytle. 2015. *Inquiry as Stance: Practitioner Research for the Next Generation*. New York: Teachers College Press.

Coe, Elisabeth. 2003. "Creating Optimal Environments for Adolescents." *Montessori Life* 15 (3): 31–6.

Damore, Sharon, and Barbara S. Rieckhoff. 2021. "School Leader Perceptions: Coaching Tool and Process." *Journal of Research on Leadership Education* 16 (1): 57–80. https://doi.org/10.1177/1942775119868258.

De Neve, Debbie, and Geert Devos. 2016. "The Role of Environmental Factors in Beginning Teachers' Professional Learning Related to Differentiated Instruction." *School Effectiveness and School Improvement* 27 (4): 557–79.

Debs, Mira, and Katie E. Brown. 2017. "Students of Color and Public Montessori Schools: A Review of the Literature." *Journal of Montessori Research* 3 (1): 1–15. https://doi.org/10.17161/jomr.v3i1.5859.

Debs, Mira, Jaap de Brouwer, Angela K. Murray, Lynne Lawrence, Megan Tyne, and Candice von der Wehl. 2022. "Global Diffusion of Montessori Schools: A Report From the 2022 Global Montessori Census." *Journal of Montessori Research* 8 (2): 1–15. https://doi.org/10.17161/jomr.v8i2.18675.

DeLuca, Christopher, M. Searle, K. Carbone, J. Ge, D. La-pointe-mcewan. 2021. "Toward a Pedagogy for Slow and Significant Learning about Assessment in Teacher Education." *Teaching and Teacher Education*, 101: 103316. https://doi.org/10.1016/j.tate.2021.103316.

Denervaud, Solange, Jean-François Knebel, Mary Helen Immordino-Yang, and Patric Hagman. 2020. "Effects of Traditional Versus Montessori Schooling on 4- to 15-Year Old Children's Performance Monitoring." *Mind, Brain, and Education* 14 (2): 167–75. https://doi.org/10.1111/mbe.12233.

Dijk, Rogier, Paige M. Bray, and Joshua A. Russell. Forthcoming. "Third Plane Teacher in an Urban Environment: Montessori Competencies and an Invitation to Co-construct a Montessori Glossary." *AMI Journal*.

Donahoe, Marta, Penny Picuki, Sheila Coad-Bernard, Betsy Coe, and Barb Scholtz. 2013. "Best Practices in Montessori Secondary Programs." *Montessori Life* 25 (2): 16–24.

Earl, Dennis. 2021. "UNgrading: Why Rating Students Undermines Learning (and What to Do Instead)." *Teaching Philosophy* 44 (4): 556–60. https://doi.org/10.5840/teachphil2021444159.

Edwards, Carolyn P., Lella Gandini, and George E. Forman. 1993. *The Hundred Languages of Children: The Reggio Emilia Approach to Early Childhood Education*. Norwood, NJ: Ablex Publishing Corporation.

Evans, Ronald. 2018. "Old, New, and Newer: Historical Context of the New Social Studies." In *Constructivism and the New Social Studies: A Collection of Classic Inquiry Lessons (A Collection of Classic Inquiry Lessons)*, edited by G. Scheurman and R. W. Evans, 21–54. Charlotte, North Carolina: Information Age Publishing, Inc.

Goodnough, Karen. 2010. "The Role of Action Research in Transforming Teacher Identity: Modes of Belonging and Ecological Perspectives." *Educational Action Research* 18 (2): 167–82.

Hazel, Cynthia E., and Wendy B. Allen. 2013. "Creating Inclusive Communities through Pedagogy at Three Elementary Schools." *School Effectiveness and School Improvement* 24 (3): 336–56. https://doi.org/10.1080/09243453.2012.692696.

Hobson, Andrew J. 2016. "Judgementoring and How to Avert It: Introducing ONSIDE Mentoring for Beginning Teachers." *International Journal of Mentoring and Coaching in Education* 5 (2): 87–110.

hooks, Bell. 1994. *Teaching to Transgress: Education as the Practice of Freedom*. New York: Routledge Press.

Hsu, Yu-Chang, Sally Baldwin, and Yu-Hui Ching. 2017. "Learning through Making and Maker Education." *TechTrends* 61 (6): 589–94.

Hutchinson, David. 2013. "Teaching Nature: From Philosophy to Practice." In *Montessori Voices: Guided by Nature*, edited by D. Kahn, 191–8. Burton, OH: The NAMTA Journal.

Kahn, David. 2016. "The Farm, Nature and Civilisation—the Roots of Social Change." *Montessori Australia* 1 (March). https://www.bms.qld.edu.au/wpcontent/uploads/MAFeArticle1601.pdf.

Katz, Lilian G., and Sylvia C. Chard. 1989. *Engaging Children's Minds: The Project Approach*. Norwood, NJ: Ablex Publishing Corporation.

Koehler, Adrie A., and Sally Meech. 2022. "Ungrading Learner Participation in a Student-Centered Learning Experience." *TechTrends* 66: 78–89.

La Faille, Jessy. 1996. "Montessori en Haar Revolutie der Waarden." Thesis, the Netherlands: Leiden University.

Lee, Icy. 2007. "Preparing Pre-Service English Teachers for Reflective Practice." *ELT Journal* 61 (4): 321–9. https://doi.org/10.1093/elt/ccm022.

Mertler, Craig. 2020. *Action Research: Improving Schools and Empowering Educators (6th edition)*. Los Angeles: Sage.

Mitchell, Kim M. 2021. "Ungrading: Why Rating Students Undermines Learning (and What to Do Instead)." In *Discourse and Writing/Rédactologie*, edited by Susan D. Blum, 121–5. WV (West Virginia): West Virginia University Press.

Montessori, Maria. 1988. *The Absorbent Mind*. Oxford, England: Clio Press Ltd.

Montessori, Maria. 1989. *To Educate the Human Potential*. Oxford, England: Clio Press Ltd.

Murray, Angela, Carolyn Daoust, and Jan Mallett. 2021. "Designing the Montessori Coaching Tool Elementary Rubric for Early-Career Professional Development." *Journal of Montessori Research* 7 (2): 25–61. https://doi.org/10.17161/jomr.v7i2.15866.

Oesting, Tammy, and Ashley Speed. 2019. "Exploring Diversity and Inclusivity in Montessori (Part 3)." *Montessori Life: A Publication of the American Montessori Society* 31 (1): 46–53.

Rasfeld, M. 2017. Changing Education System. https://youtu.be/uoGFaJXhnqE.

Resch, Katharina, and Ilse Schrittesser. 2021. "Using the Service-Learning Approach to Bridge the Gap between Theory and Practice in Teacher Education." *International Journal of Inclusive Education* 1–15. https://doi.org/10.1080/13603116.2021.1882053.

Roser, Max. 2017. "Teachers and Professors." https://ourworldindata.org/teachers-and-professors.

Rundgren, Carl-Johan. 2018. "Implementation of Inquiry-Based Science Education in Different Countries: Some Reflections." *Cultural Studies of Science Education* 13 (2): 607–15.

Salam, Maimoona, Dayang Nurfatimah Awang Iskandar, Dayang Hanani Abang Ibrahim, and Muhammad Shoaib Farooq. 2019. "Service Learning in Higher Education: A Systematic Literature Review." *Asia Pacific Education Review* 20 (4): 573–93.

Scheurman, Geoffrey. 2018. "Renaissance of Social Studies." In *Constructivism and the New Social Studies: A Collection of Classic Inquiry Lessons*, edited by G. Scheurman and R. W. Evans, 101–28. Charlotte, NC: Information Age Publishing.

Scott, Katharine, and James A. Graham. 2015. "Service-Learning: Implications for Empathy and Community Engagement in Elementary School Children." *Journal of Experiential Education* 38 (4): 354–72. https://doi.org/10.1177%2F1053825915592889.

Stavredes, Tina. 2011. *Effective Online Teaching*. San Francisco, CA: Jossey-Bass.

Subban, Pearl K., and Penny Round. 2015. "Differentiated Instruction at Work. Reinforcing the Art of Classroom Observation through the Creation of a Checklist for Beginning and Pre-Service Teachers." *Australian Journal of Teacher Education* 40 (5): 117–31. http://dx.doi.org/10.14221/ajte.2015v40n5.7.

Tomlinson, Carol Ann, and Caroline Cunningham Elsdon. 2002. *Differentiation in Practice: A Resource Guide for Differentiating Curriculum, Grades K–5*. Alexandria: Association for Supervision & Curriculum Development.

Trust, Torrey, Robert W. Maloy, and Sharon Edwards. 2017. "Learning through Making: Emerging and Expanding Designs for College Classes." *TechTrends* 62 (1): 19–28. https://doi.org/10.1007/s11528-017-0214-0.

Vasconcelos, Teresa. 2007. "Using the Project Approach in a Teacher Education Practicum." *Early Childhood Research and Practice* 9 (2).

Ward, Gay, and Michael Miller. 2019. "Action Research: A Tool for Transformation." *Montessori Life* 31 (3): 38–43.

Ward, Gay, Cate Epperson, Janet Mallett, Nancy Lindeman, Theresa Ripple, Elizabeth Park, and Melina Papadimitriou. 2019. "Action Research in Montessori Classrooms." In *Montessori Event 2019*. Washington, DC: American Montessori Society.

Zhang, Lin. 2016. "Is Inquiry-Based Science Teaching Worth the Effort? Some Thoughts Worth Considering." *Science & Education* 25: 897–915.

Zugelder, Bryan S. 2019. "Beyond New Teacher Mentoring: The Role of Instructional Coaching." *Kappa Delta Pi Record* 55 (4): 181–3. https://doi.org/10.1080/00228958.2019.1659074.

Chapter 55
Montessori Education and Gender: Recasting Gender in Montessori Contexts

Sid Mohandas

Gender in the early years has been variously theorized, researched, and conceptualized over the past few decades (Blaise 2005; Davies 1989; Hodgins 2019; MacNaughton 2000; Osgood 2006). Despite this rich legacy of scholarship, there is a lack of research that has critically engaged with gender in Montessori contexts. In fact, Montessori spaces and materials in previous research have often been framed as "gender neutral" or devoid of gendering practices (Gustafsson 2018). Notwithstanding this research framing, initiatives such as *the Male Montessorian, Queer Consultants*, and *blossoming beyond the binary* have made efforts to bring gender and sexuality into the conversation in Montessori circles. At a more institutional level, in response to the UK Department for Education's efforts to diversify gender in the early years workforce (DfE 2017), Montessori training organizations such as the former Montessori Centre International (MCI) put strategies in place to recruit more men into Montessori education. In 2016, MCI extended financial aid worth £3000 to up to three male applicants per year to recruit more men into their training program (Marcus 2016). While this is commendable, the challenges in relation to gender inequalities and injustices are comparable to the sector more widely (Osgood and Mohandas 2019).

The research literature that has dominated Montessori circles tends to be concerned with validating Montessori theory and practice (Lillard 2013, 2012; Lillard and Taggart 2019; Lillard et al. 2017), often dismissing gender as not contributing "significantly to any of the difference reported" (Lillard and Else-Quest 2006, 1893) without considering how gender is conceptualized or theorized. These feed into notions that position the Montessori approach as gender neutral or devoid of gendering practices. Using Maria Montessori's feminist legacy as a springboard, the need for a sustained engagement with contemporary feminist research to complicate understandings of gender is justified. By utilizing contemporary feminist lens, the gender-neutral status of Montessori materials is ruffled and gender within Montessori practice and theory is re-thought as performative, relational, multiple, situated, and complex.

Montessori and Feminisms

Feminist activism and research has historically been concerned with, as in the words of Chimamanda Ngozi Adichie (2014, 15), "the specific and particular problem of gender." It is committed to the task of unsettling narrow and reductive framings of gender to hold space for liberation, justice, and care. Montessori's involvement in the early feminist movement was founded upon this commitment to destabilize traditional views of gender and reimagine more equitable presents and futures. Her feminist resistance was evident quite early when as a young girl and woman she managed to jump various structural, familial, and societal hurdles to forge her way into places and spaces that were traditionally inaccessible to girls and women of her time (Kramer 1988). Moreover, she was an active participant in the early women's congresses, including the 1896 International Women's Congress in Berlin, the 1899 International Congress of Women in London, and the 1908 National Congress of Italian Women, where she spoke on matters related to unequal pay, poor working conditions, and legal issues such as the right to vote and own property (Trabalzini 2011).

The period of feminism that Montessori was engaged in, which was chiefly concerned with suffrage and property rights, is now known as the "first wave" of feminism. While the women's congresses were primarily concerned with the plight of women who owned properties, in the 1896 Congress in Berlin, Montessori brought attention to the challenges of working-class women whose lives were "made even more oppressive as a result of poverty." Montessori argued, "We are blind if we believe that the very same reforms are useful to them as they are to ourselves, and if we assume that they have, as do we, ample time to wait. It is an entirely different women's question, which is united with our own" (Povell 2010, 37). Montessori's acknowledgment of diverse struggles within feminisms[1] is noteworthy. Contrary to popular feminist historiographies that frame feminist progress in a singular and linear manner through discrete wave metaphors, feminisms have always emerged in multiple and conflicting ways (Laughlin et al. 2010). Concurrently, the numerical wave depiction tells important stories of Global North feminist hegemony, even as lesser-known feminisms inhabit pasts and presents as crosscurrents, undercurrents, and eddies (Arvin et al. 2013; Chamberlain 2017).

Notwithstanding Montessori's feminist legacies, contemporary feminist theories, research, and activism have expanded and deepened understandings of gender over the course of time, demanding a renewed engagement with how gender is theorized and practiced in contemporary Montessori classrooms. Feminist theorists such as bell hooks (1984) and Audre Lorde (1984) succinctly point out how feminist theories and activisms are imbued with white middle-class values and experiences and thus do not resonate with issues perceived as priority by women of color in diverse geopolitical locations. Other feminist scholars have offered a critical reminder that relations of power need to be analyzed through the lens of intersectionality with considerations given to coloniality of gender, i.e., how cis-white heteropatriarchy plays a pivotal role in imposing Western gender differentials on non-Western and Indigenous people (Lugones 2007; Mohanty 1991). It is crucial to note here that the Western gender binary was framed as deterministic, "neutral," and "natural," thereby resulting in the criminalization and pathologizing of gender formations that threw Western gender binaries into question, which Morgensen (2011, 66) refers to as "Indigenous possibilities." These find further relevance in contemporary debates around gender variability in trans and genderqueer feminisms (Leavy and Harris 2019). Taking the coloniality of gender into consideration underscores the inseparability of ontology, epistemology, and ethics, which feminist particle physicist and philosopher Karen Barad (2003) has conceptualized as ethico-onto-epistemology, i.e., the intertwinement and inseparability of being, knowing, and doing. A feminist ethico-onto-epistemology prompts us to ask questions such as *what is valid knowledge? Who gets to decide what valid knowledge is? What does a feminist re-appraisal do?* While the Montessori early childhood sector is relentlessly framed as "female-dominated,"[2] Mohandas (2022, 18) asserts:

> The dominant theories and knowledge frames (i.e., the theories of European male philosophers), the low pay and status (an outcome of women's contributions being historically undervalued), as well as the masculinist neoliberal machinery, reproduce and sustain cis white heteropatriarchy.

Feminist theorizations not only expose the self-invisible "modest" status of cis-white heteropatriarchy (Haraway and Goodeve 2018); they open different ways of knowing and doing research that foreground an ethic of justice and care. It is with similar intentions that Montessori founded the National League for the Care and Education of Mentally Deficient Children in 1899—training and empowering women teachers to embrace a "scientific feminism" to oppose men's scientific monopoly and invite the critical gaze of feminism (Babini 2000, 54). Honoring the feminist roots of Montessori, this chapter considers what the critical gaze of feminism can offer in transforming contemporary Montessori theory and practice. As Colebrook (2000, 8) stresses, "[f]eminism has asked an intensely active question, not 'What does it mean?', but 'How does it work?, What can this concept or theory do?'"

Beyond the Gender Neutral

According to Gustafsson (2018, 1454), "an important feature of Montessori's didactic material is that it is gender-neutral and that her educational principles transcend cultural factors." The view that Montessori environments and materials are gender neutral is widely embraced in Montessori circles. The didactic materials seen in Montessori contexts are distinctively designed with specific pedagogical intentions in mind. Gendered play objects often seen in conventional nursery spaces, such as dolls, princess dresses, superhero costumes, etc., are absent in traditional Montessori spaces. This absence accentuates the perception of gender neutrality. In this section, by tracing some feminist theoretical advancements, I question the notion of gender neutrality. To do this, I will briefly touch upon feminist post-structuralist conceptualizations of gender, following which I will dwell on more recent scholarships framed by feminist "new" materialist thinking.

Feminist Post-structuralisms

For a time, the notion of gender neutrality was lauded in education, particularly in early childhood spaces, and was seen to have transformative potential. Granger et al. (2017) assert that gender-neutral activities in preschool have a pivotal role in later academic achievements, with traditionally gender-typed activities contributing to the emergence of gender disparity in educational outcomes in the future. Feminist researchers have problematized such an atomistic view, instead arguing for gender to be understood through relations of power (Mohandas 2020). Feminist post-structuralisms,[3] for instance, conceptualize gender as performative, instituted through the "stylized repetition of acts" and materialized through discursive[4] processes

(Butler 1988, 179). It foregrounds the pivotal role language and discourse play in shaping practices. In fact, multiple and often contradictory discourses circulate in everyday educational spaces. These discursive formations work to legitimize and normalize certain knowledges and practices as common-sense truth while marginalizing others (Burn and Pratt-Adams 2015). According to feminist post-structuralism, the activities are therefore not gender typed; rather, children and adults are enmeshed in gendered relationalities. They do not passively absorb these gender relations; instead, they actively negotiate, subvert, constitute, and perpetuate gendered narratives (Blaise 2005).

Questions related to power and agency are central to feminist post-structuralist concerns. While contradictory discourses circulate and compete in early childhood spaces, it is important to acknowledge that some discourses dominate to produce moral systems that privilege certain gender formations. Rather than eliminating gender altogether (which is nearly impossible), feminist post-structuralists argue that it is possible to co-create a classroom that fosters a critical consciousness and invites an experimentation with what gender can *do* for both children and adults in Montessori spaces. This is possible by contesting, subverting, and resisting dominant narratives of gender and by illuminating and welcoming alternative narratives through means of dialogue and storytelling (Osgood and Robinson 2017). Beyond the realms of everyday practice, research identifies Montessori training and continual professional development to play a key part in sensitizing practitioners to how gendered discourses circulate in educational spaces (Burn and Pratt-Adams 2015; Osgood and Mohandas 2019; Warin 2018; Warin et al. 2020). As of present, gender-sensitive pedagogy and training is mostly absent in Montessori training and practice, whereas these discussions began decades ago in mainstream education circles (Osgood and Mohandas 2019). Incorporating gender-sensitive pedagogy in training and practice can prepare practitioners to be attuned to children's gender knowings by fostering an awareness of the various gender discourses and power relations circulating in spaces and by developing ways to co-construct with children alternative, more transformative understandings of gender.

Feminist "New" Materialisms

More recently, there has been a philosophical and scholarly shift away from language and discourses to a re-attunement to how matter comes to matter. Barad (2003, 801) contends: "Language matters. Discourse matters. Culture matters. There is an important sense in which the only thing that does not seem to matter anymore is matter." There are multiple theoretical strands that have ushered this shift away from an exclusive focus on language, including feminist "new" materialisms, actor network theory (ANT), complexity theory, science and technology studies (STS), posthumanism, animal studies, affect theory, and assemblage theory, amongst others. While all these theories intermingle and overlap, this last section will explore feminist "new" materialisms to encapsulate most current trends in gender research.

In recent research, feminist "new" materialisms[5] have been employed to open out investigations around gender in Montessori contexts by attending to mundane materials, such as Pink Towers (Osgood and Mohandas 2019), animal figurines (Osgood and Mohandas 2021), child-sized chairs (Mohandas 2022), and cameras (Mohandas forthcoming). As Osgood and Robinson (2017) stress, this is not to put feminist post-structuralisms in opposition to "new" materialist thought or to assume a radical break with past feminist interventions; rather, it is to see them as both continuous and discontinuous, or, to use Barad's (2010) neologism, "dis/continuous." Feminist "new" materialists hold onto the advances made by feminist post-structuralists while expanding the focus beyond just discourse and language.

A fundamental aspect of materialist ontology is that it rejects the dualisms of Western thought (human/nonhuman, body/mind, matter/meaning, object/subject, nature/culture, etc.) for a monist view of the world where entities do not pre-exist interactions; rather, they form and un-form through processes of intra-action[6] (Barad 2003). According to "new" materialisms, matter is not passive; it is agentic, indeterminate, and in a constant state of "becoming." Moreover, discourse does not act on inert materials. Instead, matter and discourse simultaneously co-constitute phenomena and produce agencies, expressed in the concatenated term "materialdiscursive." Interestingly, one can find traces of this materialist ontology in Montessori's own work where she understood the active role of matter in affecting change. For instance, she refers to the materials and the environment as the "principal agent" (Montessori 1997, 150), "active" (Montessori 2008, 11), "the inanimate teacher," and "informer" (Montessori 1997, 105). She argues,

> The material acts directly on the child and the child responds according to his inner activities to the material ... This material liberates the inner life of the child.
> *(Montessori 2008, 11)*

Moreover, Montessori's feminist sensibilities were apparent in her critique of the contemporary, mechanistic form of materialism that was practiced under the banner of *scientific education*. These "scientific" practices divorced education from feminine virtues of care and were interested in controlling children's behavior and movement through the implementation of large, heavy benches and tables (Babini 2000; Montessori 1997). Angered by the effect these had on children's bodies, she provoked the design and manufacture of lightweight, child-sized furniture with the hope of enhancing children's autonomy, liberty, and learning. Montessori clearly understood the agentic potential of matter to affect and transform. These feminist and materialist sensibilities are worth holding onto in reconfiguring gender in contemporary contexts.

However, despite these traces, Montessori's approach is deeply entrenched in humanist ideals that rely heavily on Western dualist traditions and position the enlightened "Man" at the apex of the developmental path (Montessori 1997), a process that results in what Sylvia Wynter (2003, 267) calls "the overrepresentation of Man." Feminist "new" materialism, in contrast, deprivileges the human, viewing the human as only a part of the many assemblages that produce worlds. Viewed in this manner, gender is not simply located within the impermeable humanist subject; it is inextricably woven into the fabric of everyday life in the Montessori classroom. Gender is iteratively materialized and rematerialized through the intra-action of bodies (human and nonhuman), places, spaces, meanings, histories, presents, affects, structures of power, etc. A shift away from an exclusive focus on human bodies allows for more-than-human[7] accounts of our world and exposes how gender has been coded into the production of worlds. Scholarship centered on the more-than-human rejects the methodological individualism that shapes Montessori theory and practice, which argues that knowledge is produced through detachment, severing the individual from the gendered relations that they are enmeshed in. More-than-human scholarship sees that relations, not individuals, are the basis for analysis. As opposed to seeing the world as "units plus relations," these scholarly advances argue that it is "relationality all the way down," where "layers are inherited from other layers, temporalities, scales of time and space, which don't nest neatly but have oddly configured geometries" (Haraway 2019, 10).

A relational view of the world is particularly important in the context of the ecological crises that have destabilized ecosystems, evidenced by ongoing anthropogenic effects that have decimated plants and animals; caused climate destruction, extinctionism; forced displacement of nonhuman and human actors; created diverse inequalities; and so forth. This calls for new ways of researching and new ways of relating. Feminist "new" materialisms invite a trans-corporeal sensibility (Alaimo 2010), where corporeal theories, environmental studies, and science studies mingle in productive ways. This transdisciplinary commitment profoundly complicates understandings of gendered subjectivities, even as the sense of gendered selfhood is transformed by the recognition that the material self is intermeshed in vast networks that are simultaneously personal, biological, economic, ecological, social, political, and industrial—impossible to entirely map or understand (Alaimo 2012).

Final Thoughts

Using Montessori's feminism as a springboard and building on her commitment to reconceptualize gender, knowledge, and practice, this chapter draws on current scholarly trends to question taken-for-granted assumptions of gender neutrality in Montessori spaces. A gender-neutral framing obscures cis-white, heteropatriarchal power relations and has the potential to let gender completely fall off the research agenda in and around Montessori education. Feminist theorizations illuminate how gender is indeed part of ordinary relations in the classroom. Feminist post-structuralisms, for instance, conceptualize gender by analyzing discursive formations in the classroom and use language to contest, subvert, negotiate, and co-create gender relations. More recent scholarly work developed in response to the exclusive focus on language and discourse, such as feminist "new" materialisms, has acknowledged matter as an active component in shaping gendered realities. Gender is thus seen as an outcome of more-than-human entanglements that is constantly shifting, emerging, and re-constituting. The intensities transform depending on the "who," "what," "when," and "where" of the assemblages. Researching gender in this manner does not render a neat set of stories, nor does it prescribe a step-by-step solution to tackle gender inequalities in Montessori settings. Instead, it invites Montessori practitioners to commit to ongoing practices of knowing, responding, and caring even as gender is materialized, sensed, and reconfigured in each encounter. Finally, honoring Montessori's feminist roots, this chapter encourages Montessori training organizations, teacher trainers, and leaders of various Montessori institutions to invite the critical gaze of feminisms by incorporating gender-sensitive pedagogy as an integral part of Montessori teacher training and continual professional development.

Notes

1. The plural use indicates that feminism is by no means a monolithic movement but encompasses diverse, multiple, and evolving perspectives.

2. There is currently no data available on the gender composition of the Montessori workforce for other planes of development.
3. Feminist post-structuralisms are theoretical approaches that highlight the social construction of gender and the circulation of power by examining matters such as language, discourse, subjectivity, and agency.
4. Discursive relates to modes of discourse, i.e., ways of speaking, writing, thinking, feeling, or acting that incorporate some ideas as "truths."
5. The "new" in feminist "new" materialism is an attempt to distinguish itself from older forms of materialism such as Marxist-inflected materialism, where material reality is believed to produce consciousness and ideology. Furthermore, the notion of "new" can be contentious as Indigenous philosophies and cosmologies in diverse locations have subscribed to similar views for centuries and millennia (Dungdung 2019; George and Wiebe 2020; Moreton-Robinson 2017; Todd 2016).
6. Intra-action is Karen Barad's term where agency is not viewed as an inherent property of the bounded individual or human; instead, all bodies (human and nonhuman) in a particular phenomenon together produce agencies.
7. "More-than-human" is a term that includes the nonhuman world—i.e., other animals, things, objects, trees, land, rivers, physical forces, etc.—as well as humans.

References

Adichie, Chimamanda Ngozi. 2014. *We Should All Be Feminists*. London: 4th Estate.
Alaimo, Stacy. 2010. *Bodily Natures: Science, Environment and the Material Self*. Bloomington: Indiana University Press.
Alaimo, Stacy. 2012. "States of Suspension: Trans-corporeality at Sea." *Interdisciplinary Studies in Literature and Environment* 19 (3) (Summer): 476–93.
Arvin, Maile, Eve Tuck, and Angie Morril. 2013. "Decolonizing Feminism: Challenging Connections between Settler Colonialism and Heteropatriarchy." *Feminist Formations* 25 (1) (Spring): 8–34.
Babini, Valeria. 2000. "Science, Feminism and Education: The Early Work of Maria Montessori." *History Workshop Journal* 49 (1) (Spring): 44–67.
Barad, Karen. 2003. "Posthumanist Performativity: Toward an Understanding of How Matter Comes to Matter." *Signs* 28 (3) (Spring): 801–30. https://doi.org/10.1086/345321.
Barad, Karen. 2010. "Quantum Entanglements and Hauntological Relations of Inheritance: Dis/continuities, SpaceTime Enfoldings, and Justice-to-Come." *Derrida Today* 3 (2): 240–68. https://doi.org/10.3366/E1754850010000813.
Blaise, Mindy. 2005. *Playing It Straight: Uncovering Gender Discourses in the Early Childhood Classroom*. New York, NY: Routledge.
Burn, Elizabeth, and Simon Pratt-Adams. 2015. *Men Teaching Children 3–11: Dismantling Gender Barriers*. London: Bloomsbury Academic.
Butler, Judith. 1988. "Performative Acts and Gender Constitution: An Essay in Phenomenology and Feminist Theory." *Theatre Journal* 40 (4) (December): 519–31.
Chamberlain, Prudence. 2017. *The Feminist Fourth Wave: Affective Temporality*. Cham, Switzerland: Palgrave Macmillan.
Colebrook, Claire. 2000. "From Radical Representations to Corporeal Becomings: The Feminist Philosophy of Lloyd, Grosz and Gatens." *Hypatia* 5 (2) (Spring): 76–93. DOI:10.1111/j.1527-2001.2000.tb00315.x.
Davies, Bronwyn. 1989. *Frogs and Snails and Feminist Tales: Preschool Children and Gender*. Sydney: Allen and Unwin.

DfE (Department for Education). 2017. *Early Years Workforce Strategy*. London: DfE. https://assets.publishing.service.gov.uk/government/uploads/system/uploads/attachment_data/file/596884/Workforce_strategy_02-03-2017.pdf.

Granger, Kristen L., Laura D. Hanish, Olga Kornienko, and Robert H. Bradley. 2017. "Preschool Teachers' Facilitation of Gender-Typed and Gender- Neutral Activities during Free Play." *Sex Roles* 76 (7–8): 498–510. https://doi.org/10.1007/s11199-016-0675-1.

Gustafsson, Christina. 2018. "Montessori Education." In *International Handbook of Early Childhood Education Volume I*, edited by Marilyn Fleer and Bert van Oers, 1439–56. Dordrecht: Springer Nature.

Haraway, Donna. 2019. A Giant Bumptious Litter: Donna Haraway on Truth, Technology, and Resisting Extinction. *Logic* 9. Accessed October 8, 2020. https://logicmag.io/nature/a-giant-bumptiouslitter/.

Haraway, Donna and Thryza Goodeve. 2018. Modest_Witness@Second_Millenium. FemaleMan©_Meets_OncoMouse™: *Feminism and Technoscience*. New York: Routledge.

Hodgins, B. Denise. 2019. *Gender and Care with Young Children: A Feminist Material Approach to Early Childhood Education*. New York, London: Routledge.

hooks, bell. 1984. *Feminist Theory: From Margin to Center*. Boston, MA: South End Press.

Kramer, Rita. 1988. *Maria Montessori: A Biography*. Boston, MA: Da Capo Press.

Laughlin, Kathleen A., Julie Gallagher, Dorothy Sue Cobble, Eileen Boris, Premilla Nadasen, Stephanie Gilmore, and Leandra Zarnow. 2010. "Is It Time to Jump Ship? Historians Rethink the Waves Metaphor." *Feminist Formations* 22 (1) (January): 76–135.

Leavy, Patricia, and Anne Harris. 2019. *Contemporary Feminist Research from Theory to Practice*. New York: The Guildford Press.

Lillard, Angeline S. 2012. "Preschool Children's Development in Classic Montessori, Supplemented Montessori, and Conventional Programs." *Journal of School Psychology* 50 (3): 379–401. https://doi.org/10.1016/j.jsp.2012.01.001.

Lillard, Angeline S. 2013. "Playful Learning and Montessori Education." *The NAMTA Journal* 38 (2) (Spring): 137–74.

Lillard, Angeline S., and Jessica Taggart. 2019. "Pretend Play and Fantasy: What if Montessori Was Right?" *Child Development Perspectives* 13: 85–90. https://doi.org/10.1111/cdep.12314.

Lillard, Angeline, and Nicole Else-Quest. 2006. "Evaluating Montessori Education." *Science* 313 (5795): 1893–4. https://doi.org/10.1126/science.1132362.

Lillard, Angeline S., Megan J. Heise, Eve M. Richey, Xin Tong, Alyssa Hart, and Paige M. Bray. 2017. "Montessori Preschool Elevates and Equalizes Child Outcomes: A Longitudinal Study." *Frontiers in Psychology* 8: 1783. https://doi.org/10.3389/fpsyg.2017.01783.

Lorde, Audre. 1984. *Sister Outsider: Essays and Speeches*. Trumansburg, NY: Crossing Press.

Lugones, María. 2007. "Heterosexualism and the Colonial/Modern Gender System." *Hypatia* 22 (1) (Winter): 186–209.

MacNaughton, Glenda. 2000. *Rethinking Gender in Early Childhood Education*. St. Leonards, NSW: Allen and Unwin.

Marcus, Laura. 2016. "Montessori Offers £3,000 Bursaries for Male Students." *NurseryWorld*. Accessed September 27, 2019. https://www.nurseryworld.co.uk/nursery-world/news/1158110/montessori-offers-gbp3-000-bursaries-for-male-students.

Mohandas, Sid. 2020. "Reclaiming Feminism in the Early Years." *Montessori International* 127 (January): 16–19.

Mohandas, Sid. 2022. "Beyond Male Recruitment: Decolonizing Gender Diversification Efforts in the Early Years by Attending to Pastpresent Material-Discursive-Affective Entanglements." *Gender and Education* 34 (1): 17–34. DOI: 10.1080/09540253.2021.1884202.

Mohandas, Sid. Forthcoming. "More-Than-Just-Cameras: Posthuman Gendered Subjectivities in Early Childhood Spaces." *Subjectivity*, edited by Lisa Blackman, Valerie Walkerdine. London: Palgrave Macmillan.

Mohanty, Chandra. 1991. "Under Western Eyes: Feminist Scholarship and Colonial Discourses." In *Third World Women and the Politics of Feminism*, edited by Chandra Talpade Mohanty, Ann Russo, and Lourdes Torres, 51–80. Bloomington: Indiana University Press.

Montessori, Maria. 1997. *The Discovery of the Child*. Translated by M. Joseph Costelloe. Oxford: ABC-Clio.
Montessori, Maria. 2008. *The Californian Lectures of Maria Montessori, 1915: Collected Speeches and Writings*. Amsterdam: Montessori-Pierson Publishing Company.
Morgensen, Scott Lauria. 2011. *Spaces between Us: Queer Settler Colonialism and Indigenous Decolonization*. Minneapolis, MN: University of Minnesota Press.
Osgood, Jayne. 2006. "Deconstructing Professionalism in Early Childhood Education: Resisting the Regulatory Gaze." *Contemporary Issues in Early Childhood* 7 (1): 5–14. https://doi.org/10.2304/ciec.2006.7.1.5.
Osgood, Jayne, and Sid Mohandas. 2019. "Reconfiguring the 'Male Montessorian': The Mattering of Gender through Pink Towering Practices." *Early Years* 40 (1): 67–81. https://doi.org/10.1080/09575146.2019.1620181.
Osgood, Jayne, and Sid Mohandas. 2021. "Figuring Gender in Early Childhood with Animal Figurines: Pursuing Tentacular Stories about Global Childhoods in the Anthropocene." In *The SAGE Handbook of Global Childhoods*, edited by Nicola J. Yelland, Lacey Peters, Nikki Fairchild, Marek Tesar and Michelle S. Pérez, 205–18. London: SAGE Publications Ltd.
Osgood, Jayne, and Kerry H. Robinson. 2017. "Celebrating Pioneering and Contemporary Feminist Approaches to Studying Gender in Early Childhood." In *Feminism(s) in Early Childhood: Using Feminist Theories in Research and Practice*, edited by Kylie Smith, Kate Alexander and Sheralyn Campbell, 35–48. Singapore: Springer.
Povell, Phyllis. 2010. *Montessori Comes to America: The Leadership of Maria Montessori and Nancy McCormick Rambusch*. Lanham: University Press of America Inc.
Trabalzini, Paola. 2011. "Maria Montessori through the Seasons of the 'Method.'" *The NAMTA Journal* 36 (2) (Spring): XI–218.
Warin, Jo. 2018. *Men in Early Childhood Education and Care: Gender Balance and Flexibility*. Cham, Switzerland: Palgrave Macmillan.
Warin, Jo, and Vina Adriany. 2017. "Gender Flexible Pedagogy in Early Childhood Education." *Journal of Gender Studies* 26 (4): 375–86. https://doi.org/10.1080/09589236.2015.1105738.
Warin, Jo, Joann Wilkinson, Jeremy Davies, Helen Greaves, and Rebecca Hibbin. 2020. *Gender Diversification of the Early Years Workforce: Recruiting and Supporting Male Practitioners*. London: GenderEYE. https://gendereye.files.wordpress.com/2020/10/gendereye-final-end-of-project-report-28-oct.pdf.
Wynter, Sylvia. 2003. "Unsettling the Coloniality of Being/Power/Truth/Freedom: Towards the Human, after Man, Its Overrepresentation—An Argument." *The New Centennial Review* 3 (3) (Fall): 257–337. https://doi.org/10.1353/ncr.2004.0015.

Additional Resources

Chapman, Rachel. 2021. "Moving beyond 'Gender-Neutral': Creating Gender Expansive Environments in Early Childhood Education." *Gender and Education* 34 (1): 1–16. https://doi.org/10.1080/09540253.2021.1902485.
Dungdung, Gladston. 2019. *Adivasis and Their Forest*. Ranchi: Adivasi Publications.
George, Rachel Yacaaʔał, and Sarah Marie Wiebe. 2020. "Fluid Decolonial Futures: Water as a Life, Ocean Citizenship and Seascape Relationality." *New Political Science* 42 (1): 498–520. https://doi.org/10.1080/07393148.2020.1842706.
Moreton-Robinson, Aileen. 2017. "Relationality: A Key Presupposition of an Indigenous Social Research Paradigm." In *Sources and Methods in Indigenous Studies*, edited by Chris Andersen and Jean M. O'Brien, 69–77. London: Routledge.
Todd, Zoe. 2016. "An Indigenous Feminist's Take on The Ontological Turn: 'Ontology' Is Just Another Word for Colonialism." *Journal of Historical Sociology* 29 (1): 4–22. https://doi.org/10.1111/johs.12124.

Chapter 56
Montessori Education and Inclusion

Jennifer D. Moss and Ann Epstein

Inclusion and inclusive classrooms refer to the practice of serving disabled learners in environments with learners who do not have special needs (Lowry 2020). Montessori educators view inclusion as an integral component of the method, as Maria Montessori's first classrooms were designed to provide sensorial stimulation and learning experiences for students deprived of these opportunities due to perceived disabilities (Kramer 1976). Much has been written on how Montessori's work began with disabled children and work is underway to address disabilities to include all children more seamlessly (AuCoin and Berger 2021; Awes 2014; Lane-Barmapov 2016; Marks 2016). Still, over time the evolution of inclusive practices in schools and the fuller breadth of children included in education globally mean that all schools, including Montessori schools, have room to improve and grow their inclusive practices. This chapter traces the chronology of inclusion in Montessori pedagogy and practice beginning with its historical underpinnings and continuing with a discussion of contemporary practice. We focus on early childhood (ages 3 through 6), while noting practices that apply to all ages of learners. Finally, we are US researchers and want to acknowledge our positionality. Our goal is to provide global examples of research and effective practices, but we recognize that the scope and length of the chapter is limited especially as it pertains to global practice and encourage readers to use this as one starting, rather than exhaustive end point in their learning about inclusion in Montessori education. We close with current research and future opportunities.

We acknowledge that disability terms can be confusing and controversial (Rolfe 2020). After consulting with a variety of members of the disabled community and disability experts, we use identity-first, such as "Deaf student," rather than person-first language, "student who is Deaf," language throughout this chapter (Flink 2021). We refer to non-disabled children as typically developing or TD.

Foundations of Inclusion in Montessori Education

As a newly minted medical doctor and anthropologist in the late 1800s, Montessori worked for the University of Rome's psychiatric clinic. When visiting psychiatric hospitals, Montessori encountered disabled children housed alongside adults with serious mental illnesses (Kramer 1976). Influenced by a variety of contemporary educational theorists, including Jean-Marc Itard (1802) and his protégé Édouard Séguin (1846), Montessori came to believe the children she met needed education and sensorial stimulation more than they needed hospitals and medicine

(Kramer 1976). After returning to school to study pedagogy and education, Montessori focused her attention on the need for schools to address issues such as cognitive disability and delinquency, both of which at the time were believed to be congenital rather than the result of inadequate care and education. At the 1898 Pedagogical Congress in Turin, Italy, Montessori argued that children who were being ignored by the educational system deserved proper schools. In 1900, she was appointed as the director of the Orthophrenic School, a new school for disabled children (Kramer 1976). Montessori implemented a precise observation-based approach to determine learning and development opportunities, one that is parallel to and valued in special education communities today, built on Itard and Seguin's work (Standing 1959). In 1907, Montessori established her first Casa dei Bambini (Children's House) in an impoverished district of Rome, creating learning materials to assist young children in exploring size, color, shape, weight, and textures. Montessori observed that children's aggressive behaviors and crying changed to extended periods of concentration when they engaged with Sensorial materials in a carefully designed space (Seldin and Epstein 2003). Older children cared for younger children. Some asked to learn to read and write. Observing this interest, Montessori developed materials such as letters made of sandpaper which provided continuing opportunities for sensory exploration (Standing 1959).

Even as Montessori moved from educating only disabled children to educating all children, others working with disabled children implemented Montessori methods and curricula in the early to mid-twentieth century. For example, Anna Margulies assisted Deaf children in learning to speak using Montessori materials (*New York Times* 1929). Similarly, Lena Gitter, an Austrian teacher trained by Montessori, adapted presentations to address the needs of cognitively and physically disabled children in both Europe and the United States (Gitter 1967).

Later in the twentieth century, strides were made worldwide to better meet disabled children's educational needs. In the United States, a 1975 law mandated free and appropriate education for all children regardless of their disability (US Department of Education n.d.). Canada, Germany, and China implemented similar protections in the 1980s, while Denmark, Japan, and Mexico began programs of inclusion for disabled students in the 1990s and 2000s (Agrawal et al. 2019). Notably, in 1994 the World Conference on Special Needs Education issued the "Salamanca Statement" calling on nations to prioritize inclusive education and providing a roadmap for educators globally to consider how special needs students should be integrated into all types of mainstream education environments. Ninety-two unique governments and twenty-five global organizations were represented at the conference (UNESCO 1994). It is not known if Montessori organizations were represented at the conference, nonetheless the influence of the Salamanca Statement on attentiveness to inclusion, particularly in non-American contexts, is still important to our discussion here and a noteworthy historical inflection point. Today, some two decades beyond the Salamanca Statement, there is still a long way to go in geographic reach of education advocacy for disabled individuals. Within practices that are enacted and where services do exist, inclusion experts agree that attention is still warranted including a focus on inclusive curriculum design, assessment, teacher training, community involvement and cultural sensitivity (UNESCO 2020). Montessori education has a role to play in the need for continued advocacy.

Especially important to the inclusion movement globally is the recognition that various barriers including entry requirements, curricular inflexibility, and a lack of teacher expertise in the arena of disability education still need to be remedied. Thompson et al. (1993) emphasized that expecting disabled students to meet certain criteria prior to inclusion eliminates participation opportunities for children who, for example, need toileting assistance or have significant mobility issues. Shanks (2014) reminds teachers that children do not need to be "fixed" before they benefit from the Montessori community. Montessori herself felt that rational methods, such as systematic observation and structured lessons and materials, allowed disabled students to learn. This experience uniting her medical education with her work on learning has been referred to as medical pedagogy (Bobbio 2021).

Modern Examples of Montessori Inclusion

Public Montessori programs began in some larger US cities in the mid-1970s to address racial disparities via desegregation programs which opened up a new era of scrutiny on inclusion in American public Montessori schools (AuCoin and Berger 2021; NCMPS 2014). Legislation at this time allowed disabled children to be educated alongside their TD peers (Lowry 2020). Private Montessori schools in the United States also took similar strides toward inclusion during the second half of the twentieth century. For example, in collaboration with the University of Kansas, Raintree Montessori School in Lawrence, Kansas, welcomed TD children and children with severe cognitive, motor, and sensory disabilities in 1973 in alignment with the 1959 United Nations Declaration of the Rights of the Child (Thompson et al. 1993; Thompson and Shanks 2020; UN General Assembly 1959). Raintree and the University of Kansas promoted the right all children have to develop relationships with one another serving as an example for other schools to follow (Shanks 2014).

Simultaneously, in 1968, Mario Montessori and Theodore Hellbrugge created Aktion Sonnenschein (Sunshine Project), a full-service inclusion program in Munich, Germany (Nehring 2014; Willingham 2019). Today the school is affiliated with a children's clinic and hospital, which allows therapeutic staff to observe children in classrooms. This environment addresses the medical pedagogy that Montessori created by integrating structured lessons and observations while providing on-site intervention. This eases the stress families encounter of shuttling to various locations for their children's services. Hellbrugge established a foundation and conducts Montessori inclusion teacher training in Germany (Willingham 2019).

Similarly the Penfield Children's Center has provided early intervention services for disabled children from birth to age 3 before they enter the public-school system for decades (Ayer 2016; Thomas 2016). Penfield grew out of what was originally the Via Marsi Montessori school which opened in 1967 and claimed to be the first Montessori school in the US exclusively serving disabled students (Penfield Children's Center 2022). After being renamed Penfield Children's Center in 1974 (Penfield Children's Center 2022), the program lost its Montessori focus with the last Montessori classroom closing in the 1980s (Ayer 2016). The program rediscovered its Montessori roots in 2016 when the Penfield Children's Center opened Penfield Montessori Academy, a public charter school that now serves children in both early childhood and elementary classrooms with 25 percent of the student population currently having an Individualized Education Plan (IEP) (Penfield Montessori Academy 2020/2021). Penfield, along with the Montessori Medical Partnerships for Inclusion, has brought Montessori inclusion to Milwaukee (Willingham 2019).

While public schools and many private Montessori schools in the United States welcome students with varying abilities, some take an even more focused stance on working with disabled students. For example, the June Shelton School and Evaluation Center, a Montessori-based school, opened in Dallas, Texas, in 1976 specifically for students at risk for learning difficulties (Shelton School n.d.). Teachers and therapists currently provide support for over a 1000 children with learning and speech/language disabilities through the Montessori curriculum and philosophy. The Shelton School offers training in the MACAR Model (Montessori Applied to Children at Risk; Pickering and Richardson 2019) and professional development for Montessori educators. The Shelton School does not include TD children, focusing entirely on children with identified disabilities. Other examples of Montessori schools in the United States serving specific populations of disabled students include Blossom Montessori School for the Deaf in Clearwater, Florida, and Alexander Graham Bell Montessori School in Wheeling, Illinois, which serves both Deaf and hearing children (AGBMS n.d.; BMSD n.d.). Both spoken English and American Sign Language are used in classrooms, providing children with a bilingual as well as a bi-cultural (hearing and Deaf) Montessori learning experience.

It is important to recall too that not all students with disabilities or learning differences are identified before entering school. Observations are key to early identification and intervention and the areas of coordination, language, attention, and perception are all easily seen as children navigate the Montessori classroom (Pickering 2017). Pickering added that while all children benefit from Montessori education, those who learn differently benefit even further from the multisensory curriculum and close observation by the teachers. Furthermore, as parents learn about their child's disability or potential disability, Montessori teachers in inclusion settings promote the child's strengths and work with the family to develop solid strategies for consistent support (Dattke 2014; Perolman 2020). Small, attainable goals that demonstrate success provide parents with confidence in their child and Montessori inclusion (Dattke 2014). As a self-paced, collaborative pedagogy, Montessori education is well situated to navigate individualized needs and feedback (Rolfe 2020).

Montessori Inclusion Research

Current research on inclusion in Montessori settings focuses on three themes: the benefits for both disabled and TD students, the role of the environment in inclusion, and roles that Montessori teachers play in classroom inclusion.

Research indicates that both disabled and TD children in the United States benefit from inclusive Montessori classrooms (Shanks 2014; Thompson et al. 1993; Thompson and Shanks 2020). TD children in inclusive settings experience differences among their peers as natural and subsequently "grow up advocating for those who are different or less able" (Shanks 2014, 7). In addition, studies addressing inclusive programs (Lieberman et al. 2017; Noggle and Stites 2018) reveal improved social skills for TD peers. Advocating for disability justice aligns with Montessori's view of the cosmic purpose of education as a force for humanistic change (Montessori and Carter 1936), and Moretti (2021) emphasizes Montessori's role as an international peace maker and humanitarian grounded in her inclusive approach to education.

Montessori educators focus on the environment as a teacher, providing opportunities for children to learn directly from interactions with the materials (Lillard and McHugh 2019). Great care is taken to create environments that promote inclusion in the classroom, for example by offering Practical Life exercises for elementary-aged children who are developing self-care skills (Goertz 1997) and by reducing the number of materials available (Pickering 2017). Drilling down more deeply, authors also discuss supporting students with specific disabilities in Montessori classrooms. Attention issues are frequently addressed (Kristiyani 2018; Murphy-Ryan 2017; Nehring Massie 2017) with recommendations to provide consistent routines, visual choice boards, alternative seating options such as sensory cushions, exercise/movement breaks, and opportunities for engagement by working with materials that create sensory and intellectual stimulation.

Danner and Fowler (2015) add to our understanding with their work that surveyed US Montessori and non-Montessori early childhood teachers about inclusive education. They found that while both groups had very positive attitudes toward inclusion, the traditionally trained teachers felt more knowledgeable about special education practices and reported more experience with a wider variety of disabled children. The authors recommended additional professional development for Montessori teachers to increase their knowledge around disability and inclusion. Similar work using semi-structured interviews from Turkey found that Montessori teachers felt inclusion was best for most children but that they were not as prepared as they would like to implement best practices for inclusive classrooms (Ak 2019). And Cossentino (2010) reminds us that communities of practice organized along the planes of development can be a helpful way for teachers within a school to share best practices which promote inclusion.

Fortunately, information about successful inclusion practices in Montessori classrooms is becoming more and more available. Pickering (2017) presented general suggestions for teachers when working with students for whom the standard Montessori presentations are not successful, including reducing the difficulty of the activity, adding more tactile input, and increasing the structure of the lesson.

Finally, McDonell (2017) argued in her research on special education schools in Hyderabad, India that students benefit from Montessori environments because of the non-competitive nature of Montessori education. Allowing children to work at their own pace and experience the social atmosphere of the Montessori classroom encourages more advanced students to assist others and model appropriate behaviors.

We lack empirical Montessori research for families to consult when making educational decisions for disabled children, including autistic learners (Lane-Barmapov 2016). However, the limited findings thus far indicate that families are drawn to the individual educational experiences that Montessori classrooms provide for all students (Epstein 2020). In a review of the literature, Fulton (2014) argued that, while Montessori education can be a model for teaching social skills, it is not a panacea for all the needs of autistic children. She also recommends that Montessori schools develop inclusion policies that specifically support students on the autism spectrum.

Overall, these findings support an important takeaway from this chapter—additional research building on extant work and extending beyond case studies is imperative for the Montessori community to grow in their understanding of inclusion and inclusive practices including the training of educators, pragmatic implementation of inclusive practices, and attention to familial relationships and cultural difference in how disabled children are perceived and integrated into Montessori environments. Perhaps most important of all, Montessori teachers must reflect on their biases and work to eliminate their assumptions and prejudices about disabled students (McDonell 2017).

Conclusion and Future Directions

The shared history of Montessori and disability education, from the early days of the Orthophrenic School to the modern era of inclusive Montessori schools such as Penfield and Aktion Sonnenschein, demonstrate that inclusive programming can be a key facet of Montessori education when Montessori communities and educators choose to be intentional about inclusion. The commitment of the Declaration on the Rights of the Child and the Salamaca Statement to the education of disabled children and a growing global awareness of the importance of this issue all support future growth and development in this field of education. In fact, Montessori reminds us that typically developing children also benefit when they learn alongside disabled students. As Montessori herself has said, one of the charms of life is meeting so many different people (1988). Increasing the availability of Montessori inclusion training, such as those held by the Montessori Medical Partnerships for Inclusion (MMPI n.d.) and the American Montessori Society's Montessori Inclusion Endorsement (AMS n.d.), can help current and future teachers facilitate a classroom for all students.

We close our chapter with a call for studies that compare Montessori education for disabled students with other types of educational practices and additional attention to inclusive practices worldwide. The field of Montessori research would benefit from increased empirical research that demonstrates what extant case studies, program descriptions, and Montessori herself have suggested: self-directed, self-paced, and patient, structured, collaborative work is beneficial for all students and, in some ways, superior for disabled students. Furthermore, Montessori's consideration of the prepared adult invites educators to become better versions of themselves by committing to continuing education about inclusive practice.

Montessori educators and special educators respect and even admire one another's mission to support all learners (AuCoin and Berger 2021). However, research is needed to go beyond the surface of shared values to evaluate, examine, and compare specific interventions and practices within Montessori environments. An even more robust and empirical pool of studies for researchers and practitioners to reference would bring greater efficacy to our work and more attention to inclusion within Montessori education in the service of creating communities where all students can learn—and learn together.

References

AGBMS (Alexander Graham Bell Montessori School). n.d. "Our Programs." https://www.agbms.org/our-programs.html#/.

Agrawal, Jugnu, Brenda L. Barrio, Benikia Kressler, Yun-Ju Hsiao, and Rebecca K. Shankland. 2019. "International Policies, Identification, and Services for Students with Learning Disabilities: An Exploration across 10 Countries." *Learning Disabilities: A Contemporary Journal* 17 (1): 95–113.

Ak, İdil Seda. 2019. "Investigating the Views of Montessori Preschool Teachers on Inclusive Education in Montessori Approach." Master's thesis, Middle East Technical University.

AMS (American Montessori Society). n.d. "Montessori Inclusion Endorsement." American Montessori Society. https://amshq.org/Educators/Montessori-Careers/Become-a-Montessori-Educator/Montessori-Inclusion-Endorsement.

AuCoin, Dena, and Brian Berger. 2021. "An Expansion of Practice: Special Education and Montessori Public School." *International Journal of Inclusive Education*. https://doi.org/10.1080/13603116.2021.1931717

Awes, Alison. 2014. "Supporting the Dyslexic Child in the Montessori Environment." *The NAMTA Journal* 39 (3) (Summer): 171–207.

Ayer, David. 2016. "Penfield Montessori Academy: A New Chapter in Milwaukee Montessori." *Montessori Public* (blog). August 10, 2016. https://www.montessoripublic.org/2016/08/penfield-montessori-academy-new-chapter-milwaukee/.

BMSD (Blossom Montessori School for the Deaf). n.d. "About Us." https://www.blossomschool.org/about-us/.

Bobbio, Andrea. 2021. "Maria Montessori between Medicine and Pedagogy: Roots, Actuality and Educational Perspectives." *Ricerche Di Pedagogia e Didattica. Journal of Theories and Research in Education* 16 (2): 23–39. https://doi.org/10.6092/issn.1970-2221/12161.

Cossentino, Jacqueline. 2010. "Following All the Children: Early Intervention and Montessori." *Montessori Life* 22 (4): 38–45.

Danner, Natalie, and Susan Fowler. 2015. "Montessori and Non-Montessori Early Childhood Teachers' Attitudes Towards Inclusion and Access." *Journal of Montessori Research* 1 (1): 28–41. https://doi.org/10.17161/jomr.v1i1.4944.

Dattke, Joachim. 2014. "A Montessori Model for Inclusion." *NAMTA Journal* 39 (3) (Summer): 107–19.

Epstein, Ann (ed.). 2020. *Montessori Inclusion: Strategies and Stories for Learners with Exceptionalities*. Santa Rosa, CA: Parent Child Press.

Epstein, Ann, Nancy Lindeman, and Shamby Polychronis. (2020). "Montessori: A Promising Practice for Young Learners with Autism Spectrum Disorder." *Montessori Life* 31 (4): 38–47.

Flink, Patrick. 2021. "Person-First & Identity-First Language: Supporting Students with Disabilities on Campus." *Community College Journal of Research and Practice* 45 (2): 79–85. https://doi.org/10.1080/10668926.2019.1640147.

Fulton, Jennifer A. 2014. "Evidence Based Social Skills Interventions for Young Children with Asperger's Syndrome and the Montessori Educational Method: An Integrative Review." PhD diss., University of Pennsylvania.

Gitter, Lena L. 1967. "The Promise of Montessori for Special Education." *The Journal of Special Education* 2 (1): 5–13. https://doi.org/10.1177/002246696700200101.

Goertz, Donna Bryant. 1997. "Embracing Learning Diversity in the Montessori School." *NAMTA Journal* 22 (1) (Winter): 204–34.

Itard, Jean Marc Gaspard. 1802. *An Historical Account of the Discovery and Education of a Savage Man: Or, the First Developments, Physical and Moral, of the Young Savage Caught in the Woods near Aveyron in the Year 1798*. London: R. Phillips. http://archive.org/details/bub_gb_E63cRcnV2hIC.

Kramer, Rita. 1976. *Maria Montessori: A Biography*. New York: Putnam.

Kristiyani, Christina. 2018. "Materials and (Language) Learning Environment Based on Montessori Concepts." *LLT Journal: A Journal on Language and Language Teaching* 21 (1): 46–54. https://doi.org/10.24071/llt.v21i1.1041.

Lane-Barmapov, K. Michelle. 2016. "Montessori and Autism: An Interpretive Description Study." Master's Thesis, Athabasca University.

Lieberman, Lauren J., Lauren Cavanaugh, Justin A. Haegele, Rocco Aiello, and Wesley J. Wilson. 2017. "The Modified Physical Education Class: An Option for the Least Restrictive Environment." *Journal of Physical Education, Recreation & Dance* 88 (7): 10–16. https://doi.org/10.1080/07303084.2017.1340203.

Lillard, Angeline S., and Virginia McHugh. 2019. "Authentic Montessori: The Dottoressa's View at the End of Her Life Part I: The Environment." *Journal of Montessori Research* 5 (1): 1–18. https://doi.org/10.17161/jomr.v5i1.7716.

Lowry, Christine. 2020. "An Overview of a Montessori-Based Multi-Tiered System of Support." In *Montessori Inclusion: Strategies and Stories of Support for Learners with Exceptionalities*, edited by Ann Epstein. Santa Rosa, CA: Parent Child Press.

Marks, Laura. 2016. "Playing to Learn: An Overview of the Montessori Approach with Pre-School Children with Autism Spectrum Condition." *Support for Learning* 31 (4): 313–28. https://doi.org/10.1111/1467-9604.12140.

McDonell, Janet. 2017. "Inclusive Education: A Montessori Perspective." *Montessori Australia* 1 (February): 1–8. https://montessori.org.au/publications/maf-earticle/2017-issue-1.

MMPI (Montessori Medical Partnership for Inclusion). n.d. "Learn More About MMPI and Join Today." *Montessori 4 Inclusion* (blog). https://montessori4inclusion.org/about-us/.

Montessori, Maria. (1949) 1988. *The Absorbent Mind*. Madras, India: Theosophical Publishing House. Reprint, Oxford, England: Clio Press, Ltd.

Montessori, Maria, and Barbara Barclay Carter. 1936. *The Secret of Childhood*. London and New York: Longmans, Green and Co.

Moretti, Erica. 2021. *The Best Weapon for Peace: Maria Montessori, Education, and Children's Rights*. Madison, WI: University of Wisconsin Press.

Murphy-Ryan, Maureen. 2017. "Helping Children with Attentional Challenges in a Montessori Classroom: The Role of the Physician." *The NAMTA Journal* 42 (2) (Spring): 355–423.

NCMPS (National Center for Montessori in the Public Sector). 2014. Growth of Montessori in the Public Sector: 1975–2014. Washington, DC: National Center for Montessori in the Public Sector. http://www.public-montessori.org/white-papers/growth-of-public-montessori-in-the-united-states-1975-2014/.

Nehring, Catherine. 2014. "Implementing Inclusion Theory into Practice." *The NAMTA Journal* 39 (3) (Summer): 39–63.

Nehring Massie, Catherine. 2017. "Appendix A: Doing Great Things with ADHD." *The NAMTA Journal* 42 (2) (Spring): 385–7.

New York Times. 1929. "Anna R. Margulies, Educator, Is Dead; She Founded and Headed Montessori (Later Ann-Reno) School Here—Taught Deaf to Speak." July 8, 1929. https://timesmachine.nytimes.com/timesmachine/1929/07/08/94167817.html.

Noggle, Amy K., and Michele L. Stites. 2018. "Inclusion and Preschoolers Who Are Typically Developing: The Lived Experience." *Early Childhood Education Journal* 46: 511–22. https://doi.org/10.1007/s10643-017-0879-1.

Penfield Children's Center. 2022. "Celebrating 50 Years of Penfield Children's Center." https://penfieldchildren.org/penfield-childrens-center/celebrating-50-years-of-penfield-childrens-center/

Penfield Montessori Academy. 2020/2021. Annual Report. https://penfieldmontessori.org/wp-content/uploads/2022/01/PMA-Annual-Report-2020-21.pdf

Perolman, Cathie. 2020. "How Can I Tell Her Parents?" In *Montessori Inclusion: Strategies and Stories of Support for Learners with Exceptionalities*, edited by Ann Epstein. Santa Rosa, CA: Parent Child Press.

Pickering, Joyce. 2017. "Montessori for Children with Learning Differences." *Montessori Life* 29 (1) (Spring): 49–53.

Pickering, Joyce S., and Sylvia O. Richardson. 2019. *Montessori Strategies for Children with Learning Differences: The MACAR Model*. Santa Rosa CA: Parent Child Press.

Rolfe, Andrée. 2020. "What New (and Not So New) Montessori Teachers Need to Know About Special Education." In *Montessori Inclusion: Strategies and Stories of Support for Learners with Exceptionalities*, edited by Ann Epstein. Santa Rosa, CA: Parent Child Press.

Séguin, Édouard. 1846. *Traitement Moral, Hygiène et Education des Idiots et des Autres Enfants Arriérés*. Paris: J.B. Baillière. http://archive.org/details/traitementmoral00segugoog.

Seldin, Timothy and Paul Epstein. 2003. *The Montessori Way: An Education for Life*. Sarasota, FL: Montessori Foundation Press.

Shanks, Pam. 2014. "Building the Inclusive Montessori School." *The NAMTA Journal* 39 (3) (Summer): 5–36.

Shelton School and Evaluation Center. n.d. "About Us." https://www.shelton.org/about-us.

Standing, Edwin Mortimer. 1959. *Maria Montessori, Her Life and Work*. Fresno, CA: Academy Library Child.

Thomas, Patrick. 2016. "New Montessori School to Open at Former Urban Day Location." *Milwaukee Journal Sentinel*. July 11, 2016. http://www.jsonline.com/news/education/new-montessori-school-to-open-at-former-urban-day-location-b99759605z1-386342291.html.

Thompson, Barbara J., and Pamela Shanks. 2020. "Including Children with Severe Disabilities in Raintree Montessori School: The Circle of Inclusion." In *Montessori Inclusion: Strategies and Stories of Support for Learners with Exceptionalities*, edited by Ann Epstein. Santa Rosa, CA: Parent Child Press.

Thompson, Barbara J., Donna Wickham, Jane Wegner, Marilyn Mulligan Ault, Pamela Shanks, and Barbara Reinerston. 1993. *Handbook for the Inclusion of Children with Severe Disabilities: Strategies for Implementing Exemplary Full Inclusion Programs*. Lawrence, KS: Learner Managed Designs.

UN General Assembly. 1959. Resolution 1386(XIV), UN Declaration of the Rights of the Child, A/RES/1386(XIV). https://digitallibrary.un.org/record/195831?ln=en.

UNESCO. 1994. Final Report: World conference on special needs education: Access and quality. Paris: UNESCO. https://www.european-agency.org/sites/default/files/salamanca-statement-and-framework.pdf

UNESCO. 2020. Towards Inclusion in Education: Status, Trends and Challenges: The UNESCO Salamanca Statement 25 Years on. Paris: UNESCO. https://unesdoc.unesco.org/ark:/48223/pf0000374246

U.S. Department of Education. n.d. "About IDEA." *IDEA: Individuals with Disabilities Education Act*. https://sites.ed.gov/idea/about-idea/.

Willingham, Trisha. 2019. "Foundations for Montessori Inclusion." *Montessori Public* (blog). October 5, 2019. https://www.montessoripublic.org/2019/10/foundations-for-montessori-inclusion/.

Chapter 57
Montessori Education in a Plurilingual World

Susan Feez and Anne-Marie Morgan

Within the field of Montessori education, the contribution of multiple languages and cultures to the provenance, dissemination, and implementation of the Montessori approach is commonplace. Montessori educators—those who are affiliated with the Association Montessori Internationale (AMI) founded by Maria Montessori in 1928—are members of an international community that build on an international educational legacy more than a century in the making (AMI 2021a). Montessori teacher training courses typically enroll a multicultural and multilingual student body and open global employment opportunities. Montessori educators routinely interact with international colleagues through regular personal communication, conferences, and professional development activities across the globe. This means interacting with people from different cultures, moving between languages or working with interpreters or translations—all echoing the multilingual, multicultural environments in which Montessori worked.

In Montessori education, the commonplace nature of working within and across different cultures and languages is perhaps the reason so little attention has been paid to this distinctive feature of the Montessori experience. In recent years, scholars and practitioners in education have increasingly turned their attention to the benefits of applying *plurilingual* approaches, that is, approaches that draw on the full linguistic repertoires of both students and teachers—all the languages and dialects they use in all the ways they use them—to enhance learning outcomes (Baker and Wright 2017; Council of Europe 2014; Council of Europe 2020; Cummins et al. 2015; Ellis 2016; García-Mateus and Palmer 2017; Rafi and Morgan 2021). It is perhaps time to look more closely at how a *pluricultural* worldview and the use of multiple languages impact the ways children and teachers experience Montessori education. Such a view recognizes that, with hybrid cultures and languages now evident in many school settings across the globe, distinct language and cultural boundaries for identification and use become less marked and frequent *translanguaging* occurs. It is also worth considering what the everyday practice of working across languages and cultures in Montessori school settings can offer the wider educational community in a rapidly changing world that is more culturally and linguistically aware.

The chapter begins with a brief survey of concepts used by educators concerned with making full use of the enormous cultural and linguistic potential of students in classrooms. These concepts will then be applied as "tools for thinking" (Bodrova and Leong 2007) about the ways many languages and cultures have contributed to the genesis of Montessori education and to current Montessori practice. The chapter will conclude with recommendations for research that investigates manifestations of plurilingualism in Montessori learning environments around the world, and how such a research trajectory might benefit not only Montessori education, but the education community more widely.

Plurilingualism in the Twenty-First Century

Language use and learning, their political and cultural implications, and the consequential impacts on education have never been more complex or more critically examined. At least two-thirds of the world's population use two or more languages, a number that is said to be growing in the twenty-first century with increased migration, globalization, and digital connectivity (Baker and Wright 2017; Grosjean 2008). Much of the world's population lives in plurilingual communities and hence is exposed to different languages and language mixing in the natural settings of everyday lives. Part of the complexity of language use and additional language learning relates to the *growth* in people speaking languages beyond those used in their home settings. This is the result of people learning a standardized variety of a *lingua franca*—a language used for communication between groups of people who speak different languages, such as English, Spanish, or Chinese (Mandarin)—to expand their education, employment, and business opportunities and to connect with others beyond regional and national boundaries. Language policies also contribute to the growth of language learning. Many nations or regions have adopted outward-looking policies and promoting additional language learning, such as the European Union's "1+2" policy (first language and two others, minimally), the UK's various additional and "foreign" language-learning policies, Asian and African nations' multilingual policies, Canada's bilingual plus policy, and the rise of mandated bilingual preschools internationally (Morgan et al. 2019; Morgan 2021a, 2021b). These policies increasingly highlight the *entitlement* of young people to plurilingual learning in a globalized world and correlated opportunities for education and employment.

Ironically, and perhaps paradoxically, growth in the learning of accepted *lingae francae* also contributes to the marginalization and subsequent loss of local languages and dialects already diminished by colonization and its aftermath. Language revitalization movements, especially for First Nations' and Indigenous languages around the world, are striving to reclaim as many endangered languages as possible and to show that linguistic and cultural diversities beyond the use of *lingae francae* are as critical to the future of humanity as biological diversity (Crystal 2014; Skutnabb-Kangas 2003).

One of the threats to linguistic and cultural diversity is the still-pervasive "monolingual mindset," a worldview that sees everything "in terms of a single language" (Clyne 2008, 348). This view is particularly prevalent where English (the language of this chapter) is dominant, even if the community is multi- or plurilingual. Evidence for the value of plurilingual capabilities across social, educational, cultural, and cognitive domains is unequivocal (Morgan et al. forthcoming). In educational settings around the world, the monolingual mindset is currently being challenged for a range of reasons: It leads to education policies and practices that constrain the educational outcomes of students who live plurilingual and pluricultural lives in their homes and communities. It simultaneously denies their monolingual peers access to an array of culturally, linguistically, and intellectually rich learning and reciprocal sharing. It also limits the professional contribution of teachers from diverse cultural and linguistic backgrounds (Ellis 2016; Ortega 2013). Moreover, valuing the interaction and interdependence of the languages in plurilingual classrooms acknowledges the cultural and linguistic knowledge of those who speak Indigenous, migrant, heritage, and additional languages. These valuable linguistic and cultural resources are too often wasted, and consequently lost, when language and literacy education policy and classroom practices are based on a monolingual mindset.

Importantly, a plurilingual perspective emphasizes the value of bilingualism and multilingualism as a means for advancing more equitable educational outcomes among those whose first languages have not been traditionally recognized as an asset worth developing and building (Ellis et al. 2010; Rafi and Morgan 2021). A plurilingual view also recognizes that bilinguals and multilinguals use their languages in dynamic, expansive, and interdependent ways that have the potential to reap social, intellectual, and economic benefits for themselves and for those they interact with, including peers who use one language only (García and Wei 2014).

Plurilingual language practices are best described "along a continuum of language rather than as a binary between first and second language" (Menken 2013, 446). The practice of speakers using their full repertoire of plurilingual resources dynamically and flexibly to make meaning has become known as *translanguaging*. When applied in classrooms, this practice is transformative, transcending conventional barriers presumed in language, in hierarchical social structures, and across learning domains (García 2009; García and Wei 2014; Rafi and Morgan 2022). Translanguaging is one aspect of the variability in meaning making covered by "multiliteracies," a term which widens the terrain to account for the way twenty-first-century humans use combinations of multiple spoken and written languages, image, sound, gesture, space, and 3D modeling for meaning making in real-life and digital environments (Greene et al. 2018; Kalantzis et al. 2016; Kellner 1988).

Two types of translanguaging are recognized. Universal translanguaging refers to the typical ways bilinguals move between languages in everyday communication (Lewis et al. 2012; Rafi and Morgan 2022). Intentional classroom translanguaging occurs when teachers provide opportunities for serendipitous language movement in classrooms and plan for the use of multiple languages to achieve pedagogical purposes, potentially activating students' full linguistic repertoires to enhance meaning-making and understanding (Durán and Palmer 2014; García-Mateus and Palmer 2017; García and Kleyn 2016; Karlsson et al. 2019; Rafi and Morgan 2022).

A Multilingual Life and Career

Maria Montessori was born in 1870, the year Italy became a unified nation-state. With the emergence of European nation-states in the eighteenth and nineteenth centuries came the idea of promoting a single standardized language to unify a national population (Gogolin 1997). By the late 1880s, despite the gender barrier, Montessori was studying modern European languages, mathematics, and natural sciences at a boys-only technical high school, aiming to become an engineer. At the Sapienza University of Rome, she studied natural sciences, Latin, and Italian. After graduating in 1896, she specialized in pediatric medicine and psychiatry, becoming well known for her clinical work and for her advocacy on behalf of socially disadvantaged women and children (Kramer 1976). She spoke regularly at women's congresses across Europe, foreshadowing the international orientation of the Montessori movement to come:

> The political style of the international conference, the exhilaration of meeting people from many countries, the generation of commitment among those present, of faith that they could return home to effect change, these were the characteristics that Montessori recreated in the Montessori movement.
>
> *(Burstyn 1979, 145)*

While excelling in the study of the natural sciences and mathematics and later in the emerging social sciences, especially anthropology and psychology, Montessori used her knowledge of languages and culture to develop and disseminate her educational method (see Chapter 59: "Beyond Authenticity: Indeginizing Montessori Education in Settler Colonial United States" and Chapter 60: "Montessori Education and Multilingualism"). This included researching the work of past educational reformers across Europe, including Aristotle, Quintilian, Comenius, Locke, Rousseau, Pestalozzi, Froebel, and Herbart. She was famously inspired by two nineteenth-century French doctors, Jean Itard and Édouard Séguin, whose books she translated into Italian (Kramer 1976; Montessori 1964). In this feat of translanguaging, Montessori applied her own multilingual interpretation to the Italian rendering:

> I felt the need of meditation. I did a thing which I had not done before, and which perhaps few students have been willing to do—I translated into Italian and copied out with my own hand, the writings of these men, from beginning to end, making for myself books as the old Benedictines used to do before the diffusion of printing.
>
> I chose to do this by hand, in order that I might have time to <u>weigh the sense of each word</u>, and to read, in truth, the *spirit* of the author
>
> *(Montessori 1964, 41; see also Kramer [1976], 95. Emphasis added)*

A Linguistically and Geographically Diverse Literature

The use of multiple languages shaped the Montessori movement from the beginning. Montessori's first description of her method of education was published in Italian in 1909. An English translation by an American elementary school teacher, Anne George, was published under the title the *Montessori Method* in 1912 (Kramer 1976, 162–6). In 1914, *Dr. Montessori's Own Handbook* was published in English to coincide with her visit to the United States. *The Advanced Montessori Method* was first published in Italian in 1916 and in English in 1918. During this period, Montessori's publications were translated into many languages by students and colleagues rather than by professional translators, reflecting perhaps the need for the translations to make sense to fellow practitioners across different language settings.

In 1916, Montessori moved to Barcelona, where she would live and work for twenty years, publishing detailed accounts of specific elements of Montessori pedagogy in Spanish; some were later translated into Italian and English. After 1920, Montessori publications tended to be articles in the popular press or second- or third-hand derivatives of notes from her original Italian lectures recorded in other languages, a fascinating resource of translanguaged and interpreted meaning (see, for example, Montessori 1973). Key collections of Montessori's talks and lectures were originally presented in India using local interpreters before being published in English by the Theosophical Society (Kramer 1976).

Montessori's lecture and writing style have been described as florid and old-fashioned, especially when translated into a language such as English (Kramer 1976). Montessori often used the technical terms of her era, drawn from a range of disciplines, to express the ideas about child development and pedagogy she was only just developing from her own observations and experiments. Many of these terms are now obsolete and clouded by interpretations; over the last century, direct—and not always accurate—translations of these terms into a variety of languages have generated an idiosyncratic vocabulary. This vocabulary is used to express meanings shared by Montessori educators around the world, but it can appear arcane or incoherent.

In recent years, critical reviews of Montessori's publications "have highlighted a previously unacknowledged complexity" in her ideas (Romano 2020, 203). Much of this work emerges from close readings of primary sources by Italian scholars in education; these sources have not been easily accessible for those who do not read Italian (see, for example, Foschi 2008; Foschi et al. 2019; Moretti 2021; Tornar 2001). There is a parallel body of work in English in which scholars evaluate Montessori theory and practice against contemporary perspectives across a range of disciplines—including philosophy, psychology, educational linguistics, history of education, and studies in pedagogy (see Debs 2019; Feez 2020; Frierson 2019; Lillard 2017; Lillard 2018; Marshall 2017; Whitehead and Feez 2018). A significant secondary Montessori literature also exists in German, Dutch, and Swedish.

Since 2006, the Pierson-Montessori Publishing Company has been publishing updated translations of Montessori's lectures, publications, and previously unpublished Montessori writing in Dutch, English, and Spanish. These translations can include notes prepared by contemporary plurilingual editorial teams about the provenance of idiosyncratic Montessori terms and concepts to illuminate their meaning and current use (for example, Montessori 2013). Scattered over a century and across languages, Montessori literature is distinguished by its diversity of purpose and quality. Developing and weaving together in principled ways the multilingual and multidisciplinary strands of this literature will continue to depend on a plurilingual and transdisciplinary community of scholars that offers the potential for re-interpretation through translanguaged meaning-making lenses.

Training Montessori Teachers from around the World

The first international Montessori teacher training course, held in Rome in 1913, attracted students from Europe, the Americas, Asia, and Australia. Montessori delivered the lectures in Italian, interspersed with an English translation provided almost sentence by sentence by Anne

George, the translator of the *Montessori Method*. To communicate personally with Anne George and many of the students, Montessori used French, which was as much an international *lingua franca* as English (Kramer 1976).

The use of multiple languages for communication between Montessori teacher trainers and their students remains a routine feature of many Montessori teacher training centers around the world, as Montessori educators working in multilingual contexts have reported to the authors through frequent and varied personal communication. For example, teams of trainers using two or three languages to deliver current Montessori teacher training courses is a feature of AMI training courses in Italy (Italian, English), the Czech Republic (Czech, Russian, English), and Thailand (Thai, Chinese, English). Lectures and presentations are typically delivered in one language by the trainer who pauses regularly for the interpreter, a situation described by one trainer as "not ideal" (Amy Kirkham, pers. comm., July 1, 2021). While making the lecture content accessible, this approach opens training course content to cultural interpretation; thus, as the trainee Montessori teachers make sense of what they hear within their own linguistic and cultural interpretative frames, the intended meaning may shift.

Outside formal lectures and presentations, multiple languages are typically used among trainers and students—i.e., in social interactions, the creation of albums, and practice sessions with the materials. Some multilingual Montessori teacher trainers deliver courses in one language in one setting and in another in a different setting. Montessori student teachers work with labels and booklets duplicated in multiple languages while materials used to teach writing and reading are adapted for different languages. For example, Montessori materials were originally designed to teach children to write and read Italian, a language with a consistent correspondence between the sounds of the language and the letters of the alphabet; these have been adjusted and augmented to teach children to write and read English, which has less consistent sound-letter correspondence (see also Dwyer 2004; Feez 2010).

In Montessori Chinese language programs, sandpaper strokes and radicals used to form Chinese characters have been developed so children can imitate, feel, and experience the lightness of touch and direction used to form the characters. Chinese characters represent a whole word, idea, or concept; there is no straightforward correspondence between the characters and the individual sounds of the language, so there are no sounds given for the strokes and radicals. Before children can control writing instruments or remember the strokes, children use moveable characters to express themselves in writing. As much as possible, moveable characters are offered to children gradually and casually to allow them to absorb each symbol and the concept it represents but usually—as far as can be determined from current correspondence and the literature—without any cross-lingual referencing for bilinguals or emerging bilinguals in the class. A similar approach is used to provide children with the keys to reading and writing in Thai and Japanese (Amy Kirkham, PC, July 1, 2021).

As the examples above illustrate, in Montessori training courses, the content is routinely interpreted and exemplified in more than one language to illustrate and illuminate knowledge about language and Montessori principles. This approach resonates with and has the potential to be enhanced by the accumulating evidence of the intellectual advantages of plurilingual approaches and intentional classroom translanguaging practices (García and Wei 2014; Ortega 2013). Montessori teacher trainers around the world use diverse approaches to integrate multiple languages into their training courses, and, as graduates of these courses anecdotally report, a plurilingual orientation enriches the experience of Montessori teachers in training. These approaches and orientations are worthy of close, systematic investigation.

Multilingual Montessori Classrooms across the World

The graduates of the first international Montessori training courses in 1913 and 1914 must have had an international and plurilingual worldview to participate successfully in the course. These graduates returned to their countries of origin to establish Montessori schools in their home languages. These first courses established the tendency for graduates of Montessori training courses to be scattered around the world, working in multiple languages; this trend continues to this day.

Some Montessori schools celebrate their multilingual school community, promoting the use and learning of more than one language as a valued feature of the school. These schools are plurilingual by design and hence are ripe for the use of universal and intentional classroom translanguaging. For others, the use of more than one language is experienced as an everyday feature of the setting and school community; for example, children from First Nations or migrant backgrounds and children who use nonstandard dialects bring their home language to school, making these languages part of the learning environment. In the last few decades, a great deal of research has documented the pedagogical benefits of using home languages in classrooms of all types, not just Montessori, as indicated by references throughout this chapter. Multilingual practices have been taken for granted as a part of many Montessori schools and training centers for a long time, perhaps as a by-product of the nature of Montessori education. This chapter proposes that these practices and their potential should be given a higher profile both within the Montessori community and in its research literature.

In Brussels, the multi-campus International Montessori Schools promote learning environments that are "rich in languages and cultures" (IMS n.d.). All children enrolled in these schools learn in a "complete and consistent bilingual English-French environment" from infancy to age eleven with the aim that they become bilingual in spoken and written language. Each classroom has two teachers, one who always speaks French and one who always speaks English, an approach known as "one person, one language" (OPOL). While OPOL continues the old tradition of separating (national) languages and identities, it also provides teachers and students with a helpful guide when planning and choosing which language to use in formal learning situations (De Houwer 2020). Both languages are used to teach across all learning areas, an approach well supported by evidence (Morgan et al. forthcoming; Rafi and Morgan 2022). Lessons are delivered in French or English, depending on the teacher, and young children can be observed "switching" languages effortlessly as needed (Amy Kirkham, pers. comm., July 1, 2021). What is not reported, however, is how frequently the language use was not a direct "switch" but instead incorporated elements—phrases, words, idioms—of both languages, as has been well-documented occurs in ordinary life settings. In a delightful translanguaging anecdote, a visitor reported being told firmly by very young children that the school dog only responded to commands if they were in Friesian, a minority language of the Netherlands.

As is typical in plurilingual Montessori environments, the Language materials in the International Montessori Schools classrooms are organized into a French language area and an English language area, with materials such as Grammar Boxes and Sentence Analysis available in both languages. These materials draw attention to differences not only in vocabulary but also in the ways words are organized into structures and texts (Feez 2008, 2020). The school provides the following evaluation of the program:

> This bilingual and multilingual environment has been put into practice at our school over an extended period of time. Our experience is that this approach has a very positive outcome. By living and learning amongst such a wealth of languages, and simultaneously working within multi-age groups that function with appropriate freedoms and limits, the students become multilingual and develop an openness to different cultures and habits. **Multilingualism has an extra bonus in that it assists the logical mind** [emphasis in original]. Being able to speak several languages means you have several "answers" to any particular issue. Each answer has a slightly different connotation. The user therefore refines the analytical capacities and abstract thinking abilities!
>
> *(International Montessori Schools n.d.)*

This approach raises the question about how much more might be achieved through intentional translanguaging, where those comparative capabilities can play out in real time across the classroom community in all available languages, rather than for private introspection only before being expressed in one language.

While OPOL is a designed-in feature of the multilingual program at this and other bilingual Montessori schools, incidental translanguaging must be an inevitable feature of these plurilingual environments, especially given the freedom within limits at the core of the Montessori approach. Children are free to move around the classroom and to choose their own work, as well as to choose where, with whom, and how long they work. These freedoms are limited by the features of the physical space and the need to maintain social harmony and conditions that support learning (Feez 2010). Offering children this type of freedom contributes to the development of their independence and executive control (Diamond 2014). In a plurilingual and pluricultural setting, it nurtures intercultural awareness and an awareness of the value of plurilingual repertoires and identities; these dispositions are interwoven with successful learning of additional languages, curriculum content in general, and diverse world views (García and Wei 2014; Morgan et al. forthcoming).

Even in conventional classrooms where OPOL is applied, translanguaging occurs organically and can be used as a resource for learning. When a classroom teacher in a German bilingual elementary school intentionally incorporated translanguaging into the pedagogy, "allowing" children to use all their language resources at all times, learning outcomes and social and identity indicators were enhanced (Wiles 2019). Drawing on students' full language repertoires in principled ways expands the terrain in which students can co-construct knowledge in a "dialogic way," leading to deeper understanding and intellectual achievement (Lo Bianco 2021).

In Montessori environments, a further contribution to expanding plurilingual repertoires for children ages 6 to 12 is the study of etymology, which apprentices children into the Graeco-Latin terms that represent knowledge in academic disciplines. Using additional linguistic and semiotic resources in this way increases both children's interest in language itself and their power and agency as language users.

Future Directions for Research

A systematic study of the use of multiple languages in high-fidelity Montessori schools, such as the International Montessori Schools in Brussels, would enable scholars to gain insights into the ways Montessori environments enhance the development of plurilingual knowledge, skills, and attitudes. In addition, researchers would learn more about the nature and impact of translanguaging on learning when children at different ages and stages of development are given the opportunities and freedoms to deploy their full linguistic and cultural repertoires and identities.

A study by Holmes (2018) examines the freedom in Montessori environments to harness children's linguistic and cultural repertoires in the service of their education. This study, which took place in a remote Australian Aboriginal early childhood setting, revealed the potential for Montessori pedagogy to align more harmoniously with the cultural dispositions of the children and their community. The lack of alignment between the culture of their community and conventional English language education is often cited as a barrier to school achievement for many Aboriginal students (see Smith et al. 2018). Holmes (2018, 34) notes that children in this community traditionally learn "by observation, imitation, and talking in Ngaanyatjarra, their home language, with their family. ... If children's first culture and language are not recognized, valued, or integrated into the school curriculum, the children are set up to fail."

The children in the community grow up in a culturally and linguistically rich environment in which children's independence and autonomy are encouraged from an early age, just as they are in Montessori early childhood environments. When children entered the Montessori setting, importantly, they could continue using their home language to learn because the Montessori teacher was a proficient user of Ngaanyatjarra. The results of the study showed that the children's response to Montessori pedagogy, in tandem with the use of their home language in the Montessori environment, was characterized by high levels of concentration, interest, engagement, autonomy, and independence, suggesting an alignment with Australian Aboriginal ways of learning.

Children's first cultures and languages are integrated into Montessori educational settings in AMI Educateurs sans Frontières (EsF) international development initiatives worldwide (AMI 2021b). However, when these initiatives are reported, multicultural and multilingual practices are revealed only in passing. Examples include using Hindi, Urdu, and English moveable alphabets in Montessori early years settings in rural areas of Andhra Pradesh in India; encouraging imprisoned mothers in the UK to speak to their babies in their first language; integrating the local language (isiXhosa) into Montessori teacher training in Kayamandi, a suburb of Stellenbosch, South Africa; and children in a Corner of Hope Montessori class in Nakuru, Kenya, using their home language in a culturally meaningful performance. A systematic study of the diverse language practices that characterize EsF programs may reveal the extent to which students using their full linguistic and cultural repertoires in Montessori environments can transcend barriers to educational achievement.

Conclusion

The provenance and nature of Montessori pedagogy have the potential to provide children with all the benefits of bilingual/multilingual development. Researching plurilingual contexts, translanguaging practices, and developing methodologically and ethically acceptable studies to understand language use, and language use potential, across and between languages and cultures is a rich field for Montessori education, with its already multilingual and multicultural history. Montessori's original aims of enhancing educational opportunities for all children, and especially disadvantaged and marginalized children and communities, surely require current and future generations of Montessori educators to respond to the recent plurilingual turn in education, so that it might be more thoroughly explored, and learnings applied within and beyond Montessori classrooms.

Note

In plurilingual settings, language users draw on their full linguistic repertoire, including all the languages and dialects they use.

References

AMI (Association Montessori Internationale). 2021a. "We Connect Montessori to the World." https://montessori-ami.org/.
AMI (Association Montessori Internationale). 2021b. "Educateurs sans Frontières." https://montessori-esf.org/.
Baker, Colin, and Wayne Wright. 2017. *Foundations of Bilingual Education and Bilingualism*, 6th ed. Bristol, UK: Blue Ridge Summit.
Bodrova, Elena, and Deborah J. Leong 2007. *Tools of the Mind: The Vygotskian Approach to Early Childhood Education*, 2nd ed. Columbus, OH: Merrill/Prentice Hall.
Burstyn, Joan N. 1979. Review of *Maria Montessori*, by Rita Kramer. *History of Education Quarterly* 19 (1) (Spring): 143–9.
Clyne, Michael. 2008. "The Monolingual Mindset as an Impediment to the Development of Plurilingual Potential in Australia." *Sociolinguistic Studies* 2 (3): 347–65. https://doi.org/10.1558/sols.v2i3.347.
Council of Europe. 2014. *Languages for Democracy and Social Cohesion: Diversity, Equity and Quality*. Strasbourg: Council of Europe Publishing. https://rm.coe.int/CoERMPublicCommonSearchServices/DisplayDCTMContent?documentId=090000168069e7bd.
Council of Europe. 2020. *Common European Framework of Reference for Languages: Learning, Teaching, Assessment—Companion Volume*. Strasbourg: Council of Europe Publishing. http://www.coe.int/lang-cefr.
Crystal, David. 2014. *Language Death*, 2nd ed. Cambridge, UK: Cambridge University Press.
Cummins, Jim, Shirley Hu, Paula Markus, and M. Kristiina Montero. 2015. "Identity Texts and Academic Achievement: Connecting the Dots in Multilingual School Contexts." *TESOL Quarterly* 49 (3): 555–81. https://doi.org/10.1002/tesq.241.
Debs, Mira. 2019. *Diverse Families, Desirable Schools: Public Montessori in the Era of School Choice*. Cambridge, MA: Harvard Education Press.

De Houwer, Annick. 2020. "Why Do So Many Children Who Hear Two Languages Speak Just a Single Language?" *Zeitschrift für Interkulturellen Fremdsprachenunterricht* 25 (1): 7–26.

Diamond, Adele. 2014. "Understanding Executive Functions: What Helps or Hinders Them and How Executive Functions and Language Development Mutually Support One Another." *Perspectives on Language and Literacy* 40 (2) (Spring): 7–11.

Durán, Leah, and Deborah Palmer. 2014. "Pluralist Discourses of Bilingualism and Translanguaging Talk in Classrooms." *Journal of Early Childhood Literacy* 14 (3): 367–88. https://doi.org/10.1177%2F1468798413497386.

Dwyer, Muriel I. 2004. "A Path for the Exploration of Any Language Leading to Writing and Reading." *The NAMTA Journal* 29 (3) (Summer): 15–40.

Ellis, Elizabeth. 2016. *The Plurilingual TESOL Teacher: The Hidden Language Lives of TESOL Teachers and Why They Matter*. Boston and Berlin: de Gruyter Mouton.

Ellis, Elizabeth, Ingrid Gogolin, and Michael Clyne. 2010. "The Janus Face of Monolingualism: A Comparison of German and Australian Language Education Policies." *Current Issues in Language Planning* 11 (4): 439–60. https://doi.org/10.1080/14664208.2010.550544.

Feez, Susan. 2008. "Multimodal Representation of Educational Meanings in Montessori Pedagogy." In *Multimodal Semiotics: Functional Analysis in Contexts of Education*, edited by Len Unsworth, 201–15. London, New York: Continuum.

Feez, Susan. 2010. *Montessori and Early Childhood*. London: Sage Publications.

Feez, Susan. 2019. "Multimodality in the Montessori Classroom." In *Multimodality Across Classrooms: Learning About and Through Different Modalities*, edited by Helen de Silva Joyce and Susan Feez, 30–48. New York and London: Routledge.

Feez, Susan. 2020. "Bringing More Than a Century of Practice to Writing Pedagogy in the Early Years." In *Developing Writers across the Primary and Secondary Years: Growing into Writing*, edited by Honglin Chen, Debra Myhill, and Helen Lewis, 60–77. London and New York: Routledge.

Foschi, Renata. 2008. "Science and Culture Around the Montessori's First 'Children's Houses' in Rome (1907–1915)." *Journal of the History of the Behavioral Sciences* 44 (3) (Summer): 238–57. https://doi.org/10.1002/jhbs.20313.

Foschi, Renata, Erica Moretti, and Paolo Trabalzini, eds. 2019. *Il Destino di Maria Montessori*, Rome, Italy: Fefè Editore.

Frierson, Patrick. 2019. "Situationism and Intellectual Virtue: A Montessori Perspective." *Synthese* 198 (5): 4123–44.

García, Ofelia. 2009. *Bilingual Education in the 21st Century: A Global Perspective*, Malden, MA: Wiley and Blackwell.

García, Ofelia, and Li Wei. 2014. *Translanguaging: Language, Bilingualism and Education*. Basingstoke, UK: Palgrave Macmillan.

García, Ofelia, and Tatyana Kleyn. 2016. *Translanguaging with Multilingual Students: Learning from Classroom Moments*, London and New York: Routledge.

García-Mateus, Suzanne, and Deborah Palmer. 2017. "Translanguaging Pedagogies for Positive Identities in Two-Way Dual Language Bilingual Education." *Journal of Language, Identity and Education* 16 (4): 245–55. https://doi.org/10.1080/15348458.2017.1329016.

Gogolin, Ingrid. 1997. "The 'Monolingual Habitus' as the Common Feature in Teaching in the Language of the Majority in Different Countries." *Per Linguam* 13 (2): 38–49.

Greene, Stuart, Kevin J. Burke, and Maria K. McKenna. 2018. "A Review of Research Connecting Digital Storytelling, Photovoice, and Civic Engagement." *Review of Educational Research* 88 (6): 844–78. https://doi.org/10.3102/0034654318794134.

Grosjean, François. 2008. *Studying Bilinguals*. Oxford, UK: Oxford University Press.

Holmes, Catherine Claire. 2018. "Introduction of Montessori Education to a Remote Indigenous Early Childhood Program: A Study of the Ways in Which Aboriginal Students Respond." *Journal of Montessori Research* 4 (2): 33–60. https://doi.org/10.17161/jomr.v4i2.6715.

IMS (International Montessori Schools). n.d. "Bilingualism/Multilingualism." Accessed July 27, 2021. https://www.international-montessori.org/schoolinfo/bilingualism-multilingualism/.

Kalantzis, Mary, Bill Cope, Eveline Chan, and Leanne Dalley-Trim. 2016. *Literacies*, 2nd ed. Melbourne: Cambridge University Press.

Karlsson, Annika, Pia Nygård Larsson, and Anders Jakobsson. 2019. "The Continuity of Learning in a Translanguaging Science Classroom." *Cultural Studies of Science Education* 15 (3): 1–25.

Kellner, Douglas. 1988. "Multiple Literacies and Critical Pedagogy in a Multicultural Society." *Educational Theory* 48 (1): 103–22. https://doi.org/10.1111/j.1741-5446.1998.00103.x.

Kramer, Rita. 1976. *Maria Montessori: A Biography*. Oxford: Basil Blackwell.

Lewis, Gwyn, Bryn Jones, and Colin Baker. 2012. "Translanguaging: Developing its Conceptualization and Contextualization." *Educational Research and Evaluation* 18 (7): 655–70.

Lillard, Angeline Stoll. 2017. *Montessori: The Science behind the Genius*, 3rd ed. New York, NY: Oxford University Press.

Lillard, Angeline S. 2018. "Rethinking Education: Montessori's Approach." *Current Directions in Psychological Science* 27 (6): 395–400. https://doi.org/10.1177%2F0963721418769878.

Lo Bianco, Joseph. 2021. "The Discourse of the Edge: Marginal Advantage, Positioning and Linguistic Entrepreneurship." *Multilingua: Journal of Cross-Cultural and Interlanguage Communication* 40 (2): 261–75.

Maffi, Luisa. 2005. "Linguistic, Cultural, and Biological Diversity." *Annual Review of Anthropology* 34: 599–617.

Marshall, Chloë. 2017. "Montessori Education: A Review of the Evidence Base." *npj Science of Learning* 2 (11): 1–9.

Menken, Kate. 2013. "Emergent Bilingual Students in Secondary School: Along the Academic Language and Literacy Continuum." *Language Teaching* 46 (4): 438–76.

Montessori, Maria. 1964. *The Montessori Method*. Translated by Anne E. George. New York: Schocken Books.

Montessori, Maria. 1973. *From Childhood to Adolescence, including Erdkinder and the Function of the University*. Translated by the Montessori Educational Research Center. New York: Schocken Books.

Montessori, Maria. 2013. *The 1913 Rome Lectures: First International Training Course*. Edited by Susan Feez, Larry Quade, Carolina Montessori, and Joke Verheul. Amsterdam: Montessori-Pierson Publishing Company.

Moretti, Erica. 2021. *The Best Weapon for Peace: Maria Montessori, Education, and Children's Rights*. Madison, WI: University of Wisconsin Press.

Morgan, Anne-Marie. 2021a. "Australian Perspectives on Trends in Languages Learning Internationally, 1969 and 2019: A Sonata Form Case Study." *Babel* 55 (1–2): 5–20.

Morgan, Anne-Marie. 2021b. "International Perspectives on Trends in Languages Learning in the 2020s: Part One: Profiling the UK and the Republic of Ireland." *Babel* 55 (3): 2–32.

Morgan, Anne-Marie, John Hajek, Elizabeth Ellis, and Joseph Lo Bianco. 2019. "Starting Young: Early Years Language Learning in Australia." Australian Research Commission Discovery Project. Unpublished manuscript.

Morgan, Anne-Marie, Nick Reid, and Peter Freebody. Forthcoming. "Literacy and Linguistic Diversity in Australia." In *Global Variation in Literacy Development*, edited by L. Verhoeven, S. Nag, C. Perfetti, and K. Pugh. Cambridge, UK: Cambridge University Press.

Ortega, Lourdes. 2013. "SLA for the 21st Century: Disciplinary Progress, Transdisciplinary Relevance, and the Mi/multilingual Turn." *Language Learning* 63 (1): 1–24. https://doi.org/10.1111/j.1467-9922.2012.00735.x.

Rafi, Abu Saleh Mohammad, and Anne-Marie Morgan. 2021. "Translanguaging and Academic Writing: Possibilities and Challenges in English-Only Classrooms." In *Creating a Transnational Space in the First Year Writing Classroom*, edited by W. Ordeman, 17–40. Wilmington, DE: Vernon Press.

Rafi, Abu Saleh Mohammad, and Anne-Maria Morgan. 2022. "Translanguaging as a Transformative Act in a Reading Classroom: Perspectives from a Bangladeshi Private University." *Journal of Language, Identity and Education* (March 21, 2022): 1–16. https://doi.org/10.1080/15348458.2021.2004894.

Romano, Andrea. 2020. "Maria Montessori: A Complex and Multifaceted Historiographical Subject." *History of Psychology* 23 (2): 203–7.

Skutnabb-Kangas, Tove. 2003. "Linguistic Diversity and Biodiversity: The Threat from Killer Languages." In *The Politics of English as a World Language: New Horizons in Post-Colonial Cultural Studies*, edited by Christian Mair, 31–52. Amsterdam, New York: Rodopi.

Smith, James A., Michael Bullot, Veronica Kerr, Dean Yibarbuk, Mille Olcay, and Fiona Shalley. 2018. "Maintaining Connection to Family, Culture and Community: Implications for Remote Aboriginal and Torres Strait Islander Pathways into Higher Education." *Rural Society* 27 (2): 108–24. https://doi.org/10.1080/10371656.2018.1477533.

Tornar, Clara, ed. 2001, *Montessori Bibliografia Internazionale/International Bibliography 1896–2000*. Rome: Opera Nazionale Montessori.

Trabalzini, Paola. 2011. "Maria Montessori through the Seasons of the 'Method.'" *The NAMTA Journal* 36 (2) (Spring): XI–218.

Whitehead, Kay, and Susan Feez. 2018. "Transnational Advocacy in Education: Maria Montessori's Connections with Australian Women." *Annali di Storia Dell'educazione e Delle Istituzioni Scolastiche* 25: 181–96.

Wiles, L. 2019. "Challenging the Monolingual Mindset of a Bilingual School: Introducing Plurilingual Pedagogy into a Fifth Grade Classroom." MEd diss., University of New England, Armidale, Australia.

Chapter 58
Montessori Education and Critical Race Theory in the United States

Lucy Canzoneri-Golden and Juliet King

Building off a large body of research examining stratified racial structures in education generally, this chapter explores critical race theory (CRT) within Montessori contexts. It will do so from the perspective of people of the global majority[1] who reside in the United States with implications for other oppressed groups globally. CRT developed out of American legal scholarship in the 1970s to explain the persistence of racism after the apparent successes of the Civil Rights movement (Bell 2016; Harris 1993; Ladson-Billings and Tate 1995; Leonardo 2013; Taylor et al. 2016). CRT theorists remind us that the legacies of racism persist in the United States, and they provide an analytical lens to examine the ways that racism pervades various facets of life, including education. Furthermore, they assert that stratified racial structures of society, rooted in colonialism, are inherent in the history, policies, legal practices, property ownership, and ideals of American society. These structures were created and expanded to maintain wealth and power for a limited subset of American society.

As the United States rose to prominence in the global community, its leaders spread colonial ideas, including racism, across the globe. As Christian (2019, 170) notes, countries and groups "negotiate and position themselves within a global relational racial field by producing internal structural and ideological racial practices that create specific racial order." The historical legacies of slavery, colonization, and consolidation of wealth in the United States live on in de facto stratified racial structures even today and continue to be embedded in our educational institutions (Ladson-Billings and Tate 1995). In the context of persistent structural racism in education generally and Montessori more specifically, researchers have suggested that two types of approaches—culturally relevant pedagogy (CRP) and anti-bias/anti-racist (ABAR) practices—can support making meaningful changes to reduce harm inflicted on children of the global majority in the classroom.

In the next section, we define both practices and discuss their alignment and potential contribution to Montessori pedagogy. We also examine how Montessori education infused with CRP and ABAR curricula can be a viable alternative to educational systems that perpetuate white supremacy and fail our students of the global majority and other marginalized groups. Curriculum is often designed to uphold and maintain a white supremacist narrative. Instructional strategies are often based on a cultural deficit theory. Assessments are known to be culturally biased, seeking to legitimize cultural deficiency under the guise of scientific objectivity. Thus, it is incumbent upon those of us interested in ameliorating these trends to explore innovative means of remediating these issues, including alternative forms of education (such as Montessori education) and the requisite access to those other forms of schooling.

According to the National Assessment of Educational Progress (NAEP), Black and Hispanic children in the United States continue to lag behind their white counterparts in standardized testing in both reading and mathematics (NAEP n.d.). These lags must be contextualized in the history of marginalization presented here, not simply attributed to individual ability or family circumstance, especially because Black and Hispanic children may even believe the deficit stories about themselves. As Leonardo (2013, 604) notes, "they created their own predicament, even as they may help reproduce it, is like saying that the impoverished life of the slave is his own doing." Sampson and Garrison-Wade (2011, 282) argue, "CRT acknowledges the power, privilege, and inequalities inherent in society, and specifically in school settings that impact the miseducation of African American children." In seeking ways to bring more relevancy and equity to the education of all children, including Black students, a child-centered pedagogy like Montessori holds promise for addressing these inequalities.

Terms to Consider: CRP and Anti-bias/Anti-racism

CRP is important to the work of this chapter and warrants a stand-alone explanation. CRP empowers students intellectually, emotionally, and politically by using cultural references specific to students' home communities to impart knowledge, skills, and attitudes within an educational context. Underlying the concept of CRP are academic success, cultural competence, and sociopolitical consciousness. Cultural competence refers to the ability to help students appreciate and celebrate their cultures of origin while gaining knowledge and fluency in at least one other culture. Sociopolitical consciousness is the ability to take learning beyond the confines of the classroom, using knowledge and skills to identify, analyze, and solve real-world problems (Ladson-Billings 2014). Other useful terms used for this work are "culturally sustaining pedagogy" and "culturally revitalizing pedagogy" (Paris 2012).

Like CRP, ABAR practices use instructional strategies and classroom practices that reflect students' backgrounds, cultural contexts, needs, and interests to meaningfully enhance learning. ABAR practices give explicit lessons about racism early on to develop awareness, critical reasoning, and dialogue. This gives students the tools to stand up to prejudice, stereotyping, bias, and eventually institutional and structural racism (Derman-Sparks and Edwards 2010; Pollock 2008). Montessori education has the capacity to integrate practices that can benefit students of color, especially when incorporating both CRP and ABAR practices (Debs and Brown 2017).

Montessori Education and Race in the United States

By 2018, the majority of the students enrolled in US public schools (53 percent) were students of color (Irwin et al. 2021). Montessori education is the largest alternative educational pedagogy in US public schools, with over 500 schools adopting its practices. Additionally, the majority of students attending public Montessori are students of color (Debs 2016). At the same time, most

Montessori schools in the United States are private (Debs et al. 2022), and little demographic information on student enrollment is available. Relatedly, 82 percent of the American public school teacher workforce is white, and American Montessori organizations have not yet begun collecting racial/ethnic demographic information about their members (Debs 2019). Therefore, when considering Montessori education, there is a need to look more critically at how demographics are collected, how training is conducted with relationship to equity and inclusion, and how the needs of diverse students are being addressed—particularly in the context of teacher diversity.

A Critical Race Lens in Montessori Research

On the one hand, Montessori education can be a credible alternative for students of color whose learning styles tend to be more congruent with Montessori pedagogy, as students can move, use hands-on learning, and research subjects that interest them (Hall and Murray 2011). On the other hand, parents and students of color often feel isolated or concerned about the perceived lack of academic rigor. Despite a frequently repeated claim that Montessori educators are inclusive and color-blind in their ability to observe without judgment (Banks and Maixner 2016), some Montessori schools have been found to be guilty of racial bias, even if the extent is less than that of traditional schools (Brown and Steele 2015; Debs 2019). In one of the few studies of public Montessori schools around issues of race and inclusion, Stansbury (2014) found evidence of institutional racism and racially disparate disciplinary practices in the classroom. Recent research seems to corroborate this, though noting that the frequency of such practices is less than in traditional public schools (Lebouef 2022).

In another research undertaking, Canzoneri-Golden and King (2020) conducted a qualitative case study examining CRP-ABAR in three public Montessori charter schools across the United States. The purpose of the study was to examine the perceptions of the administrators, teachers, and parents of CRP-ABAR and how these practices operated in three urban public Montessori schools whose population of students was 51 percent or more students of color. Findings noted that, even with a multiyear commitment to CRP-ABAR, staff at the three schools varied widely in their implementation of CRP-ABAR practices. While the schools were consistent in connecting CRP-ABAR to the Montessori practices of peace education, global education, and preparing the teacher and the environment, the largest variation in the findings centered on whether CRP-ABAR was delivered solely as a part of the classroom curriculum or implemented as a means of structural changes to the school or work in the surrounding community.

Parents at all three schools reported that Montessori connected with CRP-ABAR principles by sending a strong message for inclusion—that is, recognizing and accepting differences, building equity, celebrating diversity, being culturally aware, and learning the "why" of racism. Parents also believed these practices meant the schools demonstrated a respect for all, the embracing of varied cultures, self-exploration, talking openly about race, and viewing the world from the perspective of marginalized people. At all three schools, the administrators believed CRP-ABAR was part of their mission and vision and was intended to address the inequities in education for students of color.

The study also notes that, although the Montessori educators hoped to see increased academic progress from their implementation in CRP-ABAR, they primarily saw results in students' social-emotional growth. Even with professional development for the Montessori educators around CRP-ABAR, the perceptions of many non-Black teachers continued to include deficit theory thinking. Furthermore, educator perceptions that CRP-ABAR impacted students of color positively through social and emotional growth did not translate into fewer disciplinary issues; the behavioral referral data displayed a disparity between the disciplines of Black and white children.

While parents and teachers were generally positive about the CRP-ABAR work, there were discrepancies in teacher engagement of students (white students being called on more often than children of color), regardless of the racial identity of the teacher. Some parent concern about incidences of bias was recorded. Interview data also noted that some educators did not make connections between their implicit perceptions of their students of color and academic outcomes or participation in the Montessori classroom setting. Nonetheless, educators in the study did discuss the need for Montessori to align itself more with ABAR practices and acknowledge systemic racism.

Importantly, educator transformation is a major component of Montessori philosophy. The ongoing preparation of the adult as a conduit for preparing the environment for students is a hopeful and essential aspect of the discussion at hand in this chapter. It provides the framework for continued engagement with CRP and ABAR work, regardless of an educator's career stage. The educator's individualized journey is unique, as was evidenced in the varied responses around comfort and application of ABAR work in the educators' classrooms. Administrators at all three schools within this study also echoed these sentiments.

Montessori schools, like other educational settings, are not immune to institutionalized racism or to individual educators resistant to considering personal bias. Given the historical contexts of American education, all education in the United States—Montessori or otherwise—has been (and still is) impacted by systemic racism (Canzoneri-Golden and King 2020; Ladson-Billings 1998; Ladson-Billings and Tate 1995). As critical race theorist Ladson-Billings (2012, 115) notes, "[u]ntil educators begin to carefully examine the way race and racialized thinking influence their work, they will continue to perpetuate destructive thinking about the capabilities of learners based on race."

Progress and Important Interventions

One such response to this color-blind dilemma is the practitioner community Montessori for Social Justice (MSJ). The concept for MSJ began in 2013 in the United States to address the lack of conversation and action around topics of social justice and equity within the mainstream Montessori organizations. Their work included national conferences organized between 2014 and 2019 and a day-long workshop on "Introduction to Structural Racism" led by Crossroads Anti-Racism. MSJ also sponsored a "Montessorians of Color" retreat and held affinity/solidarity groups for white Montessori educators (MSJ n.d.). MSJ hosts a variety of networks and spaces where Montessori communities share best practices for ABAR work and discuss how to improve the climate and practices of Montessori education for all students and educators, especially those of color.

Additionally, MSJ has gained attention and influence for profoundly impacting the established organizations of mainstream in the US Montessori, the American Montessori Society (AMS) and the Association Montessori International/USA (AMI/USA). As of 2021, both organizations now have educators of color in leadership positions (Ayize Sabatier of AMI/USA and Munir Shivji of AMS) and educators of color on their boards. For the first time in the history, each group also recently articulated strategic diversity, equity, and inclusion (DEI) efforts. Currently, both organizations have had ABAR training conducted by Black coordinators, dedicated sessions and research to support DEI efforts at their annual conferences, and issued statements on recent racially and politically motivated events in the United States in the early 2020s. However, there is still work to do in recruiting and funding Montessori educators and trainers of color.

Lessons on Implementing CRP and ABAR in Montessori Classrooms

Beyond individual educator preparation and school-level challenges faced in the implementation of CRP and ABAR practices, it is difficult to enact change on a larger scale because policies reifying structural racism are embedded in the educational fabric of the United States and elsewhere. Current challenges are the resulting legacy of historical atrocities: the American Slave Codes prohibited enslaved people from learning to read; Jim Crow laws maintained segregation and prevented participation in the political life even after the official end of slavery; economic disenfranchisement via sharecropping and redlining prevented Blacks in the United States from obtaining a mortgage or owning property. In each of these instances, the education of Black and brown children was impacted in negative ways. Contemporary polices like exclusionary admissions or dress code policies, discriminatory school discipline policies, and a lack of culturally sustaining curriculum perpetuate this racial inequality in schools (George 2021). The results of these policies have served to create disadvantages for those who are not white and of European descent (see Chapter 59: "Beyond Authenticity: Indigenizing Montessori Education in Settler Colonial United States"). To eliminate these disparities and create schools that can disrupt cycles of exclusion, these policies must be examined through the lens of CRT. This includes continuous, critical examinations of race and identity-based practices in Montessori education.

Leonardo (2013) maintains that the narrative that has been woven around the lives of Black students—such as the culture of poverty, deficit thinking, and the general education of students from the global majority—has consequences that are now social facts. Montessori schools are not immune to racist practices. It is imperative that Montessori educators, administrators, and trainers can critique their teaching and administrative practices from a CRT perspective for the good of all children and our society. This is as Montessori (2007) wished it to be: "Either education contributes to a movement of universal liberation by showing the way to defend and raise humanity or it becomes like one of those organs which have shriveled up by not being used during evolution of the organism (62)." Importantly, we leave it to others to take up a more thorough examination of the ways Montessori was complicit in deficit-minded thinking around race, ethnicity, and language. However, we understand that our work now is impacted by Montessori's thinking and writing about children from non-Western European backgrounds.

Finally, as we round out this chapter, we aim to home in on storytelling a particularly salient facet of Montessori education. One of the theoretical assumptions of the CRP-ABAR curricula and Montessori education is the narrative through which the world is viewed (Ladson-Billings 1999; Lillard 2005). Storytelling has been an important part of formal and informal educational tradition from the beginning of time; to tell stories is to be human. Montessori understood this fact deeply and used story in effective and important ways in her work. We appreciate this and recognize storytelling as a valid and valuable mode of communication, cultural transmission, and even research (Paris and Winn 2015; Yosso 2005).

However, in Montessori environments, many of the stories we share are from a Eurocentric perspective to the exclusion, even erasure, of the contributions: other cultural, racial, and linguistic groups. European narratives especially marginalize Indigenous groups through omission or misrepresentation of their worldview and inaccuracies of their priorities. Love (2019, 138) asserts that CRT "centers knowledge that derives from dark people's experiences with racism by using counter-stories, challenging the normalization of the white world view of knowledge while affirming the personal and family histories of dark people." Going forward, it is the work of the Montessori community to reflect, consistently and critically, on the ways in which their storytelling is life giving, inclusive, and reflective of a truthful inquiry into the past and present. Similarly, one must consider these stories and narratives when considering work at the secondary level of Montessori, which is focused less on storytelling and more on production and exchange. It is only when the Montessori community owns the process of ongoing reflection that CRP and ABAR practices will truly become embedded into the modern Montessori ethos.

As Montessori continues to grow around the globe, Montessori educators must decide how to inform practice and progress by addressing contemporary challenges around inclusive practices, including the limitations around implementing and educating with a CRT lens.

Implications for a Global Perspective

Working to create and implement ABAR Montessori environments requires a great deal of intentional work. In some geographical locations with deeper histories of racism (and/or economic, linguistic, or religious biases), more is needed to achieve a culturally responsive Montessori school or classroom space. Montessori educators must consider the historical, geographic, and cultural contexts of bias and segregation in their training, hiring, curricular planning, outreach, and administration. They must consider how these histories have infiltrated and impacted school formats, policies, locations, and student base, especially if they are private schools.

Furthermore, to focus on anti-bias/anti-racism and culturally responsive pedagogy means to be consistently thoughtful about implementing every practice within an educational setting. In this way, ABAR and culturally responsive CRP practices are thoroughly consistent with Montessori's focus on teacher transformation and prepared environments for children. As centerpieces of the Montessori philosophy and pedagogy, both facets must include attention to issues of disenfranchisement, bias, and exclusion. CRT allows Montessorians a lens with which to examine their educational environment with the hope of creating inclusive Montessori school environments.

Conclusion

Education has long been a contested site for varied political, economic, and social narratives and agendas across the world. In the United States, as a nation with no national curriculum in public education and state-level politics playing ever-stronger roles in the national political landscape, this has never been truer. Montessori education must continue to respond, and even lead, in the arena of inclusive practices.

Finally, we note that the problem of exclusion and systemic racism is bigger than singular classrooms or schools, though these matter a great deal in practice. Montessorians must be ready to address larger, systemic problems of exclusion. We must call for massive restructuring of our educational systems across the world to include more factual narratives, critical analyses of our shared histories, data/media literacy skills, and practices of inclusion. We are aware of the magnitude of this challenge. Nonetheless, Montessori's aspirations for the power of education have compelled us to dream of a more just, equitable, and peaceful society for all children and families. This work cannot be done without a CRT consciousness. The urgency, necessity, and relevance of this work cannot be overstated.

Note

1. "People of the global majority" is used instead of terms like "minority" or "people of color" to reflect the fact that non-white people form the majority of the global population.

References

Banks, K. H., and A. Maixner 2016. "Social Justice Education in an Urban Charter Montessori School." *Journal of Montessori Research* 2 (2): 1–14. https://doi.org/10.17161/jomr.v2i2.5066.

Bell, D. A. 2016. "Who's Afraid of Critical Race Theory?" In *Foundations of Critical Race Theory in Education*, 2nd ed., edited by E. Taylor, D. Gillborn and G. Ladson-Billings, 15–30. New York, NY: Routledge.

Brown, K. E., and A. S. L. Steele 2015. "Racial Discipline Disproportionality in Montessori and Traditional Public Schools: A Comparative Study Using the Relative Rate Index." *Journal of Montessori Research* 1 (1): 14–26. https://doi.org/10.17161/jomr.v1i1.4941.

Canzoneri-Golden, Lucy and Juliet King. 2020. "An Examination of Culturally Relevant Pedagogy and Antibias-Antiracist Curriculum in a Montessori Setting." PhD diss., Lynn University. https://spiral.lynn.edu/etds/360.

Christian, Michelle, 2019. "A Global Critical Race and Racism Framework: Racial Entanglements and Deep and Malleable Whiteness." *Sociology of Race and Ethnicity* 5 (2): 169–85. https://doi.org/10.1177/2332649218783220.

Debs, Mira. 2016. "Racial and Economic Diversity in U.S. Public Montessori Schools." *Journal of Montessori Research* 2 (2): 15–34. https://doi.org/10.17161/jomr.v2i2.5848

Debs, Mira. 2019. *Diverse Families, Desirable Schools: Public Montessori in the Era of School Choice.* Cambridge, MA: Harvard Education Press.

Debs, Mira, and Katie Brown. 2017. "Students of Color and Public Montessori Schools: A Review of the Literature." *Journal of Montessori Research* 3 (1): 1–15.

Debs, Mira, Jaap de Brouwer, Angela K. Murray, Lynne Lawrence, Megan Tyne, and Candice von der Wehl. 2022. "Global Diffusion of Montessori Schools: A Report From the 2022 Global Montessori Census." *Journal of Montessori Research* 8 (2): 1–15. https://doi.org/10.17161/jomr.v8i2.18675.

Derman-Sparks, Louise, and Julie Olsen Edwards. 2010. *Anti-Bias Education for Young Children and Ourselves.* Vol. 254. Washington, DC: National Association for the Education of Young Children.

George, Janel. 2021. "Critical Race Theory Isn't a Curriculum. It's a Practice." *Education Week* May 26, 2021. https://www.edweek.org/leadership/opinion-critical-race-theory-isnt-a-curriculum-its-a-practice/2021/05.

Hall, H. R., and Angela Murray. 2011. "Intersections between Montessori Practices and Culturally Based Curriculum for African American Students." American Montessori Society Research Committee [White Paper].

Harris, Cheryl. 1993. "Whiteness as Property." *Harvard Law Review* 106 (8): 1707–91.

Irwin, Véronique, Jijun Zhang, Xiaolei Wang, Sarah Hein, Ke Wang, Ashley Roberts, Christina York et al. 2021. "Report on the Condition of Education 2021. NCES 2021–144." *National Center for Education Statistics.*

Ladson-Billings, Gloria. 1998. "Just What Is Critical Race Theory and What's It Doing in a Nice Field Like Education?" *International Journal of Qualitative Studies in Education* 11 (1): 7–24.

Ladson-Billings, Gloria. 1999. "Preparing Teachers for Diverse Student Populations: A Critical Race Theory Perspective." *Review of Research in Education* 24: 211–47.

Ladson-Billings, Gloria. 2012. "Through a Glass Darkly: The Persistence of Race in Education Research and Scholarship." *Educational Researcher* 41 (4): 115–20.

Ladson-Billings, Gloria. 2014. "Culturally Relevant Pedagogy 2.0: a.k.a. the Remix." *Harvard Educational Review* 84: 74–84. https://doi.org/10.17763/haer.84.1.p2rj131485484751.

Ladson-Billings, Gloria, and William Tate. 1995. "Toward a Critical Race Theory of Education." *Teachers College Record* 97: 47–68. (EJ519126)

Lebouef, Lee. 2022. "Examining Discipline Disproportionality in Montessori and Non-Montessori Title 1 Schools." Paper presented at the Annual Meeting of AERA, San Diego, CA.

Leonardo, Z. 2013. "The Story of Schooling: Critical Race Theory and the Educational Racial Contract." *Discourse: Studies in the Cultural Policies of Education* 34: 599–610. https://doi.org/10.1080/01596306.2013.822624.

Lillard, A. S. 2005. *The Science behind the Genius.* Oxford, UK: Oxford University Press.

Love, Bettina L. 2019. *We Want to Do More Than Survive: Abolitionist Teaching and the Pursuit of Educational Freedom.* Boston, MA: Beacon Press.

MSJ (Montessori for Social Justice). n.d. "About." Retrieved from https://www.montessoriforsocialjustice.org/about.

Montessori, Maria. 2007. *The Formation of Man.* Amseterdam: Montesrrori-Pierson.

Montessori, Maria. 2020. *The Formation of Man*, Vol. 3 (kindle edition). Amsterdam: Montessori-Pierson.

NAEP (National Assessment of Educational Progress). 2015. *Mathematics and Reading Assessment (2015).* Nation's Report Card. Retrieved from https://www.nationsreportcard.gov/reading_math_2015/#?grade=4.

Paris, D'Jango. 2012. "Culturally Sustaining Pedagogy: A Needed Change in Stance, Terminology, and Practice." *Educational Researcher* 41 (93): 93–7. https://doi.org/10.3102/0013189X12441244

Paris, D'Jango, and Manisha Winn. 2015. *Humanizing Research Decolonizing Qualitative Inquiry with Youth and Communities*. Thousand Oaks, CA: Sage

Pollock, Mica, ed. 2008. *Everyday Antiracism: Getting Real about Race in School*. New York: The New Press.

Sampson, D., and D. F. Garrison-Wade 2011. Cultural vibrancy: Exploring the Preferences of African American Children toward Culturally Relevant and Nonculturally Relevant Lessons. *Urban Review* 43 (2): 279–309. (EJ922705)

Stansbury, J. 2014. *Dealing with Diversity: Administrator, Teacher, and Parent Perceptions of the Responsiveness of Montessori Schools to Racial and Ethnic Diversity* Master's thesis. Chicago, IL: DePaul University.

Taylor, E., D. Gillborn, and G. Ladson-Billings 2016. *Foundations of Critical Race Theory in Education*. New York, NY: Routledge.

Yosso, Tara. 2005. Whose Culture Has Capital? A Critical Race Theory Discussion of Community Cultural Wealth. *Race, Ethnicity, and Education* 8 (1): 69–91. https://doi.org/10.1080/1361332052000341006

Chapter 59

Beyond Authenticity: Indigenizing Montessori Education in Settler Colonial United States

Trisha Moquino, Nacole Walker, and Katie Kitchens

Indigenous children are sacred. In many Indigenous languages, this is a term to describe children imbued with reverence. This reverence is also embedded in our languages and our stories as evidenced by the way children are spoken about and treated. This deep sense of care emerges in our ceremonies and prayers that either involve and center or protect children by honoring their innocence through lack of direct participation. There are naming ceremonies, coming of age ceremonies, ceremonies and practices just for females and just for males, and a multitude of others. These ways of honoring children, central to many Indigenous nations have existed for millennia, long before Maria Montessori first articulated ideas around *following the child* or the sacredness of childhood.

This chapter centers Indigenous epistemologies, or ways of knowing, while exploring the use of the Montessori method as a pathway for educational sovereignty. It is grounded in the context of contemporary settler colonial[1] North America (Deloria and Wildcat 2001; Narvez et al. 2019). We focus on truth telling and the idea of educational reclamation in countries living out the ongoing reality of settler colonial violence. Montessori leaders must publicly recognize that education, particularly in the United States, including Montessori education, is rooted in these ideologies often aimed at erasing Indigenous people (Grande 2015). The chapter begins by naming reasons Indigenous communities utilize Montessori practices for reclamation of their children's education. We then confront the necessity of truth telling about how Montessori has been and, in some instances, continues to be weaponized against Indigenous children and their communities. Finally, we articulate a vision for an Indigenized Montessori practice as a tool for creating culturally sustaining environments honoring, uplifting, and centering the languages, cultures, values, and knowledge of the Tribal Nations and global Indigenous communities in which it is utilized.

Author Positionality

Author positionality refers to the specific, unique intersection of identities (race, gender, ability, etc.) that each author represents (Hull 2020). This information is often included in qualitative educational research. By including our own positionalities, we hope to disrupt the notion of academic objectivity or neutrality. Positionality also visibly centers and uplifts Indigenous Montessori practitioners who are often made invisible, tokenized, spoken over, spoken for, used, and oftentimes dismissed.

Trisha Moquino comes from the tribes of Cochiti, Kewa, and Ohkay Ohwingeh, three of the Pueblo Nations of the nineteen Indian Pueblos located in settler colonial New Mexico in the settler colonial United States. She grew up with her grandparents from all three villages—a gift she cherishes. Her grandparents appreciated and had a fierce love for their respective Pueblo and their respective beautiful languages (Keres and Tewa). As a mother, daughter, granddaughter, auntie, and teacher in her grandmother's tribe of Cochiti Pueblo, she believes every child should know, live, and love their history, culture, language, and community which translates into loving one's self.

Nacole Walker is Dakota and Lakota from the Standing Rock Sioux Tribe in North Dakota and South Dakota. She was raised with her sister by her grandmother, mother, and father. She grew up learning to love and connect with the land; she spent her summers with her family swimming in the Missouri river, riding horses, picking berries, and digging wild turnips on the plains. She heard her language in the community since she was a young child and began seriously learning it as an adult. She now teaches the Dakota and Lakota languages in her communities at Standing Rock.

Katie Kitchens is a white, queer, Jewish teacher and student who grew up on unceded Tongva land in so-called Southern California. They were raised by their mother and father with their younger sister. Katie currently works as the English-speaking elementary guide at Keres Children's Learning Center.

By sharing our positionality, we honor the experiences and wisdom of whole Tribal Nations that have raised Trisha and Nacole and resist assimilation into dominant white culture. We do so for ancestors and communities that protected languages, cultures, and ways of life despite the unrelenting violence of settler colonialism. And to honor that they did so with deep love and joy. We share Katie's positionality as a way of demonstrating the role non-Indigenous individuals can play in dismantling settler colonial power structures.

Why Montessori?

We know at this point in our history and our Tribal Nations' migration stories that the space of schooling, specifically Montessori education, can support our children, families, and communities in the ways and languages (when possible) of our ancestors and respective Tribal Nations. Despite the ways schooling has been used as a tool for assimilation and violence, we recognize the potential and opportunity of culturally sustaining schools as a pathway for us to exercise and protect our sovereignty (Paris and Alim 2017). We recognize schooling in the United States often aims to assimilate Indigenous children, and children of color more broadly, into whiteness. We know that to create learning spaces honoring Indigenous children, pedagogy must recognize and honor their full humanity in the same way that our communities do.

By way of example, at Keres Children's Learning Center (KCLC),[2] the Montessori approach was selected in service of the mission of Keres language revitalization. KCLC is a non-profit Keres-language revitalization school founded in 2006 using intergenerational educators to offer dual-language immersion with Montessori pedagogy for children ages 2.5 to 12. It is located on the Cochiti Pueblo in New Mexico, USA, with the blessing of the Cochiti Tribal Council (KCLC 2022a, 2022b). Keres Children's Learning Center "strives to reclaim our children's education and honor our heritage by using a comprehensive cultural and academic curriculum to assist families in nurturing Keres-speaking, holistically healthy, community minded, and academically strong students" (KCLC 2022c).

At first glance, it might be difficult to discern that KCLC is a Montessori program. This choice is an intentional one, centering the Keres language and thereby centering worldviews, knowledge, and deep love inextricably woven throughout. While not immediately obvious, the *comprehensive cultural and academic curriculum* to which we refer is Montessori education. We use the Montessori approach for many reasons, the most important being Montessori's philosophy regarding respect for the child's spirit, as well as her recognition that all children have a cosmic task. These facets of her work match our deep belief that Indigenous children are sacred and must be treated accordingly. Of cosmic education, Montessori stated,

> Thus the way leads from the whole via the parts back to the whole. In this way the child learns to appreciate the unity and regularity of cosmic events. When this vision is opened up he will be fascinated to such an extent that he will value the cosmic laws and their correlation more than any simple fact. Thus the child will develop a kind of philosophy, which teaches him the unity of the universe. This, the very thing to organize his intelligence and to give him a better insight into his own place and task in the world, at the same time presenting a chance for the development of his creative energy.
>
> *(Montessori, as quoted in Grazzini 2013, 113)*

Here, Montessori recognizes the sacredness of the individual child, acknowledges personal will, and names children as connected to the entire universe. This belief guides many Indigenous communities and has since time immemorial. In addition to a philosophical alignment with many Indigenous worldviews, Montessori education also provides both the structure and the flexibility necessary to cultivate language immersion classrooms. Montessori observed what contemporary neuroscientists affirm as a unique ability for language acquisition in a child's earliest years (Kuhl 2000).

The languages that are most present in children's environments during early childhood are those which they will be able to speak in later years with the fluency of native speakers. Unfortunately, for many Indigenous parents today, the language most prevalent in many households is now English. This is a direct result of assimilationist policies of violent boarding school policies and practices which sought to remove children from their families to acculturate them into whiteness (see Adams 1996). This was a particularly effective form of epistemicide, the destruction of Indigenous ways of knowing. Languages contain the worldviews, prayers, and cultures of the communities to which they belong. Language also dictates culture and relationships as much as culture shapes the language. For these reasons, language loss is a particularly devastating outcome of assimilative schooling in the United States. Globally, scholars estimate there are between 4,000 and 7,145 Indigenous languages, and many are in danger of extinction because younger generations have been systemically denied the opportunity to continue these languages, thus not having the opportunity to learn their languages (Jacob et al. 2015). To heal the ongoing harm left in the wake of boarding schools, many Tribal Nations have dedicated their full effort to language revitalization.

The flexibility of the Montessori Language curriculum provides a foundation that language revitalization programs can be built on. Montessori's emphasis on spoken language instruction supports learning a language like Keres, an entirely oral language. The intentional scaffolding of reading and writing, as well as materials that can be adapted to a variety of languages, supports learning Indigenous languages. At the Lakȟól'iyapi Wahóȟpi, a Lakota language immersion school on the Standing Rock reservation, the Montessori method is also used as the main teaching medium. Students learn to read and write Lakota with scaffolded Montessori Language materials adapted to the Lakota language.

Additionally, Montessori's insistence on an intentionally prepared environment, cultivated to meet the unique developmental needs of the child, provides rich opportunities for establishing culturally sustaining learning spaces. In his writing, Mario Montessori shares three factors determining a child's self-construction: the child's own personality, the material world to which the child must adapt, and the culture of the community to which the child is born. He also notes that "it is the prevailing order of this community that permits the child to achieve an inner harmony" (Montessori 2008, 18). Through connection to their community, children can develop a deep knowledge of self, a connection to the world, and a sense of their own purpose within it. Unless the prepared environment honors the languages, values, and culture of the child's community, it cannot effectively support their harmonious self-construction. The prepared environment houses our hopes for Indigenous languages to be revitalized.

Finally, Montessori education is used in Indigenous language restoration because of the potential that it holds to serve as a pathway for humanization, justice, and, perhaps, liberation. Overall, Montessori supports the missions of our schools by providing a setting where children can access academic knowledge in a manner that does not require them to choose between being excellent students or fully participatory members of their families and communities. They do not need to sacrifice their Indigenous identities to succeed in school. Rather, identities are celebrated and nurtured through intergenerational learning, supporting children in becoming their full selves.

As authors, we celebrate Montessori pedagogy but also recognize it has faults. Montessori as a pedagogy is neither inherently liberatory nor oppressive. A pedagogy is breathed into life by the human beings who practice it. This process of animating an abstract pedagogy necessitates the diligent preparation of the guide. Emancipatory Montessori practices require systemic analysis of the ongoing realities of settler colonialism, racism, and white supremacy culture that dictate life in the United States and elsewhere around the globe. Without it, Montessori practitioners can unwittingly replicate and reify systems of oppression undermining the method's liberatory potential.

Truth Telling

One way Montessori can be harmful is through the articulation of the Montessori pedagogy as a new discovery. While this may have been true for Europeans and settlers in the United States who had moved away from child-rearing practices rooted in honoring the humanity of children,

Indigenous communities have been honoring the spirit of the child long before Maria Montessori began the process of outlining her teachings. Indigenous peoples such as the Pueblo and Lakota peoples have been practicing child-centered, reverent child-rearing for millennia. Montessori education is often heralded as revolutionary and novel while Indigenous approaches to caring for children have been historically erased and ignored, echoing narratives of colonialism. Given the context of child labor, exploitative conditions, and control-centered narratives that dominated collective thought about children in Europe during the first part of the twentieth century, Montessori's work does appear like a revelation. But within the global context, many communities had held values of respect, reverence, and awe for children at the core of their beliefs long before the first Pink Tower was created (Cajete 1994).

This lack of recognition emerges frequently within Montessori teacher education, which, like much of the educational training landscape, often systemically fails to authentically address the legacy of systemic racism, settler colonialism, and imperialism. Erasure of Indigenous practices and histories continue to shape modern realities. This lack of recognition also furthers erasure of Indigenous peoples in general. While this chapter focuses on the United States specifically, the United States is not the only country wrestling with these truths. There is other work to do in this arena globally. Moreover, worldwide, when Montessori training centers attempt to present a politically neutral version of peace education, they betray Montessori's own vision for an active peace that tears out the roots of injustice (Moquino and Han 2018). Until the Montessori community acknowledges these realities and "as long as such a profound misunderstanding [of peace] continues to exist, peace will definitely fail to fall within the range of human possibilities" (Montessori 1992, 7). The following section practices Indigenous truth telling by highlighting examples of Montessori education used to practice historic and contemporary harm on Indigenous children.

Past and Present Harm

Using the Montessori method in Indigenous communities requires interrogating how Montessori education has been and continues to be used as an assimilative tool, both historically and contemporarily, as part of the ongoing settler colonial schooling project. Just as the settler colonial United States began with violence against Indigenous peoples, the early history of Montessori education in the United States does as well. We know that Montessori education was used in Indigenous boarding schooling in the United States as early as 1913. In 1879, Richard Pratt founded the Carlisle Indian Industrial School with the foundational idea of "kill the Indian, save the man" (Adams 1996; Marr n.d.). The boarding school era ushered in assimilationist violence centered on the removal of children from their families, languages, land, cultures, and communities, and the role of Montessori education cannot be ignored in that context. It is not exempt from perpetuating this same type of racial harm either then or now. In 1913, a Montessori classroom was established at the Tulalip Indian Boarding School in Washington state.

The white educators utilizing the Montessori method for assimilation at the Tulalip Indian Boarding School celebrated its effectiveness (Hurlbut 1919). Their reflections stand in stark

Figure 59.1 Tulalip children work with Montessori letters at the Tulalip boarding school, ca. 1919. From *the Indian School Journal*, 1904–1926, National Archives ID 2745572. Retrieved from the National Archives Catalog, Department of the Interior, Office of Indian Affairs.

contrast to those of the children that experienced their teaching, including Tulalip Leader Celum Young who shared,

> They wanted me to forget my way of life and learn to be civilized and learn to be a good white person. I still don't know what a good white person is. All I know is that I learned to march, march, march, and not speak my language. You got in big trouble for that. I got many whippings and confinement.
>
> *(Marr n.d.)*

Hurlbut (1919) espoused the freedom of the Montessori method, noting that this was a controlled sort of freedom that allowed neither idleness nor disorder. Looking at this now, we ask: What kind of freedom can exist in a school seeking to strip children of their language, culture, and connection to their people? What kind of freedom presupposes idleness and disorder? What kind of freedom demands assimilation into whiteness? Before there can be peace, there must be reconciliation, and before there can be reconciliation, there must be truth telling. This truth telling includes wrestling with the reality that the Montessori method has often been used in ways that betray its liberatory aspirations. To utilize Montessori education as a tool for culturally sustaining practices the Montessori community must commit to reckoning with the past legacy of harm and the ways harm continues to be committed.

Contemporary Harm

In Fall 2013, Jeanne Oxendine-Eagle Bull (Oglala Lakota) and James Oxendine (Lumbee) were living in San Diego with their children. One afternoon, their daughter came home with a flyer advertising her Montessori school's upcoming Thanksgiving celebration which would include creating caricatures of Indigenous cultures such as feather headdresses and drums, a practice considered deeply offensive by many Indigenous peoples. When the Oxendine-Eagle Bull family expressed their concern about these events and offered to share about their own communities, they were dismissed. When they continued to raise concerns, they were silenced. Ultimately, their scholarship to the school (given in part because of their identity as Indigenous people) was revoked. Despite raising their concerns, the school continued with these culturally harmful practices. After the Oxendine-Eagle Bull family shared this story with various news outlets, the school filed a $20,000 defamation lawsuit against the family (Dadigan 2014). This story is one example, but it is neither unique nor is it isolated based on our experiences and expertise in Montessori and Indigeneity. In many ways, the example is representative of the Montessori community's practices—a veneer of inclusivity around Indigeneity rooted in good intentions but lacking critical analysis and, ultimately, demonstrating a complete disregard for the humanity of contemporary Indigenous people and communities. Regardless of intention, instances such as these serve to reify structures of white dominance, contributing to the legacy of erasure and harm.

Another example we bring to this work occurred at the Indigenous Montessori Institute, a teacher training program, hosted at KCLC that combines Indigenous knowledge systems and the Montessori philosophy (KCLC Montessori 2022c). In the spring of 2019, the inaugural cohort,[3] of which author Nacole Walker was a part, had a visit from an experienced non-Indigenous Association Montessori Internationale (AMI) early childhood level trainer. She was a guest lecturer intending to teach the cohort about song and dance to use in the classroom. It became clear quickly that the main focus of her lesson was on Western music in English, which made participants uncomfortable and did not fit the contours of the training program. Participants' comments about teaching children music from their own Indigenous nations were dismissed.

Later, the cohort of guides in training were led outside and introduced to Indigenous-themed dances. The first dance introduced was a round dance, an actual dance performed by some Indigenous peoples, particularly at powwows. The performance of this appropriated dance by a non-Indigenous person to a group of Indigenous people was wrought with stereotypical comments about Native American spirituality and vague concepts of peace. The next dance prompted more generic, stereotypical comments about Native American beliefs. Finally, the guide began dancing as an eagle in a very offensive way—a caricature of actual Indigenous spiritual dances. When the Indigenous students in the group refused to continue with the lesson, the guest lecturer expressed feeling hurt. She did not understand the harm that she had caused nor did she honor their needs, putting her own feelings at the forefront.

This example of fragility was predictable. It is common in education writ large. Montessori education, training, and implementation are not immune to this deflection and fragility which can emerge when Indigenous people address issues of settler colonialism and white supremacy directly. While to some these instances appear benign on the surface, they function to obfuscate real harm and do little to center Indigenous people's feelings and needs. These specific examples illustrate larger, structural issues within the Montessori community, including Indigenous erasure and the centering of whiteness more broadly. It reflects the ongoing reality of settler colonialism which feeds on the erasure and exploitation of Indigenous communities (Tuck and Yang 2012).

Following the state-sanctioned murders of George Floyd, Breonna Taylor, and Amaud Arbery in the United States, it appeared that there was new commitment to reckoning with racial justice. Suddenly, Montessori organizations who regularly expressed resistance to undertaking racial justice work were now positioning themselves as leaders. However, the history of anti-racism and liberation work in the Montessori community began long before the summer of 2020. It began with Mae Arlene Gadpaille and the Montessori Family Center in Roxbury, MA, in 1964 among others (Debs 2019). It began with Keres Children's Learning Center and Lakȟól'iyapi Wahóȟpi. It began with the Montessori for Social Justice learning community established in 2015. Each of these grassroots, people of the global majority-led organizations were committed to anti-racism without the support of national and international Montessori groups.

Since the mid-2010s, there has been an increase in cosmetic commitment to justice work within the Montessori community, such as the inclusion of books featuring diverse characters, Black Lives Matter webinars, the occasional keynote speaker of the global majority, and even the appointment of anti-bias/anti-racist (ABAR) directors or consultants. And yet training for both teachers and trainers of the global majority has not caught up with these efforts. More recently, both Association Montessori International/USA (AMI/USA) and American Montessori Society (AMS) have appointed leaders and board members of color and now offer specific ABAR training and certification. Nonetheless, both major global training organizations (AMI and AMS) lack specific curricular requirements related to anti-racist teaching. This perpetuates the perception of Montessori education, in the United States and elsewhere, as being for wealthy, white children and families.

Moving forward, if the global Montessori community hopes to truly move toward liberation, it must wrestle with the ways in which the culture of white supremacy and whiteness are baked into the structure of Montessori education. There are examples of individual training centers, like IMI, or individual schools, like the Pear Tree School in Oakland committing themselves to racial justice work. However, for true systemic change to occur, there needs to be a commitment at the highest levels of Montessori leadership. We acknowledge that AMI/USA, AMS, Montessori Public Policy Initiative (MPPI), and the National Center for Montessori in the Public Sector would all note that they are working on these efforts. However, we believe that true systemic change necessitates addressing the still present and very real inaccessibility of Montessori training opportunities for members of the global majority and the lack of trainers reflective of the global majority. This commitment would also include a critical examination of the materials being presented in training, with several specific examples examined in the following section.

Myths and Materials: Examples of a Need for Continued Change

Indigenous peoples know intimately the violence of settler colonialism. Although official US policies bar explicit physical violence against Indigenous peoples today, continued attempts at epistemicide through erasure, assimilation, land theft, and white-centric forms of state-sanctioned schooling continue this legacy. Montessori material companies, training centers, and online sources such as Teachers Pay Teachers still abound with harmful classroom materials created by non-Indigenous educators where Indigenous input, collaboration, and rethinking are often warranted. Furthermore, when presented in training centers, these materials become enshrined with a prescribed scope and sequence from which Montessori educators are discouraged from straying.

While these materials and lessons are often created with the intention of honoring Indigenous peoples, they instead serve to perpetuate harmful stereotypes about Indigenous peoples while participating in the continued erasure of these nations. We hope this chapter challenges others interested in Montessori education to critically examine and change practices within Montessori education and Montessori training that erase or marginalize Indigenous peoples around the globe, including their use of unexamined, incomplete puzzle maps, which represent settler colonial borders, historical timelines as with US history, and even the Great Lesson/Story centered on Language. With regard to the latter, the lesson unintentionally imparts a hierarchy of language, placing greater value on the written rather than the spoken word. For Indigenous communities whose languages do not have a written component (like the language of Keres), this is yet another form of marginalization. Even for languages with a written alphabet (like Lakota), such stories can unintentionally undermine the oral tradition that many Indigenous nations hold dear. Utilizing the Montessori method in Indigenous communities requires critically analyzing the ways in which there is misalignment between Indigenous languages, cultures, values, and traditions and Montessori as it is traditionally practiced and feeling empowered to change or abandon them. This process, which we will refer to as *Indigenizing the Montessori curriculum*, is an arduous, labor-intensive undertaking but one that is necessary in creating learning environments that truly affirm Indigenous children in their full humanity.

Indigenizing the Montessori Curriculum

In the process of using Montessori as a tool for educational sovereignty, we do recognize and appreciate all the ways in which it is in alignment with our communities' values. We believe it has the capacity to support language revitalization. But we are also acutely aware of how dominant and persistent narratives about Indigenous peoples in Montessori contribute to our erasure and erect barriers that impede our growth. Ultimately, we want to be able to fully focus our energy on fulfilling the missions of our respective schools and organizations in service to our language revitalization efforts and work with our children. And we continue to be grateful to those non-Indigenous Montessori colleagues who take responsibility for unlearning their own internalized anti-Indigeneity through concrete action. This includes following Indigenous leadership, ceding space and resources, and continually taking on the work of tackling white supremacy and settler colonialism in all Montessori spaces. For example, an effort currently underway involves Montessori curricular reform. During the summer of 2021, IMI gathered a group of predominantly BIPOC (Black, Indigenous, and people of color) Montessori educators to begin the process of Indigenizing the Montessori elementary curriculum. Decolonizing curriculum goes beyond simply inserting lessons about Indigenous peoples. It requires a radical reorientation which centers Indigenous epistemologies and redefines success within the context of the values, languages, and traditions of each Indigenous community (Gaudry and Lorenz 2018).

As Indigenous peoples, as Tribal Nation community members, we are not interested in conforming ourselves to a narrow vision of *authentic* Montessori practice determined by white-centric notions of fidelity. We do not care to adapt to Montessori pedagogy and philosophy in its entirety. Instead, we choose to adapt Montessori education for our needs. We do not exist to be in service of Montessori; rather, we use Montessori in service to our languages, children, and Tribal Nations. We encourage practitioners, researchers, and evaluators involved in Montessori education to consider the narratives and data within this chapter as they engage with Montessori in their own cultural, geographic, and social contexts. We remain committed to exploring how Montessori education can be a tool to restore balance in the lives of our people, especially our children. Our goal is ultimately to see our children thrive and live out life in a way that encourages each of us to become whole Indigenous people—a people who are intimately connected to their ancestral ways, languages, cultures while still interfacing with contemporary settler colonial society.

Creating schools that redefine success on Indigenous terms also requires radically reimagining teacher education. As one example, KCLC's Indigenous Montessori Institute (IMI) was created to fulfill KCLC's need for its own teacher preparation pathway. IMI was also created due to the lack of existing teacher training programs, regardless of pedagogical approach, that prioritize Indigenous Education and hold anti-bias and anti-racism as some of their core training principles. IMI strives to develop teachers who will serve the whole child by honoring a child's language, values, and the beliefs of their community while providing comprehensive academic training.

While the work of Indigenization is first and foremost for our Indigenous children, it also supports all children by providing an emancipatory, truth-centered educational model. The Indigenizing Montessori Elementary curriculum group acknowledged that a logical first step in this process was to start by examining the philosophy and theories of Montessori and determine how to center Indigenous thoughts, beliefs, and worldviews while decentering Montessori philosophies that do not align or benefit Indigenous peoples. Indigenous lands, languages, and histories have long been ignored and silenced in education. This Indigenization process is the first step in a long but needed evolution of the Montessori curriculum to stop the erasure of our people and children which further marginalizes us. This Indigenization process serves to hold all Montessorians accountable to truth telling and to disrupt the settler colonial narrative.

Conclusion

Indigenous children are sacred. As we continue to be grateful to the Montessori approach, we also highlight the ongoing need for confronting anti-Indigeneity in Montessori schools, Montessori training centers, and various national and international Montessori organizations. Part of this work includes committing to ongoing truth telling in classrooms and organizations with non-Indigenous children and adults so that they can be equipped to combat the erasure of Indigenous people that allows settler colonialism to flourish. As Indigenous peoples, we are reclaiming the education of our children and creating a pathway to use a pedagogy that is in alignment with our respective Tribal Nations' values. Despite the reality, and in our experience, it is still the most hopeful.

Montessori writes in *Education and Peace* that one of the ultimate goals of Montessori education is universal liberation. Because this is so, we must lovingly and compassionately hold the national and international Montessori community accountable to reckoning with truth and to follow the lead of Indigenous-trained Montessorians and Indigenous-led education efforts.

Notes

1. Here we refer to the ways in which individuals and groups deliberately and invasively repress Indigenous culture and perpetuate genocide on Indigenous people. See Alicia Cox's Oxford Bibliography and the Journal of Indigenous Research among others for more information.
2. KCLC is supported by foundations, individuals, the Administration for Native Americans, and New Mexico's Indian Affairs Department (KCLC Montessori 2022b).
3. The Indigenous Montessori Institute offers AMI primary and elementary training in partnership with the Southwest Institute of Montessori Training.

References

Adams, David Wallace. 1996. *Education for Extinction: American Indians and the Boarding School Experience, 1875–1928*. Lawrence, KS: University Press of Kansas.

Cajete, Gregory. 1994. *Look to the Mountain: An Ecology of Indigenous Education*. Skyland, NC: Kivaki Press.

Dadigan, Marc. 2014. "Family Sued for Standing against School's Racist Thanksgiving Curriculum." *Indian Country Today*, May 28, 2014. https://indiancountrytoday.com/archive/family-sued-for-standing-against-schools-racist-thanksgiving-curriculum.

Debs, Mira. 2019. *Diverse Families, Desirable Schools: Public Montessori in the Era of School Choice*. Cambridge, MA: Harvard Education Press.

Deloria Jr., Vine, and Daniel R. Wildcat. 2001. *Power and Place: Indian Education in America*. Golden, CO: Fulcrum Publishing.

Gaudry, Adam, and Danielle Lorenz. 2018. "Indigenization as Inclusion, Reconciliation, and Decolonization: Navigating the Different Visions for Indigenizing the Canadian Academy." *AlterNative: An International Journal of Indigenous Peoples* 14 (3): 218–27. https://doi.org/10.1177/1177180118785382.

Grande, Sandy. 2015. *Red Pedagogy: Native American Social and Political Thought*. Lanham, MD: Rowman and Littlefield.

Grazzini, Camillo. 2013. "Maria Montessori's Cosmic Vision, Cosmic Plan, and Cosmic Education." *The NAMTA Journal* 38 (1) (Winter): 107–16.

Hull, Andrew G. D. 2020. Researcher Positionality—A Consideration of Its Influence and Place in Qualitative Research: A New Researcher Guide. *Shanlax International Journal of Education* 8 (4): 1–10. https://doi.org/10.34293/education.v8i4.3232.

Hurlbut, Nina M. 1919. "The Montessori Class at the Tulalip Indian Boarding School." *The Indian School Journal* 19 (7): 249–53.

Jacob, W. James, Jing Liu, and Che-Wei Lee. 2015. "Policy Debates and Indigenous Education: The Trialectic of Language, Culture, and Identity." In *Indigenous Education: Language, Culture, and Identity*, edited by W. James Jacob, Maureen K. Porter and Shen Yao Cheng, 39–62. London: Springer.

KCLC Montessori. 2022a. "About our Method." Accessed February 14, 2022. https://kclcmontessori.org/about-our-method/.

KCLC Montessori. 2022b. "Our Mission." Accessed February 14, 2022. https://kclcmontessori.org/our-mission/.

KCLC Montessori. 2022c. "About Indigenous Montessori Institute." Accessed December 14, 2021. https://kclcmontessori.org/about-imi/.

Kuhl, Patricia, 2000. A New View of Language Acquisition. *PNAS* 97 (22): 11850–7. https://doi.org/10.1073/pnas.97.22.11850.

Marr, Carolyn J. n.d. *Between Two Worlds: Experiences at the Tulalip Indian Boarding School 1905–1932*. Tulalip, WA: Hibulb Cultural Center and Natural History Preserve. https://www.hibulbculturalcenter.org/assets/pdf/Between-Two-Worlds.pdf.

Montessori, Maria. 1972. *Education and Peace*. Translated by Helen Lane and A. M. Joosten. Chicago: Regnery.

Montessori, Mario M. 1992. *Education for Human Development: Understanding Montessori*. Oxford: Clio.

Montessori, Maria. 2008. *The Montessori Method*. St. Paul, MN: Wilder Publications, Incorporated

Moquino, Trisha, and Daisy Han. 2018. "Moving Beyond Peace Education to Social Justice Education," *AMI/USA Journal* 2018 (Spring): 8–10.

Narvez, Darcia, Four Arrows (Don Trent Jacobs), Eugene Halton, Brian S. Collier, and Georges Enderle, ed. 2019. *Indigenous Sustainable Wisdom: First Nation Know-how for Global Flourishing*. New York: Peter Lang.

Paris, Django, and H. Samy Alim. 2017. *Culturally Sustaining Pedagogies: Teaching and Learning for Justice in a Changing World*. New York: Teachers College Press.

Sabzalian, Leilani. 2019. *Indigenous Children's Survivance in Public Schools*. London: Routledge.

Tuck, Eve, and K. Wayne Yang. 2012. "Decolonization Is Not a Metaphor." *Decolonization: Indigeneity, Education and Society* 1 (1): 1–40.

Chapter 60
Montessori Education and Multilingualism

Kateri Carver

Throughout *The Absorbent Mind*, the seminal work published at the end of her career, Maria Montessori (1995) repeatedly uses the evidence of language acquisition to illustrate the child's astounding power of "absorption," a term that refers to the ways in which infants take in everything around them and make it part of their personhood. Montessori describes a "special language mechanism" (119) that enables the child to develop receptive and productive language and characterizes this linguistic feat as both "mysterious" and "miraculous" (119, 121). Young children learn language from their environment at a rate and with an efficiency not repeated in later periods of human development. Despite the thematic example of learning one's native language as testament to the absorbent mind, Montessori approaches language acquisition not from a linguist's perspective but from an anthropological one (Pouzar-Kozak 2008). For her, the development of language leads to the development of civilization and culture. Had she approached language acquisition as a linguist, it is almost certain that twentieth-century linguists from Jakobson to Chomsky would have looked to Montessori's understanding of the "special language mechanism" for how the mind performs one of its most incredible accomplishments—learning one's first language.[1]

Many languages are spoken in Montessori classrooms around the world, and a number of these settings formally incorporate a second language into the prepared environment. Montessori educators who offer exposure to a second language (L2) along with the first language (L1) do so understanding the power of the absorbent mind and sensitive periods, particularly as they relate to learning language, which they can leverage when introducing L2 learning in the early years. It is worth noting, however, that this ability to honor multiple languages is not always up to the individual educator.

Models of Multilingualism in Montessori Environments

Before discussing models of multilingual Montessori environments and their relationship to contemporary second language acquisition (SLA) theory and practice, we acknowledge that comprehensive data on Montessori education worldwide is limited in general and also regarding the prevalence and approaches of L2 Montessori programs (Debs et al. 2022). However, job postings provide evidence that Montessori environments frequently incorporate L2, though it is unclear if it is more common than in traditional school settings. Many Montessori schools in non-English dominant countries seek English-speaking Montessori teachers. Conversely, job postings in the United States often request classroom assistants or aids who have a second language (typically Spanish) but may not have a Montessori credential. A relatively smaller number of Montessori schools in the United States with fully integrated L2 instruction—often immersion or dual-language settings—post job opportunities for bilingual Montessori guides on frequently visited Montessori websites.

One popular L2 model in Montessori environments is also the most feasible and straightforward: the inclusion of an adult who speaks a second language. This model aptly prioritizes oral language development and comprehension. For example, Escuela Montessori de Valparaíso in Santiago, Chile, has a bilingual guide (Spanish/English) in the elementary classroom to promote exposure and learning of English in addition to their native Spanish (La Escuela Montessori de Valparaíso 2022). This "one-and-one" model, as I call it, is used in Montessori classrooms; based on personal experience over the past twenty years, it is also one of the most widely endorsed practices of multiple language use in Montessori settings. This model is employed across many languages with L2 English being common outside of the United States. The one-and-one model can range from a bilingual assistant who speaks only the target language for functional speech ("please push in your chair") to an assistant who incorporates the target language at a designated time.

Language exposure from a bilingual adult, often in early childhood classrooms, is frequently supported by L2 materials on a shelf (i.e., animal objects or color card materials). However, young children interacting independently with L2 materials will not develop vocabulary, model accent, syntax, morphology, or other embedded grammatical structures particular to that language because oral language must, by definition, come from a fluent speaker. Thus, despite Montessori educators' inclinations to give young children independent L2 work, this practice has limited value. The strength of the one-and-one approach is the modeling and contextualization of language in the environment in real time. When a child learns the deep structures of L2 naturally and unconsciously, their L2 receptive and productive skills are significantly positively impacted (Cook 2010; Hurajova 2015).

While the one-and-one model is prevalent in early childhood Montessori settings, continuity at the elementary level is limited sometimes simply because many Montessori programs outside of the United States do not extend to the elementary years. The United States is unique in its extensive offerings of public, private, and independent elementary Montessori programs compared to most other countries which translates into more opportunities to consider bilingual Montessori programs as well. For example, in Paris, France, there are numerous bilingual Montessori early childhood programs, yet there are virtually no Montessori elementary schools in Paris (International School Database 2022).

Models in the United States

In this section, I share the most common models that I have encountered in the United States during my years of experience across the country. Typical L2 models span a range of offerings. *Content-focused* paradigms include total, two-way, and partial immersion programs;

language-focused paradigms include Kindergarten through sixth grade programs where the allocation of instructional time varies (30–50 minutes) but is regularly and consistently implemented (3–5 days a week) (Shrum and Glisan 2016, 112–16). Many American Montessori schools choose traditional models of Foreign Language in the elementary School (FLES) programs of L2 instruction that focus on language instruction and not the delivery of academic content in the target language. For example, language-focused instruction might take the form of thematic-based L2 teaching, such as teaching vocabulary related to the home or winter sports; content-instruction might take the form of teaching the biomes of North America and the various shelters, animals, and plants within that geographical region in the L2.

Montessori schools in the United States extensively employ a typical FLES model which offers the L2 as a cocurricular subject. The FLES model often takes two forms. It may be a *push-in* model where the L2 teacher comes into the classroom on a regular schedule and gives language lessons to a whole class or small groups, or it may employ a *pull-out* model where the teacher takes the whole class or small groups to a different setting. Both are like traditional models of L2 instruction that focus on language instruction, not content instruction in the language. Still other L2 models in the American Montessori landscape include dual language or immersion Montessori settings that offer instructional and functional language as well as comprehensive literacy in both L1 and L2. These are few, although they are anecdotally known as highly successful.

The FLES models in Montessori environments that mimic traditional L2 instruction models favor oral and communicative language and do not emphasize grammar. The increased focus on communicative competencies and decreased focus on grammatical structures aligns with a transition in SLA theory. The audiolingual or direct method used by language teachers about fifty years ago is giving way to the contemporary sociocultural approach that includes student interaction and scaffolding (Schrum and Glisan 2016, 45).

The important takeaway of this discussion of L2 models found in US Montessori schools is that there is no documentation, little to no collaboration, and, sadly, no sharing of outcomes. As said above, in some American Montessori settings, the L2 is "freely" incorporated but at times without a comprehensive, sustainable plan; this includes implementation in spaces where educators do not have first-hand knowledge of SLA theory and practice. These problems can be addressed by looking outward: many educators outside of the United States are built on plurilingual cultures and are able to implement SLA more successfully, as Feez and Morgan note (see Chapter 57: "Montessori Education in a Plurilingual World").

Montessori and SLA Theory

In this section, I enumerate a few of the ways that the Montessori classroom supports SLA. The affective-filter hypothesis, first proposed by Dulay and Burt (1977) and revisited by Krashen (1988), provides a framework for understanding the Montessori environment's particular strength in supporting language acquisition. The affective-filter theory incorporates motivation, anxiety, personality, and attitude as influences on learning another language (Shrum and Glisan 2016). This theory posits that an environment rich in motivation, low in anxiety, and high in recognition of individual attitudes directly relates to language acquisition levels. The Montessori environment aligns with these qualities through its cultivation of intrinsic motivation, its multi-age setting that acts as a motivator to imitate peers, and respect for individual interests, learning preferences, and needs.

Another useful foundation that can be applied to L2 in Montessori education is the sociocultural perspective of language learning, which maintains "that language learning is a social process rather than one that occurs within the individual and is based largely on the work of Vygotsky" (Shrum and Glisan 2016, 24). Essentially, through interaction with others, language learners gain a mastery of a second language that they could not get alone. This model emphasizes the scaffolding that comes from others in the classroom as children assist one another with work and language (Shrum and Glisan 2016, 27). The Montessori elementary classroom strongly supports this sociocultural approach to learning a language as its co-constructing culture permeates the learning process and self-reflective practices of its students.

Finally, Shrum and Glisan's (2016) work, *Teacher's Handbook: Contextualized Language Instruction,* offers a particularly apt example of binding, which applies to a Montessori Children's House context and is related to Krashen's input hypothesis (1988) and the acquisition of vocabulary. In this example, the child acquires the word "milk" by hearing their caretakers say, "Here is your milk" or by accidentally spilling their milk on the floor and hearing someone say, "Oops, you spilled your milk" (Shrum and Glisan 2016, 17). The Montessori teacher may respond with a comment and question such as "Let's clean up that milk together; could you go and get the rag for a floor spill?" When children acquire language in real time and with real objects, they are not just exposed to new vocabulary but also to various syntactic forms, verbs in different tenses and modes, and much more. This convergence of meaning and object, as in the milk above, is known as *binding*. Terrell's (1986) introduction of this term in language-learning circles reminds teachers of the need to bind meaning with an object or action and not with a translation. This is consistent with L1 acquisition in Montessori classrooms.

Accidents happen all the time in an early childhood classroom, and they are rich linguistic opportunities. It is precisely these moments that present language that is rooted in real time and true contexts. Take, for example, a moment when the contents of a bean-pouring exercise spill on the classroom floor. The verbal interactions between an assistant or a guide in a circumstance of a spilled pitcher could expose the child to (a) the past tense forms of verbs, such as "to fall," and the appropriate helping verb (*le pichet est tombé; der Krug ist gefallen; la jarra se cayó*); (b) new vocabulary of lentils or dustpan and brush; (c) prepositions used in the process of cleaning up such as far, near, here, under, on, etc.; and (d) one-on-one communicative interaction with low affect so the child feels comfortable and supported, has direct eye contact with the speaker, and participates willingly in verbal engagement.

Case Studies of US Montessori Schools with Specific Language Programs

There are doubtless examples of Montessori programs around the globe doing excellent work in SLA and learning. As a researcher and educator based in the United States, my work relies heavily on the American context. It is also instructive to look at successful American examples of multilingual learning, as multilingual learning is neither popular nor common. Looking at the three premier multilingual Montessori schools in the United States provides a window into promising practices despite challenging cultural contexts. The first of these is Pacific Rim Montessori International School (PRINTS) in San Mateo, California, which offers Japanese or Chinese and English. The Intercultural Montessori School in Oak Park, Illinois, one of the first multilingual Montessori schools in the United States, offers Chinese, Japanese, Spanish, and English. International Montessori School of North Carolina (IMSNC) in Durham, North Carolina, offers Chinese, French, or Spanish.[2]

At IMSNC, students learn to read and write in the L2 first. Then, in the final year of Children's House, they learn to read in their L1, English. This model works well for this population since most of the students speak fluent English in their home environment. These schools serve children in language immersion or dual-language settings from toddler through at least the upper elementary years, in which the children learn to read and write in two languages for all schoolwork. Many of these Montessori students start a third language in these schools.

Other US-based multilingual schools use dual-language models for cultural and linguistic heritage purposes. The Latin-American Bilingual School (LAMB) in Washington, DC, offers Spanish and English. Of note are also two Indigenous language revitalization Montessori programs: Mukayuhsak Weekuw, which serves the four Wampanoag Tribes in southeastern Massachusetts, and Keres Children's Learning Center at the Cochiti Pueblo, New Mexico.[3] These three multilingual Montessori environments, like the programs mentioned above, maintain the language consistently over the different age levels.

Materials and Multiple Languages

With children in Montessori classrooms all over the world, one must consider the philosophical and pedagogical implications of adapting the original materials to meet the demands of teaching reading and writing in the world's many languages. In this section, I outline some examples of the challenges presented by the original Montessori Language materials. The Moveable Alphabet has been reproduced for a variety of alphabetic languages including Hebrew, Arabic, and Czech. However, with languages that are character based (Mandarin and Kanji) or syllabary based (Cherokee and Japanese), a Moveable Alphabet may not be an efficient means of teaching reading and writing. Furthermore, some languages such as Keres are exclusively oral.

Continuing the question of adaptation, some Montessori materials lose their potency and the original design value when translated into non-phonetic languages. For instance, Sandpaper Letters are meant to be a multisensory approach that associates a symbol with a sound; children would have previously identified the relevant sounds aurally and produced them orally through games and language play of poetry, finger gestures, and music. Secondarily, Sandpaper Letters are indirect preparation for handwriting. Mandarin Montessori settings often include nine sandpaper strokes for the major strokes needed to write most of the language's characters. However, due to the nature of the language, they are only a direct preparation for writing since the multi-sensory (auditory/visual/motor) counterpart to the sandpaper strokes is not present. Montessori early literacy pedagogy instructs "writing before reading" (Lillard 1972, 123), implying that building words or encoding one's own thoughts precedes decoding or reading of another's words. However, evidence is needed to gauge the degree to which this principle applies for non-alphabetic languages. With communication across geographic space and time becoming increasingly easy, US-based bilingual programs with non-alphabetic languages have an opportunity to learn more about how Montessori materials are being implemented in other language contexts to address these challenges.

Montessori came across the Moveable Alphabet during her close study of the works of Itard and Séguin (Helfrich 2011, 6). Given Montessori's immediate adoption of it, we can conclude that she saw its value in teaching phonemic languages such as Italian, Spanish, and French. Today, we know that this material serves several other purposes that contribute to the overall literacy process of learning to read and write in alphabetic languages. If the Moveable Alphabet is absent in the character-based languages Montessori environments, what materials are there to support the complementary literacy skills needed for that language? This is an important issue to consider, especially as globalization increases.

There is a clear need for exchanging ideas and practices related to materials supporting varied SLA with the awareness that not all materials will be able to follow the patterns of phonemic language. Moreover, awareness of the direct aim of the lesson is equally vital to the translation process. Grammar Boxes, which have loose word cards and phrases and/or command cards, are often translated from English into other languages in part because so many Montessori materials are available in English via the internet.[4] The adaptations that have been made in the alphabetic languages for use in bilingual programs in the United States are straightforward. They include, for example, the incorporation of additional letters or letter combinations such as é (French), ll, ch, and rr (Spanish) as Sandpaper Letters.

However, if these materials are merely translated into another language, the words and sentences *do not necessarily* teach the grammar point comprehensively or even effectively. For example, the command card, "Bring the pencil to the table," could be used in an English lesson for prepositions. When translating this preposition material into a highly inflectional language,[5] simply relying on the English version of the card will not necessarily expose the child to the various prepositional forms that are impacted by presence of certain parts of speech in that language. In the French translation of the above example, *amène le crayon à la table* doesn't teach the other forms of the preposition "à"—i.e., *amène le crayon au bureau* and *amène le crayon aux enfants*—which are affected by the gender and number of the noun in the prepositional phrase. Therefore, three versions of this card are needed in French to teach the preposition fully. When translating Montessori material, then, the translator must work from a deep understanding of both the target language's morphology and syntax and the instructional aim of the Montessori materials. Without both aspects, the resulting materials will miss the point of the lesson or fail to expose the child to all the forms of that word in the language.

Finally, we must attend to novel materials that already exist to address these characteristics of non-alphabetic languages. For example, auditory works that teach the five tones in Mandarin may already exist; likewise, for languages like French, Arabic, German, Pinyin,[6] and Czech, there may already exist visual discrimination works that train the eye to look above the letter at the diacritics which impact pronunciation and meaning. Where materials that serve these needs for different languages do *not* already exist, the Montessori community must continue to consider the expansion and responsiveness of new material production.

Some of the questions raised here may have been answered by Montessori programs in countries that natively use and teach non-alphabetic languages. Thus, we should learn from schools in countries speaking the L2: How have they adapted materials to address these and similar concerns? How can we adapt the use of these novel materials for bilingual programs?

Conclusion and Future Directions

Multilingualism and Montessori education are inextricably bound together. Montessori pedagogy has proliferated worldwide and is practiced in countless languages. Further, the classroom supports the natural and effortless capacity of the young child to acquire language(s). The abilities to use hundreds of materials, see and touch real objects, and use explicit vocabulary (such a *sphere* instead of *ball*) are yet other foundational ways in which the Montessori classroom supports language acquisition; these may explain why so many Montessori environments successfully incorporate an L2. Whether learning adjectives in L2 from the Sensorial shelf or learning names of rivers in L2 with an elementary Pin Map, interaction with materials supports the learning of the language in numerous deep ways.

As Montessori bilingual programs expand, the field would benefit from accurate, global data sharing and increased collaboration with colleagues already providing Montessori environments in diverse languages. The development of a database of best practices and newly created materials aimed at SLA would be especially salient. Better data would serve several practical purposes: (a) networking among Montessori educators across borders for resources, practices, and outcome tracking; (b) contributing valuable data for SLA research based on the Montessori paradigm, which offers insights on much younger students; and (c) tracking Montessori L2 models of instruction and newly created materials by age group, school setting, and country. Databases would enable Montessori educators to share their L2 models, improve their practice worldwide and across multiple ages, and contribute to the field of SLA research. All of this would allow educators to better serve children and our increasingly connected world—services that Montessori envisioned almost a century ago.

Notes

1. As the developer of structural linguistics, Roman Jakobson is widely known in the field of anthropology; he also made many contributions to the contemporary study of phonology, morphology, and semiotics. Early in his career in linguistics, Noam Chomsky proposed his theory of the Language Acquisition Device, an interesting parallel to Montessori's special language mechanism. Linguists and neuroscientists are still learning how the human brain acquires one's native language.
2. All three of these schools use a similar practice of speaking in the target language 90 per cent of the time and welcoming the students to answer in English in the early years. At IMSNC, for example, the expectation in the immersion elementary classrooms is that the students speak only the target language except when in the English language classroom and on the playground, when all the students

are together and English is the common language. The teachers, however, continue to speak to their students in the target language whenever is reasonably possible.
3. For more information about these schools, please see:
   The Latin-American Bilingual School (LAMB) in Washington, DC:
   https://www.lambpcs.org/
   Mukayuhsak Weekuw Schools:
   https://www.wlrp.org/language-school
4. For many years, the chapter dedicated to language development with examples in Italian in *The Advanced Montessori Method* served as a source for the words to be used to teach this material. Over time, these words have been changed and updated, especially in English versions of grammar works. The choice of the words must reflect the language's deep structures and the direct aim of the lesson in addition to reflecting the local culture.
5. The degree of a language's inflection refers to its morphology—the change in a word to mark, tense, mood, case, plural, person, etc. For example, German, Latin, Spanish, and French have extensive systems of inflection and are thus known as high-inflectional or synthetic languages. In contrast, English is a low-inflectional or analytical language.
6. Pinyin is the Latinized version of Mandarin Chinese. It captures the tones using diacritics.

References

Cook, Vivian. 2010. "The Relationship between First and Second Language Learning Revisited." In *The Continuum Companion to Second Language Acquisition*, edited by Ernesto Macaro, 137–57. London: Continuum.

Debs, Mira, Jaap de Brouwer, Angela K. Murray, Lynne Lawrence, Megan Tyne, and Candice von der Wehl. 2022. "Global Diffusion of Montessori Schools: A Report From the 2022 Global Montessori Census." *Journal of Montessori Research* 8 (2): 1–15. https://doi.org/10.17161/jomr.v8i2.18675.

Dulay, Heidi C., and Marina K. Burt 1977. "Remarks on Creativity in Language Acquisition." In *Viewpoints on English as a Second Language*, edited by Marina K. Burt, H. Dulay and M. Finocchiaro, 95–126. New York: Regents.

Helfrich, M. Shannon. 2011. *Montessori Learning in the 21st Century: A Guide for Parents and Teachers*. Troutdale, OR: NewSage Press.

Hurajova, Anna. 2015. "An Overview of Models of Bilingual Education." *Mediterranean Journal of Social Sciences* 6 (6) (S1): 186–90. https://doi.org/10.5901/mjss.2015.v6n6s1p186.

International School Database. 2022. https://www.international-schools-database.com/in/paris?filter=on&language=&ages=&currency=EUR

Krashen, Stephen D. 1988. *Second Language Acquisition and Second Language Learning*. Hoboken, New Jersey: Prentice-Hall International.

La Escuela Montessori de Valparaíso. 2022. http://www.montessorivalparaiso.org/wawauta/

Lillard, Paula Polk. 1972. *Montessori: A Modern Approach*. New York: Schocken Books.

Montessori, Maria. 1995. *The Absorbent Mind*. New York: Henry Holt & Company.

Pouzar-Kozak, Tatjana. 2008. "The Montessori Method and First Language Acquisition: Early Speech, Reading and Writing." PhD Diss. Vienna: University of Vienna.

Shrum, Judith L., and Eileen W. Glisan. 2016. *Teacher's Handbook: Contextualized Language Instruction*, 5th ed. Boston: Cengage Learning.

Terrell, Tracy David. 1986. "Acquisition in the Natural Approach: The Binding/Access Framework." *The Modern Language Journal* 70 (3) (Autumn): 213–27. https://doi.org/10.2307/326936.

Additional Resources

Arnold, Jane, ed. 2000. *Affect in Language Learning*. Cambridge: Cambridge University Press.
Birsch, Judith R. 2015. *Multisensory Teaching of Basic Language Skills*. Baltimore: Brooks Publishing.
Crystal, David. 2008. *A Dictionary of Linguistics and Phonetics*, 6th ed. Malden, MA: Blackwell.
Ellis, Rod. 1994. *The Study of Second Language Acquisition*. Oxford: Oxford University Press.
Richards, Jack C., and Theodore S. Rodgers 1986. *Approaches and Methods in Language Teaching: A Description and Analysis*. Cambridge: Cambridge University Press.

Chapter 61
Montessori Education–Based Interventions for Persons with Dementia

Cameron J. Camp and Evan G. Shelton

Maria Montessori's success working with children of impoverished families at Casa dei Bambini shattered preconceived assumptions about what was possible for these supposedly unteachable children (see Part I). Today, Montessori's pedagogy is being expanded to another misunderstood population—persons living with dementia. The parallels between what Montessori faced when she first began to work with children at Casa dei Bambini and what we face today in working with persons with dementia are clear. Persons with dementia often are described as *patients* or *sufferers*. They are viewed as individuals who need continual supervision, who cannot learn or remember, and who continually exhibit challenging behaviors. Their *condition* is seen as incurable, unalterable, and continually deteriorating (Camp 2019; Lyman 1989). A common solution, like the solution for the children of the Orthophrenic School, is to confine persons with dementia to institutional settings where they can be continually monitored and their behaviors can be controlled. Such environments are often cold and impersonal with an emphasis on safety and security rather than personhood and engagement.

Montessori's approach was more than just an educational system; it was a way of life designed to improve living conditions for all human beings (Montessori 1936). To some degree, there has been progress in this regard, particularly with disabled individuals; many countries have passed legislation focused on making environments and workplaces accessible to persons with both cognitive and physical disabilities. However, when we view the status of persons with dementia today, a very different picture emerges. Persons with dementia are viewed through a lens of stigma and negative stereotyping to the extent that some physicians are reluctant to even use the term, instead using phrases like "memory problems" (Garand et al. 2009; Kissel and Carpenter 2007). What is particularly disheartening is that these stigmatizing ideas become internalized when a person receives a diagnosis of dementia, and they often withdraw from social contact, a behavior reinforced by their families. Why should there be such a discrepancy between society's views of dementia and of other disabilities?

Dementia refers to a set of cognitive symptoms, including confusion, memory loss, language difficulties, and difficulty in performing familiar tasks, which result from damage to the brain. Depending on the root cause of dementia, symptoms are sometimes reversible and sometimes progressive. Progressive dementias are generally caused by an underlying pathological process in the brain such as Alzheimer's disease, vascular dementia, and Parkinson's disease. These forms of dementia have roots in both genetics and lifestyle factors, and their prevalence increases dramatically with age. The most common form of dementia today, comprising approximately

60–80 percent of cases, is Alzheimer's disease (Alzheimer's Association 2019). In this chapter, we will focus on progressive forms of dementia and the role that Montessori interventions can play in improving quality of life for persons in these cases.

Medicalization of Dementia

While it is true that longer life expectancy and population growth have contributed to increasing rates of dementia in the modern era, dementia is not a new phenomenon. In fact, dementia has been a subject of discussion and speculation for millennia. As early as the seventh century BCE, medical texts from the Greek and Byzantine periods offered descriptions of age-related dementia. Early philosophers such as Pythagoras, Aristotle, and Plato believed that dementia was an unavoidable consequence of advanced age (Berchtold and Cotman 1998, 174). Those who lived into their 80s and beyond, they speculated, would experience regression of the mind back to infancy. Several centuries later, Cicero hypothesized that dementia was not an inevitability caused by age and that people could combat dementia with a strong will and mental engagement (Cicero 1887).

Today, 2000 years later, medical advances such as neuroimaging provide a better understanding of the various types of dementia and their presentations. Pharmaceutical companies and researchers across the globe continue work to develop drugs to prevent or reverse the course of Alzheimer's disease and related dementias. To date, no cure exists. Approved drugs for use in Alzheimer's disease claim not to cure the disease but to delay its progression with modest efficacy (Walsh et al. 2019). At present, the pharmaceutical industry focus has shifted from finding a cure to developing a drug that will provide *more good days* for persons with dementia; the implications of this shift will be discussed later in this chapter.

The race to develop a drug for Alzheimer's disease has resulted in a highly medicalized view of dementia in modern society, unique compared to other chronic conditions. In response to a dementia diagnosis, medical professionals can do little more than offer a drug with limited efficacy. For the person receiving a diagnosis, this translates to helplessness, fear, and a treatment path that is largely ineffective. Resources for training, assistance, and legislation to improve quality of life have received a lower priority than medical research, while an extraordinary amount of time, talent, and money has been allocated to the effort to cure dementia. Not only has this effort resulted in a monumental failure, but it has also resulted in a continuation of stereotyping, stigma, and diminished quality of life. The unfortunate truth is that Cicero's approach to treatment over 2000 years ago—that one should strive to continue learning, engaging, and fostering a strong will—remains a more effective course of treatment than today's status quo for someone concerned about their memory.

Fortunately, the status quo is beginning to change. Cicero's belief that cognitive impairment could be mediated by lifestyle factors now has a solid body of scientific support (Di Marco et al. 2014; Fratiglioni et al. 2020). Individuals who remain cognitively engaged later in life build what researchers call a "cognitive reserve" (Stern et al. 2020, 181). People with a greater cognitive reserve are at a lower risk of developing dementia, and those who do develop dementia maintain a higher level of functioning as the disease progresses. Additionally, diet, exercise, sleep, stress management, and meaningful social engagement all play a mediating role in the progression of dementia. When taken together, non-pharmacological approaches in these domains lead to outcomes far exceeding what can be achieved using medication. Despite the medical focus that is so prevalent in clinical practice, the scientific community now widely accepts non-pharmacological lifestyle modification as the most effective first-line treatment for Alzheimer's disease.

Learning and Dementia

The standard clinical paradigm makes two critical assumptions that are both false and dehumanizing. The first is the assumption that older adults, especially those with dementia, cannot learn, a striking parallel to assumptions about the children Montessori first worked with in Rome. The second is that the condition of such individuals results solely from internal processes that cannot be improved through environmental manipulation.

Montessori education leverages a deep faith in both the capacity of children to learn and the power of preparing an environment for optimal learning. The concept of control of error in Montessori pedagogy involves the use of materials and procedures which steer performance toward success, reduce the likelihood of making mistakes, and enable self-correction such that children can successfully complete tasks with minimal adult interference. An example of this approach in working with persons with dementia is a Montessori-adjacent teaching technique called Spaced Retrieval (SR) (see Mahendra et al. 2006).

In the late 1980s, the first author of this chapter, Cameron Camp, began using the SR technique to help persons with dementia learn new things. The concept is based on the fact that, without reinforcement, new learning tends to be forgotten. However, asking a person to immediately recall new information reinforces what was learned. Our research demonstrates that, if asked to recall the new information repeatedly with larger intervals of time between each recall, persons with dementia were able to retain newly learned information over extended periods of time (Camp and Stevens 1990). This practice is now widely used in memory care, physical therapy, and speech-language pathology to help persons with dementia learn new information and adapt to new challenges.

Spaced Retrieval relies on repetition, self-regulation, and opportunities for self-correction, which are key elements of Montessori pedagogy. Consider an elderly woman with dementia and osteoporosis who is in danger of breaking her hip if she misses the chair when she tries to sit down. In many instances, clinicians may resort to physical restraint or continual observation rather than proactive assistance or training. Such a strategy may be implemented to prevent falling, but it would result in loss of independence and a reduced quality of life. Alternatively, the clinicians could use the SR method, borrowing from the principles of Montessori education. In this model, the clinician would obtain buy-in from the woman and then train her step by step in a procedure to ensure that she will sit safely. Teaching the new procedure would involve breaking down the steps: feeling the chair with the back of the legs, practicing self-dialogue to check that the chair is in place, and feeling the chair's arms to confirm that it is safe to sit down. The strategy would be practiced at expanding intervals. Furthermore, involving tactile and kinesthetic cues

Figure 61.1 A senior with dementia works with the Montessori Binomial cube. Ryerson Clark, 2015. Courtesy of Leica Photo.

related to starting to sit encourages safe sitting procedures that are not dependent on someone else observing or warning the person to sit safely.

A conceptually similar approach involves intergenerational programming. In one approach, persons with dementia at learning stations teach preschool children Practical Life lessons such as using tools, hanging up their own clothes, folding napkins, etc. In another example, high school students create materials and activities for residents with dementia while interviewing them to learn about these older adults' life experiences. In this way, adolescents and residents embody Montessori's notions of the value of purposeful, collaborative work. Overall, it seems that employing Montessori-based principles and activities with aging populations and those with dementia shows promise across geographic, cultural, and linguistic boundaries. We find that materials and procedures designed for persons with dementia can be effectively used by other groups like older adults without dementia, activities staff members, and family members visiting with relatives.

The Environment

For a variety of medical conditions, modern medicine often looks to drug therapy before other means of intervention, especially more thoughtfully complex approaches. Historically, dementia has been seen as maladjustment to old age and a psychosocial problem. Now, as discussed above, it is understood as disease. However, this has shifted priorities in medical practice toward curing the disease rather than treating it through caregiving. Further, this shift leads to stigmatizing dementia as an untreatable problem of internal processes which results in dangerous and problematic behaviors that must be controlled (Ballenger 2017). As Montessori found with her first students, the behaviors then observed in these individuals often become self-fulfilling prophecies for those immersed in the doctrine of the standard paradigm. Rather than a lifetime sentence of dysfunction, the principles of Montessori's prepared environment provide an alternative strategy which leads to persons with dementia becoming engaged and normalized.

Montessori's prepared environments for children, which are designed to foster autonomy, cooperation, and safety (both physical and emotional), can be applied to support individuals with dementia and related challenges. Just as physical wheelchair ramps enable physically disabled persons to successfully navigate their environment, cognitive ramps can support cognitively disabled individuals. For example, external aids are an integral part of the Montessori classroom. In some classrooms, to train a child how to set their own table, teachers use a control for error in table setting: a circle for the plate, outlines of the utensils, and a smaller circle for a cup or glass is used. In this way, the table setter can match the setting piece by piece. For persons with dementia, such a tool can enable them to set their own table.

External aids also can be useful for circumventing memory deficits associated with dementia. Examples that are helpful in supporting persons with dementia can be directly tied to work records that are used in Montessori elementary classrooms. These records are typically developed in collaboration with teachers and serve both as reminders of planned work and as a record of tasks completed. Such an aid may have something that looks like this:

I TOOK MY MEDICATIONS TODAY AT:
__ BREAKFAST
__ LUNCH
__ DINNER

This aid allows the person with dementia to record with a checkmark that they received their medication at different times of the day. That way, they know what medications have been received, which relieves the worry about remembering if medications have or have not been taken. These record keeping devices are like elementary Montessori work plans that allow tracking of tasks.

Of course, such an aid could be used for a variety of things that are important to persons with dementia. Persons with dementia often express concern that clothing was stolen when they cannot find items that have been taken to be laundered. Repeated verbal assurances may be forgotten 10 or 20 minutes later. To mitigate their anxiety, a care partner may develop an external aid with the assistance of the person with dementia, using the person's wording to assist with memory. For example, the external aid may be a simple sign, a note on a whiteboard, or a slip of paper reading:

> MY CLOTHES ARE IN THE LAUNDRY. THEY WILL BE RETURNED ON FRIDAY.

When the person with dementia then expresses worry over their clothes, the care partner can help them practice going to a location where the external aid is kept (in a purse, on a whiteboard, etc.). With repetition, the person learns to go to this location, look at the external aid, and reduce their own anxiety instead of repetitively asking a care partner about the whereabouts of their clothes. Thus, deficits associated with dementia can be circumvented, and the person with dementia is freed from an ongoing anxiety about both the location of their clothes and the character of the persons they are living with.

Responding to Challenges

The previous examples are visible and powerful demonstrations of effective strategies that challenge the underlying assumptions of the standard paradigm for dementia care. When these efforts result in increased independence, it becomes newsworthy—an unfortunate symptom of how strongly held conventional beliefs are. Just as dignitaries, reporters, and educators came to see the Casa dei Bambini, visitors from many countries and continents visited some of our first Montessori for Dementia neighborhoods where individuals could live in a prepared environment that is purposefully designed, secure, and enclosed for safety and well-being. There, they witnessed how persons with dementia were empowered to live independent and meaningful lives.

Paralleling the skepticism around Montessori education for children, some visitors question the effectiveness of our approach in other situations. They believe our approaches are not relevant to the types of residents they serve or within the regulatory system in which they operate. We counter these assertions with demonstrations that this approach works in widely different settings across all stages of dementia. Other visitors question the existence of research supporting the practices. We respond with evidence of Montessori effectiveness in multiple countries as documented in peer-reviewed scientific journals (Camp 2010, 2013; Lin 2014; Lin et al. 2011, 2009; Mahendra et al. 2006; Roberts et al. 2014; Skrajner and Camp 2007; Vance and Johns 2003; van der Ploeg et al. 2013).

The final argument we encounter is related to concerns about financial feasibility and potential increased staffing needs. Addressing financial concerns involves a discussion of three key components of motivation for residential care: revenue and expenses, marketing opportunities, and oversight by regulatory agencies. In terms of financial viability, Montessori approaches have been shown to increase census and decrease staff turnover (De Witt-Hoblit et al. 2016). Expanding access to Montessori-based programs for persons with dementia requires reference to outcomes and measures relevant to the healthcare industry. First-hand accounts from those with experience implementing these programs are particularly valuable in response to skepticism about the viability of the model. When challenged at a presentation, the executive director of a memory care neighborhood who had adopted Montessori as the culture for his staff and residents came to the microphone and said, "Once we began to use this approach, we reduced our food costs by 40 percent."

In terms of marketing, the entire approach to promoting a community changes once Montessori practices are integrated. When family members or potential residents visit a Montessori community, they are introduced to members of the Welcoming Committee for new residents and are co-led on the tour by a member of the Visitor's Committee, all of which are led by current residents. Thus, the differences between this community and those managed under the standard paradigm become obvious. (Not coincidentally, the welcoming committee is like how guests are treated when entering a Montessori classroom for children.) Waiting lists develop, and the advertising budget, which can be significant, is reduced due to the use of Montessori practice within the long-term care system. Regulatory inspections become another chance to display the benefits of Montessori methods for persons with dementia. In one such case, a nursing home in Neuchâtel, Switzerland, took the idea of having residents lead activities a step further; their residents led the inspectors through the process of inspecting their community. At the end of their tour, the community received its first perfect inspection report and later won an award for excellence in dementia care from a Swiss foundation (Camp et al. 2017).

In addition, the application of the Montessori method also leads to outcomes such as significant reductions in the use of psychotropic medications to control behaviors and the use of hypnotics (sleeping aids) (De Witt-Hoblit et al. 2016; Gaspar and Westberg 2020). Residents who are engaged in meaningful, purposeful activity during the day display fewer problematic behaviors and are more likely to sleep at night without the need for medication. Just as Montessori's prepared environment reduces behavior problems by providing optimal conditions for children (Lillard and Else-Quest 2006), the prepared long-term care environment has a powerful effect on the behavior of its residents.

Conclusion

Several years ago, Dr. Camp presented a three-day training seminar in France at the Université Paul Valéry Montpellier 3 on applications of the Montessori method for persons with dementia. University students and senior care professionals from a variety of countries were in attendance. At the end of the third day, a student raised her hand and said, "Now I understand. This is not about dementia—it is about changing civilization." Camp responded, "Now you are beginning to see the deep meaning and true purpose of Montessori education." In the long-term care industry, we have an opportunity to embrace Montessori's teachings and demonstrate that the final years of our lives can be defined not by dependency and disengagement but by meaningful participation in a supportive community. When we can create prepared environments for all older adults, we will create a better world for all humankind.

References

Alzheimer's Association. 2019. "2019 Alzheimer's Disease Facts and Figures." *Alzheimer's & Dementia* 15 (3): 321–87. https://doi.org/10.1016/j.jalz.2019.01.010.

Ballenger, Jesse F. 2017. "Framing Confusion: Dementia, Society, and History." *AMA Journal of Ethics* 19 (7): 713–19. https://doi.org/10.1001/journalofethics.2017.19.7.mhst1-1707.

Berchtold, Nicole C., and Carl W. Cotman. 1998. "Evolution in the Conceptualization of Dementia and Alzheimer's Disease: Greco-Roman Period to the 1960s." *Neurobiology of Aging* 19 (3): 173–89.

Camp, Cameron J. 2010. "Origins of Montessori Programming for Dementia." *Non-Pharmacological Therapies in Dementia* 1 (2): 163–74.

Camp, Cameron J. 2013. "The Montessori Approach to Dementia Care." *Australian Journal of Dementia Care* 2 (5): 10–11.

Camp, Cameron J. 2019. "Denial of Human Rights: We Must Change the Paradigm of Dementia Care." *Clinical Gerontologist* 42 (3): 221–3.

Camp, Cameron J., and Alan B. Stevens. 1990. "Spaced-Retrieval: A Memory Intervention for Dementia of the Alzheimer's Type." *Clinical Gerontologist* 10: 58–61.

Camp, Cameron J., Vince Antenucci, Alice Roberts, Tim Fickenscher, Jérôme Erkes, and Trudy Neal. 2017. "The Montessori Method Applied to Dementia: An International Perspective." *Montessori Life* 29 (1) (Spring): 40–7.

Cicero, Marcus. 1887. *On Old Age (De Senectute)*. Translated by Andrew P. Peabody. Boston: Little, Brown, and Company.

De Witt-Hoblit, Iva, Mary Neal Miller, and Cameron J. Camp. 2016. "Effects of Sustained, Coordinated Activities Programming in Long-Term Care: The Memory in Rhythm® Program." *Advances in Aging Research* 5 (1): 1–8.

Di Marco, Luigi Yuri, Alberto Marzo, M. Miguel Muñoz-Ruiz Arfan Ikram, Miia Kivipelto, Daniel Ruefenacht, Annalena Venneri et al. 2014. "Modifiable Lifestyle Factors in Dementia: A Systematic Review of Longitudinal Observational Cohort Studies." *Journal of Alzheimer's Disease* 42 (1): 119–35.

Fratiglioni, Laura, Anna Marseglia, and Serhiy Dekhtyar. 2020. "Ageing without Dementia: Can Stimulating Psychosocial and Lifestyle Experiences Make a Difference?" *The Lancet Neurology* 19 (6): 533–43.

Garand, Linda, Jennifer H. Lingler, Kyaien O. Conner, and Mary Amanda Dew. 2009. "Diagnostic Labels, Stigma, and Participation in Research Related to Dementia and Mild Cognitive Impairment." *Research in Gerontological Nursing* 2 (2): 112–21.

Gaspar, Phyllis M., and Katie Westberg. 2020. "Evaluation of the Montessori-Inspired Lifestyle® as the Foundation of Care in Assisted Living Memory Care." *Journal of Gerontological Nursing* 46 (5): 40–6.

Kissel, Emily C., and Brian D. Carpenter. 2007. "It's All in the Details: Physician Variability in Disclosing a Dementia Diagnosis." *Aging and Mental Health* 11 (3): 273–80.

Lillard, Angeline and Nicole Else-Quest. 2006. "Evaluating Montessori Education." *Science* 313 (5795): 1893–4. https://doi.org/10.1126/science.1132362.

Lin, Li-Chan. 2014. "Efficacy of Spaced Retrieval Only Compared to a Combination of Spaced Retrieval with Montessori-Based Activities in Improving Overeating of Residents with Dementia." *Alzheimer's & Dementia* 10: 739.

Lin, Li-Chan, Man-Hua Yang, Chieh-Chun Kao, Shiao-Chi Wu, Sai-Hung Tang, and Jaung-Geng Lin. 2009. "Using Acupressure and Montessori-Based Activities to Decrease Agitation for Residents with Dementia: A Cross-Over Trial." *Journal of the American Geriatrics Society* 57 (6): 1022–9.

Lin, Li-Chan, Ya-Ju Huang, Roger Watson, Shiao-Chi Wu, and Yue-Chune Lee. 2011. "Using a Montessori Method to Increase Eating Ability for Institutionalised Residents with Dementia: A Crossover Design." *Journal of Clinical Nursing* 20 (21–22): 3092–101.

Lyman, Karen A. 1989. "Bringing The Social Back In: A Critique of the Biomedicalization of Dementia." *The Gerontologist* 29 (5): 597–605. https://doi.org/10.1093/geront/29.5.597.

Mahendra, Nidhi, Tammy Hopper, Kathryn A. Bayles, Tamiko Azuma, Stuart Cleary, and Esther Kim. 2006. "Evidence-Based Practice Recommendations for Working with Individuals with Dementia: Montessori-Based Interventions." *Journal of Medical Speech-Language Pathology* 14 (1): xv–xxv.

Montessori, Maria. 1936. *The Secret of Childhood*. Translated by Barbara Barclay Carter. London and New York: Longmans, Green and Co.

Roberts, Gail, Catherine Morley, Wendy Walters, Sue Malta, and Colleen Phillips Doyle. 2014. "Caring for People with Dementia in Residential Aged Care: Successes with a Composite Person-Centered

Care Model Featuring Montessori-Based Activities." *Geriatric Nursing* 36 (2): 106–10. https://doi.org/10.1016/j.gerinurse.2014.11.003.

Skrajner, Michael J., and Cameron J. Camp. 2007. "Resident-Assisted Montessori Programming (RAMP™): Use of a Small Group Reading Activity Run by Persons with Dementia in Adult Day Health Care and Long-Term Care Settings." *American Journal of Alzheimer's Disease & Other Dementias* 22 (1) (February/March): 27–36.

Stern, Yaakov, Eider M. Arenaza-Urquijo, David Bartrés-Faz, Sylvie Belleville, Marc Cantilon, Gael Chetelat, Michael Ewers et al. 2020. "Whitepaper: Defining and Investigating Cognitive Reserve, Brain Reserve, and Brain Maintenance." *Alzheimer's & Dementia* 16 (9): 1305–11.

van der Ploeg, Eva S., Barbara Eppingstall, Cameron J. Camp, Susannah J. Runci, John Taffe, and Daniel W. O'Connor. 2013. "A Randomized Crossover Trial to Study the Effect of Personalized, One-to-One Interaction Using Montessori-Based Activities on Agitation, Affect, and Engagement in Nursing Home Residents with Dementia." *International Psychogeriatrics* 25 (4): 565–75.

Vance, David E., and Rebekah N. Johns. 2003. "Montessori Improved Cognitive Domains in Adults with Alzheimer's Disease." *Physical & Occupational Therapy in Geriatrics* 20 (4): 19–33.

Walsh, Sebastian, Elizabeth King, and Carol Brayne. 2019. "France Removes State Funding for Dementia Drugs." *The BMJ* 367: l6930. https://doi.org/10.1136/bmj.l6930.

Chapter 62
Montessori Education: Ecoliteracy, Sustainability, and Peace Education

Maria K. McKenna

The 2030 Agenda for Sustainable Development (ASD) was adopted by all 193 member states of the United Nations in 2015 (UN 2015). The aspirational 2030 *Agenda* consists of seventeen aims related to human flourishing.[1] This work builds on decades-long conversations within the United Nations around the care of the planet and the cultivation of a symbiotic relationship between humans and the natural world. A successor to the UN Earth Summit in 1992, alongside other intermittent climate justice efforts of the United Nations over subsequent decades, ASD reminds us of the relationship between the natural world, human progress, and global well-being. Montessori, who was keenly aware of these relationships, integrated a focus on interdependence and reciprocal flourishing into her writing, teaching, and pedagogical plans for children. Taken alongside her precept that peacemaking begins in childhood, her attentiveness to just stewardship of resources allows us to begin to see the relationship between her vision for a more peaceful world and sustainable living. She coined this aspect of her philosophy cosmic education (see Chapter 3). It is part of the fabric of Montessori philosophy and visible in a variety of ways within Montessori environments. The purpose of this chapter is to outline ways Montessori education supports ecoliteracy and sustainability but also to connect environmental stewardship to her larger vision of education for world peace.

Cosmic Education: Ecoliteracy, Sustainable Living, and Peace Education

Long before anyone was writing about contemporary climate science and before issues of gender parity, economic inequity, or environmental degradation were being debated in earnest, Montessori understood the centrality of education in helping the world grasp the relationship of the Earth and its inhabitants. Montessori coined all the various parts of the world created by humans supernature (sometimes also called supranature). Her plan of cosmic education invited educators and students to explore humans' relationships to supernature, develop a vision of the whole of human culture and nature, and consider their own unique tasks in that larger world (Ewert-Krocker 2013; Grazzini 2013; Hayes 2005[2]; Leonard 2013). Social and biological independence is at the center of Montessori education, and it is central to ecological literacy.

Montessori argued that progress must be guided by a moral compass and a desire for peaceful living for all, for without this core, progress could be dangerous (Grazzini 2013; Montessori 2003, 2008). In *The Formation of Man,* Maria Montessori writes, "man has unchained forces by his own creative action but has not been able to keep pace with them in terms of adaptation and development ... (there is) a lack of balance between man and his environment from which humanity must deliver itself by strengthening its own resources, developing its own values, healing its own madness, and becoming conscious of its own power" (quoted in Montessori 2008, 80). Montessori understood the development of the child to be the central means of restoring balance and healing "its own madness," as noted above. From the outset, her pedagogical work was connected to a philosophy of human and ecological well-being, whereby we must cultivate a world in which "the child has felt a strong love for his surroundings and for all living creatures, who has discovered joy and enthusiasm in work, (and) gives us reason to hope that humanity can develop in a new direction" (2007, 58).

At this point, however, we must pause briefly. While this chapter focuses on the ways Montessori was particularly prescient in her understanding of the relationships between the environment, human flourishing, and peace, we acknowledge that the work of sustainable development and peacemaking has been going on for as long as humans have existed. Hunter-gatherer populations aligned themselves as individuals and communities to take only what they needed to survive and rely on one another in nested evolutionary communities (Narvaez 2020). Similarly, early Indigenous communities across the world saw their lives as integrally connected to the land, water, weather, and creatures with which they shared a given locale. Ecoliteracy[3] was, and continues to be, woven into the fabric of their very lives. Mazzocchi (2020, 78–9) reminds us of such communities' powerful relationship with the Earth when he states, "Indigenous knowledge embodies a wealth of wisdom and information gained over centuries from empirical observations and transmitted over generations. It includes multiple environmental practices, which are linked to cultural norms and social protocols, and contributes to shaping Indigenous identity." To discuss Montessori's forward-thinking nature without acknowledging these communities would be a mistake. Indigenous communities with their deeply principled and sophisticated ways of knowing across time and space are critical interlocuters to recognize in this conversation (see Chapters 40 and 59). Otherwise, we miss the point Montessori raises about the interconnectedness of life, time, and peace. And so, to acknowledge an all-too-frequent, historical erasure of indigeneity, we contextualize Montessori's thinking within that of the larger chronosphere of time and culture (Bronfenbrenner 1979).

Returning to the *Agenda for Sustainable Development* (ASD), we acknowledge that the UN's efforts in this document are largely symbolic in nature. And yet, even the recognition that the planet has a finite supply of resources and that our individual actions impact the collective is a critical step toward sustained peace. The act of forming solidarity around a common idea, be it the challenge of climate change or the quest to protect individual health and well-being, is a welcome sign that people are waking up to the significant environmental crises in our midst. More than that, these kinds of collective frameworks—dare we say aspirations—are essential to our survival as a planet and our disposition toward a hopeful future. Consider Barnett and Adger's (2007, 640) worrisome summation of the contemporary environmental crisis:

> First ... climate change may undermine human security by reducing access to, and the quality of, natural resources that are important to sustain livelihoods. Second,

it suggests that the kinds of human insecurity that climate change may affect can in turn increase the risk of violent conflict. Third, it argues that climate change may undermine the capacity of states to act in ways that promote human security and peace.

Researchers estimate that without significant interventions, over 250,000 additional people are likely to die of climate-related disease every year (WHO 2022). Extreme and unpredictable weather events, agricultural impacts, and threats of rising sea levels will also impact the livelihoods and quality of life for people around the world. Montessori, writing with the industrial revolution in the background and through a series of global wars, was clear about the impact instability and human insecurity played in human behavior.

Perhaps because of her extensive travels, or perhaps because of her deeply interdisciplinary education, Montessori understood the complexity of our interdependency and, by extension, the complexity of issues like climate change. Importantly, she was never afraid to complicate educational pedagogy, seeing it as more than just a means to help people gain control of their bodies, become literate, or enter the work force. Montessori's vision of education was, and remains at its best, rooted in sustained peace and the potential of the child to influence the world for the better.

Sustainability and Ecoliteracy: Peace Education in Action

In *Education and Peace* (2007, 58), Montessori declares, "[W]hen individuals develop normally[4], they plainly feel a love not only for things, but for all living creatures. This love is not something that was taught; it is the natural result of leading the right kind of life." Montessori was an advocate for a relational, deliberative education, one where adults have carefully cultivated learning environments to support children's independence and autonomy. As climate change continues to impact the daily lives and livelihoods of more people—including their capacity to move freely, work, and meet their nutritional and shelter needs—the exigency for education with an aim of peace and a respect for human and environmental vulnerability has never been more important (Barnett and Adger 2007; Brantmeier and McKenna 2020; Catholic Church and Sean McDonagh 2016).

Central to the work that Montessori proposes are patience, compromise, forward thinking, freedom of movement, intrinsic motivation, self-control, care for others, and even silence. These skills and dispositions are crucial for the complex problem solving that is required to address a challenge as complicated and far-reaching as climate change. Montessori argued that, within a properly prepared environment, where freedom of movement and curiosity are encouraged, the child uses their energy toward that which they need the most for sustained growth. She argued that the educational path for each child will look different even within the same environment, and a child often knows what they need better than the adults around them (Montessori 1972). In this way, Montessori (1951, 4) honors the forgotten citizen, as she calls school children in her 1951 lecture to UNESCO:

> It is not yet realized that there are two powerful forces in human life: that which drive the formation of man (childhood) and that which drives the construction of

society (adulthood). These forces are so closely meshed that, if one is neglected, the other cannot be obtained. There is no awareness that the rights of the adult are necessarily dependent on those of the child.

Praxis

Montessori's theoretical and philosophical support for peace education and the natural world extended into her writings and lectures early in her scholarship. Her attentiveness to work in nature developed more fully as her pedagogical imagination grew, and many followers came to see the use of the outdoors, nature, and movement as an integral part of a Montessori classroom and also her vision of peace through education (Maria Montessori 1972, 2007, 2018, 2020).

In 1914, Montessori wrote *Dr. Montessori's Own Handbook*, where she outlined many of her materials and procedures for children ages three to six. She shared insights on various activities, structures, and facets of an education designed to support this plane of development. She honed in repeatedly on practical activities of daily life, including working outdoors and with nature writing, "and, above all, each child should have a little flower pot, in which he may sow the seed of some indoor plant, to tend and cultivate as it grows" (2018, 10). She continued a while later, "Again, gardening and manual work are a great pleasure to our children. Gardening is already a well-known as a feature of infant education" (19). In each instance, Montessori understood activity through nature serves multiple purposes: strengthening children's bodies, learning patience and consistency of caretaking, and developing an appreciation for growth and development vis-à-vis the natural world (Ramani 2013; see Chapters 13 and 14).

Montessori also understood that children at the elementary level need to expand their engagement with the world outside of the classroom. In her seminal work, *From Childhood to Adolescence* (2020), Montessori wrote extensively about the move from concrete to abstract thinking that children make between the ages of seven to twelve. She highlighted the value of complex work that required more than just oneself to complete, and she encouraged "Going Out" to explore the complexity of the larger world. For Montessori, work in this plane of development was to be interdisciplinary and lean heavily toward pure and social sciences (1939); thus, subject matter might include geography, biology, history, economics, and commerce. Montessori (2020) writes, "[T]he second period child is living two parallel existences, his home existence and his existence in society. This is new … Practical experience is also useful at this age. These children, when hiking, observe the objects left for a purpose by those who preceded them … this is an active exercise which habituates the children to observe, to seek" (24). Montessori was clear in her teaching that thoughtfully crafted opportunities whereby children engage with the wider world were crucial preparation for the next plane of development (see Chapters 15, 26, and 27 for additional relevant information). Thus, the elementary child is ripe for both introductions to environmental stewardship and considerations of the pragmatic and moral questions related to sustainability and sustainable development.

In considering sustainability, ecoliteracy, and environmental justice, Montessori's appendices in *From Childhood to Adolescence* (2020) are quite valuable. It is here that she elaborates on her vision of *Erdkinder* (children of the earth) and a philosophy of education that required adolescents to meld labor and studies, putting theory to practice in a more concrete way. For Montessori, preparing young people's minds and hands for the adult world of economic independence was a critical component of their education. However, even more important than intellectual or pragmatic preparation, Montessori understood adolescence as a most tender period for young people—a period where equal attention must be given to the development of the adolescent's heart and emotional life as to intellectual or physical tasks. She understood that for an individual to be disposed to peace they needed to be peaceful themselves.

In "Appendix A: Erdkinder," Montessori gave her fullest description for her vision of a Center for Work and Study on the Land an educational plan for adolescent children to develop a sense of competence and self-worth. Montessori's vision for a Center for Work and Study included manual labor, opportunities for self-expression via artistic means, moral education, math, language, the study of human progress, the study of earth and living things, a museum of machinery, communal living, and a deep care for the physical needs of the adolescent. All of these lend themselves to sustainability studies on a myriad of levels. Montessori believed that through meaningful work, which leads to economic independence and self-expression, adolescents would become the most complete versions of themselves. Through this type of work and the space they would be given to develop a keen sense of self-worth and purpose; each adolescent becoming capable of engaging in the adult world in peaceful ways. She called the process by which adolescents develop this healthy and lasting sense of self *valorization* (Brown 2016; Montessori 2020; see Chapters 16 and 9). Montessori also understood that care for the Earth was an integral aspect of lasting and sustained global peace but also of the valorization process. A robust focus on interdisciplinary, cooperative, nature-based work remains central for many contemporary Montessori education programs, as evidenced in Figure 62.1.

Conclusion

There is renewed and new interest in farm schools, experiential learning, environmental ethics, and land-based learning, both in response to the challenges of environmental stewardship and as a result of attentiveness to the science of learning, at all levels of Montessori education (Boyd 2018; Schmidt 2017; Siddiqui and Aqil 2014; see Part IV, including Introduction). Importantly, many contemporary manifestations of Montessori education also consider responsiveness to geographic contexts and cultural needs using oceans, deserts, rich agricultural histories, or urban centers to their advantage in this work (see Chapter 16). The steadily increasing interest in integrating environmental education into schooling across the globe is a hopeful sign for our world. As Montessori implored in *Education and Peace*, "[a]ll humanity that works for the common good, even though it may be unaware of it, is creating the new world that must be a world of peace … all the work of mankind will be seen to have had one common purpose in the world, that will be the world of peace" (2007, 115). One can forever hope that this is what we are seeing, one child, one school, and one community at a time.

Figure 62.1 Beekeeping in a Montessori Adolescent Farming Community courtesy of Good Shepherd Montessori School, South Bend, Indiana. Courtesy of Good Shepherd Montessori School.

Notes

1. The United Nations Framework Convention on Climate Change is the primary international, intergovernmental forum for negotiating the global response to climate change (United Nations 2015). Sustainable Development Goals include the following:
   Goal 1. End poverty in all its forms everywhere.
   Goal 2. End hunger, achieve food security, improve nutrition and promote sustainable agriculture.
   Goal 3. Ensure healthy lives and promote well-being for all at all ages.
   Goal 4. Ensure inclusive and equitable quality education and promote lifelong learning opportunities.
   Goal 5. Achieve gender equality and empower all women and girls.
   Goal 6. Ensure availability and sustainable management of water and sanitation for all.
   Goal 7. Ensure access to affordable, reliable, sustainable, and modern energy for all.
   Goal 8. Promote sustained, inclusive, and sustainable economic growth, full and productive employment, and decent work for all.
   Goal 9. Build resilient infrastructure, promote inclusive and sustainable industrialization and foster innovation.
   Goal 10. Reduce inequality within and among countries.
   Goal 11. Make cities and human settlements inclusive, safe, resilient, and sustainable.

Goal 12. Ensure sustainable consumption and production patterns.
Goal 13. Take urgent action to combat climate change and its impacts.
Goal 14. Conserve and sustainably use the oceans, seas, and marine resources for sustainable development.
Goal 15. Protect, restore, and promote sustainable use of terrestrial ecosystems, sustainably manage forests, combat desertification, and halt and reverse land degradation and halt biodiversity loss.
Goal 16. Promote peaceful and inclusive societies for sustainable development, provide access to justice for all and build effective, accountable, and inclusive institutions at all levels.
Goal 17. Strengthen the means of implementation and revitalize the global partnership for sustainable development.

2. Hayes's conference paper for the twenty-fifth International Montessori Congress has a beautiful collection of illustrations capturing the various facets of cosmic education. These illustrations are often difficult to find and reproduce. Having so many in one place makes Hayes's paper a very important reference for individuals interested in this aspect of Montessori education.
3. See McBride et al. (2013) for more on environmental stewardship terminology.
4. As noted in previous chapters, "normalization" was the term Montessori preferred for the natural state of young children. It included a love of quiet, order, and focused work where they develop in an environment optimally designed to facilitate long periods of concentration on freely chosen activities.

References

Barnett, Jon, and W. Neil Adger. 2007. "Climate Change, Human Security and Violent Conflict." *Political Geography* 26 (6): 639–55. https://www.sciencedirect.com/science/article/pii/S096262980700039X.

Boyd, Diane. 2018. "Early Childhood Education for Sustainability and the Legacies of Two Pioneering Giants." *Early Years* 38 (2): 227–39. https://www.researchgate.net/publication/323770726_Early_childhood_education_for_sustainability_and_the_legacies_of_two_pioneering_giants.

Brantmeier, Edward J., and Maria K. McKenna. 2020. *Pedagogy of Vulnerability*. Charlotte, NC: Information Age.

Bronfenbrenner, Urie. 1979. *The Ecology of Human Development: Experiments by Nature and Design*. Cambridge: Harvard University Press.

Brown, Maribeth. 2016. "Valorization of the Adolescent Personality." Master's Thesis, Sophia, the St. Catherine University Repository. https://sophia.stkate.edu/maed/139.

Catholic Church, and Sean McDonagh. 2016. *On Care for Our Common Home, Laudato Si': The Encyclical of Pope Francis on the Environment*. Vatican City, The Vatican.

Grazzini, Camillo. 2013. "Maria Montessori's Cosmic Vision, Cosmic Plan, and Cosmic Education." *The NAMTA Journal* 38 (1) (Winter): 107–16.

Ewert-Krocker, Laurie. 2013. "The Adolescent: Taking on the Task of Humanity—Conducting the Dialogue Between Nature and Supranature." *The NAMTA Journal* 38 (1) (Winter): 175–81.

Hayes, Mary. 2005. "Montessori's View of Cosmic Education." In *25th International Montessori Congress Papers* 1–8. http://www.mountainshadows.org/wp-content/uploads/2012/01/Montessoris-View-of-Cosmic-Education.pdf.

Leonard, Gerard. 2013. "Deepening Cosmic Education." *The NAMTA Journal* 38 (1) (Winter): 135–44.

Mazzocchi, Fulvio. 2020. "A Deeper Meaning of Sustainability: Insights from Indigenous Knowledge." *The Anthropocene Review* 7 (1): 77–93. https://doi.org/10.1177/2053019619898888.

McBride, B.B., C. A. Brewer, A. R. Berkowitz, and W. T. Borrie. 2013. "Environmental Literacy, Ecological Literacy, Ecoliteracy: What Do We Mean and How Did We Get Here?" *Ecosphere* 4 (5): 1–20. https://doi.org/10.1890/ES13-00075.1

Montessori, Maria. 1939. "The 'Erdkinder': A Scheme for a Reform of Secondary Education." *Halfyearly Bulletin of the Association Montessori Internationale* 2 (1): 5–23.

Montessori, Maria. 1951. *The Forgotten Citizen*. Amsterdam: Association Montessori Internationale.
Montessori, Maria. 1972. *The Secret of Childhood*. New York, NY: Ballantine Books.
Montessori, Maria. 2007. *Education and Peace*. Amsterdam: Montessori-Pierson Publishing Company.
Montessori, Maria. 2018. *Dr Montessori's Own Handbook*. Maroussi, Greece: Alpha Editions.
Montessori, Maria. 2020. *From Childhood to Adolescence*. Mayur Vihar Phase, Delhi: Aakar.
Montessori, Mario, Jr. 2008. *Education for Human Development: Understanding Montessori*. Amsterdam: Montessori-Pierson Publishing Company.
Montessori, Mario, Sr. 2003. *The Human Tendencies and Montessori Education*, Revised. Amsterdam: Association Montessori Internationale.
Narvaez, Darcia. 2020. "Ecocentrism: Resetting Baselines for Virtue Development." *Ethical Theory and Moral Practice* 23 (3): 391–406. https://doi.org/10.1007/s10677-020-10091-2.
Ramani, Uma. 2013. "Practical Life: The Keystone of Life, Culture, and Community." *The NAMTA Journal* 38 (2) (Spring): 47–54.
Schmidt, Thomas. 2017. "Modular Montessori: Educating towards Ecological Sustainability." Master's Thesis, North Dakota State University.
Siddiqui, Saba, and Zeba Aqil. 2014. "Building Up an Ecologically Sustainable Society by Inculcating Environmental Ethics and Values in Children." *IOS Journal of Humanities and Social Science* 19 (3): 5–9.
UNESCO. 1997. "Educating for a Sustainable Future: A Transdisciplinary Vision for Concerted Action Environment and Society." Thessalonica, Greece: United Nations Educational, Scientific and Cultural Organization, 1–44.
United Nations. 2015. *Transforming Our World: The 2030 Agenda for Sustainable Development*. A/RES/70/1. New York, NY: United Nations. https://www.un.org/en/development/desa/population/migration/generalassembly/docs/globalcompact/A_RES_70_1_E.pdf.
WHO (World Health Organization). 2022. *On Climate and Health*. Geneva, Switzerland: WHO. https://cdn.who.int/media/docs/default-source/climate-change/fast-facts-on-climate-and-health.pdf?sfvrsn=157ecd81_5.

Contributors

Editors

Mira Debs is Executive Director of the Education Studies Program and Lecturer in Sociology at Yale University, USA. Her research interests include school integration, urban education, school choice, parent involvement, international education, and progressive public schools. She is the author of *Diverse Families, Desirable Schools: Public Montessori in the Era of School Choice* (2019).

Maria K. McKenna is Professor of the Practice in the Education, Schooling and Society Program and Africana Studies at the University of Notre Dame, USA. Her academic interests include community-based, youth-centered research methods, educational equity, and peace education. She recently co-edited the volume *Pedagogy of Vulnerability* (2020).

Angela K. Murray is Assistant Research Professor at the University of Kansas (KU), USA, and is director of the KU Center for Montessori Research (CMR) within the Achievement and Assessment Institute. She is also founding Chair of the AERA Montessori Education Special Interest Group, and founding editor of the *Journal of Montessori Research*.

Eva-Maria Tebano Ahlquist is Assistant Professor of Education at Stockholm University, Sweden. Her research interests include Montessori education, didactics, and school architecture. She completed AMI elementary training from Bergamo, Italy. She is editor in chief for the open-access *Journal of Montessori Research & Education* (MoRE).

Contributing Authors

Hala Aboulela is Founder and President of the Montessori Foundation of Egypt, Egypt.

Lila A. Alhashim is a doctoral candidate at the University of South Florida, USA.

Arya Ansari is Assistant Professor of Human Development and Family Science at The Ohio State University, USA.

Valeria Paola Babini is Associate Professor of History of Science at the University of Bologna, Italy.

Abha Basargekar is a doctoral candidate and researcher at the University of Virginia, USA.

Hannah Baynham is the Director of Learning and Professional Development, American Montessori Society.

Contributors

Ilene Berson is Professor of Early Childhood Education at the University of South Florida, USA.

Joerg Boysen is President of Montessori Deutschland, Germany.

Paige M. Bray is Associate Professor of Early Childhood and Director of the Center for Montessori Studies at the University of Hartford, USA.

Katie Brown is Director of Research and Professional Learning at the National Center for Montessori in the Public Sector, USA.

Kannekar Butt is President of the Montessori Association of Thailand, Thailand.

Cameron J. Camp is Director of Research and Development at the Center for Applied Research in Dementia, USA.

Lucy Canzoneri-Golden is Co-founder and Co-director of the Coral Reef Montessori Academy Charter, USA.

Kateri Carver is Director of Graduate Montessori Teacher Education Programs and Assistant Clinical Professor at the University of Wisconsin River Falls, USA.

Jie Chen is a Psychometrician at Measurement, Inc. in Durham, North Carolina, USA.

Eder Cuevas is Executive Director of Montessori México, Mexico.

Brooke Culclasure is Research Director at the Riley Institute and Lecturer in the Department of Politics and International Affairs at Furman University, USA.

Carolyn J. Daoust is Research Associate at the University of Kansas Center for Montessori Research, USA.

Jaap de Brouwer is Researcher at the Research Group of Alternative Education at Saxion University of Applied Sciences, the Netherlands.

Solange Denervaud is a neuroscientist at the University Hospital in Lausanne, Switzerland.

Ela Eckert is Vice President of the German Montessori Society, Germany.

Noyenum Emafo is Head of School of Leikki Montessori School and a member of the Foundation for Montessori Education in Nigeria, Nigeria.

Ann Epstein is Professor of Early Childhood Education at the University of Wisconsin LaCrosse, USA.

Mara Fabri is Associate Professor of Physiology in the Department of Life and Environmental Sciences at Università Politecnica delle Marche, Ancona, Italy.

Susan Feez is Adjunct Associate Professor of English, Literacies and Languages Education at the University of New England in Australia.

Hans Forsberg is Senior Educator at Learning beyond Borders, Sweden.

Kerstin Forsberg is Senior Educator at Learning beyond Borders, Sweden.

Carmela Franzese is Adjunct Professor of Psychology at John Cabot University, Italy.

Patrick R. Frierson is Paul Piggott and William M. Allen Professor of Ethics and Philosophy at Whitman College, USA.

Ana María García Blanco is Co-founder and Executive Director of Instituto Nueva Escuela, Rio Piedras, Puerto Rico, and Chair of Para la Naturaleza Advisory Board.

Paige Geiger is Executive Director of the Centro de Educação Montessori de São Paulo, Brazil.

Per Gynther is Assistant Professor in the Department of Education at Stockholm University, Sweden.

Fay Hendriksen is Head of Outreach at Association Montessori Internationale, the Netherlands.

Sara Honegger is a writer and a trainer in the educational field based in Castellanza, Italy.

Barbara Isaacs is President of Montessori Europe.

Jaroslaw Jendza is a researcher and lecturer at the Social Sciences Faculty of the Institute of Education at the University of Gdańsk in Poland.

Kimiko Kai is Professor Emeritus of Early Childhood Education & Care at Toyo Eiwa University, Japan, and a board member of Japan Association Montessori (JAM).

Juliet King is Co-founder and Co-director of the Coral Reef Montessori Academy Charter, USA.

Francescah Kipsoi is Program Director of Montessori for Kenya, Kenya.

Katie Kitchens is a Montessori educator and doctoral researcher at the Keres Children's Learning Center, USA.

Elida V. Laski is Associate Professor of Applied Developmental and Educational Psychology at Boston College, USA.

Contributors

Hélène Leenders is Associate Professor of Pedagogy at Fontys University of Applied Sciences, the Netherlands.

Angeline S. Lillard is Professor of Psychology and Director of the Early Development Laboratory and the Montessori Science Program at the University of Virginia, USA.

Yu Liu is Associate Professor at College of Children Development and Education at Zhejiang Normal University, China.

William (Biff) Maier is Director of Faculty and Curriculum Development at Lexington Montessori School, USA, and Co-director of the Montessori Elementary Teacher Training Collaborative (METTC).

Saket Malhotra is a research assistant in the Education Studies Program at Yale University, USA.

Jan Mallett is Research Assistant Professor at Southern Methodist University, USA.

Karen Manship is a principal researcher with the American Institutes for Research, USA.

Joyce Philbert Mbuya is an educator at the Ngaruma Parish School, Tanzania.

Katherine Miranda is an independent researcher and scholar of Caribbean education, literature, and culture.

Sid Mohandas is a guest lecturer at Middlesex University, UK, and founder of The Male Montessorian and the Montistory platform.

Trisha Moquino is Co-founder and Education Director at the Keres Children's Learning Center, USA.

Erica Moretti is Assistant Professor of Italian Studies at the Fashion Institute of Technology-SUNY, USA.

Anne-Marie Morgan is Dean of Programs, Education Futures at the University of South Australia, and Adjunct Professor at the University of New England in Australia.

Sally Morris Cote is Director of Nonprofit Strategic Learning at the Riley Institute at Furman University and Co-Director of the Furman Prison Education Partnership at Furman University, USA.

Jennifer D. Moss is Assistant Professor of Psychology at Emporia State University, USA.

Amelia J. Murray was a research assistant for the *Handbook of Montessori Education* and a student at the University of Oklahoma, USA.

Mai P. Nghiem is the founder and president of the Vietnam Montessori Education Foundation (VMEF), Canada and the Vietnam AMI Montessori Initiative (VAMI), Vietnam.

Shose Dalton Ngowi is a Montessori coordinator and trainer at the Evangelical Lutheran Church of Tanzania, Northern Diocese, Tanzania.

Joel Parham is an independent archivist and researcher with JRP Consulting & Research.

Elizabeth K. Park is Associate Professor of Early Childhood Education and Director of Early Childhood and Montessori Programs at Chaminade University of Honolulu, USA.

Lesley Payne is Educational Director of the Montessori Institute of Western Australia, Australia.

Christine Quarfood is Professor of History of Ideas at the University of Gothenburg, Sweden.

Rossella Raimondo is Assistant Professor of History of Education at the University of Bologna, Italy.

Rukmini Ramachandran is a managing trustee of the Indian Montessori Foundation and Director of Training at the Navadisha Montessori Foundation, India.

Uma Ramani is Director of Training at the Montessori Institute of North Texas, USA.

Kevin Rathunde is Professor of Family and Consumer Studies at the University of Utah, USA.

Raniero Regni is Professor of Social Pedagogy at LUMSA University in Rome, Italy.

Lesli Romero is a research assistant at the University of Notre Dame, USA.

Aicha Sajid is Founder and Head of School of Ecole Montessori Casablanca, Morocco, and President of AMI Morocco.

Petter Sandgren is Assistant Professor of Education at Stockholm University, Sweden.

Laura Saylor is Dean of The School of Education and an Associate Professor at Mount St. Joseph University, USA.

Benedetto Scoppola is Associate Professor of Mathematical Physics at the University of Rome Tor Vergata, Italy.

Evan G. Shelton is Innovation Officer at The Center for Applied Research in Dementia, USA.

Patrick Sins is Professor of Alternative Education at Thomas More University of Applied Sciences, the Netherlands, and Professor of Learning at Rotterdam University of Applied Sciences, the Netherlands.

Contributors

Kate Stephens is an educator and a member of the Association of AMI Teachers of Ireland.

Astrid Steverlynck is a project leader and researcher at Fundación Patrick Sins Argentina María Montessori, Argentina.

Clara Tornar is Senior Professor of Education Sciences at Roma Tre University, Italy.

Paola Trabalzini is Associate Professor of the History of Education at LUMSA University in Rome, Italy.

Rich Ungerer is Executive Director Emeritus of the American Montessori Society and Board Chair of the National Center for Montessori in the Public Sector, USA.

Stephanie Van Hook is Executive Director of the Metta Center for Nonviolence, USA.

Joke Verheul is AMI's Director of Legacy and managing editor of the *Association Montessori Internationale (AMI) Journal*, the Netherlands.

Elske Voermans is coordinator of Educateurs sans Frontièrs at Association Montessori Internationale, the Netherlands.

Nacole Walker is Director of the Standing Rock Sioux Tribe Language and Culture Institute.

Marion Alice Wallis is Pedagogical Director of the Centro de Educação Montessori de São Paulo, Brazil.

Muanjing Julia Wang is a doctoral candidate and researcher in the Counseling, Developmental and Educational Psychology Department at Boston College, USA.

Gay C. Ward is Professor Emeritus of Literacy, Child Development and Montessori Studies at the University of Wisconsin River Falls, USA.

Margaret Whitley is a speaker, writer, and Montessori consultant with Educating Human Potential.

Tia Williams is a research assistant at the University of Notre Dame, USA.

Susan Zoll is Associate Professor and Coordinator of Early Childhood Education at Rhode Island College, USA.

Glossary

A

absorbent mind: Unique tendency of young children to absorb information seamlessly from experiences in the environment which ultimately serves as the basis for their mental self-construction.

Association Montessori Internationale (AMI): Organization founded in 1929 by Maria Montessori and her son Mario Montessori initially in Rome but relocated to Amsterdam in 1935 where it remains today.

auto-education: Process whereby children in Montessori classrooms teach themselves through using didactic learning materials that incorporate the control of error so that they can self-correct without intervention from the teacher.

B

Black, Indigenous, and People of Color (BIPOC): A term that has become popular in the United States in preference to the terms "minority" and "people of color." BIPOC purposely separates out the distinctive experiences of Black and Indigenous people in the foundational injustices they have experienced in the American historical context.

C

Children's House/Casa dei Bambini: Refers to early childhood 3–6 year-old classrooms because Montessori named her first school Casa dei Bambini (Children's House).

cis-white heteropatriarchy: Term representing the cultural dominance of people who are white, cis-gender (those whose identity corresponds to their gender at birth), heterosexual, and male over individuals with other sexual orientations and gender identities.

control of error: Feature embedded into many classic Montessori materials which make errors apparent to children so they can correct errors without adult involvement.

cosmic education: Foundation of Montessori elementary education which focuses on revealing social and biological interdependencies, inspiring gratitude, and fostering a sense of wonder in the universe.

D

decolonizing education: An educational process that works to reverse the colonial influence over school structures and in particular values Indigenous knowledge and traditions through interventions that may include modifying educational content, whose expertise is valued and the structures in which children learn.

didactic materials: Description of the materials Maria Montessori designed which teach concepts through the child's hands-on engagement without direct involvement from a teacher.

E

ecoliteracy: The recognition and understanding of ecosystems and principles for creating sustainable human communities and societies (see Chapter 62).

Erdkinder: Name that Montessori gave to her educational environment for adolescents (ages 12–18), which translates to "children of the earth."

F

fidelity: A term used in research to reflect the degree to which a particular program, such as Montessori education, follows the original or authentic design in its implementation.

Froebel/Froebelian: Refers to the approach developed by Friedrich Froebel (1782–1852), German educator who created the kindergarten.

G

global majority, people of (PGM): This term is used in preference to terms like minority or people of color to reflect the fact that non-white people form the majority of the global population.

Going Out: Activity in which a small group of Montessori elementary children independently plan and execute an outing or field trip to further study a chosen topic of interest.

Global North: Regions often characterized as wealthy, industrialized economies located primarily in the Northern hemisphere of Europe and North America. Used as an alternative to the terms "first world," or "developed/industrialized world."

Global South: Regions that are often politically, economically, or culturally marginalized including Latin America, Asia, Africa, and Oceania. Used as an alternative to terms "third world," "developing/industrializing world."

Grace and Courtesy: Lessons for children in Montessori classrooms designed to develop social skills and support healthy community functioning both within and outside of school.

Great Lessons: A group of five elementary Montessori lessons narrated as stories early in the academic year focusing on the creation of the universe, the origin of species, humans, writing, and numbers serving as the foundation of the Montessori cosmic curriculum.

guide: Another term sometimes used to refer to a Montessori classroom teacher which emphasizes their guiding role instead of teaching content.

H

hegemony: Dominance of a privileged social, cultural, or racial group over others within a society.

I

intersectionality: The idea that individuals have multiple intersecting identities (e.g., race/gender/ability) that should be studied together rather than separately.

isolation of difficulty: Characteristic of Montessori lessons in which a teacher breaks down a task into small, distinct steps so the child can focus only on the primary goal of the exercise.

isolation of qualities: Incorporated into Maria Montessori's design of learning materials so that every aspect is consistent except the one attribute which is the intended focus of the lesson.

M

materialized abstraction: Design principle of Montessori's didactic materials which offers physical form to abstract concepts enabling young children to grasp ideas which may otherwise be inaccessible to them.

Montessori method: The educational approach developed by Maria Montessori (1870–1952), also called Montessori education or Montessori pedagogy.

Montessorian: Individual who is involved in the field of Montessori education, often refers to those who have completed training to become a Montessori teacher.

N

Normalization: Montessori's term for the natural state of young children when they arrive at a state of quiet, focused work through being in an environment optimally designed to facilitate long periods of concentration on freely chosen activities.

O

Orthophrenic School: Institution where Montessori served as co-director and conducted experiments to develop and refine her learning materials.

P

pedagogy: Referring to the method and practice of teaching.

planes of development: Four phases of human development theorized by Montessori based on human tendencies and characteristics and which are broken down by ages: 0–6, 6–12, 12–18, 18–24.

prepared environment: Description of the Montessori classroom which provides physical, social, and psychological space that is appropriate for the needs of each plane of development.

Primary level: Used in a variety of contexts with differing interpretations including: 1) referencing the early childhood (3– to 6–year old) level in Montessori education particularly related to AMI training, or 2) referencing elementary level education in some national discourses.

psycho: A term sometimes placed before other nouns in Italian to signal the cognitive nature of the named construct (i.e., psychogrammatica, psychogeometry, psychomimetic).

S

self-construction: The active process of development where a child's innate potentials are realized through the interaction of the individual with the environment.

sensitive period: Particular developmental phases identified by Maria Montessori when children are particularly receptive to growth in a specific area and which provide a basis for the educational approach Montessori constructed. Neuroscience today uses the term critical periods for the phases when children are especially receptive to particular experiences which are essential for normal development and lead to permanent changes in brain performance.

Sensorial material: Instructional materials Montessori designed to facilitate young children's intellectual development by engaging their senses to discern isolated differences in the quality of particular objects.

spontaneous discipline: Children's engagement in productive, self-directed work, which produces sustained focus, joy, and peace, without teacher direction or need for correction.

T

Theosophy: A belief system developed in 1875 and expanded globally through the Theosophical Society rooted in spiritual transformation, truth seeking, and tolerance for all with the aim of appreciative inquiry and communal well-being.

three-period lesson: Lessons designed for young children to learn vocabulary and concepts in three parts: through first naming, then recognizing, and finally recalling a particular term or concept.

timelines: Implemented especially in elementary classrooms to build off the Great Lessons and convey the concept of time as students explore history across a variety of subjects from evolution, prehistory and contrasting historic cultures to the emergence of language and math concepts.

V

Valorization: A process through which adolescents develop and internal and external sense of self and value.

W

work: Term used to describe children's activities in a Montessori classroom rather than play.

Work and Study: Term used to describe the educational plan of adolescent children which aims to help each individual develop a sense of competence and self-worth. Work and Study included manual labor, opportunities for self-expression, moral education, math, language, the study of human progress, the study of earth and living things, a museum of machinery, communal living, and a deep care for the physical needs of the adolescent.

Index

The Abba's Orchard, Philippines 161–2, 165 n.3
Abbotsholme School, England 159
absorbent mind 41, 55, 72, 76–8, 98, 137–40, 143, 153, 241, 525
abstraction process 31, 64, 66, 99, 140, 242, 245, 247
abstract thinking 241–3, 245, 496, 548
academic achievement/performance 191, 193–4, 202, 251, 253, 256, 262–3, 406, 463, 471
academic skills 209–13, 400
accessibility 16, 202, 307, 311, 394–6, 450
accountability 95, 226, 284, 387, 389, 461
accreditation 17, 204, 210, 338, 351, 401–2, 413, 427, 453, 465
achievement gap 212, 358, 450
action research 226, 459–60
active child 117, 123, 135, 160, 253
activities/tasks for children 41, 44, 55, 60 n.3, 69, 73–6, 82, 86–7, 99, 105–6, 116, 120–2, 134, 137–8, 140, 151, 170, 190–1, 219, 221, 226–7, 236, 253, 264–5, 277, 459.
   See also work
   academic 266–7, 277
   beekeeping in Montessori adolescent farming 550
   Cultural Extensions 140, 144
   Cylinder Blocks 39, 73, 222
   follow-up practice 150–1
   gender-neutral 471–2
   geometric shapes 82, 122, 142, 152
   Going Out 67, 101, 123, 154, 548
   Grace and Courtesy 44, 125, 254
   hands-on 265, 448, 458
   Language Exercises 140, 142, 382–3
   Mathematics Exercises 140, 143
   motor and sensory 140–2, 183–4, 246, 262, 272
   Moveable Alphabets 86, 142, 497, 529–30
   physical 157, 183, 253
   Practical Life 123, 140–2, 202, 253, 293, 374, 483, 537
   Sandpaper Letters 121–2, 142, 222, 225, 480, 529–30
   Silence Game 43
Adams, Madonna 42
Adger, W. Neil 546
Adichie, Chimamanda Ngozi 469

adolescence/adolescents 66–9, 110, 115–16, 124, 157–65, 167–9, 181, 220, 233, 236, 252, 262, 267, 401, 465, 549
   educational technology 452–3
adult(s) 9, 13, 26, 31, 41, 50, 72, 74–6, 93, 98–9, 102–3, 108, 110, 121, 134–5, 139–40, 142, 144, 163, 234, 237–8, 261, 276, 547–9
   adult-child relationship 59, 71, 93–4
   adult learners 457–60, 465, 466 n.1
   negative affective reaction 231, 233–4
   prepared 138–9, 484
   transformation 167–72
adulthood 4, 49, 53, 67, 76–7, 115, 158, 181, 231, 241, 251, 452–3
aesthetics 11, 34, 76, 123
affective and cognitive process 275
affiliations 16, 204, 256, 286, 300, 311–12, 319, 322, 324, 329–30, 335, 338–40, 352, 368, 378–9, 382–4, 411, 413, 418, 420, 427, 436, 448, 481, 489
Africa 305, 349, 355
Aga Khan Foundation 334, 343
Agazzi Carolina 293–4
Agazzi Rosa 293–4
Agenda for Sustainable Development (ASD) 545–6
agriculture 123, 158–9, 164, 453
Aguerrí, Josefa Toledo de 416
Ahmedabad 15, 79 n.2
Aistear (Journey) curriculum 312
Akabane, Keiko 382
Aktionsgemeinschaft deutscher Montessori-Vereine (ADMV, Action Community of German Montessori Associations) 324
Aktion Sonnenschein (Sunshine Project) 481
Aktion Sonnenschein Thüringen (Action Sunshine Thuringia) 323
Alba, Domingo 411–12
Aldersbrook Primary school, Wanstead 307
Alexander Graham Bell Montessori School (AGBMS), Wheeling 482
Aljude, Saleha 363
Almeida, Miguel Calmon du Pin e 425
alternative educational model 299–300, 318, 340, 368, 393, 418, 427, 504

Index

Alzheimer's disease 535–7
American Educational Research Association (AERA) 177, 403, 457
American Montessori Society (AMS) 11, 16–17, 202, 210, 220, 257, 330, 339, 379, 383, 399, 402, 413, 419, 426, 461, 507, 520
   Montessori Inclusion Endorsement 484
   Research Committee 402
American Psychological Association 451
American Slave Codes 507
amotivation (absence of motivation) 262–3
Amsterdam 13–16, 297–9
Andhra Pradesh 368, 497
anganwadis (courtyard garden) preschool 367–8
Anglia Ruskin University 307
Anh Vu Kindergarten, Saigon 373
animal behavior studies 110, 179, 182, 472
Annecke, Eve 338
anthropology 8, 17, 23–4, 56, 108, 115, 117, 125, 177, 492, 531 n.1
anti-bias/anti-racist (ABAR) practices 503–8, 520–1
anxiety 148, 211, 214, 262, 527, 539–40
apartheid regime in South Africa 338
Aquila Nidus, Nigeria 339
Aristotle 37, 492, 536
Around the Child journal 367
Arthur Waser Foundation 345
Aruba and Region International Montessori Association 420
Arundale, George Sydney 97
Arundale, Rukmini Devi 15
Arvidsson, Stellan 317
Asia 355, 371–6, 383, 438–9, 493
Asian American children 268
Asociación de Escuelas Montessori de Puebla (Montessori Schools Association of Puebla) 413
Asociación Montessori Argentina (AMA) 431
Asociación Montessori de Chile 420
Asociación Montessori de México A.C. (AMMAC, Montessori Association of Mexico) 413
Asociación Montessori Mexicana A.C. (AMME, Mexican Montessori Association) 413
Asrary School, Saudi Arabia 361
assessments 65, 212–13, 220–1, 457, 462, 464–5, 480, 503
   authentic 223, 465
   classroom 219–22, 226
   documentation/record-keeping (tools) 222, 225–7
   embedded 223, 226
   formative 219–21, 223, 226–7, 462–4
   performance-based 464
   self-assessment 225, 464–5
   students' learning observation 223–5
   summative 219–20
   teacher-directed 222–3, 225
   of teacher educators 463–5
   work plans and portfolios 226–7
assimilation 242, 514, 517–18, 520
Associação Brasileira de Educação Montessori (ABEM, Brazilian Association of Montessori Education) 426
Associação de Educadores Católicos (AEC, Association of Catholic Educators) 426
Associação Montessori do Brasil (AMB, Montessori Association of Brazil) 426
Association Civile (A.C.), Mexico 414 n.1
Association for Educational Communications and Technology (AECT) 448–9
Association for the Development of Montessori Education 330
The Association Maria Montessori de Côte d'Ivoire 337
Association Montessori Internationale (AMI) 14, 16–17, 66, 201–2, 204–5, 212, 283, 286, 288, 294–5, 299, 304, 321–4, 327, 329–30, 333–5, 338–9, 350, 352, 355–6, 371–3, 379, 381, 389, 391, 399–400, 402, 411, 420, 519
   AMI-affiliated Sociedad Afiliada México A.C. (SAMAC, Mexican Affiliated Society) 413
   AMI Certificate Course 340
   AMI Korea Montessori Institute 372
   AMI Montessori Center Korea 372
   AMI Montessori Special Education Course 322
   AMI Nippon 383
   AMI Training Center Munich 322
   standards 210, 212, 311, 339
Association Montessori International/USA (AMI/USA) 204, 256, 400, 402, 461, 507, 520
Association Montessori Morocco (AMM) 337, 340
Association of AMI Montessori Teachers of Ireland (AATI) 311–12
Association of Montessori Nigeria (AMEN) 337, 339
Assunta LUMSA University 295
Auburn House Trust, Cape Town 338
Aurin, Margarete 322–3
Australian Aboriginal 497. *See also* Indigenous people/communities (Indigeneity)
Australian Curriculum and Reporting Authority 390
Australian Montessori Teacher Education Foundation (AMTEF) 390
Australian National Curriculum 390
Australian Schools Commission 389

Index

Australian Thai Montessori (ATM) 372
Austria/Austrian 5, 12, 15, 120, 285, 459
authentic/authenticity 42, 65, 75, 117, 147, 159, 192–3, 199, 202–3, 205, 223, 253, 257, 274, 363, 374, 399, 401, 407, 458–9, 465, 517, 522
authoritarian 12, 171, 297, 303, 311, 327
authoritative parents 171, 275
auto-education (Autoeducazione) 11, 13, 223
autonomy/autonomous 12, 21–2, 63, 74, 76, 99–100, 133, 151, 169, 226, 237, 262–8, 338, 362, 368, 394, 407, 460, 473, 497, 539, 547
Auxiliary Montessori Education Secretariat (SAEM) 407–9

Bachelard, Gaston 118
Badheka, Gijubhai 16, 286, 365
Bahrain 361
Balak (Child) Journal 367
balwadis (children's garden) preschool 367
Bangkok 371–2
Bangalore 368
Bangladesh 439
Bapoo, Khatoon 334
Barad, Karen 470, 472–3, 475 n.6
Barcelona 11–12, 15, 58, 81, 130, 293, 493
Barnett, Jon 546
Barrameda, Christopher 161
Baumrind, Diana 275
Bavaria 323
Beebe, Beatrice, *Infant Research and Adult Treatment: Constructing Interactions* 131
begreifen (grasp) 122
behavioral science 450
Beijing Normal University (BNU) 378–9
Bell, Alexander Graham 393
Bell, Mabel Graham 393
Benedictine Sisters of Kaunas 328
Benincasa Special School 311–12
Bergamo 294–5, 411
Berlin 7, 14, 17, 21, 159, 201, 321, 323, 325, 470
Bhutan 438–9
Bildungsakademie (Educational Academy) of the Bavarian Regional Montessori Association 322–3
bilingualism 395, 418, 482, 490–1, 494–6, 498, 526, 530–1. *See also* multilingualism
biological development 179–80
biological liberty 9
BIPOC (Black, Indigenous, and people of color) 521
Black children 212, 334, 337, 403, 504, 506–7

Blackfriars Practising School 387–8
Black Montessori Education Fund 403
blossoming beyond the binary initiative 469
Blossom Montessori School for the Deaf in Clearwater, Florida 482
Blume, Wilhelm 159
boarding schools 159, 515–18
body movement 38, 59, 82, 183, 246
    hands/hand movements 179, 184
    mind-body interaction 17, 38, 88, 122, 135, 246, 451
Bonfigli, Clodomiro 6–7
Born Inside initiative 356, 358
Borruat, Luis 429
Bourneville, Désiré Magloire 8
Bowlby, John 13, 130, 182
brain 43, 78, 84–6, 98, 101, 122, 132, 137, 157–8, 180–3, 231, 233–7, 246, 251, 531 n.1, 535. *See also* error monitoring mechanism
    brain plasticity 233, 236
    cerebral development 181
    cerebral maturation 237
    dimensions of mind (narrative and paradigmatic) 101
    engram 246
    functional brain imaging studies 234
    hand as an organ of 184
    during math task 234
    movement for brain development 179
Brazilian Common Curriculum 427
Brazilian Montessori Congress 426
British Columbia 393–6
British Journal of Education (*El Monitor de la Educación Común*) 429
British Montessori Society 11–12
Bruh Tesfa Kindergarten Teacher Training Institute, Ethiopia 335
Bruner, Jerome 101–2
Brussels 495, 497
Buarque, Ciridião 425
Buarque, Mary 425
Buckleitner, Warren 447–8
Buenos Aires 430–2
Bulgaria 327, 329–30
Burg, Cecile 394
Burt, Marina K. 527
Butt, John 372
Buytendijk, Frederick 121

Caballero, Agustín Nieto 416
Cairo 340
Caldeira, Eny 426

Calgary 201, 291
Calgary Montessori School (CMS) 393
California 11, 401
The Call of Education Journal 13
Cambi, Franco 33
Canadian Association of Montessori Teachers (CAMT) 394
Canadian Council of Montessori Administrators (CCMA) 394–5
Canova, Marisa 431
Caranza, Matilda 416
Carballo, Connie 431
Carbonneau, Kira J. 245
caregivers/caregiving 71–2, 75, 79, 95, 130–2, 147, 171–2, 182, 539
Carnegie School of Education 307
Casa da Infância, São Paulo 425
Casa dei Bambini (Children's House) 8–9, 25, 53, 55, 57–9, 66, 101, 111 n.6, 118–19, 135, 137–44, 147, 199, 291, 297, 315, 321, 382, 394, 409, 451, 480, 528–9, 535, 540
Casa del Niño María de Nazareth organization 431
Casa Montessori 366
Castro, Margarita 416
Catalan government 11–12, 130
Catechesis of the Good Shepherd (CGS) 312
The Catholic Church 11–12, 14, 22, 57, 60 n.6, 312, 335, 349, 382, 428
Catholics/Catholicism 58–9, 92, 108, 111 n.6, 291, 293, 297, 310–12, 321, 334, 345, 382, 390, 394, 399, 401
Cavalletti, Sofia 312
Celli, Angelo 6–7
Center for Montessori Teacher Education, New York 406
"Center for Work and Study on the Land" 158–64, 549
centralized educational system 309, 315, 318–19
Centro de Estudios de Educación Montessori A.C. (CEMAC/*El Centro*, Center for Studies of Montessori Education) 411–12
Centro Nascita Montessori (Montessori Birth Center) 295
certification of Montessori teachers 286, 299, 402, 457
Chalmers, Diana 393–4
charismatic leadership 285–6
charter schools 318, 400–1, 408, 481, 505
Chennai 365–6, 368
childcare 306–7, 343, 345, 356, 385, 387, 389–91, 391 n.4, 395, 449
child-centered system 74, 95, 184, 227, 272, 288, 298, 372, 381, 385, 388, 391, 394, 504, 517
Child Developers Programme 349

child development 16, 38, 50, 65–9, 74, 86, 98, 101–2, 108–9, 115, 147, 170–2, 177, 179–80, 184, 221, 225, 237, 291, 336, 361, 385, 445, 493
  planes of development (*see* planes of development (developmental phases))
  stages of 180–1
childhood 5, 17, 24, 30–1, 34, 43, 57, 59, 60 n.3, 63, 71–2, 75–6, 79, 98–9, 101–3, 170, 251–2, 513, 545
Child, Phoebe 286, 304, 311
child-rearing methods 9, 12, 18, 97, 129–31, 135, 171, 297, 336, 516–17
Children's House. *See* Casa dei Bambini (Children's House)
The Children's Laboratory school, Canada 393
Chinese Education 377
Chisnall, Nicola 438
Chomsky, Noam 85, 182, 525, 531 n.1
Christian, Michelle 503
Christian mission schools 335
Cicero, Marcus 536
Città di Castello, Perugia 53–4, 56, 293, 355
civilization 29, 69, 103, 158–60, 334, 381, 525, 541
Claremont, Claude 303
Clark, Koren 336
classic Montessori approach 16, 43, 205, 223, 257, 300
climate change/disruption 95, 103, 162, 546–7, 550–1 n.1
Clodd, Edward 86
Cochiti Pueblo 514–15, 529
cognition 43–4, 85, 99, 122, 138, 167–8, 246
  cognitive development 9, 81, 160, 167, 177, 194, 242, 297
  cognitive flexibility 213, 251–2, 255–8
  cognitive reserve 536
  cognitive science 241, 243, 246
cohesion 43, 107, 144, 167, 268
Cold, Birgit 120
Colebrook, Claire 471
Colegio del Rosario school 430
Colegio Montessori de Luján 430–1
collaborations, Montessori's 8, 14, 16, 18, 29, 32, 39, 102, 117, 130, 152, 192, 284, 291, 293, 299, 346, 356, 367, 369, 372–3, 402, 408, 413, 430–1, 459–60, 481–2, 521, 531, 539
Collecott, Clare 338
collective governance model 406, 408–9
Comité Hispano Montessori (Hispanic Montessori Committee). *See* Consejo Interamericano Montessori (Inter-American Montessori Council)

commercialization and marketing 159, 257, 288, 363, 433, 540
communal living 165, 458, 460–1, 549
communication 31, 109, 142, 154, 287, 489–90, 494, 508, 530
communist/communism 14, 284, 327, 329–30, 426
competition 10–11, 307
compulsory education 304, 317, 418, 421
concentration 73–4, 76, 78–9, 105–6, 109, 134, 137, 169, 191, 252–3, 271–4, 276, 278, 343, 395, 445, 451, 480, 551 n.4
concrete materials 143–4, 241–5
concrete representation 82, 143, 221, 243, 246–7
concrete-to-abstract development 241–3, 246
confidence 31, 56, 142, 151, 172, 223, 254, 482
Connecticut 211, 399–400, 411
consciousness 22, 91, 94, 123, 153, 472, 475 n.5, 504, 509
Consejo Interamericano Montessori (Inter-American Montessori Council) 419, 421 n.3
Constantin-Hansen, Thora 315
control of error 65, 222–3, 257, 537
conventional programs 205, 257, 266, 496
Copenhagen 15, 91, 315–16
Corcoran, Timothy 311
Corner of Hope Montessori 350, 352, 356–8, 436, 497
cosmic education 16, 29–34, 67, 99, 110–11, 123, 154, 159, 366, 459, 465, 482, 545–7.
  See also universe
  in childhood pedagogy 30–1
  cosmic agents 30, 99, 102
  cosmic fables (Great Lessons) 29, 31–3, 101, 152
  cosmic plan 30, 33, 38, 59, 99–101
  cosmic vision 30, 33, 66, 99–101
  mystical dimension 100
cosmos 29–30, 34, 92, 94, 99–102
Cossentino, Jacqueline 399, 483
Costa Gnocchi, Adele 130, 135
Council of Protestant Churches of Nicaragua (CEPAD) 419
COVID-19 pandemic 195, 287, 307, 346, 356, 368, 409, 453–4, 463
creative energy 39, 78, 106
creativity 21–2, 119, 123, 191, 204, 210, 213–14, 236, 263, 278, 329, 362
Credaro, Luigi 37, 293
Creel, Maria Luisa Ryan de 411
Crianza Juntos (Parenting Together) project 432
critical periods 13, 179–81, 251
critical race theory (CRT) 503–4, 507–9
critical thinking skills 362, 461
Cromwell, Mary 435

Crossroads Anti-Racism 506
Crow, Jim 507
Csikszentmihalyi, Mihaly 276, 278
Cuevas, Guadalupe 430–1
culturally relevant pedagogy (CRP) 503–8
Cultural Revolution (1966–1977) 378
culture(s)/cultural 30, 39, 55–7, 60 n.3, 68–9, 98–101, 108, 115, 117, 123, 139–40, 144, 152, 242, 268, 286, 309, 333, 337, 352, 362–4, 395, 436, 439, 448, 451, 489, 490–2, 497–8, 503, 505, 515–16, 518, 520, 525, 528, 540
  cofigurative 171
  comprehensive cultural 515
  cultural codes 329
  cultural competence 504
  cultural context 10, 16, 55, 179, 202, 210, 267–8, 271, 362–3, 437, 440, 504, 529
  cultural critique of Montessori 5, 12–13
  cultural diversity 490
  cultural responsiveness 202, 336–7, 350, 352, 374, 403, 420, 508
  diffuse 139, 144
  multicultural 108, 396, 489, 497–8
  pluricultural 489–90, 496
  postfigurative 171
  prefigurative 171–2
Cunningham, Allen 171
curriculum 9, 12, 17, 40, 50, 63, 66, 77, 81, 99–100, 109, 144, 151–4, 159–61, 189, 204–5, 210, 225–6, 232, 243, 246, 252–3, 256, 262, 265, 267, 286, 295, 312, 317, 319, 323–4, 337–8, 346, 351–2, 361–4, 366, 372–4, 390, 395, 431, 458, 460–1, 465, 480, 482, 496, 505, 507, 509, 515–16, 521–2
Czech Republic 327–30, 494

Dąbrowski, Kazimierz 168–9
Daem Training, Riyadh 364
The Dalton Plan teaching method 111 n.9, 201, 299
Damore, Sharon 463–4
Đạm Phương nữ sử, *Giáo Dục Nhi Đồng* (*To Educate the Child*) 373
Danish Montessori Society 316
Danner, Natalie 483
Das Kind in der Familie (The Child in the Family) series 13
data collection 192, 266, 276, 287, 457
daycare center 322, 337, 345, 395
d'Azeglio, Massimo 5
de Almeida, Talita 426
de Azevedo, Edith Dias Menezes 426

Debs, Mira 461
decision-making 148, 151, 158, 161, 165, 223, 253, 406, 450–1, 458, 464
Declaration of the Rights of the Child 13, 64, 426, 481, 484
decolonizing education 340, 403, 521
Decroly Method 109, 416
Decroly, Ovide 111 n.8, 299, 439
deficit-minded thinking 462, 507–8
Dehaene, Stanislas 102
  The Number Sense 84
de Lacerda, Piper 426
de Lenval, Lubienska 426
Delhi 367–8
De Marco, Allison 190
dementia 535–41
de Saint-Exupéry, Antoine 238
Descartes, René 122
design/setup (classroom/school) 109, 118–20, 139, 144, 212, 225, 241, 254, 309, 330, 357, 367, 421, 458, 462
Deutsche Montessori Gesellschaft (DMG, German Montessori Society) 321–3
Deutsche Montessori-Vereinigung (DMV, German Montessori Association) 322–3
Deutschsprachige AMI-Pädagogen (DAMIP, Association of German-Speaking AMI Pedagogues) 322
developmental psychology 17, 124, 137, 165, 373
deviations 8, 68, 106, 147
de Vries, Hugo 9, 13, 138, 180
Dewey, John 11, 275, 378, 387, 425, 445, 458
dictatorial regime 284, 426, 430
dictatorship 12, 94, 426
didactics 8–9, 50, 63, 67, 115–17, 121, 124
  didactic materials (hands on learning material) 9, 11, 118, 122–3, 147–50, 190–1, 200, 209, 222, 232–3, 343, 471
Dietrich, Irene 323
differentiated curriculum 252, 257
differentiated instruction (DI) 256, 462–3, 465
The Dimensional Change Card Sort (DCCS) 255–7
diplomas 200, 299, 311, 323, 368, 372, 379, 391, 402
disability/disabled children 53, 59, 315, 322, 385, 420–1, 445–6, 450, 479–84, 535
  autism/autistic children 483
  deaf 479–80, 482
  intellectual disability 53, 59
  medical-pedagogical institutes for 7–8
discipline 17, 21, 274–5, 345, 375
Discovery House Montessori 339
distance-learning model 304, 307, 311, 453

distractions 225, 255, 272–4
Distretto Montessori Perugia (Montessori Perugia District) 295
diverse/diversity 5, 13, 56, 84, 93, 107–8, 152, 154, 177, 202, 210, 235–6, 287, 329, 333, 437, 457, 461, 469, 490, 497, 505, 507, 520, 531
diversity, equity, and inclusion (DEI) 461, 507
ĐỔI MỚI (Renovation) policy 373
Do Minh Training Center 373
Donohue, Chip 450
Do Phuong Khanh 373
driving ideas, object's 82, 122
drugs 163, 536, 538
Drunothaya School, Hua Chang Bridge (Bangkok) 371
Dublin 201, 311–12
Dubovoy, Silvia 431
Dulay, Heidi C. 527
Dutch Montessori Association 298–300
Dutch Montessori schools 299–300
Dwyer, Muriel 305, 334, 343–4, 349–50
The Dynamic Indicators of Basic Early Literacy Skills 220

Early Childhood 16, 30, 98, 118–20, 123–4, 148, 180, 182, 199, 210, 214, 220, 223, 225–6, 306, 309, 324–5, 361, 363–4, 395, 418, 421, 427, 451, 497, 526, 528
Early Childhood education (ECE) 102, 284, 288, 295, 303, 306–7, 312, 322–3, 333–5, 338, 351, 361, 365, 367, 372, 378, 381–2, 385, 387, 402, 415–16, 420, 429–31, 433
early (personal) life and family of Montessori 5, 8, 11
Eastern Europe 285, 327–30
East London 303–4, 307
East London University 307
eclectics/eclecticism 12, 291, 399, 430
Ecole Montessori Casablanca (EMC) 340
ecoliteracy 545–50
economic independence 22, 158, 160, 165, 549
Educación con Participación de la Comunidad (EDUCO) 420
Educateurs Sans Frontierès (EsF), AMI 286–7, 335, 355–8, 368, 431, 497
  advocacy for children's rights 355–6
  Community Rooted Education (CoRE) program 338, 356, 368
  Corner of Hope model 350
  EsF Assembly 355, 413
  Voices of EsF program 356

educational technology 105, 447–54
   for adolescent (ages 12–18) 452–3
   COVID-19 impacts on 453–4
   for early childhood (birth through age 6) 451–2
   for elementary (ages 6–12) 452
   evolution and guidelines 448–50
   in Montessori programs 451
   position statement 449–50
   teacher education programs 453
   technology integration 450–1
educere (to draw out) 94
Egypt 150, 333, 337, 340, 341 n.2, 361, 439
El Boletín 419–20, 422 n.4
Elementary Alumni Association (EAA) 402
elementary education/schools 11, 63, 66, 81, 86, 99–101, 117, 123–4, 132, 147–54, 159, 180–1, 213, 220, 226, 262, 294, 303, 321–3, 325, 345, 357, 366, 372, 389, 411, 429–31, 448, 452, 526, 528, 531 n.2, 539, 548
El Salvador 415, 420
Else-Quest, Nicole 211, 214, 256
embodied cognition 43–4, 246
embodied learning 120, 253
embodiment 43–4, 122–3, 307
embryology 77
Emilia Erichsen Kindergarten, Curitiba 425
emotional recognition skills 214, 235
emotional regulation 254–5
engagement, children's 82, 147, 152, 225–6, 261, 264, 268, 273, 276, 548
English and American Sign Language 482
English First Language (EFL) system 394
environment 7–9, 17, 37, 41, 57, 68, 71–2, 78–9, 85, 88, 98–9, 103, 106, 109–11, 115–26, 167–8, 179, 225, 232, 236, 241, 253–4, 257, 261–2, 265–6, 267, 343, 356–8, 447, 451–2, 462, 481, 483–4, 497, 509, 513, 525–6, 528, 531, 535, 545, 551 n.4
   domestic 74
   enriched/stimulating 181–2
   learning 64–5, 72, 75–6, 106–7, 116, 122, 124–5, 151, 159–61, 165, 252, 274, 450, 495, 521, 547
   non-anticipatory 132–3
   ordered 106, 191
   outdoor 120, 123, 139
   for people with dementia 538–40
   prepared 5, 59, 74–5, 138–40, 163, 170, 273–4, 385, 453, 458–9, 508, 516, 525, 539, 540–1, 547
   psychological 139–40
   and self-learning 64
   social 139, 232, 266
   stewardship 545, 548–9
environmental concerns 30, 32, 34, 40, 59, 66, 93–4, 101, 131, 153, 233, 246, 251, 272–4, 291, 336, 479, 515
epistemology 38, 40, 42, 44, 100, 470
equity 159, 380, 403, 450, 460–1, 504–7
Erdkinder (children of the Earth) model 69, 123, 157–65, 324, 368, 549
error monitoring mechanism 231–8
Escola Experimental center 426
Escola Modelo Montessori (Montessori Model School) 11
Escuela Argentina Modelo 430
Escuela del Pueblo Trabajador 405
Escuela Maternal preschool 416
Escuela Montessori de Valparaíso, Santiago 526
Escuela Normal Roque Saenz Peña, Buenos Aires 429–30
Escuelas Normal (teacher training schools) 429
Ethiopia 14, 335, 341
ethnicity 446, 450, 508
Europe/European 3, 5, 10, 16, 18, 22, 85, 119, 159, 200, 225, 283, 293–4, 298, 311, 321, 324, 334, 343, 345, 355, 381, 385, 387–9, 394, 416, 419–21, 425, 429–30, 437, 439, 480, 491–3, 516–17
   European American children 268
   European Montessori movement 11–14
Evans, Tony 393
evidence-based teaching 125, 219, 465
executive control 234, 496
executive functional skills 141, 144, 151, 194, 209–10, 213–14, 236–7, 251–8
experiential learning 458, 465, 549
experiential perspective on education 272–4
experiential sampling method (ESM) 275–8
experimentation 9, 13, 57, 87, 101, 133, 294, 299, 472
exploration 66, 78, 86, 101, 122, 142–4, 237, 363, 458, 465
   exploratory wandering 133–4

fairy tales 107–9, 121
faith 92, 94, 99–100, 108, 172, 243, 309, 401, 457, 537
family-style classroom 148
Fan, Bingqing, *Ms. Montessori and Her New Teaching Method* 377
Faria, Heloisa Marcondes de 425
Farmer, Marjorie "Marge" 419, 421

farm-school approach 161–2, 549. *See also Erdkinder*
Farm School La Granja, Philippines 161–2
fascism/fascists 13–14, 18, 50, 55, 57–8, 283–4, 293–4
Faure, Pierre 426
Fausek, Yulia Ivanovna 327
feedback 65, 219–20, 223, 225–6, 234, 237, 276, 295, 307, 461, 465, 482
feminism/feminists 469–71, 474, 474 n.1. *See also* women's rights
　critical gaze of 471, 474
　first wave 7, 470
　Italian 7, 21–4
　militant 21, 23
　new materialisms 471–4, 475 n.5
　post-structuralisms 471–4, 475 n.3
　scientific 21–6, 26 n.1, 471
fidelity 12, 177, 192–3, 199, 202–6, 209–13, 256, 258, 287–8, 312, 363, 369, 371, 379, 427, 522. *See also* implementation fidelity
Finnish Montessori Association 318
Finnish Montessori Training Enterprise 319
First World War 9–12, 201, 388, 399, 435
Fisher, Dorothy Canfield, *A Montessori Mother* 297
The Flanker Inhibitory Control and Attention Test 255, 257
flexible error monitoring system 231, 236–7
flow experience 253, 271, 275, 277–8
flow theory 271–8
folwark (feudal relations) 329
The Fondazione Centro Internazionale Studi Montessoriani (International Foundation for Montessori Studies) 294
Foreign Language in the Elementary School (FLES) 527
formal operations cognitive development 242
Fornaca, Remo 34, 57
Fortuna, Stefania 185
Foundation Degree Program 307
Foundation for Montessori Education in Nigeria (FMEN) 337, 339–40
The Foundation for Paedological Lectures, Hague 297
Fowler, Susan 483
France 57, 75, 204, 212, 214, 328, 381, 426, 429, 439, 526
Franchetti, Alice Hallgarten 54–5, 60 n.3, 293
Franchetti, Baron Leopoldo 53–4, 60 n.3, 293
Frank, Anne 298
Fred, Doreen 345
Fred Rogers Center 449–50, 452
free choice 55, 109, 133–4, 202, 276

freedom 9, 12, 17, 37–8, 41–4, 56, 58, 63, 82, 93, 100, 106, 109, 120, 124–5, 135, 139–40, 169, 172, 204, 274–5, 286, 297, 315, 420, 496–7, 518, 547
"Freedom of Education Act," Dutch Constitution 297, 299–300
free schools 315, 318
free-tuition preschool program, Irish 312
Freire, Paulo 409 n.1, 426
French First Language (FFL) system 394
French public school system 205
Friends School of Newtown, Waterford 309
Froebel, Friedrich (Froebelian) 9, 56, 303, 316, 321, 381, 387, 429–30, 439, 492
Frondizi, Arturo 430
Frondizi, Elena 430
Fruitful Orchard School, Lagos, Nigeria 244, 285, 339
Fukakusa Children's House, Kyoto 383–4
Fundación Argentina María Montessori (FAMM) 420, 431
Fundación del Rosario 430
Fundación Eco-Educativa Montessori Colombia (FEMCO) 420

Gadamer, Hans-Georg 125
Galton, Francis 8
Gambia 335–7
Gandhi, Mahatma 15, 365, 367
Garzanti, Aldo 53
Garzanti, Sofia Ravasi 53
Gatehouse school (St. Bartholomew's church as a classroom) 304–6
Gebhardt-Seele, Peter 322
gender 445, 469, 530
　coloniality of 470
　gender identity 446, 450
　gender-neutral 121, 469, 471, 474
　gender-sensitive pedagogy 472, 474
　Western gender binary 470
General Regulations for the Formation of an Authorized Montessori Society (1915) 201
Geneva 14, 58
Gentile, Giovanni 3, 13
George, Anne 492–4
Gerbich, Penny 418
Germany/German 12, 69, 105, 200, 285–7, 321–5, 345, 381–2, 459, 480–1, 493, 496, 530
Gimnasio Moderno school, Bogotá 416
Giroux, Henry 170
Gitter, Lena 480

Glisan, Eileen W., *Teacher's Handbook: Contextualized Language Instruction* 528
global influence on Montessori education 283–8
global majority, people of 503, 507, 509 n.1, 520
global Montessori research 435–40
Global North 288, 445, 470
Global South 202, 284, 288
Gobbi, Gianna 312
Goldsbrough, Binda Mary 438
Goldschmied, Elinor 133
Goodnough, Karen 464
Good Shepherd Training Center, Colombo 438
Gould, Katherine Clemens 377
government-funded Montessori programs 202, 286, 297, 300, 303–4, 307, 330, 333, 365, 368, 390, 435–6
Graham, James A. 460
grammar/grammar exercises 66, 81, 85–7, 150, 153, 527, 530
    Grammatical Boxes 86
    Sorting Tray exercise 150
Grazzini, Camillo 100, 515
The Great Leap Forward (1958–1960) 378
Great Lessons (cosmic fables) 31–3, 152
Grossman, Carolina 425
Grunwald, Clara 286, 321
Guatemala 416, 418, 421
guide 22, 106, 139, 147, 151, 154, 160, 225–6, 336, 407, 459, 495, 519, 528
Guidelines for the Learning and Development of Children (aged 3–6) 379–80
Gujarat 365, 367
Gunning, Johannes Herman 298

The Hague 16, 297–9
Haiti 336, 356
Hall-Dennis Report 394
Hall, Sally 338
Hall, Stanley 67
The Hamilton Spectator 393
Handmaids of the Holy Child Jesus 334
hands-on learning modalities 8, 86, 122, 159, 161, 241, 253, 265, 272, 304, 395, 448, 452–3, 458, 505
Hanrath, Cato "Nan" 411
Harold Simmons Foundation 401
Hassan School, Saudi Arabia 363
Hawker, Bertram 303
Hayes, Mary 551 n.2
Hecker, Hilde 321
Hegel, Georg Wilhelm Friedrich 37, 42
Heidrich, Petro 382

Heilman, Victoria Marwa 345
The Heilpädagogische Vereinigung (HPV, Therapeutic Education Association) 323
helicopter parenting style 171
Hellbrügge, Theodor 322, 481
Helming, Helene 322, 324
Helms, Marie 315
Helsingør 316, 421 n.2
Helvetius, Claude Adrien 56
Hendricksen, Fay 288 n.1
Hershey Foundation 401
Hershey Montessori School, Huntsburg 159
Hertha magazine 315
Hertzberger, Herman 120
heuristic game 133
high-fidelity Montessori programs 205, 211–13, 215, 252, 254, 256, 337, 339, 365, 368, 402, 497
The Hilda Rothschild Foundation 420
Hiratsuka, Masunori 381–2
Hispanic children 504
Hội Tâm lý Giáo dục học Hà Nội (Association of Psychology in Education) 373
holistic learning 373, 457, 460, 465
Holland. *See* The Netherlands
Holliday Montessori School, Kansas 119
Holmes, Catherine Claire 497
Holmes, Edmond G. A. 303–4
Holsen, Ingrid 190
Holtstiege, Hildegard 324
Homfray, Margaret 286, 304, 311, 389
Honduras 418, 420
Honegger Fresco, Grazia, study on newborns 129–35
hooks, bell 470
horme 77–8
House of Childhood, Inc. 200
Hubel, David 180
human development 42, 57, 67, 69, 99, 107, 122, 137–8, 177, 271–2, 446, 525
    flourishing 42–3, 226, 545–6
humanity 24–6, 30, 33–4, 50, 60, 68–9, 91–5, 97, 99–103, 110–11, 154, 158, 170, 172, 291, 294, 445–6, 460, 490, 507, 514, 516, 519, 521, 546, 549
Hunt, J. McVicker 261
Hurlbut, Nina M. 518
Husén, Torsten 316–17
Hutchinson, David 460
Hutchinson, Lilly 303
Hyderabad 356, 367–8, 483
hydroponics 161–2
hygiene and anthropology 8, 23, 119

Ibn Khaldun Schools 364
Ida Sjögren's Montessori school, Norrköping 316
imagination 31–3, 40, 65, 67, 99, 101, 108–9, 121, 144, 148, 152–3, 172, 454, 459, 548
Imanishi, Yoshizo 381
immersive experiences 272, 275
immigrants 389, 429
implementation fidelity 199, 203–5, 209, 213, 255–6, 258, 266. *See also* fidelity
implementation science 202
Inanda Montessori School and Training Centre 338
inclusion/inclusive education 203, 385, 403, 406, 457, 461, 479–84, 505, 507, 509, 520
The Indaba Foundation 338
The Indaba Institute in the Cape Winelands 338
independence 50, 74, 76, 98, 120, 124, 131–2, 134, 140, 144, 191, 223, 264, 266, 284, 318, 330, 336, 340, 346, 387, 426, 428, 459, 497, 547
Independent School Act 394
independent schools 311–12, 338, 389–90, 399, 403. *See also* private schools
India 5, 14–16, 31, 59, 76, 79 n.2, 97–9, 111 n.3, 201–2, 294, 304, 311, 394, 438–9, 447, 493
Indian Montessori Centre (IMC) 368
Indian Montessori Training Course (IMTC) 367
Indigenous Montessori Institute (IMI) 519–22, 523 n.3
Indigenous people/communities (Indigeneity) 286, 336, 355, 389, 395, 418, 446, 470, 508, 513–23, 546
   author positionality 513–14
   genocide on 523 n.1
   Indigenizing Montessori curriculum 521–2
   Indigenous children 418, 513–15, 517, 521–2
   myths and materials 520–1
   truth telling 516–17
   violence against 517–20
individualism/individuality 38, 102, 169, 191, 278, 329, 473
   individual development 40, 94, 139, 324, 385
   individualized learning 191, 449
   individual work 12, 109
Individualized Education Plan (IEP) 481
Indonesia 267, 371, 437–8
infants/infancy 16, 57, 68, 74, 78, 131, 133, 135, 194, 220, 242–3, 252, 265, 273, 358, 387, 395, 401, 406, 449, 495, 525, 536
Information Age 448, 454
inhibitory control 251–3, 255–8
inquiry-based learning 123, 459, 465

Institute of Education Sciences 210, 214
Instituto Nacional de Estadística y Geografía (INEGI) 413
Instituto Nueva Escuela (INE) 406–8
Integrated Child Development Services (ICDS) 367
integrity of Montessori method 16, 50, 199–203, 206, 420
intellectual development 66, 78, 144
interconnectedness/interconnections 33, 38–40, 44, 67, 88, 98, 123, 236, 458–61, 546
Intercultural Montessori School, Oak Park 529
interdependence 29, 32–3, 39–40, 94, 101, 123, 144, 153–4, 274, 322, 491, 545, 547
interdisciplinarity 31, 457
interdisciplinary 29, 101, 158–60, 164, 236, 446, 460, 462, 465, 547–9
internally displaced people (IDP) 350, 357–8
International Association for Montessori Education (IAME) 17
International Baccalaureate (IB) 162, 164, 283
International Congress of Women, London 303, 470
International Montessori Congress 29, 66, 91, 130, 294, 304, 421 n.2, 551 n.2
International Montessori Council (IMC) 14, 15, 29, 66, 83, 91, 130, 294, 304, 402, 421 n.2, 426, 551 n.2
International Montessori Foundation 401
International Montessori Institute 307
International Montessori School of North Carolina (IMSNC), Durham 529, 531 n.2
International Montessori Schools (IMS) 495–7
International Montessori Training Center, Fukuoka 383
International Organ of the Montessori Movement 13
International Society for Technology in Education (ISTE) 449–50
International Women's Congress, Berlin 7, 470
intersectionality 470, 513
interventions 77, 135, 172, 189, 190–1, 199, 210, 237, 252, 256, 418, 473, 481–2, 484, 506–7, 536, 538, 547
intra-action 473, 475 n.6
"Introduction to Structural Racism" workshop 506
Inuit people 286, 395
Iran 214
Ireland 287, 309–13, 394
Irish Montessori Association. *See* Association of AMI Montessori Teachers of Ireland (AATI)
Irish Montessori Education Board (IMEB) 311–12
Irish National Teachers' Organization Conference (1924) 309
Irish Preschool Playgroups Association 311

Irwin, Sophia Arbella 381
Islamic Education Psychology 363
Islam/Islamic 361–4, 401
isolation of difficulty 143
isolation of quality 64, 82
Istituto Romano dei Beni Stabili (IRBS, Roman Association of Real Estate) 8, 291
Italian National Institute of Statistics (ISTAT) 295
Italy/Italian 5, 10–12, 23, 49–50, 53, 56–8, 63, 85, 105, 117, 132–3, 135 n.2, 205, 303, 327, 355, 411, 425, 436, 492–4
  Italian feminism 7, 21, 23
  Italian Montessorism, politicization of (1924–1934) 13–14
  Italian Montessori Society 13
Itard, Jean-Marc 8, 56, 479–80, 492, 530
Iyengar, Sheena S. 268

Jackson, Maggie 451
Jakobson, Roman 525, 531 n.1
James, William 37, 56, 64
Jank, Werner 115
Januszewski, Alan 449
Japan 285, 480
Japan Association Montessori (JAM) 382–4
Japan Montessori Research Institute 382
Japan Montessori Society 382
Jenaplan School 159, 299
Jericho Nursery School, Nairobi 349
Jewish school 401
Johnson, Mark 122
Joosten, Albert Max 367, 438
Jordan, Nancy 311
Journal of Education 377
Journal of Montessori Research 403
Journal of Montessori Research and Education 319
Joyce, David E, *Euclid's Elements* 82–4
Juan Ponce de León (JPL) school 405–6, 409 n.1
June Shelton School and Evaluation Center, Dallas 482
junior high school 220, 384
justice-oriented learning 461

Kahn, David 159, 356, 458
Kaminski, Christa 322
The Kansas Reflection-Impulsivity Scale for Preschool (KRISP) 255–6
Kant, Immanuel 37, 42
  On Education 56
Karnataka 368
Kashamba, Gaspara 334, 344
Kaul, Claus 322

Kaunas 328
Kawano, Kiyomaru 381
Kayılı treatment group 203
Keleher, Julia 407–8
Kellogg, W. K., *Logic Model Development Guide* 190
Kenya Institute of Curriculum Development 352
Kerala 368
Keres Children's Learning Center (KCLC) 403, 514–16, 519–21, 523 n.2, 529
Kilpatrick, William Heard 11, 111 n.5, 399
kindergarten 213, 257, 294, 316, 322–3, 329, 343, 345, 362, 373, 377–9, 381, 387, 415–16, 425, 429–30, 527
Kindergarten Modelo at the Colegio de Señoritas de Managua (Women's College of Managua) 416
Kindergarten Nacional program 416
Kinderzentrum (Children's Center) 322
Kindezi, Congolese educational practice 336
Kira, Bertha 344
Kodaikanal 294, 366
Kohlberg, Lawrence 167–8
Kolkata (Calcutta) 367–8
Kòsmos (order) 99
Kožíšková, Božena 328
Kramer, Rita 8
Krashen, Stephen D. 527–8
KRB Consultant Australia 372
Krieger, Ana 430
Kurahashi, Sozo 381
Kuraitytė-Varnienė, Marija 328

Labanca, Maria 431
Lachmann, Franck M., *Infant Research and Adult Treatment: Constructing Interactions* 131
Lafferty, Carolyn K. 190
LaForett, Doré R. 190
Lagos Montessori School 339
Laínez, Don José 415
Lakȟól'iyapi Wahóȟpi 516, 520
Lakota people 517
Landerziehungsheime (country education homes) 69, 159
language(s) 85–6, 98, 108, 123, 140–2, 179, 181, 189, 200, 209, 211, 223, 242, 333, 337, 343, 352, 363, 394–5, 437–9, 445–6, 448–50, 472, 489–90, 492, 508, 515. *See also* linguistics/linguistic development
  activities 382–3
  alphabetic 529–30
  Arabic 361–3, 530
  Chinese 490, 494, 529, 532 n.6

Dakota and Lakota 514, 516
dual-language models 515, 526, 529
English 3, 45, 115, 212, 349, 437, 490, 492–7, 515, 526, 529, 531–2 n.2, 532 n.5
  examples of Montessori programs 528–9
  first language 446, 479, 490–1, 497, 525, 528
French 394, 494–6, 529–30, 532 n.5
Gambia's national 337
German 115, 530, 532 n.5
and hand activity 184
Hindi 365, 497
home language 495, 497
Indigenous 395, 403, 490, 513, 515–16, 521, 529
Inuktitut 395–6
Italian 3, 86
Japanese 494, 529
language acquisition 86, 122, 142, 182–3, 242, 515, 525, 527, 531, 531 n.1
language development 179, 184, 526, 532 n.4
Language Exercises 140, 142
language-focused paradigm 527
language materials 496, 516, 529–31
learning 81, 337, 490, 528
Mandarin 490, 529–30, 532 n.6
Ngaanyatjarra 497
non-alphabetic 530–1
oral 78, 516, 526
phonemic 530
Pinyin 530, 532 n.6
"1+2" policy, European Union's 490
revitalization 490, 514, 516, 521, 529
second language 86, 181, 491, 525–9, 531
Spanish 413, 416, 421, 429–30, 490, 492–3, 526, 529–30, 532 n.5
switching 495
Thai 494
Urdu 497
vocabulary 49, 82, 142, 153, 205, 493, 496, 526–8, 531
Language Acquisition Device 531 n.1
La Obra (The Work) journal 430
Larsen, Torill Bogsnes 190
La Sapienza (The University of Rome) 6, 8, 24, 56, 293
Las Nereidas (The Sea Nymphs) 405
Latin-American Bilingual School (LAMB), Washington DC 529
Law 85 (education law) 407–8
Law 277 (education law) 409
Lawrence, Lynne 355
learning differences 148, 482
learning materials 66, 121, 141, 148, 210, 222–3, 243, 253, 274, 283, 293, 337, 480

The Learning Project, Gauteng 338
Leeds Beckett University 307
legacy, Montessori's 3–4, 16–18, 31, 38, 76, 201, 307, 313, 356, 438, 446, 469–70, 489
Lega nazionale per l'educazione e la cura dei deficienti (National League for the Care and Education of Mentally Deficient Children) 22, 471
Lekki Montessori 339
Leonardo, Z. 504, 507
Lepper, Mark R. 268
Lê Thị Tuất 373
Lexington Montessori School 149
Liang, Zhishen 378
liberation 12, 99, 403, 426, 470, 507, 516, 520, 523
Libera Università Maria SS 295
Liceo Montessoriano del Caribe 405–6
L'idea Montessori magazine 293
Lietz, Hermann 69, 159
lifelong learning 271–2, 278
Lillard, Angeline S. 205, 211, 214, 256
lingua franca 490, 494
linguistics/linguistic development 78, 81, 85–7, 98, 286, 489–94, 497, 508, 525, 528–9, 531 n.1, 538
Lithuanian Montessori Society 328
live-model Montessori class (1915), San Francisco Panama-Pacific Exposition 11
Lochhead, Tessa 395
Loeb, Jacques 138
logic model of Montessori education 189–95
Loko, Angela 344
London 7, 12, 16, 21, 66–7, 92, 200–1, 303–4, 307, 311, 316, 321, 338, 393, 416
London County Council 303
London Montessori Centre 305
Longmore, Lydia 387
Lorde, Audre 470
Lorenz, Konrad 13, 180
lottery-based studies 204, 214, 266
Lowry, Mother de Sales 309
Ludwig, Harald 108, 125, 159, 324
Luhmer, Klaus 382
Lu, Leshan, *Montessori's Early Childhood Education* 378
Lumin Education 356
Lutheran sisters 344
Lynedoch Children's House, South Africa 339
Lyra, Carmen 416

MACAR Model (Montessori Applied to Children at Risk) 482

Maccheroni, Anna Maria 11, 53, 292
Macias, Geraldine O'Leary de 419
Magdalene, Sister Mary Charles 334
magnetic resonance imaging (MRI) 233–4, 236
Magyarországi Montessori Egyesület (Hungarian Montessori Society) 330
Mahoney, Colleen A. 190
Make a Difference (MAD) Projects 163
maker movement 458
Malaysia 371
Maldano, Dora (Tina) 419
The Male Montessorian initiative 469
Malva, Zarin 368
Mầm Non Khai Tâm school 374
Mantere, Oskari 315
Maragh, Beverley 358
Marenah, Nnaceesay 336–7
marginalization 403, 490, 504, 521
Margulies, Anna 480
Maria Montessori Institute (MMI) 305, 307, 334, 346, 358
market-based economic system 377–8
Marley, Scott C. 245
Marriott, Constance 334
Marstrand, Elna 316
Martini, Ferdinando 5
Marxist 37, 42, 294
Marxist-inflected materialism 475 n.5
Maslow, Abraham H. 275–6
Mason, Charlotte M. 303
mastery orientation 213–14, 266–7
materialist ontology 473
materialized abstractions 31, 141
material-making 350–1, 357, 363
Maternal, Escuela 416
maternity 22, 24–6, 130, 190, 291, 367. *See also* motherhood
mathematics/mathematical (materials) 81–6, 121–3, 150, 212, 243–4, 247, 412, 491–2, 504. *See also* Psychoarithmetic; Psychogeometry
  arithmetic operations 242–3
  Bead Frames 149, 244–5
  Cards and Counters 143
  color-coded materials 121, 148–9
  curriculum 243, 246
  Decimal Checkerboard 149
  decimal system 143, 148, 244–6
  Euclidean geometry 82–3
  Golden Beads 143, 148–9, 244–5
  manipulatives 148, 150, 243–6
  Mathematics Exercises 140, 143

Multiplication Checkerboard 149
  natural numbers 82–4
  number rods 83–4, 143, 246
  Pythagoras's theorem 83
  Sandpaper Numerals 84, 143, 246
  Spindle Box 143, 245
  Stamp Game 149
Matiso, Nomonde 338
Matsumoto, Hisako 382
Matsumoto, Shizuko 382
Mattle, Denise 345
Matuurai, Kimitoshi 382
McCaffrey, Barney 418
McCaffrey, Pat 418
McClure, Samuel 60 n.5
McClure's Magazine, promotion campaign for Montessori 10, 399
McDermott, John 17
McDonell, Janet 483
McHugh, Virginia 448
McNamara, John 451, 454
Mead, Margaret 171
measurement instruments 192–3
The Measures of Academic Progress (MAP) 220
media 447, 449
medical pedagogy 481
Mehta, Dinoo 366
memory 183–4, 234, 236, 246, 255, 445, 535–7, 539. *See also* working memory
Merleau-Ponty, Maurice 121
Metodo (Montessori Method) 24–6
Meyer, Hilbert 115
Международный институт Монтессори-педагогики (International Montessori Pedagogy Institute) 330
The Middle East 361, 364, 439
middle school 123–4, 212, 266, 271, 276–7, 405. *See also* junior high school
migration/migrants 304, 387, 389, 429, 490–1, 495, 514
Milan International Exposition 118
military-style education 425
Milwaukee (Wisconsin) 211–12, 481
minds 98, 109, 122, 131, 138, 153, 246, 253
  dimensions of (narrative and paradigmatic) 101
  mind-body interaction 17, 38, 88, 122, 135, 246, 451
  and movement 98–9
The Minnesota Executive Function Scale (MEFS App) tool 255
mixed-age group of children 123, 161, 164, 202, 204, 209, 235, 262, 265, 395

575

Moberg, Maria 316
Moche, Patricia 430
Modak, Tarabai 16, 286, 365, 367
Modernism movement 60 n.6
modernity 24, 88, 327, 381
modernization 10, 56, 324, 329
Möller, Wiebe 164
monolingual mindset 490–1
Montesano, Giuseppe 7–8
Montessori Academy for International Children, Poland 330
Montessori Accreditation Council for Teacher Education (MACTE) 17, 394, 401–2, 453
MACTE-recognized training centers 339
Montessori adolescent programs 266–7
Montessori, Alessandro 5
Montessori AMI College, Dublin 311
Montessorian 11–15, 17, 53, 55, 58, 102, 131, 135, 221, 335, 461, 509, 522–3
Montessori Association in the United Arab Emirates 361
Montessori Association of Romania 328
Montessori Association of Thailand 372
Montessori Association Peru 420
Montessori Atlas 60 n.2
Montessori Biberkor 322
Montessori Bibliography Online (MBO) 421 n.1, 435, 439
Montessori Bundesverband Deutschland (German Federal Montessori Association) 322, 325
Montessori Census 401, 436
Montessori Center for Newborns 132
Montessori Centre for Work and Study 319
Montessori Centre International (MCI) 305, 307, 469
Montessori Community of Tanzania (MCT) 337, 346
Montessori Dachverband Deutschland (MDD, German Montessori Organization) 324–5
Montessori de Chihuahua 411
Montessori de la Ciudad de México 411–12
Montessori del Sol 405
Montessori education 177, 209, 284
in Africa 333–41
in Argentina 200, 283, 286, 415, 420, 429–33
in Australasia 437–8
in Australia 200, 226, 283, 286, 372, 387–91, 437, 493
in Austria 12, 15, 120, 285, 459
in Belarus 327, 329
in Belgium 71, 439, 495, 497
in Bolivia 419–20
in Brazil 283, 285, 287, 310, 415, 420, 425–8
in Britain 10, 12, 57, 99, 159, 190, 303–7, 334, 371
in Canada 286, 393–6
in Caribbean 437
in Central America 418, 420–1
in Chile 415–18, 420, 430
in China 200, 268, 286, 371, 377–80, 480
in Costa Rica 415–16, 421
in Côte d'Ivoire 335, 356
in Dar es Salaam 343–6, 349
in Denmark 12, 315–16, 318, 421 n.2, 480
in Eastern Europe 285, 327–30
in Europe (*see* Europe/European)
in Finland 315, 318–19
in Germany 200, 287, 321–5 (*see also* Germany/German)
in Göttingen 164
in Iceland 315
in India 200, 283, 286, 356, 365–9, 436, 483, 497 (*see also* India)
in Ireland 309–13
in Italy 117, 273, 284, 291–5, 436 (*see also* Italy/Italian)
in Japan 200, 371, 381–5
in Kenya 286, 335, 341, 349–52, 357–8, 436, 497
in Latin America 415–21
in Lithuania 328
in London 200–1, 304, 309, 311, 316, 321, 346, 358 (*see also* London)
in Mexico 200, 411–14, 420
in Morocco 333, 337, 340
in Nepal 439
in the Netherlands 120, 266, 286, 297–300, 436 (*see also* The Netherlands)
in New Zealand 200, 436–8
in Nicaragua 415–16, 419
in Nigeria 244, 285, 333–5, 339–40, 349
in Nordic Countries 315–19
in North America 355, 393, 446, 513, 527
in Norway 315–16, 318–19
in Panama 415–16, 419
in Peru 415, 417–20
in Philippines 161–2, 371
in Poland 327, 329–30
in Puerto Rico 286–7, 401, 405–9, 420
in Romania 327–8, 330
in Rome 130–2, 200–1, 283, 295, 315, 327–8
in Russia 283, 327, 329–30
in Saudi Arabia 287, 361–4
in Singapore 371–3, 375
in South Africa 333–5, 337–8, 341, 497
in South Asia 438–9
in Southeast and East Asia 200, 371–6
in South Korea 371–2

in Sri Lanka 366, 394, 438
in Sweden 315–19, 345, 436
in Switzerland 232–3, 345, 373
in Tanzania 334–5, 337, 341, 343–6, 349
in Thailand 286–7, 371–2, 375
in Treland 286
in Turkey 214, 256–7, 436–7, 439, 483
in the United Kingdom 190, 286, 303–7
in the United States 503–9 (*see also* The United States)
in Vienna 71, 162–4
in Vietnam 371, 373–5
Montessori Educational Programs International (MEPI) 401–2
Montessori Education Special Interest Group (SIG) 177
Montessoriförbundet, Svenska (website of) 319
Montessori for Dementia and Ageing 391
Montessori for Kenya (MfK) 337, 352
Montessori for Social Justice (MSJ) 403, 506–7, 520
Montessori Foundation of Egypt (MFE) 337, 340
Montessori-Fröbel synthesis 298–9
Montessori Group 307
Montessori Home School in Rondebosch, South Africa 334
Montessori Infants' Assistants (AIM) school, Rome 130, 132
Montessori-inspired programs 312, 338, 361, 363, 401
Montessori Institute in Cairo 340
Montessori Institute of Bucharest (MIB) 330
"A Montessori Integrated Approach to Science, Mathematics, Technology, and the Environment," NAMTA conference 452
Montessori Jewish Day School, Toronto 395
Montessori Kalpilli 411
Montessori-Komitee (Montessori Committee) 321
Montessori Labor Berlin 323
Montessori Leaders Collaborative (MLC) 402
Montessori-Lubienska program 426
Montessori Magazine journal 367
Montessori, Maria, writings of 50 n.1, 105
  The Absorbent Mind 16, 50, 71, 76–7, 111 n.3, 525
  "Address to the World Fellowship of Faiths" 91–2
  Advanced Montessori Method (*I* and *II*) 11, 50, 63–6, 70 n.1, 81, 85–6, 492, 532 n.4
  Antropologia Pedagogica (Pedagogical Anthropology) 8, 38, 59
  From Childhood to Adolescence 50, 63, 66–9, 110, 275, 548
  The Child in the Church 111 n.7
  The Child in the Family 50, 71–2, 77

The Child, Society and the World: Unpublished Speeches and Writings 105–11
  "Alternative Comprehensive School" 109
  "Child and Society" 110
  lectures to parents and teachers 105–7
  "Lesson of Silence" 107–8
  "Man's Place in the Cosmos" 110–11
  On Recurring Themes 107–9
De l'enfant à l'adolescent (From Childhood to Adolescence) 66
The Discovery of the Child 37, 49–50, 53, 111 n.6
Dr. Montessori's Own Handbook 81, 492, 548
To Educate the Human Potential 97, 99–102
Education and Peace 34, 50, 91, 95, 547, 549
Education for a New World 97–9
The Forgotten Citizen 445
The Formation of Man 97, 102–3, 546
How to Educate Human Potential 32
Il metodo della pedagogica scientifica applicato all'educazione infantile nelle Case dei bambini (The Montessori Method: Scientific Pedagogy as Applied to Child Education in "The Children's House") 9, 49, 53–60, 60 n.1, 60 n.4, 81, 97, 102, 241, 297, 303, 328
Il segreto dell'infanzia (The Secret of Childhood) 411
"The Importance of Education in Bringing about Peace" 91
L'autoeducazione nelle scuole elementari: Continuazione del volume il metodo della pedagogia scientifica applicato all'educazione infantile nelle Case dei Bambini (auto-education in elementary school) 11, 13, 63, 292
The Montessori Method 10, 64
Psychoarithmetic 50, 66, 81–5
Psychogeometry 50, 66, 81–5
Psychogrammar 50, 66, 81, 85–7
Scientific Pedagogy 425
The Secret of Childhood 13, 37, 50, 75–7, 132, 382
Sulla Morale Sessuale (On Sexual Morals) 26
Von der Kindheit zur Jugend 165 n.2
"When Your Child Knows Better Than You" 172
Montessori, Mario M. 11–17, 24, 31–2, 58, 200–2, 304–5, 322, 328, 331 n.1, 366, 371, 382, 394, 399, 481, 516
Montessori materials 120, 122–3, 202–5, 210, 214, 256–7, 286, 337, 344, 346, 351, 356–7, 361, 363, 371–2, 374, 378, 382–3, 385, 419, 425, 430, 465, 469, 480, 494, 521, 529–30

Montessori Medical Partnerships for Inclusion (MMPI) 481, 484
Montessori Model United Nations (MMUN) 164
The Montessori movement 12–13, 16–17, 286–7, 297, 304, 321–2, 325, 343, 355, 411, 413, 419, 421 n.1, 430, 439, 461, 492
  1911–1918 9–11
  ban in Nazi Germany (1936) 14
  history of the US 399–401
  public Montessori movement (2000–2016) 406–7, 409
  sustaining through crisis (2016–2022) 407–9
Montessori National Curriculum 390–1
Montessori National Opera institution. *See* Opera Nazionale Montessori
Montessori-Pierson Publishing Company 373
Montessori preschool and elementary programs 204
Montessori Public Fund 330
Montessori Public Policy Initiative (MPPI) 402, 520
Montessori, Renilde 355, 394
Montessori, Renilde (Stoppani) 5, 8, 11
Montessori Research Working Group 193
Montessori School of Moscow, Russia 330
Montessori Schools Association (MSA) 306–7
Montessori Sierra Madre School, Monterrey 413
Montessorism 11–14, 17–18
Montessori Teachers Association of Kenya (MTAK) 337, 349, 352
Montessori Teacher Training College 12, 351
Montessori Training and Research Trust, Hyderabad 368
Montessori Training Association of Tanzania (MTAT) 337, 345
Montessori Training Centre (MTC) 344–6
Montessori-Zentrum Münster (Montessori Center Münster) 324, 435
Monti, Veronica 431
Moonflower Montessori school, Gambia 336
Moore, Jennifer 338
moral development 160, 167–8
moral education 24, 69, 160, 549
moral intellectual 170
morality 26, 38, 110, 168
more-than-human 473–4, 475 n.7
Morgensen, Scott Lauria 470
Morioka, Tunezou 381
morphology 526, 530, 532 n.5
mother-child bond 131–2
motherhood 22–6. *See also* maternity; social motherhood
motivation 262–3, 265, 272, 277, 445
  in academic activities 266–7
  autonomous 262–5
  controlled 262
  intrinsic 82, 152, 226, 253, 261–8, 271, 273–4, 276–8, 460, 528, 547
motor skills 73, 75, 78–9, 85, 132, 140, 253
Moudry, Ben 453
Mozzoni, Anna Maria 23–4
Mukayuhsak Weekuw program 529
Müller-Hohagen, Ingeborg 322
multiage classrooms 148, 204, 232, 237, 253–4, 375, 427, 462
Multidisciplinary University Research Initiative (MURI) 79
multilingualism 490–2, 494–8, 525–31. *See also* bilingualism
multiliteracies 491
multisensory 78, 149, 482, 529
Mumbai 366, 368
Munich Montessori Model 322
Muñoz, Jose Antonio 419–20
Murji, Khatoon 349
Murray, Angela K. 403
music and dance education 11, 69, 144, 236, 278, 519, 529
Mussolini, Benito 13–14, 57–8, 284, 293
Mwendopole, Hilda 334
Myanmar 366, 371, 436
Myrdal, Alva 316, 319 n.1

Nagasaki Junshin Catholic University 383
Nairobi 349
Nakuru 350–2, 357, 497
narratives 59, 101, 142, 152, 189, 287, 448, 508
Nasgaard, Sigurd 316
National Agency for Education, Sweden 106
National Assessment of Educational Progress (NAEP) 504
National Association for the Education of Young Children (NAEYC) 226, 401, 449–50, 452, 520
National Center for Montessori Education (NCME) 419
National Center for Montessori in the Public Sector (NCMPS) 401–2, 226, 520
National Congress of Italian Women (1908) 470
National Education Plan (PNE) 427
National Education policy (2020) 368
National Education Technology Plan (NETP) 450
National Institute for Educational Policy Research 382
The National Institutes of Health Toolbox (NIH Toolbox) 255, 257
Native American 519. *See also* Indigenous people/communities (Indigeneity)

natural disasters 407, 409
natural sciences 13, 32, 53, 160, 491–2
nature/nature education 23, 29, 100–1, 120, 460, 465
Nazi Germany 14–15, 50
Nebula Children's Home, Vietnam 374
negative affective reaction 231, 233–4
neoliberal education reform 288
neoliberal rationality 329–30
NEPSY-II 255
The Netherlands 12, 16, 85, 204, 436, 495
 school-admission lotteries 266
neural circuits 84, 180
neural plasticity 184
neuroimaging techniques 233, 235, 536
neurological development 254
neurons 99, 183–4
neuropedagogy 88
neuroscience 64, 81–2, 84–6, 88, 98, 102, 134, 137, 158, 165, 177, 179–85, 445, 450, 457
newborns 77, 98, 116, 129–33
New Education Fellowship 102, 159, 316, 416, 421
new man 24, 93–4
New York Times 201
The New York Tribune 10, 55
Nghiêm Phương Mai 373
Nguyễn Phúc Vĩnh Bang 373
Nguyễn Thị Khang 373
Nietzsche, Friedrich Wilhelm 37, 42, 56
The Nitte Foundation 336–7
No Child Left Behind 400
nongovernment organizations (NGOs) 330, 335, 337, 356, 372–3, 414, 420–1, 427, 431
nonrandom studies 212–14, 255
normalization 9, 42, 68, 76, 101, 106–7, 109, 111 n.3, 141, 147, 169, 508, 551 n.4
North American Montessori Teacher Association (NAMTA) 400, 402, 452
The Northern Diocese of the Evangelical Lutheran Church of Tanzania 345
Norwegian Montessori Society 318
not-for-profit organizations 401, 421
Notre Dame University 287
nurseries/nursery school 9, 25, 132–5, 294–5, 303, 306–7, 337, 343, 382, 418
Nutan Bal Shiksan Sangh (NBSS, New Child Education Society) 365
Nutarak, Karen 395
Nyerere, Julius 343

observation-based approach 480
Ochs, Else 321
O'Connell, Bridgid 419–20

O'Dwyer, Alison 393
Office of Basic Education Commission of Thailand 372
Office of Intellectual Labor 23
Olivos Montessori School 430–1
one person, one language (OPOL) approach 495–6
Ontario 394–5
open-ended period 153, 243
Opera Nazionale Balilla organization 14
Opera Nazionale Montessori (ONM, Italian National Montessori Organization) 13–14, 55, 293–4
Operation Upgrade in the Eastern Cape 338
Oppenheimer, Orcillia 338
optimal development and learning 64, 147, 183, 210, 261, 271, 275
optimal experience 177, 271, 273–8
Organização Montessori do Brasil (OMB, Montessori Organization of Brazil) 420, 427
Organization for Economic Co-Operation and Development (OECD) 220
orphanages 11, 130–1, 346, 413, 419–20
Orthophrenic School 8, 273, 480, 484, 535
Oswald, Paul 324
Oxendine-Eagle Bull, Jeanne 519
Oxendine, James 519

Pacific Rim Montessori International School (PRINTS), San Mateo 529
Pädagogische Akademie (Teachers College), Essen 324
Padilla, Migdalia 409
Paedological Society of Amsterdam 297
Paez-Barrameda, Maria Angelica 161
Pakistan 439
Pallin, Anna 316
Palmieri, Estela 411
Panama Pacific International Exposition 377
Pankhurst, Emmeline 303
parenting styles 171–2, 358, 363
parent-led private Montessori schools 323
parents 16, 74–5, 95, 103, 105–7, 130, 147, 160, 162, 167–8, 170–2, 182, 201, 203, 233, 275–6, 288, 291, 297, 299–300, 303, 306–7, 311, 318, 323–4, 334, 340, 345, 356, 363, 373, 375–6, 378, 385, 387, 389, 405–6, 409, 431, 463, 482, 505–6, 515
Paris 8, 435, 526
Parkhurst, Helen 111 n.9, 201, 286
patents 200, 206 n.2
peace, education and 91, 93–5, 119, 517, 523
 ecoliteracy and sustainability 545–50

positive/negative peace 93
religious experience 92
science of peace 91
Pear Tree School, Oakland 520
Pedagogical Congress (1898), Turin 480
pedagogy 21–2, 24, 26, 30–1, 37–41, 43–4, 50, 64, 71, 74, 82, 84, 93, 97, 101–2, 105, 115–17, 120, 125–6, 132, 139, 168, 170, 177, 179, 189, 195, 227, 235–7, 243, 272, 278, 285, 288, 291, 293, 297, 299, 303, 307, 312–13, 318, 323, 327, 330, 336–7, 352, 361, 405–6, 409, 416, 427, 429, 445–6, 457, 460, 462, 492, 516, 531, 535, 537
   abstract 516
   psycho-pedagogy 13, 100
   radical 26, 97
   scientific 53–60, 118, 130, 402
peer-to-peer learning 232, 235, 237
Penfield Children's Center 481
Penfield Montessori Academy 481
Penfield, Wilder 184, 481, 484
Pensiero e Azione (Thought and Action) society 23
perceived competence 265, 267
Perón, Juan 430
Perón, Eva 430
Perry, Celma 426–7
Persichitte, Kay A. 449
personality 9, 34, 41, 50, 60, 68, 72, 92, 135, 138, 147, 157, 165, 169, 276, 516, 527
personalized learning 79, 449
person-environment relationship 273
person-first language 446
Perugia 53, 295, 426
Pestalozzi, Johann Heinrich 102, 430, 492
Peter Hesse Foundation 335, 356
Petersen, Peter 159
pharmaceutical industry 536
philanthropic/philanthropy 21, 288, 333, 343, 346, 387, 438
Philip, Ruth 315
philosophy 37–8, 43–4, 99–101, 111, 118, 124, 159, 170, 177, 179, 220, 241, 271, 275–6, 286, 363, 372, 380, 408, 419, 428, 448, 452, 462, 482, 493, 509, 515, 519, 521–2, 545–6, 549
   embodiment 43–4, 122–3, 307
   epistemology 38, 40, 42, 44, 100, 470
   freedom (*see* freedom)
   metaphysics 38–40
   moral (character, respect, and solidarity) 38, 42–4
The Phumelela Community Training Programme 338
physical development 78, 181, 223

physical education (sports) 85, 236
physical materials 243, 246
physics 39, 82, 101
Piaget, Jean 14, 102, 242, 272, 373, 445, 458
   De la logique de l'enfant à la logique de l'adolescent (The Growth of Logical Thinking from Childhood to Adolescence) 67
Pickering, Joyce 482–3
Piga, Arturo 416, 418
Pikler, Emmi 132–3
Piruvik Preschool, Nunavut 395–6
Pitisuka School, Chiang Rai 371
place-based learning 460
planes of development (developmental phases) 32, 100–1, 107, 115–16, 137–8, 140, 143–4, 147, 352, 356, 457, 466 n.1, 475 n.2, 483, 548
   first plane 116, 137–44
   second plane 32, 101, 147–54
   fifth plane 465, 466 n.1
Plato 445, 536
play 4, 65, 92, 99, 121, 134, 143–4, 293, 312, 321, 384. *See also* activities/tasks for children; work
playbook 226
pluricultural 489–90, 496
pluridisciplinary 177
plurilingualism 489–90, 493–8, 527
   in the twenty-first century 490–1
Pokot 350, 352, 358
Polangkul, Chalopchalai Maha Niranon 371
policy 167–9, 203, 215, 219, 226, 288, 415–16
Polish Solidarity movement 329
Polskie Stowarzyszenie Montessori (Polish Montessori Association) 330
Polski Instytut Montessori (Polish Montessori Institute) 330
Pong, Khamkaew Kraisorn 371
Poolpat, Jiraphan 371
Pope Benedict XV 58
Portugal 460
positivism 8, 13, 37, 57–8
Potts, Margaret 393
Powell, Mark 451
power relations 170, 329–30, 471–2, 474
pre-K (pre-kindergarten) 212, 294, 402–3
preschool children/education 8–10, 75, 116, 118, 120, 124, 204, 209, 211–14, 253, 256–8, 266, 293, 295, 298–9, 303–4, 312, 316, 319, 345–6, 352, 361, 365–8, 373–4, 377–8, 385, 403, 415–16, 418–19, 427, 471, 490, 538

The Preschool Self-Regulation Assessment 255–7
pretest-posttest design 256–7
preventive medicine 7, 22
primary education/schools 8, 13, 72, 262, 297, 299, 312, 352, 389, 416, 430. *See also* elementary education/schools
Prins-Werker, Jo 297
private schools 205, 286, 288, 295, 303, 307, 312–13, 323, 351, 365, 368, 372, 385, 394, 401–2, 405, 408, 415, 420, 427–31, 436, 481, 505, 508
problem-solving 45, 152, 184, 205, 209, 214, 223, 252, 458, 460
professional development 190, 225, 300, 307, 375, 407, 449, 459, 465, 472, 474, 482–3, 506
Programa Hondureño de Educación Comunitaria (PROHECO) 420
progressive education 283–4, 329, 394, 399, 415–17, 425, 429–30
project-based learning 365, 459–60
Project Nicaragua 419
prophet Mohammed 363
psychiatry 56, 177, 199, 492
psychic hygiene 154
psycho 81
psychoanalysis 50, 131
Psychoarithmetic 50, 66, 81–5, 87
psychobiological development 179–80
Psychogeometry 50, 66, 81–5, 87
Psychogrammar 50, 66, 81, 85–7
psychological development 69, 71, 115, 124, 137, 180, 182
psychology 9, 57, 87–8, 98, 108, 120, 130, 177, 221, 224, 247, 261, 272, 445, 492–3
psychophysiology 64
puberty 157–8, 180
public education 312, 325, 338, 372, 403, 405, 409, 416, 418, 509
public funding 286, 312–13, 394–6, 408, 584
public-private partnership 365, 375
public schools 11, 41, 211–14, 232, 295, 297, 318, 351, 399–401, 405–7, 427, 429, 436, 481, 505
Pueblo 514, 517
Puerto Rican Charter Management Organization (CMO) 408
pull-out/push-in model 527
Pythagoras 83, 536

Quality Framework, MDD 324–5
quasi-experimental studies 211–12, 214
Quebec 394

Queer Consultants initiative 469
The Quran 363

race/racial/racism 190, 202, 212, 334, 403, 446, 450, 481, 503–9, 513, 516–17, 520
Radice, Sheila, *The New Children: Talks with Maria Montessori* 12
Raintree Montessori School, Lawrence, Kansas 481
Rambusch, Nancy McCormick 16, 202, 286, 394, 399–400
Ramsay, Prudence 338
randomization 256
randomized controlled trials (RCTs) 210–11
random-lottery design 256, 401
Rasfeld, Margaret 459
rationality 22, 170, 329–30
receptive language skills 142
reciprocity 132
reconstruction 58, 92, 95, 97, 170, 172, 294
Red Montessori Solidario (RMS) 286, 431, 433
reflective practitioner 169–70, 458, 460
Reform Act of 1999 (Thailand) 372
refugee 352, 357, 435–6, 439
Regia Scuola Magistrale di Metodo Montessori (Royal Teacher Training College for the Montessori Method) 14, 58
regulation 181, 237, 254–5, 286, 312, 341, 362, 374, 389, 395, 413
relatedness 263, 265–7
religion/religious 56–9, 91–2, 97, 100, 107–8, 111 n.6, 283, 309–12, 337, 345–6, 361–4, 387, 399, 415, 418, 421. *See also specific religions*
religious education 56, 58–9, 92, 107–8, 111 n.6
religious orders 387, 399
Renaissance of Montessori Education 322–4
repeated-measures methodology 224
repetition 55, 73, 134, 141, 222, 232, 243, 272, 471, 537, 540
rewards for children 26, 76, 82, 234, 237, 262, 264, 266, 274, 363, 459
Richardt, Marguerite 340
Rieckhoff, Barbara S. 463–4
Rifbjer, Sofie 316
Rizzolatti, Giacomo, *Mirrors in the Brain: How Our Minds Share Actions, Emotions, and Experience* 85
Robertson, Isa H. 393
Rodriguez, Arturo Alessandri 418
Roman Catholics 297, 394
Rome 6, 8, 10, 14, 21, 23–4, 29, 44, 53, 58, 60 n.5, 118, 291, 293, 377, 381, 387, 393, 409, 493, 537

Roth, Maria 322
Rotten, Elisabeth 14
Roubiczek, Lili 120
Rousseau, Jean Jacques 56, 445, 492
Rudolph, Norma 338
Ruijs, Nienke 266
Rural Montessori school, Muquiyauyo, Chile 417
Rushbrook Primary Academy, Manchester 307

Sackett, Ginni 452
Sagara, Atsuko 385
Saigon 373–4
Salamanca Statement 480, 484
Salás, Darío 416
salience 277, 369
Samburu 350, 352, 358
San Lorenzo 8, 25, 53–4, 57, 59, 98, 118–19, 137, 291, 355, 379, 409
Santa Fe province 429–30
Santiago Atitlán 418
Sanzio, Raffaello, *Madonna della Seggiola* 57
São Paulo 425–6
Saudi Vision 2030 initiative 361
scaffolding 75, 252–3, 274, 465, 516, 527–8
Scalco, Joana Falce 425
Scheid, Paul 322
Scheurman, Geoffrey 459
schism 18, 200, 202, 286, 369, 399
Schjetnan, Christian 413
Schjetnan, Tete 413
scholarships 3, 102, 355, 371, 395, 439–40, 469, 471, 473, 503, 519, 548
Schomburg, Roberta 450
Schön, Donald 170
school choice 284, 288, 315, 318, 400, 436
School Community Law (Ley 18) 406
Schopenhauer 37
Schuldhei, Anna 315
Schulfarm Insel Scharfenberg 159
Schulz-Benesch, Günter 105, 107–8, 324
Schulze, Friedemann 323
Schwarz, Elizabeth 321
science and technology studies (STS) 472
Science Council of Japan 383
scientific education 11, 53, 473
Scocchera, Augusto 33
Scocchera, Rita 33
Scott, Katharine 460
secondary education/schools 6, 23, 66, 68–9, 158, 213, 266, 299, 322, 324, 345, 374, 389, 458
second language acquisition (SLA) 86, 525, 527–8, 530–1

Second World War 97, 130, 284, 303–4, 311, 329, 366, 371, 388, 426
Séguin, Edouard 8–9, 56, 152, 222, 479–80, 492, 530
self-confidence 68–9, 345
self-construction 137–9, 452, 516
self-control 236, 251–2, 265, 547
self-correction/self-correcting materials 10, 76, 191, 223, 232–3, 235–7, 465, 537
self-determination 169, 261–8
self-determination theory (SDT) 262–3, 265, 267
self-discipline 9, 76, 105, 169
self-discovery 82, 454
self-education 11, 298
self-expression 69, 160, 549
self-guided learning 13, 362–3
self-reflection 139, 144, 401, 463–4
self-regulation 72, 131, 152, 213, 237, 251, 256–7, 537
self-reliance 329, 343, 358, 387
Senegal 335, 356
sense of competence 265, 549
sensibilities 59, 107, 138, 273, 473
sensitive periods 13, 40, 55, 68, 75, 77–8, 98–9, 101, 132–3, 137–41, 225, 233, 235–7, 525
sensorial materials 118, 134, 141, 148, 480
sensorimotor 86, 101, 122, 181, 184, 242, 246, 253
sensory affective stimulation 181–2, 184
sensory education/training 7, 9, 11, 31, 117, 233, 372
sensory perception 40, 138, 140–2
Šeracký, František 328
Sergi, Giuseppe 8–9, 37–8, 117
service learning 458, 460–1, 465
settler colonialism 513–14, 516–17, 520–3
sex education 24, 26
sexuality 22–4, 26, 26 n.2, 469
Shanks, Pamela 481
Shan, Weiru 379
shared responsibility 25, 167
Shrum, Judith L., *Teacher's Handbook: Contextualized Language Instruction* 528
silence 43, 76, 107, 547
Simpson, Martha 387
sinicization 377, 379, 380 n.2
Sinigaglia, Corrado, *Mirrors in the Brain: How Our Minds Share Actions, Emotions, and Experience* 85
Sivaramakrishnan, Meenakshi 368
Sjögren, Ida 316
Skinner, B. F. 445
Smith, Huston 92
social education 107
social-emotional development 132, 151, 252, 257, 506

social-emotional learning 148, 214
social interactions 140, 254, 453, 494
socialist(s) 283, 297, 299, 321, 373
social justice 170, 403, 405, 409, 452, 465, 506
social motherhood 24–5. *See also* motherhood
social problem-solving skills 205, 209, 214
social reform/reformers 75, 283, 387, 415–17
social sciences 195, 492, 548
social skills 205, 210, 214, 235, 254, 459, 482–3
social studies 68, 212–13, 459
Social Welfare Vocational School 382
Sociedad Amigos de la Infancia 429
Società Umanitaria (Humanitarian Society) organization 292
society by cohesion 43, 107
sociobiological degeneration theory 9
socioemotional focus 254
Sonnenschein, Aktion 322, 481, 484
Sophia University 382
Sorge Affair 14
SOS Children's Villages 335
South Africa Montessori Association (SAMA) 337–8
The South African Montessori Society (SAMS) 338
South Carolina 212, 214, 401
sovereignty 513–14, 521
Spaced Retrieval (SR) technique 537
Spain 11–12, 14, 85, 284, 439
special education 8–9, 325, 480, 483
specialized schools 406
special language mechanism 525, 531 n.1
special needs 222, 385, 479, 480
Spencer, Herbert 9, 37
spiritual/spirituality 3–4, 16, 33, 38, 57–8, 60 n.6, 92, 95, 97, 98, 99, 107, 139, 147, 254, 293, 310, 362, 411, 446, 519
  spiritual embryo 39, 77, 180
  spiritual reconstruction of humanity 92, 95
  spiritual research 60 n.6
Spitz, René 130
Spitz syndrome 182
Společnosti Montessori ČR (Montessori Society Czech Republic) 330
spontaneous discipline 55
spontaneous manifestation 124
Sri Ramacharan Charitable Trust 368
stage-environment fit 261, 267
stage-specific approach 267
Standing Rock Sioux Tribe 514
Stanford Achievement Test 220
St. Ann's Montessori College, Nakuru 349, 351
Stephenson, Susan Mayclin 418
Stern, Daniel 131

St. Irene's Montessori College, Kenya 349
St. Joseph's School, Catholic convent in Calabar 334–5
St. Nicholas Montessori College 311
St. Nicholas Montessori Society of Ireland 311
St. Nicholas Training Centre in London 389
St. Nicholas Training Organization 304–7, 312
Stockholm 315–16
Stockholm University 319
storytelling 152, 472, 508
St. Otteran's school, Waterford 309–10
Strait Start initiative 391 n.3
Strand, Mark 278
student-centered classroom assessment 221, 449, 462
student-centered learning 117, 123, 373, 405, 463–4
student choice 147, 151, 153, 252, 257
student-directed education 276, 284
subjective experience 271–2, 274
Sulea-Firu, Illie 328, 331 n.1
supplemental materials 205, 210
supplemented Montessori programs 257–8
supportive family context 274–5
supportive of learning 213–14
supranature 545
Suriname 417
sustainability 153, 158, 345, 356, 368, 460, 465, 545–50
  sustainable development 111, 338, 352, 546, 548
  Sustainable Development Goals 550–1 n.1
  sustainable schools program 190
The Sustainability Institute 338
Swamy, S. R. 367–8
Swedish Montessori Society 317–19
Swiss Little Sisters of St. Francis of Assisi Msimbazi Mission 344
Swiss Montessori society 14
Switzerland 12, 55, 541
Sydney Montessori Teachers' College 389, 391 n.2
The Sydney Montessori Training Centre 391
syllabus. *See* curriculum
systemic racism 506, 509, 517

tacit knowledge 170
tacit parenting ideology 171–2
Tagore, Rabindranath 15, 365
Taiwan 213, 371
Taiwanese Montessori Education Research Foundation 379
Takane, Fumio 385
Talamo, Edoardo 8, 291
talent development 278
Tamil Nadu 365, 368

teacher education/preparation 390, 420, 426, 457–66, 517, 522
  assessment 463–5
  curiosity in 459–60
  differentiated instruction (DI) 462–3
  early childhood teachers 106, 152, 363, 449, 483
  hands-on learning 458–9
  interconnectedness 460–1
  service learning 458
  technology 463
teacher education programs (TEPs) 225, 402, 427, 453, 458, 460–1, 463–5
Teacher Questionnaire of Montessori Practices 204
Teachers Pay Teachers 521
Teacher training at the Social Pedagogical Seminary (1939–1945) 316
teacher training centers 8, 11–12, 14, 299, 304, 307, 318, 329, 338, 346, 364–5, 368, 372, 394, 406, 411–12, 494, 517, 520–1
teacher training courses 5, 10, 14, 16–18, 97, 168, 200–4, 293–5, 297–8, 304–5, 307, 309, 311, 319, 321–5, 327, 334, 343, 346, 361, 379, 381–3, 411, 419, 489, 493–5
teaching-learning process 66, 85–6
technique of isolation 122
technology and digital media 447–54. *See also* educational technology
teleology 38–40
telluric economy 30
Terrell, Tracy David 528
Thailand Montessori Association 371
theory of mind 210, 213–14
Theosophical Society 15, 60 n.6, 97, 366–7, 421, 493
theosophy 60 n.6
Thomas, Miriam 393
Thomas More University of Applied Sciences 300
Thompson, Evan 246
three-period lesson 152–3, 222, 224–5
Tibetan Children's Villages (TCV) 436
Tibetans 286
time
  role of time in Montessori classrooms 151–3
  and space 153, 160, 453, 474, 546
timelines 68, 71, 123, 150, 152, 521
Times Educational Supplement 12, 201
toddlers 73–4, 101, 130–1, 133–5, 194, 394–5, 401, 529
Tokyo Montessori Educational Research Institution. 382
Tolstoy, Leo 102
Toronto Montessori School (TMS) 394

Toshio, Nogami 381
totalitarian/totalitarianism 14, 329
Tozier, Josephine 60 n.5
transdisciplinary 177, 460, 474, 493
transformation 25, 42, 68, 138, 180–1, 224, 362, 405, 448, 454, 461
  of parent and caregiver 171–2
  of teachers/educators 116, 167–72, 506, 508
transformative intellectual 169–70
transitional phases of development 67, 75, 115, 132, 152, 157
translanguaging 489, 491–8
Tribal Nations 513–14, 516, 522–3
truth-centered educational model 522
truth telling 513, 516–18, 522
Tsuzumi, Tsuneyoshi 382
tuition-based schools 313, 421
Tulalip Indian Boarding School 517–18

Ulibarri, Pilar 413
Underhill, Evelyn 92
Union international de sécours aux enfants (UISE, International Union of Care for Children) 13
The United Nations 356, 545
United Nations General Assembly 64, 164
United Nations Educational, Scientific and Cultural Organization (UNESCO) 356, 382, 547
The United Nations Framework Convention on Climate Change 550–1 n.1
The United States 9–10, 16–17, 55, 57, 60 n.5, 63, 130, 189–90, 200–2, 204–5, 209–14, 225, 256–7, 266, 283, 286, 318, 324, 345, 356, 358, 378, 381, 393–5, 399–403, 416, 420–1, 429, 449–50, 459, 462, 465, 480–2, 503–9, 513–17, 520, 526–30
Universal Design for Learning and Response to Intervention practices 462
universe 31–2, 38–9, 67, 99–101, 154, 275, 515. *See also* cosmic education
Universidad Torcuato Di Tella 432
Università degli Studi di Foggia 295
Università degli Studi di Verona 295
University of Chile 416
University of Hartford 403
University of Kansas 403, 439, 481
University of Oklahoma 287
University of Social Sciences and Humanities (USSH) 373
University of South-Eastern Norway 319
Ursuline Convent, Waterford 309

Uruguay 417–18
Ushirika wa Neema (Fellowship of Grace) 345
Uttal, David H. 243

valorization 68, 549
van Reesema, Cornelia Philippi Sieuwertz 298
Vargas, Getulio 425–6
variability 199, 202, 205, 209–10, 363, 470, 491
variation theory 122–3
Varnas, Adomas 328
Vasconcelos, Teresa 460
Vera Peñaloza, Rosario 429
Verein Montessori-Pädagogik Deutschland (German Society of Montessori Pedagogy) 321
Via Marsi Montessori school 481
video monitoring 172
Vidot, Vargas 409
Vienna Erdkinder model 164
Vietnam AMI Montessori Initiative (VAMI) 373–4
Vietnam Montessori Education Foundation (VMEF) 373
violence 50, 91–4, 357, 405, 513–14, 517, 520
Vujs, Robert 349
Vygotsky, Lev S. 65, 242, 265, 445, 528

Wallbank, Phyllis 304
Walton Family Foundation 401
Wampanoag Tribes 529
Wasserzug, Herminia 430
Waterman, Alan S. 276
Weill, Rita 418
Weipa State School, Cape York Peninsula 389
Welcoming Committee 540–1
Wend Collective 401
Western civilization 381
Western missionaries 286
What Works Clearinghouse website (Institute of Education Sciences) 210
Whitby School, Greenwich, Connecticut 399–400
White Cross organization 13, 436
Whitehead, Alfred North 152
whiteness 514–15, 518, 520
Whitescarver, Keith 399
white supremacy 503, 516, 519–21
Wiesel, Torsten 180
Wikramaratne, Lena 335, 438

Wissenschaftliches Zentrum für Montessori-Pädagogik (Scientific Center for Montessori Pedagogy) 324
Wittgenstein, Ludwig 97
Women's Indian Association Montessori School 365–6
women's rights, Montessori's support for
  demands for equal rights 7
  domina and *mater* 25
  emancipation of 21–4
  new woman 22, 56
  suffrage 7, 22–3
Wonderkids Montessori in Kwa Zulu Natal 338
Wong Sun Yue Clemens 377
Wong Sun Yue Montessori House of Childhood in Beijing 377
work 8–9, 39, 41–2, 54, 57, 69, 74, 88, 99, 106, 109–11, 121–3, 125, 137, 139–40, 148–9, 151–4, 161–4, 221–4, 226, 232, 264–5, 276–7, 293–4, 298, 366, 396, 438, 458–9, 479, 483–4, 518, 521–2, 526. *See also* activities/tasks for children
Work and Study 159–65, 319, 549
work cycle 140, 224–5, 268, 374, 431
working memory 184, 213, 251, 255–8. *See also* memory
Working Memory Test 255
World Conference on Special Needs Education (1994) 480
World Health Organization 130
Wundt, Wilhelm 56
Wyndham-Stewart, Pamela 358

Xiuying Lu 378

Yale University 287
Yorozutyoho newspaper 381
Yoshioka, Tsuyoshi 381
Young, Celum 518

The Zama Montessori Center 338
Združenja Montessori Slovenje (Slovenian Montessori Association) 330
Zhejiang Montessori Institute of Child Development 379
zone of proximal development 265, 274
Zurich, Switzerland 213

Printed in the USA
CPSIA information can be obtained
at www.ICGtesting.com
LVHW010722011123
762517LV00006B/44